Communication, Relationships and Practices in Virtual Work

Shawn D. Long
University of North Carolina at Charlotte, USA

BUSINESS SCIENCE REFERENCE

Hershey · New York

Director of Editorial Content:	Kristin Klinger
Director of Book Publications:	Julia Mosemann
Acquisitions Editor:	Lindsay Johnston
Development Editor:	Joel Gamon
Publishing Assistant:	Thomas Foley
Typesetter:	Michael Brehm
Production Editor:	Jamie Snavely
Cover Design:	Lisa Tosheff
Printed at:	Yurchak Printing Inc.

Published in the United States of America by
    Business Science Reference (an imprint of IGI Global)
    701 E. Chocolate Avenue
    Hershey PA 17033
    Tel: 717-533-8845
    Fax: 717-533-8661
    E-mail: cust@igi-global.com
    Web site: http://www.igi-global.com

Library of Congress Cataloging-in-Publication Data

Communication, relationships and practices in virtual work / Shawn Long,
editor.
    p. cm.
 Includes bibliographical references and index.
 Summary: "This book provides exploration of the opportunities, benefits and costs associated with virtual work, addressing several communicative, relational and practical issues associated with virtual work"--Provided by publisher.
 ISBN 978-1-61520-979-8 -- ISBN 978-1-61520-980-4 (ebook) 1. Telecommuting. 2. Virtual work. I. Long, Shawn.
 HD2336.3.C66 2010
 658.3'123--dc22
                 2010006729

British Cataloguing in Publication Data
A Cataloguing in Publication record for this book is available from the British Library.

All work contributed to this book is new, previously-unpublished material. The views expressed in this book are those of the authors, but not necessarily of the publisher.

Table of Contents

Section 1
Communication in Virtual Work

Section 3
Practices in Virtual Work

Detailed Table of Contents

Section 1
Communication in Virtual Work

Chapter 1

Jennifer L. Gibbs, Rutgers University, USA
Craig R. Scott, Rutgers University, USA
Young Hoon Kim, Rutgers University, USA
Sun Kyong Lee, Rutgers University, USA

This chapter examines workplace policies related to virtual work, with a specific focus on telework policies. Such policies are important to successful telework in communicating rules and expectations and providing a basis for negotiation between individual telecommuters and their employers. A content analysis of 35 state government telework policies revealed that such policies are characterized by two major tensions between autonomy and control and between flexibility and rigidity. The first tension relates to issues such as individual versus organizational responsibility for monitoring performance, providing equipment, and ensuring physical and data security, while the second tension relates to the standardization of working hours and eligibility criteria, whether rules are clear or left ambiguous, and the degree of work/family balance. Although explicit contradictions between stated benefits and realities of telework implementation may be problematic, most of the policies used tension productively by providing enough ambiguity to allow for competing individual and organizational interests to co-exist. Practical implications for teleworkers and their managers are suggested.

Chapter 2

Tyler R. Harrison, Purdue University, USA
Elizabeth A. Williams, Purdue University, USA

Conflict is just as common in virtual teams as it is in collocated teams. However little is known about the process of conflict in these teams. This study presented in this chapter analyzed conflict in three inter-organizational teams. The purpose of this research is to identify primary types of conflict in virtual teams, examine the role that the structure of communication plays in the conflict, and examine the influence of the social context. Specifically, this chapter 1) reviews the extant literature on conflict in virtual teams and organizational conflict in general; 2) presents results from a study of three inter-organizational virtual team collaborations; and 3) offers an outline of potential future research in this area and provides best practices and potential pitfalls for practitioners to consider when structuring inter-organizational virtual teams.

Chapter 3

Online teaching and learning has been adopted throughout higher education with minimal critical attention to the challenges it poses to traditional definitions of academic labor. This chapter explores four areas where the nature of academic labor becomes contestable through the introduction of online instruction: (1) the boundaries demarcating work from personal time; (2) the relative invisibility of online labor; (3) the documentation, recognition, and rewards attendant to online instruction; and (4) the illusory empowerment of online students as consumers. The theory and practice of what constitutes "legitimate" labor in higher education require substantial reconsideration to incorporate the online dimension.

Chapter 4

Ethical issues due to the following four major factors inherent to virtual work are examined: 1) organizational culture, 2) trust, 3) cross-cultural diversity, and 4) monitoring. The author proposes that the negative ethical implications of the virtual work environment can be overcome by following the suggested steps and proposed guidelines. Areas for potential future research are included and are followed by an overall discussion of the issues covered and some closing remarks.

Chapter 5

This chapter explores the role of surveillance in virtual work. With the modern societal shift as well as the increased global market, working virtually is becoming more necessary and even a requirement at times. With the removal of physical interaction, questions of how to properly ensure productivity arise. This chapter suggests the panopticon, as developed by Bentham (1791) and expounded upon by

Foucault (1977), is very influential in the surveillance of virtual activity. This chapter will ultimately explore theoretical underpinnings of the panopticon, work place surveillance, virtual surveillance in practice, ethical issues created by virtual surveillance, and consequences of virtual surveillance.

Section 2
Relationships in Virtual Work

Chapter 6

Huiyan Zhang, Schouten China, People's Republic of China
Marshall Scott Poole, University of Illinois Urbana-Champaign, USA

This chapter reports the results of a multiple case study which investigated how virtual teams appropriated multiple media to facilitate the construction of group identity and manage group boundaries. It focuses on relationships within and between virtual teams. The study found five processes that shaped group identity, including clarification of goals and mission, developing regularized pattern of interaction, group norms for media use, and negotiation of task jurisdiction with interlocking groups. The study discovered that groups managed boundaries in terms of clarity distinctness, and permeability. It indicated that group boundaries were blurred and maintained simultaneously through purposeful use of communication technologies.

Chapter 7

Stacey L. Connaughton, Purdue University, USA
Elizabeth A. Williams, Purdue University, USA
Jennifer S. Linvill, Purdue University, USA
Elizabeth J. O'Connor, Purdue University, USA
Troy Hayes, Ingersoll-Rand plc., USA

Temporary virtual teams are common organizing forms across industries and sectors, and their members often span national, functional, and other boundaries. Many times temporary virtual team members have no prior experience working with one another, may seldom if ever meet face-to-face, and may never work together again, thus team development may occur differently than it does in long-term or in tact teams. Yet little is known about the development of temporary virtual teams and the process challenges therein. The purpose of this chapter is to contribute to this body of research by revealing how individuals who are members of a temporary virtual team experience team development. Specifically, this chapter (a) reviews two often-cited models of team development and discusses the limited body of research on virtual team development; (b) presents findings from a study of one organization's business intelligence teams that were temporary, virtual, and global in nature; and (c) advances a research agenda for scholars in this area and recommendations to practitioners who are working in these contexts.

Chapter 8

Communication between members of decision-making teams has long been known to be strongly influenced by member status. However, we still know relatively little about how status and status-driven influence processes change with the implementation of technologically-mediated virtual teams and mobile collaborative enterprises. Early predictions were that technologically-mediated communication would essentially flatten the status hierarchy of groups and teams (Kiesler, Siegel, & McGuire, 1984), allowing all members, regardless of position, social identity, or other characteristics, to have equal access to the decision-making process. A review of relevant theoretical approaches and prior empirical findings indicates that in all likelihood, status processes and influence are maintained in these settings, at least in some cases to the detriment of team effectiveness. This chapter examines, through the manifestations and functions of interpersonal status, the effects of technological mechanisms of collaboration on communication processes, relationships, and practices.

Chapter 9

Sense of virtual community (feelings of identity, belonging, and attachment) is an essential component of virtual communities. In this chapter, the authors develop a model of how sense of virtual community develops in professional virtual communities. Based on sense of virtual community models in social virtual communities, they expect that the exchange of support, development of a group identity, and group norms will lead to a stronger professional sense of virtual community. Unlike social virtual communities, they also predict that employee/members occupational identification will increase professional sense of virtual community, particularly when the virtual community can provide support and information not available in the employee/member's face-to-face life. Finally, they propose that increased occupational commitment, professional networks, and employee performance are outcomes of sense of virtual community in professional virtual communities.

With the proliferation of information technology and its saturation within homes, classrooms, and organizations, the traditional landscape of mentoring relationships is quickly becoming a faceless phenomenon. Virtual mentoring is rapidly being the more preferred way to initiate mentor and protégé relationships because of constraints that prevent people from meeting face-to-face. It is through this computer-mediated method of interaction where benefits surface that increase computer-mediate dialogue, allow for the free exchange of knowledge and information regardless of an individual's role within the interaction, and provides women a channel to voice their opinions and ideas free from gender bias. Outside of these benefits; however, limitations do exist that should be closely monitored so that the continued success of virtual mentoring can remain a viable option.

Chapter 11

Shawn D. Long, University of North Carolina at Charlotte, USA
Marla D. Boughton, University of North Carolina at Charlotte, USA
Rachel Widener, University of North Carolina at Charlotte, USA

Due to their hierarchical structure and limited resources, organizations are inherently political. Employees need to know how to "play the game" in order to get ahead. This chapter provides provide a background on politics, examining how the study of politics has evolved over time. The authors also examine the relationship between politics and similar constructs, such as authority, power, and influence. The authors then apply politics to an increasingly common organizational structure—virtual teams. Based upon research on trust, resource allocation, and influence in virtual teams, the authors suggest that, rather than being attenuated in the virtual environment, politics may in fact become exacerbated by the use of computer-mediated communication. The chapter ends with suggestions for future research on politics in virtual teams.

Section 3
Practices in Virtual Work

Chapter 12

Stephen C. Yungbluth, Northern Kentucky University, USA
Zachary P. Hart, Northern Kentucky University, USA

This chapter examines how power dynamics are manifested in virtual work. It starts with a look at how power is demonstrated in traditional decision making, and progresses to an exploration of how some organizations are experimenting with different forms of e-participation. Two cases are presented to illustrate some of the decisions associated with the implementation of information and communication technology (ICT), and the consequences of those choices. The first case looks at President Obama's platform on technology and how his administration has embraced it to expand his vision of democracy in the information age. The second case portrays a utility company seeking to increase the involvement of its stakeholders through the creation of a blog site for the exclusive use of its community council. Both cases reveal a complex view of how organizations attempting to increase participation can paradoxically find themselves stifling it.

Chapter 13

Virtual work is increasingly prevalent in organizational settings. Many corporations communicate virtually to reduce travel and facility costs and expedite production. Benefits of employees communicating virtually are recognizable and advantageous, but the benefits can come at a price—decreased human interactions. This study explored engineers' perceptions of relational limitations inherent to virtual work. Engineers enrolled in a communication course who use virtual work methods on the job comprised the sample. Qualitative content analysis revealed engineers perceive virtual work as a convenient and easy-to-use medium that bridges geography, curtails expenses, expedites meetings, and allows flex time. Conversely, engineers reported several relational limitations associated with virtual work, including reduced personal interactions, diminished nonverbal cues, increased miscommunications, added interference, and weakened interpersonal skills. Engineers exercise supplemental face-to-face communication, occasional on-site meetings, and social activities to counter virtual relational limitations. A social exchange theoretical perspective explains engineers' continued use of virtual work.

How we work in an increasingly computer-mediated world requires new ways of understanding the construction of teams, their co-construction of tacit knowledge to make sense of the organization, and their use of emergent technologies. The authors of this chapter posit an alternative research perspective –that of the communities of practice construct – allows a fuller understanding of the relationships of power and trust in team behaviors and processes. The communities-of-practice model provides an avenue to examine the intricate dance that trust and power perform in virtual environments, with people as the focal point. It is how people interact with each other, with in technology, to be or become successful virtually that is the focus of this chapter. The authors explore trust and power in virtual or blended work environments using a reflexive autoethnographic narrative, comprised of three case studies, grounded in the larger context of the organizational communication literature.

Chapter 15

This chapter focuses on a multi-institutional shared curricular-build project (2009) out of Kansas State University, Johnson County Community College, Kansas City Kansas Community College, and Dodge City Community College. This project involved the building of a range of digital learning objects for modules for an online course that will be taught at the various institutions in both online and hybrid formats. This collaboration is unique in that it brought together experts from cross-functional domains (from both the empirical sciences and the humanities) for an interdisciplinary freshman level course. The team collaborated virtually through computer mediated communications and built e-learning based on instructional design precepts. The curriculum was built to the standards of the public health domain field, the Quality Matters™ rubric (for e-learning standards), federal accessibility guidelines, intellectual property laws, and technological interoperability standards (with the curriculum to be delivered through three disparate learning / course management systems). This chapter focuses on the sociotechnical structuring of a local virtual work ecology to support this "Pathways to Public Health" project.

Chapter 16

Marinita Schumacher, Ecole Centrale Paris, France
Julie Stal-Le Cardinal, Ecole Centrale Paris, France
Jean-Claude Bocquet, Ecole Centrale Paris, France

Virtual instruments and tools are future trends in Engineering which are due to the growing complexity of engineering tasks. Individuals who are working in Virtual Teams must be equipped with spanning competencies that provide a basis for Virtual Team building. In the first step this chapter gives a broad insight to the field of Competence Management and Virtual Teams. The second step responds to the need of a method of Competence Management to build Virtual Teams that are active in virtual design projects in the area of New Product Development (NPD).

Preface

Virtual work is rapidly becoming an essential element in contemporary organizations. The traditional brick and mortar organizational structure is rapidly shifting to one that is dislocated, virtual and geographically dispersed. While the traditional structural work paradigm is characterized by face-to-face work with robust physically-present task and social interactions; this structure is rapidly surrendering to a more disjointed, rarely physically present, internet-based connected structure. This new work paradigm relies less upon physicality, but with a greater reliance on connectivity. Connectivity, both technological and interpersonal, is imperative to virtual work.

The increasing costs associated with working today are forcing organizations to rethink how work is accomplished across all industries and sectors. Due to the significant cost savings associated with virtual work (e.g. real estate, travel, supplies, space, capital expenses, etc.), organizations are embracing this new remotely-connected work structure. Organizations are recasting their thoughts about work design, employees, organizational place, space, and its members. Although the traditional ways of working with tethered employees to a physical campus or building, is still the most common organizational structure. These hierarchical physical structures are being replaced by a leaner, swifter, organic, time-sensitive, globally-focused, team-based, electronic aesthetic. This shifting organizational paradigm centers on the expanding and dominant use of information technologies as the key structural bedrock for virtual organizational functioning.

The virtual work paradigm has been spurred by local, national and global economics, societal changes with the use of technology, employees' attitudes of increased individual agency, employee pressure for greater work autonomy, deliberate focus on work-life balance, and reliance for "on-demand" services rather than the standard business operating hours. Intertwine these factors with rapid globalization, outsourcing, right-sizing, offshoring, cross-cultural and (inter)national collaborations and the ability to connect remote individuals and teams, it leaves no doubt as to why the world of virtual work is fertile ground for applied and academic study.

Organizations are increasing their integration of communication technologies to facilitate the growing appetite by consumers, employees, stockholders and various constituents groups to work smarter, faster, more efficiently and with greater levels of information access. This hunger, contrasted with decreasing resources and calls for greater levels of accountability, creates an inherent conflict between various organizational stakeholders. Although the virtual work paradigm is an intriguing structural mandate that creates significant opportunities and new work arrangements. Virtual work also poses significant dilemmas and organizational issues, for organizations and employees working in this electronic terrain.

This book provides entrée into the exploration of the opportunities, benefits and costs associated with virtual work. The sixteen chapters that follow will address several communicative, relational and practical issues associated with virtual work. The chapters reflect a broad range of conceptual, theoretical, empirical, methodological and pragmatic points of view. In developing this book, my hope was to facilitate spirited interdisciplinary and international conversations across industries and institutions among academic, management and professionals about the act, process and implications of virtual work. By drawing attention to the communicative, relational and pragmatic concerns operating in the world of virtual work, this book offers a different opportunity for academics and organizational leaders to engage in the ongoing conversations about the changing nature of work driven by technology and the future of organizations as we tumble through the information-age.

DEFINING VIRTUAL WORK

In centering this book on issues associated with virtual work, I am making clear distinctions between the *virtual workplace, working virtually* and *virtual work*. These concepts are certainly interrelated, interchangeable and often overlap in their descriptions. However, I think it is critical to identify, define, deconstruct, extrapolate and distinguish these concepts by their functions, usage and intent within the organization by organizational members.

First, the virtual workplace is broadly defined as a non-traditional workplace that is not located in the same physical space. Easily conceptualized, the virtual workplace is operationalized as two or more work spaces that are connected by internet-based technology, without regard to the bounded space or geographical co-located structures indicative of the traditional workplace. The virtual workplace allows employees to engage in work tasks away from an organizational campus. These tasks may be accomplished individually, collaboratively, but most often remotely. Employees are able to communicate and interact with one another regardless of their location in the world. The traditional workplace characterized by physical desks, corrals, telephones, offices and break rooms are replaced by smart phones, instant messaging, electronic mail, internet access and teleconferencing software. I consider the virtual workplace an organizational "noun" due to its alternative work arrangement. The virtual workplace, like traditional workplaces or objects, may be objectively observed and described. There is no inherent value placed on the virtual workplace initially; it is just another way of doing ones work through a different configuration. The virtual workplace serves as a structural counter to the traditional workplace because employees are not physically tethered to a desk or cubicle. However, they are certainly tethered remotely through the electronic nature of the virtual workplace. A virtual workplace is increasing because it decreases unnecessary costs by integrating technological processes, people processes and online processes.

On the other hand, I consider working virtually an organizational "verb" due to its inherent action-oriented position. Working virtually indicates "doing" something. The most common term used in working virtually is teleworking. Teleworking has increased dramatically as communication technologies have become more advanced and less expensive (Leonardi, Treem and Jackson, 2010). Much like the virtual workplace, working virtually is an alternative work arrangement. One can work traditionally (face-to-face constant interaction) or work virtually (minimal physical face-to-face contact with peers, supervisors and subordinates). Working virtually is not necessarily value-free. One works virtually due to a number of antecedent and motivational issues: reduction in overhead, decreasing the costs of real estate, flexibility for greater work-life balance, right-sizing, becoming a leaner organization by extracting the costs of doing business associated with the physical workplace, moving toward a "greener" workspace by minimizing the carbon footprint via working virtually.

Finally, the concept of virtual work is much more complex to define and describe. I consider virtual work as both an organizational noun and verb. There are inherently objective and subjective components associated with virtual work. Virtual work is a value-laden, politically rich, nuanced form of organizational functioning that has significant ecological considerations and implications. Virtual work is complicated by the constant energy given to tasks, social concerns, informal and formal communication, labor (emotional, psychological and physical), impression management, face-saving techniques, virtual dramaturgy, managing up and down, motivating employees, rewarding and punishing virtual work behaviors, decision-making, socializing, organizational change, diversity issues, leading a virtual work team/group, etc. In essence, virtual work is work! In light of the electronic terrain, this virtual work is structurally complex due to the lack of nonverbal cues that are heavily relied upon and taken for granted in traditional face-to-face work arrangements.

Virtual work is much more than dislocated space. Virtual work is much more than just "doing" something. Virtual work is a state of being in a dislocated space operating under a new and emerging (and always changing) social contract between the organization and its members. Virtual work is political, social, economic, cultural, financial, legal and ecologically paradoxical. Virtual work can be viewed as tacit and overt, confusing and stable, local and global, rational and irrational, dynamic and static and fraught with similar tensions that enable and inhibit this emerging work arrangement. This book offers the first social scientific/humanistic definition of virtual work.

The title of this book, *Communication, Relationships and Practices,* is inspired by the socio-humanistic intersections between organizations, technology and humans that have typically been underserved in the research literature. By focusing our attention on extant communication theories, relational concepts and practices underpinning virtual work in contemporary society, my hope is that individuals will have more robust decision and sense making models about their engagement and management of this technological enterprise. Indeed, this is a great time to study organizations and how individuals engage and interact within and between them. I hope that this book adds a distinct perspective to the various conversations about organization and their rapid expansion in the virtual work terrain.

ORGANIZATION OF THE BOOK

This book is organized into three sections with 16 chapters. The three sections are: communication in virtual work, relationships in virtual work and practices in virtual work. The sixteen chapters embedded in the sections will shed light on the opportunities, dilemmas, complexities and costs associated with virtual work.

Section 1: Communication in Virtual Work

The chapters in this section represent how communication explicitly and implicitly operates in virtual work. Communication is an embedded and essential theme in organizations and virtual work is no exception. The following five chapters illuminate the role and impact of communication in virtual work.

Chapter 1: Gibbs, Scott, Hoon Kim, & Kyong Lee in their chapter *"Examining Tensions in Telework Polices"*, studies workplace policies related to virtual work, with a specific focus on telework polices. The authors conducted a content analysis of 35 state government polices that revealed that telework polices have underlying tensions between autonomy and control; as well as flexibility and rigidity. They found that most of the policies used these tensions productively by providing enough ambiguity for individual and organizational competing interests to co-exist.

Chapter 2: Harrison and Williams analyzed conflict in three inter-organizational teams in their study *"Communication, Structural Links, and Conflict in Three Inter-Organizational Virtual Collaborations."* Their chapter identifies the various types of conflict in virtual teams, the role communication plays in these conflicts and they contextualize these conflicts in the social domain.

Chapter 3: In their chapter *"Online Teaching as Virtual Work in the New (Political) Economy"*, Schwartzman and Carlone critically examines the hidden costs of academic labor in online teaching in higher education. The authors explore the boundaries demarcating work from personal time; the relative invisibility of online labor, the cost-rewards associated with online instruction and the illusory empowerment of online students as consumers.

Chapter 4: In *"The Ethical Implications of the Virtual Work Environment"*, Byers examine four major ethical factors inherent to virtual work. The four factors are culture, trust, cross-cultural diversity and monitoring. The author advances a normative approach in this chapter by suggesting that the negative ethical consequences of virtual work can be countered by following appropriate guidelines.

Chapter 5: Long, Goodman and Clow in their chapter *"The Electronic Panopticon: Organizational Surveillance in Virtual Work"* explore the role surveillance in virtual work. The authors examine the theoretical underpinnings of the panopticon, work place surveillance, the practice of surveillance in virtual work ethical concerns of virtual surveillance and the implications of this virtual work management strategy.

Section 2: Relationships in Virtual Work

The chapters in this section cover relational issues in virtual work.

Chapter 6: Zhang and Poole in their chapter *"Virtual Team Identity Construction and Boundary Maintenance"* reports the results of a multiple case study which investigated how virtual teams appropriated multiple media to facilitate the construction of group identity and manage group boundaries. The chapter focuses on relationship within and between virtual teams. The authors found five processes that help shape group identity.

Chapter 7: In *"Temporary Virtual Teams: An Empirical Examination of Team Development"*, Connaughton, Williams, Linvill, O'Connor and Hayes highlights two common models of team development as a basis to illustrate the dearth of scholarship in virtual team development. Additionally, the authors present their findings from a study of global virtual team and advance a research agenda for scholars and pragmatic platform for practitioners working within and between virtual teams.

Chapter 8: *"Status and Influence Processes in Virtual Teams and Mobile Collaboration"* examine the effects of technological mechanisms of collaboration on the communication processes, relationships and practices of virtual teams. Ravlin reviews various theoretical approaches and prior empirical findings and posits that status processes and influence are maintained many times at the detriment of team effectiveness.

Chapter 9: In their chapter *"Sense of Community in Professional Virtual Communities"* Blanchard, Askay and Frear develop a model of how professional virtual communities facilitate a perception of community. Through support exchange, development of group identity and leveraging group norms, the strength of professional communities are realized with increased occupational identification, occupational commitment, expanding professional networks and increased employee performance.

Chapter 10: Punyanunt-Carter and Hernandez closely examines a critical organizational leadership element of mentoring in their chapter *"Virtual Mentoring."* The authors suggest that virtual mentoring is becoming the more preferred way to initiate mentor and protégé relationships in organizations due to time and space constraints. The authors provide limitations and implications of virtual mentoring in this chapter.

Chapter 11: Long, Boughton and Widener explore the implicit and tacit role of organizational politics in their chapter *"Organizational Politics in Virtual Work"*. The authors examine how the study of politics has evolved over time. Additionally, the authors illustrate the relationship between politics and authority, power and influence. The authors conclude that organizational politics are exacerbated in virtual work rather than attenuated.

Section 3: Practices in Virtual Work

The chapters in this section cover practices in virtual work.

Chapter 12: Yungbluth and Hart examine how power dynamics are manifested in virtual work in their chapter *"The Amplification of Power Dynamics in Virtual Work."* The authors present two case studies to illustrate decisions regarding the implementation of information and communication technologies and the implications of those choices. The cases presented reveal a complex view of how organizations seeking to increase participation through technology may find that their decisions actually stifle participation and active communication.

Chapter 13: In this chapter, Gilchrist explores engineers' perceptions of relational limitations inherent to virtual work. *"Engineers' Perceptions of Relational Limitations Intrinsic to Virtual Work"* studies engineers enrolled in a communication course whose primary work consists of virtual work. Results of the study reveal that virtual work is viewed as convenient and easy-to-use. However, there are several relational limitations associated with using this medium. Gilchrist additionally reports how engineers supplement their virtual work through a number of strategic methods.

Chapter 14: In *"Power and Trust in the Virtual Workplace: Team Development as Communities of Practice"*, Hanson, Engel and Gobes-Ryan suggest utilizing a communities of practice construct, an alternative research perspective, in understanding the construction of virtual teams and the power and trust issues in team behaviors and processes. They advance the communities of practice model through the use of a reflexive autoethnographic narrative, comprised of three case studies.

Chapter 15: Hai-Jew focuses on a multi-institutional common curricular-build project between four Midwest institutions in his chapter *"Structuring a Local Virtual Work Ecology for a Collaborative, Multi-Institutional Higher Educational Project: A Case Study."* This chapter illustrates through the case study approach how bringing together experts from cross-functional domains via computer mediated technologies assisted in building an e-learning platform based on instructional design precepts. The chapter focuses on the socio-technical aspects important in structuring virtual work ecology.

Chapter 16: In *"Aided System of Competence Management for Virtual Team Building Adapted to Specific Needs of Design Projects"*, Schumacher, Stal-Le Cardinal and Bocquet present an Aided Competence Management for Virtual Team Building System (Aided CMVTB System) that permits it to be adapted not only to organizations but to design projects without a physical structure. This chapter gives broad insight to the field of Competence Management and Virtual Teams.

REFERENCES

Leonardi, P. M., Treem, J. W., & Jackson, M. H. (2010). The connectivity paradox: Using technology to both decrease and increase perceptions of distance in distributed work arrangements. *Journal of Applied Communication Research, 38*, 85-105.

Acknowledgment

There are several people that I would like to acknowledge who were involved in this process. I would like to thank all of the authors and contributors to this book for their insightful and well executed chapters.

Many thanks to my editorial board: Dr. Brenda J. Allen-University of Denver; Dr. Mark P. Orbe-Western Michigan University; Dr. Clifton W. Scott- The University of North Carolina at Charlotte; Dr. Tyler Harrison-Purdue University; Dr. Stacey Connaughton-Purdue University; and Dr. Gaelle Picherit-Duthler-Zehid University, UAE.

I would like to thank the numerous reviewers who blind reviewed each of the chapters and offered insightful and instructive feedback to the contributors. Special thanks to my research team- Rachel Widener, M.A., Richie Goodman, M.A., and Jamon Flowers, M.A.. I would also like to thank Dr. Richard Leeman and Dr. Steven Rogelberg for their important insights on this project.

The support of the Department of Communication Studies and Organizational Science Program at the University of North Carolina at Charlotte has been invaluable in completing this project. The intellectual and interdisciplinary climate at this vibrant institution makes working a pleasure.

Special thanks to IGI Global and the competent and energetic team with whom I worked closely with to complete this project. A special thanks to Elizabeth Ardner and Joel Gamon for their expert guidance and support throughout this process.

Finally, and most importantly, I wish to thank my family and friends for their ongoing and tireless support of me in all of my endeavors and lending a willful ear and support to this project.

Shawn D. Long
University of North Carolina at Charlotte, USA

Section 1
Communication in Virtual Work

Chapter 1
Examining Tensions in Telework Policies

Jennifer L. Gibbs
Rutgers University, USA

Craig R. Scott
Rutgers University, USA

Young Hoon Kim
Rutgers University, USA

Sun Kyong Lee
Rutgers University, USA

ABSTRACT

This chapter examines workplace policies related to virtual work, with a specific focus on telework policies. Such policies are important to successful telework in communicating rules and expectations and providing a basis for negotiation between individual teleworkers and their employers. A content analysis of 35 state government telework policies revealed that such policies are characterized by two major tensions between autonomy and control and between flexibility and rigidity. The first tension relates to issues such as individual versus organizational responsibility for monitoring performance, providing equipment, and ensuring physical and data security, while the second tension relates to the standardization of working hours and eligibility criteria, whether rules are clear or left ambiguous, and the degree of work/family balance. Although explicit contradictions between stated benefits and realities of telework implementation may be problematic, most of the policies used tension productively by providing enough ambiguity to allow for competing individual and organizational interests to co-exist. Practical implications for teleworkers and their managers are suggested.

INTRODUCTION

There is little debate about the growing importance of virtual work (e.g., telework, virtual teams) in organizations. In some cases these virtual forms represent a type of alternative work arrangement driven predominantly by employee needs and in other instances they reflect management efforts to leverage global expertise in dealing with organi-

DOI: 10.4018/978-1-61520-979-8.ch001

zational challenges—but in all situations, virtual forms present several key communication challenges for organizations and their members. From a communication perspective, there has been an interest in issues such as communication technology use (Scott & Timmerman, 1999; Timmerman & Scott, 2006), cross-cultural communication (Cramton & Hinds, 2004; Gibson & Gibbs, 2006; Grosse, 2002), distanced leadership (Connaughton & Daly, 2004; 2005), fostering identification and shared identity (Hinds & Mortensen, 2005; Sivunen, 2006; Wiesenfeld, Raghuram, & Garud, 1999), and creating trust (Jarvenpaa, Shaw, & Staples, 2004; Walther & Bunz, 2005) among virtual workers and teams (for a review, see Gibbs, Nekrassova, Grushina, & Abdul Wahab, 2008).

One additional communication topic that has not yet received adequate attention concerns the policies and guidelines surrounding virtual work. Organizations have historically developed policies surrounding issues such as operating procedures, governance, member rights and duties. One function of socialization efforts in most organizations (see Jablin, 2001) is to introduce new members to the formal policies and guidelines of the organization. Even though important informal communication may not always align with these formal policies—which sometimes go unread or are even unknown to organizational members—one should not underestimate the importance of these policies. They do communicate official guidelines and rules relevant to rewards/sanctions so that members know how to act; thus, they represent a type of directive in Speech Act Theory (see Putnam & Fairhurst, 2001). Even when unknown or unfamiliar, they are legally forceful. They are often produced in response to organizational practices and may in turn shape various practices. A wide range of organizational members are involved in the creation of such documents—and an even greater percentage are impacted by them. They may also serve as a starting point for ongoing

dialogue about issues or even as something to be communicatively resisted.

Although the growth in information and communication technologies (ICTs) has led to increased development of policies governing communication—occurring in various types of organizations, with policies developed by multiple stakeholders, and producing online policies that are discussed and updated with greater regularity than ever before—it is not clear how extensive or adequate those policies addressing virtual work are. Regardless, such policies may matter greatly. The success of teleworking, for example, largely depends on whether organizations effectively communicate its necessity and benefits to their employees, which can be done partially by "the provision of carefully crafted organizational policies" (Perez, Sanchez, & Carnicer, 2003, p. 68). However, when policies do not communicate effectively, are not carefully crafted, or otherwise suggest inconsistencies, virtual work practices are almost certainly influenced. As we attempt to illustrate in this chapter through the use of a dialectical framework applied to virtual work (Gibbs, 2009), these policies regularly reveal contradictions and tensions that challenge virtual workers and the organizations for which they work.

Thus, one objective of this chapter is to establish the importance of workplace policies related to virtual work, focusing most specifically on telework policies. We then describe the methods used to analyze a set of telework policies from U.S. state governments—which allows us to meet our second objective of describing policies and articulating tensions that exist within and across them. Finally, we seek to offer some scholarly and practical implications from this work. Better understanding of the nature of virtual work policies as a form of communication is essential for describing virtual work behaviors, organizational rewards, and several other workplace dynamics.

WORKPLACE POLICIES

Although most of the interest in what is broadly called communication and information policy research has centered on "how regulators, governments, and public policies shape communication-information industries and social practices" (Mueller & Lentz, 2004, p. 155), this type of large scale policy research has not examined policies in the more local for-profit, nonprofit, or government workplaces where communication policies are developed and enforced. Our focus is to examine those workplace policies as organizational messages (see Scott & Choi, 2009) and to focus on the content of those documents as they reveal and create tensions. This is consistent with Corman's (2006) call for organizational communication scholars to focus more on messages. It also aligns with a recognized tradition of examining written forms of communication produced by the organization and its members as an important means of constituting organizational life (see Cheney, 1983).

Not only do work-related policies represent a form of organizational communication, but they also regularly address communication rights and responsibilities. Prior studies have examined communication policies in contexts such as school board meetings (Castor, 2007), work-family benefits (Kirby & Krone, 2002), and school meal programs (Legreco, 2007). For example, adopting structuration theory and using discourse tracing methods, Legreco examined the talk, texts, and larger discourse that operate during a major policy change in the state of Arizona school meal programs designed to promote healthier eating habits. By showing how different "policies are formulated through dialogue and deliberation, implemented through negotiation between consumer and producer, and evaluated against other initiatives and programs" (p. iii), Legreco's research highlights the important communicative role played by policies in the organization of everyday experiences. Kirby and Krone also used a structurational approach to examine ways in which organizational members' discourse about the issues addressed by formally stated work-family policies may work to undermine the actual use of such policies.

ICT Policies

More related to virtual forms of work, policy-related research on new ICTs exists as well and most commonly examines privacy policies (see D'Urso, 2006; Townsend & Bennett, 2003), telecommunication policies (see Whitman, Townsend, & Alberts, 1999), and/or acceptable use policies (see Barnes, 2002; Simbulan, 2004). However, also included here are various security policies, online access guides, records retention policies, netiquette standards, computer ethics codes, Internet use policies, technology management guidelines, intellectual property/copyright/trademark policies, technology checkout and personal use guidelines, and more. As Scott and Choi (2009) argue, concerns about issues such as cyberslacking and records retention—especially in light of the Sarbanes-Oxley legislation following the Enron scandal (Lange & Nelson, 2005)—have resulted in various ICT policies becoming increasingly common in the workplace (American Management Association, 2006). Despite this, surprisingly little research has focused on these messages directly.

Organizations have now begun to actively draft such policies, partly in response to perceived misuse of such tools in organizations (Zetter, 2006). Indeed, Simmers (2002) suggests explicit and clearly communicated policy is key in addressing issues related to loss of intellectual property, sexual harassment lawsuits, productivity losses due to online activity, security threats, and network overload. The 2006 Workplace E-Mail, Instant Messaging & Blog Survey from the American Management Association (2006) revealed that 76% of organizations have e-mail usage and content policies, with another 68% using policy to control personal e-mail. Thirty-one percent of organizations have instant messaging policy in place. In each case, these numbers reflect notable increases from surveys done in previous years.

Thus, organizational policies specifically related to ICT use have become increasingly common in recent years. Although research on them from any organizational perspective remains relatively limited, it does exist. For example, Pollach's (2006) study of privacy policies from 50 commercial websites notes that such policies often omit critical information and fail to communicate in a transparent manner. Simmers (2002) reports case studies of eight diverse organizations, each of which illustrates the important role of Internet usage policies—but also the delicate balance in how restrictive they are and the necessity to communicate such directives clearly. Simbulan (2004) examined employee's perceptions of their organization's Internet use policy—noting that policies must be clear and that specific time frames were needed for personal use of technology. In one of the more extensive works in this area, Siau, Nah, and Teng (2002) examined the acceptable Internet use policies (AIUP) of three groups of organizations (i.e., educational institutions, Internet service provider, and non-Internet service providers). These authors conclude that policies were generally not comprehensive and contained a number of gray areas. Collectively, these studies suggest both the relevance of this type of policy research and the potential for such policies to be problematic.

TELEWORK POLICY

Telework

One set of policies clearly linked to virtual forms is what are known as teleworking or telecommuting policies. The terms telecommuting and teleworking have often been used interchangeably (Ellison, 1999) to refer to using ICTs to perform work 'at a distance' (Mokhtarian, Salomon, & Choo, 2005), but they were distinguished by

Nilles (1998) who defined teleworking as "any form of substitution of information technologies for work-related travel" and telecommuting as "periodic work out of the principal office, one or more days per week, either at home, a client's site, or in a telework center" (p. 1). Whereas telecommuting emphasizes a reduction in physical travel, telework is a broader category that emphasizes the crucial role of ICTs in reducing or overcoming spatial and temporal limitations in performing work (Garrett & Danziger, 2007; Halford, 2005). We focus on the broader term 'telework' here, and define it as an alternative work arrangement in which workers are allowed to perform their tasks elsewhere, usually outside conventional offices using communication technologies to interact with others (Bailey & Kurland, 2002; Baruch, 2001). This academic definition is also in line with that of the Telework Enhancement Act of 2009, which provided a formal definition of telework as a "work arrangement in which an employee regularly performs officially assigned duties at home or other worksites geographically convenient to the residence of the employee" (The Telework Enhancement Act of 2009, p.2).

The need to study telework policy is heightened by the number of people engaged in this form of virtual work. Even with the significant difficulty in accurately counting teleworkers (Mokhtarian et al., 2005), low end estimates suggest it includes 8.6 million U.S. households (Makower, 2009). Other marketing research reported a jump to 17.2 million in late 2008 (WorldatWork, 2009) and estimated that another 29 million telecommuters will enter the U.S. workforce between 2009 and 2016, totaling to nearly 43% of all U.S. employees (Suitecommute, nd). A recent agreement between the U.S. General Services Administration and the American Federation of Government Employees regarding a new national telework policy supporting broad use of telework by federal employees (McCrehin, 2008) could further raise those numbers.

The current numbers and potential growth of these virtual workers—not to mention variations in how often they telework and from where they do remote work—create several opportunities and challenges for organizations and their members (both those who are and are not teleworking). One of those concerns development of policy for such programs, which can be viewed as attempts to formalize and clarify expectations and practices regarding teleworking.

Practitioner Perspectives on Policy Development

A number of trade publications as well as telework consultants and groups have specifically pointed to the need for policy. "As more and more employees clamor for the ability to telecommute, it is imperative for companies to have in place a viable telecommuting policy" (Hoskins, 2006, p. 1). For some, the focus of such policies is on minimizing risk and liability for the employer (Prince, 2000; Suitecommute, nd; Thibodeaux, 2003). "The more precise you can be, within the law, the better you will be at controlling your risk exposures," claims one expert (Prince, p. 22). For others, the emphasis is on cost and productivity issues (Donaldson, 2002; Mills-Senn, 2006). "To avoid those problems [performance issues], work-from-home policies must be well-defined" (Mills-Senn, p. 24).

In fact, industry practitioners and other telework experts suggest a wide range of issues that might be covered in telework policies (see Hoskins, 2006; Prince, 2000; Suitecommute, nd). Hoskins suggests these fall into three categories: work concerns, location concerns, and policy concerns. *Work concerns* may include amount of work expected, setting hours for work and tracking time/attendance, measuring performance, and communication expectations. *Location concerns* include who owns and provides equipment, who covers what costs, safety issues, and securing intellectual property. *Policy concerns* address eligibil-

ity requirements, termination requirements, and number of days one can/must telework. Of course, other issues such as arrangements for child and pet care cut across categories. Thus, developing sound policy that appropriately covers a range of issues in this growing area likely presents many organizations with a challenge.

Scholarly Perspectives on Policy Development

Scholarly efforts to examine policy as it relates to teleworkers take several different forms. For some, the connections have been at broader societal levels where social policies encouraging telework are examined (World Wide Waves, 1999). In other cases, the focus has been on policies related to the environment (Nelson, Safirova, & Walls, 2007), IT/broadband (Trkman, Jerman-Blazic, & Turk, 2008), and trade unions (Horner & Day, 1995) as they might then influence telework practices. Baker, Moon, and Ward (2006) specifically examined workplace accommodation policies related to telework, noting that "less examined are the policy and regulatory barriers preventing effective telework outcomes for people with disabilities" (p. 424).

In general, however, specific scholarly examinations of actual telework policies appear extremely rare. Igbaria and Tan's (1998) edited volume on the virtual workplace does not include the term *policy* in the index, and none of the several specific chapters examining telework look specifically at policy. McCloskey and Igbaria's (1998) chapter providing a detailed review of existing empirical pieces suggests no prior focus on policy, although some findings had implications for policy. As a more recent illustration of that, Major, Verive, and Joice's (2008) examination of telework and dependent care produced agency policy recommendations from federal home-based teleworkers they surveyed. These included a desire for more flexibility in types and arrangements, permitting dependent care tasks while teleworking, improving fairness and consistency related to telework eligibility, and training managers how to accept and support teleworkers.

These recommendations for policy, like much of what is suggested by telework consultants and trade publications, are about specific workplace policies that directly impact teleworkers and other organizational members. Indeed, Baker et al. (2006) conclude that an appropriate focus for telework-related research is not on broad societal policies, but on more localized ones:

…available evidence suggests that telework at present remains a practice customized to the needs and capabilities of a particular employer and employee. …In particular, relatively little is known about the range of current telework practices and policies among employers, and research gaps persist in the documentation of actual implementation outcomes. (p. 426)

The research reported here attempts to provide some of that focus. In looking specifically at telework policies, we also recognize the complexity and challenges of constructing such communication. As Major et al. (2008) and Kirby and Krone (2002) both note, policies and practices are not always aligned. We suspect in part that this relates to potential inconsistencies, contradictions, uncertainties, and other variations within and across telework policies. We turn next to a framework useful for analyzing these sorts of organizational tensions.

DIALECTICAL TENSIONS IN TELEWORK AND TELEWORK POLICIES

A growing body of literature focuses on articulating contradictions and tensions in various organizational settings (Pepper & Larson, 2006; Poole & Van de Ven, 1989; Seo, Putnam, & Bartunek, 2004; Tracy, 2004; Trethewey & Ashcraft, 2004). Grounded in Bakhtin's (1981) dialogism, dialectical theory was originally applied to the

study of interpersonal relationships (Baxter & Montgomery, 1996), but it has been extended to organizational settings as well and recent studies have focused on communicative tensions in contexts as varied as correctional facilities (Tracy, 2004), information technology use (Jian, 2007) and family farm succession planning (Pitts, Fowler, Kaplan, Nussbaum, & Becker, 2009).

A framework of organizational tensions is helpful in analyzing the necessary contradictions and dualities that arise whenever competing goals and interests exist in organizations (Tretheway & Ashcraft, 2004). Tensions or dualities are defined as bi-polar opposites that often work against each other; rather than being simple alternatives between mutually exclusive options, the choice to focus on one pole elicits tension and makes it difficult to enact both ends of the continuum at once (Seo et al., 2004). Rather than regarding tensions or contradictions as anomalies or exceptions, a tensional approach situates tensions and ambiguity – rather than clarity, stability, consensus, and rationality – as normal, routine features of organizational life (Eisenberg, 1984; Tretheway & Ashcraft; Weick, 1979). Further, rather than necessarily being problematic features of organizing that need to be reconciled or eliminated, tensions may be productive in that focusing on contradictions rather than consistency helps surface inconsistencies in our logic and assumptions and presents researchers with "opportunities to discover different assumptions, shift perspectives, pose problems in fundamentally different ways, and focus on different research questions" (Poole & Van de Ven, 1989, p. 564). Research has distinguished dialectical tensions from simple contradictions (which involve an either-or choice between two opposing alternatives) and paradoxes (which are dilemmas that require impossible choices between mutually exclusive or non-existent options). While simple contradictions and pragmatic paradoxes have been found to limit options and constrain action (Tracy, 2004), complementary dialectics are more productive in that they generate new, creative options and transform or transcend the given opposition by enabling the merging of opposites through embracing both alternatives as "both-and" options (Putnam & Boys, 2006; Tracy).

Processes of global and virtual organizing, in particular, have been found to be fraught with tensions due to the complex nature of virtual work and the fact that virtual workers are embedded in multiple organizational, geographical, and cultural structures (Gibbs, 2009). Gibbs identified three major tensions in interaction in a global software team: autonomy versus connectedness, inclusion versus exclusion, and empowerment versus disempowerment, and found that such tensions were managed through responses of selection, transcendence, and withdrawal.

Tensions in Telework

Participatory and democratic work practices and structures have been characterized as fraught with communicative tensions (Stohl & Cheney, 2001). As such, telework comprises one such high-involvement participatory organizational arrangement. The popular discourse of telework often touts its alleged benefits to individual employees, organizations, and society more broadly. News articles and reports on telecommuting repeatedly cite organizational benefits such as reduced employee turnover and increased productivity as well as individual benefits of higher job satisfaction (Barett, 2008; Goluboff, 2006; Sedgewick, 2009). Telecommuting is also associated with societal benefits such as reduced commuting costs (Makower, 2009) and is often regarded as a strategy for combating high gas prices, reducing dependence on foreign oil, and easing road congestion (Barett). Similar claims are made in the academic literature about reduced traffic and increased time and energy efficiency (Novaco, Kilewer, & Broquet, 1991) and greater productivity as well as many individual level benefits such as enhanced worker autonomy, flexibility, work-life balance, and work-family relationships

(e.g., DuBrin, 1991; Golden, 2006; Kurland & Bailey, 1999; Lautsch, Kossek, & Eaton, 2009). Employees' greater autonomy and flexibility in choosing where and when work takes place are also thought to have a positive impact on job satisfaction, productivity, and health conditions (e.g., reduced stress) (Gajendran & Harrison, 2007; Golden, Veiga, & Simsek, 2006).

Such unqualified benefits are not always empirically observed, however. For example, many indicators point to the fact that travel and congestion continue to increase (rather than decrease) along with the rise of telecommunication (Mokhtarian, 2009). Other studies have challenged the promised benefits of telework by showing that such anticipated results are not always evident in reality or that conflicting consequences are evident. Perhaps these conflicting findings are the result of inherent contradictions in telecommuting. Telecommuting has been identified as inherently paradoxical (Hylmo & Buzzanell, 2002); for example, many organizations claim to be supportive of telework yet fail to widely embrace it as part of organizational life (Khaifa & Davidson, 2000). Further, telework can function as both success and threat to organizational practices and individual outcomes. On one hand, it can enable organizations to be more flexible, reduce costs, and respond to changing workforce needs, and enable teleworkers to better manage personal and work demands (Pinsonneault & Boisvert, 2001). On the other hand, telecommuting poses a threat by dissolving attachments based on face-to-face communication and leaving teleworkers socially isolated and physically, temporally, and psychologically disconnected (Golden & Veiga, 2005; Hylmo & Buzzanell).

Telework has been framed as a mysterious alternative work arrangement in which questions arise as to what teleworkers are doing (and whether they are working) and how to maintain relationships without routine interactions (Hylmo & Buzzanell, 2002). Hylmo and Buzzanell's study of telecommuters revealed a variety of tensions and paradoxes: teleworkers routinely worked more hours than in-house employees and faced a paradox of control as the systems that were designed to allow for more autonomy ended up limiting their freedom and flexibility, as well as being marginalized by in-house employees due to their lack of physical presence. Further, telecommuters expressed confusion over how to do their job, how to advance in the organization and how to maintain relationships with co-workers and they faced a tension in being expected to perform well without sufficient resources (p. 344). Another empirical study of teleworkers identified a tension between perceived organizational demand versus personal life objectives, which produced a secondary tension between autonomy/comfort and control/anxiety (Jian & Rosiek, 2009).

Tensions in Policies

Work analyzing organizational policies has also found them to reflect tensions. An analysis of 300 U.S. state government policies regarding the use of ICTs revealed nine tensions related to issues of anonymity and identifiability (Scott & Choi, 2009). These tensions were largely associated with the revealing of personal information and dealt with issues such as privacy and confidentiality, identification of personal information, use of names/passwords, anonymity, and signing of documents. For example, policy messages suggested that anonymity was to be prohibited, but not ignored; that personal information should not be collected, but that information should be collected that is personally identifying; and that user identity should be protected, but that users should be identifiable. The contradictory messages contained in these policy documents illustrate the complexity of such policy and the challenges associated with developing reasonable ICT policy due to disagreements over issues such as what constitutes personally identifying information.

Similarly, we suspect some of the tensions surrounding telework generally may both result from and lead to problematic telework policies. Despite the demonstrated importance of tensions in global and virtual organizing, telework, and in organizational policies about ICTs, research has yet to examine tensions in telework policy. This chapter represents an attempt to fill this gap, as we address the following research question: *What types of tensions are evident in U.S. state telework policies?*

METHODS

Among many possible virtual work policies, we looked at U.S. state government telework policies (including the District of Columbia). The data collection for this study was part of a larger policy-based research project conducted in the spring of 2008 in which publicly available ICT policies were collected for analysis on a number of research topics. This policy database was composed of a variety of ICT-related policies—including, but not limited to, those addressing telework. As Scott and Choi (2009) argue, state governments seem an appropriate context for such work because (a) policy may be better developed here given constitutional protections applicable to public employees, (b) they represent sizable employers who have historically made use of ICTs, and (c) as a public entity their policies are more readily available online. Furthermore, many state governments have regularly offered telework to some degree for the past few decades.

We found 35 states having some sort of telework policy through an extensive search for the web-published policy documents. We included a variety of search terms including telework, telecommuting, flexible and alternative work arrangements, flextime, and flexplace, in order to capture as many related policies as possible. We recognize that these terms are not synonymous but wanted to cast a wide net in light of the varying ways in which telecommuting has been labeled and defined (Mokhtarian et al., 2005). Most state governments had their search functions linked to the Google search, but when we could not locate any relevant policy from a state government website, we tried an independent search from the Google website using the same search terms with the name of the state.[1] If we could not locate any policy documents after at least 30 minutes to an hour searching for one, we concluded that the particular state government did not provide them specifically on its website.[2]

Analysis

We employed a qualitative content analysis to examine the identified telework policy documents of the state governments, and three co-authors openly and independently coded those policy documents using ATLAS.ti software. The software is particularly designed for coding sizable amounts of qualitative data; it lets individual coders access documents and code the content by any unit of analysis (i.e., word, sentence, or paragraph) electronically. All three coders initially coded several policies in common in order to establish major coding categories and ensure consistency in coding. We then discussed these major codes and repetitive themes found in those documents. Based on the discussion, the coding framework was established and all 35 state policies were divided among the coders and coded independently.

Our analysis resembled the general process of grounded theory regarding constant comparison and coding steps (Strauss & Corbin, 1998). However, our coding was directed by the broader dialectical theoretical framework; we focused on dialectics as the central phenomenon around which we formulated relationships among the codes. The first step in our data analysis was line-by-line open coding, which helped classify the data into different categories and themes. During this initial coding, we started observing dialectical tensions in policy documents of the state governments. Following open coding, axial coding was used to identify primary and secondary dialectical tensions.

FINDINGS

Overall, our analysis indicated that state telework policies ranged from a few to 20 or more pages, although most were between 5-10 pages long. The two most commonly used terms were 'telework' and 'telecommuting.' Most followed a common format and contained the three categories set forth by Hoskins (2006): work concerns (rules for work hours and measuring performance), location concerns (ownership and provision of equipment and security issues), and policy concerns (eligibility and termination requirements). Telework policies generally started with a preamble addressing the purpose and benefits of telecommuting (to the individual, organization, and community), and went on to address specific eligibility criteria and rules for telework implementation. There was variation, however, in the degree to which policies spelled out specific requirements and guidelines versus leaving room for agencies to work out the details. In response to our research question, the analysis of state telework policies revealed two major sets of tensions: autonomy versus control and flexibility versus rigidity. These primary tensions will now be discussed along with the secondary tensions associated with them.

Autonomy vs. Control

In any workplace, a tension between employee autonomy and supervisor or employer control of employee work performance exists. However, due to the shift in workspace and the possibility of reduced communication between employees and their supervisors, the autonomy versus control tension seems to be more prominent for teleworking as a work format; employers still expect teleworkers to observe the same requirements as in the office whereas employees inevitably view telework as an opportunity to be free from a controlled office environment. Teleworkers may want to enjoy some of the autonomy in their home or non-office workspace. On the other hand, due to the nature of telework, it is hard for managers to monitor whether teleworkers actually observe the job requirements that are enforced in the office and they may need to impose additional controls to ensure this.

A major tension was evident in the telework policies we studied between allowing for this individual autonomy of teleworkers while maintaining organizational control. This tension was reflected in the framing of telework as (a) a management option versus an employee choice, (b) in the degree to which teleworkers are monitored by the agency versus self-managed, and (c) in the delegation of responsibility for telework infrastructure and security to agencies versus individual teleworkers.

Voluntary, But Not a Choice

There was a high degree of consensus in the policy wording that telework was to be a management option rather than an employee choice, privilege or a universal benefit—although most policies simultaneously stressed that telework was to be voluntary for employees. In this sense, an implicit tension existed in that telework was something seen as voluntary for employees yet not up to them to decide. The slippage in language here can be interpreted to mean that employers decide who is eligible to telework, although they cannot oblige employees to telework (except in rare cases of mandating telework).

For example, the New York state government's telework policy highlighted the positive aspects of telework in general. Several of the employee benefits were to provide "greater empowerment," "improve morale and flexibility," and "increase family interaction." However in another provision, it emphasized the understanding of telecommuting as another management tool to "improve agency operations." Ultimately, this policy ended up

stressing what was of foremost value: the options of management. This tension can also be seen in the following policy statements:

Offering state employees the opportunity to telework is a management option and employees must follow the policies established by their agency… Teleworking is not an employee entitlement. When employee participation is voluntary, telework may be terminated with reasonable notice by the employee or by the agency. Note: some positions include telework as a condition of employment. In these cases, unilateral termination of telework will not be possible. [Washington]

Offering the opportunity to work at home is a management option; telework is not a universal employee benefit. An employee's participation in the State's telework program is entirely voluntary. The employee, supervisor or manager may terminate teleworking without cause. [Arizona]

Organizational Surveillance vs. Self-Surveillance

Efforts to monitor the telework arrangements also reflected a tension between individual and organizational surveillance. Some policies included on-going monitoring efforts by the agencies with further reporting to higher levels of the state, while others provided more of an expectation for employee self-monitoring. Due to the shift to a remote workspace, supervisors' monitoring of teleworking performance became a critical issue. Many state governments' policies mentioned that maintaining constant and clear communication between teleworkers and their supervisors or coworkers was important in order to keep them apprised of their work performance and maintain a connection with the main office. Many policies emphasized supervisors' responsibility for monitoring teleworkers' remote work performance—and when supervisors were concerned about a teleworker's ability to work independently or about whether certain tasks were suitable for virtual work, it was suggested that they not implement telecommuting for their work divisions.

While working away from the central office, the primary modes of communication for telework employees will be by telephone and e-mail systems. The teleworker and supervisor will work together to create a reasonable communication plan, including when and how they will communicate daily. Teleworkers are responsible for informing their supervisor and others, in accordance with existing practice, of how to reach them. [California]

Supervisors approving a telework arrangement for their employees must ensure that: the teleworker's position description is up to date; the performance appraisal is up to date and that the teleworker has at least a satisfactory performance evaluation; provide a signed telework agreement that itemizes state equipment and supplies to be used, designations for work hours and location; provide clear understanding of job duties and standards of how work is to be monitored and evaluated. [Indiana]

Some state governments suggested that suitable jobs for teleworking were those that could be done independently without frequent observation by supervisors. North Carolina's policy stated that there should be no demand for constant and in-person contact by supervisors, co-workers and/or customers in teleworking. However, such a general statement seems to be inconsistent with a more specific level of provision that indicates the same level of control for teleworking sites as in the government office. The specific provision says that "management reserves the right to require the employee to report to the central workplace

on scheduled telework days." There was some overly intrusive control appearing in several state governments' telework policies. Beyond the extent of reasonable guidelines, these statements reveal an excessive level of control that may create discomfort for teleworkers. The following illustrates this kind control of teleworkers:

Managers...need to decide whether or not to require the same dress code for work at home. [Montana]

Although the policy does not mandate that a particular dress code be enforced for teleworkers, raising this as an issue for discussion may be perceived as intrusive by teleworkers, who are not accustomed to having their employer dictate what they wear in the privacy of their home. In addition to dress code, other state government policies expected teleworkers to observe work norms in the same way they did in a traditional office. Although most state government policies required teleworkers to set aside some time during the day to be reached by their supervisors, Arizona's more rigid policy explicitly stated,

While teleworking, employees should be reachable via telephone, within reason, during agreed upon work hours. Teleworkers must notify the office if they leave their telework location, much like they would inform the receptionist when leaving the traditional office during the work day. [Arizona]

To the contrary, Colorado's policy took into consideration some concerns for teleworkers. Its policy explicitly mentioned that "teleworkers are reluctant to leave their phone on their telecommute days, even to use the restroom or take a break, because someone who called might think they are not working." Colorado's policy emphasized trust between the state government and the teleworkers as essential for the successful implementation of its telework program:

Managerial trust is also critical. The employee must be trusted to do the work assigned and manage time appropriately and the supervisor must be trusted to manage by results or outcomes. The manager must trust or be open to the arrangement itself. [Colorado]

Organizational vs. Individual Responsibility

Finally, autonomy versus control was evident in a tension over whose responsibility it was to provide and maintain office equipment and ensure security of the home office and data. Due to the shift in teleworkers' main workspace from the state government office to their home or other alternative places, provision of equipment and establishment of a remote office were issues. There was a great variety in state governments' telework policies in terms of who was to provide necessary equipment for teleworking including communication technologies; some allowed teleworkers to use their personal equipment, but required them to be responsible for any maintenance and liability even if they were used for work purposes. The issue became more complicated when it came to installing state-owned software into employee-owned computers. Most policies discussed the safety of home workspaces and requested teleworkers to self-certify that their home office was safe and free from health hazards. Some state governments were willing to provide any equipment needed for working at home, but also required teleworkers to secure work-related data including confidential information and limit the use of equipment for work purposes and by authorized users only.

Provision of Equipment

State policies varied in terms of whose responsibility it was to provide the equipment, supplies, and telephone/data connection for telework. Some

stated clearly that agencies were to provide all equipment:

Agencies remain liable for state-owned equipment located at the employee's telework location and assume the risks associated with the equipment... Office supplies for use by teleworkers at their alternate worksites should be provided by the state and should be obtained during the teleworkers' in-office work time. [Washington]

Others did not clearly specify who should provide such equipment, merely that

The agency should ensure that the employee has appropriate equipment to safely perform the job without increased risk of injury and should establish minimum safety requirements...All equipment used by the employee, whether provided by the agency or the employee, should be ergonomically correct. [Wisconsin]

Still others, such as Tennessee, distinguished between full-time and part-time teleworkers, stating that the agency should provide necessary equipment, supplies, and telephone/data connection for full-time telecommuters, but that part-timers were responsible for providing their own equipment. Policies also differed on whether agencies were to be held liable for job-related injuries or illnesses. While some left this unclear, others stated clearly that agencies were not responsible:

The State shall not be liable for injury or property damage to third persons at the telecommuting work site. Telecommuter agrees to indemnify and hold harmless the State, its agents and employees, from and against any and all claims, demands, judgments, liabilities, losses, damages or expenses resulting or arising from any injury or damage to any person, corporation or other entity caused directly or indirectly by the telecommuter's acts, omissions, bad faith, willful misconduct or neg-

ligence excluding acts within the scope of the telecommuter's employment pursuant to Tennessee Code Annotated Section 9-8-307(h). [Tennessee]

Physical and Data Security

Tensions were also evident in designated responsibility for maintaining security and confidentiality of data, with most policies regarding this as a joint effort in which teleworkers were responsible for safeguarding and protecting company information and materials from unauthorized disclosure or damage, while following security procedures developed by the agency. This dual responsibility can be seen in the following statement:

Materials, documents, etc. transported from the official work station are the telecommuter's responsibility. The telecommuter will protect the Department records and documents from unauthorized disclosure or damage and will comply with the Department policies and procedures regarding such matters…To protect confidentiality and guard against data contamination, telecommuters will follow Department approved data security procedures. [Tennessee]

These differences illustrated a tension in determining the responsibility for maintaining a safe, secure home office environment between state entities and individual teleworkers. By assigning dual responsibility, it was unclear who would be to blame if a violation should occur and to what extent individual teleworkers could be held accountable.

Overall, the autonomy-control tension suggested that the relationship between the individual telecommuter and the employer was not clear-cut in terms of the decision to telework, the degree to which performance monitoring was to be handled by the supervisor or the teleworker, and whether the organization or the individual held more responsibility for the provision of equipment

and the security of the physical office and data. Although a few policies were clear in specifying organizational control, the ambiguous wording of most of them implied that this tension was to be negotiated between the individual teleworker and his or her supervisor.

Flexibility vs. Rigidity

A second major tension could be seen between flexibility and rigidity. Policies varied in the rigidity versus flexibility of their wording, in terms of standardized versus ad hoc eligibility criteria and guidelines for teleworkers, the degree to which rules were clearly stated versus left ambiguous, and in how much leeway they allowed telecommuters to balance work and family.

Standardized vs. Ad Hoc

The tension between flexibility and rigidity was evident in the criteria for eligibility to telework as well as the degree of specificity of the rules regarding what teleworkers were and were not allowed to do. First, there was a tension related to eligibility to telework. Some policies provided extensive lists of criteria for teleworkers, such as "no pending personnel related disciplinary action, portable job duties, availability of a work site suitable for telecommuting, not in probationary status…supervisor agreement and approval, nature of the work to be accomplished, job duties with clearly defined performance requirements that are measurable and results oriented, willingness to participate in telecommuter training and Department surveys…" as well as personal qualities such as "dependable, self motivated and responsible, good organizational skills, effective communicator, adaptable to change, results oriented" (Tennessee). Despite these detailed criteria, Tennessee's policy also included a statement that "An employee is selected to participate at the sole discretion of the Department," indicating that telecommuting arrangements cannot be completely standardized but are somewhat ad hoc or determined on a case-by-case basis. This was evident in other policies as well:

It is anticipated that approval to allow telecommuting will be on a case-by-case basis. [Wisconsin]

Most policies noted that not all state employees were eligible for teleworking, but certain criteria should be met such as quality of previous work performance, suitability of individual task, and employees' general and independent work skills. Even when these criteria were provided to determine one's eligibility, it was often stated that teleworking requests were to be evaluated case by case for each individual worker and the eligibility of a position could be changed depending on the circumstances. Therefore, we identified this somewhat inconsistent application of policy rules as another example showing the tension between standardized rules versus ad hoc application of them.

The Department has identified the job classes and positions considered appropriate for telecommuting. Requests will be considered on an individual basis to determine if the incumbent has the necessary skills and abilities to be a telecommuter and if the duties of the incumbent's position can adequately be performed by telecommuting or telework. [Florida]

Eligible position - A position having measurable quantitative or qualitative results-oriented standards of performance that is structured to be performed independently of others and with minimal need for support and can be scheduled at least one day a pay period to participate in teleworking without impacting service quality or organizational operations. The eligibility of a position may change depending on circumstances. [Georgia]

Statements about eligibility requirements to telework may be the most ambiguous part of telework policy. As discussed previously, in most state governments, telework was pronounced as the management's option, not the employees' privilege or right. The fact that state governments view telework as a management option may be related to the fact that they are intentionally or strategically ambiguous (Eisenberg, 1984) with respect to the eligibility of telework and the jobs that are suitable for telework. Employers, in this case state governments, did not seem to be specific about the extent to which the policies included standardized statements regarding who was eligible to telework and what kind of jobs were suitable. Although an individual employee may satisfy the publicly stated eligibility conditions, under certain circumstances, state governments cannot accept all eligible applicants from their point of view. As a result, whether an employer permits certain employees to telework is fully dependent on the employer's managerial evaluation. For employers, such a managerial judgment may not be appropriately represented in these policy statements. Thus, a tension between standardization and ad hoc occurred when state governments tried to define the eligibility of teleworkers and the boundaries of eligible work.

The tension between standardization vs. ad hoc emerged further when state governments' telework policies specified the provision for equipment:

The division director shall determine, with information supplied by the employee and the supervisor, the appropriate equipment needs for each telecommuting arrangement on a case-by-case basis. [North Dakota]

The decision to provide equipment will be made on a case-by-case basis based on funding availability and whether or not a business case can be made to fund equipment for the employee. [North Carolina]

Georgia's telework policy also took an ad hoc approach regarding workspace. Contrary to some states that rigidly defined what a workspace should be (e.g., Colorado), Georgia's policy only mentioned that the state government needed to make "on-site visits at mutually agreed-upon time." But, basically, this state's approach to this issue operated upon "a case-by-case basis." Such an ad hoc approach may or may not appear to be more rigid than teleworkers expect. In some way, this approach may provide some room for teleworkers to negotiate for more favorable telework conditions. The degree of the negotiation may be dependent upon the specific relationship between employer and employee.

Clear vs. Ambiguous Statement of Rules

Similar to eligibility and equipment issues, it seemed that there was a tension between formally and clearly stating the rules or expectations for teleworkers and leaving some ambiguity in what was allowed. First, policies varied in terms of how clearly they spelled out expectations about the work schedules and working hours of teleworkers. Many policies stated that the same policies and number of work hours applied to teleworkers as when they worked in the office.

The total number of hours that employees are expected to work will not change, regardless of work location. Employees agree to apply themselves to their work during work hours. [Virginia]

Each agency must establish internal policies and procedures related to telecommuting. [Virginia]

Other policies left it vague and requested agencies to come up with their own policies, sometimes providing suggestions for what types of issues such policies could include.

A mutually established telecommuting schedule must be defined and agreed upon by the telecommuter and supervisor and remains on file in the Department. However, the Department's needs take precedence over the telecommuting schedule…The telecommuter must be reachable during the periods outlined in the telecommuting work schedule. [Tennessee]

Some policies were rather rigid in their flexibility. Other policies negotiated work schedules differently, but with a similar mix of flexibility and rigidity. For example, the following policy allowed for employees and supervisors to agree on a work schedule, but with a rigid requirement to specify detailed working times in writing:

Work schedule, i.e. number of times per week/ month, hours, specific day(s), etc. Include a statement that any hours worked outside of the agreed to work schedule or changes in the agreed to work hours (including working additional hours) must be pre-approved in writing. [Washington]

Finally, some policies seemed to be excessively rigid in their specification of rules and guidelines for teleworkers. For example, Wisconsin's policy was quite restrictive, explicitly prohibiting activities such as "non-work activities, including basic homemaking tasks such as dishes, laundry, etc." and discouraging visitors, and requiring that:

Employees who see clients should be subject to drive by checks of the residence to ensure visitor safety. If deficiencies are found in the maintenance/upkeep of accessible areas (such as the driveway, sidewalk, and stoops), the employee should be given a reasonable amount of time (60-90 days) to make corrections/improvements, with no visitors allowed until the corrections are made. [Wisconsin]

Wisconsin's policy also provided three detailed worksheets to administer related to (a) employee eligibility, (b) a telecommuting agreement form (including detailed items such as how often to check email!), and (c) a safety checklist. These worksheets provided little room for flexibility of interpretation, and such restrictive policies could be seen as imposing additional constraints on teleworkers (such as ensuring home maintenance) that would not normally be expected of in-house employees.

Work/Family Balance

A final sub-theme under the tension between flexibility and rigidity of policy documents related to work-family balance is an inconsistency between the suggested benefits of teleworking and the application of the rules in practice. Although many policy documents stated the benefit of flexible scheduling for individual teleworkers, which could assist with coordination of their family obligations, most policies mandated that teleworkers have a separate arrangement for dependent care.

Tennessee's policy cited "assistance with family obligations" as an employee benefit of telecommuting; however later in the policy, it stated that "The telecommuter shall have family arrangements, which allow the telecommuting work site to be a productive working environment." There is considerable ambiguity here in terms of what constitutes a "productive working environment." Other policies explicitly prohibited attending to family or other personal responsibilities during work.

Telecommuting is not intended to serve as a substitute for child or adult care. If children or adults in need of primary care are in the alternate work location during employees' work hours, some other individual must be present to provide the care. [Virginia]

Family pets/animals should be restricted from the work area. Child care/elderly care activity

or related responsibilities should occur outside of the workday and not within the dedicated work area. [Wisconsin]

Other policies, however, acknowledged that teleworkers may take advantage of telework in order to take care of their dependents, at least at certain times.

Telework should not be used as a regular substitute for full-time dependent care. The state recognizes that one advantage of working at home is the opportunity to have more time with dependents, but it is the teleworker's responsibility to ensure that he or she is fully able to complete work assignments on time. [Montana]

Employee will also not undertake to provide primary care for an adult.... In some case... the manager may give approval, on a temporary basis, for a teleworker to provide primary care for another family member. [Montana]

Hawaii's policy explicitly stated that telework contributes to "minimizing work/home conflicts." Such an orientation on a broad level does not materialize at the specific level. When it comes to dependent care, it is required of teleworkers "to agree not to undertake to provide primary care of children/others during core hours." Although this state's policy does not state that teleworkers should not take care of their dependents at any time, it adds additional conditions:

Telecommuters shall not undertake to provide primary care during core hours for a child (or children) under twelve (12) years of age or a person who has a serious health condition or disability. If such person will be present during that time, another individual shall be present to provide primary care, and if such person is ill and care is required on a temporary basis by the

Table 1. Primary and secondary tensions in telework policies

Primary Tension	Secondary Tensions	Issues
Autonomy vs. Control	1) Management option vs. employee choice 2) Organizational surveillance vs. self-surveillance 3) Organizational vs. individual responsibility	1) Eligibility to telework 2) Monitoring performance 3) Equipment and physical/data security
Flexibility vs. Rigidity	1) Standardized vs. ad hoc 2) Clear vs. ambiguous statement of rules 3) Work/life balance	1) Eligibility to telework and provision of equipment 2) Work schedules and working hours 3) Dependent care

telecommuter, prior approval by the supervisor shall be obtained. [Hawaii]

Whereas tensions in specifying eligibility criteria to telework and working hours were more productive in allowing for managerial discretion and for teleworkers to negotiate with their supervisors, the tensions around work-family balance seemed to be more problematic as they involved contradictions within policies between what was promised and what was allowed in practice. The primary and secondary tensions are summarized in Table 1. The implications of these findings will now be discussed.

DISCUSSION

Our analysis of state government telework policies revealed two key tensions in the form of autonomy vs. control and flexibility vs. rigidity. The autonomy-control tension pertains to the degree to which employee autonomy was maintained relative to organizational control, relating to issues of organizational monitoring versus self-surveillance, the extent to which the decision to telework was a management option versus an employee choice, and the degree to which providing equipment for the home office and ensuring physical and data security were the responsibility of the individual teleworker or the state agency. The second tension of flexibility-rigidity encompasses the extent to which policies were standardized versus ad hoc, whether rules were clearly stated or left ambigu-

ous, and the degree to which work and family were explicitly separated or allowed to blend. Although the tensions were evident in different ways, they both represent facets of the larger tension between individual freedom (in the form of autonomy and flexibility) and organizational constraint (through control and rigidity). We will now discuss the implications of such tensions for telework policies and for virtual work more broadly.

Our findings revealed that most tensions arose in the form of discrepancies across different state policies rather than explicit contradictions within the same policy. This suggests that state governments take different approaches to telecommuting and the degree to which they mandate its terms rather than leaving them open to interpretation by agencies and individual teleworkers. Such tensions are likely to be less problematic than contradictions within a single policy, as state governments operate relatively independently and their employees are unlikely to work interdependently with those of different states. They do indicate competing perspectives on how telework should be implemented, however, which reflect inconsistencies in our understanding of telework processes more broadly.

When considering the broader discourse about telework, however, a number of policies did suffer from internal tensions between the stated benefits of telework (such as greater flexibility in balancing work and family care) and the realities of telework implementation, which included fairly rigid rules about not caring for dependents and other specific prohibitions of performing domestic work during work hours. There are differences in the extent to which state governments allow teleworkers to exercise their discretion with regard to what they can and cannot do at home. At the very least, overly rigid stipulations of telework policies may be at odds with what teleworkers anticipate as some degree of flexibility while teleworking. This disconnect calls into question the extent to which telecommuting and other virtual work arrangements provide more individual freedom or more control of workers' home lives, and the extent to which the realities of telework live up to its often-cited promise of providing more freedom, flexibility, and work-life balance. Whereas much of the popular and academic discourse on telework emphasizes these individual benefits (e.g., Barett, 2008; Gajendran & Harrison, 2007; Golden & Veiga, 2005), telework policies seemed to focus more on providing mechanisms to ensure organizational control in ways that may in fact impose additional constraints on teleworkers by regulating their actions within the home rather than enabling autonomy and flexibility. Taking a tensional perspective enables us to account for both individual and organizational needs/goals and ways in which they are inter-related, as well as encouraging us to develop creative responses to transcend polar oppositions and attend to both poles (see Gibbs, 2009; Putnam & Boys, 2006). It is also helpful in understanding the complexities of telework processes, rather than classifying their outcomes into simple categories of positive or negative.

Further, although few policies contained striking contradictions, the majority did use ambiguous language that did not clearly specify rules and eligibility criteria. While contradictions regarding dependent care may be confusing or problematic, our findings suggest that most telework policies used tension effectively by providing enough ambiguity to bridge diverse individual and organizational interests and allow them to co-exist (Gibbs, 2009). Literature on dialectical tensions has found that productive tensions allow for both

alternatives to be embraced rather than forcing the selection of one or the other (Putnam & Boys, 2006; Tracy, 2004). In this sense, telework policies need to be worded to allow for autonomy of state agencies and individual teleworkers as well as organizational control (at both the state and agency levels); they should allow for both flexibility and standardization in interpretation and implementation. Successful policies can thus be expected to strike a balance between these opposing poles and incorporate both. Although prior research on organizational tensions has focused mainly on the lived experiences of organizational members (e.g., Gibbs; Jian & Rosiek, 2009; Tracy), this chapter makes an important contribution by examining formal communication in the form of policy messages and establishing that communicative tensions exist in such messages as well—and that such tensions may even be necessary and useful.

Practical Implications

Our findings have practical implications for the implementation of virtual work policies in organizations. Although prior literature on telework (Mills-Senn, 2006; Prince, 2000) would prescribe that policies be written to eliminate ambiguity and provide the utmost degree of clarity, telework practices and virtual work practices more broadly involve inherent oppositions between diverse organizational and individual goals and the need to maintain both autonomy and control, flexibility and standardization. As such, effective policies are not necessarily those that provide the greatest level of clarity (which would select poles of control and rigidity while ignoring the simultaneous need for autonomy and flexibility), but rather incorporate enough ambiguity to allow for these conflicting needs and interests to be mutually attained. While we are not advocating unclear policies or vague guidelines, our findings do suggest that state governments and other organizations should develop strategically ambiguous policies that allow for these tensions to coexist and do not overclarify or overspecify the terms and conditions, in order to allow for more autonomy and flexibility of interpretation and execution of terms and rules. Further, teleworkers and managers should use policy as a guide and point of departure for conversations about virtual work—— not the final word.

Across these state governments, the findings here suggest several differences in some of their telework policies. Although we cannot label some policies as preferable to others, this does point to an opportunity for these organizations to compare policies and work toward development of some best practices. For both managers and individual teleworkers, our findings would suggest the value in fully knowing the policies that do exist. Not only does such knowledge provide one with guidance about organizational expectations, but also the tensions in such policies can reveal space for negotiation and opportunities to create desirable virtual work arrangements. Further, understanding the tensions and contradictions inherent in telework policies may help to reduce potential conflict between managers and the employees surrounding the interpretation of telework policies by making each side aware of the interests and concerns of the other. The mere presence of a formal policy in an organization does not necessarily guarantee effective communication between managers and teleworkers.

The high level of ambiguity in many policies leaves much of the implementation of telework rules and procedures up to individual managers to negotiate with individual telecommuters. This suggests that successful telecommuting arrangements may require managers to develop supportive, trusting relationships with teleworkers rather than simply enforce policy and rules in a uniform way. Our findings suggest that enacting organizational policy should not be considered a fixed process, but rather an ongoing process involving all parties. The tensional view we take draws attention to the constitutive role of policies in shaping interaction as they are continuously

interpreted and enacted through the participation of all involved organizational members. It is often implicitly accepted that enforcing policies is solely the responsibility of management. But making sense of the ambiguity in such policies raises the necessity of employees' participation in the process of enacting such policies.

FUTURE RESEARCH

Future research should explore ways in which various forms of telework discourse coincide or conflict, by comparing the communication of managers, teleworkers, and non-teleworking coworkers to the discourse contained in telework policies to identify further tensions. The impact of such formal policies and the degree to which policies are followed and shape telecommuting arrangements should also be assessed. The communicative responses to policies and the tensions they contain also warrant study, as well as the ways in which policy is a relational construction, in that the employer-employee relationship influences how policies are interpreted and implemented. Of course, we have only examined policy in one type of organization here; thus, future research should extend this analysis by examining policy in the private sector and in organizations whose members are more globally dispersed.

CONCLUSION

As telework and other forms of virtual work become more and more prevalent, policies related to such work have become increasingly important to organizations. Yet, scholarly analysis of these important organizational documents has often lagged behind. Our objectives in this chapter were to establish the importance of workplace policies related to telework and to articulate tensions that exist within and across them. Our dialectical framework relies on the premise that telework policies contain tensions and ambiguity that may be necessary in order to balance conflicting individual and organizational interests, and that the existence of such tensions may allow space for specific procedures to be interpreted and negotiated within the context of particular employer-employee relationships. Our findings identified tensions in the form of ambiguity within and across policies themselves, as well as disconnects between affordances provided by the policies and the larger discourse of telework. We believe the communicative tensions we discuss here offer both practical implications and guidance for future scholarly efforts in this area.

REFERENCES

American Management Association. (2006). *2006 Workplace E-Mail, Instant Messaging & Blog Survey*. New York: Author.

Bailey, D. E., & Kurland, N. B. (2002). A review of telework research: Findings, new directions and lessons for the study of modern work. *Journal of Organizational Behavior, 23*, 383–400. doi:10.1002/job.144

Baker, P. M. A., Moon, N. W., & Ward, A. C. (2006). Virtual exclusion and telework: Barriers and opportunities of technocentric workplace accommodation policy. *Work (Reading, Mass.), 27*, 421–430.

Bakhtin, M. M. (1981). *The dialogic imagination: Four essays* (Holquist, M., Trans.). Austin, TX: University of Texas Press.

Barett, A. (2008, October 17). Making telecommuting work. *Business Week SmallBiz*. Retrieved September 29, 2009, from http://www.businessweek.com/magazine/content/08_70/s0810048750962.htm?chan=smallbiz_smallbiz+index+page_best+of+small+biz+magazine

Barnes, S. B. (2002). *Computer-mediated communication: Human-to-human communication across the Internet*. Boston: Allyn & Bacon.

Baruch, Y. (2001). The state of research on teleworking and an agenda for future research. *International Journal of Management Reviews, 3*, 113–129. doi:10.1111/1468-2370.00058

Baxter, L. A., & Montgomery, B. M. (1996). *Relating: Dialogues & dialectics*. New York: Guildford Press.

Castor, T. (2007). Language use during school board meetings: Understanding controversies of and about communication. *Journal of Business Communication, 44*, 111–136. doi:10.1177/0021943606298828

Cheney, G. (1983). The rhetoric of identification and the study of organizational communication. *The Quarterly Journal of Speech, 69*, 145–158. doi:10.1080/00335638309383643

Connaughton, S. L., & Daly, J. A. (2004). Leading from afar: Strategies for effectively leading virtual teams . In Godar, S. H., & Ferris, S. P. (Eds.), *Virtual and collaborative teams: Process, technologies, and practice* (pp. 49–75). Hershey, PA: Idea Group Publishing.

Connaughton, S. L., & Daly, J. A. (2005). Leadership in the new millennium: Communicating beyond temporal, spatial, and geographical boundaries . In Kalbfleisch, P. (Ed.), *Communication yearbook, 29* (pp. 187–213). Mahwah, NJ: Erlbaum.

Corman, S. R. (2006). On being less theoretical and more technological in organizational communication. *Journal of Business and Technical Communication, 20*, 325–338. doi:10.1177/1050651906287256

Cramton, C. D., & Hinds, P. J. (2004). Subgroup dynamics in internationally distributed teams: Ethnocentrism or cross-national learning? *Research in Organizational Behavior, 26*, 231–263. doi:10.1016/S0191-3085(04)26006-3

D'Urso, S. C. (2006). Toward a structural-perceptual model of electronic monitoring and surveillance in organizations. *Communication Theory, 16*, 281–303. doi:10.1111/j.1468-2885.2006.00271.x

Donaldson, S. A. (2002). Who should work from home? *Black Enterprise, 33*(1), 42.

DuBrin, A. J. (1991). Comparison of the job satisfaction and productivity of telecommuters versus in-house employees: A research note on work in progress. *Psychological Reports, 68*, 1223–1234. doi:10.2466/PR0.68.4.1223-1234

Eisenberg, E. M. (1984). Ambiguity as strategy in organizational communication. *Communication Monographs, 51*, 227–242. doi:10.1080/03637758409390197

Ellison, N. B. (1999). Social impacts: New perspectives on telework. *Social Science Computer Review, 17*, 338–356. doi:10.1177/089443939901700308

Gajendran, R. S., & Harrison, D. A. (2007). The good, the bad, and the unknown about telecommuting: Meta-analysis of psychological mediators and individual consequences. *The Journal of Applied Psychology, 92*, 1524–1541. doi:10.1037/0021-9010.92.6.1524

Garrett, R. K., & Danziger, J. N. (2007). Which telework? Defining and testing a taxonomy of technology-mediated work at a distance. *Social Science Computer Review, 25*, 27–47. doi:10.1177/0894439306293819

Gibbs, J. L. (2009). Dialectics in a global software team: Negotiating tensions across time, space, and culture. *Human Relations, 62*, 905–935. doi:10.1177/0018726709104547

Gibbs, J. L., Nekrassova, D., Grushina, Y., & Abdul Wahab, S. (2008). Reconceptualizing virtual teaming from a constitutive perspective: Review, redirection, and research agenda . In Beck, C. S. (Ed.), *Communication yearbook, 32* (pp. 187–229). New York: Routledge.

Gibson, C. B., & Gibbs, J. L. (2006). Unpacking the concept of virtuality: The effects of geographic dispersion, electronic dependence, dynamic structure, and national diversity on team innovation. *Administrative Science Quarterly, 51*, 451–495.

Golden, T. D. (2006). The role of relationships in understanding telecommuter satisfaction. *Journal of Organizational Behavior, 27*, 319–340. doi:10.1002/job.369

Golden, T. D., & Veiga, J. F. (2005). The impact of extent of telecommuting on job satisfaction: Resolving inconsistent findings. *Journal of Management, 31*, 301–318. doi:10.1177/0149206304271768

Golden, T. D., Veiga, J. F., & Simsek, Z. (2006). Telecommuting's differential impact on work-family conflict: Is there no place like home? *The Journal of Applied Psychology, 91*, 1340–1350. doi:10.1037/0021-9010.91.6.1340

Goluboff, N. B. (2006, August 6). Taxing telecommuters. *New York Times*. Retrieved September 30, 2009, from http://www.nytimes.com/2006/08/06/opinion/nyregionopinions/06CTgolubuff.html

Grosse, C. U. (2002). Managing communication within virtual intercultural teams. *Business Communication Quarterly, 65*(4), 22–38. doi:10.1177/108056990206500404

Halford, S. (2005). Hybrid workspace: Re-spatialisations of work, organization and management. *New Technology, Work and Employment, 20*, 19–33. doi:10.1111/j.1468-005X.2005.00141.x

Hinds, P. J., & Mortensen, M. (2005). Understanding conflict in geographically distributed teams: The moderating effects of shared identity, shared context, and spontaneous communication. *Organization Science, 16,* 290–307. doi:10.1287/orsc.1050.0122

Horner, D., & Day, P. (1995). Labour and the information society: Trade union policies for teleworking. *Journal of Information Science, 21,* 333–341. doi:10.1177/016555159502100501

Hoskins (2006, July 10). *Understanding the importante of a telecommuting policy.* Retrieved May 7, 2009 from http://articles.tecrepublic.com.com/5100-10878_11-6070340.html

Hylmo, A., & Buzzanell, P. (2002). Telecommuting as viewed through cultural lenses: An empirical investigation of the discourses of utopia, identity and mystery. *Communication Monographs, 69,* 329–356. doi:10.1080/03637750216547

Igbaria, M., & Tan, M. (Eds.). (1998). *The virtual workplace.* Hershey, PA: Idea Group.

Jablin, F. M. (2001). Organizational entry, assimilation, and disengagement/exit . In Jablin, F. M., & Putnam, L. L. (Eds.), *The new handbook of organizational communication* (pp. 732–818). Thousand Oaks, CA: Sage.

Jarvenpaa, S. L., Shaw, T. R., & Staples, D. S. (2004). Toward contextualized theories of trust: The role of trust in global virtual teams. *Information Systems Research, 15,* 250–264. doi:10.1287/isre.1040.0028

Jian, G. (2007). "Omega is a four-letter word": Toward a tension-centered model of resistance to information and communication technologies. *Communication Monographs, 74,* 517–540. doi:10.1080/03637750701716602

Jian, G., & Rosiek, S. (2009, May). *Understanding the paradox of autonomy and control: Toward a dialectical model of telework.* Paper presented at annual conventions of the International Communication Association, Chicago, IL.

Khaifa, M., & Davidson, R. (2000). Exploring the telecommuting paradox. *Communications of the ACM, 43*(3), 29–31. doi:10.1145/330534.330554

Kirby, E. L., & Krone, K. J. (2002). "The policy exists but you can't really use it": Communication and the structuration of work-family policies. *Journal of Applied Communication Research, 30,* 50–77. doi:10.1080/00909880216577

Kurland, N. B., & Bailey, D. E. (1999). Telework: The advantages and challenges of work here, there, anywhere, and anytime. *Organizational Dynamics, 28,* 53–67. doi:10.1016/S0090-2616(00)80016-9

Lange, M. C. S., & Nelson, M. D. (2005, March 29). Preservation perils: Updating your corporation's document retention policy for the digital age. Retrieved on November 2, 2008 from http://sw-micropublishing.com/wpdload/preserv-perils.pdf

Lautsch, B. A., Kossek, E. E., & Eaton, S. C. (2009). Supervisory approaches and paradoxes in managing telecommuting implementation. *Human Relations, 62,* 795–827. doi:10.1177/0018726709104543

Legreco, M. E. (2007). Consuming policy: Organizing school meal programs to promote healthy eating practices. Doctoral dissertation, Arizona State University. Retrieved September 24, 2009 from *Dissertations & Theses: A&I* (Publication No. AAT 3270597).

Major, D. A., Verive, J. M., & Joice, W. (2008). Telework as a dependent care solution: Examining current practice to improve telework management strategies. *The Psychologist Manager Journal, 11,* 65–91. doi:10.1080/10887150801967134

Makower, J. (2009, February 2). In recession, business keeps going green. *Business Week*. Retrieved September, 29, 2009 from http://www.businessweek.com/bwdaily/dnflash/content/feb2009/db2009022_982216.htm

McCloskey, D. W., & Igbaria, M. (1998). A review of the empirical research on telecommuting and directions for future research . In Igbaria, M., & Tan, M. (Eds.), *The virtual workplace* (pp. 338–358). Hershey, PA: Idea Group.

McCrehin, C. (2008, September). GSA, AFGE sign national agreement on telework. *American Society for Public Administration, 13*.

Mills-Senn, P. (2006). Can home work work? *H&HN . Hospitals & Health Networks, 80*(6), 24.

Mokhtarian, P. L. (2009). If telecommunication is such a good substitute for travel, why does congestion continue to get worse? *Transportation Letters: The International Journal of Transportation Research, 1*, 1–17. doi:10.3328/TL.2009.01.01.1-17

Mokhtarian, P. L., Salomon, I., & Choo, S. (2005). Measuring the measurable: Why can't we agree on the number of telecommuters in the U.S.? *Quality & Quantity, 39*, 423–452. doi:10.1007/s11135-004-6790-z

Mueller, M., & Lentz, B. (2004). Revitalizing communication and information policy research. *The Information Society, 20*, 155–157. doi:10.1080/01972240490456773

Nelson, P., Safirova, E., & Walls, M. (2007). Telecommuting and environmental policy: Lessons from the ecommute program. *Transportation Research Part D, Transport and Environment, 12*(3), 195–207. doi:10.1016/j.trd.2007.01.011

Nilles, J. (1998). *Managing telework: Strategies for managing the virtual workforce*. New York: John Wiley.

Novaco, R. W., Kliewer, W., & Broquet, A. (1991). Home environmental consequences of commute travel impedance. *American Journal of Community Psychology, 19*, 881–909. doi:10.1007/BF00937890

Pepper, G. L., & Larson, G. S. (2006). Cultural identity tensions in a post-acquisition organization. *Journal of Applied Communication Research, 34*, 49–71. doi:10.1080/00909880500420267

Perez, M. P., Sanchez, A. M., & Carnicer, M. (2003). Top manager and institutional effects on the adoption of innovations: The case of teleworking. *Prometheus, 21*, 59–73. doi:10.1080/0810902032000051018

Pinsonneault, A., & Boisvert, M. (2001). The impacts of telecommuting on organizations and individuals: A review of the literature . In Johnson, N. J. (Ed.), *Telecommuting and virtual offices: Issues and opportunities* (pp. 163–185). Hershey, PA: Idea Group.

Pitts, M. J., Fowler, C., Kaplan, M. S., Nussbaum, J., & Becker, J. C. (2009). Dialectical tensions underpinning family farm succession planning. *Journal of Applied Communication Research, 37*, 59–79. doi:10.1080/00909880802592631

Pollach, I. (2006). Privacy statements as a means of uncertainty reduction in WWW interactions. *Journal of Organizational and End User Computing, 18*, 23–49.

Poole, M. S., & Van de Ven, A. (1989). Using paradox to build management and organizational theories. *Academy of Management Review, 14*, 562–578. doi:10.2307/258559

Prince, M. (2000). Telecommuters present unique risks to employers. *Business Insurance, 34*(20), 22–23.

Putnam, L. L., & Boys, S. (2006). Revisiting metaphors of organizational communication . In Clegg, S., Hardy, C., & Nord, W. (Eds.), *Handbook of organizational studies* (2nd ed., pp. 541–576). London: Sage.

Putnam, L. L., & Fairhurst, G. T. (2001). Discourse analysis in organizations: Issues and concerns . In Jablin, F. M., & Putnam, L. L. (Eds.), *The new handbook of organizational communication* (pp. 78–136). Thousand Oaks, CA: Sage.

Scott, C. R., & Choi, S. (2009, May). *Communication policies in the workplace: Tensions surrounding identifiability and anonymity of technology users*. Paper presented at the annual convention of the International Communication Association, Chicago, IL.

Scott, C. R., & Timmerman, C. E. (1999). Communication technology use and multiple workplace identifications among organizational teleworkers with varied degrees of virtuality. *IEEE Transactions on Professional Communication*, *42*, 240–260. doi:10.1109/47.807961

Sedgewick, R. (2009, June 1). Green and beyond: The hard and soft benefits of telecommuting. *ITBusinessEdge*. Retrieved September 28, 2009, from http://www.itbusinessedge.com/cm/community/features/guestopinions/blog/green-and-beyond-the-hard-and-soft-benefits-of-telecommuting/?cs=32987

Seo, M., Putnam, L. L., & Bartunek, J. M. (2004). Dualities and tensions of planned organizational change . In Poole, M. S., & van de Ven, A. H. (Eds.), *Handbook of organizational change and innovation* (pp. 73–107). New York: Oxford University Press.

Siau, K., Nah, F. F., & Teng, L. (2002). Acceptable Internet use policy. *Communications of the ACM*, *45*, 75–79. doi:10.1145/502269.502302

Simbulan, M. S. R. (2004). Internet access practices and employee attitudes toward Internet usage policy implementation in selected Philippines financial institutions. *Gadjah Mada International Journal of Business*, *6*, 193–224.

Simmers, C. A. (2002). Aligning Internet usage with business priorities. *Communications of the ACM*, *45*, 71–74. doi:10.1145/502269.502301

Sivunen, A. (2006). Strengthening identification with the team in virtual teams: The leaders' perspective. *Group Decision and Negotiation*, *15*, 345–366. doi:10.1007/s10726-006-9046-6

Stohl, C., & Cheney, G. (2001). Participatory processes/paradoxical practices: Communication and the dilemmas of organizational democracy. *Management Communication Quarterly*, *14*, 349–407. doi:10.1177/0893318901143001

Strauss, A., & Corbin, J. (1998). *Basics of qualitative research: Grounded theory, procedures and techniques*. Newbury Park, CA: Sage.

Suitecommute (no date). *Suitecommute: A complete telework solutions provider*. Retrieved May 7, 2009 from http://www.suitecommute.com.

Telework Enhancement Act of 2009. Retrieved October 1, 2009, from govtrack.us website http://frwebgate.access.gpo.gov/cgi-bin/getdoc.cgi?dbname=111_cong_bills&docid=f:s707is.txt.pdf

Thibodeaux, P. (2003). Telecommuters weather storm. *Computerworld*, *37*(8), 1–2.

Timmerman, C. E., & Scott, C. R. (2006). Virtually working: Communicative and structural predictors of media use and key outcomes in virtual work teams. *Communication Monographs*, *73*, 108–136. doi:10.1080/03637750500534396

Townsend, A. M., & Bennett, J. T. (2003). Privacy, technology, and conflict: Emerging issues and action in workplace privacy. *Journal of Labor Research*, *24*, 195–205. doi:10.1007/BF02701789

Tracy, S. J. (2004). Dialectic, contradiction, or double bind? Analyzing and theorizing employee reactions to organizational tensions. *Journal of Applied Communication Research, 32*, 119–146. doi:10.1080/0090988042000210025

Tretheway, A., & Ashcraft, K. L. (2004). Special issue introduction. Practicing disorganization: The development of applied perspectives on living with tension. *Journal of Applied Communication Research, 32*, 81–88.

Trkman, P., Jerman-Blazic, B., & Turk, T. (2008). Factors of broadband development and the design of a strategic policy framework. *Telecommunications Policy, 32*, 101–115. doi:10.1016/j.telpol.2007.11.001

Walther, J. B., & Bunz, U. (2005). The rules of virtual groups: Trust, liking, and performance in computer-mediated communication. *The Journal of Communication, 55*, 828–846. doi:10.1111/j.1460-2466.2005.tb03025.x

Weick, K. E. (1979). *The social psychology of organizing* (2nd ed.). New York: McGraw-Hill, Inc.

Whitman, M. E., Townsend, A. M., & Alberts, R. J. (1999). Considerations for an effective telecommunications-use policy. *Communications of the ACM, 42*(6), 101–108. doi:10.1145/303849.303868

Wiesenfeld, B. M., Raghuram, S., & Garud, R. (1999). Communication patterns as determinants of organizational identification in a virtual organization. *Organization Science, 10*, 777–790. doi:10.1287/orsc.10.6.777

World Wide Waves. (1999, October). Policy makers need the facts on global effects of telework. *Management Services, 43*(10), 7.

WorldatWork. (2009). *Telework trendlines 2009: A survey brief.* Scottsdale, AZ: WorldatWork.

Zetter, K. (2006, October). Employers crack down on personal net use. *PC World Magazine.*

ENDNOTES

[1] When we found more than one telework policy document within a given website, the priority choice was a state-wide policy and the most recently updated version of the policy.

[2] There needs to be a cautionary interpretation about the fact that no policy document was available for a state government because we found these cases: (a) restricted access to the government materials in which the policy document might exist in a different format (e.g., written document, handbook) but not be publicly available, (b) departmentalization of telework implementation (i.e., telework adopted and applied by each agency of a state government but no state-wide policy available, and/or (c) the establishment of a general guideline or policy under consideration.

Chapter 2
Communication, Structural Links, and Conflict in Three Inter-Organizational Virtual Collaborations

Tyler R. Harrison
Purdue University, USA

Elizabeth A. Williams
Purdue University, USA

ABSTRACT

Conflict is just as common in virtual teams as it is in collocated teams. However little is known about the process of conflict in these teams. The study presented in this chapter analyzed conflict in three inter-organizational teams. The purpose of this research is to identify primary types of conflict in virtual teams, examine the role that the structure of communication plays in the conflict, and examine the influence of the social context. Specifically, this chapter (1) reviews the extant literature on conflict in virtual teams and organizational conflict in general; (2) presents results from a study of three inter-organizational virtual team collaborations; and (3) offers an outline of potential future research in this area and provides best practices and potential pitfalls for practitioners to consider when structuring inter-organizational virtual teams.

INTRODUCTION

Conflict in virtual teams is as inevitable as it is in collocated teams. Although a growing body of literature examines conflict in virtual teams (e.g., Hinds, & Mortensen, 2005; Mortensen & Hinds, 2001; Paul, Samarah, Seetharaman, & Myktyn, 2005; Shin, 2005), little is known about *processes*

of conflict management in virtual teams and the influence that team structure has on conflict within the team. Much of the research on conflict in virtual teams focuses on the antecedents to conflict or the conditions necessary to prevent conflict and the implications of said conflict. In other words, extant research examines the inputs and outputs of conflict. This study, however, seeks to explore how individuals experience conflict and how they

DOI: 10.4018/978-1-61520-979-8.ch002

are constrained and enabled by various relational structures to deal with that conflict. Exploring these experiences allows us to understand the nuances of conflict in virtual teams. Ultimately we seek to answer three questions about the nature, manifestation, and management of conflict in three inter-organizational collaborative projects: (1) What are the primary types of conflict in virtual inter-organizational collaborations? (2) How does the structure of communication influence virtual team conflicts and dynamics? (3) What is the influence of social context on communicative practices and conflict in virtual teams?

The data for this study come from three health intervention projects. The projects varied systematically on a number of fronts, but were similar in that teams consisted of core members from two or three organizations (academic, community health, and political), and several team members were consistent across all three projects. Additionally, the ultimate goals of the projects were similar. The team dynamics varied based on the structures of communication linkages, relational history, and degree of collocation. While the projects ultimately shared similar goals, the participating organizations had very different missions, roles, expertise, and power that influenced team member interaction, and ultimately, conflict. Overall, the structure of communication (the formal and informal rules that regulated who could talk to who, how communication occurred)[1] and the division of tasks across team members represented the degree to which the teams integrated across the organizations and the level to which they became interdependent versus continuing to operate as largely autonomous organizations.

The chapter begins with a brief review of the theoretical perspectives relevant to conflict in virtual teams. Processes of data collection and analysis are presented in the methods section. Then, an overview of each collaborative project is provided. Each overview situates the broad nature of the participating organizations, describes the teams, and offers a history of relational development and collocation. The structure of each collaborative project and communication linkages between participating teams are illustrated. Similarities and difference related to conflict between cases based on structural linkages, relational history and levels of collocation are explored. The chapter concludes by offering a set of "best practices" for practitioners to use when structuring virtual teams and also provides a set of "potential pitfalls" for forming virtual teams and developing interaction practices within these teams.

BACKGROUND

Review of Virtual Team Conflict

We draw on multiple definitions of conflict (e.g., Pondy, 1967; Putnam & Poole, 1987; Walls & Callister, 1995) and advance the following working definition: Conflict involves grievances between interdependent people that arise from incompatible values, attitudes, goals, and/or beliefs.

Geographic dispersion further complicates team conflict. Although studies have suggested that there is not necessarily more conflict in geographically dispersed teams (Mortensen & Hinds, 2001), the nature of conflict is different. Theorists have posited that there are four ways that distance perpetuates conflict: (1) teams no longer have a shared context, meaning they no longer "have access to the same information and share the same tools, work processes, and work cultures" (Hinds & Mortensen, 2005, p. 293); (2) team members are not familiar with one another because of the decreased informal interactions; (3) friendship relationships do not form because there is a lack of spontaneous interaction; and (4) because distance increases the heterogeneity of the team (Hinds & Bailey, 2003). However, conflict can be mitigated if teams can form a shared identity and have a shared context, which is often accomplished through spontaneous communication (Hinds & Mortensen, 2005). In their empirical study, Hinds and Mortensen (2005) found that shared identity is more important for the management of relationship conflict while shared context is more important for managing task conflict. The emphasis on shared context is echoed by Montoya-Weiss, Massey and Song (2001) who argue that the interaction patterns and structures of virtual teams "may require deliberate creation of the social norms that regulate communication and work" (p. 1259). Furthermore, research has linked virtual team structure to how the teams performed through conflict and has offered support for nonhierarchical structures (Liu, Magjuka & Lee, 2008). In summary, communication patterns and structure in virtual teams are different than in collocated teams. This necessitates emphasis on creating a shared identity and shared context for team members which may be accomplished through nonhierarchical structures.

The Relevance of Structure and Context

While literature on conflict in virtual teams provides key insight, the focus is limited in scope and concentrates largely on the impact of distance and time. Although these elements are obviously critical to understanding conflict in virtual teams, only by examining broader theoretical perspectives that explore conflict can we appreciate the nuanced nature of social context surrounding working relationships and how they relate to processes of conflict in these types of team collaborations.

We consider social context to consist of the following dimensions: organizational resources and power, relational history, the nature of social ties, shared normative and cultural information and values, communicative links and practices, and degrees of collocation.

Social context is influential in approaches to managing conflict (Harrison & Morrill, 2004). Black (1976; 1984) argues that those with organizational power and resources are more likely to act unilaterally and less likely to engage in

negotiation to solve conflicts, while those with equal resources are more likely to engage in negotiation. Similarly, relational history and social ties are believed to influence both the likelihood and nature of engaging in manifest conflict, those conflicts that actually emerge in discourse between individuals (Pondy, 1967). Those with stronger relational history and multiplex social ties (ties that span both task and personal relationships) have stronger incentives to work toward productive resolution of conflict, while those with little relational history and uniplex ties feel less pressure to manage conflicts in productive or proactive manners (e.g., Harrison & Morrill, 2004, Morrill, 1995). Similar patterns occur with degrees of shared normative information and cultural values. Organizations that value similar working styles, that know more about their collaborators, and share similar organizational cultures are more likely to engage in processes like negotiation, while those with limited knowledge, different cultural values and norms, and different working styles are more likely to engage in unilateral or forceful conflict management (Morrill, 1995; Nader, 1990). These arguments are similar to those advanced in the virtual teams literature, but provide more specificity to the concept of social context.

In addition to the social context, communication practices are also argued to be influential in the enactment and experience of conflict. The pragmatics of everyday interaction are thought to be isomorphic with the pragmatics of conflict; in other words, patterns that we engage in for everyday tasks often carry over when we are faced with conflict (Morrill, 1995; Swidler, 1986). Additionally, the ability to build relationships and coalitions through open communication can shift power in a conflict with dramatic effects. Finally, processes that hinder the flow of important information can be a source of conflict and frustration, unnecessarily slowing down decision-making and collaboration.

Ultimately, understanding how social context and the structures of relationships and communication in virtual teams influence conflict processes will allow for more strategic decision making in designing virtual collaboration communication protocols that facilitate effective task and relational performance and the effective management of conflict. Such approaches to design have been utilized and recommended for dispute resolution processes in organizations (Harrison & Morrill, 2004; Jackson, 1998) and other contexts (Aakhus, 2007; van Eemeren, Grootendoorst, Jackson, & Jacobs, 1993).

To address these issues, a study of three inter-organizational collaborations was conducted. The following section details the methods used in our approach.

METHOD

This study attempts to identify the influence of specific patterns of communication on conflict in three inter-organizational health campaigns. This is a retrospective examination of conflict that previously occurred. To recreate these conflict "trouble cases" (e.g., Llewellyn & Hoebel, 1983) and analyze the interactions and structures, we relied on focus group data, interviews, analysis of archived emails, and analysis of structural communication linkages.

Participants

The participants in this study consisted of all the members of the academic team. This included the leaders of the projects and most of the graduate student assistants who worked on the projects and who had some interaction with the community partner(s). There were seven research assistants and two professors (i.e., the project leaders) who participated. Involvement in the projects varied from participant to participant. The two leaders and one of the research assistants were involved with all three projects, one research assistant was involved with two of the projects, and the remain-

ing five research assistants were each involved with one of the three projects. The first author served as a project leader on one of the studies and was intimately involved in the other two projects. The second author was involved in two of the projects as a research assistant.

Data Collection

This study employs a multi-methodological approach which was designed to enable triangulation. According to Lindlof and Taylor (2002), triangulation seeks a "convergence of meaning from more than one direction" (p. 240). The first source of data for this chapter was archived emails from the three projects. While these emails provided rich data about conflict in the moment and allowed patterns of conflict to emerge, they could not reveal how team members experienced the conflict. Therefore, the second author conducted a focus group with the research assistants and interviews with each of the projects' leaders.

Archived Emails

The primary source of data for this chapter was archived emails sent during the course of the projects. Over 5000 total emails were analyzed for instances of manifest/expressed conflict. Overall there were an average of thirteen categories of significant conflict per project (range = 11 – 15), with most categories having multiple instances of conflict. Email chains addressing the conflicts ranged from short, one or two response messages directly between the individuals involved to chains involving upwards of fifteen exchanges, drawing all team members into the discussion.

Focus Group

As a qualitative method, focus groups are situated between participant observation and interviews (Morgan, 1997). That is focus groups allow for group interaction but the focus is still driven by the researcher. Focus groups let participants compare and contrast their experiences with those of other participants (Morgan & Krueger, 1993). This is especially relevant in this study as we are looking for patterns *across* projects. The seven student research assistants participated in the focus group. The focus group lasted for one hour and ten minutes and produced eighteen pages of single-spaced transcripts. A semi-structured interview protocol that focused on participants' experiences of conflict with the community partners was used.

Interviews

The final method of data collection was interviews. Interviews allow researchers to access and "understand the social actor's experience and perspective" (Lindlof & Taylor, 2002, p. 173). Because of differences in roles and power with other team members, the two project leaders did not participate in the focus groups. Both project leaders were interviewed using the same semi-structured protocol that was used in the focus groups. The interviews lasted one hour and fifteen minutes and one and a half hours and produced 37 pages of single-spaced transcripts.

Structural Linkages

Structural links were estimated based on analysis of email chains, participant observation, and interview and focus group data. The network charts are not meant to be direct representations of the distance or strength of ties, but represent dominant patterns of interaction.

Data Analysis

A grounded theory approach was used for data analysis. Those using grounded theory seek to "identify categories and concepts that emerge from text and link these concepts into substantive and formal theories" (Ryan & Bernard, 2003, pp. 278-279). Grounded theory develops

rich concepts from the textual data that exists. The researchers each read through all the data individually and noted themes that emerged. The authors paid special attention to how the social context, relational history, and structural links (e.g., Black, 1976; Morrill, 1995; Harrison & Morrill, 2004) influence communication but did not limit themselves to these categories during the initial stages of analysis. Analysis continued as the researchers remained immersed in the data and participated in axial and selective coding (Strauss & Corbin, 1998). Throughout the analysis, the researchers created memos documenting their findings (Lindlof & Taylor, 2002). They discussed their findings with one another until they came to a mutual agreement on the themes in the data.

DESCRIPTION OF PROJECTS

The Context and Structure of Virtual Collaborations

There are important similarities and differences in the working relationships and structures of the three virtual collaborations that are influential in the enactment of communication patterns and conflict.

First, the academic team (Communicating Health)[2] was relatively stable. The two project leaders frequently worked as a team, with one leading two of the projects while the other led the third project. Additionally, there was one research assistant team member in common across all three projects, while several team members were involved in various capacities across multiple projects.

Second, the health issue addressed in all three projects was the same, although the campaigns and the contexts where the campaigns were enacted were different. Third, all projects had two goals: increase the desired health related behavior and establish the efficacy of certain principles of health communication campaigns. Fourth, each project involved a non-profit community health organization. These organizations were all similar in that they were strictly regulated by the federal government, but they were very different in how they approached their mission. The inclusion of these partner organizations in these projects represents a growing trend towards inter-organizational collaborations. As the problems facing society have become more complex, it has become evident that a single organization may not have the resources to adequately address the issue at hand. In this case, the academic team had the knowledge about campaign design but did not have the access needed to implement campaigns. The partner organizations had this access. By collaborating, both organizations were able to further their agendas and help meet a societal need.

Communicating Health had a very different working style and structure than partner organizations. The team was project-focused and while there was an ultimate authority when it came time to make decisions, problems were seen as opportunities for collaborative problem solving. Roles were specified but not strict. Any member of the team could talk to any other member of the team, and all team members helped out wherever needed, whenever needed, including nights and weekends. This project was the primary priority for Communicating Health, and the attitude was characterized by the motto "whatever it takes." Communicating Health had a very flat organizational hierarchy. As each project's partner organization had a unique style, they are described in the relevant sections below.

There were various degrees of relational history and collocation between members of the three projects. Two of the projects began with existing relational ties while the final project did not have a relational history. All three teams had face-to-face meetings during the creation and/or start-up phases of the projects and most shared close enough physical proximity that they had semi-regular (i.e., semi-annually, if not quarterly)

face-to-face meetings. However, all of the projects are considered virtual. Virtuality has been characterized as a continuum of varying degrees of geographical separation, temporal separation, and communication media richness (Connaughton & Daly, 2004). These projects are virtual because in each of them the teams were at least partially distributed geographically, not all communication was synchronous, and a variety of media was used to enable team interactions (i.e., face-to-face meetings, conference calls, email, etc.).

Finally, the structure of communication varied by project. In two of the projects all team members directly involved in implementation had direct lines of communication to all other team members (although there were distinct barriers to communication with the extended team in one of the projects). In the final project, interaction tended to flow through the gatekeepers of each of the organizations involved in the team.

Project 1: Corporate Campaigns

The Corporate Campaigns project was a collaboration between a non-profit community health organization (Health Initiatives) and the Communicating Health academic team. The organizations involved were geographically near enough for regular face-to-face meetings for the first half of the project, but the second half of the project shifted to a solely virtual relationship when all but one member of the Communicating Health team moved out of state. Members of both teams had worked together on a previous project. The Health Initiatives organization was the most corporate and hierarchical of the community partner organizations.

The organizations had very different working styles, structures, and goals. Health Initiatives structured its organization as a corporate entity rather than a traditional non-profit organization. The chains of command were very formal and hierarchical. There were "tried and true" ways

Figure 1. Communication network structure for the corporate campaigns project

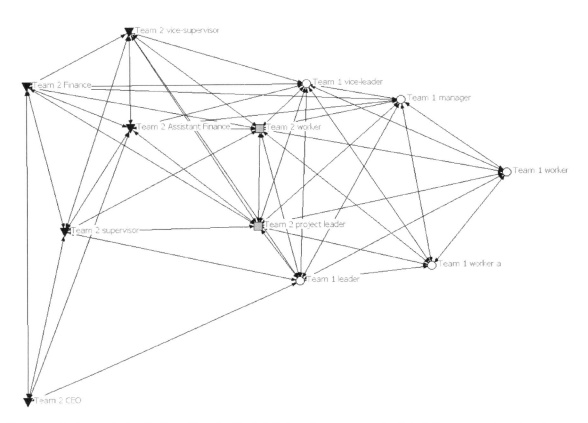

Note: Team 1 is Communicating Health and Team 2 is Health Initiatives. Gray squares are Health Initiative team members whose time was dedicated solely to the project, while black upside down triangles represent Health Initiative team members who had influence on the project regardless of their lack of official involvement

of doing things, and any challenge to those established methods was blocked. Finally, Health Initiatives only showed concern with the health behavior outcome and did not appear to see any real merit to the side of the project focused on advancing knowledge of health campaigns related to this health issue.

There is one other characteristic of this project that made it unique from the other two cases presented below. Two Health Initiatives team members became embedded in a dual-authority matrix system, a system that required them to

answer to both the Communicating Health team leader as well as the supervisors in their chain of command at Health Initiatives. These two team members had weekly face-to-face meetings with Communicating Health, socialized with the Communicating Health team, and the Communicating Health team worked in direct and close contact with them for the first year and a half of the project. Ultimately they became socialized into Communicating Health as well as Health Initiatives. Below is a graphical representation of the communication structure of the project.

Figure 2. Communication network structure for the 12 county intervention

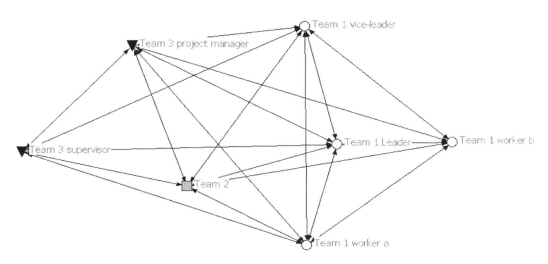

Note: Team 1 is Communicating Health, Team 2 is Southern Health Affiliates, and Team 3 is The Public Trust

Project 2: The 12 County Intervention

Project two involved three organizations, Communicating Health, the community partner (Southern Health Affiliates), and an outreach organization (The Public Trust) created by a political body to operate in conjunction with a specific branch of government. Members of Communicating Health and Southern Health Affiliates had a strong relational history, and Members of Southern Health Affiliates and The Public Trust also shared relational history. There was no existing relational connection between Communicating Health and The Public Trust. This project was designed to promote the health behavior in 12 counties across the state utilizing a combination of media campaigns and interventions in government offices with high public traffic.

The working styles of Communicating Health and Southern Health Affiliates were similar in many ways, with both having flattened hierarchies and a strong sense of mission The Public Trust operated on a much tighter budget with fewer resources and support staff. Much of The Pubic

Trust's working style was based on developing relationships and doing whatever satisficing was necessary to accomplish a goal. Conflict in this case arose primarily over lack of reciprocal information exchange and competing organizational goals, with The Public Trust placing organizational goals ahead of project goals. Below is a graphical representation of the communication structure between members of the teams.

Project 3: The Politics of Health Campaigns

The third project consisted of Communicating Health, the community partner (Great Lakes Health Promotion), and a political office (Political Ambitions) in charge of the intervention sites. This project is different from the other two in the respect that there was no relational history between Communicating Health and the other two organizations, although there was relational history between Great Lakes Health Promotion and Political Ambitions. Additionally, the entire project was developed and implemented virtually, with the exception of a face-to-face meeting as

Figure 3. Communication network structure for the politics of health campaign

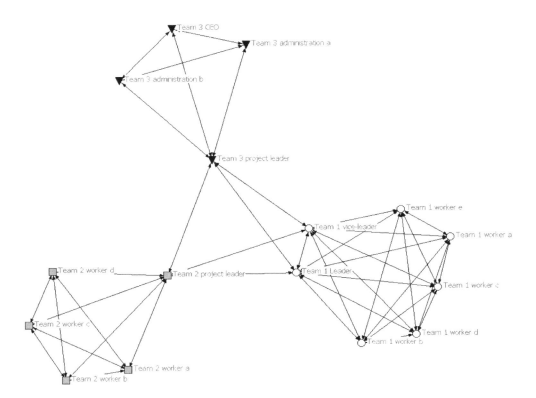

Note: Team 1 is Communicating Health, Team 2 is Great Lakes Health Promotion, and Team 3 is Political Ambitions.

the project was about to begin, and a couple of training sessions attended by key members of all three organizations. This project was similar to the 12 County Intervention in that it focused on promoting health behaviors in numerous counties across the state and in governmental offices, but the specifics of the campaign and interventions were different.

While the initial preference for this project was to have open information exchange between all members of all teams, it quickly became apparent that this was not the best working model. During the initial face-to-face team building meeting it became clear that several key members of Great Lakes Health Promotion were not on board with the goals or scope of the project, or trusting of the expertise or involvement of Communicating Health (similar to the first project, they expressed

resentment at "academics telling them how to do their jobs"). When the issue was broached by the leaders of Communicating Health with the leader of Great Lakes Health Promotion, the response was for Communicating Health not to worry about it, she would control her team, and Communicating Health should simply direct all communication to her team through her. Additionally, Great Lakes Health Promotion was trying to rebuild a constructive relationship with Political Ambitions (a relationship that had been contentious and problematic for many years), so she requested that any feedback or information seeking about problems or issues that required approval beyond Political Ambitions' designated project leader go through her. Given the long term goals of improving health behaviors and outcomes, Communicating Health agreed to this structure, which in essence created

Table 1. Nature of project conflicts

Larger Organizational Conflict	Immediate Team Member Conflict
Budgetary issues/billing/federal reporting Use of organizational resources Decision making and project control Access to information Design decisions Use and control of project personnel Approval of proposals Approval of campaign materials Control of messages Attempts to influence larger campaign Lack of communication Unilateral decisions Timing of campaign interventions Communication styles	Use of project resources and personnel Hiring, salary, and personnel roles Lack of communication about key issues Media buys Data collection issues Task completion and deadlines Inaccurate information for materials Delays in implementation Design of messages and materials Screening of volunteers Recruiting of volunteers Task completion Deadlines Project implementation issues Standards of campaigning Role boundaries

a set of three highly isolated teams rather than a single integrated team, with communication patterns as illustrated below. This is the only project where communication practices were intentionally designed to be restricted. While the goals of employee control and conflict minimization were explicitly stated, this design did result in unanticipated consequences as well.

RESULTS

At the beginning of the chapter we identified three questions we hoped to answer regarding conflict in virtual collaborations: (1) What are the primary types of conflict in inter-organizational collaborations? (2) How does the structure of communication influence team conflicts and dynamics? (3) What is the influence of social context on communicative practices and conflict?

The answers to the three questions are intertwined in that the types of conflict are often directly linked to the structure of the group, the social context, and communicative practices. However, brief answers to these questions will be offered before discussing the relationship between them.

Types of Conflict

Ultimately, all conflicts in the projects were directly related to the accomplishment of tasks and the running of the projects. The conflicts can be categorized into two types – those experienced with direct members of the team, and those arising from interaction with the larger organizations. Conflict with immediate team members tended to focus on the day-to-day work such as meeting timelines, designing materials, and meeting specific goals. When the larger organization became involved, issues tended to focus on decision making authority, control of finances, and organizational image and identity. While there were attributions made about the motivations of others involved in the conflicts, they all revolved around meeting the goals of the projects. Table 1 summarizes the types of conflicts encountered in the projects.

The Influence of Structure

Research question two asked how the structure of communication influenced conflict and team dynamics. The structure of communication norms and practices influenced team dynamics in a multitude of ways. First, when teams were tightly connected, the flow of information made the accomplishment of tasks easier, and team members felt more connected. Conflict was open and issues were discussed until they were (or appeared to be) resolved. For example when issues arose surrounding distribution of surveys with the Corporate Campaigns project, a series of emails went back and forth between the entire team attempting to solve the problem. Eventually, as it looked as if the issues were solved, the team member from Health Initiatives offered some playful banter at the end of her email, writing, "I'll defer to the rest of you nerds [referring to the academic team] to discuss the surveys/identifiers/confidentiality." This interaction not only illustrates how problems were solved by the team, but it also shows the relationship that had developed between Communicating Health and the immediate members of Health Initiatives.

However, when patterns of conflict related to lack of communication or lack of task accomplishment continued, conflict became more direct and confrontational with fewer pleasantries, and non-conflict communication decreased.

Next, when teams were not tightly connected and had to communicate through gatekeepers, the accomplishment of tasks was even more difficult and frustrating. One of the Communicating Health research assistants explained his frustration on the Politics of Health Campaigns project:

So in order for me to just get the simple answer of whether that was the way into which the state did its work, I was not allowed to directly contact the Great Lakes Health Promotions. I had to ask my questions to [the leader of Communicating Health]. He then had to ask the questions to Great Lakes Health Promotions. Great Lakes Health Promotions would tell him. He would forward the answer to me and the issue would always be it was never the complete response or I would always have follow up questions where if I could

have just directly picked up the phone and called somebody.

While conflict between team members in this gatekeeper system was minimal, occasionally the gatekeepers were bypassed. The same research assistant shared his experience when questioning whether a process was part of Great Lakes Health Promotions protocol or state law:

But there were several times where I just did the simplest reaching out to Great Lakes Health Promotions, wanting a simple response to a simple question and you know it blew up in my face [...] I received the most hostile email response from a Great Lakes Health Promotions' team member. To quote to me line and verse of the law and to tell me that they have never broken the law and that if I had any accusations that I wanted to make. My jaw was hanging open. I was like "All I wanted to know is this law or policy?" So that was one of the times when I was just asking a simple, harmless stupid question, and thought "Oh, I don't need to go through Communicating Health's leader, let me just ask somebody." And it blew up in my face.

While the structure of communication between teams influenced conflict and team dynamics, conflict also influenced communication processes, especially in the two projects that were virtual from inception. When conflicts arose in the Politics of Health project, initial attempts to resolve the grievances were very cordial, included pleasantries, and attempted to reason with logic. As the lack of communication and unilateral decision making continued and developed into serious problems for the integrity of the project, the pleasantries became fewer, the emails became more confrontational, and the conflicts escalated to the use of threats by both Political Ambitions and Communicating Health. For example, the leader of Political Ambitions sent the following in an email:

We may not completely understand the theoretical issues and arguments (and I point out that is not our goal here), [...The gatekeepers of the organization] insist on the right to review the materials and when necessary, edit them. The alternative is to not allow the materials on our premises.

Ultimately as a result of these conflicts, Communicating Health professed an unwillingness to engage in certain tasks and turned much of the responsibility for success and failure of the project to Great Lakes Health Promotion.

Similar patterns were seen in the 12 County Intervention project as well. While it would appear conflicts were resolved and understandings had been reached, more serious grievances kept arising over the course of the project. The emails became more direct and conversations more confrontational between the academic team and the point person, but pleasantries were always proffered by the Communicating Health team leader. They were reciprocated in only the most general sense by The Public Trust team leader, and eventually dropped off significantly. Ultimately, Communicating Health largely withdrew its interaction with Great Lakes Health Promotion, with only the team leader communicating with the partner teams, and then only when absolutely necessary. As the vice leader from Communicating Health shared:

The 12 Counties Intervention was a little unique that way though in that there hit a certain point where we just didn't care anymore because they had screwed things up so badly. And so I respond to almost no emails. I have almost nothing to say on the calls with them. I've really kind of removed myself from all communication with them except for the most necessary type of things.

As we see in this quote, there came a point in team relations where maintenance of the relationship was no longer a goal.

The Influence of Social Context

Research question 3 explored the influence of social context on communicative practices and conflict. The causes and enactment of conflict are largely a function of the social context. While all conflicts were task-oriented, they stem from issues of power and control, roles, goals, lack of communication, task accomplishment, and expertise. Many of these issues vary based on organizational values and culture and mission. Shared history led to more attempts at relational maintenance, while shared working styles and normative information led to conflict being handled directly and with humor, with little threat to relationships, as we saw in the above example when the Health Initiatives team member referred to the academic Communicating Health team members as "nerds." Yet, the distance associated with being geographically dispersed meant there were fewer opportunities for monitoring activities, and also fewer opportunities to develop personal attributions for behavior. As one of the leaders stated:

So I had to get to the point where I had to kind of let go. You know, it's going to be what it's going to be and I had to recognize that I couldn't control everything, unless I was going to fly back every month, which I wasn't going to do.

However, face-to-face meetings were enough for team members to begin to make judgments about the motivations and actions of others. Notice in the quote below how one of the research assistants who worked on the Corporate Campaigns project attempted to explain the experiences of the Health Initiative team members who were assigned to the implementation of the campaigns (i.e., those who were also acculturated into Communicating Health):

I think...the community outreach workers, definitely felt like they were, not serving two different bosses, but at the same time they were because there was such a struggle for control. I think they definitely had to work hard to be part of Communicating Health and I think they were personally there with our goals and what we were doing and enjoyed being part of the grant team but then when they had to go back and work as part of their own larger organization, because they still retained some element of their jobs in that organization, there was a totally different feel and they wanted to be able to regain those jobs they had to kind of compromise but definitely they felt the power struggle and they were torn. [...] I would say interpersonally we had an easy time developing trust and that helped us when the task trust wasn't always there also.

The nature of these conflicts and their manifestations and consequences has implications for the design of virtual collaborations. Conscious choice about designing and developing structures for virtual collaboration become possible when looking at communication structure and relationships. Early socialization and shared tasks across team members from different organizations involved in the collaboration creates a stronger sense of team and facilitates the development of shared norms and cultural values. This early socialization also allows conflict to be addressed openly and productively (assuming that is the culture of the organization they are being socialized into), with concern for relationships remaining intact, even as projects shift to more virtual interactions and more discrete tasks. One of the research assistants pointed out the importance of relationships on the Corporate Campaign project:

I guess, we all really liked each other and we all did get pretty close so even when that conflict arose, I think that everybody for the most part came to the table willing to get through that and willing to hear the other's point of view simply because we liked each other. And although it became more difficult when we moved to a mediated

setting, I don't think I had a bad experience with the mediated setting. I think that we already laid a solid foundation.

Relational history and face-to-face interactions, along with open communication patterns between team members from different organizations, can have very positive consequences for teams and conflict. For example, some of the early patterns of the 12 County Campaign project demonstrated both concern for relationships and concern for tasks. There was development of shared norms among many of the team members. One of the leaders shared the following about his face-to-face meetings with the individual responsible for project implementation for the 12 County Campaign:

I think the only useful part about having face-to-face meetings was in the early stages when we were trying to get the project manager sort of in her role, and being able to communicate with her what those were and what our expectations were and that we were actually on her side trying to help her. And I think they were very useful at that point in time. One of the first big meetings I had with her about those kinds of issues she actually was in tears most of the meeting. She was so upset about the whole process. She was so afraid we didn't like her. She was resentful at her boss for the way he had brought her in and he was using her in different ways than he was supposed to be so it was a very intense emotional thing that we had to spend a couple of hours talking through and working through, just she and I sitting in a bar. So I think those parts were very important.

It is primarily because of the actions of one key player (i.e., the leader of The Public Trust) with specific power and assumed expertise that the project is threatened and relationships become less social and friendly. In this particular case, collocation may have been an effective way to resolve task related conflict, but would have required a level of micro-management that may not have been feasible even if collocated. While it is possible to design systems of interaction to promote the sharing of norms and tasks, and that facilitate relationship building, it is difficult to design a system to overcome the self-interested actions of a single individual who has power and is determined to promote organizational goals at the expense of project goals.

Ultimately the structure of communication and relational history between the Communicating Health and the Southern Health Affiliates served to facilitate attempts to manage conflict and keep tasks on track, but the lack of oversight of daily tasks as a result of being geographically distributed proved a stronger influence when one partner chose to place organizational goals ahead of project goals. One Communicating Health team member noted the difference between being collocated and being virtual:

It's like you don't have to watch yourself so much when you know no one is coming to knock on your door sort of thing and they can't come into your office saying "Let me see this, let me see this."

Finally, and perhaps surprisingly, when there is no relational history and when organizations have distinct and varied working styles and goals, the process of restricting communication may actually reduce conflict in a fairly functional way. This closed system of communication can still be very frustrating and can cause delays in the effective accomplishment of tasks, but reduces the potential for normative conflict between individual team members. Since they have limited information and ability to communicate, the focus is necessarily oriented to task accomplishment. As one of the research assistants pointed out, there was the potential for a lot of conflict in the Politics of Health Campaigns project, but the conflict did not have the opportunity to occur. Note in his response that this structure also resulted in decreased satisfaction with the team:

We just didn't know what was going on. I was very dissatisfied with the inter-team communication but I don't say whose fault that is. It's irrelevant. Maybe we could have done something but we were instructed not to. And for that reason I think there were a lot of conflicts or a lot of passive aggressive tension that never played out or actually a lot of passive aggressive possibilities that never played out because we didn't even have the chance to do it and that was probably not a bad thing that we didn't have chance to be passive aggressive, it just seems that it led to a lot of fake interactions with individuals.

A Confluence of Issues

There are issues that seem to be beyond the ability of a communication design perspective to solve, though. The complications caused by larger organizational issues, such as when key decisions or influence are enacted by powerful organizational members who are, at best, only tangentially involved in the development or implementation of the project, are relatively impossible to overcome or plan for in any systematic way. This is evident across all three projects. In the Corporate Campaign project the actions of finance, indirect supervisors, and even the CEO were more disruptive to the project than any actions by team members involved in the implementation of the project. As one of the leaders of Communicating Health shared about the Corporate Campaign project:

[The CEO] was absolutely the problem. And it got to the point that I had to sit down with him and say that I was going to send the money back, I was going to decline the grant, I was going to send back 1.7 million dollars and say I'm not going to do this project unless this changes, this changes, this changes. And I brought out all my bad words[...]You know I was extremely unprofessional but he finally got the message, I wasn't asking, I was telling.

In the 12 County Campaign, the leader of The Public Trust provided a rationale and defense of unilaterally made key decisions that was placed squarely on the board of directors of the organization. Finally, in the Politics of Health Campaigns project, the gatekeepers to the Political Ambitions leader held the most influence and enacted the most power. According to a team member of Communicating Health:

And then when Political Ambitions started jerking the leader of Great Lakes Health Promotion around and saying, "Oh no, you can't [do this and you can't talk to them and you can't put that up]" We were like, what the hell is going on here…and it would take months to get approval on something. That's not professional respect. That's just sadism.

These problems occurred as a direct result of distinct organizational goals and work styles, lack of understanding of key project goals, and different organizational structures, and are likely to occur regardless of how specific roles and project tasks are delineated in advance. These problems tend to be exacerbated by closed communication systems and restrictions on information, but because of power, organizational structure, and competing goals, those lines of communication are not always able to be opened.

DISCUSSION

Overall these findings point to patterns of conflict in virtual collaborations that are focused almost exclusively on task and work related behavior. While conflict in teams is common and often even desirable, conflict in inter-organizational collaborations is compounded by the differences in organizational cultures, goals, communication patterns, and working styles. While virtual teams are likely to develop their own sets of norms, many virtual teams are intra-organizational and at least share a sense of larger organizational goals and have shared norms and understandings of the organizational culture. Creating these shared norms and understandings in inter-organizational virtual teams is much more difficult. In these three projects, the only project that developed shared norms was the Corporate Campaigns project, and those norms developed during the early stages of the project while the teams were collocated and had significant face-to-face interactions.

In the other projects, the nature of virtual relationships precluded close interpersonal relational development and interpersonal trust that is often developed through spontaneous interactions that occur when teams and individuals are collocated. This is both problematic and beneficial. Having limited social connections did reduce conflicts that arise from personal differences, but when conflicts inevitably arose, the shared trust that is often necessary for positive conflict resolution was missing. This lack of trust, combined with different goals and work styles and cultures meant that when significant conflict did arise, relationships and communication became strained, and communication became less frequent, more direct, and lacked standard relational discourse.

While much of the conflict in these projects can be traced to differences in organizational goals and cultures, the communication structure of the projects and the virtual nature of the collaborations also contributed to difficulties in the projects. Having flatter team structures with direct communication links between all team members facilitates the sharing of information and the completion of tasks in a more timely fashion. However, this is only true if parties are willing to share the necessary information. Having structural patterns the limit interaction between team members, such as the utilization of gatekeepers evident in the Politics of Health project, both delayed and complicated information sharing, ultimately leading to more conflict and less trust of other team members. This often led to a sense of "us versus them" rather than "we are all in this together." Additionally, because of the virtual nature of the projects, monitoring of tasks and garnering needed information is more difficult, and it is necessary to rely on team partners to share relevant information and complete their tasks.

Best Practices and Pitfalls

Communication design (e.g., Aakhus, 2007; Harrison & Morrill, 2004) provides a compelling framework for the design of inter-organizational team development and communication structures and patterns. This approach advocates examining the intended and unintended consequences of communication protocols, and framing them within the social context of work. By doing so, it is possible to design better systems of interaction to achieve desired goals. The findings from this project suggest the following best practices, with unintended consequences representing the pitfalls.

First, communication network structure should be open with all team members directly connected to and in communication with all other team members. This has the intended consequences of enhanced and more rapid sharing of information and ideas, less filtering of information that may cause distortion, and the ability to connect and form direct working relationships with other team members. It is also likely to reduce ambiguity in decision-making authority, with team leaders able to step in and mediate when decisions are unclear. However, having the open lines of communication may have pitfalls that arise from certain social contexts. For example, in the Politics of Health, when direct communication was attempted with team members who were less vested in the project, conflict escalated and relationships became less trusting.

This leads to the second recommendation for best practices. Team members who are assigned to a project on a full time basis are likely to become more committed to the overall project goals and develop more shared norms as a team. Without competing demands of other organizationally separate tasks, integration of all team members should be more easily accomplished. Therefore, when negotiating inter-organizational collaborations, each organization should be upfront about the level of commitment that can be expected from its members. Furthermore, these organizations should make necessary compromises to allow some or all of the project members to shift work responsibilities to others in the organization so that focus can be given to the project. This may also reduce the burdens of dual reporting often found in matrix organizational structures.

Third, inter-organizational virtual collaborations operate better if there is one clear leader of the project. Many of the more serious conflicts in the projects presented in this study arose from the involvement of organizational team members not directly connected to the projects. Leadership and decision boundaries need to be clearly delineated and negotiated in advance, with clear procedures in place to address any outside interference. Unfortunately, this is not always easily accomplished. One of the biggest pitfalls in these projects occurred as a result of larger organizational concerns overriding agreements that were already negotiated. Perhaps one way to address this pitfall is to build meta-communication about shared goals and organizational agreements into messages and meetings on a consistent basis. Creating a norm of explicit discussion about roles and expectations as part of everyday conversations rather than only when conflict occurs may result in lower levels of non-productive conflict and insure individual team member commitment to the project.

Finally, having face-to-face meetings to help establish shared norms and working relationships can have positive results. However, the experiences in these projects suggest that for those meetings to be effective they have to happen early and frequently. When face-to-face meetings are infrequent, they may serve to provide just enough personal information for team members to bring personal attributions about behavior into their sensemaking schemas when conflicts arise.

FUTURE RESEARCH DIRECTIONS

The findings in this project point to several avenues of future investigation. Much of the interpretation and management of conflict in these projects have an undertone of trust that has not been fully explored. While there is research on how trust affects conflict processes (e.g., Harrison & Doerfel, 2006) and literature on trust in virtual teams (e.g., Benoit & Kelsey, 2003; Crossman & Lee-Kelley, 2004), the data in this project did not support a full exploration of trust. While Liu, Magjuka, and Lee (2008) provide an initial investigation, these concepts are in need of further development.

Additionally, the findings on face-to-face interactions to support virtual team development show both promise and problems. The overall success of the projects in terms of meeting project goals was neither enhanced nor hindered directly as a result of face-to-face relational maintenance. Instead, what these projects suggest is that the experience of working on these teams is more enjoyable for many team members when they have the opportunity for developing closer interpersonal relationships. Ultimately, this area would benefit from additional systematic research on the role of face-to-face interactions in managing conflict as well as enhancing relationships and accomplishing project goals.

Finally, while these projects demonstrate the nature and enactment of conflict in inter-organizational virtual collaboration, there is little on the processes of resolution of the grievances. Research exploring different mechanisms for managing and resolving conflict would add to understanding how virtual teams can more successfully manage conflict.

CONCLUSION

This chapter explored conflict in three inter-organizational collaborations. Overall conflict was prevalent in the projects, and differences in the enactment of conflict are related to both the social context of the inter-organizational relationships as well as the structural communication linkages between team members. Additionally, relational history plays an important role in how conflicts are enacted, with members who have stronger ties and more shared norms able to express conflict directly with little threat to the relationship. Conflict in the absence of those ties tended to escalate more, do more relational damage, and decreased overall interaction between team members. Conflicts with team members tended to focus on task accomplishment, role, or authority, while conflicts with extended organizational members tended to focus on competing organizational goals, resources, and use of personnel.

REFERENCES

Aakhus, M. (2007). Communication as design. *Communication Monographs*, *74*, 112–117. doi:10.1080/03637750701196383

Benoit, A. A., & Kelsey, B. L. (2003). Further understanding of trust and performance in virtual teams. *Small Group Research*, *34*, 575–618. doi:10.1177/1046496403256011

Black, D. (1976). *The behavior of law*. New York: Academic Press.

Black, D. (1984). Social control as a dependent variable . In Black, D. (Ed.), *Toward a general theory of social control* (*Vol. 1*, pp. 1–36). New York: Academic Press.

Connaughton, S. L., & Daly, J. A. (2004). Leading from afar: Strategies for effectively leading virtual teams . In Godar, S., & Ferris, S. P. (Eds.), *Virtual & collaborative teams: Process, technologies, & practice* (pp. 49–75). Hershey, PA: Idea Group Inc.

Crossman, A., & Lee-Kelley, L. (2004). Trust, commitment and team working: The paradox of virtual organizations. *Global Networks, 4*, 375–390. doi:10.1111/j.1471-0374.2004.00099.x

Harrison, T. R., & Doerfel, M. L. (2006). Competitive and cooperative conflict communication climates: The influence of ombuds processes on trust and commitment to the organization. *The International Journal of Conflict Management, 17*, 129–153. doi:10.1108/10444060610736611

Harrison, T. R., & Morrill, C. (2004). Ombuds processes and disputant reconciliation. *Journal of Applied Communication Research, 32*(4), 318–342. doi:10.1080/0090988042000276005

Hinds, P. J., & Bailey, D. E. (2003). Out of sight, out of sync: Understanding conflict in distributed teams. *Organization Science, 14*, 615–632. doi:10.1287/orsc.14.6.615.24872

Hinds, P. J., & Mortensen, M. (2005). Understanding conflict in geographically distributed teams: The moderating effects of shared identity, shared context, and spontaneous communication. *Organization Science, 16*, 290–307. doi:10.1287/orsc.1050.0122

Jackson, S. (1998). Disputation by design. *Argumentation, 12*, 183–198. doi:10.1023/A:1007743830491

Lindlof, T. R., & Taylor, B. C. (2002). *Qualitative communication research methods*. Thousand Oaks, CA: Sage.

Liu, X., Magjuka, R. J., & Lee, S. (2008). An examination of the relationship among structure, trust, and conflict management styles in virtual teams. *Performance Improvement Quarterly, 21*, 77–93. doi:10.1002/piq.20016

Llewellyn, K., & Hoebel, E. A. (1983). *The Cheyenne Way: Conflict and Case Law in Primitive Jurisprudence*. Norman, OK: Oklahoma University Press.

Montoya-Weiss, M. M., Massey, A. P., & Song, M. (2001). Getting it together: Temporal coordination and conflict management in global virtual teams. *Academy of Management Journal, 44*, 1251–1262. doi:10.2307/3069399

Morgan, D. L. (1997). *Focus groups as qualitative research*. Thousand Oaks, CA: Sage.

Morgan, D. L., & Krueger, R. A. (1993). When to use focus groups and why . In Morgan, D. L. (Ed.), *Successful Focus Groups: Advancing the State of the Art*. Thousand Oaks, CA: Sage.

Morrill, C. (1995). *The executive way: Conflict management in corporations*. Chicago: University of Chicago Press.

Mortensen, M., & Hinds, P. J. (2001). Conflict and shared identity in geographically distributed teams. *The International Journal of Conflict Management, 12*, 212–238. doi:10.1108/eb022856

Paul, S., Samarah, I. M., Seetharaman, P., & Myktyn, P. P. (2005). An empirical investigation of collaborative conflict management style in group support system-based global virtual teams. *Journal of Management Information Systems, 21*, 185–222.

Pondy, L. R. (1967). Organizational conflict: Concepts and models. *Administrative Science Quarterly, 12*, 296–320. doi:10.2307/2391553

Putnam, L. L., & Poole, M. S. (1987). Conflict and negotiation . In Jablin, F. M., Putnam, L. L., Roberts, K. H., & Porter, L. W. (Eds.), *Handbook of Organizational Communication: An Interdisciplinary perspective* (pp. 549–599). Newbury Park, CA: Sage Publications.

Ryan, G. W., & Bernard, H. R. (2003). Data management and analysis methods . In Denzin, N. K., & Lincoln, Y. S. (Eds.), *Collecting and interpreting qualitative materials* (pp. 259–309). Thousand Oaks, CA: Sage.

Shin, Y. (2005). Conflict resolution in virtual teams. *Organizational Dynamics, 34,* 331–345. doi:10.1016/j.orgdyn.2005.08.002

Strauss, A., & Corbin, J. (1998). *Basics of qualitative research: Techniques and procedures for developing grounded theory.* Thousand Oaks, CA: Sage.

Swidler, A. (1986). Culture in actions: Symbols and strategies. *American Sociological Review, 51,* 273–286. doi:10.2307/2095521

van Eemeren, F. H., Grootendorst, R., Jackson, S., & Jacobs, S. (1993). *Reconstructing argumentative discourse.* Tuscaloosa: University of Alabama Press.

Walls, J. A. Jr, & Callister, R. R. (1995). Conflict and its management. *Journal of Management, 21,* 515–558. doi:10.1177/014920639502100306

ADDITIONAL READING

Dani, S. S., Burns, N. D., Backhouse, C. J., & Kochhar, A. K. (2006). The implications of organizational culture and trust in the working of virtual teams. *Proceedings of the Institution of Mechanical Engineers. Part B, Journal of Engineering Manufacture, 220,* 951–960. doi:10.1243/09544054JEM415

DeRosa, D. M., Hantula, D. A., Kock, N., & D'Arcy, J. (2004). Trust and leadership in virtual teamwork: A media naturalness perspective. *Human Resource Management, 43,* 219–232. doi:10.1002/hrm.20016

Felstiner, W. L. F., Abel, R. L., & Sarat, A. (1980-81). The emergence and transformation of disputes: Naming, blaming, claiming.... *Law & Society Review, 15,* 631–654. doi:10.2307/3053505

Greenberg, P. S., Greenberg, R. H., & Antonucci, Y. L. (2007). Creating and sustaining trust in virtual teams. *Business Horizons, 50,* 325–333. doi:10.1016/j.bushor.2007.02.005

Jarvenpaa, S. L., Knoll, K., & Leidner, D. E. (1998). Is anybody out there? Antecedents of trust in global virtual teams. *Journal of Management Information Systems, 14,* 29–64.

Jarvenpaa, S. L., & Leidner, D. E. (1999). Communication and trust in global virtual teams. *Organization Science, 10,* 791–815. doi:10.1287/orsc.10.6.791

Jarvenpaa, S. L., Shaw, T. R., & Staples, D. S. (2004). Toward contextualized theories of trust: The role of trust in global virtual teams. *Information Systems Research, 15,* 250–267. doi:10.1287/isre.1040.0028

Kolb, D. M., & Putnam, L. L. (1992). Introduction: The dialectics of disputing . In Kolb, D. M., & Bartunek, J. M. (Eds.), *Hidden conflict in organizations: Uncovering behind-the-scenes disputes* (pp. 1–31). Newbury Park, CA: Sage.

Kolb, D. M., & Putnam, L. L. (1992). The multiple faces of conflict in organizations. *Journal of Organizational Behavior, 13*(3), 311–324. doi:10.1002/job.4030130313

Krebs, S. A., Hobman, E. V., & Bordia, P. (2006). Virtual teams and group member dissimilarity: Consequences for the development of trust. *Small Group Research, 37,* 721–741. doi:10.1177/1046496406294886

Morrill, C. (1995). *The executive way: Conflict management in corporations.* Chicago: University of Chicago Press.

Morrill, C., Zald, M. N., & Rao, H. (2003). Covert political conflict in organizations: Challenges from below. *Annual Review of Sociology, 29,* 391–415. doi:10.1146/annurev.soc.29.010202.095927

Nader, L. (1990). *Harmony Ideology: Justice and Control in a Zapotec Mountain Village*. Stanford, CA: Stanford University Press.

Pinkley, R. L. (1990). Dimensions of conflict frame: Disputant interpretations of conflict. *The Journal of Applied Psychology, 75*(2), 117–126. doi:10.1037/0021-9010.75.2.117

Poole, M. S., & Garner, J. T. (2006). Perspectives on workgroup conflict and communication. In Oetzel, J. G., & Ting-Toomey, S. (Eds.), *The Sage Handbook of Conflict Communication* (pp. 267–292). Thousand Oaks, CA: Sage Publications.

KEY TERMS AND DEFINITIONS

Collaboration: The process of multiple individuals, teams, or organizations working together to accomplish a shared goal.

Collocation: In inter-organizational collaborations this is when teams are geographically near enough to allow for frequent face-to-face meetings, and those meetings become part of the routine working arrangements of the project.

Communication Design: The process of deliberately designing systems of communication to help achieve the desired goals of interaction.

Conflict: Involves grievances between interdependent people that arise from incompatible values, attitudes, goals, and/or beliefs.

Social Context: Consists of the following dimensions: organizational resources and power, relational history, the nature of social ties, shared normative and cultural information and values, communicative links and practices, and degrees of collocation.

Structural Links: The ties or network nodes that connect individuals and teams together. These may be deliberately designed or they may occur organically.

ENDNOTES

[1] The concept of communication structure is distinct from formal organizational structure in that organizational structure typically delineates who reports to whom (i.e., the formal chain of command) and communication structure refers to who can communicate with whom. Communication structure is also slightly different from network structure as it focuses on the formal rather than the emergent connections and it also consists of how communication occurs.

[2] Pseudonyms are used for all organizations.

Chapter 3
Online Teaching as Virtual Work in the New (Political) Economy

Roy Schwartzman
The University of North Carolina at Greensboro, USA

David Carlone
The University of North Carolina at Greensboro, USA

ABSTRACT

Online teaching and learning has been adopted throughout higher education with minimal critical attention to the challenges it poses to traditional definitions of academic labor. This chapter explores four areas where the nature of academic labor becomes contestable through the introduction of online instruction: (1) the boundaries demarcating work from personal time; (2) the relative invisibility of online labor; (3) the documentation, recognition, and rewards attendant to online instruction; and (4) the illusory empowerment of online students as consumers. The theory and practice of what constitutes "legitimate" labor in higher education require substantial reconsideration to incorporate the online dimension.

INTRODUCTION

Online teaching occupies a contested site for the definition, performance, recognition, and reward of labor in higher education. Contestability in this context refers to public documents, policies, and practices that promote or embrace online teaching and learning (OTL) while also inviting questions about the role of online teaching as academic labor. Online teaching is conditioned by the context in which it is implemented. Several features of the contemporary context warrant discussion.

The first feature is an enduring concern for the interaction between corporate-oriented and public-oriented communication and organizing. A series of scholars have examined, using a colonization model, the impact of managerial rhetoric and practice on the public sphere, or on public goods, such as education (Giroux & Myrsiades, 2001). The key issue in these works is colonization of the lifeworld by the system (Deetz, 1992, 1995; Habermas, 1987), of the public sphere by the corporation (Sproule, 1988,

DOI: 10.4018/978-1-61520-979-8.ch003

1989, 1990), or of a value logos by an instrumental logos (Sayer, 1999; Tompkins, 2005).

Stanley Deetz offers a particularly eloquent account of this concern. For Deetz (1992, 1995), organization leaders and members, particularly those in corporate organizations, suffer from managerialism, or an ideology that lays out what managers should believe, say, and do, and the legitimate role of managers in organizations and society. Defined by managerialism, managers make decisions based on narrow meanings of the world, such as control and efficiency. As well, managerialism conditions non-managers to accept the authority of managers and their decisions based on control and efficiency. Today, managerialism likely influences much university decision making (Giroux & Myrsiades, 2001), shaping the meaning and implementation of online teaching.

The second feature is the broader cultural, political, and economic context. Key aspects of this context in the US include economic disinvestment in public institutions and structures, political cynicism, an embrace of the market as a solution to destabilized cultural authority (Grossberg, 2005), and increasing economic inequality (Munger, 2002). Public policy informed by neoliberalism has sought to turn labor into a fixed cost and a principal site for locating economic risk, while increasing rewards for finance capital and industries (Grossberg, 2005). Finally, capitalist commodities and value routinely stem from the direct exploitation of cultural knowledge and human connection (Lazzarato, 1996; Thrift, 2006).

Developments such as these broadly affect university operations. In the specific case of online teaching, these developments help position online teaching as, simultaneously, a way to improve human capital, widen access to higher education (to improve human capital), and contain costs in times of inadequate public funding. Thus, although OTL may be shaped in progressive ways, the current context exerts considerable influence, pushing online teaching in directions that systematically devalue or marginalize academic labor performed by teachers and students.

BACKGROUND

Before proceeding, the terminology of OTL requires clarification. In this chapter, references to online teaching and learning denote fully computer-mediated courses and programs rather than online components that supplement traditional classroom teaching. We would argue, however, that the labor-related issues discussed herein become incrementally more salient as more instructional work migrates toward computer-mediated communication and away from face-to-face interpersonal interactions.

One of the most comprehensive national surveys of faculty who teach online courses asked respondents to rank the importance of factors that will most likely determine the success of online instruction (Kim & Bonk, 2006). The results revealed a clear mismatch between faculty's educational preparation and the skills faculty themselves associated with successful online teaching. The top four factors, in order of importance, were: monetary support, pedagogical competency, technical competency, and improvements in online technologies (Kim & Bonk, 2006). A major challenge these and other online instructors face is how some of these factors might remain unrecognized or under-acknowledged within the definitions of labor that higher education institutions deem "legitimate" academic work.

Regarding labor issues associated with OTL, extant research concentrates on comparing the relative workload of online versus on-ground teaching (Shedletsky & Aitken, 2001). By contrast, we posit that online education introduces *qualitative* differences in the nature of academic work, differences that often escape institutionalized practices of managing and monitoring labor in higher education. The central issue becomes less a matter of sheer workload than one of understanding the nature of work itself. The following sections describe various dimensions of OTL where instructors and students confront tensions between the prevalent standards governing traditional academic labor and the emergent types of labor involved in online education.

Online education presents important challenges to the traditional scope of what qualifies as labor appropriate for academic workers. The standard Marxist theme of alienation traces the separation of workers from the products of their labor (Marx, 1978). The expansion of work-related roles and expectations in OTL magnifies the risk of worker alienation as the skills for doing the job diverge from the knowledge base necessary for teaching in an academic field. Positive identification with one's own labor also could become problematic the more that labor encroaches on spheres of activity (such as family) customarily sequestered from the realm of academic work. In addition, discontent with institutional recognition may discourage faculty from engaging in online teaching. These factors could converge to provide negative legitimation (Berger & Luckmann, 1967) for online instruction by systematically failing to recognize its incompatibility with the prevailing narrow definitions of teaching that were shaped within a paradigm of face-to-face, synchronous classroom instruction.

Problematic notions of labor also affect students. The entrepreneurial lure of online education touted as infinitely flexible to schedules and geographic locations gives an impression of consumer control. Such portrayals obscure the labor of learning that requires self-discipline to meet due dates, monitor course content updates, and adapt to schedules of other students when engaged in collaborative assignments. The illusory independence of online learning provides potent promotional material but obscures the accountability that accompanies such freedom.

The conundrums of online instruction discussed in this chapter risk alienating online laborers from the social and academic milieu of higher education. Paradoxically, this alienation that occurs in academic practice accompanies simultaneous public affirmations of the centrality and importance of OTL. This study examines four locales where online teaching and learning become publicly contestable as labor: the boundaries demarcating work from personal time; the relative invisibility of online labor; the documentation, recognition, and rewards attendant to online instruction; and the illusory empowerment of online students as consumers.

DISJUNCTIONS IN THE LABOR OF ONLINE TEACHING AND LEARNING

The subsequent sections navigate the contested terrain of online teaching by examining several discontinuities between the theoretical promise and the actual practice of such academic labor. These disjunctions occur on multiple levels. Each set of paradoxes foregrounds underlying tensions between prevailing conceptions of labor operant in higher education and the way academic labor becomes altered in an online educational context.

Burgeoning Economies of Scale, Blurring Bounds of Labor

An attractive feature of online courses has been their presumed capability of accommodating more students using two economies of scale: reaching students who cannot readily access traditional campus instruction and expanding the size of sections beyond the physical limitations of classroom structures. Advocates of online teaching seek to use information and communication technology to deliver education to a wider array of students at lower cost (Hewett & Powers, 2007). As the classroom walls tumble, the enrollment capacity of online courses supposedly can expand to accommodate more students (Draves, 2000). Essentially, online teaching may increase instructional revenues, measured as the difference between the tuition generated by students enrolled and the costs associated with the course. To date, however, this promise has proven elusive. For example, The University of North Carolina's report on distance education throughout its 16 campus system cited costs unrelated to instructor salaries of online courses at $437 per student per course compared to $326 for their face-to-face counterparts (UNC Board of Governors, 2004). These costs, additionally, do not include the expenses involved in training, hardware and software upgrades, instructional technology specialists, or other expenditures beyond what the traditional version of a course requires. The report noted that the average size of online courses in its study was only 20 compared to a face-to-face class average of 77 students. If online class size reached parity with traditional classes, direct costs per student should decline proportionately. Current methods of cost calculation have difficulty accounting for technology and support costs. The University of North Carolina (2004) report notes:

The additional costs of technical expertise (often in the form of instructional technology specialists), training, hardware and software required to adapt courses for technology-mediated delivery add further to course development costs. This represents a new category of costs not present in traditionally-taught courses and not anticipated by our current funding model. (p. 14)

Online teaching, then, holds appeal for its (perhaps unrealized) potential to increase both access to and revenue for higher education institutions.

Justifying online teaching on the basis of cost containment subtly foregrounds the production of surplus labor; the difference between an instructor's teaching-related salary and tuition generated by the instructor's students may be considered surplus labor. Indeed, an economy of scale presumes increasing output while maintaining cost. Conceiving the academic labor of online teaching in terms of surplus labor raises the questions of to

whom and for what the value of the surplus labor should flow (Curtis, 2001).

In addition, attention to the production of surplus labor helps us to consider not just how much surplus labor is produced, but how that surplus labor is produced (Gibson-Graham, 1996). For example, comparisons of face-to-face and online teaching often fail to distinguish adequately between the labor involved in each form of pedagogy. The well-documented "no significant difference phenomenon" consistently documents equivalent learning outcomes in online and face-to-face courses (Russell, 2001). Setting aside any methodological concerns, such studies measure outcomes such as test scores, student satisfaction, and demonstrable skills independently of the instructional inputs invested to achieve these results.

This lack of differentiation between the labor of classroom versus online teaching glosses over the ways online teaching alters traditional practices of academic work, obscuring possible struggles over the meaning, practice, and value of teaching. Thus, online teaching represents a particular configuration of economic activity, as well as a new way to organize teaching.

Considerations of online teaching, then, should consider questions of economic and social value. However, growth in economies of scale may highlight economic value and obscure social value. In particular, the "illusion of infinite scalability" (Schwartzman, 2007a) fails to acknowledge encroachment of the online workplace into heretofore personal or private domains and the implications this has for what counts as academic labor. Rather than simply growing enrollment, as with, say, movement from a discussion-based course to a lecture-based course, much of the work of online teaching is generated by the ease of use of electronic means of communication. In other words, as "seats" are added to online courses, the amount of labor conducted in typically personal space and time may increase dramatically. According to one online instructor, "The students expect me to be online 24/7. I find myself glued and much more dependent on my computer" (Vanhorn, Pearson, & Child, 2008, p. 31).

The ease and speed of electronic information production has outstripped the capacity to process that information. Online instruction accelerates student expectations for responses. The speed of online communication and the ease of creating messages foster the belief that instructor response time should shrink accordingly. The development of electronic communication tools, especially in computer-mediated communication, has proceeded by using a production-focused economic model based on quantity of output (outgoing messages). In addition, a technological imperative mentality emerges: as new technological tools become available—such as new means of interacting with students through social networking tools embedded in courseware—instructors feel compelled to use them. As a result, the technological imperative drives online course instructors to maximize the opportunities for interaction so the course stays current with technological innovation and appears more engaging to tech-savvy students. Multiplying these interactive tools, however, also multiplies the channels of communication that the instructor must monitor. The newest release of Blackboard, for example, embeds wikis, blogs, discussion boards, chats, whiteboards, and podcasts as communication options in addition to conventional tools such as e-mail.

The efficacy of computer-mediated communication relies on concomitant improvements in the quality of sorting, interpreting, and evaluating messages. Many of the information overload woes expressed by online instructors reflect the asymmetry between information production capacity and information processing capacity. Focusing on a "production" metaphor to describe online instruction may exacerbate this problematic imbalance between the quantity of incoming information and the quality of its processing. Reconfiguring online instructors more as information managers could at least call attention to the risk and consequences of information proliferation (Rosenberg, 2001).

The production bias that infuses the world of online instruction relies on the questionable assumption that information plenitude contributes to better quality. Unrestricted multiplication of data without sufficient means for assimilating, comprehending, or evaluating that data may plunge instructors into a pedagogical miasma. A producer-oriented bias in OTL may qualify as symptomatic of a larger focus on production as the prevailing descriptor of academic labor, at least from the instructional side. The best scholars are presumably those who are most prolific, an equation that privileges quantity of publications even when quality measures such as "impact factors" are included.

While online teaching may be promoted as a cost-saving measure for universities and governments, its practice redefines "teaching" in ways that colonize personal areas traditional definitions of teaching have preserved. By shrinking expected feedback time for evaluating student work, rendering the teacher a worker constantly "on call," and relying on manufactured participant motivation (through various interactive tools) rather than spatio-temporal discursive generators (arriving simultaneously to a regular meeting place), online teaching may expand the extent and range of labor involved in teaching.

Online teaching, coupled with the ease of use of new forms of electronic communication (e.g., email, instant messaging, blogging), affords the teaching audience (students) with considerable access to the instructor, making online teaching more closely resemble the creative work found in the arts, such as painting, music, or fashion design. In these, the creators of art must rely upon the judgments of an audience to determine the quality and value of their works (Adkins, 2005; Currid, 2007). Though this process may be a positive outcome, for it engages students in the active creation and negotiation of knowledge, we note countervailing forces.

First, the active creation and negotiation of knowledge requires large commitments of time and energy on the part of instructors. When performed online, often with single students rather than with groups of students, the process may exhaust even the most enthusiastic teacher. Second, the positioning of students as consumers (Cheney, McMillan, & Schwartzman, 1997) may mitigate the positive possibilities of engaging in knowledge creation and negotiation; students may simply want the "right answer." Finally, organization scholars have noted the ambiguous nature of knowledge and the intense activity that often occurs around it. For instance, knowledge workers routinely manage their identity, image, and social relations to be seen by others as "knowledgeable" (Alvesson, 2001; Alvesson & Wilmott, 2002). In one extreme example, Deetz (1998) reports on organization consultants who, to show their loyalty to their clients, slept on cots in the client offices rather than returning to their own homes. Online teaching, then, may erode traditional barriers between work and non-work as online instructors work intensively to manage their courses, relations with students, and images.

Since much of the work of online teaching may occur in what is typically referred to as "private" time (early mornings, lunch hours, evenings, weekends), it may be more likely that instructors will need the support of a partner or domestic services, as the domestic labor of cooking, cleaning, or child care are displaced. Online teaching may increase access to higher education for students, but decrease career access for instructors. In this way, online teaching may resemble other forms of new economy work. For example, post-Fordist models of work that emphasize, and are often celebrated for, decentralization, flexibility, autonomy, and creativity, very often re-emphasize traditional gender roles (Adkins, 1999; Van Echtelt, Glebbeek, Lewis, & Lindenberg, 2009).

Transparency of Learning, Invisibility of Teaching

Online teaching confronts a paradox of visibility. On the one hand, interactive tools such as blogs, threaded discussions, and chats enable instructors to see student deliberative processes, especially when they conduct virtual meetings for collaborative projects. Furthermore, monitoring tools such as statistics tracking make student usage patterns visible so instructors can diagnose patterns of course-related behavior and intervene to improve performance (Schwartzman, 2007a). On the other hand, this relative transparency of student labor contrasts with the instructional labor that can become invisible in online teaching, especially if not consistently captured, evaluated, or recognized (Shedletsky & Aitken, 2001; Vanhorn, Pearson, & Child, 2008).

In fact, evidence suggests there is considerable difficulty in making the labor of online teaching visible. For example, those who teach online courses report difficulty convincing their peers and supervisors that online teaching is valid instruction and legitimate work (Shedletsky & Aitken, 2001; Vanhorn, Pearson, & Child, 2008). In traditional institutions, the more one teaches online, the more one may become physically invisible by not occupying a classroom or hosting lines of students during office hours. The relations are highly visible, and potentially quite meaningful, for students and instructors. Yet, these same relations remain rather invisible for instructors' colleagues, who cannot readily witness them. As instruction moves online and the social relations comprising the instruction fade from the view of colleagues, the instruction may come to resemble a commodity as described by Marx; the social relations among people may appear as social relations among things (Marx, 1967). In other words, faculty members not involved in online teaching may come to believe that online teaching is largely a matter of posting materials to folders, automating quizzes, and sending announcements.

Such belief may be enabled, in part, due to the common view that communication that lacks bodily presence is inferior.

Though online teaching may appear as a commodity to those outside of the virtual environment, primary aspects of online teaching include responding to students' needs and concerns, often around the clock (Vanhorn, Pearson, & Child, 2008). Becoming invisible to professional colleagues may be particularly troublesome as the demands of being "on call" escalate. Since students may use the online system at any time on any day, requests of the instructor may also come at any time on any day. Conversely, some students may begin to disappear, lacking any online presence. For the conscientious teacher, both kinds of students demand attention (Vanhorn, Pearson, & Child, 2008). Perversely, as the online presence escalates, the in-person presence fades.

However, we wish to acknowledge that being on call may not only be demanding. For instance, research on call center and customer service work has shown that these forms of work may be quite stressful *and* personally satisfying. For instance, call center workers often report satisfaction from the ability to demonstrate care and concern for others (Carlone, 2008; Shuler & Sypher, 2000; Wray-Bliss, 2001). Importantly, deriving satisfaction from such intensive interpersonal work, not to mention simply avoiding burnout, requires the ability to talk with colleagues about the experiences (Shuler & Sypher, 2000; Wray-Bliss, 2001). Sense making with others allows for reflection, alternative perspectives, venting, humor, and other forms of support. In situations where online teaching is invisible or seen as illegitimate, we might also expect increasing levels of dissatisfaction or frustration as those who teach online find it difficult to talk with sympathetic, supportive colleagues.

Online teaching may also be "unseen" due to its intangible qualities, such as subjectivity, affect, or image. Maurizio Lazzarato (1996) captures this development with the concept of immaterial labor. One form of immaterial labor "involves a series of activities that are not normally recognized as 'work'—in other words, the kinds of activities involved in defining and fixing cultural and artistic standards, fashions, tastes, consumer norms, and, more strategically, public opinion" (p. 133). Online teaching assumes the form of immaterial labor when instructors set performance standards for the virtual environment, establish community norms for discussion, or nurture relationships with students.

Traditional face-to-face instruction also often involves such immaterial labor. However, in the online environment, this labor is perhaps even more intangible as fewer people, particularly other faculty and administrators, witness these activities. As well, various other constituents, such as prospective students, legislators, community members, or parents, can visit physical classrooms and experience the work being done there. The online course visitor, if she/he can gain access to secure sites, has no host or guide, privately navigating the attenuated space that "guest" access might allow.

Institutional recognition and reward structures have difficulty capturing the labor involved in creating an online version of an existing course. The conceptual equipment and vocabulary of "new" course preparation leaves the status of classroom-to-online course conversions ambiguous. Online teaching is highly creative, requiring the invention of motivation and assessment strategies, the development of new instructional materials, and the development of norms for appropriate and successful behavior. The more online teaching is allowed to recede into invisibility, the more it will become distanced from what counts as genuine labor.

Expansive Outreach, Elusive Traces of Labor

A powerful argument in favor of OTL has been its capacity for outreach, bringing academic coursework to students who could not feasibly attend campus classes (Schwartzman, 2007b). This increased availability of education accompanies challenges in documenting the investment in building student-teacher relationships. Much of the actual labor involved in online instruction recedes from public view, thereby escaping institutional acknowledgment or recognition as labor at all. Goffman's (1959) classic work on self-presentation distinguishes the "front region" of public performance from the "backstage" of private behavior. Teaching in cyberspace involves an analogous distinction as the relational labor invested in online teaching shifts heavily to the instructor's backstage. Instead of reserving office space and time for consultations—a highly visible way of personalizing instruction—online consultations reduce opportunities for external observation and recognition. Personal comments to an individual during an online chat, for example, are not archived in most courseware. Individual consultations occur via e-mail or other means that elude public notice. The selfless and very visible sacrifice of the theatre instructor at daily rehearsals lasting until midnight earns praise and demonstrates commitment. Meanwhile, the online instructor's megabytes of archived e-mails sit silently in private mailboxes and ephemeral instant messages evaporate in cyberspace.

Responses to an open-ended survey of 240 online communication course instructors (Vanhorn, Pearson, & Child, 2008) reflect concern about three themes related to redefinitions of work: performance expectations that stretch beyond academic training, redistribution of time away from content delivery, and lack of institutional support. All three concerns reflect a larger labor-related paradox. As online courses alter and extend the scope of instructional labor, instructors are ill-prepared to undertake and document it while educational institutions are ill-equipped to recognize and reward it.

First, instructors notice the skill sets required for successful online course development extend beyond their academic training. Some educational institutions engage in online course development and maintenance practices that expand the instructor's labors far beyond traditional academic work. On the developmental side, instructors may be delegated full responsibility for developing course components such as simulations, reusable interactive digital resources known as learning objects (Kraus & Ally, 2005), or other resources that call for technical skills unrelated to the instructor's academic training. Some institutions provide support for such endeavors with instructional technology personnel that partner with faculty. These collaborative arrangements team technical specialists with subject matter specialists to create online educational tools that deliver interactive content (Schwartzman, Runyon, & von Holzen, 2007). Such pooling of labor enables development of course resources to span departmental divisions, enabling technicians to document their role in building course content while keeping faculty focused primarily on delivering content. Successful development and implementation of online courses may require a combination of technical skills (e.g., writing program code), subject matter expertise, and graphic design skills (for user interfaces) that extends beyond the capacities of one individual (Polsani, 2005).

Second, insufficient training in the technological tools and in course management skills redistributes workload toward technical tasks and away from actual instruction. Instructors complain that they spend excessive time maintaining course tools and monitoring student communication on multiple channels such as e-mails, chats, and discussion boards. The point about monitoring multiple communication channels reflects the challenge of adapting to different modalities of an information-based environment. That issue can be addressed by instructional redesign that places more explicit parameters on the type and frequency of communication within the course (Schwartzman, 2006). The course maintenance issue, however, has direct bearing on the nature of instructional labor.

As for course maintenance, distance education faculty express frustration at often having to perform technical support tasks they feel incompetent to address (Schoenfeld-Tacher & Persichitte, 2000; Vanhorn, Pearson, & Child, 2008). Many campuses provide minimal in-house support for online course delivery programs, relying on the courseware vendor to handle maintenance and malfunctions. Instructors face a double bind when confronting course maintenance issues. If they assume extensive technical maintenance tasks, they effectively become surrogate technical support staff. The ability to "fix" technical problems students encounter may earn praise and appreciation from the students. This perk, however, carries a price. Time spent in these maintenance tasks competes with time that could be devoted to other course activities that intellectually engage students, such as posting on threaded discussions, conducting online chats, or providing feedback on student work. Furthermore, maintenance tasks remain utterly invisible as coursework because they have no clear analogue in traditional teaching. Critics of online teaching might observe that fixing the air conditioning in a classroom improves the learning environment, but such tasks fall within the purview of physical maintenance. Revamping the technical machinery of an online course shell simply keeps the course functional without visibly contributing new course content. Yet, course maintenance can materially improve student experiences with an online course by altering user interfaces and improving functionality of course components.

The problem with the classroom analogy is that the malfunctioning air conditioner and its repair have no inherent relationship to delivery of content in a particular course. Every campus also has maintenance staff dedicated to resolving challenges in the physical environment. In addition, the classroom instructor has simple alternatives to circumvent the problem, such as switching classrooms, holding class outdoors, or moving to a more comfortable off-campus location.

The physical plant that fixes classrooms does not invite comparison to the "mental plant" that delivers instruction. For the online instructor, the sole instructional lifeline between students and teacher is the online course itself. If it becomes inaccessible or if components malfunction, no practical alternatives exist. The economic realities of course delivery platforms position the instructor more and more as a surrogate technician. Large courseware conglomerates such as Blackboard (especially since its acquisition of WebCT) cannot offer rapid, personal responses to technical malfunctions on individual campuses. Smaller, in-house online course delivery systems developed on individual campuses may offer more personal attention but they also tend to have minimal staff devoted to ongoing technical maintenance of course sites.

The online instructor can render these invisible and necessary maintenance tasks more apparent. For performance appraisals, the instructor could document the nature of various functionality problems with the course. Producing student e-mails complaining about the problem would demonstrate the connection between the technical issue and delivery of quality instruction. The instructor's activity report could detail each major problem, its impact on instructional quality, and the measures (including time spent) taken to resolve the problem. This kind of report would demonstrate responsiveness to students (thereby enhancing instructional quality) and restore time spent behind the scenes as directly related to the labor of teaching.

Third, online instructors raise concern about institutional recognition and support (Vanhorn, Pearson, & Child, 2008). The elusiveness of online labor also arises after course design and administration, when the time comes for the labor to "count" in a performance appraisal. The very terminology of "counting" adopts a vocabulary that emphasizes tabulating observable products. Boshier and Onn (2000) recognize that discourse shapes the instructional experience of OTL. They note that discursive patterns, when unexamined, can perpetuate or exacerbate misconceptions regarding online instruction. For example, treating web-based instruction as an utterly novel, radical paradigm shift in education reduces the likelihood of reconciling the different types of labor involved in traditional teaching and OTL. Moreover, the binary opposition of face-to-face versus online (Boshier & Onn, 2000) hampers discussions about how to expand definitions of academic labor to accommodate OTL. As Deetz (1992) notes, discourse plays a major role in shaping organizational culture. The power relationships observable in discourse reflect and reinforce the power structures in the organization. If the labor involved in OTL does not receive recognition in institutional evaluation procedures, then online education becomes marginalized by its absence.

Aside from marginalization by absence, the method of evaluating online instruction may unnecessarily imperil an instructor's career. Online courses may garner lower student evaluations compared to their face-to-face counterparts—and not because of anything to do with the quality of instruction. Despite their myriad limitations, often sloppy construction, and problematic validity, student evaluations of instruction still serve as the mainstay of evaluating instructional quality (Snare, 2000). Unfortunately these instruments may systematically underrate the quality of OTL. Self-selection bias occurs in some online sections that become the refuge for students who previously failed and then could not reschedule the classroom version of the course (Schwartzman, 2007a). Online sections of public speaking courses may attract students with high levels of performance anxiety who believe that online sections would have fewer performance components. Unless these differences receive attention, online instructors could earn systematically lower ratings simply because the evaluative instruments were designed to assess different kinds of academic labor.

MacDonald et al. (2005) report a chilling effect from the perceived risk of lower student evalua-tions in online courses. They contend that faculty become reticent to risk high performance ratings in face-to-face teaching because the online environment requires different skills sets yet uses the same evaluative criteria. Using evaluative measures specifically designed for classroom instruction (mis)applies one set of performance measures to a different line of work. Unless evaluations reflect the realities of the online course environment, they will generate at best inapplicable and at worst systematically poorer results for online instructors. For example, until it redesigned course evaluations, one university included questions about instructors keeping regular office hours. Naturally, all the online instructors received abysmal ratings for accessibility because none of the online students sought the instructor's office.

Consumer Convenience, Student Responsibility

Thus far, this chapter has focused on academic labor primarily from the instructor's perspective, treated in traditional economic models as the producer. This section deals primarily with the student side of online instruction. If academic work follows the path of a business model, then the master metaphor of the market defines the roles of student and teacher. The limitations of this framework for describing the labor of online teaching have been noted already. On the other side of the keyboard, student labor becomes just as problematic. Several conundrums arise as students occupy the role of consumers to complement the instructor's role as producer.

The metaphor of the student as consumer has received sharp criticism from many quarters (Schwartzman, 1995; McMillan & Cheney, 1996; Cheney, McMillan, & Schwartzman, 1997). While the details of these objections will not be reviewed here, the consumer role in online learning accentu-ates the perilous intersection between commerce and coursework. Writing in 1918, Thorstein Veblen voiced trepidation about this very matter. Veblen

(1918/1976) worried that success in business was taken as an indicator of wisdom, so the proof of knowledge lay in its conversion to economic gain. Based on this tenuous argument, businesspeople were invested with the trusteeship of academic institutions—a perilous prospect indeed given the highly constrained grounds for managerial decision-making (Deetz, 1992) and the current economic climate.

Configuring students as customers carries important implications for online instructional practice. The managerial mantra to stay close to the customer (Peters & Waterman, 1982) has a pedagogical analogue: build immediacy with the student. Immediacy describes the perceived physical or psychological distance between interactants. The more immediacy one feels toward someone—the greater the sense of closeness and approachability—the more positive the perception of the other person becomes (Mehrabian, 1971). Immediacy has received extensive attention in instructional communication research, which consistently finds that high levels of immediacy increase student affinity for the instructor, enhance attitudes toward the course, and sometimes improve learning outcomes (Andersen, 1979; Kelley & Gorham, 1988; Christophel, 1990; Richmond, 1990; Skow & Whitaker, 1996). Nonverbal immediacy deserves special attention, as it highlights how online instruction adds new layers to academic labor.

A sense of human contact, such as an aura of the instructor's personal presence, proves critically important to "pedagogical quality and effectiveness" in online learning (Wolff, Hanor, & Bulik, 2000, pp. 146-147). Nonverbal immediacy, the subject of most research in instructional contexts, consists of behaviors relatively simple to initiate in personal interactions, such as: reducing physical distance, wearing non-intimidating attire, smiling, open rather than defensive posture and body language, and direct eye contact. The mechanisms for achieving immediacy in cyberspace are not as obvious and may require the instructor to

manufacture novel means of initiating closeness. Passive affective indicators such as emoticons have minimal impact, especially given their ubiquity. Emotional indicators in real time, such as the "tweets" in Twitter or instant messaging, require almost constant updating, thereby extending course-related time expenditure and further colonizing non-work life. Many interactive tools designed to generate a sense of immediacy, such as the "friending" feature in Facebook, spread the labor of creating immediacy in ways that colonize more of everyone's lifeworld. A friend request carries with it a social imperative of response—not mere response, but acceptance. Ignoring a friend request counts as a direct snub, but accepting a friend request enables an ever-expanding social network to send e-mails and friend requests, thereby adding to the incoming information glut and again shifting labor from teaching to information management.

Technology is not necessarily antithetical to immediacy (Witt & Schrodt, 2006). Instructors can convey immediacy successfully in a fully online course format. The reasons for immediacy in online courses are as varied as for more traditional course formats, but one important factor may be that the online environment induces students and instructors to participate more actively in a collective effort to stimulate interaction (Arbaugh, 2001). Immediacy in online classes, however, must be manufactured in ways that could require one or more kinds of labor beyond traditional instruction, such as: management of new communicative tools (such as social networking sites), monitoring additional communication channels (such as a Facebook group that accompanies a course), or sending personal messages that proliferate indefinitely because of expected direct response. While traditional courses may also include some of these features, online courses lack other more readily available means of inducing nonverbal immediacy. Absent the familiar nonverbal channels to convey immediacy, those who engage in OTL must develop and use tools that classroom instruction would classify as optional or superfluous.

Student usage patterns of online courses may intensify the instructional labor of creating immediacy in cyberspace. The relative anonymity of the online environment enables reticent students to feel more confident about participating. For example, research has shown that many Japanese and Chinese students who tend to remain quiet in American college classrooms become full participants in electronic learning environments (Warschauer, 1999). The availability of online communication tools, especially when without the availability of face-to-face interaction, increases the likelihood that students will interact with instructors beyond the class (Kelly, Keaten, & Finch, 2004). Since frequency of interaction can boost immediacy, instructors may reciprocate to cultivate a welcoming, inclusive environment. Thus students and instructors not only build momentum toward increasing interactions, but these interactions migrate toward the recesses of instructional backspace. Even when interactions percolate to the forefront, immediacy behaviors may portray dimensions of instructional labor that seem frivolous or embarrassing to outside observers. Consider, for example, the photos and "wall" graffiti that could appear on a course group's Facebook page. Engaging one's audience in these ways is both necessary (Adkins, 2005) and not typically classified as "work" (Lazzarato, 1996).

A major "selling point" of online education is its purported convenience. Promoting the ease and flexibility of online learning, however, also deflects attention from the student labor involved in adapting to the online educational environment. This labor extends beyond mere technical skills, but encompasses the self-discipline and initiative to stay current with assignments, ask questions without being called on, and meet obligations to other students on collaborative work when classmates are not physically present. The failure to acculturate students into the world of online educational labor may account for the disappoint-

ingly low retention rates in many online courses. While the number of students taking courses online continues to grow, non-completion rates remain disturbingly high: national studies estimate non-retention at 20-50 percent (Herbert, 2006). One of this chapter's authors experienced non-retention rates in online courses of at least 25 percent over five years compared to less than 5 percent in the same courses taught face-to-face during that time. Any product in the traditional marketplace that experienced a 20-50 percent return rate would be scrapped or recalled and thoroughly redesigned. Part of the problem may stem from promoting online coursework as a commodity.

Closer examination reveals that marketing online learning primarily as a convenience actually remains quite faithful to the etymology of "commodity" (Baldwin, 1994). Online education often gets promoted as commodious rather than rigorous, offering the convenience of flexible hours and delivery of course content directly to wherever the student accesses a computer. Lofty descriptions of the easy-to-use, convenient "product" of online courses rarely accompany any explanation of the investment of labor that online courses require. The educational relationship, rather than a mutual investment of time and intellectual effort (which fits poorly with the bifurcation of students and teachers into the roles of knowledge producer and consumer), resembles more the delivery of a ready-made product to a consumer that need only passively enjoy its benefits. Ritzer (1996) labels this educational mentality a "McDonaldized" system that emphasizes speed of product delivery (analogous to student expectations of instant electronic responses), favors efficiency over quality, and values the satisfaction of consumers over their well-being.

For example, one of the authors continually encountered online students who rejected the concept of assignment deadlines. They argued that the courses were "sold" to them as allowing more flexible time, accommodating work, family, and social obligations. Due dates that occurred at inconvenient times seemed to violate the implied promise to accommodate their schedules. Many of these students either dropped the course or stopped doing any work and earned a failing grade. This example demonstrates that high attrition rates could signify student alienation, not so much with education or with the online environment, but with expectations of labor greatly at odds with promotional emphasis on the ease of online learning.

The brand of consumerism operant especially in online educational settings is allied to entitlement (Sacks, 1996, p. 160). As long as the consumers in some sense pay for an education, they have absolute sovereignty (du Gay, 1996) over how to dispose of it. In this formulation, the decisions of how, when, or whether to consume, as well as the effects on others and the environment, are value-neutral. Consumerism is not immoral; it is simply amoral, with the individual consumer invested with authority to decide the ends and means of education.

Consumerism also finds comfortable company in the mentality of victimization (Sacks, 1996, p. 161). If consumers are to be served, then they function as the recipients of whatever caters to their desires. Failure to meet these desires equates with being cheated or ill-served. The demand to satisfy individual desires leaves little room for deferring to the desires of others or recognizing that the consumer should give as well as get. Sacks (1996) vigorously opposes this position: "The same hyperconsumerism that has taken hold of the larger American culture has also gripped higher education by the throat, threatening to render meaningless such traditional notions as hard work, responsibility, and standards of excellence" (p. 161). Despite the perhaps overly dramatic language, the limitations of a market-based approach to OTL should generate serious questions regarding the suitability of this metaphoric framework, especially the suitability of the producer/consumer dichotomy.

FUTURE RESEARCH DIRECTIONS

Further research should explore the transformation of academic labor in the online context. Several interwoven intellectual threads deserve additional attention. Examination of these research themes aligns with each of the four problem areas discussed in this chapter.

First, more extensive data needs to be collected on how instructors experience and manage online versus face-to-face teaching. Purported cost savings from online instruction might also devalue the labor expended in achieving economies of scale. Since the online educational environment blurs boundaries between being "at work," "on call," and "off duty," workloads need to be reviewed to reveal faulty equivalencies among different kinds of labor. The activity of "teaching" as a category of labor may need further specification and clarification to incorporate the various modes of instruction. Perhaps this realm requires the kind of reconceptualization that Ernest Boyer's *Scholarship Reconsidered* (1990) brought to research.

Second, the elusiveness of online academic labor points to the need to realign intellectual work with theories of labor that move beyond industrial models. The virtual work world in cyberspace presents thorny challenges for defining and assessing the relationship between laborers and the work they produce. Consider the ongoing debates about copyrights, ownership, and technology transfer agreements relating to online course content. To what degree is the online instructor a creative freelancer who designs educational resources? Or should those who teach online courses qualify as deliverers of content? Answers to these and other troublesome questions may call for theories of labor more firmly grounded in post-industrial labor practices.

Third, innovative ways to manage, document, and acknowledge the instructional labor of online teaching deserve attention. The freedom to reclaim authority over one's own time and the flexibility to teach and learn anywhere make OTL a potent educational method. Unfortunately the academic and social context wherein online education operates can undermine the liberatory opportunities. Additional studies might examine the ways online courses and programs become instruments of limiting as well as extending educational practices. These studies could illuminate the inconsistencies between the theoretical liberties attendant to OTL and how they might be fostered rather than fettered within the institutionalized practices of higher education. Such research clearly would bring a reformist agenda that requires healthy but potentially uncomfortable self-reflection regarding the species of power and control operant in academia.

Finally, the promotion and justification of OTL requires more critical scrutiny. Institutions with high online student retention rates could provide models for cultivating a sense of inclusion and immediacy in online environments. In addition, research could explore alternative rationales for recruiting students and faculty to OTL. Despite the dominance of market-rooted metaphors, they do not offer the only or the most felicitous means of portraying the full dimension of labor online education requires from students and instructors. Even within an economic frame, discourse that emphasizes the investment of effort could counteract the disproportionate highlighting of simplicity and convenience.

While the research on student performance and perceptions of online coursework has burgeoned in recent years, far less scholarly attention has been devoted to OTL from the instructor's standpoint (Santilli & Beck, 2005). Rapid expansion of online courses has outpaced the development of educational paradigms and evaluative methods, which remain entrenched in face-to-face models that poorly fit the online environment (Santilli & Beck, 2005). Viewed through the lens of online instruction, Boyer's (1990) discussion of the scholarship of teaching could qualify as a call to treat OTL as a scholarly activity by documenting, recognizing, and rewarding it as valid intellectual labor.

The intellectual labor of OTL may not fall within the purview of traditional physical labor quantified by sheer numbers of student credit hours generated. Reconsidering online education as intellectual labor would require acknowledging that online pedagogy demands engagement not only with students, but with the theories pertinent to how computer-mediated communication operates. An online instructor could document, in traditional scholarly publications or in internal documents such as a self-assessment prepared in an annual report or tenure review, how the structure and administration of specific online coursework relates to state-of-the-art research in computer-mediated communication. For example, an instructor might explore how incorporation of social networking features into a course confirms or challenges findings of current research on interactive media.

Rendering the labor of OTL more visible may open attractive opportunities for observing and evaluating performance. Online courses are especially well suited for external peer review because each course's entire content, structure, and interactive patterns between teachers and students are readily observable. In an era of increasing budget consciousness, the old, expensive, and laborious practice of bringing external reviewers in to observe courses becomes less justifiable. Instead, external review of online courses can proceed by enabling reviewers to access a course, especially upon its completion. Observation of the completed course would permit examination of interactive components, such as threaded discussions, throughout the duration of the term. Alternatively, an evaluator could be enrolled in a course from the outset, which would permit exposure to course-wide e-mails and *in situ* observation of course administration. This kind of longitudinal observation within a course would be impractical to conduct in a traditional classroom.

External reviewers also could observe multiple online courses taught by the same instructor, which could document the instructor's development as a teacher and adaptation to different levels of students and varying course content. Such sustained observation affords a deeper, more nuanced understanding of the actual labor expended in OTL. Used judiciously, ongoing observations of online instruction offer far richer documentations of educational labor than the standard one-shot classroom visit to a face-to-face setting. More thorough, ongoing observations of online education "from the inside" could alleviate what interviews with online instructors reveal as the most commonly expressed concern about online instruction: "they do not feel there is adequate recognition of how time consuming online teaching can be" (Gonzalez, 2009, p. 307).

CONCLUSION

This chapter has argued that online teaching occupies a contested site; faculty, students, administrators, and policy makers struggle over the definition, performance, recognition, and reward of OTL, specifically, and academic labor, generally, in higher education. In no way should the arguments in this chapter bolster categorical indictments of online education. To the contrary, the challenges online education poses for defining, recognizing, and benefiting from academic labor offer the potential for needed refinements in theories of work in post-industrial capitalism. The conundrums attendant to online education invite considerations of how to understand the problematic and paradoxical outcomes of treating intellectual labor within the theoretical, discursive, and regulatory frameworks derived from physical labor. Far from criticizing computer-mediated communication or online education, this essay uses emergent educational technologies as fulcrums to open existing labor practices to constructive critique and improvement.

Importantly, though disagreements persist over specific elements of online courses, programs, and supports, struggles over the meaning and practice of online teaching are conditioned by its context of implementation. For us, the contemporary context includes attention to the contemporary political economy, featuring consumerism, labor devaluation, managerialism, and neo-liberalism. Often, this context pushes online teaching toward four ambiguous outcomes: (1) an expansion in economy of scale for teaching and the labor required to teach online, (2) making student learning more visible and obscuring the labor of teaching, (3) wider outreach and access to higher education and difficulty in tracking the labor involved in this access, and (4) an embrace of online teaching as convenient for consumers and the diminishment of student responsibility for learning.

As this chapter on online teaching and learning concludes, we offer some practical advice for OTL instructors and their colleagues. As discussed, OTL acquires meaning and specificity in contexts of enactment. The general context identified above pushes OTL in directions that cause concern. Still, we recognize that there are some good reasons for implementing OTL. Thus, even as we hope to raise serious questions about the prevalence and practice of online education, and work to change the dominant context for its implementation, we believe it important to provide practical lessons for those participating in OTL in less-than-ideal circumstances. The advice focuses on matters of socialization.

Socialization may be conceptualized as an ongoing process, one requiring interaction with other organization members (Jablin, 1987), in which group members learn the ways of being and knowing preferred by a group. Within this process, newcomers should be seen as active participants (Miller & Jablin, 1991), not only recipients of information and meaning.

We first note, then, an important element of socializing educators for online teaching and learning. To the extent that OTL represents a new way of being and knowing in higher education, socialization might be usefully thought of as re-socialization. In other words, many problems associated with OTL stem from extension or direct transfer of taken-for-granted meanings and practices of face-to-face education to education in virtual spaces. As we have sought to demonstrate, using existing meanings and instruments to develop and assess OTL may result in a poor fit for educators and students.

Socialization involves learning values and norms (Bullis & Bach, 1989). Hence, OTL-related socialization may serve several functions. First, it may assist instructors in learning "new" values and norms of teaching. Hopefully, these values and norms will improve outcomes for instructors and students. Second, these "new" values and norms may help all instructors, whether participating in OTL or not, to reflect critically on the prevailing values and norms of teaching, typically derived from face-to-face instruction. In other words, socialization may help OTL educators handle the demands of their instruction while also prompting and informing campus-wide discussions of what counts and matters in and across various forms of teaching. Third, with a focus on socialization as an ongoing process, participation in OTL may represent turning points for educators, moments at which already existing understandings of teaching and learning come in for scrutiny and reflection. Turning points are important because they are moments that signal changes in relationships, moments at which organization members may affiliate or distance themselves from their organizations (Bullis & Bach, 1989). Socialization, done well, helps people become and remain valuable members of their groups.

Foremost, then, OTL instructors must have access to others to make sense of their experiences. As discussed above, work satisfaction often derives, in part, from the ability to talk with colleagues about work experiences (Shuler & Sypher, 2000; Wray-Bliss, 2001). Additionally, organization scholars know that new hires seek information from co-workers as a way to cope with the realities of their situations (Miller & Jabin, 1991). Thus, it seems likely that those new to OTL may also desire information from co-workers. Universities should provide mechanisms to ease information seeking and sense making, particularly given the isolation that may arise from working in virtual space. Information seeking and meaning construction might be achieved through cohorts of instructors new to OTL, or matching such instructors with OTL-experienced mentors. Since online instruction is not the same as traditional classroom instruction, discussants should come from the ranks of those teaching online. Drawing from lessons on emotional labor (Shuler & Sypher, 2000), those who have successfully managed the stresses of such work have much to teach those who come to it anew. Inviting administrators to participate in these conversations, especially those involved in crafting tenure and promotion policies, would alert policy makers to the challenges and opportunities involved in the labor of online education.

As part of socialization, efforts should be made to let people know what they are in for before/when they take on teaching in an online environment. Such anticipatory socialization (Jablin, 1987) should foreground how OTL labor is different from traditional instructional labor. Because OTL is not a simple matter of translating classroom practices to an online presence, faculty should have up front training in the differences. For example, discussion might consider the meanings of university education and how those intersect with or alter within the online environment. Instructors might also benefit from specific definition of what is needed for OTL success, such as fast and reliable Internet connections, portable or multiple computers, and flexible personal and professional schedules. Finally, prospective teachers of online courses could shadow established online instructors by being "enrolled" in one or more online courses to observe techniques of task management and ways to stimulate interaction. Ultimately, faculty should have access to resources that help them decide whether and when OTL makes sense for them, their courses, and their students.

Given the relatively recent emergence of and questions about OTL, we believe socialization has the ability not only to enculturate into existing values and norms, but also to serve as a site for creation of the norms and values appropriate for OTL. Ongoing socialization should provide opportunity to engage with evolving meanings of and reactions to OTL. For instance, how do face-to-face instructional faculty view OTL faculty (e.g., as a colleague, threat, slacker, etc.)? How should they be viewed? Frank conversation about OTL might help all of us to re-think OTL, especially in light of the demands acknowledged here. It might also help us all reflect on contemporary university life.

Online teaching and learning appears now to be firmly established as a part of the agenda and practice of higher education. Indeed, we acknowledge its potential to broaden access to higher education, diversify pedagogical methods, and enhance course offerings. To achieve this progressive potential, those in higher education must assess and develop OTL in ways that respond to the political economic context, even as they work to reshape that context. For online teaching and learning to fulfill its promise, we must acknowledge the full range of investments teachers, students, and staff make in its practice.

REFERENCES

Adkins, L. (1999). Community and economy: A retraditionalization of gender? *Theory, Culture & Society*, *16*, 119–139.

Adkins, L. (2005). The new economy, property and personhood. *Theory, Culture & Society*, *22*, 111–130. doi:10.1177/0263276405048437

Alvesson, M. (2001). Knowledge work: Ambiguity, image, and identity. *Human Relations*, *54*, 863–886. doi:10.1177/0018726701547004

Alvesson, M., & Willmott, H. (2002). Identity regulation as organizational control: Producing the appropriate individual. *Journal of Management Studies*, *39*, 619–644. doi:10.1111/1467-6486.00305

Andersen, J. (1979). Teacher immediacy as a predictor of teaching effectiveness. In Nimmo, D. (Ed.), *Communication yearbook 3* (pp. 543–559). New Brunswick, NJ: Transaction Books.

Arbaugh, J. B. (2001). How instructor immediacy behaviors affect student satisfaction and learning in web-based courses. *Business Communication Quarterly*, *64*, 42–54. doi:10.1177/108056990106400405

Baldwin, G. (1994). The student as customer: The discourse of 'quality' in higher education. *Journal of Tertiary Educational Administration*, *16*, 125–133.

Berger, P. L., & Luckmann, T. (1967). *The social construction of reality: A treatise in the sociology of knowledge*. New York: Anchor.

Boshier, R., & Onn, C. M. (2000). Discursive constructions of Web learning and education. *Journal of Distance Education*, *15*, 1–16.

Boyer, E. (1990). *Scholarship reconsidered: Priorities of the professoriate*. Princeton, NJ: Carnegie Foundation for the Advancement of Teaching.

Bullis, C., & Bach, B. W. (1989). Socialization turning points: An examination of change in organizational identification. *Western Journal of Speech Communication*, *53*, 273–293.

Carlone, D. (2008). The contradictions of communicative labor in service work. *Communication and Critical . Cultural Studies*, *5*, 158–179.

Cheney, G., McMillan, J. J., & Schwartzman, R. (1997). Should we buy the 'student-as-consumer' metaphor? *The Montana Professor*, *8*(3), 8–11.

Christophel, J. L. (1990). The relationships among teacher immediacy behaviors, student motivation and learning. *Communication Education, 39*, 323–340. doi:10.1080/03634529009378813

Currid, E. (2007). *The Warhol economy: How fashion, art, and music drive New York City.* Princeton, NJ: Princeton University Press.

Curtis, F. (2001). Ivy-covered exploitation: Class, education, and the liberal arts college . In Gibson-Graham, J. K., Resnick, S., & Wolff, R. (Eds.), *Re/Presenting class: Essays in postmodern Marxism* (pp. 81–104). Durham, NC: Duke.

Deetz, S. A. (1992). *Democracy in an age of corporate colonization: Developments in communication and the politics of everyday life.* Albany: State University of New York.

Deetz, S. A. (1995). Transforming communication, transforming business: Building responsive and responsible workplaces. Cresskill, NJ: Hampton.

Deetz, S. A. (1998). Discursive formations, strategized subordination and self-surveillance . In McKinley, A., & Starkey, K. (Eds.), *Foucault, management and organizational theory* (pp. 151–172). London: Sage.

Draves, W. A. (2000). *Teaching online.* River Falls, WI: LERN Books.

du Gay, P. (1996). *Consumption and identity at work.* London: Sage.

Giroux, H. A., & Myrsiades, K. (Eds.). (2001). *Beyond the corporate university: Pedagogy, culture, and literary studies in the new millennium.* Lanham, MD: Rowman and Littlefield.

Goffman, E. (1959). *The presentation of self in everyday life.* Garden City, NY: Doubleday Anchor.

Gonzalez, C. (2009). Conceptions of, and approaches to, teaching online: A study of lecturers teaching postgraduate distance courses. *Higher Education, 57*, 299–314. doi:10.1007/s10734-008-9145-1

Greene, R. W. (2004). Rhetoric and capitalism: Rhetorical agency as communicative labor. *Philosophy and Rhetoric, 37*, 188–206. doi:10.1353/par.2004.0020

Grossberg, L. (2005). *Caught in the crossfire: Kids, politics, and America's future.* Boulder, CO: Paradigm.

Habermas, J. (1987). The theory of communicative action: *Vol. 2. Lifeworld and system.* Cambridge, MA: MIT Press.

Herbert, M. (2006). Staying the course: A study in online student satisfaction and retention. *Online Journal of Distance Learning Administration, 9*(4). Retrieved March 28, 2009 from http://www.westga.edu/~distance/ojdla/winter94/herbert94.htm

Hewett, B. L., & Powers, C. E. (2007). Guest editors' introduction: Online teaching and learning: Preparation, development, and organizational communication. *Technical Communication Quarterly, 16*, 1–11. doi:10.1207/s15427625tcq1601_1

Jablin, E. M. (1987). Organizational entry, assimilation, and exit . In Jablin, E. M., Putnam, L. L., Roberts, K. H., & Porter, L. W. (Eds.), *Handbook of organizational communication: An interdisciplinary perspective* (pp. 679–740). Newbury Park, CA: Sage.

Kelley, D., & Gorham, J. (1988). Effects of immediacy on recall information. *Communication Education, 37*, 198–207. doi:10.1080/03634528809378719

Kelly, L., Keaten, J., & Finch, C. (2004). Reticent and non-reticent college students' preferred communication channels for interacting with faculty. *Communication Research Reports, 21,* 197–209.

Kim, K.-J., & Bonk, C. J. (2006). The future of online teaching and learning in higher education: The survey says…. *Educause Quarterly, 29*(4). Retrieved March 28, 2009 from http://www.educause.edu/EDUCAUSE+Quarterly/EDUCAUSEQuarterlyMagazineVolum/TheFutureofOnlineTeachingandLe/157426

Krauss, F., & Ally, M. (2005). A study of the design and evaluation of a learning object and implications for content development. *Interdisciplinary Journal of Knowledge and Learning Objects, 1,* 1–22.

Lazzarato, M. (1996). Immaterial labor. In Virno, P., & Hardt, M. (Eds.), *Radical thought in Italy: A potential politics* (pp. 133–147). Minneapolis: University of Minneapolis Press.

MacDonald, C. J., Stodel, E., Thompson, T. L., Muirhead, B., Hinton, C., Carson, B., & Banit, E. (2005). Addressing the eLearning contradiction: A collaborative approach for developing a conceptual framework learning object. *Interdisciplinary Journal of Knowledge and Learning Objects, 1,* 79–98.

Marx, K. (1967). Capital: *Vol. 1. A critical analysis of capitalist production.* New York: International.

Marx, K. (1978). Economic and philosophic manuscripts of 1844. In Tucker, R. C. (Ed.), *The Marx-Engels reader* (2nd ed., pp. 66–125). (Milligan, M., Trans.). New York: Norton.

McMillan, J. J., & Cheney, G. (1996). The student as consumer: The implications and limitations of a metaphor. *Communication Education, 45,* 1–15. doi:10.1080/03634529609379028

Mehrabian, A. (1971). *Silent messages.* Belmont, CA: Wadsworth.

Meyer, K. A. (2002). *Quality in distance education: Focus on on-line Learning* ([). San Francisco: Jossey-Bass.]. *ASHE-ERIC Higher Education Report, 29*(4).

Miller, V. D., & Jablin, F. M. (1991). Information seeking during organizational entry: Influences, tactics, and a model of the process. *Academy of Management Review, 16,* 92–120. doi:10.2307/258608

Peters, T. J., & Waterman, R. H. (1982). *In search of excellence: Lessons from America's best-run companies.* New York: Harper and Row.

Polsani, P. R. (2003). Use and abuse of reusable learning objects. *Journal of Digital Information, 3*(4). Retrieved June 14, 2005 from http://jodi.ecs.soton.ac.uk/Articles/v03/i04/Polsani/

Richmond, V. P. (1990). Communication in the classroom: Power and motivation. *Communication Education, 45,* 293–305.

Ritzer, G. (1996). *The McDonaldization of society* (Rev. ed.). Thousand Oaks, CA: Pine Forge Press.

Rosenberg, M. J. (2001). *E-learning: Strategies for delivering knowledge in the digital age.* New York: McGraw-Hill.

Russell, T. L. (2001). *The no significant difference phenomenon* (5th ed.). Montgomery, AL: International Distance Education Certification Center.

Sacks, P. (1996). *Generation X goes to college.* Chicago: Open Court.

Santilli, S., & Beck, V. (2005). Graduate faculty perceptions of online teaching. *Quarterly Review of Distance Education, 6,* 155–160.

Sayer, A. (1999). Valuing culture and economy. In Ray, L., & Sayer, A. (Eds.), *Culture and economy after the cultural turn* (pp. 53–75). London: Sage.

Schoenfeld-Tacher, R., & Persichitte, K. A. (2000). Differential skills and competencies required of faculty teaching distance education courses. *International Journal of Educational Technology, 2*(1). Retrieved April 1, 2009 from: http://www.outreach.uiuc.edu/ijet/v2n1/schoenfeld-tacher/index.html

Schwartzman, R. (1995). Are students customers? The metaphoric mismatch between management and education. *Education, 116*, 215–222.

Schwartzman, R. (2006). Virtual group problem solving in the basic communication course: Lessons for online learning. *Journal of Instructional Psychology, 33*, 3–14.

Schwartzman, R. (2007a). Electronifying oral communication: Refining the conceptual framework for online instruction. *College Student Journal, 41*, 37–49.

Schwartzman, R. (2007b). Refining the question: How can online instruction maximize opportunities for all students? *Communication Education, 56*, 113–117. doi:10.1080/03634520601009728

Schwartzman, R., Runyon, D., & von Holzen, R. (2007). Where theory meets practice: Design and deployment of learning objects. In Koohang, A., & Harman, K. (Eds.), *Learning objects: Theory, praxis, issues, and trends* (pp. 1–44). Santa Rosa, CA: Informing Science Press.

Shedletsky, L. J., & Aitken, J. E. (2001). The paradoxes of online academic work. *Communication Education, 50*, 206–217. doi:10.1080/03634520109379248

Shuler, S., & Sypher, B. D. (2000). Seeking emotional labor: When managing the heart enhances the work experience. *Management Communication Quarterly, 14*, 50–89. doi:10.1177/0893318900141003

Skow, L., & Whitaker, T. (1996). It's what you say *and* what you do! Nonverbal immediacy behaviors: A key to effective communication. *NASSP Bulletin, 80*(584), 90–95. doi:10.1177/019263659608058414

Snare, C. E. (2000). An alternative end-of-semester questionnaire. *PS: Political Science and Politics, 33*, 823–825. doi:10.2307/420922

Sproule, M. J. (1988). The new managerial rhetoric and the old criticism. *The Quarterly Journal of Speech, 74*, 468–486. doi:10.1080/00335638809383854

Sproule, M. J. (1989). Organizational rhetoric and the public sphere. *Communication Studies, 40*, 258–265.

Sproule, M. J. (1990). Organizational rhetoric and the rational-democratic society. *Journal of Applied Communication Research, 18*, 129–140.

Thrift, N. (2006). Re-inventing invention: New tendencies in capitalist commodification. *Economy and Society, 35*, 279–306. doi:10.1080/03085140600635755

Tompkins, P. K. (2005). *Apollo, Challenger, Columbia: The decline of the space program.* Los Angeles: Roxbury.

UNC Tomorrow Commission. (2007). *University of North Carolina Tomorrow Commission final report.* Chapel Hill, NC: University of North Carolina General Administration.

University of North Carolina Board of Governors. (2004). *Report on expanding access to higher education through state-funded distance education programs.* Retrieved March 27, 2009 from http://intranet.northcarolina.edu/docs/aa/planning/reports/DERpt2004.pdf

Van Echtelt, P., Glebbeek, A., Lewis, S., & Lindenberg, S. (2009). Post-Fordist work: A man's world?: Gender and working overtime in the Netherlands. *Gender & Society*, *23*, 188–214. doi:10.1177/0891243208331320

Vanhorn, S., Pearson, J. C., & Child, J. T. (2008). The online communication course: The challenges. *Qualitative Research Reports in Communication*, *9*, 29–36. doi:10.1080/17459430802400332

Veblen, T. (1976). The higher learning. In Lerner, M. (Ed.), *The portable Veblen* (pp. 507–528). New York: Penguin. (Original work published 1918)

Warschauer, M. (1999). *Electronic literacies: Language, culture, and power in online education*. Mahwah, NJ: Lawrence Erlbaum.

Witt, P. L., & Schrodt, P. (2006). The influence of instructional technology use and teacher immediacy on student affect for teacher and course. *Communication Reports*, *19*, 1–15. doi:10.1080/08934210500309843

Wray-Bliss, E. (2001). Representing customer service: Telephones and texts. In Sturdy, A., Grugulis, I., & Wilmott, H. (Eds.), *Customer service: Empowerment and entrapment* (pp. 38–59). New York: Palgrave.

Wulff, S., Hanor, J., & Bulik, R. J. (2000). The roles and interrelationships of presence, reflection, and self-directed learning in effective world wide web-based pedagogy. In Cole, R. A. (Ed.), *Issues in web-based pedagogy: A critical primer* (pp. 143–160). Westport, CT: Greenwood Press.

ADDITIONAL READING

Aune, J. A. (2001). *Selling the free market: The rhetoric of economic correctness*. New York: Guilford.

Bok, D. (2003). *Universities in the marketplace: The commercialization of higher education*. Princeton: Princeton University.

Cheney, G., Zorn, T. E. Jr, Planalp, S., & Lair, D. J. (2008). Meaningful work and personal/social well-being: Organizational communication engages the meanings of work. In Beck, C. (Ed.), *Communication Yearbook 32* (pp. 137–186). Thousand Oaks, CA: Sage.

Damrau, J. (2008). Communication and cooperation in the virtual workplace: Teamwork in computer-mediated-communication. *Technical Communication*, *55*, 73–74.

du Gay, P., & Salaman, G. (1992). The cult(ure) of the customer. *Journal of Management Studies*, *29*, 615–633. doi:10.1111/j.1467-6486.1992.tb00681.x

Geiger, R. L. (2004). *Knowledge & money: Research universities and the paradox of the marketplace*. Stanford: Stanford University Press.

Gibson-Graham, J. K. (2006). *The end of capitalism (as we knew it): A feminist critique of political economy*. Minneapolis: University of Minnesota.

Giroux, H. (2005). *Schooling and the struggle for public life*. Boulder, CO: Paradigm Publishers.

Giroux, H. (2007). *The university in chains: Confronting the military-industrial-academic complex*. Boulder, CO: Paradigm Publishers.

Hanigan, M. (2008). Managing virtual teams: Getting the most from wikis, blogs, and other collaborative tools. *Technical Communication*, *55*, 89–90.

Hesmondhalgh, D., & Baker, S. (2008). Creative work and emotional labour in the television industry. *Theory, Culture & Society*, *25*, 97–118. doi:10.1177/0263276408097798

Hyllegard, D., Heping, D., & Hunter, C. (2008). Why do students leave online courses? Attrition in community college distance learning courses. *International Journal of Instructional Media, 35,* 429–434.

Kirp, D. L. (2003). *Shakespeare, Einstein, and the bottom line: The marketing of higher education.* Cambridge, MA: Harvard University.

Pickering, K. W. (2009). Student ethos in the online technical communication classroom: Diverse voices. *Technical Communication Quarterly, 18,* 166–187. doi:10.1080/10572250802708303

Schultz, D. (2005, Fall). The corporate university in American society. *Logos: A journal of modern society & culture, 4*(4). Retrieved April 28, 2009 from http://www.logosjournal.com/issue_4.4/schultz.htm

Sennett, R. (1998). *The corrosion of character: The personal consequences of work in the new capitalism.* New York: W. W. Norton.

Starke-Meyerring, D., & Andrews, D. (2006). Building a shared virtual learning culture. *Business Communication Quarterly, 69,* 25–49. doi:10.1177/1080569905285543

Thrift, N. J. (2005). *Knowing capitalism.* London: Sage.

Washburn, J. (2005). *University, Inc.: The corporate corruption of higher education.* New York: Basic Books.

KEY TERMS AND DEFINITIONS

Colonization: The domination of various life pursuits by corporate values and logics.

Commodification: Social relations and goods are turned into objects for exchange.

Consumerism: The belief that the consumption of goods and services is the primary way to participate in society. Often accompanied by the belief that consumers know best, and that consumer choices decide what is good in a society.

Immediacy: The perceived physical or psychological distance between people as they interact.

Neo-Liberalism: A political-economic project committed to de-regulation of markets, the use of free markets as systems of democratic choice, and individualism.

No Significant Difference Phenomenon: Research that compares online and face-to-face teaching of the same course and finds equivalent learning outcomes.

Production Bias: Producing more of something is always better; emphasizes quantity over quality.

Surplus Labor: Value created by labor that is greater than the cost of that labor.

Technological Imperative: The view that availability of a technological tool warrants its use.

Chapter 4
The Ethical Implications of the Virtual Work Environment

Rachel N. Byers
Byers, Byers, and Associates P.C & University of South Alabama, USA

ABSTRACT

Ethical issues due to the following four major factors inherent to virtual work are examined: (1) organizational culture, (2) trust, (3) cross-cultural diversity, and (4) monitoring. The author proposes that the negative ethical implications of the virtual work environment can be overcome by following the suggested steps and proposed guidelines. Areas for potential future research are included and are followed by an overall discussion of the issues covered and some closing remarks.

INTRODUCTION

Technology is booming. The business world is changing. Rapid globalization is prevalent. These factors, among many others, have given rise to what some researchers have referred to as the "new economy" (Argandona, 2003; Paulre, 2000). Argandona (2003) describes the new economy as a technological revolution involving the information and communication technologies that affects almost all aspects of the economy, business, and our personal lives (p. 3).

Specific to the business world, this technological revolution has opened the door to the development and implementation of "virtual work" in organizations around the world. How many people do you know that work from home? How about someone who works for a company located in another country? You may not have realized it, but virtual work is all around us. That father with a laptop in the stands at his son's baseball game, for instance, is most likely engaging in some form of virtual work. Virtual work, which is commonly referred to as virtual team work (Anawati & Craig, 2006; Lu, Watson-Manheim, Chudoba, & Wynn, 2006; Malhotra, Majchrzak, & Rosen, 2007; Powell, Piccoli, & Ives, 2004) or "telework" (Moustafa-Leonard, 2007), has been defined in many ways. However, researcher's (Hughes, O'Brien, Randall, Rouncefield, & Tolmie, 2001; Malhotra et al., 2007) most

DOI: 10.4018/978-1-61520-979-8.ch004

common definitions resemble that of Powell et al. (2004) in which they describe virtual teams as "groups of geographically, organizationally, and/or time dispersed workers brought together by information and telecommunication technologies to accomplish one or more organizational tasks" (p. 7). The terms virtual organization and virtual corporation refer to new organizational forms that are characterized by this type of work and will be used interchangeably throughout this chapter.

Virtual work has given organizations the opportunity to work across the traditional boundaries of time, space, and geographical location. Subsequently, businesses world wide are jumping on board the "virtual" ship and setting sail for territories unknown. In 2001, Wiesenfeld, Raghuram, and Garud referenced estimates from a 1999 issue of Work Week stating that nearly 18 million U.S. workers spent at least a portion of their work week in virtual mode (p. 213). Further, 51% of North American companies at that time had virtual work programs, and almost two-thirds of the Fortune 1000 companies offered employees an opportunity to work virtually (p. 214). Imagine the comparable numbers today, nearly a decade later.

The prevalence of virtual work has sparked an increase in research on various topics within, surrounding, and in part due to the nature of this type of work. One area that has not seen specific attention is the area of ethics. While virtual work has presented numerous opportunities and provided the potential for rapid growth and significant decreases in costs, one must consider the ethical implications of the virtual work environment. It is important to note that traditional organizations are not immune to ethical issues. However, virtual organizations face many ethical dilemmas specific to the virtual work environment in addition to those traditional problems.

This chapter explores the internal and external ethical implications of the virtual work environment. Specifically, this chapter analyzes and evaluates traditional organizational practices and theories as they compare to those of the virtual

organization. First, background information is presented to aid in developing the needed understanding of what might be foreign concepts. Next, the internal implications explored are the numerous issues surrounding the development and maintaining of organizational culture and its importance to individual and organizational ethical development, as well as the development of trust in virtual organizations with almost zero face-to-face interaction. The external implications explored are the ethical issues arising from cross-cultural distribution of employees and the highly criticized issue of monitoring. While the ethical dilemmas are substantial, they can be managed. So, at the conclusion of each listed factor, guidelines will be proposed and suggestions will be offered to effectively minimize the negative effects the ethical dilemmas might have on virtual organizations.

Before diving into the vast sea of the ethical implications of the virtual work environment, it should be noted that this chapter is based on the underlying assumption that a virtual work environment is SOLELY virtual (i.e. all employees work virtually full-time). While this may not always be the case, this chapter suggests that those employees working virtually sporadically or part-time should be considered working in a "semi-virtual" environment. In addition, another primary reason for writing this chapter based on this assumption is the subject matter which it addresses, ethics. In order to highlight some of the critical shortfalls of the virtual work environment with regards to ethical concerns, it is necessary to examine the environment in its most extreme sense (i.e. solely virtual).

BACKGROUND

In order to accurately assess the ethical implications of the virtual work environment one must be knowledgeable on the underlying fundamental concepts involved in such an assessment. These fundamentals include business ethics, organizational culture, trust, cross-cultural diversity, and monitoring. An understanding of business ethics requires a familiarity of basic ethical theories. To evaluate the potential shortfalls of virtual work with regards to the ethical implications of organizational culture and trust, one must have a general awareness of what these two factors are and their effects on organizations. Similarly, a broad understanding of cross-cultural diversity and monitoring is vital to accurately address these issues in the unexplored virtual business world. Therefore, a broad description of these factors and brief literature reviews concerning each is presented.

Ethics

Webster's dictionary defines an ethic as "a set of moral principles" (Ethic, 2003). Further, the plural form of the word, which is often used in the singular sense, is defined as "the study of the general nature of morals and of the specific moral choices to be made by a person" (Ethic, 2003). Velasquez (2006) defines ethics as "the discipline that examines one's moral standards or the moral standards of a society" (p. 10). The common factor within these definitions is the focus on moral standards or moral principles. So, what is a moral standard? Velasquez (2006) states, "Moral standards include the norms we have about the kinds of actions we believe are morally right and wrong as well as the values we place on the kinds of objects we believe are morally good or morally bad" (p. 9). A common misconception about ethics is that it is the study of whether something is right or wrong. This is not the case. As the definitions elude, ethics is the study of the underlying moral principles or standards actually applied to any given situation. Ethics is "the process of examining the moral standards of a person or society to determine whether these standards are reasonable or unreasonable in order to apply them to concrete situations and issues" (p. 11).

In order to evaluate the relevancy or validity of certain moral principles many ethical theories have been developed. The most widely used theories include utilitarianism, Kantian rights theory (or formalism), justice based theories, and the ethic of care.

A utilitarian approach to ethics defines ethical actions or decision as those that will provide the greatest net benefit for the greatest number of people. Brady (1985, 1996) labels this type of approach as outcome oriented. In contrast, a formalist approach is process oriented (Brady, 1985; Brady & Wheeler, 1996; Schminke, Ambrose, & Noel, 1997). Schminke et. al (1997) states, "Under formalism, individuals subscribe to a set of rules or principles for guiding behavior" (p.19) They continue by noting that "actions are ethical or unethical in and of themselves, to the extent that they conform to these rules" (p. 19). These rules are based off the foundation for moral rights provided by Immanuel Kant (Velasquez, 2006). Kant's ethical theory is based on two moral principles- (1) no action should be taken unless that person is willing to have that action taken on everyone including themselves (i.e. universalizability), and (2) every person should be treated as an end not just as a means to an end. Formalism and utilitarianism are labeled as "the two major ethical principles" by Kohlberg (1984, p. 579). Initial research would deem these two approaches as opposite ends of a spectrum. Individuals were thought to possess tendencies to utilize one or the other. However, this notion has evolved to the empirically supported proposition that the two are "independent dimensions of ethical reasoning that each individual possesses" (Schminke & Wells, 1999). This evolution in thought was mostly due to the influential research done by Brady (1985) and Brady and Wheeler (1996).

Often times, ethical conflicts tend to involve issues related to justice or fairness. Because of this, ethical theories based on *justice* developed. These theories have been used for ages to evaluate the ethicality of certain situations. Standards of justice can usually be divided into three distinct categories. First, distributive justice involves "fair distribution of society's benefits and burdens" (Velasquez, 2006: p. 88). Secondly, retributive justice deals with "the justice impositions of punishments and penalties on those who do wrong" (p. 88). And lastly, compensatory justice concerns the restoration to a person of what they lost when wronged by someone else.

The approaches to ethics highlighted above all assume that ethics should be impartial and that, consequently, and special relationships that one may have with particular individuals, such as relatives, friends, or one's employees, should be set aside when determining how one should act (Velasquez, 2006). In contrast to these approaches is an *ethic of care* approach to ethics. This view holds that we as humans "have an obligation to exercise special care toward those particular persons with whom we have valuable close relationships, particularly relations of dependency."

These theories do not represent an "either-or" approach to evaluating moral principles. They simply provide an underlying framework for assessing ethical situations. An action can be deemed ethical by the standards of one theory and unethical by the standards of another. When faced with the challenge of labeling an action or decision ethical or unethical, these theories are the starting point.

The ethical theories described are used in various situations in a number of fields. At a more micro level, researchers have focused their attention on a specific field of ethics called business ethics. Velasquez (2006) describes the field as "a specialized study of moral right and wrong that concentrates on moral standards as they apply to business institutions, organizations, and behavior" (p. 9). Sinclair (1993) describes the ethics of organizations as "those principles of right and wrong that govern the exchanges of members of the organization when they are engaged in organizational activities" (p.64). As the description implies, the topics that the field

of business ethics attempts to address range from corporate or organizational issues to individual ethical issues and how they affect an organization as a whole. While previous research is relevant to virtual organizations, critical analysis of the applications of these theories and other underlying ethical concepts to virtual work has not been extensively researched.

Organizational Culture

In an attempt to address the ethical issues in traditional organizations, researchers have focused their studies on the causes or influential factors in ethical decision making. These include individual factors, situational factors, and organizational factors, among others. Researchers suggest that organizational culture plays an important role in promoting and encouraging ethical behavior (Ambrose, Arnaud, Schminke, 2007; Chen, Sawyers, & Williams, 1997; Deshpande and Joseph, 2008; Douglas, Davidson, & Schwartz, 2001; Ford and Richardson, 1994; McCuddy, Reichardt, & Schroeder, 1993; Reidenbach & Robin, 1991; Sinclair, 1993; Valentine and Barnett, 2007; Verbos, Gerard, Forshey, Harding, & Miller, 2007). In fact, many suggest that organizational culture is the most important factor in influencing an organization's ethical environment. Organizational (or corporate) culture is defined as "the shared values and beliefs of organizational members, specifically beliefs about what works within an organization, and values about preferred end states and the … approaches used to reach them" (Reidenbach & Robin, 1991: p. 273). Essentially, culture is a sense of "how we do things around here" that governs the behavior of management and employees. The link between governing employees' behavior and ethical organizations is obvious. Some researchers propose that ethical behavior is related to the ethical climate of an organization, which is a dimension of corporate culture (Verbos et al., 2007; Wimbush & Shepard, 1994). While the research on organizational culture and its ethical connotations are vast, there has been little focus on its effects on virtual work.

Trust

In order to examine the role of trust in virtual work from an ethical perspective, one must understand the importance of trust and its ethical involvement within traditional organizations. The influence of trust on teams and organizations has been studied on many levels. Trust is defined as "a positive expectation that another will not – through words, actions, or decisions – act opportunistically" (Robbins, 2005: p. 318). Similar definitions resemble that of Barney and Hansen (1994): "trust is the mutual confidence that no party to an exchange will exploit another's vulnerabilities" (p. 176). This vulnerability and dependancy, which is especially present in virtual teams, is a primary ethical concern as noted above in the discussion of an *ethic of care* approach to ethics. Further, the topic of trust concerns characteristics of honesty, loyalty, and integrity. The assumption that a person whom is honest and loyal will act ethically is the basis for the existence of trust in many relationships within organizations. Robbins (2005) states, "Because top executives set the moral tone for an organization, they need to set high ethical standards, demonstrate those standards through their own behavior, and encourage and reward integrity in others" (p. 335). In addressing the issue of trust in virtual work, consider the methods of establishing, developing, and maintaining trust in traditional organizations and how those techniques fit in to the virtual work environment.

Monitoring

The term *monitoring* is an all inclusive reference to actions taken to measure the extent to which a certain variable complies with what is thought to be standard or protocol. While there are many forms of monitoring in the business world, their core purpose is to "provide performance feedback to employees and implementing controls over activities" (Alder, Schminke, Noel, & Kuenzi, 2007: p. 483). With the increase in information and communication technology (ICT), researchers have become increasingly concerned with electronic monitoring and its ethical implications in the traditional organizational setting (Alder, et al., 2007) as well as the virtual organizational setting (Wiesenfeld et al., 1999). A 2005 American Management Association (AMA) survey reported that 76% of companies in the United States engage in regular electronic monitoring of their employees, and that internet monitoring is one of the fastest growing segments of this type of monitoring (as cited Alder et al., 2007). The most obvious ethical concern with electronic monitoring is the issue of the right to privacy, which is defined as "the right people have to determine what, to whom, and how much information about themselves shall be disclosed to others (Velasquez, 2006). This issue arises on many levels -- an employee's right to privacy and a employer's right to keep the business private from outsiders. Virtual work amplifies these pre-existing problems in many ways. For instance, effective performance measurements may be unattainable (Leung, 2008), virtual employees work from home which blurs the lines of the home life and the work life, and the fact that company needs must be balanced with the right to privacy. Therefore, they must be considered in order to successfully develop ethical monitoring techniques and policies.

While the research on the effects of monitoring efforts have focused primarily on traditional organizational structures, its findings are still relevant to the virtual work environment. Friedman and Reed (2008) note that often times monitoring efforts are counter-productive when employees perceive a violation of privacy because this perception leads to decreased employee morale and motivation. This result, the perception of a violation of privacy and its affect on employees, will likely be more prevalent in the virtual environment. As Friedman and Reed (2008) state,

"Negative reactions to organizational monitoring are likely to increase when employees perceive that it extends beyond the workplace" p.82. This is far more likely to occur in the virtual setting since in many cases an employees' workplace and their home are one in the same.

ETHICAL IMPLICATIONS

As discussed, virtual work is characterized by a technology-mediated and geographically dispersed structure. These characteristics, along with the nature of virtual work, pose an immediate need for an evaluation of the ethical implications of such an environment. In order to do so, one must analyze the traditional organizational practices and theories as they compare to those of the virtual organization. Ethical dilemmas surrounding the difficulty of developing and maintaining organizational culture as well as trust in virtual organizations with almost zero face-to-face interaction is explored. In addition, ethical issues arising from cross-cultural distribution of employees and the highly criticized issue of monitoring are examined.

Organizational Culture

The belief that organizational factors influence the ethical development of individuals and organizations is not new. Numerous researchers have studied this notion and many suggest that organizational culture plays an important role in promoting and encouraging ethical behavior (Chen et al., 2001; Ford & Richardson, 1994; McCuddy et al., 1993; Reidenbach & Robin, 1991; Sinclair, 1993; Verbos et al., 2007). Due to the fact that organizational culture has such a vast and direct affect on the ethical development of an organization and its employees, it is important to explore this concept in depth.

With regards to individual ethical development, research has consistently shown that the more ethical the culture of an organization, the more ethical individual employees' decisions will be (Chen et al., 1997; Ford & Richardson, 1994; Schminke & Wells, 1999; Sinclair, 1993). Verbos et al. (2007) discusses the importance of an ethical organizational identity-- a special form of social identity that is socially constructed through the thoughts, feelings, and behaviors of individual and group members embedded in the organizational context-- for promoting ethical behavior. Another example is McCuddy et al.'s (1993) study on the prevalence of the pressures to act unethically in business found that external (or organizational) pressures had a more substantial impact on ethical decision making than individual pressures did. The results of the 1,365 survey respondents, of the 2,400 surveys sent out to members of the Institute of Management Accountants, revealed that pressures to behave unethically may be related more to attributes of the organization than they are to attributes of individual employees. Moreover, attempts to reduce unethical behavior "should focus on the organization and its culture rather than on the individual members of the organization" (p. 59). Similarly, Chen et al. (1997) argues that the "ability of individuals to respond ethically is related to the reinforcement and support the organization provides for ethical behavior" (p. 856). In another study, one hundred sixteen business students were surveyed to measure the extent to which group work affected individual ethical predispositions (Schminke & Wells, 1999). Like the other research, the study revealed that "groups play an important role in molding individuals' ethical frameworks" (p. 376). In contrast, O'Leary and Pangemanan's (2007) study of the factors impacting ethical decisions of accountancy students found that "individuals free from the constraints of group pressure appear more inclined to take a more ethical stance...when faced with an ethical dilemma" (p. 224). This may prove to be an advantage of virtual work over traditional organizational forms from an ethical standpoint.

While a large portion of the research has focused on organizational culture's influence on individual ethical development, some research has focused on its influence on the ethical development of the organization as a whole. Reidenbach and Robin (1991) stated, "The moral development of a corporation is determined by the organization's culture" (p. 273). Building on the individual moral development model created by Kohlberg (1984), Reidenbach and Robin (1991) developed the model of corporate moral development. In order to allow researchers to recognize different stages in organizational ethical development, they state, "the classificatory variables include management philosophy and attitudes, the evidence of ethical values manifested in their cultures, and the existence and proliferation of organizational cultural ethics, and artifacts (i.e., codes, ombudsmen, reward systems)" (p. 274). The model is made up of five stages. Starting from the bottom the stages are labeled as follows: the amoral organization; the legalistic organization; the responsive organization; the emergent ethical organization; and the ethical organization. Based on the variables used to classify organizations into different stages of ethical development, it is obvious that organizational culture is a significant determining factor.

Now that it has been established that organizational culture plays an important role in promoting and encouraging ethical behavior in traditional organizations, considers its affect on the virtual work environment. While the research has not specifically addressed virtual work, the notion that organizational culture affects individual and organizational ethical development applies to traditional and non-traditional businesses alike. However, the nature of the virtual environment creates several problems that could potentially damage the ethical development of the company. These problems include limited, or lack of, socialization; the effect of differing perceptions of organizational culture due to culturally dispersed employees; and, most importantly, the methods used to establish, develop, and maintain an ethical corporate culture.

Problems with Establishing and Developing Organizational Culture

Creating an effective organizational culture is no easy task, not even in traditional organizations. The task of doing so becomes increasingly more difficult as ICT's infiltrate the corporate world allowing for boundary-less organizations. Before we know how to establish an *ethical* culture, we have to understand how organizational culture in its broadest sense is created.

So, how is culture created? Where do these "social norms" come from? Robbins (2005) states, "An organization's current customs, traditions, and general way of doing things are largely due to what it has done before and the degree of success it has had with those endeavors" (p. 492). This statement provides the foundation for his assessment of the ultimate source of a traditional organization's culture: its founders.

The founders of an organization set the tone for how things are to be done in the future. This is done in three ways. The first step in doing so is hiring and keeping employees who "think and feel the same way they do" (p. 493). Ambrose et al.'s (2007) study of the fit between employees' moral development and the ethical work climate of their organizations found that ethical person-organizational (P-O) congruence needs to be considered for training, development, and selection of employees. "Recruitment and selection procedures attempt to identify a match between the potential employee and the organization" (p. 331). In traditional organizations judging potential employees based on how they "think and feel" is already difficult, even with the help of face-to-face interaction rich with non-verbal and observable cues. Further, consider the hiring process of virtual workers. In many cases, management is not given the opportunity to meet the potential employee face-to-face. Most of the communication is done via electronic communication devices. Subsequently, the lack of face-to-face interaction in the virtual work environment puts management at a disadvantage with regards to assessing the moral values of prospective employees.

The second way that founders facilitate the creation of organizational culture is by indoctrinating and socializing new employees to their way of thinking and feeling (Robbins, 2005: p. 493). Verbos et al.'s (2007) article on positive ethical organizations notes that socialization is vital to creating a positive ethical organization. Douglas et al. (2001) defines socialization as "the process by which individuals are molded by the society to which they seek full membership" (p. 104). In their study of the relationship between organizational ethical culture, personal values, and ethical judgments, they examined over 300 survey responses in an attempt to gauge the correlation of the three variables. Results were consistent with the socialization theory which initially led the researchers to "expect an eventual convergence of personal values with those of the organization" (p. 111). They stated, "Firms mold their members to fit the organizational environment, or select and promote individuals who already fit into the prevailing culture and cause those that do not fit to leave" (p. 111). This "molding" process is done by means of communication vertically and laterally, as well as formally and informally throughout the organization. However, similar to the issues noted above, lack of face-to-face interaction limits this process (Schlenkrich and Upfold, 2009). Mello (2007) notes that the nature of virtual work (referred to as telework) alters coordination, communication, and feedback, and therefore, organization-related identification and verification can become more ambiguous for employees. Similarly, Wiesenfeld et al. (2001) state, "Virtual workers are often separated from coworkers, supervisors, and other organization members, leadings to feelings of isolation... and sometimes greater stress" (p. 214). Relating this statement back to the original definition of socialization presented above, it is important to note that a "feeling of isolation" contradicts one of the critical factors of the socialization theory- that

employees are actively seeking full membership into that society (or in this case, that organization).

While socialization is limited in the traditional sense, it is not entirely impossible. "Several scholars have argued that an important way in which socialization occurs is through social interactions between newcomers and "insiders," or more experienced members of their new organization" (Morrison, 2002; p. 1149). This process involves "molding" new employees as noted above, but it also include individual "new comers" attempts to define an acceptable role for him/herself in an organization. Miller and Jablin (1991) suggest that "information-seeking efforts during organizational entry are of critical importance to newcomers' successful organizational assimilation" (p. 92). With that said, new comers are faced with the challenge of seeking out this type of interaction virtually. The limits of the socialization process in virtual organizations create potential ethical risks. By not being able to consistently hire and retain employees whose values line up with those of management, virtual organizations are more susceptible to unethical behavior by employees.

The third and final way founders go about developing organizational culture in traditional organizations is setting an example. Robbins (2005) states that "the founders' own behavior acts as a role model that encourages employees to identify with them and thereby internalize their beliefs, values, and assumptions" (p. 493). For example, imagine a newly hired employee in a traditional organization over hears a conversation among fellow employees about the employee whom he/she replaced. The co-workers discuss an incident involving questionable accounting practices and go on to reveal that management quickly terminated the prior employee for taking part in it. Immediately the new employee is aware that questionable accounting practices are not acceptable at that particular company. Further, the new employee is likely to identify with the beliefs and core values the termination was based. Therefore, the "tone-at-the-top" has infiltrated the lower employee levels. Unfortunately, this example is relevant to traditional organizations and not virtual organizations. Once again, lack of face-to-face interaction poses a problem.

Proposed Guidelines and Suggestions

The problems virtual organizations face in creating and developing organizational culture are many and must be addressed in order to ensure effectiveness. Possible solutions or ways to minimize the negative effects of these dilemmas come in many forms.

First, in hiring employees, management might consider requiring at least one face-to-face interview. In doing so, management would be provided with an opportunity to effectively gauge the extent to which they believe the potential employee is a "good fit" in the company. If this were not possible, management could resort to live-streaming video conference calls. Again, this would allow management to pick up on the non-verbal cues usually present in a traditional interview, subsequently leading to a better understanding and perception of the underlying values and principles on which the perspective employee stands. Directly related to the selection of employees is the process in which that employee is indoctrinated into the virtual organization and its existing culture. An employee orientation program is necessary to facilitate this process. Verbos et al. (2007) state "employee orientation programs typically include some discussion of organizational history and founder ideology, and give the organization an opportunity to express the unique values and beliefs that underlie its artifacts, including how serious an organization is about ethics" (p. 24). Virtual workers should take part in this type of orientation to ensure congruence between the individual employee and the organization.

Next, in an attempt to encourage and facilitate the socialization process, one might consider having an annual gathering in which all employees travel to a central location and take part in team building activities and festival like get-togethers (Hayes-Brown & Massiello, 2009). By creating an environment that promotes teamwork and allows individual employees to interact with one another, the annual gathering would most likely be effective in minimizing the feelings of isolation. However, if this is not feasible, other options are available. For instance, the virtual organization might offer an open online chat arena designated solely for the purpose of building and enhancing relationships among employees (Schlenkrich & Upfold, 2009). Instead of limiting communication to strictly business interactions, it would be beneficial to promote this sort of informal communication. This too could potentially minimize the isolation factor that leads to limited or lack of socialization.

Also, referring to the individual employee's role in the socialization process, management should encourage new comers to facilitate the process by initiating communication with "insiders" (Morrison, 2002). Further, managers should offer these new comers ideas on how to effectively do so. For example, give the new comer access to informal chat rooms or instant messaging software, provide him/her with a time schedule of when existing employees are usually available for informal communication, and consider facilitating a telephone or video conference introduction of the new employee to the existing team.

Lastly, with regards to management's ability to set an example, virtual organizations are again at a disadvantage. One suggestion to diminish the shortcoming would be to dedicate portions of the organization's website to recognizing and rewarding ethical behaviors. For instance, a forum could be created that allows employees to post stories of fellow employees or supervisors engaging in ethical behaviors. While communication in this manner is far more formal than in a traditional organizational setting, it still effectively portrays the message that the particular behavior was rewarded. This forum could essentially replace the example of the overheard conversation described earlier in the chapter. Another possible way managing founders might go about setting a good example would require the annual gathering suggested above. These meetings would provide management and employees the opportunity to share stories and give examples of their experiences, specifically those in which the ethical principles of the company were upheld.

Proposed Guidelines and Suggestions for Creating and Developing an Ethical Organizational Culture

In addition to the techniques for creating organizational culture already discussed, there are additional steps that must be taken to ensure that the culture is one centered on ethical and moral values. Sinclair (1993) discusses two approaches to the management of organizational culture to improve organizational ethics – creating a unitary culture approach and the subculture approach.

Sinclair (1993) describes the unitary approach by stating that "management can create a unitary and cohesive organizational culture around core ethical values" (p. 67). Chen et al. (1997) labels this approach the "strong" approach and states, "it is characterized by...a culture in which values and norms are shared by all employees" (p. 858). Moreover, these values and norms are "deeply-felt" as opposed to simply being adhered to (Sinclair, 1993: p. 67). This approach relies heavily on management to create a culture that induces consistent ethical responses. This is done in many ways. First, by "clear articulation of a corporate strategy... [which] does not confine itself to economic goals but includes statements about what kind of organization the company will be – its character, the values it espouses, its relationships to customers, employees, communities, and shareholders" (p.68). Next, "systems of rewards, selection, appraisals... rituals and ceremonies, should all be designed to reinforce organization values and norms" (p. 68). This is extremely important because, as Bobek and

Radtke (2007) note, rewards for ethical behavior and punishments for unethical behavior are critical to reinforcing ethical behavior. This approach essentially creates a set of moral values that must be adhered to across the organization.

Some researchers argue against the unitary approach and opt for one that focuses more on individual moral autonomy (Maclagan, 2007). He states, "There are limits to managerial control, for example due to the ambiguity of language used in policies and codes, while the conflicting ethical demands that...confront individuals means that sometimes they will have to take responsibility for their own moral actions; in other words, to exercise a degree of autonomy in any case" (p. 49). This sort of moral autonomy, or free from the influence of others, coincides with Sinclair's (1993) sub-cultural approach which would recognize a "plurality of conflicting values and would nurture individual processes of self-inspection, critique and debate" (Maclagan, 2007: p. 53). This approach, similar to O'Leary and Pangemanan's (2007) notion describe earlier, represents an advantage of the virtual work environment. Being that individual employees are separated from one another, virtual workers rely on their own individual moral development to make decisions, freeing them from the constraints of group influence (O'Leary and Pangemanan's, 2007).

In addition to these techniques, Robbins (2005) makes a few supplementary suggestions. In order to create an ethical culture, Robbins (2005) suggests communicating ethical expectations by means of an organizational code of ethics, providing ethical training to reinforce the organization's standard of conduct, visibly rewarding ethical acts and punishing unethical ones, and providing protective mechanisms so employees can report unethical behavior without the fear of reprimand.

Unlike the problems in creating organizational culture as a whole, the techniques and steps taken to ensure that culture is ethical can be directly applied to the virtual organization. Clearly, with well articulated organizational missions in combination with a focus on values of integrity, honesty, and loyalty, virtual and traditional organizations alike can effectively create an ethical organizational culture; thereby, enhancing individual and organizational ethical development.

Trust

Building on the concept of organizational culture, Brien (1998) states that professional ethics requires a culture that "seeks to promote trust in the profession and trustworthiness as a virtue exemplified in each individual" (p. 391). The reference to trust in describing ethically strong organizations and individuals is widespread. For example, Lu et al. (2006) states, "trust is pivotal to effective team performance" (p. 8). The concept of trust involves individual and corporate virtues of honesty, integrity, and commitment. Unlike the research on organizational culture, some focus has been on the issue of trust in the virtual work environment. At a more micro level, researchers have focused on the means used to establish, develop, and maintain trust in virtual organizations (Jones & Bowie, 1998; Malhotra et al., 2007; Powell et al., 2004). Virtual work is subject to significant challenges in this area.

Two of the techniques used to develop trust in traditional organizations are far less effective in the virtual corporation (Jones & Bowie, 1998). "Sincere manner and reputation" are exchanged primarily through face-to-face interaction. Sincere manner is described as "behavioral cues evident in voice patterns, physical gestures, perspiration, facial and eye movements – body language in general" (p. 277). Reputation involves the perception of the trustworthiness and competence of a fellow employee. These reputations are traditionally developed through lasting relationships. Subsequently, new employees are "likely to be viewed with considerable skepticism" (p. 277). In the case of the new employee, reputation can be established through actual interaction with the other party. However, these types of interactions

are not frequently present in the virtual work environment.

Creating and Developing Trust

So, how can trust be established in virtual organizations? Research in the area has given rise to a swift trust model. "The swift trust [model] suggests that, when [team members] don't have enough time to slowly build trust, [they] assume that others are trustworthy and begin working as if trust were already in place while seeking confirming or disconfirming evidence throughout the duration of the project" (Powell et al., 2004: p. 10). In this model, trust is essentially automatic and implied. However, Jones and Bowie (1998) argue that "the existence of swift trust requires… an ethical account of trust" (p. 285). This argument is based on the notion that "trust is an element of moral character." This ethics based trust strongly resembles the "strong form" or "hard-core" trust Barney and Hansen (1994) describe. Hard core trust comes from the reflection of values, principles, and standards of the party involved. The person is thought to be trustworthy because "that is who or what they are" (p. 179). The need for an ethics based trust is most necessary in the virtual work environment, because "for many relationships necessary to the formation of a virtual corporation, neither trust based on rational calculation nor trust based on the norms of stable relationships is adequate" (Jones & Bowie, 1998: p. 287). Therefore, in order for members of a virtual organization to gain sufficient trust in one another, those members must base their actions on moral principles of loyalty, commitment, honesty, and integrity.

Other Suggestions on Developing Trust

While ethics based trust is necessary, there are other viable options for overcoming the increased difficulty of establishing trust in the virtual work environment. For instance, one possible solution to the issue of trust building in virtual organizations is "an early face-to-face meeting with the intent of developing a strong foundation of trust between members" (Powell et al., 2004: p. 11). While some argue that "face-to-face interactions are irreplaceable for trust building among dispersed team members" (Lu et al., 2006: p. 8), others suggest that the lack there of can be compensated. Chan (2002) introduces the concept of a "virtual work contract" which is a legally binding contract that includes provisions addressing many of the uncertainties inherent to the virtual work environment. By requiring all parties involved to "assert in the contract that he or she has the requisite qualifications, skills, and experience to undertake the assigned tasks" (p. 28), the implied or automatic trust that the other parties will not exploit their vulnerabilities is confirmed and validated.

Breaches of Trust

It is important to note that, "trust within a team can be harmed by breaches of confidentiality outside of the team" (Malhotra et al., 2007: p. 62). Being that most of the interaction among employees is through communication technologies such as the internet, virtual organizations are comparably more vulnerable to security threats than traditional organizations. These types of threats can be addressed through norms which regulate what can and cannot be shared outside of the team or through the virtual work contract described above. The contract would legally require all parties involved to obtain and maintain adequate "security technologies and appropriate organizational policies to ensure that all systems are secure" (Chan, 2002: p. 28).

Cross-Cultural Diversity

One dominant characteristic of a virtual organization is the geographical dispersion of employees and managers. Because virtual workers reside in differing parts of the world, they are likely to live in different cultures. The ethical issues of having culturally diverse employees can be broken down into many different areas. Some of the primary ethical concerns are communication and individual ethical development.

Issues in Communication

Effective communication is a vital component to the success of any organization. Ethical problems arising from cross-cultural communication can range from language issues and timing differences to online communication and differing perceptions. Robbins (2005) describes four problems related to language difficulties in cross-cultural communication: (1) barriers caused by semantics, (2) barriers caused by word connotations, (3) barriers caused by tone differences, and (4) barriers caused by differing perceptions. These challenges in communication can lead to conflict, misattribution, or difficulty with team building (Lu et al., 2006). Consider the following example. An employee receives an email about his most recent work on a project from a fellow employee who speaks another language. The email has been translated to English via translation software. However, a few words are mistranslated and the reader is left with either a jumble of text that makes absolutely no sense or even worse, a paragraph that expresses negative feelings or dislike for his work when in fact the writer was entirely impressed. Subsequently, the perception of the fellow employee is tainted. Beliefs about that person's moral principles and values change due to the fact that this one particular email was misinterpreted. This type of communication error can lead to distress and conflict.

Another aspect of the communication issue is the use of computer-aided technology. With the absence of non-verbal cues the structure, tone, and style of online communication becomes increasingly important. Typing in all caps, for instance, is usually seen as yelling or speaking with an angry tone. In traditional organizations relaying bad news such as a failed experiment or even notification of termination, the wielder will most likely utilize non-verbal cues such as body language to express emotions reflecting their character. For example, if a supervisor is forced to fire a valued employee because of the recent economic crisis, that supervisor would most likely embody sadness and remorse for their employee. For example, their facial expressions might exhibit sadness or a soft touch on the arm or back might exemplify an attempt to comfort the employee. The employee who is being fired is likely to recognize these clues and subsequently affirm their belief that their supervisor is of good moral character. In virtual organizations, the lack of face-to-face interaction puts a strain on an organization's ability to harbor effective communication (Anawati & Craig, 2006; Kayworth & Leidner, 2000; Powell et al., 2004).

While the lack of face-to-face interaction can be a disadvantage, studies have shown that in some cases communication via the internet is more effective. Es, French, and Stellmaszek's (2004) found that negotiations concerning ethical issues through asynchronous Internet connections tend to be more effective, meaning it will produce a greater percentage of successful resolutions, than those done face-to-face. This is primarily due to more time for reflection on prior statements as well as a dramatic decrease in the amount of emotion involved in the conversation. Therefore, the virtual work environment provides the perfect setting for discussion ethical issues.

Proposed Guidelines and Suggestions

The results of a 2006 study done by Anawati and Craig on the ways team members should adapt their behavior in cross cultural teams revealed that "team members can adapt their behavior in both spoken and written communication" (p. 44). By recognizing the importance of communication early in the development process, virtual organizations can create effective ways to mitigate

these issues. Guidelines should be implemented that require employees to be conscious of fellow employees religious beliefs, differing translations and semantics issues involved with other languages, standard styles of writing in electronic communication (such as all caps for urgent messages), and frequency requirements. By creating and enforcing these norms, virtual organizations can overcome the difficulties that are faced due to cross-culture communication, thereby reducing the negative ethical effects of such.

Affects of Cultural Diversity on Individual Moral Development

There has been extensive research on the impact of differing cultural value systems on individual moral development (Lopez, Rechner, & Olson-Buchanan, 2005). Individuals do not operate in a vacuum. They are subject not only to organizational cultures, but also to their specific national cultures. Robbins (2005) states, "national culture has a greater impact on the employees than does their organization's culture" (p. 489). Subsequently, a group of culturally diverse virtual workers will often perceive and approach ethical situations differently.

Proposed Guidelines and Suggestions

The Global Leadership and Organizational Behavior Effectiveness (GLOBE) research program is an ongoing cross-cultural investigation of national culture. Using data from 825 organizations in 62 countries, the GLOBE team identified nine dimensions on which national cultures differ—assertiveness, future orientation, gender differentiation, uncertainty avoidance, power distance, invidualism/collectivism, in-group collectivism, performance orientation, and humane orientation. By taking into consideration individual employees' national cultures, managers of virtual workers can gain insight into their employees' differing perspectives when facing an ethical dilemma. For example, and employee who is thought to be highly individualistic, which means they prefer to act as an individual rather than as a member of a group, might choose to handle an ethical situation on their own rather than depending on the aid of management or fellow employees. An employee from a culture that exhibits high uncertainty avoidance, which is a society's reliance on social norms and procedures to alleviate the unpredictability of future events, would likely prefer a highly structured procedure for addressing ethical dilemmas. As you can see, the affects of cultural diversity on an individual's moral development are substantial. However, if it is positively managed, diversity can "increase creativity and innovation in organizations as well as improve decision making by providing different perspectives on problems" (p. 19).

Other Ethical Problems

As noted earlier, the issues arising from culturally diverse employees are not limited to communication and compensation. Problems due to time differences and distributing work loads are equally important. For example, a meeting scheduled at 2:00 p.m. in one country might require an employee in another country to take part at 4:00 a.m. Theories of distributive justice would require that benefits and burdens be distributed fairly among the employees. So, what is fair? Egalitarianism requires that every person be given equal shares of the organization's benefits and burdens (Velasquez, 2006). Therefore, management and leaders of virtual organizations should rotate times at which meetings are held to ensure that all employees "suffer" the burdens of virtual work equally. Similarly, by distributing work equally among employees, management is ensuring that everyone is fairly treated even though they are geographically dispersed and cannot visually observe such a distribution.

Monitoring

A critical ethical dilemma faced by virtual organizations is the issue of monitoring. The most prevalent ethical issue involving the monitoring of employees surrounds the employee's right to privacy. Velasquez (2006) defines this right as "the right people have to determine what, to whom, and how much information about themselves shall be disclosed to others. Relevant to all types of organizations (virtual and traditional), "the employee's right to privacy has become particularly vulnerable with the development of recent technologies" (p. 375). While employees do have this right, it is important to note that it must be balanced against the rights of the organization as a whole.

Electronic Monitoring

Managers are entrusted with the task of supervising their subordinates' behaviors and ensuring that work be completed in a timely manner. In traditional organizations this is done through visual observation of employee's work ethic, performance evaluations, evaluating productivity levels, etc. In virtual organizations managers are unable to supervise their employees because they are unable to see or keep track of their actions (Wiesenfeld et al., 1999). Therefore, computerized methods of monitoring employees are utilized to overcome this shortfall. Consider an employee who does all of their work via a personal laptop computer, should management be given access to that computer in its entirety? If yes, is this ethical? If not, how is management going to achieve the task bestowed upon them to ensure productivity is maintained and make certain subordinates' behaviors are in line with those morally acceptable in the company?

Other Forms of Monitoring

In contrast to the electronic monitoring of current employees' actions, other forms of monitoring are focused on the potential employee. The utilization of background checks is extremely common among organizations worldwide (Friedman & Reed, 2008). While some might argue that this is still a violation of privacy, most agree that the organization has a legitimate right to know whether or not a potential employees could pose a significant risk to the company. For instance, background checks ensure that the perspective employee has not been arrested for embezzlement from a previous employer or that the employee is not prone to frequent drug or alcohol binges. While this form of monitoring is widely accepted, the needs of virtual organizations can far exceed those of traditional organizations. With the lack of face-to-face interaction and limited relationships between supervisors and subordinates, managers are not given sufficient information to make a sound judgment on their employees' character or work ethic. Because of this disadvantage, would it be ethical to require potential employees to fill out questionnaires that would give managers a better idea of that person's moral characteristics or tendencies?

Proposed Guidelines and Suggestions

Although some forms of monitoring are justified because of their protective and enabling functions, there has to be a line drawn between the unethical and the ethical. How is this done? To answer this and the questions noted above, leaders of virtual organizations must consider three elements when collecting information about employees: relevance, consent, and method (Velasquez, 2006). Velasquez (2006) states, "The employer must limit inquiry into the employee's affairs to those areas that are directly relevant to the issue at hand" (p. 376). This element would limit virtual manager's access in an employee's personal computer to those programs and information that is directly related to the work done for the organization. With regards to consent, only those monitoring or information gathering techniques

that have been directly consented to may be used. McCarthy (1999) suggests implementing policies that alert employees of the monitoring techniques employed. By notifying employees of these policies and receiving consent in employment agreements, these monitoring techniques would be deemed ethical from the formalist perspective and the utilitarian perspective. By giving consent, the employee's right to be treated only as he or she has agreed to be treated is upheld, thereby meeting the formalism requirements. Further, by eliminating the potential risk of litigation costs the organization is minimizing the burden of that particular action subsequently creating a net benefit which fulfills the utilitarian requirements. The last factor that must be considered when considering monitoring techniques and their ethical inferences is the method used to gather information or observe the employee. Prior to implementation, an organization should distinguish between reasonable and unreasonable methods of investigation (Velasquez, 2006). An example of an unreasonable method would be a program or software that can infiltrate an employee's personal email account. In fact, this method would be deemed unethical when considering the relevancy, consent, and method elements. These factors should be considered, especially in the virtual work environment, in order to successfully develop ethical monitoring techniques and policies.

FUTURE RESEARCH DIRECTIONS

The recent phenomenon of virtual work is open to research in many directions. Some ethical areas that warrant specific focus are the numerous issues surrounding affirmative action and its relevance to the virtual organization. Another potential topic could be to investigate the increased focus on the social responsibility of organizations to "go green" and how the virtual organization fits into this responsibility. Without brick and mortar business locations, organizations are actively fighting the war against global warming and simultaneously conserving energy. These are just a few of the many ethical areas that can be explored with regards to the virtual organization.

CONCLUSION

While virtual work has given organizations the opportunity to work across the traditional boundaries of time, space, and geographical location, there are many issues that must be addressed before the virtual organization can be deemed an effective business structure. Specifically, the numerous ethical implications of the virtual work environment that have been explored in this chapter are extremely important and must be considered to prevent detrimental repercussions. We took an in depth look at the important ethical issues involved in creating an ethical organizational culture in a virtual work environment. We explored the issue of trust development and its noteworthy ethical implications. In addition, we examined the ethical issues surrounding cross-cultural communication, culturally diverse employees and their compensation, and monitoring techniques. While the challenges we discussed were many, if adequate measures are taken and the proposed guidelines are followed, the ethical dilemmas faced in the virtual work environment can be overcome.

In closing, I hope the information provided in this chapter has provided you, the reader, with sufficient knowledge to adequately consider and address the ethical issues arising from, and in part due to, the virtual work environment.

REFERENCES

Alder, G. S., Schminke, M., & Noel, T. W. (2007). The Impact of Individual Ethics on Reactions to Potentially Invasive HR Practices. *Journal of Business Ethics, 75*(2), 201. doi: 1337619411.

Ambrose, M., Arnaud, A., & Schminke, M. (2008, February). Individual moral development and ethical climate: The influence of person-organization fit on job attitudes. *Journal of Business Ethics, 77*(3), 323–333. .doi:10.1007/s10551-007-9352-1

Anawati, D., & Craig, A. (2006). Behavioral Adaptation Within Cross-Cultural Virtual Teams. *IEEE Transactions on Professional Communication, 49*(1), 44-56. doi: 1003825671.

Argandona, A. (2003). The new economy: Ethical issues. *Journal of Business Ethics, 44*(1), 3-22. doi: 470202181.

Barney, J. B., & Hansen, M. H. (1994). Trustworthiness as a source of competitive advantage. Strategic Management Journal: Special Issue, 15, 175. doi: 8926192.

Bobek, D., & Radtke, R. (2007, Fall). 2007). An experiential investigation of tax professionals' ethical environments. [from Business Source Complete database.]. *Journal of the American Taxation Association, 29*(2), 63–84. Retrieved April 19, 2009. doi:10.2308/jata.2007.29.2.63

Brady, F. N. (1985). A Janus-headed model of ethical theory: Looking two ways at business/society issues. *Academy of Management Review, 10*, 568–576. doi:10.2307/258137

Brady, F. N., & Wheeler, G. E. (1996). An empirical study of ethical predispositions. *Journal of Business Ethics, 15*, 927–940. doi:10.1007/BF00705573

Brief, A. P., Dukerich, P. R., & Doran, L. I. (1991). Resolving ethical dilemmas in management: Experimental investigations of values, accountability, and choice'. *Journal of Applied Social Psychology, 21*, 380–396. doi:10.1111/j.1559-1816.1991.tb00526.x

Brien, A. (1998). Professional ethics and the culture of trust. *Journal of Business Ethics, 17*(4), 391-409. doi: 27409633.

Chan, S. (2002). Getting the virtual work contract done - Practicalities and organizational dynamics. *Employment Relations Today, 28*(4), 27-35. doi: 108932704.

Chen, A.Y. S., Sawyers, R. B.,& Williams, P. F. (1997). Reinforcing ethical decision making through corporate culture. *Journal of Business Ethics, 16*(8), 855-865. doi: 12622777.

Deshpande, S., & Joseph, J. (2009, April). Impact of emotional intelligence, ethical climate, and behavior of peers on ethical behavior of nurses. *Journal of Business Ethics, 85*(3), 403–410. .doi:10.1007/s10551-008-9779-z

Douglas, P.C., Davidson, R. A., & Schwartz, B.N. (2001). The effect of organizational culture and ethical orientation on accountants' ethical judgements. *Journal of Business Ethics, 34*(2), 101-121. doi: 90060318.

(2003). *Ethic* (11th ed.). Merriam-Webster's Collegiate Dictionary.

Ford, R.C., & Richardson, W. D. (1994). Ethical decision making: A review of the empirical literature. *Journal of Business Ethics, 13*(3), 205. doi: 572059.

Friedman, B., & Reed, L. (2007). Workplace privacy: Employee relations and legal implications of monitoring employee e-mail use. *Employee Responsibilities and Rights Journal, 19*(2), 75–83. .doi:10.1007/s10672-007-9035-1

Hayes-Brown, T., & Massiello, L. (2009). Keep your virtual employees IN THE LOOP. [Retrieved from Business Source Complete database.]. *Incentive, 183*(6), 34–35.

Hughes, J., O'Brien, J., Randall, D., Rouncefield, M., & Tolmie, P. (2001, March). Some 'real' problems of 'virtual' organisation. [from Business Source Premier database.]. *New Technology, Work and Employment, 16*(1), 49. Retrieved March 11, 2009. doi:10.1111/1468-005X.00076

Jones, T., & Bowie, N. (1998, April). Moral hazards on the road to the virtual corporation. [from Business Source Complete database.]. *Business Ethics Quarterly, 8*(2), 273–292. Retrieved January 29, 2009. doi:10.2307/3857329

Kayworth, T. Leidner, D. (2000). The global virtual manager: A prescription for success. *European Management Journal, 18*(2), 183-194. doi: 53926014.

Kohlberg, L. (1984). *The psychology of moral development*. San Francisco: Harper & Row.

Leung, C. (2008). Handling teleworkers. [from ABI/INFORM Global database.]. *Canadian Business, 81*(5), 34. Retrieved March 21, 2009.

Lopez, Y., Rechner, P., & Olson-Buchanan, J. (2005, September 15). Shaping ethical perceptions: An empirical assessment of the influence of business education, culture, and demographic factors. *Journal of Business Ethics, 60*(4), 341–358. .doi:10.1007/s10551-005-1834-4

Lu, M., Watson-Manheim, M., Chudoba, K. M., & Wynn, E. (2006). Virtuality and Team Performance: Understanding the Impact of Variety of Practices. *Journal of Global Information Technology Management, 9*(1), 4-23. doi: 999471691.

Maclagan, P. (2007, January). Hierarchical control or individuals' moral autonomy? Addressing a fundamental tension in the management of business ethics. *Business Ethics . European Review (Chichester, England), 16*(1), 48–61. .doi:10.1111/j.1467-8608.2006.00468.x

Malhotra, A., Majchrzak, A., & Rosen, B. (2007, February). Leading virtual teams. [from Business Source Premier database.]. *The Academy of Management Perspectives, 21*(1), 60–70. Retrieved March 11, 2009.

McCarthy, M. J. (1999, October 21). Virtual Morality: A New Workplace Quandary. *Wall Street Journal* (Eastern Edition), p. B1. doi: 45699514.

McCuddy, M. K., Reichardt, K. E., & Schroeder, D. L. (1993). Ethical pressures: Fact or fiction? Management Accounting, 74(10), 57. doi: 654037.

Mello, J. A. (2007). Managing telework programs effectively. [from ABI/INFORM Global database.]. *Employee Responsibilities and Rights Journal, 19*(4), 247. Retrieved March 21, 2009. doi:10.1007/s10672-007-9051-1

Miller, V., & Jablin, F. (1991). Information seeking during organizational entry: influences, tactics, and a model of the process. [Retrieved from Business Source Complete database.]. *Academy of Management Review, 16*(1), 92–120. doi:10.2307/258608

Morrison, E. (2002). Newcomers' relationships: The role of social network ties during socialization. [Retrieved from Business Source Complete database.]. *Academy of Management Journal, 45*(6), 1149–1160. doi:10.2307/3069430

Moustafa-Leonard, K. (2007). Trust and the manager-subordinate dyad: Virtual work as a unique context. [from ABI/INFORM Global database.]. *Journal of Behavioral and Applied Management, 8*(3), 197–201. Retrieved January 23, 2009.

O'Leary, C., & Pangemanan, G. (2007, October 15). The effect of groupwork on ethical decision-making of accountancy students. *Journal of Business Ethics, 75*(3), 215–228. .doi:10.1007/s10551-006-9248-5

Panteli, N., & Sockalingam, S. (2005). Trust and conflict within virtual inter-organizational alliances: a framework for facilitating knowledge sharing. *Decision Support Systems, 39*(4), 599-617. doi: 842383101.

Paulre, B. (2000). Is the New Economy a Useful Concept? Matisse UMT CNRS No. 8595, Paris.

Powell, A., Piccoli, G., & Ives, B. (2004, January). Virtual teams: A review of current literature and directions for future research. [from ABI/INFORM Global database.]. *The Data Base for Advances in Information Systems, 35*(1), 6–36. Retrieved January 29, 2009.

Reidenbach, R. E., & Robin, D. P. (1991). A conceptual model of corporate moral development. *Journal of Business Ethics, 10*(4), 273. doi: 572503.

Robbins, S. (2005). Organizational Behavior. In Capella University (Ed.), Managing and Organizing People (11th ed.). Boston, MA: Pearson Custom Publishing.

Schlenkrich, L., & Upfold, C. (2009). A guideline for virtual team managers: the key to effective social interaction and communication. [Retrieved from Business Source Complete database.]. *Electronic Journal of Information Systems Evaluation, 12*(1), 109–118.

Schminke, M., Ambrose, M. L., & Noel, T. W.. (1997). The effect of ethical frameworks on perceptions of organizational justice. *Academy of Management Journal, 40*(5), 1190-1207. doi: 22006305.

Schminke, M., & Wells, D. (1999). Group processes and performance and their effects on individuals' ethical frameworks. *Journal of Business Ethics, 18*(4), 367-381. doi: 40195392.

Sinclair, A. (1993). Approaches to organisational culture and ethics. *Journal of Business Ethics, 12*(1), 63. doi: 571826.

Trevino, L., Butterfield, K., & McCabe, D. (1998, July). The ethical context in organizations: Influences on employee attitudes and behaviors. [from Business Source Premier database.]. *Business Ethics Quarterly, 8*(3), 447–476. Retrieved March 10, 2009. doi:10.2307/3857431

Valentine, S., & Barnett, T. (2007, Fall). 2007). Perceived organizational ethics and the ethical decisions of sales and marketing personnel. [from Business Source Complete database.]. *Journal of Personal Selling & Sales Management, 27*(4), 373–388. Retrieved April 19, 2009. doi:10.2753/PSS0885-3134270407

van Es, R., & French, W., & Stellmaszek, F. (2004). Resolving Conflicts Over Ethical Issues: Face-to-face Versus Internet Negotiations. *Journal of Business Ethics: Building Ethical Institutions for Business*, 165-172. doi: 707261411.

Velasquez, M. (2006). *Business Ethics Concepts and Cases*. New Jersey: Pearson Prentice Hall.

Verbos, A., Gerard, J., Forshey, P., Harding, C., & Miller, J. (2007, November 15). The positive ethical organization: Enacting a living code of ethics and ethical organizational identity. *Journal of Business Ethics, 76*(1), 17–33. .doi:10.1007/s10551-006-9275-2

Wiesenfeld, B.M., Raghuram, S., Garud, R. (1999). Managers in a Virtual Context: The Experience of Self-threat and its Effects on Virtual Work Organizations. *Journal of Organizational Behavior*: Trends in Organizational Behavior, 6, 31-44. doi: 1393566161.

Wimbush, J. C., & Shepard, J. M. (1994). Toward an understanding of ethical climate: Its relationship to ethical behavior and supervisory influence. *Journal of Business Ethics, 13*, 637–647. doi:10.1007/BF00871811

KEY TERMS AND DEFINITIONS

Compensatory Justice: Concerns the restoration to a person of what they lost when wronged by someone else.

Distributive Justice: Concerns the fair distributions of society's benefits and burdens.

Ethics: The study of moral standards to evaluate the relevancy and applicability to various situations.

Formalism: View of ethics that evaluates actions and decisions based on the degree to which they conform to a prescribed set of rules.

Moral Standard: The social norms about what actions are considered morally right and wrong as well as the relative value of those objects we deem morally good or bad.

New Economy: A technological revolution involving information and communication technologies and their affect on numerous aspects of our everyday lives.

Organizational Culture: The shared values and beliefs of an organization; a sense of "how we do things around here."

Retributive Justice: Concerns the punishments and penalties imposed on those who do wrong.

Socialization: The process in which individuals are molded by a group.

Utilitarianism: View of ethics that evaluates actions and decisions on the basis of their costs and benefits imposed on society.

Chapter 5
The Electronic Panopticon:
Organizational Surveillance in Virtual Work

Shawn D. Long
University of North Carolina at Charlotte, USA

Richie A. Goodman
University of North Carolina at Charlotte, USA

Chase Clow
Arizona State University, USA

ABSRACT

This chapter explores the role of surveillance in virtual work. With the modern societal shift as well as the increased global market, working virtually is becoming more necessary and even a requirement at times. With the removal of physical interaction, questions of how to properly ensure productivity arise. This chapter suggests the panopticon, as developed by Bentham (1791) and expounded upon by Foucault (1977), is very influential in the surveillance of virtual activity. This chapter will ultimately explore theoretical underpinnings of the panopticon, work place surveillance, virtual surveillance in practice, ethical issues created by virtual surveillance, and consequences of virtual surveillance.

INTRODUCTION

George Orwell, in his landmark book *1984*, wrote about a futuristic world that was fully controlled by the government through surveillance. The premise was that no actions occurred in society without the government's or "Big Brother's" awareness. This awareness was achieved by a constant and overt gaze. Although not quite to the extremes as Orwell described in his fictional book, the increasing role of surveillance in contemporary society .is well established and engrained in individuals' daily lives.

DOI: 10.4018/978-1-61520-979-8.ch005

Information technology (IT) fosters an environment where surveillance can flourish, and as will be explored here, working virtually is an ideal platform for organizational control and close monitoring of employees' communication and behavior.

The rapid and vast proliferations of Internet-based technologies in the workplace have provided prime opportunities for employers to (in) directly monitor the communication activities and behaviors of its employees, in both professional and personal spaces. Orthmann (1998) reported that at least two-thirds of organizations have integrated some type of employee monitoring and surveillance technology in their operations (e.g. computer, email, video monitoring). This technology, also known as employee monitoring and surveillance technologies (MST), is used to measure, shape, and/or control the behavior of employees. Details of sales, deliveries, contact with customers, phone calls, time taken to complete tasks are routinely logged on computer systems and the information used by bosses to evaluate their staff and make sure performance targets are hit (Telegraph.co.uk, Jan. 2008). Employee surveillance is so pervasive in the workplace that one study found managers in a fifth of British workplaces admit to monitoring their employees using computer-based systems (Telegraph, Jan 09, 2008). The structure of the contemporary workplace, with the integration of computers and IT systems and more individuals working remotely and virtually, increases the likelihood that organizations will track employees' workplace and personal communications and behaviors in both overt and covert ways.

The organizational discourse framing the use of MST is compelling. Implementing technology in the workplace has some real advantages: increased productivity, rapid access to robust and timely information, increased safety with video surveillance, theft deterrence, prompts good behavior (e.g., this call is being recorded "for training purposes"), objective evidence of productivity (number of sales, etc.) and curtailing inappropriate uses of the electronic equipment, email and the Internet. However, there are some striking disadvantages of utilizing information technology, mainly MST in the workplace including, but not limited to: potential invasion of privacy, lowering of morale, inhibition of creativity for fear of retribution for not following protocol, reduction of agency, and the blurring of personal and professional boundaries with the ubiquitous use of social networking platforms by individuals and organizations alike.

It must be noted that organizational surveillance is not a new phenomenon. Employee and individual monitoring by organizations has a long and storied history. This chapter provides a brief historical glimpse at organizational surveillance; carries forward historical conceptual and theoretical aspects of surveillance to assist in framing the use of MST in organizations today; discusses employee resistance of information technology and surveillance; and concludes with practical, relational and theoretical implications of the use of technology in the workplace and the surveillance implications.

THEORETICAL FRAMEWORK

Bentham and Foucault's concept of the panopticon provides a useful framework to ground the discussion of surveillance in the workplace. The panopticon is a prison building developed by Jeremy Bentham, an English philosopher and social theorist in 1785. Bentham (1791) developed the panopticon as an apparent omnipresence for prisoners where the hope was that if prisoners were under constant surveillance, they would behave more appropriately. In Bentham's prison, a guard tower equipped with venetian blinds was to stand in the center of the windowed cells armed with a guard for surveillance. This constant source of surveillance was hypothesized to produce better behavior from prisoners. Bentham's ultimate goal was for the guard tower to become a reminder of surveillance so prisoners would begin to practice self surveillance. The threat of the guard would eventually be enough by itself, removing the need for an actual physical presence in the tower. The prisoners' belief that there was a guard would produce the desired results. Once this process is engrained, the prisoners' practice of self policing will render a better behaved, productive prison environment.

Foucault (1977) takes the panopticon a step further, applying it to situations outside of the prison/guard scenarios. Foucault concentrates on issues of power, the primary reasons for the panopticon's success. He argues that the panopticon must "be a generalizable model of function;

a way of defining power relations in terms of the everyday life of men" (Foucault, 1977, p. 205). For Foucault, the concept of self surveillance was the key function. The generalizability of this self surveillance Foucault argues is essential and it can be argued to be a basic function in our culture. Once the concept is established, "the surveillance is permanent in its effects, even if it is discontinuous in its action… the perfection of power should tend to render its actual exercise unnecessary. (Foucault, 1977, p. 205).

Thus, with self surveillance at the heart of the panoptic lens, a prison setting is not the only setting for panoptic gaze. In Foucault's words, "it is polyvalent in its applications; it serves to reform prisoners, but also to treat patients, to instruct schoolchildren, to confine the insane, to supervise workers, to put beggars and idlers to work" (Foucault, 1977, p. 201). Societal structures then are produced based upon the panoptic idea, and individuals become its participants. Panoptic surveillance is a strategic and powerful socialization technique that has the potential to tacitly shape the behaviors and actions of individuals throughout their lives. Due to the normalization of constant surveillance individuals experience throughout life, the expectation of complete privacy in contemporary society should no longer be an expectation, the normalcy of the panoptic gaze is reified through the constant monitoring occurring in our daily lives. As Lyon (2001) states, in today's society "It is hard to find a place, or an activity, that is shielded or secure from some purposeful tracking, tagging, listening, watching, recording or verification device" (Lyon, 2001, p. 1).

As Giddens' (1984) theory of structuration notes, these everyday practices become routine in our lives, as we begin to no longer consciously examine their purposes or consequences. Since we are so used to having our activities monitored on highways, in hallways, at grocery stores, at school, etc., we begin to think and assume that surveillance and monitoring is normal. With this assumption, we normalize surveillance in society;

we no longer believe it is abnormal or something to be concerned about.

This, as Foucault speculates, is what allows the panopticon to work so easily in our society. For example, organizational work settings often are managed through surveillance by wandering, where managers walk around the office to ensure productive and focused employees. This is known in the management literature as management by walking around (MBWA). This is an unstructured approach to hands-on, direct participation by the managers in the tasks of their employees. Managers spend a considerable amount of time asking questions, informally surveying the work areas and listening to employees. This provides managers an opportunity to see firsthand what is going on at the operational level (MBWA, 2006). The threat of the manager walking to a person's cubicle, or simply glancing up from his or her desk, ensures productive work from employees. As the Hawthorne effect states, people are more productive when they are being watched (Roethelisberger, 1939). Lyon and Zureik (2006) describe this industrial surveillance as labor time, where employees are expected to be productive during their hours at work. Lyon and Zureik explore industrial, organizational surveillance from a Weberian perspective where surveillance is the means that keeps the organization moving forward.

VIRTUAL WORK SURVEILLANCE

The panoptic gaze is advanced in the contemporary workplace through the use of similar electronic mechanisms that monitor and control employees' behaviors in "real time". Spitzmuller and Stanton (2006) note that current computer software allows employers to monitor employees' computer usage by recording activity logs for all software programs used on a computer, access to information of a LAN (local area network), logs of all Internet sites visited, and detailed information about keystrokes. Recent software even allows screenshots of the computer displays of employees connected to the network at anytime (Spitzmuller & Stanton, 2006). Emails may be monitored, recorded and stored by transmitting messages through the organization's servers. Anything done on office computers is legally the property of the organizations and subject to close monitoring and sometimes restriction by the organization. Typically, employees' ability to check different websites are limited while on the office computer as a number of 'counterproductive' sites are not accessible, even when working remotely, away from the office.

Our continuous association with the panoptic gaze normalizes the close monitoring of employees and reifies the technological actions of organizations as reasonable and justified. The electronic gaze is powerful and operates fairly unnoticed. Organizations have leveraged the robust electronic capabilities of the Internet to create a system where surveillance can become even more powerful. As virtual teams and the amount of people who work remotely becomes more routine (Holloway, 2007; Hylmo& Buzzanell, 2002; Tietze, 2002), the ability to closely monitor employees' communication and Internet activity is exponentially larger than the ability to monitor in person. We term this management by technological gaze (MBTG). This is an indirect and unobtrusive organizational mechanism used to closely monitor the online communication, actions and behaviors of employees. This monitoring is not limited to work-related issues, but extends to activities beyond work that can be tracked through technology such as online social networking activities, search engine usage, etc. For instance, IT specialists can easily view what you are viewing on your server-connected computer, what e-mails you are sending, what documents you are workings on and time on tasks, even if you are working remotely. This holistic monitoring is only possible with Internet-capable technology, which is widely available and many times necessary for individuals to do their work efficiently and collaboratively.

Lyon (2001) describes this phenomenon as disappearing bodies; "bodies disappear when we do things at a distance" (Lyons, 2001, p. 15). It is because of disappearing bodies that surveillance is becoming more and more in depth and common. Telephone conversations rely on voice communication, removing the physical body. Taking this a step further, e-mail and Internet work remove all trace of embodiment. Lyon states simply that "disappearing bodies is a basic problem of modernity that has been accentuated with the growth and pervasiveness of communication and information technologies" (Lyon, 2001, p. 15).

At a general level, the use of online monitoring can be seen by looking at advertisements people encounter while online. Campbell and Carlson (2002) apply the panoptical design to the Internet exploring targeted advertising. They argue surveillance is the key concept in Internet advertising; "the objective is to assess the individual's likelihood for undesirable behavior, and to monitor, categorize, and rank as to curb such behavior" (p. 587). Following what an individual's patterns are online gives advertisers an idea as to what they are interested in. Green (1999) further explores this practice terming it 'dataveillance'. Green argues dataveillance is slightly different from Foucault's panopticon. In dataveillance "only 'markers' which are secondary and often difficult to accurately interpret are seen" (Green, p. 35, 1999). However, Green's argument for surveillance without the eye when applied to one's working conditions creates a panoptic gaze.

Hertel, Geister, and Konradt (2005) explore management of virtual work describing three forms of managing: Electronic Performance Monitoring (EPM), Management by Objectives and Feedback (MBO), and Self-managing teams. EPM is "based on performance recordings by the computer hardware (number of keystrokes, claims, lo-in hours etc.) and/or service observations by a supervisor (e.g., on the telephone) of qualitative aspects such as courtesy, tone, and accuracy of information" (Hertel, Geister, & Konradt, 2005, p.

80). This form of virtual management is Foucault's panopticon explicitly at work online. Workers operate under the assumption that they are under constant surveillance, and everything they do is being watched by their employer. We argue that this is accepted by virtual workers because individuals are normalized to constant surveillance through early socialization processes and techniques (e.g. nanny cams, daycare surveillance, etc.) that reify the process as natural and rational. This is the main means of enforcement for management in regards to virtual teams. By establishing a threat of the constant monitoring, workers engage in self surveillance at home, making the necessity of a physical manager an organizational relic. This is a powerful component of MBTG. Green's (1999) description of dataveillance is very similar to the process of monitoring described here. How then can we discuss surveillance of virtual teams as an all seeing eye? Green's description of dataveillance is targeted advertising while we are exploring surveillance and virtual work. Thus, when nothing is changing on a computer screen, the 'markers' in dataveillance are unable to provide much information; however, when this occurs in a work environment it can be viewed as lack of productivity and is therefore informational for management and the organization.

ETHICAL CONCERNS

Such direct application of Foucault's panoptic gaze on virtual work prompts an ethical discussion. What is considered private? What is the right balance of employee versus employer rights? What degree of surveillance is acceptable and reasonable? What constitutes professional and personal boundaries in this vast technological era? Is there a new social and relational contract between employers and employees? All of these are interesting and highly debated questions.

The heart of this ethical issue is best summarized by Regan (2006) who posits that there is "a recent trend in workplace surveillance, which of surveillance increasingly focused on the *worker* rather than the *work* itself" (Regan, 2006, p. 21). At the center of this issue is the discussion on privacy. Lyon (2001) explores the public and private realms. Surveillance has become more individualized because work has become more individualized. Nonetheless, the question of what is still considered employee privacy is blurred with the use of new surveillance technology.

Lyon and Zureik (2006) further address the issue of privacy in their study of webcams in Finland. Finland originally sought the use of webcam technology to keep tabs on criminals, but this same technology is now used by the tourist industry for promotions. Though Lyon and Zuriek do not deliberately call this act unethical, they openly ponder its role in escalation. In other words, if the technology goes from tracking criminals to tourists, is the next step tracking employees or even citizens?

Hughes (2007) explores the invasion of privacy through surveillance in discussing the panoptic gaze utilized by the American government. Hughes states,

The panopticon is a relevant model for current surveillance practices because in many ways the current statutory allowances for intercepting communications allow government agencies to watch all citizens for patterns of deviant behavior, rather than simply using "surveillance" to watch individuals that are known to be a threat to society. (p. 21)

Hughes's argument is a concern many Americans share. This is Orwell's novel brought to life. The popular film *Enemy of the State* also explores this possibility, and these capabilities, as early as 1998.

In regards to the escalation debate where online surveillance will lead to some more intrusive surveillance techniques, Regan (2006) explores genetic screening, as it relates to a "person's physical and psychological development," (p. 23) used by organizations. In this model, "surveillance moves along a continuum from work (performance) to the worker (personal characteristics)" (Regan, 2006, p. 23). Along this continuum then, through genetic screening employers are able to 'see' a candidate's performance, behavior, and personal characteristics as they may translate to their productivity in the organization. This case again highlights the public vs. private debate.

The difficulty in discussing privacy is operationalizing what private means. Perrolle (2006) presents some of the inherent fallacies in her definition, "privacy as the freedom to be left alone by other individuals and by social groups has been distinguished from privacy as freedom from the intrusions of formal institutions and authorities into personal life" (Perrolle, 2006, p. 47). Nissenbaum (1998) provides an additional account on the difficulty of operationalizing privacy,

As disturbing as the practices of public surveillance are, they seem to fall outside the scope of predominant theoretical approaches to privacy, which have concerned themselves primarily with two aspects of privacy – namely, maintaining privacy against intrusion into the intimate, private realms, and protecting the privacy of individuals against intrusion by agents of government. (Nissenbaum, 1998, p. 564)

Privacy operates in both private and public realms, making it difficult to establish rules and nearly impossible to establish laws for what is and is not private. Thus situates the ethical debate with surveillance and work. Is work inherently public? This is a difficult question to answer, and this debate is likely to remain unresolved for some time.

Lastly, it is important to remember that panopticons, panoptic technology, and surveillance are simply technologies and techniques. With that, these technologies and techniques are inherently neutral; they are not good or bad. Green (1999) notes that we need to understand and appreciate

that surveillance can be used for "control and facilitation, for social management and social empowerment" (p. 27). It is not the technology that is good or bad, but rather the uses of the technology that are positive and negative. For example, one can use surveillance to invade another's privacy by monitoring their every move (which can be considered 'bad'), but on the other hand, one can use the exact same surveillance technology to stop criminals and terrorists (which can be considered 'good'). It is important to remember that technology does not necessarily determine behavior. Technology is just a tool that can be used in a variety of manners to benefit or harm individuals, organizations, and societies.

Regarding the workplace, Guidi (2004) notes that businesses desire efficiency from their employees, and efficiency occurs when organizations have power and control. In other words, organizations need power to effectively mobilize and utilize their employees. Surveillance is one way of increasing this power and control, and the technology can be used both ethically and unethically. Guidi (2004) argues that the potential abuses of surveillance will occur regardless of whether the surveillance technology is present or not. Individuals who abuse surveillance technology and use it in unethical ways, are likely to abuse other methods of power and control as well. After all, privacy abuses existed long before the existence of online surveillance, and will most likely exist with the advent of new technologies of employee control. Thus, when examining the ethics of surveillance, it is important to closely investigate individual and societal norms and values as well.

RESISTANCE

We assert that there is an innate power struggle between organizations and its workers. Any discussion on power implies the likelihood of a struggle between parties. Those without power work to resist those who have power. Organizational settings are ideal sites to view this contested relationship. Surveillance technologies have increased largely due to the debated shift to postmodernity and the disembodiment of individuals as previously discussed. However, the grasp employers have on their employees also tightens in response to resistance and/or the potential of resistance. Due to the emerging and youthful poise of virtual work, understanding the techniques for resisting are still minimally explored and in its infancy. The dearth of empirical literature to date supports this observation.

However, the use of the Internet as a source of resistance is a widely studied topic. Lyon (2002) investigates Internet use to resist government control, movements, etc. Gossett and Kilker (2005) explore the use of hate websites to inspire organizational change. If successful, such anti-organization websites may be successful in promoting less surveillance of virtual workers or in the very least an attention getter for organizational leaders signaling the need for a discussion on the topic.

Further, Bain and Taylor (2000) researched the ways in which some call center employees have resisted the surveillance found at their workplace. At this particular call center, managers monitored employee calls to potential customers in order to evaluate performance. The call monitoring was designed to occur randomly (i.e., the employees were not supposed to know when the monitoring was occurring), which effectively created a panopticon. However, employees found a way to resist this panopticon by simply observing when the manager was in his or her office. When the manager was away from his or her office, the employees knew that their calls were not being monitored, and therefore were free to work as they pleased. Additionally, Bain and Taylor (2000) noted that employees were able to exploit the computer system that monitored their activities, by tricking it into thinking they were working when they really were not. In regard to virtual work surveillance, this research suggests that if employees are able to "fool" the system into thinking they are doing their job (when they really are not), or if the employee is able to determine when they are being monitored, they should be able to resist the panoptic surveillance.

Similarly, Kitto (2003) found students in distant-learning situations (i.e., online classes) were able to resist their electronic panopticon by simply manipulating the system. In this distant learning situation, students were required to read online for a specified time period. However, students learned that as long as they were logged into the system, the system registered them as reading the required texts (even if they were not). Thus, students simply logged on and then walked away. In regard to virtual work, this type of resistance suggests that organizations may have trouble properly training employees online, as employees may simply circumvent the system and "fool" the organization.

Aubert and Kelsey (2003) describe trust as an alternative to surveillance. Their stance is, "the formation of trust is desirable because it reduces the costs of monitoring and controlling, hence, making the transaction more efficient" (Aubert & Kelsey, 2003, p. 578). By establishing trust, the need for monitoring is greatly diminished. Of course, this solution to the surveillance ethical issues is a bit idealistic as trust takes time, and in our capitalistic society, time is very often the enemy of productivity.

Another method of resistance is the legal route, through the courts. Lyon (2001) discusses the two possibilities of approaching the legal nature of surveillance, "The strategies for resisting and limiting surveillance power have been mainly modern in style. Legislation relating to data protection (in Europe) or privacy (in North America) came to be seen as the effective muzzle on more menacing aspects or methods of surveillance" (Lyon, 2001, p. 144). The difficulty here again lies in the operationalization of what private means. In the legal realm, the inability to completely define what it means to be private makes this method of resistance very difficult.

CONSEQUENCES OF SURVEILLANCE

Given the pervasive nature of surveillance, it is vital to examine some of the consequences associated with its presence in the virtual workplace. After all, since constant surveillance is commonplace in many organizations, it is important to determine how it affects employee well-being and performance. As will be seen below, research has suggested that workplace surveillance can increase fear and stress levels in employees, which, in turn, can influence performance. Research has also shown that constant surveillance can decrease employee trust in organizations. Fortunately, many of the negative consequences associated with surveillance can be minimized by altering a few components of the workplace.

To begin, simply being under the watchful eye of surveillance can evoke the emotion of fear in individuals (Kosekela, 2000). When being monitored, individuals become self-conscious and fear negative appraisals. They fear their managers or bosses will perceive them as poor workers, deviants, or incompetent. With this increased fear also comes increased managerial control, as employees are forced to self-regulate, in an attempt to be seen as good performers. It is thought that this self-regulation will increase performance, as employees will be forced to follow organizational procedures and regulations (Guidi, 2004). Thus, a beneficial consequence of increased fear related to surveillance, is increased performance. However, an unfortunate side effect of this fear-induced self-regulation is an increase in employee stress levels (Holmes, 2001).

Aiello and Kolb (1995) note that a number of studies have reported a link between electronic performance monitoring and increased stress levels (for example in clerical employees and telecommunication workers). Employees in these studies felt more tension, anxiety and fatigue than employees who were not monitored. It was hypothesized that monitored employees felt more stress because they focused on enhancing personal productivity at the expense of meeting group goals. In other words, since the employees were so preoccupied with their own personal performance, they neglected group and organizational goals. This then increased stress levels because over-arching demands were not being met. Additionally, since managers were able to micro-manage employees to a greater extent, stress levels also increased (Aiello &Kolb, 1995).

While increased stress can result in increased performance in some cases (as it forces employees to work harder), it has also been argued that stress has the potential to decrease employee health, and therefore, decrease employee performance (Alder, 1998). Since being monitored increases stress, and stress is linked to illness, headaches, anxiety, anger and depression, it is thought that increased surveillance will also be associated with increased employee sickness and missed days at work (Alder, 1998). This negatively influences performance, because ill employees are unable to perform their jobs to the best of their abilities. At the macro-level, this can be associated with losses in organizational earnings and profitability (Alder, 1998). Thus, it is important to remember that constant surveillance in the virtual workplace may not always be associated with increased productivity.

Next, research has suggested surveillance can undermine employee trust in an organization (Kramer, 1999). For instance, when being monitored, employees may become suspicious of their supervisors and start to distrust their motives (Kramer, 1999). Employees might begin to wonder why their supervisors were monitoring them. They might assume their bosses were looking for reasons to fire them, or that their supervisors simply did not like them. This lack of trust and increased suspicion can lead to ironic consequences. As Kramer (1999) writes, "there is increasing evidence that such systems can actually undermine trust and even elicit the very behaviors they are intended to suppress or eliminate" (p. 591). For example, if employees do not trust their bosses, and feel like their bosses are actively trying to sabotage them, employees may begin to work less, find ways to fool the organization, or even find ways to damage the company (De Lara, 2006)! Thus, a drop in trust related to surveillance may actually hurt a company substantially more than help it.

Given all of the negatives associated with constant surveillance (increased fear, increased stress, decreased trust, decreased performance), it is important to examine some methods of reducing these problematic consequences. Fortunately, much work has been done in this area. Amick and Smith (1992) found that stress related to surveillance can be minimized by having employees participate in the job design process. If employees help in determining how they perform their jobs, or the types of tasks they will be required to perform, they often feel more positively about being monitored by surveillance. This is because when employees participate in the job design process they start to feel a sense of empowerment, they feel as if they have some control and agency at their workplace (Varca, 2003). When empowered, employees start to feel they are active and respected members of the organization, and they begin to understand the need for surveillance.

Similarly, Amick and Smith (1992) suggested that if employees participate in determining when and where they will be observed, stress should also decrease. For example, managers and supervisors could consult with employees to determine what types of online activities are monitored and when the monitoring will be take place. When employees understand exactly what will be monitored and when, they can prepare for the surveillance, and therefore reduce their stress levels.

Research also suggests the perceived intensity of panoptic surveillance can influence stress levels (Holman, Chissick, & Totterdell, 2002). In their study of customer service agents in the

United Kingdom, it was found that as participant-perceived surveillance intensity increased, so did exhaustion and stress. Intensity was determined by the pervasiveness of the monitoring. For example, when a supervisor intermittently monitored calls, surveillance was seen as less intense, but when the supervisor was sitting right next to the employee, surveillance was perceived as very intense. Due to the fact that supervisors were physically next to the employee, and directly monitoring him or her, employees felt increased stress because they felt their every move was being analyzed and they could not escape the glare of their bosses. However, when supervisors randomly monitored calls, employees felt less stressed, as they knew their every action and behavior was not being monitored; only a few of their actions and behaviors were. This research suggests, when possible, managers should attempt to decrease the intensity of the monitoring and surveillance, in order to reduce stress. In regard to the virtual work environment, this could mean only monitoring online activity a portion of the time, as opposed to every minute of every day. As mentioned above, decreased stress should lead to decreased employee sickness and down-time, and therefore increased performance overall.

Further, Alder, Noel, and Ambrose (2006) found when employees are provided justification for monitoring techniques, they begin to trust the organization more. Essentially, when employees understand the need for surveillance, they learn that their organization does not have ulterior motives, but rather wishes to improve the workplace in some manner. Justification can include a need for employee development, a need to reduce cyber-loafing, or a desire to improve quality control, etc. (Alder et al., 2006). All in all, simply explaining to employees why they are being monitored can have beneficial effects that can be seen all over the workplace (decreased stress, increased trust, increased performance).

CONCLUSION

The emergence and rapid increase of individuals working virtually is changing the nature of what constitutes work and how individuals do their work. Contemporary organizations are mindful of the tremendous potential to leverage opportunities and expand traditional organizational boundaries through the strategic use of powerful and wide ranging information technologies. To be sure, the Internet has ushered in the information-age of work, slowly replacing the industrial age. While embarking on this new and exciting era of rapid access and a highly collaborative and connected workplace, one should be mindful of the full impact of this technology at work. Emerging is a new social contract that has the potential to redefine the relational dynamics of employers and employees in organizations. The postmodern society we live in allows Foucault's panopticon to operate with increased ease. Couple this with the organizational shift where working virtually is increasingly commonplace and the traditional ways of doing business is under constant interrogation and threat. As employees are empowered and encouraged (sometimes mandated) to work remotely to save organizational costs and provide greater worker flexibility; the control of the organization has not lessened, but actually increased in a more insidious and viral manner. As shown, information technology and MST has the capability to monitor key strokes, view e-mails, and even view what is being shown on your screen. However, the electronic panopticon socializes workers to increase productivity and monitor their actions online, both personal and professional, as if they are constantly monitored even if they are not. The issues associated with working virtually and the ethics of surveillance is fertile ecological ground for greater exploration. As virtual work continues to emerge, so will resistance and agency redefining and positioning, as increased surveillance and control is central to contemporary work life.

REFERENCES

Aiello, J. R., & Kolb, K. J. (1995). Electronic performance monitoring: A risk factor for workplace stress . In Stauter, S. L., & Murphy, L. R. (Eds.), *Organizational Risk Factors for Job Stress* (pp. 163–180). Washington, D.C.: American Psychological Association. doi:10.1037/10173-010

Alder, G. S. (1998). Ethical issues in electronic performance monitoring: A consideration of deontological and teleological perspectives. *Journal of Business Ethics*, *17*, 729–743. doi:10.1023/A:1005776615072

Alder, G. S., Noel, T. W., & Ambrose, M. L. (2006). Clarifying the effects of internet monitoring on job attitudes: The mediating role of employee trust. *Information & Management*, *43*, 894–903. doi:10.1016/j.im.2006.08.008

Amick, B. C., & Smith, M. J. (1992). Stress, computer-based work monitoring and measurement systems: A conceptual overview. *Applied Ergonomics*, *23*(11), 6–16. doi:10.1016/0003-6870(92)90005-G

Aubert, B. A., & Kelsey, B. L. (2003). Further understanding of trust and performance in virtual Teams [Electronic verson]. *Small Group Research*, *34*, 575–618. doi:10.1177/1046496403256011

Bain, P., & Taylor, P. (2000). Entrapped by the 'electronic panopticon:' Worker resistance in the call centre. *New Technology, Work and Employment*, *15*(1), 2–18. doi:10.1111/1468-005X.00061

Bentham, J. (1791). Outline for the construction of a panopticon penitentiary house . In Mack, M. (Ed.), *A Bentham Reader*. New York: Pegasus.

Bentham, J. (1995). The Panopticon Writings. (Miran Bozovic, Ed.; pp. 29-95). London: Verso.

Cambell, J. E., & Carlson, M. (2002). Panopticon. com: Online surveillance and the commodification of privacy [Electronic version]. *Journal of Broadcasting & Electronic Media, 46*, 586–606. doi:10.1207/s15506878jobem4604_6

De Lara, P. Z. M. (2006). Fear in organizations: Does intimidation by formal punishment mediate the relationship between interactional justice and workplace internet deviance? *Journal of Managerial Psychology, 21*(6), 580–592. doi:10.1108/02683940610684418

Foucault, M. (1977). *Discipline and punishment: The birth of the prison.* New York: Pantheon Books.

Giddens, A. (1984). *The constitution of society: Outline and the theory of structuration.* Los Angeles: University of California Press.

Gossett, L., & Kilker, J. (2005). My job sucks: Counter-institutional websites as locations for organizational member voice, dissent, and resistance. *Management Communication Quarterly, 20*, 63–90. doi:10.1177/0893318906291729

Green, S. (1999). A plague on the panopticon: Surveillance and power in the global information economy [Electronic version]. *Information Communication and Society, 2*, 26–44. doi:10.1080/136911899359745

Guidi, M. E. L. (2004). My own utopia. The economics of Bentham's panopticon. *European Journal of the History of Economic Thought, 11*(3), 405–431. doi:10.1080/0967256042000246485

Hertel, G., Geister, S., & Konradt, U. (2005). Managing virtual teams: A review of current empirical research [Electronic version]. *Human Resource Management Review, 15*, 69–95. doi:10.1016/j.hrmr.2005.01.002

Holloway, D. (2007). Gender, telework and the reconfiguration of the Australian family home [Electronic version]. *Journal of Mass Media and Cultural Studies, 21*, 33–44. doi:10.1080/10304310601103919

Holman, D., Chissick, C., & Totterdell, P. (2002). The effect of performance monitoring on emotional labor and well-being in call centers. *Motivation and Emotion, 26*(1), 57–82. doi:10.1023/A:1015194108376

Holmes, D. (2001). From iron gaze to nursing care: Mental health nursing in the era of panopticism. *Journal of Psychiatric and Mental Health Nursing, 8*, 7–15. doi:10.1046/j.1365-2850.2001.00345.x

Hughes, S. S. (2007). Global panopticon: Looking at human rights in light of the U.S. and international laws [Electronic version]. *Conference Paper: National Communication Association.*

Hylmo, A., & Buzzanell, P. M. (2002). Telecommuting as viewed through cultural lenses: An empirical investigation of the discourses of utopia, identity, and mystery [Electronic version]. *Communication Monographs, 69*, 329–356. doi:10.1080/03637750216547

Kitto, S. (2003). Transplanting and electronic panopticon: Educational technology and the rearticulation of lecture-student relations in online learning. *Information Communication and Society, 6*(1), 1–23. doi:10.1080/1369118032000068796

Koskela, H. (2000). 'The gaze without eyes': Video-surveillance and the changing nature of urban space. *Progress in Human Geography, 24*(2), 243–265. doi:10.1191/030913200668791096

Kramer, R. M. (1999). Trust and distrust in organizations: Emerging perspectives, enduring questions. *Annual Review of Psychology, 50*, 569–598. doi:10.1146/annurev.psych.50.1.569

Lyon, D. (1994). *The electronic eye: The rise of surveillance society*. Minneapolis, MN: University of Minnesota Press.

Lyon, D. (2001). *Surveillance society: Monitoring everyday life*. Philadelphia, PA: Open University Press.

Lyon, D. (2002). Surveillance studies: understanding, visibility, mobility and the phonetic fix [Electronic version]. *Surveillance & Society*, *1*, 1–7.

Lyon, D., & Zureik, E. (Eds.). (2006). *Computers, surveillance, and privacy*. Minneapolis, MN: University of Minnesota Press. "Management by walking around." A Dictionary of Business and Management. Oxford University Press. 2006. Retrieved January 06, 2010 from Encyclopedia. com: http://www.encyclopedia.com/doc/1O18-managementbywalkingaround.html

Nissenbaum, H. (1998). Protecting privacy in an information age: The problem of privacy in Public [Electronic version]. *Law and Philosophy*, *17*, 559–596.

Perrolle, J. A. (2006). Privacy and surveillance in computer-supported cooperative work . In Lyon, D., & Zureik, E. (Eds.), *Computers, surveillance, and privacy* (pp. 47–65). Minneapolis, MN: University of Minnesota Press.

Regan, P. M. (2006). Genetic testing and workplace surveillance: Implications for privacy . In Lyon, D., & Zureik, E. (Eds.), *Computers, surveillance, and privacy* (pp. 21–46). Minneapolis, MN: University of Minnesota Press.

Roethelisberger, F. J. (1939). *Management and the worker; an account of a research program conducted by the Western electric company, Hawthorne works*. Cambridge, MA: Harvard University Press.

Tietze, S. (2002). When "work" comes "home": Coping strategies of teleworkers and their families [Electronic version]. *Journal of Business Ethics*, *41*, 385–396. doi:10.1023/A:1021236426657

Varca, P. E. (2006). Telephone surveillance in call centers: Prescriptions for reducing strain. *Managing Service Quality*, *16*(3), 290–305. doi:10.1108/09604520610663507

KEY TERMS AND DEFINITIONS

Panopticon: Originally a prison design establishing constant surveillance of prisoners, later adapted to societal structures relating to power and surveillance.

Information Technology (IT): A service based industry which administers, assists, and monitors, among other functions, the digital infrastructure present in both the workplace and the home.

Monitoring and Surveillance Technologies (MST): Tools and techniques used to shape and control employee production, interaction, and behavior.

Management by Walking Around (MBWA): Monitoring employee's communication, behavior, and productivity in person.

Management by Technological Gaze (MBTG): Remotely monitoring an employee's communication and Internet activity through the use of surveillance tools.

Dataveillance: Technique often used in Internet advertising where secondary markers are used to track an individual's activities online.

Section 2
Relationships in Virtual Work

Chapter 6
Virtual Team Identity Construction and Boundary Maintenance

Huiyan Zhang
Schouten China, People's Republic of China

Marshall Scott Poole
University of Illinois Urbana-Champaign, USA

ABSTRACT

This chapter reports the results of a multiple case study which investigated how virtual teams appropriated multiple media to facilitate the construction of group identity and manage group boundaries. It focuses on relationships within and between virtual teams. The study found five processes that shaped group identity, including clarification of goals and mission, developing regularized pattern of interaction, group norms for media use, and negotiation of task jurisdiction with interlocking groups. The study discovered that groups managed boundaries in terms of clarity distinctness, and permeability. It indicated that group boundaries were blurred and maintained simultaneously through purposeful use of communication technologies.

INTRODUCTION

The virtual team has become a "default" component of today's organizations (Pauleen, 2004). Several factors contribute to the increasing use of virtual teams (VTs), including the globalization of the economy, the advance of information technology, the rise of new organizational forms, and the emergence and growth of telework (Lipnack & Stamp, 1997; Poole & Zhang, 2005). Not surprisingly, there has been a dramatic increase in research on VTs in recent

years (e.g., Aubert & Kelsey, 2003; Connaugton & Daly, 2004; Cramton, 2001, 2002; Dube & Pare, 2004; Gibson & Manuel, 2003; Gluesing et al., 2003; Massey, Montoya-Weiss & Hung, 2003).

There are still some gaps in our current knowledge of virtual teaming (Poole & Zhang, 2005). For the most part, existing studies have tended to focus on internal group processes and the challenges that virtual work and diverse membership pose in terms of social cognition (e.g., Cramton, 2001), relational communication (e.g., Jarvenpaa, Knoll & Leidner, 1998; Jarvepaa & Leidner, 1999), conflict management (e.g., Montoya-Weiss, Massey

DOI: 10.4018/978-1-61520-979-8.ch006

& Song, 2001), leadership styles (e.g., James & Ward, 2001; Kayworth & Leidner, 2001/2002; Leonard, Brand, Edmondson, & Fenwick., 1998), and other internal team processes (Poole & Zhang, 2005). Less attention has been paid to how VTs function vis-à-vis external teams and individuals or considered how VTs sustain themselves in dynamic environments. The current study focuses on external aspects of virtual teaming by focusing on how VTs develop and sustain a sense of group identity and manage group boundaries when dealing with other groups and individuals in complex and dynamic environments.

Initially the focus of our research was neither on external linkages nor on group identity and boundaries, but on the role of communication in VT effectiveness. However, the importance of group identity and boundary management issues became apparent as we conducted four in-depth case studies of virtual teams in context. Our observations suggested that boundary maintenance and identity constitution were major challenges for all four teams, though for the most part the teams did not explicitly acknowledge them. Hence, we took advantage of an opportunity to add to the literature on external relations of VTs.

In this study, we define group identity as the reflexive understanding members have of the group as an entity (Giddens, 1984). In a group with a clear and well-defined identity, members perceive the group to be (a) a coherent entity with a clear boundary between itself and its environment and other small groups (b) with its own unique purpose, culture, and history. A coherent and positive group identity gives members a clear reference point that helps members understand the place of the group in the organization, gives them something to identify with, and encourages them to act as a collective whole.

Scholars such as Bormann (1980) have contributed greatly to our understanding of the role of culture in developing convergence around a common sense of values. However, we have much less understanding of group identity and boundary

processes and how they relate to culture, purpose, and history. This study specifically focuses how VTs constitute themselves as coherent entities. VTs can be seen as systems that are constantly skating the edge of existence in producing and reproducing an identity and boundary that lends them coherence.

In this study we focused on how VTs structured themselves as coherent entities and maintained their boundaries in interacting with internal and external members and with other groups. We identified several processes that contributed to the construction and maintenance of group identity and several more related to boundary management group boundaries. We conceptualized boundaries in terms of their clarity, distinctness, and permeability. *Clarity* is defined as the degree to which members perceive the group to have a clear demarcation from its environment and other groups. *Distinctness* is the degree to which boundaries are presented to outsiders as clear demarcations. Boundaries may be blurred by groups in order to signal to outside groups that they are part of the group or that the group is open to them. *Permeability* refers to the ease with which things outside the group—information, new members, material artifacts, ideas—can pass into the group. Clarity refers to how the members perceive the group themselves, while distinctness refers to how they present it to others outside the group (and thus indirectly, to themselves), and permeability is an objective property of the group that we as observers can assess.

THEORETICAL FRAMEWORKS

We employed the bona fide group perspective and structuration theory as guiding theoretical frameworks. These two theoretical perspectives complement each other well for the purpose of this study. Bona fide group theory provides a framework for understanding the challenges and problems that VTs faced in terms of maintaining identity and boundaries, while structuration theory addresses how the groups addressed these challenges through giving an account of how groups structure themselves.

The Bona Fide Group Perspective

In developing this perspective Stohl and Putnam(1994) critiqued the use of a container metaphor in small group studies and suggested that real groups have fluid and permeable boundaries, which are socially constructed in both internal and external interaction. The bona fide group perspective views groups as having two defining features, stable yet permeable boundaries and interdependence with their immediate contexts. Permeability of group boundaries occurs through several means, including "(a) multiple group memberships and conflicting role identities, (b) representative roles, (c) fluctuations in group membership, and (d) group identity formation" (Putnam & Stohl, 1996, p. 150). Specifically, the bona fide perspective recognizes that individual members may bring roles from other contexts, including other groups they belong to, into any specific group context. The perspective also indicates that when new members join a group, they bring in new information and perspectives, which in effect makes group boundaries permeable. Another defining feature of bona fide groups is interdependence with their immediate contexts, a reciprocal relationship between a given group and the environment it is embedded in (Stohl & Putnam, 1994). In other words, groups influence and are influenced by their surroundings, including the intergroup system, the social, historical, cultural, and economic contexts.

The bona fide group perspective has significant implications for VT studies, due to the increasing level of permeability and fluidity of group boundaries in the VT context. Virtual teams tend to be tightly coupled to their external environments (Bell & Kolzlowski, 2002) and frequently take the form of interorganizational collaborations (Fermandez,

2004; Majchrzak, Rice, Malhortra, King, & Ba, 2000). In addition, members of VTs tend to hold multiple memberships and their membership configurations shift frequently as the focus and needs of projects change.

As mentioned previously, existing studies of VTs have rarely addressed issues and challenges raised by the bona fide group perspective. Exceptions include Alexander, Peterson, and Hollingshead (2003), who studied online support groups and found that the existence of boundary spanners significantly impacted group processes. Through multiple memberships and providing referrals to other sources, the boundary spanners linked internal processes to the groups' external environment. In addition, through micro-analysis of transcribed notes taken from a videoconference meeting in a virtual group, Meier (2003) explored how a sense of "groupness" was achieved in communication practices.

Structuration Theory

Although the bona fide group perspective defines key problems groups in context face and the processes by which those problems are addressed, it does not provide much guidance as to how those processes operate, for example, how boundaries are maintained. Structuration theory, on the other hand, complements the bona fide group perspective and offers an account of how the processes defined in bona fide group theory are carried out by members. Structuration theory provides a way to understand how groups respond to identity and boundary problems they encounter. Through the process of technology structuring, bona fide virtual teams develop group-specific patterns of technology use as well as group norms in interaction, which help the members to manage the identity and boundary issues raised by the bona fide group perspective.

Structuration theory departs from Social Presence Theory (Short et al., 1976) and Media Richness Theory (Daft & Lengel, 1984) in its emphasis on the subjective features of technology and more importantly, its view of context as critical to technology appropriation. As Majchrzak et. al. (2000) suggested, a structurational approach to technology adoption stresses how technologies are "structured in their context of use," how users can "manipulate and reshape" those technologies for their own purposes, as well as the uses draw on rules and resources from "the particular social contexts within which they work (p. 570)." Adaptive Structuration Theory (AST), proposed by DeSanctis and Poole (1994), stresses the mutual influence between technology and social processes. The theory is concerned with the active role that users play in technology adaptation. As a result, patterns of technology use in context may vary and differ from how they are intended to be used, since users adapt systems to their particular work needs--they may choose to appropriate certain features while leaving others unrealized, or they may resist them and fail to use them at all (DeSanctis & Poole, 1994; Poole & DeSanctis, 1992).

A large body of research has explored various aspects of AST (DeSanctis, Poole, Zigurs, & Associates, 2008). Timmerman and Scott (2006), for instance, provided empirical support to AST in their empirical study of VTs in context through identifying structural and contextual features that were linked to variations in media use. In addition, Huysman et al. (2003) found the six virtual groups studied appropriated available technologies such as videoconferencing, email, and a group contribution tracking application in a variety of ways. For instance, although all groups relied mainly on videoconferencing and email for group interaction, the frequency and purposes of use varied from group to group. Videoconferencing, for example, was used for different purposes in each group, such as socialization, forcing action after email coordination, and task related communication. In addition, some groups engaged in task-related interactions mainly or exclusively,

others engaged in social interaction and developed group cohesiveness.

Structuration theory has implications for the current study, as structuring norms and patterns of technology use are an important way in which groups respond to the need to develop and maintain boundaries and a sense of identity. First, by defining how a member should think, feel, and behave in a given group context, group norms are inextricably linked to a group's identity. As Feldman (1984) claimed, "enforcing group norms gives group members a chance of expressing what their central values are, and to clarify what is distinctive about the group and central to its identity" (p. 48). Group norms are not only linked to group identity, they also set boundaries for groups. As Feldman argued, as group norms suggest the range of acceptable behaviors to a given group, they indicate the "boundaries" of a given group. Among the limited studies of norm development in VTs, Postmes et al. (2000), for instance, suggested that virtual groups tend to exhibit distinctive consistencies in media use and that observation of these consistencies allowed inference of group norms and identity. In addition, according to the authors, interaction norms set boundaries for virtual groups in that norms that structured behaviors inside a group did not apply to interactions outside it. As Frey (2003) concurred, group boundaries are constructed and reinforced through differentiating groups from other groups and recurring patterns of interaction that create and reinforce that differentiation.

To summarize, in light of the unique challenges that VTs face, our study intends to address boundary and identity issues posed by the bona fide group perspective. The purpose of the study is to explore boundary and identity processes in VTs. Specifically, we attempted to understand how members of VTs structured their group identities and managed group boundaries in their routine communication practices.

METHODOLOGY

Study Sites

We studied four virtual teams from three different organizations: the Global Research Team in a leading US Public Relations firm; the SWAT Team, a project team in a major financial group; and two committees from a major academic association, the Scholarship Committee, and the Pedagogy Committee.

Our first case study focused on the Global Research Team in Media One, a leading public relations firm in the US. The organization has a very collaborative and informal culture. Management encouraged the use of technology at work and introduced new technologies into the work process a few years before the study. The Global Research Team (GR Team) had fifteen members, with nine members collocated in organization's headquarters and six others working from remote offices in various domestic locations. The team had access to multiple media for team interaction, including phone, teleconference, electronic mail, instant messenger, and eConf groupware, which provided the team with a shared online folder for common documents, spreadsheets and other files the members wanted to make accessible to team. eConf also provided tools of computer ferencing.

e second case was the SWAT Team in a major financial services organization. he period of the study, KBC was going cultural shift in which it was changing ll, entrepreneurial organization which and had fairly open procedures to a lized, structured organization. The cultural shift on communication n-making became a more for- nd required solid justifications nentation. The SWAT Team, rged with designing a Data included over twenty core l functional departments

within the organization as well as representatives of four external vendors. The majority of the KBC members were located in two sites a hundred miles apart. The principal communication technologies used by the team were email, teleconferencing, and voicemail.

The third and fourth cases were project-oriented committees of a scholarly association, CRS. CRS is a nonprofit organization dedicated to promoting scholarship, education, and practice in a large scholarly discipline. The governing structure of CRS includes five major committees comprised of five to six members, each dedicated to managing one aspect of the organization, specifically publications, research, pedagogy, policy, and finance. Major executive decisions are made in a sixth committee, the Governing Committee, which is comprised of the past, present and future Presidents of CRS, the chairs of the five committees, and the Chief Administrative Officer. In addition, the chairs of the five committees also meet in a Coordinating Committee which manages projects that fall between the jurisdictions of the five committees. Members of the five committees are elected for 3-year terms. CRS' constitution specifies the purpose of each committee and the Governing Committee, but the committees themselves develop their own specific missions and projects. The two committees we chose to study are the Scholarship Committee, which had the general goal of promoting and facilitating research by the association and its members, and the Pedagogy Committee, whose mission was to promote education in the discipline. The Scholarship Committee had five members and the Pedagogy Committee had six members during the period of the study. The major communication technologies utilized in the two committees were email and teleconference.

The four cases differed along several dimensions that provided useful points of comparison and contrast. First the teams varied in terms of size, with the two Committees being relatively small, whereas the GR Team and the SWAT Team were emphasis on the subjective features of technology and more importantly, its view of context as critical to technology appropriation. As Majchrzak et. al. (2000) suggested, a structurational approach to technology adoption stresses how technologies are "structured in their context of use," how users can "manipulate and reshape" those technologies for their own purposes, as well as the uses draw on rules and resources from "the particular social contexts within which they work (p. 570)." Adaptive Structuration Theory (AST), proposed by DeSanctis and Poole (1994), stresses the mutual influence between technology and social processes. The theory is concerned with the active role that users play in technology adaptation. As a result, patterns of technology use in context may vary and differ from how they are intended to be used, since users adapt systems to their particular work needs--they may choose to appropriate certain features while leaving others unrealized, or they may resist them and fail to use them at all (DeSanctis & Poole, 1994; Poole & DeSanctis, 1992).

A large body of research has explored various aspects of AST (DeSanctis, Poole, Zigurs, & Associates, 2008). Timmerman and Scott (2006), for instance, provided empirical support to AST in their empirical study of VTs in context through identifying structural and contextual features that were linked to variations in media use. In addition, Huysman et al. (2003) found the six virtual groups studied appropriated available technologies such as videoconferencing, email, and a group contribution tracking application in a variety of ways. For instance, although all groups relied mainly on videoconferencing and email for group interaction, the frequency and purposes of use varied from group to group. Videoconferencing, for example, was used for different purposes in each group, such as socialization, forcing action after email coordination, and task related communication. In addition, some groups engaged in task-related interactions mainly or exclusively, others engaged in social interaction and developed group cohesiveness.

Structuration theory has implications for the current study, as structuring norms and patterns of technology use are an important way in which groups respond to the need to develop and maintain boundaries and a sense of identity. First, by defining how a member should think, feel, and behave in a given group context, group norms are inextricably linked to a group's identity. As Feldman (1984) claimed, "enforcing group norms gives group members a chance of expressing what their central values are, and to clarify what is distinctive about the group and central to its identity" (p. 48). Group norms are not only linked to group identity, they also set boundaries for groups. As Feldman argued, as group norms suggest the range of acceptable behaviors to a given group, they indicate the "boundaries" of a given group. Among the limited studies of norm development in VTs, Postmes et al. (2000), for instance, suggested that virtual groups tend to exhibit distinctive consistencies in media use and that observation of these consistencies allowed inference of group norms and identity. In addition, according to the authors, interaction norms set boundaries for virtual groups in that norms that structured behaviors inside a group did not apply to interactions outside it. As Frey (2003) concurred, group boundaries are constructed and reinforced through differentiating groups from other groups and recurring patterns of interaction that create and reinforce that differentiation.

To summarize, in light of the unique challenges that VTs face, our study intends to address boundary and identity issues posed by the bona fide group perspective. The purpose of the study is to explore boundary and identity processes in VTs. Specifically, we attempted to understand how members of VTs structured their group identities and managed group boundaries in their routine communication practices.

METHODOLOGY

Study Sites

We studied four virtual teams from three different organizations: the Global Research Team in a leading US Public Relations firm; the SWAT Team, a project team in a major financial group; and two committees from a major academic association, the Scholarship Committee, and the Pedagogy Committee.

Our first case study focused on the Global Research Team in Media One, a leading public relations firm in the US. The organization has a very collaborative and informal culture. Management encouraged the use of technology at work and introduced new technologies into the work process a few years before the study. The Global Research Team (GR Team) had fifteen members, with nine members collocated in organization's headquarters and six others working from remote offices in various domestic locations. The team had access to multiple media for team interaction, including phone, teleconference, electronic mail, instant messenger, and eConf groupware, which provided the team with a shared online folder for common documents, spreadsheets and other files the members wanted to make accessible to the team. eConf also provided tools of computer conferencing.

The second case was the SWAT Team in KBC, a major financial services organization. During the period of the study, KBC was going through a cultural shift in which it was changing from a small, entrepreneurial organization which valued risk and had fairly open procedures to a more standardized, structured organization. The impact of the cultural shift on communication was that decision-making became a more formalized process and required solid justifications and detailed documentation. The SWAT Team, an ad hoc team charged with designing a Data Capturing Campaign, included over twenty core members from several functional departments within the organization as well as representatives of four external vendors. The majority of the KBC members were located in two sites a hundred miles apart. The principal communication technologies used by the team were email, teleconferencing, and voicemail.

The third and fourth cases were project-oriented committees of a scholarly association, CRS. CRS is a nonprofit organization dedicated to promoting scholarship, education, and practice in a large scholarly discipline. The governing structure of CRS includes five major committees comprised of five to six members, each dedicated to managing one aspect of the organization, specifically publications, research, pedagogy, policy, and finance. Major executive decisions are made in a sixth committee, the Governing Committee, which is comprised of the past, present and future Presidents of CRS, the chairs of the five committees, and the Chief Administrative Officer. In addition, the chairs of the five committees also meet in a Coordinating Committee which manages projects that fall between the jurisdictions of the five committees. Members of the five committees are elected for 3-year terms. CRS' constitution specifies the purpose of each committee and the Governing Committee, but the committees themselves develop their own specific missions and projects. The two committees we chose to study are the Scholarship Committee, which had the general goal of promoting and facilitating research by the association and its members, and the Pedagogy Committee, whose mission was to promote education in the discipline. The Scholarship Committee had five members and the Pedagogy Committee had six members during the period of the study. The major communication technologies utilized in the two committees were email and teleconference.

The four cases differed along several dimensions that provided useful points of comparison and contrast. First the teams varied in terms of size, with the two Committees being relatively small, whereas the GR Team and the SWAT Team were

Table 1. Qualitative methods of data collection used in each case

	Interviews	**Field Observation**
Global Research Team	Face-to-face, phone or email interviews with 13 out of the 15 group members, each lasting about 45 minutes; One interview with the organization's eConf expert	On site visit, informal talks with some key members of the group, observation of group conference calls, group eConf use, organizational trainings mediated by WebEx, organization's intranet, access to group/organization's mass emails, collection of printed documents
SWAT Team	In-depth interviews with the core members of the group, with each one lasting from one hour to two and half hours; ongoing conversation with one key member of the group throughout the study period	N/A
The Scholarship Committee & the Pedagogy Committee	Face-to-face or phone interviews with all current members of the groups; periodic interviews with the group leaders; interviews with some previous leaders/members; interviews with two key members of the staff group in the organization	Longitudinal observation (about eight months) of email and conference call use within the two groups; observation of annual face-to-face meetings; access to all meeting agendas and minutes; access to various kinds of group documents such as project list, procedure manuals, etc.

much larger. Second the teams varied in degree of collocation. The GR Tteam and the SWAT Team had a number of people collocated at one site and other members dispersed over several other sites, while the members of the two Committees were dispersed so that there was only one person per site. Third, the teams varied in terms of their organizational contexts. The GR Team and SWAT Team operated in private sector organizations, while the Scholarship Committee and the Pedagogy Committee were part of a non-profit professional association. The GR and SWAT Teams had higher degrees of urgency than the Scholarship and Pedagogy Committees due to the emphasis of profit-making organizations on tangible results. The Global Research Team, the Scholarship Committee, and the Pedagogy Committee were long-term teams, while the SWAT Team was a short-term project team. Hence the teams could be contrasted in terms of task urgency, time perspective, and expectations for future interaction.

Data Collection

Multiple sources of qualitative data were gathered, including interview data, field notes, electronic data retrieved from online sources, and written documents. As a result of the negotiations we had with the participants in the study, however, the level of access we obtained in each case differed. Two of the four virtual teams gave us nearly full access to the process of team interaction for an extended period of time. With respect to the two other teams, we collected in-depth interview data from both teams and conducted limited, but very helpful non-participant observation in one of the two teams (see Table 1).

Data Analysis

In coding the qualitative data, we utilized the constant comparative method discussed by Lincoln and Guba (1985) and the techniques for developing grounded theory proposed by Strauss and Corbin (1990, 1998). In view of our adoption of the theoretical frameworks prior to data collection and analysis, our approach should be better viewed as a modified grounded theory approach. The bona fide group and structurational frameworks offer general conceptual schemes, which must be specified by the researcher for each particular type of group and context. Hence, an open, grounded approach was applied to determine which aspects of bona fide groups were in play in the teams studied and the structuring processes employed to address them.

We developed an initial conceptual understanding of the interview data and field notes through line-by-line reading. Subsequently, we started to relate "categories to subcategories along the lines of their properties and dimensions" (Strauss & Corbin, 1990, 124). The next stage consisted of thematic analysis (Harry, Sturges, and Klingner, 2005). Understanding of the general patterns as well as identification of connections between and among the themes started during open coding and expanded during axial and selective coding, and continued through the writing process.

Although we have described the coding process as if each step occurred in a linear fashion, the actual coding process was more complex. In coding the data, we constantly found ourselves going back and forth between open coding and axial coding. In other words, any significant idea about patterns or connections necessitated another reading of relevant interview data and field notes. In addition, the initial coding also informed the later interviews and redirected our research questions. As the inductive analysis of the data progressed, we collected more data to confirm the significance of existing categories/themes or to revise already-developed categories. In addition, following the constant comparative method, we continually compared certain parts/types of the data with other parts/types and with the literature to achieve triangulation. For example, in one of the case studies, we learned that email interaction within that team tended to happen among subcommittees. Going back to the archive of the email messages exchanged among the members of that team helped us to verify that pattern. In addition, as categories, themes, and linkages were identified, we constantly compared them to the interview and the observation data to ensure the coding process was grounded in the data.

We attempted to increase the validity of the study not only through data triangulation discussed above, but also through "member checks" (Lincoln & Guba, 1985). During all four case studies, we maintained ongoing conversations with our contact for a team and talked to the key members periodically. We discussed the emerging ideas and themes with those contacts or key informants to test our interpretations against the participants' perspectives. Subsequently, this testing either gave us more confidence in our interpretations, or, in some cases, led us to revise or reject initial findings. In addition, interpretive adequacy (Lincoln and Guba, 1985) was further guaranteed through sharing the results (which is always an ongoing process) with some of the members.

FINDINGS

In synthesizing findings from all four case studies, we identified several common factors that fostered a sense of identity within the VTs. In addition, we analyzed the boundary processes within those teams in terms of clarity, distinctness, and permeability. In the following section, we discuss identity and boundary processes respectively. Throughout our discussions, we suggest how the communication practices in managing both boundary and identity issues helped the teams to deal with challenges specific to VTs.

Managing Group Identity

In view of the challenges that are specific to virtual teaming, the VTs in this study made extra efforts to develop a sense of identity, as reflected in the following processes: developing common goals and mission, interdependence, regularized interactions, group norms, and a self perception through the perceptions of other interlocking groups. We report each of those processes leading to the development of a collective identity in this section.

Developing and Reinforcing Common Goals

Common goals are an important constituent of group identity. Larson and LaFasto (1989), for example, found that effective teams had clear, inspirational goals. Given their geographic dispersion, VTs face daunting challenges in developing and maintaining clear goals and a sense of mission. Members of VTs are constantly exposed to other contexts which suggest goals different from that of the VT. For instance, Fernandez (2004) found that the diverse and sometimes conflicting goals of the organizations that were represented in a large VT made planning and control of the project difficult. Dispersed as they are, members of VTs may feel more involved with others they can directly interact with in their immediate contexts and the goals connected to these other immediate situations are likely to seem more salient and real to them than the goals of the VT.

In this study, we found that the VTs developed team-specific communication practices to deal with challenges associated with maintaining clear goals and a sense of mission in the virtual context. Our data suggested that sensemaking regarding group goals was important to the structuring of group identity.

In the case of the GR Team, for example, the team leader explicitly discussed how he purposefully stressed the importance of repetitively communicating a common goal to team members. He explained:

I try to make sure that everybody has a good sense of our goal and has a good sense of the progress against those goals. And we talk about that and you see that all the time and you realize you're a part of the team, because you know what the goals of the teams are. Even though we're not sitting together, we are part of the team.

In practice, the team leader used multiple channels repetitively to communicate team goals to his members, including annual face-to-face meetings, periodic group meetings via conference calls, and bi-weekly newsletters sent to all members on the team. For instance, the group started their 2002 offsite meeting (i.e., their annual face-to-face meeting) with discussions of what the group had accomplished in the past year and what their goals were for the upcoming year. The members considered those discussions as being instrumental for the development of a consensual view of the team's collective goal.

A clear set of common goals and mission also unified the members of the Scholarship Committee. The organization that the two scholarly committees were embedded in had very vague and inclusive goal definitions for each of the committees. Thus, each committee was left with the task of specifying its own goals and thus, differentiating itself from other interrelated committees in the same organization. Additionally, as full time university professors, the members evidently had multiple roles and hence, competing goals in their immediate context. Nevertheless, the Scholarship Committee developed a very clear sense of its mission. In particular, the committee stressed its role in publicizing the organization and in serving as a liaison to external funding agencies. The members of the committee felt strong commitment to their goals. In effect, as a result of its task effectiveness, the committee was perceived to be the "strongest committee" in the organization, which evidently strengthened the members' sense of groupness and became part of their group identity.

In contrast, in the case of the Pedagogy Committee, the team experienced some confusion and ambiguity with regard to its mission. Given the long-term nature of their projects and the periodic rotation of its membership, the members of the committee felt ambiguity and a lack of consistency with regard to their goals and mission. They were unsure what the committee had accomplished in the past or where it fit in the organization. Members managed this goal ambiguity in the virtual context through technological tools, inventing a fairly complex numbering system to notate their projects and keeping a project portfolio online that listed all past, ongoing, and pipeline projects as well as their status. This online portfolio made it clear what the group had accomplished in the past and enabled members to begin to discern consistent patterns among its project. The effort devoted to recording the group's history in the portfolio helped members to make sense of their goals and mission. This contributed to their sense of the group's identity and how it could be differentiated from other committees in CRS.

The SWAT Team experienced goal ambiguity due to the many contextual factors that worked against the team and made its task extremely challenging, including the need to complete the project rapidly, a constantly changing legal environment, and the necessity of dealing with new domestic and international vendors. The project was ill-defined, as the team was expected to reach as far and wide as possible, to collaborate with as many vendors as they could find, and to collect as much information as possible from the customer database. As a result, one member described how the "playing field" changed constantly:

I think one of the reasons that this project was unique was that the goals were changing quickly. You would get more information, which, as a result, would change the direction you wanted to go. All of a sudden, a legal expert might say, "You can't do this," and as a result of knowing that, we would change the direction we were going. We had many quick shifts. We might find out some IT system wasn't available and we counted on the IT system being available. So as a result of knowing it wasn't available, we had to come up with a different solution.

Given the fast pace of the project and its goal ambiguity, the key members of the team met at 10:00 AM everyday during the project period via teleconferencing, with the collocated members sitting in a conference room and dispersed members dialing in from various domestic and international locations. Among other functions that those daily meetings served, they allowed the team opportunities to make sense of the changing scope of the project on a daily basis and to figure out—for the time being—what the current goals for the group would be. While the overall goal of the team was fairly stable, the intermediate goals through which they would attain the main goal were constantly shifting.

To summarize, in face of the challenges in maintaining common goals and mission in the virtual context, the VTs made purposeful efforts to develop and communicate a clear set of goals to their members. In cases when goals were ambiguous, the VTs either engaged in ongoing sensemaking activities or developed creative ways of interpreting group history that made their goals and mission clear and consistent. This "goal-making" activity produced a situated and temporary certainty for several of the VTs, as changing circumstances required them to rework and redefine their goals over time. These efforts helped to maintain a sense of group identity among the members of the VTs.

Creating and Maintaining Interdependency

Past research shows that an important source of group identity is interdependence among the team members (Gluesing et al., 2003; Henry, Arrow, & Carini, 1999). When working at distance, members of VTs tend to develop a habit of working in solo and become less aware of other members' activities. For this reason, some researchers advocate selecting independent and self-steering individuals as members to enhance the effectiveness of VTs (Kirkman, Rosen, Gibson, Tesluk and McPherson, 2002; McDonald, 1999; Murphy, 2004). However, it may be more difficult for independent-minded members to develop a collaborative climate and interdependence. Our case studies suggested that certain procedural structures could be used to purposefully foster a sense of interdependence in the VTs, which subsequently contributed to the members' sense of group identity.

In the case of the GR Team structural procedures facilitating knowledge sharing and task collaboration strengthened the members' sense of interdependence and groupness. For example, normative practices during conference calls included having each member give project updates and having everyone indicate his/her availability to help or alternatively to request help from other members. Interdependence was also reinforced through a shared space online in the team eConf. This served, first, as a knowledge depository. Information such as completed projects, focus group study results, useful links, etc. were shared in the eConf. The eConf thus provided a common space to bridge team members. Second, the members kept a shared group schedule online in the eConf so that everyone's schedule and vacation times were shared. These procedural structures clearly helped the members of the GR Team to be more connected with one another, increasing interdependence. This yielded dividends in terms of team effectiveness. An external vendor described the GR Team:

First of all, everyone is sharp, in terms of intelligence. The know how to use a vendor. They are very passionate about their jobs because they do it so effectively and correctly. Yes, this is this person's job and that's that person's job. Yet they are so helpful to each other. I see XXX going into XXX's office and ask for help. They do the best they can, yet they don't compete. They act as a genuine team with one goal.

We observed a similar connection between interdependence and a sense of groupness within the SWAT Team. At the outset, the team's project was collaborative in nature. As the project leader put it, "We have this goal, but none of us could achieve the goal working in solo." Additionally,

the project manager elaborated the multiple facets of the project in great detail,

…but the way that KBC is structured, myself, as the Project Manager, I don't have all the knowledge to go out and communicate with the vendors. Or I don't have the ability to know how to set up the contract…you got other groups who are experts in the way of passing data back and forth. So I don't know anything about the portfolio on our platform, segmenting and having the right information sent in a table format, passing that off through a file transfer process, making sure that it was secure… So we've got another group that was responsible for drafting the script…It has a legal piece of pie in the project. There was sensitive information that we were collecting. So we had legal guidelines to work through…So they [the legal experts] had to be part of the project team as well.

Consequently, the team developed procedural structures to ensure that information was equally distributed among all team members. The team shared information via multiple channels, including daily conference calls, mass emails sent to all members, and an online project folder that stored all important project information. Information sharing was deemed so important within the team that the members developed the habit of "replying all" in emailing (which caused information overload). Nevertheless, the use of these structures allowed the team to evolve a sense of interdependence reflected in both task division and information sharing.

VTs can benefit in terms of group building when procedural structures are in place to facilitate interdependence and collaboration. In our cases, the effective use of simple and advanced communication technology such as eConf and online project folder facilitated information and knowledge sharing. In addition, regular conference meetings with highly collaborative climates provided another occasion for sharing and collaboration. When members of VTs are more aware of geographically dispersed members' activities and count on each other to get work done, their sense of the group evolves naturally.

Regularized Interactions

Collaborative interaction is an important element in VT maintenance in general and in the development of group identity specifically. With members working at a distance, communication can be a daunting challenge for VTs. As research (Cramton 2001; Jarvenpaa, Knoll, & Leidner, 1998) indicates, when not properly structured, communication within VTs tends to break down and member uncertainty increases. When this happens, it may break down trust and weaken group cohesiveness. In contrast, as illustrated by our case studies, regularized interactions glued members of the VTs together, a finding consistent with the findings of Connaughton and Daly (2004), Kayworth and Leidner (2001-2002), Knoll and Jarvenpaa (1998) and Yoo and Alavi (2004).

Regularized interaction via multiple media bound the members of the GR Team together. At the outset, the team held periodic FtF meetings of the entire team,. Dispersed members particularly valued these and reported that they felt "energized" after each FtF meeting. Periodic conference calls also helped to keep dispersed members in the communication loop. As it is easier for the collocated members to know what was going on within the team, the members in satellite offices counted on those meetings to get an update on project status, personnel changes, new policies, etc. When these meetings were cancelled, the members in remote locations felt lost or disconnected with the rest of the team. Another effective way the GR Team used to keep lines of communication open, particularly to the geographically dispersed members, was to hold weekly phone meetings between the team leader and individual members in satellite offices. Because these meetings were private and individual, they enabled members in remote locations to voice their concerns or problems.

In the case of the SWAT Team, all members stressed the importance of their daily conference call meetings. For instance, a project manager who planned and facilitated the daily meeting explained the positive feedback he got from the members of the team as follows,

...I had a lessons learned session way after we did all the work. And all the groups that were part of the daily meeting came ...so that was the first time that someone got to meet face-to-face. Every group member that was there said that the one thing held the project together was having the teleconference.

The team members relied on their daily meetings to serve a number of purposes, including information sharing, brainstorming, sense-making and goal redefinition, problem solving, etc. The team would not have become a team without its daily meetings.

Similarly, in the case of the Scholarship Committee, as both the leader and members indicated, the monthly conference calls really "got the committee together." The team used these regular conference calls for discussion of strategically important group issues, such as group goals, internal and external interaction processes, budget concerns, selection of future members, etc. The team managed multiple projects which were carried out by subgroups that often included additional members from outside the Scholarship Committee. The work of subgroups tended to occur primarily through email exchanges, and the intensity of project work had the potential to undermine group identity through encouraging members to identify more with their subcommittees than with the Scholarship Committee as a whole. The groupwide conference calls, however, mitigated this problem. Members agreed that the monthly conference calls were their most significant channel of communication. Regular discussions of topics of general concern to all members helped them to enhance their sense of group identity.

The members of the Pedagogy Committee relied on periodic email exchanges as well as sporadic conference calls to stay connected with each other. Email exchanges were used primarily for task purposes, while the sporadic conference calls were reserved for boosting team morale and developing team identity. As one member indicated, it simply felt "too long not to talk to each other and hear [other members'] voices" between their two annual face-to-face meetings.

In general, the members described the crucial role that regularized conference calls played in bringing their teams together. In addition, each team evolved unique patterns of regular interaction so that the members could stay in touch with each other. When patterns of interaction became routinized and predictable, uncertainly embedded in mediated interaction was reduced and as a result, trust and team cohesiveness came more easily, resulting in increased sense of group identity.

Developing Common Norms

We suggested earlier that structuring norms are important to group maintenance, as these norms indicate the central values and provide a unification point for a group. Previous research (Lea & Spears, 1991; Leonard, et al, 1998; Zigurs, 2003) indicated that VTs often lack norms and protocols for electronically-mediated team interaction. As Zigurs put it, traditional teams typically operate within a shared culture that includes deeply-buried assumptions about basic communication practices. Virtual teams, however, have to take explicit steps, during the early stage of team formation in order to surface those assumptions (Zigurs, 2003, p.341). Hence, we focus in this section on discussing how the emergence of unique structuring norms within each VT helped the members to evolve a sense of their group.

Common norms that indicated the "personality" of the GR Team included being responsive in interaction and relational communication. For instance, several members mentioned "getting back to people quickly" as a norm of the PR industry. Another norm expressed the value of relational communication. For instance, while the study was being conducted, a new member joined the group. The team leader formally introduced her to the entire team via email and his half of his message described her hobbies. A member of the GR Team located in one of the remote offices explained why socializing was important:

I also call people, just say "hi" and ask what was going on, how was their weekend, their dog, etc. It helps me to keep perspective and helps with work--you want to know their other responsibilities outside their work.

Unlike the GR Team, given its tight deadline, the SWAT Team had little time for social interaction. Nevertheless, the members evolved a sense of the group through common values such as task focus and effectiveness. For example, one members explained norms for their conference calls as follows:

I'm not saying people were mean. People got focused. It wasn't about personality. It wasn't about your way versus my way. It's about finding the best way to accomplish the task. One key factor contributing to the success of the project was that people really focused on the task and ego was left at the door. It's just a proposal and if it can be made better, let's make it better. I would say, that was the attribute of about just everyone on the team.

Another member commented on the group norm of "being effective" in handling conference calls as follows,

...Our conference calls were very effective, I thought. Anybody could sit in, including senior managers, our conference calls and after an hour, know exactly where our project was at any point of time.

While the VTs in the private sector organizations often drew their norms from those typical for industrial and organizational contexts, we found the two committees in the nonprofit organization negotiated and evolved unique norms. For instance, when faced with information overload due to an overwhelming amount of email messages, members of the Scholarship committee negotiated group norms to regulate email use, including "cutting back" on acknowledgement notes and changing the "subject line" as topics shifted. In the case of the Pedagogy Committee, members differentiated this group from other committees in the organization through their valuation of a "high level of group maintenance." For instance, the Chair explicitly commented, "you can't be on the committee unless you are a fun person." Additionally, one member described socializing as an important group norm:

Just the friendliness. We enjoy one another's company. We enjoy laughing and relaxing with one another. And I think that facilitated the work that we did in the committee. I think that's important norm, we enjoyed fun, relaxing time together in addition to our working time together.

In summary, unique norms emerged in each of the VTs. These norms expressed the shared values of the members and therefore solidified group identity through expressing the common and unique features of membership in the group. Their sense that they had developed unique norms (even if they were not unique in actuality) helped members feel that their group was differentiated from other groups.

Relationships with Other Groups

As discussed previously, one formidable challenge that VTs face is their exposure to other groups, including multiple interlocking groups (Fernandez 2004; Krikorian and Kiyomiya, 2003; Peterson, and Hollingshead, 2003). The permeability of the group's boundary can either threaten the existence of a group or, when managed effectively, enhance the sense of the group as an entity. For instance, Krikorian and Kiyomiya (2003) examined newsgroups as bona fide groups and concluded that a newsgroup's ability to respond to external forces that threaten group stability was critical for its survival. In the same vein, we found that how the VTs managed their relationships with the interlocking groups affected their efforts to maintain a sense of identity.

At the outset, the case of the GR Team provided an excellent example of maintaining a sense of groupness while engaging in interaction with parties external to the group. In its close collaboration with account groups in the organization, members managed to preserve the group boundary through stressing the distinction between in-group versus out-group interactions. Members of GR Team reported that they employed "richer media," such as face-to-face meetings, in interacting with members of the account groups than when they interacted with one another. In addition, group boundaries were also reinforced through showing different levels of trust to in-group versus out-group members. The following comment illustrates how the members differentiated in-group members from out-group members.

I think we [the members of the research team] are very honest with each other. We can call and say, "Look, I'm really in a crunch, and I really need help with this." We don't take advantage of each other, and we only do what is necessary. So there is the level of trust there. With other people in the organization, we fear they're going to do something [that requires us] to make their life easier. But there is no such fear within our group.

In addition, as suggested by the concept of the "looking glass self" (Cooley, 1902), the GR Team also made sense of its collective identity through reading others' perceptions of the team. For example, with regard to its strategic significance, the leader indicated that the group perceived itself to be strategically important because the organization's clients ranked research as the second or third most important factor in differentiating PR firms. Similarly, the Scholarship Committee reinforced its collective identity through others' perceptions of the group. The previous Chair of the committee recalled that when others commented that the group was very effective and coupled that comment with the committee's outreach and promotion mission, it solidified his sense of the group. These two cases suggest that if others' perceptions and reactions seemed to be fairly consistent and made sense to the members of the group in light of their self conception, they reinforced it in a continuing cycle of structuration of the group's identity.

Interestingly, in the case of the Pedagogy Committee, the identity prescribed by others, that it was "the weakest committee," and a "dumping ground" for odd issues, did not fit with the group's self conception. This led to a struggle on the part of the Pedagogy Committee to reclaim a preferred group identity and redefine group boundaries. The committee rejected its ascribed identity through turning down projects that did not fit its mission and announcing its avowed identity (Martin & Nakayama, 2006). Field observation of the organization's annual retreat indicated that the Pedagogy Committee announced its unique identity to others by being the only group that laughed raucously and put posters in the hallway claiming to be the best group. Specifically, through joking around with the Scholarship Committee with regard to which group was the best in CRS, the Pedagogy Committee strengthened its members' sense of identity. The chair indicated that there was also a serious layer in those jokes. The Chair's plan to shift the committee from being reactive to proactive, combined with the addition of three active new members, led to a new identity for the committee as more influential in the organization. This change in identity was expressed through the joking claim that "we're the best group." Thus,

external interactions provided the group with an opportunity to reject the identity ascribed by others and reclaim a sense of itself as a proactive entity.

Summary

For the convenience, we discussed each identity process as if they exist in isolation. However, it is clear that these processes interact, that they reinforce each other or exist in tension. In terms of reinforcement, a clear sense of common goals and mission clearly strengthened members' sense of interdependence. In addition, a sense of interdependence can also be enhanced through regularized patterns of interaction through certain procedural structures, such as "replying all" in email, and normative practices related to information sharing during conference calls.

On the other hand, these processes could contradict each other, creating tensions that the groups had to respond to. For example, the Pedagogy Committee made tremendous efforts to make sense of its goals and mission so that members could differentiate the groups from other interlocking committees. Nevertheless, the members of the committee constantly felt that others considered them as a "dumping ground." Although the Chair and members shared the structuring norm of being proactive in interaction, the committee was viewed by members of other groups as a relatively weak committee. The members of the Pedagogy Committee resisted this external definition through managing this tension. Members developed a unique system of prioritizing each possible project against their stated mission and goals and rejected assigned projects that they considered to be inconsistent with their sense of their primary mission. In addition, members consciously excluded one external member from participating in their conference calls, as he tended to suggest inconsistent ideas and divert the group from focusing on its mission. Moreover, as our previous discussion indicated, when there was a disagreement between members of the group and those external to the group on group identity, the team managed its communication practices to project a desired image.

Boundary Processes

We now turn to a consideration of boundary processes in terms of three properties of boundaries that were defined in the introduction: their clarity, distinctness, and permeability.

The bona fide group perspective implies that group boundaries present a dilemma for groups. On the one hand, groups must allow ideas, resources, and people from outside the group across their boundaries in order to remain viable and get their work done. There are a number of benefits associated with being open to external influences for the VTs in this study, including fast and convenient acquisition of relevant knowledge, the creation of opportunities for business and service, and improvement in group processes through introduction of new procedures or norms. On the other hand, opening the group to the outside runs the danger of eroding group boundaries to an extent that group identity began to break down. In the following we discuss how the groups managed these tensions.

Clarity

We defined clarity as the degree to which members perceive the group to have a clear demarcation from its environment and from other groups. The bona fide group perspective stresses that all group boundaries as potentially blurry and permeable. To maintain a clear identity groups must construct and maintain a sense of clarity regarding boundaries in the face of events and issues that erode boundaries. VTs are particularly subject to challenges in terms of defining group boundaries clearly, because their members are constantly exposed to other groups and members in their local contexts. As we noted in the previous section, members of

all four teams related constantly to other groups and individuals in their immediate context and virtually. These interactions had the potential to

For both the GR Team and the Scholarship Committee, group boundaries were clearly delineated, and this could be traced largely to the clarity of their missions and goals. Although the turnover rate within the GR Team was high and there were yearly rotations of members into and out of the Scholarship Committee, their distinct and consistent missions and goals enabled the members of both teams to discern a clear demarcation between the teams and their surrounding environment. Unique mission and goals enabled both teams to differentiate themselves from other groups they interacted with. In addition, in the case of the GR Team, the members reinforced the clarity of group boundaries through internal and external interactions, as they developed a very collaborative climate within the group and evolved distinct patterns of interaction with out-group members.

Because their boundaries were clear, the GR Team and the Scholarship Committee admitting inputs from outside the group had little effect on group identity. Both groups interacted easily with other groups and with individuals external to the group.

In contrast, both the SWAT Team and the Pedagogy Committee struggled with clarity of their boundaries. In the case of the SWAT Team, goal ambiguity and shifting membership negatively affected members' clarity on boundaries. The SWAT Team was interlocked with other groups and individuals, including the customer service team, the escalation team, the public relations team, and senior management. The participants in SWAT Team activities and team goals shifted depending on which other groups they interacted with, and since the others involved shifted throughout the project, it was difficult to stabilize clear boundaries. Members of the SWAT Team delineated core members through observing interaction patterns within the team, including those included on the team's internal email list and those who attended the team's daily conference calls. Initially, lack of consistent goals and mission also prevented the members of the Pedagogy Committee from achieving clarity on group boundaries. Over time, through persistent sense making, the group evolved a clearer sense of mission. The members of the Pedagogy Committee further reinforced the clarity of its boundary by rejecting projects that were deemed inconsistent with its mission, hence reinforcing the clarity of the group's mission.

Distinctness

Distinctness refers to the degree to which boundaries are presented to outsiders as clear demarcations. Our cases suggested that the VTs often purposefully blurred their boundaries to signal others that they are open to external influence, while in other cases they made them more distinct to underscore group identity. Our case studies suggested several ways in which the VTs managed distinctness.

The GR Team recognized the importance of their linkage to their internal clients, the account teams, and intentionally blurred their group boundaries through frequently putting themselves "in front of their faces." The members of the GR Team made themselves open to the account teams through using "richer" media in interacting with them so that ties between groups were strengthened and boundaries between them blurred. The team also blurred its boundary through promoting seamless collaboration with its external clients utilizing advanced information and communication technology, as indicated by the following statement:

People upload drafts and final versions of documents. We used the eConf to house information, save drafts and clips, and post brochures in PDF format. We even used the voting tool when we do creative things. For example, when we design graphics for our campaign, our client can click

the button and vote among, for instance, nine graphics and we will discuss the ones they like.

This openness enabled the GR Team to explore new business opportunities and to better serve the needs of their clients.

In SWAT Team, members indicated their openness to interrelated groups and individuals through including them "in the loop." Specifically, the SWAT Team copied the minutes of their daily meetings to some members of senior management and provided daily voicemail updates to the management of related groups who were affected by their data collection activities. Leaving voicemails to the members of interrelated groups allowed the team to maintain its boundaries while remaining open to external parties, as those voicemails provided them with basic information about the group's activities so that they would not feel the need to intervene (and thus become an active part of the group).

The members of the Scholarship Committee both reinforced and blurred their group boundaries in interacting with other members and groups. For instance, although the organization created group email lists for each of the five committees, the previous Chair indicated that he kept two separate email lists, one with the staff members on it which was used for open discussions, and the other with only the committee members which was used for private discussions. The private email list was especially used when the committee was trying to figure out how to frame things so the staff would understand and/or support them. In addition, members agreed to have their chair filter messages from external parties. The Scholarship Committee maintained linkages to external groups and members by maintaining an email list with external members and by allowing external members to send emails to the group. At the same time, members filtered messages and kept another email list for private discussions, which helped the group maintain its distinctness.

Permeability

When VTs open themselves to external influences, a natural consequence is that things outside the group, such as information, new members, material artifacts, and ideas, are likely to be passed into the group. The ease with occurs is permeability. Findings from our case studies indicated that permeability of group boundaries allowed VTs to borrow norms, glean knowledge, and introduce new members and practices into internal processes.

Earlier we noted that its relationship with external groups and members reinforced the GR Team's identity. This suggests that permeability of group boundaries can be functional. In addition, the GR Team also connected to external groups through its members' multiple group memberships, information sharing with other member of the organization, and through importing group norms from the organization and other groups. For example, one member who was welcomed into the group was from an outside vendor's group. Through providing onsite services to the team, she became an integral part of the team while maintaining her affiliation with the vendor's group. As a boundary spanner, she was a member of both organizations, and her presence rendered the group's boundary permeable. In addition, permeability was also reflected in how its members imported industrial as well as organizational values and norms into the process of team interaction. When discussing the norm of "being responsive" and "getting back to people quickly," for instance, members frequently referred to the ethics of the public relations industry. One member of GR Team compared Media One with another PR firm she had worked with, commenting, "There are a lot of similarities. Working in the PR industry, people share work ethics, such as getting back to people quickly."

Similarly, the SWAT Team imported norms from its organizational context, which affected the patterns of email interaction within the team. SWAT Team members were facing an organiza-tion in flux, as KBC was changing its organizational culture to move from a small, risk- taking enterprise to one that placed more emphasis on standardization and formalization. To enact this change at the team level, members of the SWAT Team utilized electronic mail as one of their primary communication tools, since it allowed them to document in great detail the process of team interaction as well as the results. One project manager explained how email was used within the SWAT Team as follows:

Any issues that came up, any progress that came up. So it was technical information that needed to be documented. So issues that everyone needed to have a record of, it went by email. Any results that came out went by email. So people can be kept up with results. Any deliverables. So anything that needed to be documented, for whatever reason, was put into email.

In order to collect customer information, the team used external vendors to make phone calls to its customers. The team gave vendors scripts for their calls and adjusted the scripts constantly according to feedback they received from ven-dors. These calls sometimes triggered customer responses and complaints. As a result, other groups in the organization, such as the escalation team and the public relations team, were involved in the process and their feedback reached the SWAT Team, whose internal activities were thus altered and constrained.

The Scholarly Committee enacted permeability of boundaries in several ways. First, in view of the fact that all members of the Scholarship Committee had full-time university positions, permeability occurred within this team as the members of the team imported norms and transferred roles and identities from their work contexts into the team,. For example, in terms of transference of roles, members indicated how the existence of differ-ences in rank, relative influence in the field, and previous experience with certain issues influenced and shaped the interaction patterns and decision-making within the committee. Interviews with the Chair of the committee suggested that she believed that norms of the committee's monthly business meetings via conference call were similar to the norms of departmental meetings in university settings. Moreover, holding multiple memberships in more than one committee within the organization also allowed the chairs of the committee to import procedures from other committees into the team. The previous chair of the committee indicated that he initiated the process of drafting a Procedures Manual for the committee as a result of conversing with the chair of another committee that had developed such a manual. Finally, project subgroups, which often included external members, offered a way to bring new ideas and thinking into the group.

The group boundary of the Pedagogy Committee was permeable due to new members rotating in while old members rotated out each year. These new members brought with them new group norms and redefined the group's patterns of interaction. With two members leaving and three new members joining the group in 2004, the committee experienced a significant membership change in the middle of the study. Interaction among members increased and interaction patterns of the group changed dramatically. Previously, the group used email primarily for task purposes and conference calls were used sparsely and mainly for group maintenance purposes. After the membership change, however, different patterns of combining the two media emerged. One member explained the change: "The emails are preparation-focused and the calls are action-focused." In addition, new norms emerged such that members expected each other to take initiative in interaction. One new member discussed this norm:

The Pedagogy Committee members want you to be responsible for your actions. Be assertive. If you have things to say, say them. Participate on your own initiative. Don't wait for others to respond.

Be self-motivated. The group does not tolerate a passive member.

These emergent interaction patterns and norms seemed to be quite consistent with the Chair's vision to change the committee from being reactive to being more proactive. Thus, the permeability of the group boundary became salient when the newly joined members brought into the group new practices and norms, through which the committee redefined its boundary and voiced its changing identity.

Summary

Like identity processes, boundary processes also interact with each other in terms of being either complementary or in tension. At the beginning of this section we noted that processes generating clarity, distinctness, and permeability were potentially in tension with each other. This is most likely to occur if one of three processes is over-emphasized. However, if properly balanced, these processes complement each other. For instance, the boundaries of the group might be quite clear to members, and this gives them a sense of identity that in turn makes them confident enough to make their boundaries less distinct to those outside the group in order to foster external linkages. If boundaries become too indistinct, then members may come to thinkers think differently about the group, and this may have repercussions for clarity. We observed this balancing act in the Scholarship Committee, when the members perceived clarity of the group boundary and this enabled them to open up outside members. The group managed this through keeping two separate email lists and thus, maintained its boundary in the eyes of members, while simultaneously opening itself to other members and groups. Similarly, through leaving voicemails for management, the SWAT Team indicated its openness to external feedback but at the same time, preserved its boundaries by lowering the probability that managers would intervene. In the end all four teams in the study were able to manage boundaries in ways that contributed to their identities.

Relationships between Identity Construction and Boundary Management Processes

There were also tensions in the relationship between identity and boundary processes. On the one hand, the VTs employed a variety of communicative practices in routine interaction to maintain a sense of their group. This allowed the teams to constitute themselves as coherent entities, to differentiate themselves from outsiders, and to evolve a sense of group identity. At the same time, the VTs were embedded in an intergroup system which introduced ambiguities. These ambiguities emerged particularly when the groups were concerned with being open and permeable. These boundary ambiguities were handled through communication practices such as keeping separate email lists, leaving daily voicemails to the interlocking groups, and filtering messages from outside groups and members.

We also found that identity and boundary processes could reinforce each other. Communicative practices developed in boundary management preserved and reinforced group identity. For instance, members of the GR Team developed a cohesive and collaborative culture internally which reinforced their sense group identity when they worked with the account teams. Specifically, they stressed distinctive patterns of technology use and exhibited greater trust in core members than in external groups and members. In external interaction, the Scholarship Committee filtered messages from external groups and individuals, which not only preserved the group boundary, but also reinforced members' sense of the group. In turn, factors that fostered group identity also helped members to manage boundary issues. For example, common goals and mission facilitated the delineation of group boundaries. Regularized

patterns of interaction as well as structuring norms developed in each team also helped to define group boundary.

In short, although identity and boundary processes were discussed separately, these two aspects of virtual teaming are not independent processes. Instead, they often reinforce each other and, at times, they are in tension. When tensions emerged members developed creative communicative practices to manage both simultaneously.

CONCLUSION

Gluesing et al. (2003) defined a mature VT as one that has "a common task that team members believe in and are committed to, collaborative interactions with one another and with important groups outside the team, and the ability to sustain a common task focus and collaboration across multiple contexts" (p. 357). We might add to this definition that a mature VT will have a well-defined and robust group identity and effective boundary management processes.

VTs face formidable challenges in developing group identity and in boundary management, for several reasons. First, the goals of VTs must compete against other goals salient to their members in their immediate contexts. Second, interdependence in VT may be difficult to develop due to the fact that members selected for these teams may be independent individuals who have a preference for working solo. In addition, geographical dispersion is likely to make the members unaware of one anothers' activities, rendering coordination more difficult. Third, problems may emerge within VTs when the interaction processes were not well planned or regularized, which negatively affect task effectiveness, trust building, and team cohesiveness. Fourth, structuring norms that may naturally emerge in traditional FtF teams need to be consciously negotiated among VT members. Finally, though discussed only in passing in previous research, when VTs are often part of a set of interlocking groups (presumably more so than traditional FtF teams). Because of this boundary management becomes an important process in virtual teaming, as external interactions may either reinforce or threaten the existence of a given group.

Our qualitative studies of four virtual teams in context suggested that consciously dealing with these challenges is critical to developing group identity. Specifically, processes that emphasize and reinforce a common sense of mission and goals, regularized interactions, interdependence among team members, the emergence of structuring norms, and clearly defined relationships to other groups enabled the VTs to foster group identity.

According to the bona fide group perspective, there is often a tension between tendencies toward stability and the permeability/fluidity of group boundaries. Putnam and Stohl (1996) suggested the tension between stability and permeability in their following discussions.

If boundaries are too volatile and indistinct, the group risks being overwhelmed and losing its identity; if boundaries are too stable and exclusionary, the group may become isolated and ineffective. (Putnam & Stohl, 1996, p. 151)

The study indicated that clarity, distinctness, and permeability of group boundaries interrelated in a complex way.. Consistent with Putnam and Stohl's discussions, we suggested that bona fide groups faced the simultaneous needs to preserve the group boundary and to be open to external influences. Thus, the teams struggled to maintain a sense of clear demarcation from their surrounding environments and from other groups (clarity and distinctness). At the same time, the teams also maintained a degree of openness to external groups. For example, the teams used communication media to interact with interrelated groups and individuals. Their openness to external groups and individuals resulted permeable boundaries and the introduction of temporary members, ideas, and practices into the group. Then as the groups

were subject to external influences that blurred boundaries, their members felt the need to preserve and maintain the clarity of the groups' boundaries through additional communicative practices, such as filtering messages from external members or playing jokes on another team.

The interrelated processes of identity and boundary management are integral to group effectiveness. A team can only function properly if members have a sense of its identity and are able to maintain it as a coherent unity, with clear delineation of "what is" the group and "what is not." Like people, groups need identity and boundaries.

REFERENCES

Alexander, S. C., Peterson, J. L., & Hollingshead, A. B. (2003). Help is at your keyboard: Support groups on the internet. In Frey, L. R. (Ed.), *Group communication in context: Studies of bona fide groups* (pp. 309–335). Hillsdale, NJ: Lawrence Erlbaum Associates.

Aubert, B. A., & Kelsey, B. L. (2003). Further understanding of trust and performance in virtual teams. *Small Group Research, 34,* 574–618. doi:10.1177/1046496403256011

Bell, B. S., & Kozlowski, S. J. (2002). A typology of virtual teams: Implications for effective leadership. *Group & Organization Management, 27,* 14–49. doi:10.1177/1059601102027001003

Bormann, E. G. (1980). *Communication theory.* New York: Holt, Rinehart & Winston.

Connaughton, S. L., & Daly, J. A. (2004). Long distance leadership: Communicative strategies for leading virtual teams. In Pauleen, D. J. (Ed.), *Virtual teams: Projects, protocols, and processes* (pp. 116–144). Hershey, PA: Idea Group Publishing.

Cooley, C. H. (1902). *Human nature and the social order.* New York: Scribner's.

Cramton, C. D. (2001). The mutual knowledge problem and its consequences for dispersed collaboration. *Organization Science*, *12*, 346–371. doi:10.1287/orsc.12.3.346.10098

Cramton, C. D. (2002). Finding common ground in dispersed collaboration. *Organizational Dynamics*, *30*, 356–367. doi:10.1016/S0090-2616(02)00063-3

Daft, R. L., & Lengel, R. K. (1984). Information richness: A new approach to managerial information processing and organizational design . In Cummings, L. L., & Staw, B. M. (Eds.), *Research in organizational behavior* (pp. 191–234). Greenwich, CT: JAI.

DeSanctis, G., & Poole, M. S. (1994). Capturing the complexity in advanced technology use: Adaptive structuration theory. *Organization Science*, *5*, 121–147. doi:10.1287/orsc.5.2.121

DeSanctis, G., Poole, M. S., & Zigurs, I. (2008). The Minnesota GDSS research project: Group support systems, group processes, and group outcomes. *Journal of the Association for Information Systems*, *9*, 551–608.

Dube, L., & Pare, G. (2004). The multifaceted nature of virtual teams . In Pauleen, D. J. (Ed.), *Virtual teams: Projects, protocols, and processes* (pp. 1–39). Hershey, PA: Idea Group Publishing.

Feldman, D. C. (1984). The development and enforcement of group norms. *Academy of Management Review*, *9*, 47–53. doi:10.2307/258231

Fernandez, W. D. (2004). Trust and the trust placement process in metateam projects . In Pauleen, D. J. (Ed.), *Virtual teams: Projects, protocols, and processes* (pp. 40–69). Hershey, PA: Idea Group Publishing.

Frey, L. R. (Ed.). (2003). *Group communication in context: Studies of bona fide groups*. Hillsdale, NJ: Lawrence Erlbaum Associates.

Giddens, A. (1984). *Constitution of society: Outline of the theory of structuration*. Cambridge: Polity Press.

Gluesing, J. C., Alcordo, T. C., Baba, M. L., Britt, D., Wagner, K. H., & McKether, W. (2003). The development of global virtual teams . In Gibson, C. B., & Cohen, S. G. (Eds.), *Virtual teams that work: Creating conditions for virtual team effectiveness* (pp. 59–86). San Francisco, CA: Jossey-Bass.

Harry, B., Sturges, K. M., & Klinger, J. K. (2005). Mapping the process: An exemplar of process and challenge in grounded theory analysis. *Educational Researcher*, *34*, 3–13. doi:10.3102/0013189X034002003

Henry, K. B., Arrow, H., & Carini, B. (1999). A tripartite model of group identification: Theory and measurement. *Small Group Research*, *30*, 558–581. doi:10.1177/104649649903000504

Huysman, M., Steinfield, C., Chyng-Chang, J., Kenneth, D., & Huis, I., M., Jan, P., & Ingrid, M. (2003). Virtual teams and the exploration of communication technology: Exploring the concept of media stickiness. *Computer Supported Cooperative Work: The Journal of Collaborative Computing*, *12*, 411–437. doi:10.1023/A:1026145017609

James, M., & Ward, K. (2001). Leading a multinational team of change agents at Glaxo Wellcome (now Glaxo SmithKline). *Journal of Change Management*, *2*, 148–159. doi:10.1080/714042500

Jarvenpaa, S. L., Knoll, K., & Leidner, D. (1998). Is anybody out there? Antecedents of trust in global virtual teams. *Journal of Management Information Systems*, *14*, 29–64.

Jarvenpaa, S. L., & Leidner, D. E. (1999). Communication and trust in global virtual teams. *Organization Science*, *10*, 791–815. doi:10.1287/orsc.10.6.791

Kayworth, T. R., & Leidner, D. E. (2001/2002). Leadership effectiveness in global virtual teams. *Journal of Management Information Systems, 18*, 7–40.

Kirkman, B. L., Rosen, B., Tesluk, P. E., & Gibson, C. B. (2004). The impact of team empowerment on virtual team performance: The moderating role of face-to-face interaction. *Academy of Management Journal, 47*, 175–192. doi:10.2307/20159571

Knoll, K., & Jarvenpaa, S. L. (1998). Working together in global virtual teams. In Igbaria, M., & Tan, M. (Eds.), *The virtual workplace* (pp. 2–23). Hershey, PA: Idea Group Publishing.

Krikorian, D., & Kiyomiya, T. (2003). Bona fide groups as self-organizing systems: Applications to electronic newsgroups. In Frey, L. R. (Ed.), *Group communication in context: Studies of bona fide groups* (pp. 335–367). Hillsdale, NJ: Lawrence Erlbaum Associates.

Larson, C. E., & LaFasto, F. M. (1989). *Teamwork: What must go right/what can go wrong*. Newbury Park, CA: Sage.

Leonard, D. A., Brand, P. A., Edmondson, A., & Fenwick, J. (1998). Virtual teams: Using communications technology to manage geographically dispersed development groups. In Bradley, S. P., & Nolan, R. L. (Eds.), *Sense & Respond: Capturing value in the network era* (pp. 285–298). Boston: Harvard Business School Press.

Lincoln, Y. S., & Guba, E. G. (1985). *Naturalistic inquiry*. Beverly Hills, CA: Sage.

Lipnack, J., & Stamps, J. (1997). *Virtual teams: Reaching across space, time, and organizations with technology*. New York: John Wiley.

Majchrzak, A., Rice, R. E., Malhotra, A., King, N., & Ba, F. (2000). Technology adaptation: The case of a computer-supported inter-organizational virtual team. *Management Information Systems Quarterly, 24*, 569–599. doi:10.2307/3250948

Massey, A. P., Montoya-Weiss, M. M., & Hung, Y. (2003). Because time matters: Temporal coordination in global virtual project teams. *Journal of Management Information Systems, 19*, 129–155.

McDonald, T. (1999). A whole new ball game. *Successful Meetings, 48*, 19.

Meier, C. (2003). Doing "groupness" in a spatially distributed work groups: The case of videoconferences at Technics. In L. R. Frey (Ed.), Group communication in context: Studies of bona fide groups (pp. 367-399). Hillsdale, NJ: Lawrence Erlbaum Associates.

Murphy, P. (2004). Trust, rationality, and the virtual team. In Pauleen, D. J. (Ed.), *Virtual teams: Projects, protocols, and processes* (pp. 317–343). Hershey, PA: Idea Group.

Pauleen, D. J. (2004). *Virtual teams: Projects, protocols and processes*. Hershey, PA: Idea Group Publishing.

Poole, M. S., & DeSanctis, G. (1992). Micro-level structuration in computer-supported group decision making. *Human Communication Research, 19*, 5–49. doi:10.1111/j.1468-2958.1992.tb00294.x

Poole, M. S., & Zhang, H. (2005). Virtual teams. In Wheelan, S. A. (Ed.), *The handbook of group research and practice* (pp. 363–386). Thousand Oaks, CA: Sage Publications.

Postmes, T., Spears, R., & Lea, M. (2000). The formation of group norms in computer-medicated communication. *Human Communication Research, 26*, 341–371. doi:10.1111/j.1468-2958.2000.tb00761.x

Putnam, L. L., & Stohl, C. (1990). Bona fide groups: A reconceptualization of groups in context. *Communication Studies, 41*, 248–265.

Putnam, L. L., & Stohl, C. (1996). Bona fide groups: An alternative perspective for communication and small group decision making . In Hirokawa, R. Y., & Poole, M. S. (Eds.), *Communication and group decision making* (2nd ed., pp. 147–177). Thousand Oaks, CA: Sage Publications.

Short, J., Williams, E., & Christie, B. (1976). *The social psychology of telecommunications*. New York: John Wiley.

Stohl, C., & Putnam, L. L. (1994). Group communication in context: Implications for the study of bona fide groups . In Frey, L. R. (Ed.), *Group communication in context: Studies of natural groups* (pp. 248–292). Hillsdale, NJ: Lawrence Erlbaum Associates.

Stohl, C., & Putnam, L. L. (2003). Communication in bona fide groups: A retrospective and prospective account . In Frey, L. R. (Ed.), *Group communication in context: Studies of bona fide groups* (pp. 399–414). Hillsdale, NJ: Lawrence Erlbaum Associates.

Strauss, A. L., & Corbin, J. (1990). *Basics of qualitative research: Grounded theory procedures and techniques*. Newbury Park, CA: Sage.

Strauss, A. L., & Corbin, J. (1998). *Basics of qualitative research: Grounded theory procedures and techniques* (2nd ed.). Newbury Park, CA: Sage.

Yoo, Y., & Alavi, M. (2004). Emergent leadership in virtual teams: What do emergent leaders do? *Information and Organization, 14*, 27–58. doi:10.1016/j.infoandorg.2003.11.001

Zigurs, I. (2003). Leadership in virtual teams: Oxymoron or opportunity? *Organizational Dynamics, 31*, 339–351. doi:10.1016/S0090-2616(02)00132-8

Chapter 7
Temporary Virtual Teams:
An Empirical Examination of Team Development

Stacey L. Connaughton
Purdue University, USA

Elizabeth A. Williams
Purdue University, USA

Jennifer S. Linvill
Purdue University, USA

Elizabeth J. O'Connor
Purdue University, USA

Troy Hayes
Ingersoll-Rand plc., USA

ABSTRACT

Temporary virtual teams are common organizing forms across industries and sectors, and their members often span national, functional, and other boundaries. Many times temporary virtual team members have no prior experience working with one another, may seldom if ever meet face-to-face, and may never work together again, thus team development may occur differently than it does in long-term or in tact teams. Yet little is known about the development of temporary virtual teams and the process challenges therein. The purpose of this chapter is to contribute to this body of research by revealing how individuals who are members of a temporary virtual team experience team development. Specifically, this chapter (a) reviews two often-cited models of team development and discusses the limited body of research on virtual team development; (b) presents findings from a study of one organization's business intelligence teams that were temporary, virtual, and global in nature; and (c) advances a research agenda for scholars in this area and recommendations to practitioners who are working in these contexts.

DOI: 10.4018/978-1-61520-979-8.ch007

INTRODUCTION

Virtual teams are organizing forms characterized by geographic and/or temporal distribution in which members' interactions are often mediated through communication technologies (Zaccaro, Ardison, & Orvis, 2004). Although nearly all teams operate virtually to some extent (e.g., through the use of e-mail, document sharing web sites, or other resources), those labeled virtual teams conduct the majority, or even all, of their work through these channels. Organizations utilize virtual teams comprised of locally and/or globally distributed team members to attend to customer problems, develop and market products, deliver services, and address business challenges (Duarte & Snyder, 2006).

Although virtual teams can be permanent, they are often temporary in nature. Ad hoc project teams, for example, are assembled to complete a specific project and then dissolve once the task is accomplished. In this respect, temporary virtual teams are advantageous and serve important functions. However, many times temporary virtual team members have no prior experience working with one another, may seldom if ever meet face-to-face, and may never work together again. These factors may hinder team development. Further issues such as low commitment, role ambiguity, social loafing, and role overload – issues which have been shown to exist in virtual teams (O'Hara-Devereaux & Johansen, 1994) – may further adversely influence team development. Moreover, teams that primarily use computer-mediated communication have been found to be more task-oriented and to exchange less social-emotional information, which can slow the development of relationships among team members (Bordia, 1997; Chidambaram, 1996). Thus, given their prevalence across multiple industries and sectors as well as the potential process challenges this organizing form raises, temporary virtual teams constitute a topic worthy of researchers' and practitioners' attention (Chudoba, Wynn, Lu, & Watson-Manheim, 2005; Jarvenpaa, Knoll, & Leidner, 1998; Kennedy, Loughry, Klammer, & Beyerlein, 2009).

The purpose of this chapter is to understand how team members themselves experience temporary virtual team development. Of particular interest is how the global, virtual, and temporary aspects of these teams are perceived to relate to team processes. This chapter also seeks to advance a research agenda that encourages further exploration of these intersections as well as extend recommendations to practitioners who engage in this kind of organizing form. To meet these objectives, this chapter (a) reviews two often-cited models of team development and discusses the limited body of research on virtual team development; (b) presents findings from a study of one organization's business intelligence teams that were temporary, virtual, and global in nature; and (c) advances a research agenda for scholars and recommendations for practitioners who are working in these contexts.

BACKGROUND

Global, Virtual, and Temporary Teams

Although temporary virtual teams are created to capitalize on knowledge and expertise that is geographically distributed (locally and/or globally) and to address a time-sensitive need, the nature of this organizing form may present challenges to team processes. Trust, for instance, constitutes one team process variable that has been found to be fleeting in virtual teams (Jarvenpaa & Leidner, 1999; Jarvenpaa, et al., 1998). In temporary teams, researchers have argued that trust must be developed swiftly or it does not develop at all (Jarvenpaa & Leidner, 1999; Krebs, Hobman, & Bordia, 2006; Meyerson, Weick, & Kramer). Moreover, like virtual teams in general (see Picherit-Duthler, Long, & Kohut, 2004), members of temporary virtual teams may not know one another nor have previous history working together prior to their experiences on the team. In addition, team members often originate from varying national, organizational, team, and/or functional cultures, factors which may affect the ways in which they communicate and do their work (Connaughton & Shuffler, 2007; Gibson & Gibbs, 2006). And, issues surrounding the finite nature of these teams may have implications for team development. The fact that these teams exist for a short period of time suggests that temporary teams may need to develop differently from, or at least at a quicker pace than, newly forming long-term teams (Panteli & Duncan, 2004).

Little is known, however, about the development of temporary virtual teams. The current study thus, draws on two models of team development commonly cited in the teams literature (Tuckman, 1965; Gersick, 1988) as well as on existing work on virtual team development. In the paragraphs that follow, these models and research findings are presented.

Temporary Virtual Team Development

Perhaps one of the most well known models of team development is Tuckman's (1965) model that delineates four stages of team development: forming, storming, norming, and performing. This model not only serves as the foundation for several studies examining team development, but is also well known in the corporate arena. In fact, one of the participants in this study even cited Tuckman's model when describing his own experience within his team.

Tuckman's model offers a sequential explanation of team development based on stages. The first stage, forming, is when groups determine their boundaries and engage in a type of orientation, both to one another and to the project at hand. From the forming stage, teams move into the storming stage which is marked by "conflict and polarization around interpersonal issues, with concomitant emotional responding in the task sphere" (Tuckman, 1965, p. 396). In essence the storming stage is when team members test and resist those boundaries which were established in the forming stage. According to Tuckman's model, as teams move out of the storming stage they enter a period of norming. The norming stage features coherence among the group, role adoption, and the development of standards. Then, teams move into the performing stage when "interpersonal structure becomes the tool of task activities" (p. 396). In other words, the structure developed through the previous three stages allows for the task to be accomplished. Based on further research one more stage, adjourning, was added to the model (Tuckman & Jensen, 1977). The adjourning phase takes place when the group has completed its task and dissolves. Researchers have also posited that if adjournment does not happen, a group may experience de-norming, de-storming, and de-forming over time (McGrew, Bilotta, & Deeney, 1999).

Gersick (1988) offered an alternative view of team development. Gersick's model considers two factors which are absent in Tuckman's work: time and environment. Using the concept of punctuated equilibrium, Gersick asserts that there is a "pattern of continuity and change" in groups (1988, p. 38). Gersick proposes that groups develop initial frameworks for performing their task. This is followed by a period of inertia and then a transition, or a "paradigmatic shift" (p. 32) that typically occurs at the halfway point of a team's lifespan. This shift changes how the team approaches its work and sets the stage for a second phase of inertia. Finally, at completion, the group makes a "final effort to satisfy outside expectations" (p. 32). Time pressures and outside observers seem to serve as catalysts for action in Gersick's model.

One difference between Tuckman's model and that of Gersick concerns the nature of the developmental process itself. Tuckman's model proposes that development occurs in a linear fashion while Gersick's model allows for more fluidity within phases but with distinct turning points in a group's progression. Gersick's model also recognizes the influences of outside forces, factors which Tuckman's model seems to neglect.

Like Tuckman and Gersick, various researchers have depicted *virtual* team development as a linear process and a fluid one. As is illustrated below, the models focus specifically on the type of communication that is ideal in each stage. Connaughton and Daly (2003), for example, offer a stage model of how leadership relationships develop in virtual teams. Their model posits that there are two stages to this development: (a) the initial stage in which face-to-face communication is key to building trust, establishing relationships, and managing expectations; and (b) the maintenance stage which is characterized by the usage of multiple media channels, constant communication, maintenance of trust, and continued sensitivity for the individual differences unveiled during the initial stage. This work offers a linear model reminiscent of Tuckman's approach.

Other researchers draw on Gersick's framework as the foundation for their analysis of virtual teams. In one such study, Rasters, Vissers and Dankbaar (2002) examine the various communication media used in the development of a virtual team. They note, however, two key differences between their observations and the punctuated equilibrium proposed by Gersick. First, Gersick's model assumes an initial structure whereas the team observed by Raster and colleagues began as a loosely formed group of scholars from various institutions without a central organization. Next, the observed team did not have a time frame or deadline at the beginning of their project; the authors argue that this consequently renders Gersick's predictive mid-point of team life negligible. The researchers concluded that "different communication media are likely to give rise to different group formation processes and communication processes that may

be rich, poor, or something in-between" (Rasters et al., 2002, p. 750).

These models of traditional and virtual team development underscore several factors to consider when examining team development and what may influence it. Specifically, the progression of these models urges scholars to examine the larger context in which these teams operate. Tuckman's familiar mnemonic continues to be used within organizations yet its stage model orientation may be perpetuating a pattern of team development that may not be the most beneficial, or realistic, for the team or the organization. The contextual factors illuminated by Gersick's punctuated equilibrium model may be particularly salient in temporary virtual teams, for in these teams, time is of the essence and communication takes various forms. In the analysis that follows, special attention is given to these two contextual factors – time and communication – as well as to the ways in which team members themselves describe the development of their team.

THE STUDY

This section presents findings from a study of four Business Intelligence Teams (BITs) that were part of a multi-national security technologies company headquartered in the Midwestern United States. The teams were global, virtual, and temporary, and thus provided a rich opportunity for us to examine issues of team development, virtuality, and communication processes in a temporary virtual team context. Team members participated in these BITs in addition to their regular day-to-day responsibilities and members were from various functions within the organization. All team members had prior experience working on virtual teams. The following general research question guided the study: *What are the process challenges that are experienced over time in teams that are global, virtual, and temporary?*

A qualitative approach to inquiry was employed in order to gather a rich description of participants' experiences with their global, virtual, and temporary team. This qualitative approach enabled the participants to describe their experiences, perceptions, and attitudes, all of which the researchers could not directly observe (Lindlof & Taylor, 2002). Interview data were collected at three points in time using in-depth, semi-structured interview protocols that varied among the three points in time (see Appendices A, B, and C). Participants were asked about the development of their team (e.g., time 1: What are you and your Business Intelligence Team members doing to begin to develop your team?), the challenges that the team faced (e.g., time 2: What do you see is the biggest challenge to your Business Intelligence Team's effectiveness?), and they were asked to provide recommendations for future teams (e.g., time 3: What recommendations would you make to the next round of Business Intelligence Teams?). This approach allowed the researchers to cover necessary topics of inquiry and clarify meaning without limiting the participants' responses (Lindlof & Taylor, 2002). A total of forty-five interviews were conducted. Interviews were approximately 30 minutes in length. Participants for each of the three interviews were randomly selected, with some individuals participating more than once (interviewed twice n=6; interviewed three times n=6). Participants were asked various questions about team processes and perceived outcomes. Interviews were audio-recorded and later transcribed verbatim (although fillers such as "um," "uh," and "ah" were removed) by one of the researchers. The transcripts were then read and analyzed by the other researchers to be sure that each member of the research team was fully immersed in the data and that there was agreement on the findings.

It is important to note that prior to data collection, all team members had been brought from their various locations around the world to the organization's headquarters in the Midwestern United States for a formal "kickoff" event. During this five-day event, team members were given their project plans and expectations, and many team members met each other for the first time. Team members engaged in structured activities such as a workshop on effective teaming and other sessions related to business strategy. They also had some time each day to get to know one another and discuss the projects they would be working on. During the kickoff meeting, team members were briefed on the study and were encouraged to participate in interviews when contacted. Team members then traveled back to their locations, and continued work on their team projects by mainly virtual means. A few weeks later, the researchers randomly selected participants and contacted them via e-mail to request their participation. Because team members were located around the world, interviews were held via telephone. Participation was voluntary and all identifying information for participants has been concealed.

Time 1 data collection occurred soon after the BITs were formed. These interviews were conducted shortly after the team members had met at corporate headquarters and had returned to their respective geographic locations. Thirteen individuals participated in the first round of interviews (at least 3 individuals from each of the four teams). Time 2 data collection took place approximately mid-way through the BIT projects (4-6 weeks after time 1). Twenty individuals participated in the second round of interviews (at least 4 individuals from each of the four teams with as many as 7 participants from one team). Time 3 data collection occurred after the BIT projects had been completed (8-10 weeks after time 2). Twelve BIT members participated (at least two individuals from each team).

In the spirit of grounded theory, data were analyzed through a constant comparative approach (Charmaz, 2000; Strauss & Corbin, 1998) where systematic data gathering and inductive data analysis (Strauss & Corbin, 1998) enable themes to emerge (Charmaz, 2000). Comparing the data for similarities and/or differences is essential to analysis because it allows researchers to differentiate one category or theme from another, as well as to identify features specific to that category or theme (Corbin & Straus, 2008). Data analysis began early on during the interview and transcription processes when the researchers wrote field notes and memos on the data to record initial thoughts, reflections, and analytic questions (Creswell, 2003). By beginning analysis early in the data collection process, researchers have an accurate memory of what was being depicted or described in the data (Lindlof & Taylor, 2002). Furthermore, beginning analysis early allowed for initial interpretations to be made (Lindlof & Taylor, 2002) and for relationships among concepts to be explored in future data collection processes (Charmaz, 2000; Strauss & Corbin, 1998). Initial findings informed the project framework and the researchers were able to alter subsequent interview protocol and add probing questions to address initial themes that emerged. The researchers engaged in open, axial, and selective coding of the data (Lindlof & Taylor, 2002; Strauss & Corbin, 1998). Through these coding processes, the researchers further refined their analysis by revealing related themes and connecting similar experiences among participants (Lindlof & Taylor, 2002). After each phase of the coding process, the researchers came together to discuss and come to agreement on their interpretations (Creswell, 2003). This form of triangulation sought to help ensure the integrity of the findings and minimize any researcher bias (Lindlof & Taylor, 2002).

Team Development as Reflected in Participants' Talk Over Time

The data reveal interviewees foregrounding different themes in their talk over the course of their team's development and existence. Specifically, over time the team members' talk tended to focus on: (a) constraints (time 1); (b) processes (time 2); and (c) product (time 3).

Time 1: Constraints

Near the beginning of the teams' existence, participants' talk focused on the constraints they perceived their team was facing. Team members talked about various limiting factors that can be grouped into three categories: (a) time constraints, (b) environmental constraints and (c) people constraints. Talk about *time constraints* included concerns about completing the project, the limited amount of time each team member was available to dedicate to the project, and coordinating time among team members. Several participants spoke of the time it took to understand their project. One said, "We probably spent two weeks or so apart [not communicating], kind of understanding what our objective was and kind of getting into it…." Some team members talked about balancing time for their project and their regular work responsibilities. Some gave examples of team members missing conference calls and meetings due to these other time commitments. Time zone differences among team members were also cited as a challenge for scheduling group conference calls.

The category, *environmental constraints*, included talk about the spatial aspects of geographic dispersion, collaborating in a virtual environment (via telephone conference calls, document sharing, etc.), and a lack of face-to-face interaction. Interestingly, participants identified distance as a challenge but most did not believe it would affect the quality of their final projects. Most team members thought face-to-face interaction was simply more efficient than working virtually. One team member said, "It's just a different dynamic when you're not in the same room with people." Others noted feeling "disconnected," and commented that there was more room for misunderstandings and potential for technological difficulties when working virtually.

The category, *people constraints,* included areas of expertise and industry knowledge as well as varying levels of engagement among team members. On the topic of knowledge, one participant noted, "everybody, with exception of a very few people [has a] a limited knowledge base about this industry and about this market." Several other participants made similar remarks and indicated that a learning curve had to occur before they were comfortable with the project. Varying levels of perceived engagement among team members was another commonly cited constraint. Some team members expressed concern that some of their colleagues, although participating, may not be as engaged as others. As one team member put it, "there are some team members that are, every time, on the call that are heavily engaged. There are others that there are times when their contribution is higher and you know they do not participate in every session. It's really a challenge, I think, to keep everyone engaged and you know up to speed."

Time 2: Process

Time 2 interviews were conducted approximately midway between the kickoff and the project deadlines. We noted that the talk shifted from an assessment of the constraints facing the team to a focus on the processes involved in effectively meeting their team goals. Much of the talk focused on how the team communicated (i.e., frequency, methods, nature of communication), how tasks were assigned and completed (i.e., the creation of sub-teams), balancing BIT demands with other work/life responsibilities, and processes of leadership within each team.

Many participants pointed to the kickoff meeting as being crucial to their team's development. They indicated that the initial face-to-face meeting gave them the opportunity to get to know one another's strengths and weakness as well as set guidelines for communication. One team member said the time spent at the kickoff was "worth its weight in gold." Another team member described the kickoff meeting as "instrumental" to the team's success. Several teams indicated that supplemental face-to-face meetings, monthly or bi-monthly,

were essential to their team's progress because these meetings allowed everyone to work together more efficiently. When referring to face-to-face meetings, one participant said, "Whenever we meet in those face-to-face meetings, we really achieve some good progress... it is more difficult to achieve progress [virtually] compared to us together around the table [when] everybody is listening and actively involved."

Most participants described their team's communication process as structured, meaning they had an agenda or someone was guiding the interaction during virtual meetings. All teams utilized scheduled communication, usually in the form of a weekly or bi-weekly conference call. Outside of the structured communication there was also talk of spontaneous communication occurring. Participants noted this spontaneous communication was usually task-oriented, and increased in frequency near deadlines or upcoming meetings. This spontaneous communication typically was in the form of telephone calls or emails between members of sub-teams as they worked to get their tasks completed for the team meetings. At other times this spontaneous communication took the form of emails between the entire team. In these instances, the focus of the spontaneous communication was usually logistics (e.g., determining when the group could meet for a face-to-face meeting).

By time 2, all of the BITs had split members into smaller sub-teams to accomplish tasks. Participants explained that these teams formed "naturally," based on geographic location, area of expertise, or interests of individual team members. Leaders of sub-teams were also said to have emerged naturally. Most participants recognized shared leadership among their teams. One participant elaborated by saying, "everybody has taken ownership in either their specific piece or the final output."

Nearly all participants talked of the difficult process of balancing their BIT commitments and other responsibilities such as day-to-day work demands, working toward an advanced degree, and family responsibilities. One participant described the situation in this way: "Everybody is having a lot of daily duties and tasks, and the [BIT] really is asking for a lot of time and effort. So I think the balance is the most difficult thing." A few participants said they were not able to achieve balance, but were simply working extra hours to meet competing demands on their time. One said, "It isn't a balance, it's an imbalance right now."

Time 3: Product

The talk during time 3 interviews was focused on the final product (goal of project), and was characterized by a "drive to the finish line mentality." Team members were no longer as concerned with their constraints or how to overcome them through team processes. They were now focused on meeting the quickly approaching deadlines. Most team members were confident in their team's abilities, with talk concentrated on trusting each other to complete assigned tasks, the successful completion of their projects, and the presentation and resulting outcomes of their projects.

According to team members, the last four weeks were critical and it took discipline to work independently or in sub-teams while not collocated with the rest of their team. The work during this time was characterized as "tying up loose ends," and "dotting the I's and crossing the T's." Many participants said meeting face-to-face before their presentation was critical for final preparations. According to one participant, "that's when we really got our best work product done," and many echoed this belief.

Participants talked of trusting their fellow team members to come through on the final product and presentations. This trust had been established throughout the project based on performance and follow-through, and according to one participant, "a personal good feeling" about other team members. Participants explained that the sub-teams were assigned to complete specific tasks in order to prevent the team from "rehashing" or "reworking" the same material.

Additionally, there was much talk of the project presentations and what would come of their work. "We've done a lot of work and now it's time to step up in front of the senior management and not be afraid of if they disagree with you," said one participant. Others spoke of receiving feedback from upper management, and how their team's recommendations to the organization would be implemented. A few also cited the development of professional and personal relationships with team members as an outcome of participating on the BIT.

Development of the Teams' Foci on Team Relationships and Team Objective

Both models of team development discussed earlier in this essay (i.e., Tuckman, 1965; Gersick, 1988) acknowledge the importance of a team's task and the development of a team's relationship. However, both models seem to focus more on one element than the other (i.e., Tuckman focuses primarily on relationship development, whereas Gersick focuses primarily on task development). Moreover, neither model clearly delineates the *differences* between how the task and team relationships develop.

When talking about their experiences, individuals on the four BITs differentiated between task and relationship development. Furthermore, team members described the development of these two areas as occurring at different speeds. According to participants, due to the virtual and temporary nature of the team, relationships among team members had to develop quickly. This is consistent with research indicating that trust must form swiftly on virtual teams (Jarvenpaa & Leidner, 1999; Jarvenpaa, et al., 1998). Conversely, development of the task (i.e., understanding the goal and progressing toward completion) was described as a much slower and steady process.

The development of the task and the relationship are happening concurrently but are taking place at different speeds. One way to think of this variation is to consider the fable *The Tortoise and the Hare*. The task can be thought of as the tortoise, developing (relatively) slowly over the course of the BIT. The hare, on the other hand is representative of the relationship which develops quickly at the beginning of the team's existence. In this section we explore the ways that our participants talked about the development of the relationship and the task (discussed below in that order), paying special attention to their use of metaphors of movement and mention of speed which indicate the different rates of development.

"The Hare": Relational Development on the Team

The development of relationships seemed to move quickly, beginning with the kickoff meeting. Indeed, all BIT members pointed to the importance of the teams' initial kickoff meeting, indicating that this was essential for relationship formation. As one participant stated, "[the] workshop also helped us express our strengths and weaknesses. It was formally asked of us so we all got to hear each other's strengths and weaknesses, kind of bonding." When asked why this was so important, he responded, "I think because on this team we barely knew each other...the other members were from sales and different departments where we never come across each other." Almost all interviewees made similar statements about the importance of the kickoff meeting to relationship building. They cited the meeting as being central to getting all members of the team "pulling in the same direction."

After the initial kickoff meeting, relationship development, which had occurred quickly, became relationship maintenance. One participant noted that trust was continually built on the team by performance: "It was more within working and proving yourself when there's something like,

'Hey I'll get this done on this day.' And then you do." While a large effort had been placed on quickly building relationships during the kickoff meeting, after the kickoff meeting the relationship maintenance and strengthening occurred based on individuals' performance on the task and when individuals were not "in the loop" they were quickly "brought up to speed."

Furthermore, the quick formation of relationships on the team was essential in order for the team's focus to shift to the task. This is illustrated in the following response:

[T]he project has nothing to do with operations [his area], it has everything to do with marketing and sales, the level of communication and the way the team members have communicated has helped me understand the subject better and faster versus - there was no information withholding I would say. So everyone was communicating clearly and as good as they could within their own way. As well as to help me to develop and get to the same level as the rest of the team as quickly as possible. In general, I think one of the things that happened is quite clear. Because of the level of trust, there was a good discussion going on that helped the team go from the storming stage of team formation relatively pain free. It helped us get to level where challenging each other's ideas is accepted. Not only accepted, but expected also. You know, not many teams can get to that stage within a couple of months like we have. I think open communication, and not holding information, and not having hidden agenda that has helped us become more trustworthy and perform better as a team.

Note that in this statement, the participant invokes Tuckman's language of the storming stage of team formation. Tuckman's model focuses primarily on the relational stages which teams work through. In this participant's experience, which was echoed by several other BIT members, the relational formation occurred swiftly and this allowed the focus to shift to the task.

"The Tortoise": Task Development on the Team

As was alluded to in the previous section, each of the teams seemed to go through a "learning curve" period in which they spent time clarifying the goals of the project and learning about the subject matter. While they were focusing on task-related activities during the first few weeks, it took them time to get up to speed to actually make progress towards the goal. We see this in the above quotation as the participant discusses how his teammates helped bring him up to speed on the knowledge necessary for the completion of this project. We also see this in another participant's response when asked what he would have done differently had he been leading the team:

Probably just since this was a new topic really for all of us, there was probably some uncertainty on my part. I went into it not having...we spent the first three weeks or so kind of feeling our way through what the objective was and how to get to it. Maybe just identifying and being a little more clear to everyone at the beginning of our direction as opposed to kind of feeling our way through. We felt through kind of as a group.

Note in his response the time it took to determine the objective for the project and the plan of action. The participant describes the process as "feeling our way through" indicating a sense of hesitation before charging forward. Although the team may have quickly developed relationships, they still struggled to begin to make progress on the project. However, as the previous response reminds us, it is important to note that the relationship and task development are occurring concurrently.

Although *The Tortoise and the Hare* fable adequately describes the beginning stages of BIT team development, unlike in the fable, the tortoise in this story does not continue at a slow and steady pace. Rather, as the projects progressed,

we noted that our participants had an increased sense of urgency towards the task. As another participant noted:

In a certain moment I think and I saw that people put less effort. However now in this month...I feel that people in this moment really feeling the same urgency and the fact that we need to present it in front of the CEO it, I think, has a great catalyst effect.

In his response, note that there is an increased focus on the task and effort to complete it. Similarly, another participant points out the change in the nature of the communication on the team:

Team Member: I think [the communication has] become, and some of this is the nature of the state that we're in the project, but the conference calls don't necessarily last as long now. It's more of a quick update. Where are you headed? This is what we need to get done and then go off and do it.

Interviewer: Contrast that to how it was before.

Team Member: In the beginning it was a lot more, and again I think it was because of the stage of the project, we were still kind of working our way through, trying to figure out what needed to be done so it was a lot more discussion and trying to figure out where we needed to go instead of here's my update, here's the next step and here's what will be done.

This exchange points to a few things. First, it underscores that communication about the task has changed. It appears there is more doing and less talking about doing among team members. Next, note the reference to the learning curve (i.e., "trying to figure out where we needed to go") as well as how things have changed and how the pace of accomplishing tasks has increased.

Another participant echoes the sentiments found in the two previous statements in the following response. Note how he discusses the catalyst for the new found sense of urgency.

I think we have come to a very interesting stage last week....At the beginning of [month], there was a lot of work that had been done and now we need to come to a conclusion and make decisions. And this was a pretty interesting stage in the project because you needed to just nail down tangible results and decisions. And you could feel that some of the team members, they would have liked to discuss for many days, but we haven't had the time. So it was quite interesting to see this process. But finally getting people to get to a decision, get to a joint agreement on something, and now use what we have decided on to develop the final presentation and our recommendations to the executive team.

This response underscores that the urgency of the moment comes from impending deadlines. This deadline makes completion of the task paramount and to an extent changes the way that team members approach the task (i.e., "they would have liked to discuss for many days, but we haven't had the time").

Participants' responses demonstrate that while both relationships and the primary task are developed throughout the course of the project, the development of each occurs at different speeds. Relationships were developed quickly through face-to-face interaction at the kickoff meeting. They were sustained by individuals meeting their deadlines. Meanwhile, task development occurred very slowly at the beginning of the project as team members struggled to understand the project and its goals. Task development, however, sped up as deadlines drew near and as it became necessary to produce a tangible product.

An Organic Model of Temporary Virtual Team Development

These data suggest an alternative to the Gersick and Tuckman models when viewed within the context of virtual teams. In keeping with Gersick's (1988) model, the virtual nature of these teams allowed them to change and evolve. According to participants, trust and "open communication" very early on in the team's development allowed for rapid progress. This enabled the teams to develop and progress quickly and in a more fluid fashion than the models proposed by Gersick and Tuckman. For as one participant shared, "You know, not many teams can get to that stage within a couple of months like we have."

During the initial phase of development for each of the BITs (time 1 interview) individuals came together and formed a temporary virtual team. According to participants, this forming phase (similar to Tuckman's model) allowed team members to recognize the enablers, or the positive factors that each individual, the organization, and the environment brought to the team (e.g., cultural and occupational diversity, existing knowledge about various geographic area(s), organizational support and resources), and the constraints, or various potential challenges that the team members did not have control over (e.g., time, distance, diverse occupational backgrounds, skills, and cultures, leadership, varying levels of engagement/participation, work/life balance).

In keeping with Gersick's model, the teams moved through an initial phase of inertia that was bounded by these enablers and constraints. At the end of the first phase of inertia, BIT members realized that change was needed and that the team must move forward (Gersick, 1988). To do so, the teams entered into a transition period (around time 2). As one participant illustrated:

Everybody's hard charging out of the gate, the true test is 60-90 days in when it starts to get tougher;

when you start to feel the pressure to put together a substantive deliverable and a viable solution that you're presenting to leadership. I think some people run toward that and embrace [it]....

From this quotation we see the shift that occurs when the deliverable becomes the focus of the team.

In Gersick's (1988) model teams moved into the transition phase due to an environmentally-induced trigger; an "alarm" indicated that time was quickly passing and that the team must immediately act in order to move forward. The teams in Gersick's (1988) "punctuated equilibrium" model were bound by time and other various factors outside of the team members' control (e.g., environment, outside others) that set off the alarm that triggered change so that the team could enter into the second phase of inertia.

In contrast, the teams in this study progressed towards their goal in a more fluid (and less linear) nature. Whereas, in existing models of team development, factors such as time, environment, and outside stakeholders serve as external forces influencing team progress, the teams in this study were not bound by these forces. Instead, the teams changed and evolved in a more organic fashion. Instead of an environmentally induced trigger creating an "alarm" for change, participants indicated that there was a more natural transition that moved them into the second phase of inertia. This is not to say that external factors did not exist but rather that the individuals on these teams seem to engage in collective sensemaking (Weick, 1995) to define and respond to these factors. Several examples, though not exhaustive, are discussed below.

Differing from Gersick's (1988) model, a specific time constraint did not serve as a trigger to set off an alarm for change. This was due in part to the fact that the four BITs' deadlines were not fixed, but continually moving. As one participant stated, "Unfortunately, we don't have an end date set in stone." This created some frustration for this participant since he did not have a timeline for completion of the final project. It did, however, allow the teams work together to determine when they should be meeting particular milestones. This participant further shared the benefit of the changing deadline by stating, "We set our hard dates to collect all that data, [and] things have progressed very nicely." As this participant explained, the teams were able to choose their own internal deadlines and that helped them stay on track.

These teams, however, experienced a sense of urgency to accomplish their goals. The desire to be successful appears to have been the trigger that moved these teams into the second phase of inertia and allowed each team to complete their project goals. As one participant summarized, "The sense of urgency, I think, is key everywhere when you want to achieve something, especially in these days when we need to change some rule of the game." As he illustrated, a sense of urgency to accomplish the team's goal(s) is the key to triggering change and entering into the second phase of inertia.

That individuals were able to exercise agency and make meaningful decisions within these BITs helped promote a transition to the second phase of inertia. In other words, the organization did not dictate the direction that the teams had to take or the method they used to accomplish their goals. Instead, the teams worked together to make these decisions. For example, the sub-teams that each BIT created helped them complete the maximum amount of work in a shorter amount of time. The ability to make these types of team decisions greatly increased the fluid nature of the teams and their progress. Thus, each team's trigger for transition was born organically when team members came to a collective understanding of the team's enablers and constraints and determined the best way to work within these boundaries. Once this determination was made, team members were then able to exercise agency in order to make decisions necessary to achieve their goals. Importantly, team members recognized weaknesses or less than ideal characteristics of the team and/

or their work environment and moved forward in spite of these factors. As one participant further explained of this transition phase: "We're having to shift our gears a little bit and we're having to shift our focus." One participant illustrated this by sharing that team members had to "be able to distinguish good, bad, and also move forward."

Similarly, teams constructed the virtual context of the teams as a positive feature as it afforded members the ability to participate from any location. In making sense of how to manage team operations and relationships in a virtual environment, team members remained flexible and open to the innovative methods that helped them achieve their goals. This openness to different ways of interacting led to a high rate of productivity early on. Interestingly, none of the participants in time 1 viewed distance as a challenge that would affect the effectiveness or quality of the teams' work or their final product. This ability to adapt as necessary to their environment again illustrates the fluid nature of these teams in a virtual setting.

That this study was conducted longitudinally with data collected at three points in time allowed the researchers to capture the fluid nature of teams' development. Specifically, the teams developed as follows. In time 1, participants discussed various *constraints*. In time 2, teams abandoned any notions of an ideal team (i.e., characteristics and environment) and formed sub-teams in order to focus on making the *processes* more efficient and effective. And in time 3, the teams moved into a final phase where they focused primarily on the final *product* they were producing, following Gersick's (1988) model where teams "satisfy outside expectations" (p. 32). While time pressures and outside observers served as environmental catalysts for action in Gersick's (1988) model, the data in the current study suggest that the ways in which team members made sense of these environmental factors, allowed change to occur more organically and moved teams towards their collective goal.

In summary, the teams in this study were similar to those studied by Gersick and Tuckman as they conceptualized their models of team development. The BITs, like those in Gersick and Tuckman's studies, had little, if any, team history and were temporary in nature. This makes these teams especially relevant for studying temporary, virtual team development. It also makes the mismatch between our findings and subsequent model and what the Gersick and Tuckman models would suggest all the more interesting.

FUTURE RESEARCH DIRECTIONS

Findings from this study encourage researchers to investigate temporary virtual team development in greater detail and in so doing to examine the intersections of virtuality, temporality, and other variables. One of the other variables we encourage future researchers to investigate is culture (national, team, functional) and in particular, the conditions under which culture is salient in temporary virtual teams. We make this suggestion because of what did *not* appear in our data. We anticipated going into the project that, given the composition of these temporary virtual teams culture, particularly national culture, would emerge as a salient issue related to team development and team processes in general. Interestingly, in the current study, few participants commented on national cultural differences among members of their teams. This is a compelling omission given that the teams were comprised of individuals from various national cultures. That the participants in this study did not talk about national culture raises questions for future research: When do national cultural differences among team members matter? When do they not? Moreover, Connaughton and Shuffler (2007) have argued that, when focusing on culture in virtual teams, researchers have spent much time examining *national* culture and less effort ascertaining the potential influences of other aspects of culture such as team culture, functional culture, and organizational culture. Thus, future researchers should question how multiple cultures (national, team, functional) might be working together to influence team processes and outcomes in temporary virtual teams.

In addition, researchers should examine the role of uncertainties of various types (i.e., with team members; one's role) and its management in temporary virtual teams. Although the ways in which team members managed and/or reduced uncertainty was not the focus of this study, we see traces of their need and ability to do so in our data. For instance, as quoted previously in this chapter, one of our interviewees expressed uncertainty about the nature of the project. Other interviewees implicitly point to uncertainties about how to negotiate perceived constraints; others noted that having the face-to-face kickoff meeting helped to alleviate uncertainties about whom they would be working with over the course of the team's existence. Indeed, much of our participants' task and relational work appears to be about negotiating and/or managing some type of uncertainty. To be sure, uncertainty reduction theory (Berger & Calabrese, 1975) has been applied to interpersonal and organizational contexts (i.e., Jablin, 1984; 1987; Kramer, 1993; Miller & Jablin, 1991) and in virtual teams, uncertainty reduction has been proposed as a potential motivator for member identification (see Fiol & O'Connor, 2005). Yet the ways in which team members manage uncertainty has not been integrated into models of (virtual) team development. Indeed, the Tuckman and Gersick models do not sufficiently address this important communicative issue. Given that uncertainty management is central to how individuals develop their roles and their relationships in interpersonal and organizational contexts, we encourage future researchers to further explore the ways in which uncertainties are managed in temporary virtual teams.

Moreover, the extent to which virtual teams are virtual varies, and perceptions of the effects of geographic distance on team processes continues to be a topic of interest (and debate) within the virtual teams literature (see Kirkman & Mathieu, 2005). One wonders if temporary virtual development is affected more by the temporal or virtual aspects of these teams, or perhaps neither. These remain important questions for future research to address.

RECOMMENDATIONS FOR PRACTITIONERS

Findings from this study suggest several recommendations to practitioners.

Consideration 1: *If possible, the organization should bring team members together for a kickoff meeting.* Participants in this study unanimously believed that the kickoff meeting at corporate headquarters was one of the reasons their teams got off to such a strong start. The team members provided several reasons why. Some commented on how developing the project charter needed to be done face-to-face so that members could give instant feedback to one another and so that they could build on each other's ideas. Others noted that this meeting was also an extremely instrumental time for developing the strategies that would help them meet their final goal(s). Although these face-to-face meetings carry significant expense for organizations, these gatherings allow team members to get to know one another on both a personal and professional level. Our data suggest that these meetings help significantly in the formation of team dynamics and trust and are worth the expense.

Consideration 2: *Team members should take the time to get to know each others' specializations, competencies, strengths, work styles, preferred methods of communication, and other preferences and expectations early in the team's development.* The kickoff meeting may be a good opportunity for facilitating a structured activity to accomplish these tasks. These sorts of activities are not only for team building purposes, but also are helpful later on to foster effective team processes. Knowing the preferred work styles of various team members can help the individuals understand why certain team members respond in particular ways; knowing who is competent at various aspects of the team's work can be helpful in expediting the accomplishment of various team tasks.

Consideration 3: *During the team's existence, team members should try to meet face-to-face, perhaps leveraging other organizational meetings as opportunities to do so.* Periodic face-to-face communication was found to be helpful in meeting the following team process needs: (a) making sure there is progress – some teams reported that these meetings served as internal deadlines for meeting specific goals; (b) focusing *exclusively* on BIT team work – all BIT members reported that balancing BIT responsibilities with day-to-day responsibilities was challenging; face-to-face meetings ensured that team members would be focused on the BIT project exclusively; (c) facilitating effective brainstorming – some BIT members preferred brainstorming in person rather than over the phone or through email. They believed brainstorming was more effective in person because synergy was created among team members; and (d) giving BIT members additional time to bond as a team – several BIT members noted the importance of relational components to team work. Toward the end of the team's existence, these face-to-face meetings also gave BIT members a chance to celebrate all that their team had accomplished together.

Consideration 4: *Teams should schedule weekly teleconferences and full team participation on these calls is necessary.* The interview data revealed that all BIT members had at least one weekly teleconference; in some cases, teams teleconferenced twice per week. The times for these teleconferences were set by the designated team leader once he/she had gathered availability data from team members and considered time zone differences. What varied among teams, however, was the extent to which there was full participation on these calls. Of course, travel schedules were a factor from time to time. Some team members reported that if they had to miss a call due to travel, they would make a point of catching up on the content of that call with their designated team leader or another team member. But, other times, some individuals either did not catch up on team processes or did not participate during teleconferences. This lack of participation can be attributed to several factors. One factor that emerged in one of the interviews was that some individuals felt compelled to become a member of a BIT when they were asked to do so. In other words, they did not feel as though they could turn down the opportunity. For some, the level of commitment to the project was not high to begin with, thus this may have contributed to their lack of participation. Another reason for their lack of participation may have had to do with team climate. Some interviewees shared that some team members were quite vocal and monopolized the conversations. Some interviewees noted that their designated team leaders did much of the talking, especially early on in the team's development, and thus a climate for open participation may not have been fostered from the start. All of these perceptions point to the importance of (a) committed team members, (b) creating a team climate in which members feel comfortable participating, and (c) training team leaders on how to facilitate group discussion and elicit participation from even the most reticent team members.

Consideration 5: *Adopt a mindset that there is not a "one-size-fits-all" model of temporary virtual team development.* That is, no two temporary virtual teams develop in the same manner. What findings in this study reveal are some general patterns that may occur, but which future empirical research needs to examine. For instance, it is likely that team members from Team A/Organization A are likely to perceive different constraints (time 1) than Team B/Organization B based on organizational and team cultures and resources. Team leaders and members, as well as key organizational members, should recognize that team development is an organic process.

CONCLUSION

This chapter has considered how temporary virtual teams develop from the perspective of individuals who experience this organizing form firsthand. Their words underscore the tension between a linear approach to team development and a more fluid and/or organic one. Clearly, the team members who participated in the current study had a project deadline to meet (although the exact deadline fluctuated over time) and they incorporated phrasings reflective of linear team development in their talk. Yet their movement toward that deadline was anything but linear. Future research is needed to de-tangle the web of factors that emerged in this study as potentially influencing temporary virtual team processes and effectiveness.

REFERENCES

Berger, C. R., & Calabrese, R. J. (1975). Some explorations in initial interaction and beyond: Toward a developmental theory of interpersonal communication. *Human Communication Research, 1,* 99–112. doi:10.1111/j.1468-2958.1975.tb00258.x

Bordia, P. (1997). Face-to-face versus computer-mediated communication: a synthesis of the experimental literature. *Journal of Business Communication, 34*(1), 99–120. doi:10.1177/002194369703400106

Charmaz, K. (2000). Grounded theory: objectivist and constructivist methods . In Denzin, N. K., & Lincoln, Y. S. (Eds.), *Handbook of qualitative research* (pp. 509–535). Thousand Oaks, CA: Sage.

Chidambaram, L. (1996). Relational development in computer-supported groups. *Management Information Systems Quarterly, 20*(2), 143–165. doi:10.2307/249476

Chudoba, K. M., Wynn, E., Lu, M., & Watson-Manheim, M. B. (2005). How virtual are we? Measuring virtuality and understanding its impact on a global organization. *Information Systems Journal, 15,* 279–306. doi:10.1111/j.1365-2575.2005.00200.x

Connaughton, S. L., & Daly, J. A. (2003). Long distance leadership: Communicative strategies for leading virtual teams . In Pauleen, D. J. (Ed.), *Virtual teams: Projects, protocols, and processes* (pp. 116–144). Hershey, PA: Idea Group Inc.

Connaughton, S. L., & Shuffler, M. (2007). Multinational multicultural distributed teams: A review and future agenda. *Small Group Research, 38,* 387–412. doi:10.1177/1046496407301970

Corbin, J., & Strauss, A. (2008). *Basics of qualitative research* (3rd ed.). Thousand Oaks, CA: Sage.

Creswell, J. W. (2003). *Research design: Qualitative, quantitative, and mixed methods approaches* (2nd ed.). Thousand Oaks, CA: Sage.

Duarte, D., & Snyder, N. (2006). *Mastering virtual teams: Strategies, tools, and techniques that succeed* (3rd ed.). San Francisco, CA: John Wiley & Sons, Inc.

Fiol, C. M., & O'Connor, E. J. (2005). Identification in face-to-face, hybrid, and pure virtual teams: Untangling the contradictions. *Organization Science, 16,* 19–32. doi:10.1287/orsc.1040.0101

Gersick, C. J. G. (1988). Time and transition in work teams: Toward a new model of group development. *Academy of Management Journal, 31,* 9–41. doi:10.2307/256496

Gibson, C. B., & Gibbs, J. L. (2006). Unpacking the concept of virtuality: The effects of geographic dispersion, electronic dependence, dynamic structure, and national diversity on team innovation. *Administrative Science Quarterly, 51*, 451–495.

Jablin, F. M. (1984). Assimilating new members into organizations . In Bostrom, R. (Ed.), *Communication Yearbook 8* (pp. 594–626). Beverly Hills, CA: Sage.

Jablin, F. M. (1987). Organizational entry, assimilation and exit . In Jablin, F. M., Putnam, L. L., Roberts, K. H., & Porter, L. W. (Eds.), *Handbook of organizational communication* (pp. 679–740). Beverly Hills, CA: Sage.

Jarvenpaa, S. L., Knoll, K., & Leidner, D. E. (1998). Is anybody out there? Antecedents of trust in global virtual teams. *Journal of Management Information Systems, 14*, 29–64.

Jarvenpaa, S. L., & Leidner, D. E. (1999). Communication and trust in global virtual teams. *Organization Science, 10*, 791–815. doi:10.1287/orsc.10.6.791

Kennedy, F. A., Loughry, M. L., Klammer, T. P., & Beyerlein, M. M. (2009). Effects of organizational support on potency in work teams: The mediating role of team processes. *Small Group Research, 40*, 72–93. doi:10.1177/1046496408326744

Kirkman, B., & Mathieu, J. (2005). The dimensions and antecedents of team virtuality. *Journal of Management, 31*, 700–718. doi:10.1177/0149206305279113

Kramer, M. W. (1993). Communication and uncertainty reduction during job transfers: Leaving and joining processes. *Communication Monographs, 60*, 178–198. doi:10.1080/03637759309376307

Krebs, S. A., Hobman, E. V., & Bordia, P. (2006). Virtual teams and group member dissimilarity: Consequences for the development of trust. *Small Group Research, 37*, 721–741. doi:10.1177/1046496406294886

Lindlof, T. R., & Taylor, B. C. (2002). *Qualitative communication research methods* (2nd ed.). Thousand Oaks: Sage.

McGrew, J. F., Bilotta, J. G., & Deeney, J. M. (1999). Software team formation and decay: Extending the standard model for small groups. *Small Group Research, 30*, 209–234. doi:10.1177/104649649903000204

Meyerson, D., Weick, K. E., & Kramer, R. M. (1996). Early trust and temporary groups . In Kramer, R. M., & Tyler, T. R. (Eds.), *Trust in organizations: Frontiers of theory and research* (pp. 166–195). Thousand Oaks, CA: Sage.

Miller, V. D., & Jablin, F. M. (1991). Information seeking during organizational entry: Influences, tactics and a model of the process. *Academy of Management Review, 16*, 92–120. doi:10.2307/258608

O'Hara-Devereaux, M., & Johansen, R. (1994). *Global work: Bridging distance, culture, and time.* San Francisco: Jossey-Bass.

Panteli, N., & Duncan, E. (2004). Trust and temporary virtual teams: Alternative explanations and dramaturgical relationships. *Information Technology & People, 17*, 423–441. doi:10.1108/09593840410570276

Picherit-Duthler, G., Long, S. D., & Kohut, G. F. (2004). Newcomer assimilation in virtual team socialization . In Godar, S., & Ferris, S. P. (Eds.), *Virtual & collaborative teams: Process, technologies, & practice* (pp. 115–132). Hershey, PA: Idea Group Inc.

Rasters, G., Vissers, G., & Dankbear, B. (2002). An inside look – Rich communication through lean media in a virtual research team. *Small Group Research, 33,* 718–734. doi:10.1177/1046496402238622

Strauss, A., & Corbin, J. (1998). *Basics of qualitative research: Techniques and procedures for developing grounded theory.* Thousand Oaks, CA: Sage.

Tuckman, B. (1965). Developmental sequence in small groups. *Psychological Bulletin, 63,* 384–399. doi:10.1037/h0022100

Tuckman, B., & Jensen, M. (1977). Stages of small group development. *Group and Organizational Studies, 2,* 419–427. doi:10.1177/105960117700200404

Weick, K. E. (1995). *Sensemaking in organizations.* Thousand Oaks, CA: Sage.

Zaccaro, S. J., Ardison, S. D., & Orvis, K. L. (2004). Leadership in virtual teams . In Day, D., Zaccaro, S., & Halpins, S. (Eds.), *Leader development for transforming organizations* (pp. 267–292). Mahwah, NJ: Lawrence Erlbaum.

ADDITIONAL READING

Alge, B. J., Wiethoff, C., & Klein, H. J. (2003). When does the medium matter? Knowledge-building experiences and opportunities in decision-making teams. *Organizational Behavior and Human Decision Processes, 91,* 26–37. doi:10.1016/S0749-5978(02)00524-1

Ancona, D. G. (1987). Groups in organizations: Extending laboratory models . In Hendrick, C. (Ed.), *Group processes and intergroup relations* (pp. 178–202). Newbury Park, CA: Sage.

Baba, M. L., Gluesing, J., Ratner, H., & Wagner, K. H. (2004). The contexts of knowing: Natural history of a globally distributed team. *Journal of Organizational Behavior, 25,* 547–587. doi:10.1002/job.259

Bell, B. S., & Kozlowski, S. W. J. (2002). A typology of virtual teams: Implications for effective leadership. *Group & Organization Management, 27,* 14–49. doi:10.1177/1059601102027001003

Boudreau, M. C., Loch, K. D., Robey, D., & Straud, D. (1998). Going global: Using information technology to advance the competitiveness of the virtual transnational organization. *The Academy of Management Executive, 12,* 120–128.

Brannen, M. J. (2003). What is culture and why does it matter? Current conceptualizations of culture from anthropology . In Byacigiller, N. A., Goodman, R. A., & Phillips, M. E. (Eds.), *Crossing cultures: Insights from master teachers* (pp. 20–37). New York: Routledge. doi:10.4324/9780203218693_chapter_3

Brett, J., Behfar, K., & Kern, M. C. (2006). Managing multicultural teams. *Harvard Business Review, 84,* 84–90.

Chudoba, K. M., Wynn, E., Lu, M., & Watson-Manheim, M. B. (2005). How virtual are we? Measuring virtuality and understanding its impact on a global organization. *Information Systems Journal, 15,* 279–306. doi:10.1111/j.1365-2575.2005.00200.x

Cogburn, D. L., & Levinson, N. S. (2003). U.S.–Africa virtual Collaboration in globalization studies: Success factors for complex, cross-national learning teams. *International Studies Perspectives, 4,* 31–54. doi:10.1111/1528-3577.04103

Cohen, S. G., & Gibson, C. B. (2003). In the beginning: Introduction and framework . In Gibson, C. B., & Cohen, S. G. (Eds.), *Virtual teams that work: Creating conditions for team effectiveness* (pp. 1–13). San Francisco, CA: Jossey-Bass.

Connaughton, S. L., & Daly, J. A. (2005). Leadership in the new millennium: Communication beyond temporal, spatial, and geographical boundaries . In Kalbfleisch, P. (Ed.), *Communication Yearbook, 29* (pp. 187–213). Mahwah, NJ: Erlbaum.

Cramton, C. D. (2001). The mutual knowledge problem and its consequences for dispersed collaboration. *Organization Science, 12*, 346–371. doi:10.1287/orsc.12.3.346.10098

Cramton, C. D. (2003). Finding common ground in dispersed collaboration. *Organizational Dynamics, 30*, 356–367. doi:10.1016/S0090-2616(02)00063-3

Earley, P. C., & Mosakowski, E. (2000). Creating hybrid cultures: An empirical test of transnational team functioning. *Academy of Management Journal, 43*, 26–49. doi:10.2307/1556384

Gibson, C. B., & Gibbs, J. L. (2006). Unpacking the concept of virtuality: The effects of geographic dispersion, electronic dependence, dynamic structure, and national diversity on team innovation. *Administrative Science Quarterly, 51*, 451–495.

Harvey, M., Novic, M. M., & Garrison, G. (2005). Global virtual teams: A human resource capital architecture. *International Journal of Human Resource Management, 16*, 1583–1599. doi:10.1080/09585190500239119

Hinds, P. J., & Bailey, D. E. (2003). Out of sight, out of sync: Understanding conflict in distributed teams. *Organization Science, 14*, 615–632. doi:10.1287/orsc.14.6.615.24872

Hinds, P. J., & Mortensen, M. (2005). Understanding conflict in geographically distributed teams: The moderating effects of shared identity, shared context, and spontaneous communication. *Organization Science, 16*, 290–307. doi:10.1287/orsc.1050.0122

Hofstede, G. J. (1980). *Culture's consequences.* Beverly Hills, CA: Sage.

Janssens, M., & Brett, J. M. (2006). Cultural intelligence in global teams: A fusion model of collaboration. *Group & Organization Management, 31*, 124–153. doi:10.1177/1059601105275268

Kayworth, T. R., & Leidner, D. E. (2001/2002). Leadership effectiveness in global virtual teams. *Journal of Management Information Systems, 18*, 7–40.

Kiesler, S., & Cummings, J. (2002). What do we know about proximity and distance in work groups? A legacy of research . In Hinds, P., & Kiesler, S. (Eds.), *Distributed work* (pp. 57–80). Cambridge, MA: MIT Press.

Marks, M. A., Mathieu, J., & Zaccaro, S. J. (2001). A temporally based framework and taxonomy of team processes. *Academy of Management Review, 26*, 356–376. doi:10.2307/259182

Martins, L. L., Gilson, L. L., & Maynard, M. T. (2004). Virtual teams: What do we know and where do we go from here. *Journal of Management, 30*, 805–836. doi:10.1016/j.jm.2004.05.002

Maruping, L. M., & Agarwal, R. (2004). Managing team interpersonal processes through technology: A task-technology fit perspective. *The Journal of Applied Psychology, 89*, 975–990. doi:10.1037/0021-9010.89.6.975

Maznevski, M. L. (1994). Understanding our differences: Performance in decision-making groups with diverse members. *Human Relations, 47*, 531–542. doi:10.1177/001872679404700504

Maznevski, M. L., & Chudoba, K. M. (2000). Bridging space over time: Global virtual team dynamics. *Organization Science, 11*, 473–492. doi:10.1287/orsc.11.5.473.15200

McGrath, J. E., Arrow, H., & Berdahl, J. L. (2000). The study of groups: Past, present and future. *Personality and Social Psychology Review, 4*, 95–105. doi:10.1207/S15327957PSPR0401_8

Modalis Research Technologies, Inc. (2001). Meetings in America III: A study of the virtual workforce in 2001. Retrieved September 18, 2006, from http://e-meetings.mci.com/meetingsinamerica/pdf/MIA3.pdf.

Montoya-Weiss, M. M., Massey, A. P., & Song, M. (2001). Getting it together: Temporal coordination and conflict management in global virtual teams. *Academy of Management Journal, 44*, 1251–1262. doi:10.2307/3069399

Mortensen, M., & Hinds, P. J. (2001). Conflict and shared identity in geographically distributed teams. *The International Journal of Conflict Management, 12*, 212–238. doi:10.1108/eb022856

Napier, B. J., & Ferris, G. R. (1993). Distance in organizations. *Human Resource Management Review, 3*, 321–357. doi:10.1016/1053-4822(93)90004-N

Oakley, J. G. (1998). Leadership processes in virtual teams and organizations. *The Journal of Leadership Studies, 5*, 3–17. doi:10.1177/107179199900500301

Oertig, M., & Buegri, T. (2006). The challenges of managing cross-cultural virtual project teams. *Team Performance Management, 12*(1/2), 23–30. doi:10.1108/13527590610652774

Paul, S., Samarah, I. M., Seetharaman, P., & Myktyn, P. P. (2005). An empirical investigation of collaborative conflict management style in group support system-based global virtual teams. *Journal of Management Information Systems, 21*, 185–222.

Sarker, S. (2005). Knowledge transfer and collaboration in distributed U.S.-Thai teams. *Journal of Computer Mediated Communication, 10*. Accessible at: doi:10.1111/j.1083-6101.2005.tb00278.x

Saunders, C., Van Slyke, C., & Vogel, D. R. (2004). My time or yours? Managing time visions in global virtual teams. *The Academy of Management Executive, 18*, 19–31.

Townsend, A. M., DeMarie, S. M., & Hendrickson, A. R. (1998). Virtual teams: Technology and the workplace of the future. *The Academy of Management Executive, 12*, 17–29.

Uber Grosse, C. (2002). Managing communication within virtual intercultural teams. *Business Communication Quarterly, 65*, 22–38. doi:10.1177/108056990206500404

Vogel, D. R., Van Genuchten, M., Lou, D., Verveen, S., Van Eekout, M., & Adams, A. (2001). Exploratory research on the role of national and professional cultures in a distributed learning project. *IEEE Transactions on Professional Communication, 44*, 114–125. doi:10.1109/47.925514

Walther, J. B. (1996). Group and interpersonal effects in international computer-mediated collaboration. *Human Communication Research, 23*, 342–369. doi:10.1111/j.1468-2958.1997.tb00400.x

Watson-Manheim, M. B., Chudoba, K. M., & Crowston, K. (2002). Discontinuities and continuities: A new way to understand virtual work. *Information Technology & People, 15*, 191–209. doi:10.1108/09593840210444746

Workman, M. (2005). Virtual team culture and the amplification of team boundary permeability on team performance. *Human Resource Development Quarterly, 16*, 435–458. doi:10.1002/hrdq.1149

Yoo, Y., & Torrey, B. (2002). National culture and knowledge management in a global learning organization . In Choo, C. W., & Bontis, N. (Eds.), *The Strategic Management of Intellectual Capital and Organizational Knowledge* (pp. 421–435). New York: Oxford University Press.

Yoon, S. W. (2006). Two group development patterns of virtual learning teams: Linear progression and adaptive progression. *The Quarterly Review of Distance Education, 7*, 297–312.

Yuan, Y. C., & Gay, G. (2006). Homophily of network ties and bonding and briding social capital in computer-mediated distributed teams. *Journal of Computer-Mediated Communication, 11*, 1062–1084. doi:10.1111/j.1083-6101.2006.00308.x

Zakaria, N., Amelinckx, A., & Wilemon, D. (2004). Working together apart? Building a knowledge-sharing culture for global virtual teams. *Creativity and Innovation Management, 13*, 15–29. doi:10.1111/j.1467-8691.2004.00290.x

KEY TERMS AND DEFINITIONS

Virtual Team: An organizing form in which member interactions tend to be mediated through electronic communication technology.

Global Virtual Teams: Virtual teams characterized by geographic dispersion whose members span several nation-states and cultures.

Temporary Virtual Teams: Virtual teams which are bound by time; these teams have a definitive end point.

Tuckman's Model of Team Development: A description of team development that focuses on relational development which goes through four stages: forming, storming, norming, and performing.

Punctuated Equilibrium: Used in Gersick's team development model to describe how teams go through periods of inertia punctuated by paradigmatic shifts, occurring at the midway point of team development. Originally a concept within the field of natural history, Gersick (1988) uses this term to describe a shift in paradigm. Specifically, Gersick (1988) posits that teams experience "long periods of inertia, punctuated by concentrated, revolutionary periods of quantum change" (p. 16). In Gersick's model, time and environment trigger the periods of change.

APPENDIX A. TIME 1 INTERVIEW QUESTIONS

What is the primary goal of your Business Intelligence Team? What are you and your team members working toward?

What are you and your Business Intelligence Team members doing to begin to develop your team?

What do you see as potential challenges to effective teamwork on your Business Intelligence Team?

What do you believe are the biggest strengths of your Business Intelligence Team? Please give an example(s) that illustrates these strengths from your experiences with this team.

Do you believe physical distance (team members being geographically separated) will affect the quality of your team's final product? Why or why not?

Does your team communicate effectively with each other? Please give an example that describes the nature of the communication on your team.

Please describe a time when leadership was exhibited in your Business Intelligence Team. Please describe a time when leadership needed to be exhibited in your Business Intelligence Team but was not.

Appendix B. Time 2 Interview Questions

What is the primary goal of your Business Intelligence Team? What are you and your team members working toward?

What did your Business Intelligence Team do when it first developed in order to build your team? Was that successful in helping you work together as a team? Why or why not?

What do you see is the biggest challenge to your Business Intelligence Team's effectiveness? Please give an example that illustrates this challenge from your experiences with this team.

What do you believe is the biggest contributor (asset) to your Business Intelligence Team's effectiveness? Please give an example that illustrates this strength from your experiences with this team.

Would you say your Business Intelligence Team members trust each other? How has trust developed on the team? What threatens trust?

Do cultural differences (e.g., national culture, language, functional culture) among team members influence your team's ability to function effectively? Why or why not? If you believe they do, how do they impact your effectiveness?

Does physical distance (geographic separation) between you and your Business Intelligence Team members affect how effective your team is? If so, how? Please give an example of how distance does or does not affect your team.

Does your Business Intelligence Team communicate effectively with each other? Please give an example that describes the nature of the communication on your team.

Please describe a time when leadership was exhibited in your Business Intelligence Team. Please describe a time when leadership needed to be exhibited in your Business Intelligence Team but was not.

Has leadership been shared among members of your Business Intelligence Team? Why or why not?

Appendix C. Time 3 Interview Questions

Overall, what has been the most positive aspect of this team experience?

What were your biggest challenges during the last month of your Business Intelligence Team's work? In other words, what challenges did the team face in getting its Business Intelligence Team work done?

What recommendations would you make to the next round of Business Intelligence Teams?

Chapter 8
Status and Influence Processes in Virtual Teams and Mobile Collaborations

Elizabeth C. Ravlin
University of South Carolina, USA

ABSTRACT

Communication between members of decision-making teams has long been known to be strongly influenced by member status. However, we still know relatively little about how status and status-driven influence processes change with the implementation of technologically-mediated virtual teams and mobile collaborative enterprises. Early predictions were that technologically-mediated communication would essentially flatten the status hierarchy of groups and teams (Kiesler, Siegel, & McGuire, 1984), allowing all members, regardless of position, social identity, or other characteristics, to have equal access to the decision-making process. A review of relevant theoretical approaches and prior empirical findings indicates that in all likelihood, status processes and influence are maintained in these settings, at least in some cases to the detriment of team effectiveness. This chapter examines, through the manifestations and functions of interpersonal status, the effects of technological mechanisms of collaboration on communication processes, relationships, and practices.

INTRODUCTION

Collaboration conducted via computer-mediated technologies has often been acclaimed for the potential it holds to provide avenues for participation on the part of all members of an aggregate (Anson & Munkvold, 2004). This participation is particularly important because knowledge held in

such aggregates is considered to be a distinctive competence (Harvey, Novicevic, & Garrison, 2004). As compared to face-to-face groups, theoretically, teams operating virtually should be better able to facilitate broad member input in that status cues, and in some cases, even status characteristics, are not available (Driskell, Radtke, & Salas, 2003). Turn-taking no longer dictates who will speak, normative pressure for conformity is reduced, and everyone involved should have access to the same

DOI: 10.4018/978-1-61520-979-8.ch008

information via the technological system used by the team.

As organizations move into the next evolution of technology-facilitated collaboration, once again, barriers appear to be coming down with regard to influence and participation. Mobile phone-style devices are rapidly becoming the locus of technology-mediated communication, and ultimately, all who have such a device will have access, from virtually any location, to their co-workers and internet-stored information and software. Availability of information continues to increase, and presumably, access to individual members of a collaboration is increasing as well.

However, the presumed equalization (or merit basis) of influence is unlikely to occur without intervention, despite these technological changes. As noted by Wallace (2004), "the idea [use of the internet] was to make distance unimportant to teamwork," but "it did not quite work out that way" (p. 159). The purpose of this chapter is to examine, from a theoretical perspective, how technological mediation interacts with the differential status of team members to influence team communications, relationships, and practices. I argue that despite increasing access to the information and technology needed to participate in such collaborations, there are still real and relevant psychological and sociological barriers to influence for low-status members that are either not affected by or actually facilitated by these communication technologies and their common usage.

In the following background section, I initially review relevant theory regarding communication and distance. Secondly, essential elements of basic theories of identity and status are introduced. Lastly, I provide an overview of key research in the area of virtual teams.

BACKGROUND

Theories of Organizational Communication

Organizational communications have been subject to theorizing from a variety of perspectives. In general, Carlson and Zmud (1999) provide a three-pronged typology organizing this body of thought. First, researchers address what characteristics influence choice and use of particular types (channels) of communication. Secondly, studies may focus on how specific types of communication are used. Thirdly, perceptions generated from the use of different types of communication are particularly important in developing an understanding of how technology changes interpersonal interaction. I draw to some extent on all three of these areas, but focus here on two key well-known theories: social presence (Short, Williams, & Christie, 1976) and media richness (Daft & Lengel, 1986), both of which fall into the last category, and argue for varying effects on group process based on the type of communication media utilized.

Social presence is a term used by Short, et al. (1976) to indicate the extent to which a person with whom one is interacting is salient. Many nonverbal cues may be comprised by social presence (e.g., facial expression), but a central issue is the extent to which the focal person is aware of or processing the relationship with the other, as opposed to simply carrying out individually-generated task-oriented behavior. Thus, it is anticipated that when social presence is low (awareness of the other is not salient), less effort is generated toward being socially appropriate, sensitive to the relationship, or interpreting messages beyond literal meaning. Social presence is typically cast as a quality of the medium of communication; that is, if the medium is audio-only, one would have little opportunity to read non-verbal cues, and would have less sense of the presence of the other.

Media richness (Daft & Lengel, 1986) provides another approach to evaluating channel features, in that to the extent that a medium provides the opportunity for exchange of many different types of complex information, that medium can help to reduce uncertainty for the receiver. That is, one can use tone of voice, literal message, facial expression, body language, and other cues to interpretation in face-to-face communication, whereas the use of email tends to limit the message to text. Typical approaches to understanding communication effectiveness in the context of media richness suggest that the medium used should match the required richness for the message to be conveyed appropriately.

For the purposes of this chapter, these theories provide background on the key categories of variables that are affected by changes in communications technology. In general, two factors emerge. First, and most obviously, different types and amounts of information are transmitted by different technologies, affecting the cognitive availability of a variety of inputs to decision making. Second, and perhaps more importantly, different socio-emotional and motivational effects are produced by varying levels of social presence generated by technological characteristics. Here, I focus on cognitive, socio-emotional, and motivational issues in the development and effects of status and influence processes and patterns within virtual teams and mobile collaborations. Through this focus, a better understanding can be developed of potential shifts in influence patterns for lower status members.

Theories of Identity and Status

The dominant approach to understanding how groups and their members function continues to be Social Identity Theory (SIT; Tajfel, 1978) and its variants. According to SIT, individuals are motivated to perceive (possibly creating, maintaining, or enhancing) the characteristics of fellow in-group members that positively distinguish them from opposing out-group members. Perception of such distinguishing characteristics allows the

maintenance of positive identification with the in-group. Although multiple motives have been noted as forming the basis for these categorization processes, the fundamental motives underlying in-group favoritism are commonly considered to be (1) the need for self enhancement, or the search for positive comparisons that can be made with others, and (2) the need for increased certainty to maintain or increase understanding of the self in the context of social or interpersonal interactions (Reid & Hogg, 2005). A typical co-located workgroup is an ideal venue for meeting such needs, as co-workers tend to have some commonalities that can be emphasized, and common or inter-relating tasks that require some sharing of mental models.

From the standpoint of social identity approaches, hierarchy is provided to an aggregate by the prototypicality of members (Hogg & Terry, 2000). As the group comes to agree on the characteristics and behaviors of an ideal member, each individual is measured against this ideal standard. Those who are the closest to the prototype typically emerge as leaders, while those who are farthest from it are categorized as "black sheep" (Marques, Abrams, Paez, & Hogg, 2001). These members who deviate most greatly from the prototype still tend to be preferred to out-group individuals, but are often used to exemplify how members should *not* behave, or as having characteristics that members should ideally *not* have. Thus, highly prototypical individuals either appear to be, or are, highly influential. As the prototypicality of the individual diminishes, so does influence (or the appearance thereof). Prototypicality is an internal characteristic of the unit, in that it arises from depersonalized social attraction (i.e., the attraction of one member to another based on the group context as opposed to individual characteristics). The development of prototypicality is implicitly based on the existence of a strong group identity, a condition that a virtual aggregate may fail to meet.

Status characteristics theory (SCT; e.g., Berger, Cohen, & Zelditch, 1972) provides a more widely recognized summary dimension that enhances understanding of how team member characteristics affect these individuals' abilities to influence beyond specific group and social identity approaches. In general, the concept of status has received less attention in the organizational literature than might be expected, given the prominent role of authority in organizations (Ravlin & Thomas, 2005). SCT is the dominant approach to understanding status processes in sociology, and provides an avenue for the importation of status from other aggregates, relationships, or identities. The theory and its associated findings argue that all aggregates tend to quickly form status hierarchies within their membership based on perceptions of competence regarding the accomplishment of the unit's task (e.g., Fisek & Ofshe, 1970).

Status perceptions refer to the identification of distinctions in prestige and deference among members of an aggregate (Conway, Pizzamglio, & Mount, 1996; Shils, 1975). As differentiating information is categorized as "good" or "bad," the overall status hierarchy is created by weighting salient dimensions of comparison by their importance, and combining them into an overall index (Fisek, Berger, & Norman, 1995). SCT suggests that external or diffuse status characteristics, such as gender, racial, or ethnic qualities, tend to be evaluated and used to form initial status perceptions, as little else is known about the individual. In addition to these external status characteristics, over time other sources of status perceptions come to include interaction patterns, evaluations of task competence, and styles of verbal and non-verbal behavior. Research evidence indicates that external or diffuse characteristics such as gender contribute, independently of performance, to ascriptions of status (Cohen & Zhou, 1991). This finding suggests that once status orders are formulated, they are difficult to change (Berger, et al., 1980). Within a team, status orders provide members with information about their roles, such as the amount of contribution appropriate, when to

defer, and whose opinion carries the most weight (Cohen & Zhou, 1991).

Thus, perceived status is influenced by task-relevant qualities of members such as expertise (specific characteristics), but also is a function of demographic or other salient characteristics that are construed in some way to be related to team goals (diffuse characteristics). To the extent that there is perceived to be a direct link between a characteristic and task competence, the characteristic is given more weight. As the link becomes more indirect (for example, the perception is that the task requires mathematical abilities, women have weak mathematical abilities, and this member is a woman), the characteristic receives less consideration. As better evidence is collected (providing a more direct link between the individual's characteristics and his or her actual competence), it is argued that diffuse characteristics will become unimportant in determining influence. Of course, the dissipation of diffuse characteristic effects is dependent on the presence of several contingencies that are not always met (see Knottnerus, 1988 for further critique of the task-based rationale of the SCT approach): (1) that the aggregate values task competence above all other potential values; (2) that task competence is easily recognized with some experience, and (3) that there is a clear and compelling relationship between individual characteristics and task performance. If these conditions are *not* present, initial beliefs about diffuse status characteristics will often be quite tenacious.

Virtual Teams and Mobile Collaborations

Although today's virtual work can take on many forms, the most intensively studied of these is the virtual team. These structures are typically defined as task groups in which members do not work in the same location, but have interdependent functions, and in which the work is carried out using technologically-mediated communication (Driskell, et al., 2003; Martins, Gilson, & Maynard, 2004). Technologies have, in recent years, included various combinations of computerized text, visual, audio, and project- and meeting-specific applications. A significant amount of early research, reflecting the most popular options of the 1980s and early 1990s, compared text-only communication (typically email or messaging) with face-to-face options. In particular, group decision support software was often lauded as a mechanism whereby non-task-related status influences could be removed from or at least mitigated in the group decision process (e.g., Zigurs, Poole, & DeSanctis, 1988). As compared to face-to-face interaction, text-based technology-mediated processes were thought to better facilitate broader member input and open knowledge sharing by removing visible and/or audible status cues (social identity, identifiable accent). Many such technologies allow simultaneous contribution, and therefore both the need to take turns and pressure to conform are diminished or eliminated. With the addition of relevant databases, all members also should have equal access to important task-related information, further reducing status barriers.

These typical arguments with regard to the role of technological mediation in virtual collaborations suggest a leveling of the playing field over time with regard to diffuse status characteristics, and a stronger emphasis on task-relevant contributions (Driskell, et al., 2003). However, this approach minimizes findings by McLeod, Baron, Marti, and Yoon (1997) that indicate that minority members may participate more in such settings, but may actually have less influence. This finding might potentially imply that minority members feel more comfortable in stating their opinions in such settings, but that the majority still doesn't particularly care about them. Further, a number of studies have found relatively few differences in communication patterns between virtual and face-to-face teams (e.g., Bordia, DiFonzo, & Chang, 1999). In addition, technological changes

have altered the computer-mediated environment, which has typically been identified as lower in social presence and less rich in terms of prior theories of social presence and media richness. Current technology allows not only for strong feelings of presence of others and rich media for communication, but also is becoming increasingly mobile and fluid in nature (Bisoux, 2009). These factors must be considered in any analysis of the effects of virtual work.

Below, I argue that cognitive, socio-emotional, and motivational issues play important roles in how communication and influence patterns will be enacted in any given context. Further, continuing evolution of technologies interacts with the human element to produce and maintain status and influence structures that are far from perfect replications of task competence rankings in work teams. In the next section, the role of cognitive, socio-emotional, and motivational processes in decision making in virtual teams and in developing mobile collaborative structures is examined.

STATUS AND INFLUENCE PROCESSES IN VIRTUAL WORK

The Evolution to Mobile Collaboration

As technology used for distance collaboration evolves, the nature of virtual work changes with it. Technological developments that are currently having a strong influence on the work process across a broad spectrum of organizational forms are focused in three areas: (1) the mobility of the user is greatly enhanced without compromising access, (2) feelings of social presence can be dramatically increased, and (3) in conjunction, added richness of available media of communication is increased as well. Organizations are moving into this next phase of technology-facilitated collaboration, and obstacles continue to fall with regard to the potential for influence and participation.

As Personal Digital Assistants (PDAs) or small notebook and tablet computers become the locus of technology-mediated communication, the cost of access drops dramatically, and the tie to a specific location is essentially severed.

In the global business environment, typically all employees who have the need to communicate with distant others will have such a device, and will thus have access, from almost any location, to their co-workers, internet-stored information, and software. Although this situation is now commonplace, other developments also entering the mainstream depend on further technological changes. In general, these changes alter the way we view and use team structures and expatriate assignments.

The value of virtual team structures is generally considered to lie in its facilitation of the extent to which people in different locations can work efficiently and effectively together. As is constantly noted, the globalization of business and the rapidity with which change now occurs have altered the needs of organizations that conduct their activities in this world-wide community. The expatriate model used for decades, in which an individual executive, typically from the home-country headquarters operation, would be sent on an extended assignment (3 to 5 years) to a subsidiary location to ensure that headquarters' mandates were carried out is declining in use, and is in part replaced by business travel (e.g., Ward, Leong, & Low, 2004). Today, business travelers are drawn from a broader range of the organizational hierarchy, from technical professionals to top executives. The length of stay in other locations is likely to be a few days as opposed to years, and these individuals are sent to multiple locations and thus may have little opportunity to build knowledge about the countries in which they travel or the people with whom they interact. Further, project needs change rapidly, and most managers and employees find themselves switching teams frequently, and/or working on multiple teams simultaneously. Virtual teams can be constructed and reconfigured

rapidly, at least in part because the location of the redeployed human resources is irrelevant. Propinquity is now considered to be unimportant, with the help of a strong mobile collaboration model (see Allen, 1977, for a discussion of the role of distance in collaboration). This development also suggests that locating specialized competencies at specific organizational locations, as was common in the past for divisionally organized firms, is no longer required. Another advantage of virtual work may include a reduction in travel, which limits expenses and also can be an integral part of a company's approach to sustainability. In sum, virtual teams may provide organizations with the ability to respond to increased globalization and change, the knowledge intensity of today's work, and the increased expense, difficulty, and undesirability of travel.

In support of this different approach to conducting business globally, new technologies provide previously missing or reduced functions in communication. Although PDAs or cell phone devices have been available for quite some time, wireless access functionality continues to increase, and cost is diminishing. Use of PDAs as primary work tools beyond their cell phone capacity typically encountered two significant obstacles in the past. First, the ability to store data provided a serious constraint, and second, inputting information in the form of text, beyond the typical text message, was limited. Technological developments, however, are now making these constraints vanish. Most organizations have moved to a net storage model of data and software. This evolution now means that the most important aspect of the PDA is its internet access. In addition, virtual keyboard technology (in which the keyboard is typically projected onto a flat surface for the user), allows for greatly expanded use of more conveniently portable mobile devices. Further, use of a connection to a television or visionware that enables a user to access a larger view of their work is also enabling more extensive usage of small connective devices. Another issue that is being addressed is the ability of these devices to run multiple applications at once. Technology forecasters believe that the demise of the laptop as a primary virtual work component will occur in the near future (Miller, 2009). Even teleconferencing systems, primarily geared toward increasing feelings of social presence through life-size video images, have the capacity for limited mobility, in that some systems are designed to be set up temporarily in different locations.

Given these changes in the technological environment, key issues arise with regard to how status processes are affected. A natural result of these changes is an increasing expectation of instantaneous contact or access to information, which suggests that patterns of interaction may be altered based on speed of response. In addition, the social presence of some individuals will likely be greater than others, as members located at a major site for the company will have access to tele-presence systems, but those at small locations, or travelling, will not. Although social presence can be greatly enhanced, it also has some unique features relative to typical face-to-face interaction. Finally, rich communication will be more readily available to some members than others, and in a variety of formats (e.g., tele-presence, VOIP). The implications of these changes are discussed further below.

Socio-Emotional, Motivational, and Cognitive Influences on Status Processes

Virtual work at its present level of development has at least three important implications for how people perceive and respond to status and influence processes. First, perceptions of status are less likely to be shared in a virtual environment; second, technology presents a potential (and likely) overload of messages, and third, social cues are now available again in distance work, but they are unlikely to be constantly present. A broad array of status-related effects is likely to result.

Although there are clearly multiple reasons for the development of status perceptions within teams (e.g., Sidanius, Pratto, & Rabinowitz, 1994), sharing of these perceptions among team members, particularly in virtual environments, is not likely to be uniform. The fact that individual members do not share a common view leads to negative socio-emotional reactions and conflict-oriented behaviors. Three primary factors can be identified in the evolution of status disagreements within an aggregate, beyond the exacerbating effects of virtual collaboration. These factors are (1) the differentiated belief structures held by members prior to joining the team (based on heterogeneity of membership), (2) differing levels of prior familiarity within dyadic relationships in the team, and (3) individual differences related to self-esteem. These factors can lead to lack of a shared mental model of status with implications for communications, relationships, and practice.

Heterogeneous belief systems impact status beliefs in multiple ways. For example, cultural differences can carry inconsistent external evaluations of status (e.g., U.S. and Japanese beliefs about business superiority). They influence interaction patterns over time, and also have implications for beliefs about appropriate verbal and non-verbal behavior (e.g., Ravlin, Thomas, & Ilsev, 2000). In general, we would expect that homogeneous others tend to evaluate one another more positively (e.g., Byrne, 1971); however, the influence of the similarity-attraction effect (or social identity processes; Tajfel & Turner, 1986) on status perceptions will be moderated by beliefs about the connection between demographic qualities and status and the specific task at hand. In addition, differences in prior familiarity within dyads on a team may lead to individuals having a great deal of task-based information about one team member, and purely stereotypical information about another. These differences in familiarity should also lead to differences in perceptions of the appropriate status ranking each individual should hold, in part based on the development of cognitive trust, or a belief that a partner can and will do what they say they will do, among more familiar dyads (Lewis & Weigart, 1985). Lastly, individuals will evaluate themselves differently in terms of status, with a tendency toward over-evaluating their own importance within the team. Self-esteem level should play a role in exacerbating or mitigating this tendency.

Disagreement regarding the status hierarchy may imply a lack of legitimacy of the status structure as it is currently perceived, in that it is not accepted as appropriate or proper by all team members. This is a significant issue, because if the status order becomes unstable, interpersonal conflict is more likely to become manifest (Zelditch & Walker, 1989). Status perceptions of other interaction partners also act as screening and evaluating devices of these partners' communications and behaviors. That is, based on status perceptions of a team contributor, perceptions and judgments regarding the member's contribution will be affected in the following ways. First, attention will be drawn to aspects of the contribution consistent with existing status perceptions, or inconsistent information will be processed until it fits better (or is marked as an understandable exception). Second, the task- and process-based evaluation made of the contribution will be influenced by existing status perceptions as well, to the extent that the evaluation criteria contain ambiguity. Third, the resulting interpretation and evaluation will then be encoded in memory, if the evaluation suggests that the contribution merits encoding. As the team uses the information from different members, each member's contributions contain information based on the above process. Thus, both motivational and cognitive biases are likely to be apparent in overall team interaction.

If status disagreements exist within the team, we would expect the following outcomes. As incongruence in status beliefs increases, more behaviors will be labeled as illegitimate by team members (inconsistent with an individual's status role). Members will also be more likely to per-

ceive that the legitimacy of their beliefs, affect, and behavior is being challenged (Ravlin, et al., 2000). If the status structure is perceived as unstable, members will demonstrate some form of non-acceptance. In general, they may either attempt to gain more status for themselves or their sub-group (individuals high in self-perceived status and self-esteem, subgroups in a numerical majority), or may become passive because they don't know with whom they should try to affiliate themselves (individuals lower in self-perceived status and self-esteem, subgroups in a numerical minority; see also Blalock, 1957). Conflict will tend to be destructive, as opposed to constructive (e.g., Amason, 1996), because members do not agree on a status hierarchy for resolving differences of opinion, and consensus will be difficult to achieve.

Based on their lack of co-location, identification with virtual teams is more difficult to develop (Driskell, et al., 2003). Therefore, individual motives for self-enhancement and uncertainty reduction are less likely to be met by membership in a virtual team, and the processes of in-group favoritism and out-group distancing may well be exercised in reference to other social aggregations or sub-groups within the team. This lessened degree of identification should reduce the extent to which favoritism based on virtual team membership should occur. Unfortunately, in this context, location, nationality, functional area, or other salient categorizations may act as the source of self-enhancement and uncertainty reduction, leading to a lack of desire to communicate fully with other sub-groups and to form positive relationships with members of these out-groups, and a tendency to develop practices that are unique to the sub-group rather than the virtual unit.

Because of the overload of messages and information produced by technology-mediated communication, sub-groupings are likely to form an important screening device for processing messages and their attendant influence attempts. Technology-based media have reached a point where at any given moment, individuals have the ability to communicate with anyone, as long as that potential partner is receptive. In this situation, it would appear to be somewhat less likely that status barriers will fall as opposed to being maintained. As research suggests that demographic group separation is in part self-chosen, and that people connect across these barriers when "forced" to do so in the context of work or school (Martin & Ross-Gordon, 1990), the ability to communicate with essentially infinite numbers of other partners at any moment in time should increase the likelihood that individuals continue to communicate with members of their in-group or with those of higher status in an effort at self-enhancement. In the meantime, those of higher status may be targeted by many communications from below (see Blau, 1977, for example). A variety of technological screening devices allows these higher status individuals to quickly screen these lesser members out.

In cognitive and motivational terms, even the best intentions may lead team members to determine that they cannot process all the information that comes across their desktops, and to come up with rules for accessing or discarding messages based on the personal utility of the items. The perception of utility, of course, is driven primarily by the sender (via caller id, email identifications) and topic (when available). A key point to note is that these communications can now be eliminated based on sender without accessing them at all (email, smart voicemail, incoming calls and texts). Automatic processing (Bargh & Ferguson, 2000) may enhance this effect with very little cognitive or physical effort or input on the part of the screener, thus reducing the amount of information that must be processed. Both technological and human characteristics suggest that this trend should continue as technology evolves to support fully mobile collaborative efforts.

Status Characteristics Theory is based on the assumption that team members are strongly, if not entirely, task motivated. Thus, influence goes

to the most competent of teammates once these individuals are identified, and presumably, communications should be processed accordingly, with preference going to those that can best help with task accomplishment. However, if the team itself is not the locus of social identity, the success of the team, as opposed to a sub-group of the team, may be unimportant to individual members, and they may be motivated, not to identify input that is best for the team as a whole, but for the sub-group with which they identify. Beyond this motivational issue, we also know that performance is difficult to measure, and typically is more so at a distance. Members may be distracted by technological expertise, such that those who are good at using the technology, but not necessarily providing great task input, are accorded more influence (Anderson, McEwan, Bal, & Carletta, 2007). In addition, of course, member performance evaluations are likely to be biased by in-group favoritism (here, often based on sub-groupings). Therefore, virtual team members are disadvantaged in identifying their best contributors by the ambiguity of performance data and by biased information processing.

As noted above, technological developments that allow for visual, and in some cases life-sized, images have become more commonplace. These developments reintroduce the external status characteristics, turn-taking, and conformity pressures that early researchers noted were missing in technologically-mediated work communication. It should be noted, however, that these media (traditional video-conferencing, tele-presence systems, and VOIP) do *not* provide a constant presence, as sharing a location does. These tools may at times reinforce the irritations created by communicating with different others (from other sub-groups). They may require a specific meeting time, location, and more controlled social behavior than is typical in the rest of the work day. What media are available at a given location may also have implications for status (e.g., everyone with the exception of those at a specific site is available visually). While social presence (Short, et al., 1976) may require members to consider and potentially work on the relationships they have with distant others, this may be regarded as something of an intrusion on the work day, and is not fully comparable to working in the presence of an individual on a daily basis. A key issue to be considered is whether the focus of these visual meetings is on commonalities or differences, and if the focus is on differences, whether the emphasis lies on finding solutions or paths to agreement. How practices regarding such meetings evolve may determine whether they help to enhance feelings of identity among the aggregate as a whole, or whether they actually reinforce distinctions between subgroups.

In sum, it may be that early research was somewhat biased toward more equal participation by not only the limitations of the technology of the time, but also the typically experimental nature of the studies. In today's virtual work environment, the development of relationships between virtual partners is considered to be of such great importance, it is often recommended that face-to-face meetings occur at the initial start-up phase of virtual projects, and beyond this expensive alternative, purely social communication is also suggested as part of a bonding process between teammates. These tactics, of course, also open the door to typical interpersonal relationships based in part on knowledge of others' social identity and status characteristics.

SOLUTIONS AND RECOMMENDATIONS

This approach to understanding status organizing processes in virtual environments suggests that teams that either fail to extend influence beyond the typical high status participants, or to share a view of the status hierarchy, will not, of their own accord, solve their problems over time, but instead need training and guidance on developing appropriate interaction processes (Thomas, 1999).

Organizations are, of course, not helpless in the face of psychological and sociological forces on behavior. However, it would be a mistake to assume that technological communication tools will enhance access to the power structure on the part of lower status participants without active management of the process. Some approaches to helping virtual workers establish positive communications, relationships, and performance practices are provided below.

Recent research in the area of virtual work points to several opportunities for organizations to improve the function of their distance collaborations. Establishing a strong virtual team identity should aid in increasing communication among the team members and between sub-groups. The task and its accomplishment should ideally be the focus of this identity. Procedural justice appears to be a central determinant of the formation of positive social identity in virtual teams (Hakonen & Lipponen, 2004). Procedural justice is supported by having a clear understanding of what each member of the collaboration is to contribute, and why (i.e., abilities, availability, or other factors). In particular, members may not be aware of the resource limitations that exist for teammates at other sites, either in terms of the time they have available to dedicate to the joint task, or with regard to technological resources for task and communication activities. This lack of awareness may lead to negative beliefs about non-collocated members' motivation or competence that are unjustified.

Providing some opportunities for face-to-face interaction (mixed modality models) appears to be more successful in developing satisfaction and cohesion than purely virtual interaction (Gajendran & Harrison, 2007). Allowing for, and even encouraging, social interaction is important in assisting virtual partners to find commonalities and joint interests, and further, to better understand the conditions they face, either in another company location, or while travelling. As noted above, it is often assumed that all members of the aggregate have the same access to equipment and information, but although this may be the trend, it is by no means a uniform condition. Sharing such information in casual conversation is a useful way for members to develop a broader picture of the available resources and limitations faced by their teammates. In addition, these casual "conversations" remove some of the artificiality, imposed by structured meetings held using visual media, in particular standard video conferencing and tele-presence meetings. Richer media appear to increase cohesion (Hambley, O'Neill, & Kline, 2007), but managers do not always understand that "richer" communication also must include the personal and socio-emotional communication that is central to facilitating relationship building among members (Hart & McLeod, 2003).

Increased leadership behaviors within the team may also facilitate performance (Carte, Chidambaram, & Becker, 2006). Each member can be tasked with aiding in the development of norms for cooperation, inclusion, and recognition of member differences. These norms appear to be particularly important when the aggregate is dependent on less rich media such as email (Rosen, Furst, & Blackburn, 2007; Dekker, Rutte, & Van den Berg, 2008; Naquin, Kurtzburg, & Belkin, 2008). When responsibility for inclusion is distributed among members, the natural tendencies to limit communication to known or high-status sources can be overcome.

An understanding of the relationship between source (majority, minority) and valence of messages and the extent of influence will also be key to effecting change (Martin & Hewstone, 2003), given that individuals have been shown to behave differently when the source of identical information is either minority or majority (in-group or out-group). If negative information about progress on the task is provided by a smaller or more distant site, this information may well be considered subsidiary to more positive information from a larger sub-group. This tendency is potentially dangerous to task achievement, and negates the positive aspects of heterogeneous composition

of work teams. General diversity training may also be of benefit to limit or potentially overcome this influence of status organizing processes and in-group/out-group biases.

Ultimately, these findings can be utilized as levers in the continuing effort to provide avenues for input from all members. However, more research is needed to more fully understand how these practices can improve effectiveness in virtual decision making.

FUTURE RESEARCH DIRECTIONS

Research on technologically-mediated communication has thus far been based primarily on the foundations of media richness and social presence. With rapidly changing potential for both richness and social presence, more research is needed on how these advances affect communication practices. Do tele-presence systems create effects similar to face-to-face meetings? Does this then maintain typical status influence processes? How does mobility affect work? Can individuals be as productive in their collaborative efforts using mobile devices and as they travel frequently? A major issue to be considered is the immediacy with which information is available. In today's environment, and considering today's workers, expectations tend to be that information can be instantaneously shared, that work partners be constantly available, and that a bias toward immediate action is always a positive approach. The more immediately decisions are anticipated, the more important the status processes that give rise to those decisions become. As speed in decision making is typically increased when an individual decision maker acts alone, this raises a problematic issue. As collaborations become increasingly virtual, and the demands for action become more salient, will the high status individual refer decisions to the collaborative, or tend to make them him/herself? Clearly, effectiveness will be strongly affected by the answers to such questions.

CONCLUSION

This chapter addresses important issues in the future of virtual collaborations, in that the general expectation is that technology-mediated communication has the opportunity to provide influence to marginalized or under-represented groups in organizational decisions. Here, I note several reasons why this equalization of influence should not be expected. The nature of distance collaboration is changing, such that there is a reintroduction of factors that lead to status hierarchies in face-to-face groups. Basic cognitive, socio-emotional, and motivational processes tend to mitigate against the abandonment of status hierarchies. In an imperfect world, we have imperfect information about what causes high performance, and who has the best capabilities. In general, individuals are likely to continue to use heuristics based on social identity processes to determine who should have influence, and further, in virtual environments may have more difficulty agreeing on whom should have more significant decision input. Ultimately, managers are not off the hook, that is, they cannot depend on technology to sort out this problem of influence. Instead, more active management is called for in developing practices of open communication, procedurally just norms for behavior, and enhancing a positive social identity for the virtual collaborative.

REFERENCES

Allen, T. J. (1977). *Managing the flow of technology: Technology transfer and the dissemination of technological information within the R&D organization.* Cambridge, MA: MIT Press.

Amason, A. (1996). Distinguishing the effects of functional and dysfunctional conflict on strategic decision making: Resolving a paradox for top management teams. *Academy of Management Journal, 39*, 123–148. doi:10.2307/256633

Anderson, A. H., McEwan, R., Bal, J., & Carletta, J. (2007). Virtual team meetings: An analysis of communication and context. *Computers in Human Behavior, 23*, 2558–2580. doi:10.1016/j.chb.2007.01.001

Anson, R., & Munkvold, B. E. (2004). Beyond face-to-face: A field study of electronic meetings in different time and place modes. *Journal of Organizational Computing and Electronic Commerce, 14*, 127–152. doi:10.1207/s15327744joce1402_03

Bargh, J. A., & Ferguson, M. J. (2000). Beyond behaviorism: On the automaticity of higher mental processes. *Psychological Bulletin, 126*, 925–945. doi:10.1037/0033-2909.126.6.925

Berger, J., Cohen, B. P., & Zelditch, M. Jr. (1972). Status characteristics and social interaction. *American Sociological Review, 37*, 241–255. doi:10.2307/2093465

Berger, J., Rosenholtz, S. J., & Zelditch, M. Jr. (1980). Status organizing processes. *Annual Review of Sociology, 6*, 479–508. doi:10.1146/annurev.so.06.080180.002403

Bixoux, T. (2009). Making connections. *BizEd*, January/February, 16-22.

Blalock, H. (1957). Percent non-white and discrimination in the South. *American Sociological Review, 22*, 677–682. doi:10.2307/2089197

Blau, P. M. (1977). *Inequality and heterogeneity.* New York: Free Press.

Bordia, P., DiFonzo, N., & Chang, A. (1999). Rumor as group problem solving: Development patterns in informal computer-mediated groups. *Small Group Research, 30*, 8–28. doi:10.1177/104649649903000102

Byrne, D. (1971). *The attraction paradigm.* New York: Academic Press.

Carlson, J. R., & Zmud, R. W. (1999). Channel expansion theory and the experiential nature of media richness perceptions. *Academy of Management Journal, 42*, 153–170. doi:10.2307/257090

Carte, T. A., Chidambaram, L., & Becker, A. (2006). Emergent leadership in self-managed virtual teams. *Group Decision and Negotiation, 15*, 323–343. doi:10.1007/s10726-006-9045-7

Cohen, B. P., & Zhou, X. (1991). Status processes in enduring work groups. *American Sociological Review, 56*, 179–188. doi:10.2307/2095778

Conway, M., Pizzamiglio, M. T., & Mount, L. (1996). Status, communality, and agency: Implications for stereotypes of gender and other groups. *Journal of Personality and Social Psychology, 71*, 25–38. doi:10.1037/0022-3514.71.1.25

Daft, R. L., & Lengel, R. H. (1986). Organizational information requirements, media richness, and structural design. *Management Science, 32*, 554–571. doi:10.1287/mnsc.32.5.554

Dekker, D. M., Rutte, C. G., & Van den Berg, P. T. (2008). Cultural differences in the perception of critical interaction behaviors in global virtual teams. *International Journal of Intercultural Relations, 32*, 441–452. doi:10.1016/j.ijintrel.2008.06.003

Driskell, J. E., Radtke, P. H., & Salas, E. (2003). Virtual teams: Effects of technological mediation on team performance. *Group Dynamics, 7*, 297–323. doi:10.1037/1089-2699.7.4.297

Fisek, M. H., Berger, J., & Norman, R. Z. (1995). Evaluations and the formation of expectations. *American Journal of Sociology, 101*, 721–746. doi:10.1086/230758

Fisek, M. H., & Ofshe, R. (1970). The process of status evolution. *Sociometry, 33*, 327–346. doi:10.2307/2786161

Gajendran, R. S., & Harrison, D. A. (2007). The good, the bad, and the unknown about telecommuting: Meta-analysis of psychological mediators and individual consequences. *The Journal of Applied Psychology, 92*, 1524–1541. doi:10.1037/0021-9010.92.6.1524

Hakonen, M., & Lipponen, J. (2008). Procedural justice and identification with virtual teams: The moderating role of face-to-face meetings and geographical dispersion. *Social Justice Research, 21*, 164–178. doi:10.1007/s11211-008-0070-3

Hambley, L. A., O'Neill, T. A., & Kline, T. B. (2007). Virtual team leadership: The effects of leadership style and communication medium on team interaction styles and outcomes. *Organizational Behavior and Human Decision Processes, 103*, 1–20. doi:10.1016/j.obhdp.2006.09.004

Hart, R. K., & McLeod, P. L. (2003). Rethinking team building in geographically dispersed teams: One message at a time. *Organizational Dynamics, 31*, 352–361. doi:10.1016/S0090-2616(02)00131-6

Harvey, M., Novicevic, M. M., & Garrison, G. (2004). Challenges to staffing global virtual teams. *Human Resource Management Review, 14*, 275–294. doi:10.1016/j.hrmr.2004.06.005

Hogg, M. A., & Terry, D. J. (2000). Social identity and self-categorization processes in organizational contexts. *Academy of Management Review, 25*, 121–140. doi:10.2307/259266

Kiesler, S., Siegel, J., & McGuire, T. W. (1984). Social psychological aspects of computer-mediated communication. *The American Psychologist, 39*, 1123–1134. doi:10.1037/0003-066X.39.10.1123

Knottnerus, J. D. (1988). A critique of expectation states theory: Theoretical assumptions and models of social cognition. *Sociological Perspectives, 31*, 420–445.

Lewis, J. D., & Weigart, A. (1985). Trust as a social reality. *Social Forces, 63,* 967–985. doi:10.2307/2578601

Marques, J. M., Abrams, D., Paez, D., & Hogg, M. A. (2001). Social categorization, social identification and rejection of deviant group members . In Hogg, M. A., & Tindale, R. S. (Eds.), *Blackwell handbook of social psychology: Group Processes* (*Vol. 3,* pp. 400–424). Oxford: Blackwell. doi:10.1002/9780470998458.ch17

Martin, L. G., & Ross-Gordon, J. M. (1990). Cultural diversity in the workplace: Managing a multicultural workforce. *New Directions for Adult and Continuing Education, 48,* 45–54. doi:10.1002/ace.36719904806

Martin, R., & Hewstone, M. (2003). Majority versus minority influence: When, not whether, source status instigates heuristic or systematic processing. *European Journal of Social Psychology, 33,* 313–330. doi:10.1002/ejsp.146

Martins, L. L., Gilson, L. L., & Maynard, M. T. (2004). Virtual teams: What do we know and where do we go from here? *Journal of Management, 30,* 805–835. doi:10.1016/j.jm.2004.05.002

McLeod, P. L., Baron, R. S., Marti, M. W., & Yoon, K. (1997). The eyes have it: Minority influence in face-to-face and computer-mediated group discussion. *The Journal of Applied Psychology, 82,* 706–718. doi:10.1037/0021-9010.82.5.706

Miller, C. C. (2009). Sharing consumers' tastes in cellphone web surfing. *New York Times,* Retrieved February 23, 2009 from http://www.nytimes.com/2009/02/23/technology/23buzz.html?th=&emc=th&pagewanted=print.

Naquin, C. E., Kurtzburg, T. R., & Belkin, L. Y. (2008). E-mail communication and group cooperation in mixed motive contexts. *Social Justice Research, 21,* 470–489. doi:10.1007/s11211-008-0084-x

Ravlin, E. C., & Thomas, D. C. (2005). Status and stratification processes in organizational life. *Journal of Management, 31,* 966–987. doi:10.1177/0149206305279898

Ravlin, E. C., Thomas, D. C., & Ilsev, A. (2000). Beliefs about values, status, and legitimacy in multicultural groups: Influences on intragroup conflict. In P.C. Earley & H. Singh (Eds.), Innovations in international and cross-cultural management (pp. 17-51). Thousand Oaks, CA: Sage.

Reid, S. A., & Hogg, M. A. (2005). Uncertainty reduction, self enhancement, and ingroup identification. *Personality and Social Psychology Bulletin, 31,* 804–817. doi:10.1177/0146167204271708

Rosen, B., Furst, S., & Blackburn, R. (2007). Overcoming barriers to knowledge sharing in virtual teams. *Organizational Dynamics, 36,* 259–273. doi:10.1016/j.orgdyn.2007.04.007

Shils, E. (1975). *Center and periphery: Essays in macrosociology.* Chicago: University of Chicago Press.

Short, J., Williams, E., & Christie, B. (1976). *The social psychology of telecommunications.* New York: Wiley.

Sidanius, J., Pratto, F., & Rabinowitz, J. L. (1994). Gender, ethnic status, and ideological asymmetry. *Journal of Cross-Cultural Psychology, 25,* 194–216. doi:10.1177/0022022194252003

Tajfel, H. (1978). *Differentiation between social groups.* London: Academic Press.

Tajfel, H., & Turner, J. C. (1986). The social identity theory of intergroup behavior . In Worchel, S., & Austin, W. G. (Eds.), *Psychology of intergroup relations* (2nd ed., pp. 7–24). Chicago: Nelson-Hall.

Thomas, D. C. (1999). Cultural diversity and work group effectiveness: An experimental study. *Journal of Cross-Cultural Psychology, 30,* 242–263. doi:10.1177/0022022199030002006

Wallace, P. (2004). *The internet in the workplace: How new technology is transforming work*. New York: Cambridge University Press.

Ward, C., Leong, C.-H., & Low, M. (2004). Personality and sojourner adjustment: An exploration of the Big Five and the cultural fit proposition. *Journal of Cross-Cultural Psychology, 35*, 137–151. doi:10.1177/0022022103260719

Zelditch, M. Jr, & Walker, H. A. (1989). Legitimacy and the stability of authority. *Advances in Group Processes, 1*, 1–25.

Zigurs, I., Poole, M. S., & DeSanctis, G. L. (1988). A study of influence in computer-mediated group decision making. *Management Information Systems Quarterly, 12*, 625–644. doi:10.2307/249136

ADDITIONAL READING

Bowers, C., Salas, E., & Jentsch, F. (2006). *Creating high-tech teams: Practical guidance on work performance and technology*. Washington, DC: American Psychological Association. doi:10.1037/11263-000

Cascio, W. F. (2000). Managing a virtual workplace. *The Academy of Management Executive, 14*, 81–90.

Duarte, D. L., & Snyder, N. T. (1999). *Mastering virtual teams*. San Francisco: Jossey-Bass.

Maznevski, M. L., & Chudoba, K. M. (2000). Briding space over time: Global virtual team dynamics and effectiveness. *Organization Science, 11*, 473–492. doi:10.1287/orsc.11.5.473.15200

Olson, M. H. (Ed.). (1989). *Technological support for work group collaboration*. Hillsdale, NJ: Lawrence Erlbaum Associates.

Staples, D. S., & Zhao, L. (2006). The effects of cultural diversity in virtual teams versus face-to-face teams. *Group Decision and Negotiation, 15*, 389–406. doi:10.1007/s10726-006-9042-x

Walther, J. B. (1995). Relational aspects of computer-mediated communication: Experimental observations over time. *Organization Science, 6*, 186–203. doi:10.1287/orsc.6.2.186

Webster, J., & Wong, W. K. P. (2008). Comparing traditional and virtual group forms: Identity, communication, and trust in naturally occurring project teams. *International Journal of Human Resource Management, 19*, 41–62.

Weisband, S. (Ed.). (2008). *Leadership at a distance: Research in technologically supported work*. New York: Lawrence Erlbaum Associates.

Chapter 9
Sense of Community in Professional Virtual Communities

Anita Blanchard
University of North Carolina at Charlotte, USA

David A. Askay
University of North Carolina at Charlotte, USA

Katherine A. Frear
University of North Carolina at Charlotte, USA

ABSTRACT

Sense of virtual community (feelings of identity, belonging, and attachment) is an essential component of virtual communities. In this chapter, we develop a model of how sense of virtual community develops in professional virtual communities. Based on sense of virtual community models in social virtual communities, we expect that the exchange of support, development of a group identity, and group norms will lead to a stronger professional sense of virtual community. Unlike social virtual communities, we also predict that employee/members occupational identification will increase professional sense of virtual community, particularly when the virtual community can provide support and information not available in the employee/member's face-to-face life. Finally, we propose that increased occupational commitment, professional networks, and employee performance are outcomes of sense of virtual community in professional virtual communities.

INTRODUCTION

Virtual communities are groups of people who interact primarily through information and communication technologies (ICT). Virtual communities and other virtual groups have existed since the mid

1980's for people both at work (Finholt & Sproull, 1988; Sproull & Kiesler, 1986) and in their social lives (Rheingold, 1993). They exist over a wide variety of ICT, including forums such as bulletin boards and newsgroups, listservs, and even blogs (Blanchard, 2004a; Ren, Kraut, & Kiesler, 2007). Even newer social networking sites (e.g., Facebook,

DOI: 10.4018/978-1-61520-979-8.ch009

Twitter) have the potential to support virtual communities and other forms of virtual groups.

An essential characteristic of virtual communities is the members' sense of virtual community (SOVC) (Blanchard, 2008; Blanchard & Markus, 2004; De Koster & Houtman, 2008; Koh & Kim, 2003). SOVC is defined as the member's feelings of identity, belonging, and attachment with each other in their online groups. The SOVC construct is based on the sense of community (SOC) in face-to-face (FtF) groups (McMillan & Chavis, 1986). SOC has a long history as an essential component of community psychology research (Chavis & Pretty, 1999; Obst & White, 2007; Sarason, 1974) and has strong theoretical support and growing empirical base of research. Researchers have also found that SOC is important in organizations and may have a positive relationship with organizational commitment and job satisfaction (Burroughs & Eby, 1998). SOVC, therefore, may have high relevance to organizational virtual communities.

SOVC is considered a positive development for a group and its members. Like SOC, SOVC is believed to lead to outcomes such as longer membership tenure in the group, more problem-focused coping behavior, more activity, and greater social capital both in the virtual community and in members' FtF communities (Blanchard, 2004b; Burroughs & Eby, 1998; McMillan & Chavis, 1986).

SOVC, therefore, can help distinguish virtual communities from mere virtual groups. Virtual communities, as opposed to virtual groups, should have members who participate longer and more frequently, who work to solve the community's problems and who are more likely to share support and trust both in and outside of the virtual community. As will be discussed below, virtual communities should have many-to-many communications in which members continually share information and support. Virtual groups are more likely to have one-to-many communications or have more limited group interactions. The key

difference remains the development of a sense of virtual community (or not) for the members.

Previous research has primarily examined SOVC in social virtual communities. These virtual communities focus on a wide variety of topics including hobbies (e.g., gardening, Honda motorcycles, marathon training), special interests (e.g., movie reviews, parenting), or even health issues (e.g., cancer, infertility). While this line of research is informative, it may not be entirely applicable to the growing number of professional virtual communities.

Professional virtual communities are composed of employees or free-lance professionals who interact through ICT about topics related to their paid work. Professional virtual communities include employees of particular companies (e.g., Disney, Radio Shack) who discuss employment policies, problems, and experiences at their particular company as well as employees from a broad range of organizations employed in a particular profession (e.g., bankers, human resource professionals, freelance writers and even medical doctors). They likely differ from social virtual communities because of the members' valid concerns about their participation affecting their professional reputations (Constant, Sproull, & Kiesler, 1996)—either in general or coming back to their employing organization—or members' increased potential to interact FtF in professional conferences.

This chapter will focus on the latter type of professional virtual communities: virtual communities that support employees who identify with a particular profession. First, these virtual communities are likely to discuss particular topics unique to their professions making them more similar to the social virtual communities which have been more extensively researched. For example, virtual communities of bankers will focus on banking issues like virtual communities of marathon trainers that focus on training issues. We suggest that models of the antecedents and outcomes of SOVC for social virtual communities

Figure 1. Model of sense of virtual community in professional virtual communities

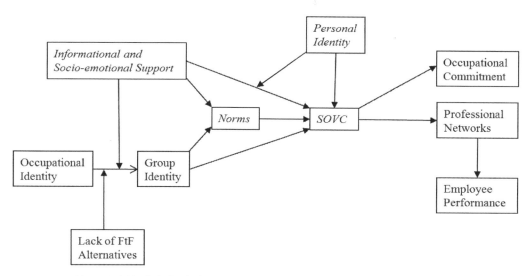

Note: Variables in italics indicate the previous SOVC model for social virtual communities.

should be more easily transferrable to these types of professional virtual communities.

Second, these professional virtual communities may have significant yet under-studied benefits to the employing organization. For example, the information and support exchanged within these professional virtual communities could provide new and innovative work practices that the employee-members can use in their own jobs (Constant, et al., 1996; Haythornwaite, 2002; Pickering, 1995). This development of social capital in the professional virtual community could have quite positive effects for the organization (Adler & Kwon, 2002; Bergquist & Ljungberg, 2001; Nahapiet & Ghoshal, 1998; Wasko & Faraj, 2005).

The goal of this chapter will be to extend the research on SOVC to properly account for professional virtual communities. We develop a model that will build upon theories and research which have examined SOVC in social virtual communities and will expand this model to account for the particulars of professional virtual communities. In particular, this model will give attention to the stronger professional identities that members of professional virtual communities may have as well

as how these virtual communities affect employees and their employing organizations.

BACKGROUND

Previous research on the antecedents of group outcomes similar to SOVC in social groups has demonstrated the importance of (a) the exchange of information and socio-emotional support,(b) the development of identity within the virtual community including both group identity and personal identity; and (c) the perception of norms (Blanchard, 2008; Blanchard & Markus, 2004; De Koster & Houtman, 2008; Michinov, Michinov, & Toczek-Capelle, 2004; Ren, et al., 2007; Spears, Lea, & Postmes, 2007). This section will review that literature and advance it to account for professional virtual communities.

Informational and Socio-Emotional Support

Exchanging informational and socio-emotional support is an important—if not essential—behavior in virtual communities (Baym, 1997; Ro-thaermel & Sugiyama, 2001; Wellman & Guilia, 1999). Members exchange support in a variety of ways in these groups. Support may be actively exchanged publicly in posts for the entire group to read or may occur privately through emails exchanged behind the scenes. Support may also be passively exchanged when members read others' exchanges, but do not participate in exchange the support themselves. Wellman and Gulia (1999) have argued that the public exchange of support may increase members' perceptions of being a supportive group when, in fact, few people are actually involved in the supportive exchange. Thus, there is a perception that the group is very supportive, even if only a few of the members actually help each other. Yet, because everyone can read the message, all group members benefit from the support exchange even if they were not active in creating it.

Using social exchange theory and theories about the norms of reciprocity, previous research has demonstrated that both participating in the exchange of support and observing the exchange of support by others are positively related to SOVC in social virtual communities (Blanchard, 2008; Blanchard & Markus, 2004; De Koster & Hout-man, 2008). The relationship between actively participating in the exchange of support and SOVC has been stronger than SOVC's relationship with passively observing support exchanges, but both relationships are independently related to SOVC in social virtual communities.

We expect that the exchange of socio-emotional and informational support will also be important for professional virtual communities (Ridings & Gefen, 2004). There may, however, be a shift in both the prevalence and importance of the types of support. For example, in some social virtual communities (e.g., health virtual communities), socio-emotional support may be as important or even more important than informational support. In professional groups, we expect informational support to be the primary form of support exchanged.

This reliance on informational support could have slightly detrimental effects on professional SOVC. Socio-emotional support may more easily create emotional bonds that tie the members together in a virtual community. However, some social virtual communities (e.g., gardening, Honda motorcycle enthusiasts) are also likely to put a premium on informational support over emotional support. They nonetheless remain virtual communities. For example, a virtual gardening community member may be less interested in receiving sympathy that aphids have destroyed his or her garden and more interested in receiving information about how to kill them. Similarly, a human resources professional will be more in learning about particular interpretations of employment law instead of sympathy for dealing with a difficult employee. Therefore, we expect social exchange of support, particularly informational support, to continue to have a positive relationship to professional SOVC. Exchanges of socio-emotional support will play an important—if somewhat weaker—role in professional virtual communities as compared to social virtual communities.

Identity

Identity issues have always had a prominent role in online research. Two important identity issues that often arise are (1) group identity, the feelings of belonging and membership in a group, and (2) personal identity, the ability to recognize and feel recognized by other members of the group. We will first consider group identity in the development of SOVC and then personal identity.

Occupational vs. Group Identity

To begin our discussion of group identity, we first want to present the differences between a super-ordinate identity (i.e., a social identity) and a sub-ordinate identity (i.e., a group identity). Although there are similarities between these two forms of identity (Hogg, Abrams, Otten, &

Hinkle, 2004), there are also differences which are important to our model.

Super-ordinate identities involve societal level groups. This can include identity with diffuse individual characteristics (e.g., gender, ethnicity, college alumnus), identity with a particular professional or occupational group (e.g., human resource professional, doctor, freelance writer), identity with hobbies and interests (e.g., marathoner, Harley Davidson rider, gardener), or even with health or family issues (e.g., cancer survivor, new mother, diabetic). The distinguishing feature of super-ordinate groups is that the members do not generally interact with each other and cannot interact with other as a whole. Nonetheless, these groups are very important to an individual's social identity (Hogg, et al., 2004; Meyer, Becker, & Van Dick, 2006), that is, her or his super-ordinate identity. For professional virtual communities, the super-ordinate identity is their members' occupational identity. This is defined as the set of central and distinctive characteristics that individuals use to define themselves in terms of their work (Ashforth & Kreiner, 1999). When we refer to super-ordinate identity in professional virtual communities, we mean the shared occupational identity for the members of the group.

Sub-ordinate identity is related to specific groups where the members interact with one another. These groups may be focused around the same super-ordinate groups listed above (i.e., individual characteristics, professional groups, hobbies and health concerns), but the members of these groups can and do interact with each other. A main difference, then, is that sub-ordinate identity is attached to a particular interacting group, even though it is likely to be related to the super-ordinate identity. For example, a doctor may feel like a member of a local professional group, but his or her overall identity as a "doctor" has not diminished. On the other hand, freelance writers may identify as a people who seeks writing assignments from a group of publications, but also be attached to the regular, local writing group that helps them improve their writing and networking skills.

In this chapter, we focus on the sub-ordinate identity of professional virtual communities, that is, group identity. We highlight this because we have noted that researchers often use the term "identity" when they are referring both to non-interacting groups (i.e., super-ordinate identity) was well as interacting groups (i.e., sub-ordinate identity). We are interested in interacting groups in order to understand what contributes to their group's professional SOVC.

In addition, the members' shared occupational identity may benefit professional virtual communities in comparison to social virtual communities. Members of social virtual communities may share little beyond the group's topic of interest. These virtual community members may over-interpret cues and perceive more similarity than is actually there, creating hyperpersonal relationships which may not last over time (Walther, 1996). Members of professional virtual communities, on the other hand, are more likely to share real educational, socio-economical, and even knowledge, skills, and abilities, as well as day-to-day work experiences. Thus, their shared occupational identities will increase the development and perception of shared norms of behavior (Hogg, et al., 2004), a very important component of SOVC (Blanchard, 2008; McMillan & Chavis, 1986). Thus, members' occupational identity should be an important antecedent to group identity in professional virtual communities.

However, this relationship is likely to be more complex than a simple, direct antecedent. Otherwise, everyone who has a strong occupational identity would likely to have a strong group identity with the professional virtual community. This is obviously not true. Many members who identify strongly with their occupation are not strongly identified with any professional virtual community. We propose two moderators to this relationship. First, we consider whether the individual has FtF alternatives for which he or she can draw upon professional advice and information. The lack of FtF alternatives has played an important role why people become involved in social and virtual communities (McKenna & Green, 2002; Weis, et al., 2003). The lack of FtF support and interaction for a professional could explain why members move from a super-ordinate to an online group specific identity. Indeed, it may play a more important role for professional virtual communities because of the flexibility of participation in the online groups. For example, members may be able to participate in the online group while still working during work hours as opposed to having to leave work for a few hours to attend a monthly luncheon or dinner.

In addition, we also suggest that the usefulness of the group, particularly, the value of the informational and socio-emotional exchange, will moderate the relationship between occupational identity and group identity. Optimal matching theory suggests that certain types of support are more beneficial for certain types of stressors (Cutrona & Russell, 1990). This theory applies here when professionals view the support from the group to be appropriate to their needs. Then they are more likely to identify with the group starting the process by which they develop a professional SOVC.

Research on optimal matching theory in health virtual communities supports both our moderators. First, it suggests that members participate more in an online group if they receive specific support that they value, but particularly when they cannot find that support FtF (Turner, Grube, & Meyers, 2001). If professionals find that the group provides the information and support they need, they are more likely to find the group attractive and to identify with the group. If the group does not meet the professional's needs, then he or she is less likely to develop a subordinate identity from his or her super-ordinate identity.

Now that we have proposed a relationship between occupational identity and group identity within professional virtual communities, we turn our attention to the outcomes of group identity. There is a substantial amount of empirical and theoretical research which considers group identity as the antecedent to other group outcomes; it finds that as members develop a stronger identity with each other in the group, they will experience stronger positive group outcomes, such as commitment, and group trust. (Postmes, Spears, Lee, & Novak, 2005; Ren, et al., 2007; Spears, et al., 2007; Tanis & Postmes, 2005). Previous researchers have not explicitly examined SOVC or professional SOVC. Nonetheless, we think it is reasonable that like group identity and SOC in FtF groups (Omoto & Malsch, 2005), there should be a strong positive relationship between group identity and professional SOVC.

Some of the research on online group identity outcomes, particularly by Postmes and his colleagues, has previously argued that online group members must remain completely anonymous in order to develop a group identity; otherwise individuation of group members will occur and the salience of group identity will break down. While this may have been true in laboratory experiments conducted in chatrooms, this mode of reasoning is no longer appropriate. Today's technologies have a wide variety of anonymity reducing technological features that indicate personalization in the virtual community (e.g., profiles, photos, signature files). Indeed, people who interact in FtF groups are not anonymous by definition and yet these groups still have a group identity. Other researchers (Ren, et al., 2007) and even Postmes himself (Postmes, et al., 2005) has started to examine group identity with the use of technology identity cues that contribute to personal identity.

Personal Identity

The lack of cues to communicators' identities was one of the first areas of research that focused on group relations (Constant, et al., 1996; Sproull & Kiesler, 1986). While cues to personal identity still remain of interest, technological features have changed so that communicators are much less likely to be anonymous to each other (Ren, et al., 2007; Walther, Slovacek, & Tidwell, 2001). Communicators are more likely to have avatars—pictures which may be real pictures of themselves or feature some characteristic about themselves; signature files—which can contain personal information relevant to the group and witticisms, their real names, and other ways to contact the communicator in "real life." All of these cues allow for communicators to make impressions of others in the group as well as allow them to make impressions about themselves to project to others.

Information about others' identities can also come from the messages that members write and exchange (Blanchard & Markus, 2004). These messages, separate from the cues provided by the technology, allow members to determine others' stances on the issues, their sense of humor, and their position or role in the professional virtual community. While members may purposefully attempt to craft their image to have a certain stance, to be witty or to have a particular place in the group, it still implies that members develop perceptions of each other apart from their available technological cues.

Previous research has proposed a direct relationship of personal identity to SOVC in social virtual communities (Blanchard, 2008). This research predicted a positive relationship for both learning others' identity and creating one's own identity to SOVC. However, the results were mixed. Only members' perceptions of creating an identity were directly related to the members' SOVC. This was interpreted to mean that when members felt "known" by and "accepted" in the group, they had a stronger SOVC. Paradoxically, there was no direct relationship from knowing others' identity to SOVC. This may provide some support to Postmes and other's arguments that the individuation of members breaks down group processes. However, as the Blanchard study was the first examination of this hypothesis in "real" virtual communities, more research needs to be conducted. This may be particularly true in professional virtual communities in which professional reputations may be more important than simply being known or identified.

In this paper, we build upon the previous research. We argue that perceptions of knowing others' will be positively related to SOVC. However, perceptions of knowing others will also moderate the relationship between exchanging support and SOVC. That is, forming positive opinions of others in the group and perceiving them as similar to the group will increase these individuals' trustworthiness. Therefore, it should strengthen the relationship between exchanging support and SOVC. The opposite is also true. Perceiving other members of the group as having negative roles and attitudes will decrease their trustworthiness as members of the group and weaken the relationship between exchange of support and SOVC. This will build on the previous research and expand our understanding of how personal identity affects SOVC.

Norms

A final important antecedent of SOVC in social virtual communities is norms. In general, norms within online groups have attracted a great deal of research attention since researchers have recognized virtual groups as a new social entity (Kollock & Smith, 1996; Kraut & Rice, 1998; Postmes, Spears, & Lea, 2000; Postmes, et al., 2005; Sassenberg, 2002) . Norms provide members with implicit rules of behavior. These rules of behavior may be more important in online groups because of the novelty of these groups and the ease with which members can sometimes violate these norms.

Norms are important in FtF SOC (McMillan & Chavis, 1986). In their original model of FtF SOC, McMillan and Chavis (1986) posited that community norms play a significant role in the development of SOC. They argue that as the community becomes more cohesive, there is a greater pressure on the community members to conform.

This pressure creates a consensual validation among the community members, essentially a feeling that "we are alike." This feeling develops into members' SOC. As members more closely adhere to the norms of the community, their bond to the community increases. Thus, development and adherence to norms closely precede SOC in FtF communities.

Previous research demonstrates that the perception of norms within a group has a strong, positive relationship to SOVC in social virtual communities (Blanchard, 2008). This research then supports that SOVC and norms have a similar relationship online as they do FtF. We expect that this relationship will hold in professional virtual communities, too.

We propose that norms will partially mediate the relationship between exchanging support and group identity with professional SOVC. That is, while there is still a direct relationship between social exchanges and SOVC, part of that relationship is also mediated by norms. Past research suggests that social identity processes, as well as social exchange processes, lead to the formation of group norms. In online research on identity and norms, members of naturally forming online groups create and then adhere to group specific norms of behavior (Postmes, et al., 2005). In particular, through learning other members' identity, they inductively create a social identity, and subsequently develop norms about what this group does and what its particular characteristics are (Postmes, et al., 2005).

Similarly, Cropanzano and Mitchell (2005) argue that one of the basic tenets of social exchange theory is that people develop and then are constrained by certain rules of exchange, norms that serve as guidelines for people's interactions. These norms of behavior can develop as people participate in the exchange (Cropanzano & Mitchell, 2005) or by merely watching other people interact (Postmes, et al., 2005). Thus, as members observe and also participate in the exchange of support, they are developing norms of behavior.

Blanchard (2008) found that norms serve as a mediator from exchanging to SOVC. Although the relationship between group identity and norms has been tested (Postmes, et al., 2000; Postmes, et al., 2005; Sassenberg, 2002), norms have not been examined as a mediator between group identity and SOVC. This research will, therefore, expand on our knowledge of group identity, norms and SOVC.

OUTCOMES OF PROFESSIONAL SOVC

In social virtual communities, outcomes include trust for other members of the virtual community and social capital both within the group and extending to members' FtF groups and communities (Blanchard, 2004b). What about the outcomes of interest for SOVC in professional virtual communities? We suggest that there are several positive outcomes that could benefit the employee, the profession, and the organization.

Occupational Commitment

First, members of professional virtual communities may have an increased occupational commitment. Occupational commitment is defined as the commitment to the actual work an employee does (Meyer, Allen, & Smith, 1993). Occupational commitment is independent of organizational commitment and is related to the job an employee performs. Meyer et al., (1993) argue that all employees, not just professionals, can be committed to the work they do above and beyond whatever commitment they feel to their organization.

We suggest that participating in a professional virtual community in which the employee develops feelings of community is likely to lead to higher levels of occupational commitment. By interacting with others in the same occupation (or profession) and developing a professional SOVC, professional virtual community members strengthen their occupational identity and, therefore, strengthen their occupational commitment. In a sense, we are proposing that the group identity and the resulting professional SOVC mediate and amplify the members' occupational commitment. There is currently still some lively debate about the relationship of identity and commitment (Meyer, et al., 2006; Redman & Snape, 2005; Ritekka, 2005; Van Knippenberg & Sleebos, 2006). Nonetheless, experts in the area generally believe that identity comes before commitment. We suggest occupational commitment is also mediated by SOVC.

Professional Networks

There are also benefits to the employee in relation to the profession. Professional virtual community members could also significantly increase their professional social networks through their online activities. Professional social networks are the other employees that an employee can call upon to help with problems or to share work issues. Without participating in a professional virtual community, employees are limited in developing their professional social networks to co-workers or members of their local city or regional professional groups such as the Society for Human Resource Managers (SHRM) local groups. This may be augmented by attending national conferences for their profession (e.g., SHRM's annual national conference).

However, by participating in a professional virtual community, members have the potential to interact with other similar professional from around the country. This could widely increase the contacts a professional has to provide information for his or her job. For some highly active members, this could enhance their professional reputation and improve their prominence in their field. These core members are likely to have their identity known by other group members. They may rise to prominence in a way not possible through traditional FtF professional groups. Indeed, improving one's reputation has been found to be a strong motivator for engaging in knowledge exchange in professional communities (Stewart 2005; Wasko and Faraj, 2005).

Employee Performance

The outcomes of a larger social network are important. However, there are positive outcomes for the employee and the organization beyond just reputation enhancement. Members can increase their professional social capital through these networks (Oh, Chung, & Labianca, 2004; Putnam, 1996; Wellman, Haase, Witte, & Hampton, 2001). This suggests that knowledge and support will travel through the virtual community and improve the employees' performance. The weak ties, that is, the other members of the professional virtual community, can provide additional information that can be used on the employee's job (Constant, et al., 1996; Pickering, 1995). The employee learns of perspectives and solutions that are outside the organization's culture and standard operating procedure. These novel approaches may be especially beneficial to the organization.

Professional virtual communities are, therefore, important for employees and their organization. This is an understudied area despite the growing number of and reliance on professional virtual communities by employees today.

FUTURE RESEARCH DIRECTIONS

Our model implies several streams of research to empirically test it. We suggest the most pressing areas for future research are as follows:

• How does group identity develop from super-ordinate/occupational identity for professional virtual communities? Which potential moderator has the strongest effect on this relationship?

• How strong are the relationships of support, group identity, and personal identity to SOVC in professional virtual communities? How do these relationships compare to previous research in social virtual communities? Does informational support play a stronger role than socio-emotional support? How strong is the moderating effect of personal identity on the relationship between support and SOVC?

- How does SOVC in professional virtual communities affect employee outcomes? How strong is the mediating effect of group identity and SOVC on the relationship between occupational identity and occupational commitment? How strong is the relationship from SOVC to employee performance through the mediator of professional networks?

Researchers may also want to pursue multi-level theories and research methods in studying SOVC in different virtual groups. These theoretical and methodological approaches may be able to take advantage of the contextual features of the virtual communities while still engaging in quantitative methods.

CONCLUSION

We have developed and presented a model which extends the theoretical and empirical research on sense of virtual community in social virtual communities to sense of virtual community in professional virtual communities. Professional virtual communities and the sense of community which develops within them are under-studied yet highly important areas of research in communications, relations, and virtual work.

REFERENCES

Adler, P. S., & Kwon, S.-W. (2002). Social capital: prospects for a new concept. *Academy of Management Review*, 22(1), 17–40. doi:10.2307/4134367

Ashforth, B. E., & Kreiner, G. E. (1999). "How can you do it?": Dirty work and the challenge of constructing a positive identity. *Academy of Management Review*, 24(3), 413–434. doi:10.2307/259134

Baym, N. (1997). Interpreting soap operas and creating community: Inside an electronic fan culture . In Keisler, S. (Ed.), *Culture of the Internet* (pp. 103–120). Manhaw, NJ: Lawrence Erlbaum Associates.

Bergquist, M., & Ljungberg, J. (2001). The power of gifts: Organizing social relationships in open source communities. *Information Systems Journal*, 11(4), 305–320. doi:10.1046/j.1365-2575.2001.00111.x

Blanchard, A. L. (2004a). Blogs as Virtual Communities: Identifying sense of community in the Julie/Julia Project . In Gurak, L., Antonijevic, S., Johnson, L., Ratliff, C., & Reyman, J. (Eds.), *Into the Blogosphere: Rhetoric*. Community and Culture.

Blanchard, A. L. (2004b). The effects of dispersed virtual communities on face-to-face social capital . In Huysman, M., & Wulf, V. (Eds.), *Social Capital and Information Technology* (pp. 53–74). Cambridge: MIT Press.

Blanchard, A. L. (2008). Testing a model of sense of virtual community. *Computers in Human Behavior*, 24(5), 2107–2123. doi:10.1016/j.chb.2007.10.002

Blanchard, A. L., & Markus, M. L. (2004). The experienced "sense" of a virtual community: Characteristics and processes. *The Data Base for Advances in Information Systems*, 35(1), 65–79.

Burroughs, S. M., & Eby, L. T. (1998). Psychological sense of community at work: A measurement system and explanatory framework. *Journal of Community Psychology*, *26*(6), 509–532. doi:10.1002/(SICI)1520-6629(199811)26:6<509::AID-JCOP1>3.0.CO;2-P

Chavis, D. M., & Pretty, G. H. (1999). Sense of community: Advances in measurement and application. *Journal of Community Psychology*, *27*(6), 635–642. doi:10.1002/(SICI)1520-6629(199911)27:6<635::AID-JCOP1>3.0.CO;2-F

Constant, D., Sproull, L., & Kiesler, S. (1996). The kindness of strangers: On the usefulness of electronic weak ties for technical advice. *Organization Science*, *7*(2), 119–135. doi:10.1287/orsc.7.2.119

Cropanzano, R., & Mitchell, M. S. (2005). Social exchange theory: An interdisciplinary review. *Journal of Management*, *31*(6), 874–900. doi:10.1177/0149206305279602

Cutrona, C. E., & Russell, D. W. (1990). Type of social support and specific stress: Toward a theory of optimal matching . In Sarason, I. G., Sarason, B. R., & Pierce, G. R. (Eds.), *Social support: An interactional view* (pp. 319–366). Oxford, England: John Wiley & Sons.

De Koster, W., & Houtman, D. (2008). 'Stormfront is like a second home to me': On virtual community formation by right-wing extremists. *Information . Communication and Technology*, *11*(8), 1155–1176.

Finholt, T., & Sproull, L. (1988). Electronic groups at work. *Organization Science*, *1*(1), 41–64. doi:10.1287/orsc.1.1.41

Haythornwaite, C. (2002). Strong, weak, and latent ties and the impact of new media. *The Information Society*, *18*(5), 385–401. doi:10.1080/01972240290108195

Hogg, M. A., Abrams, D., Otten, S., & Hinkle, S. (2004). The social identity perspective: intergroup relations, self-conception and small groups. *Small Group Research*, *35*(3), 246–276. doi:10.1177/1046496404263424

Koh, J., & Kim, Y.-G. (2003). Sense of virtual community: A conceptual framework and empirical validation. *International Journal of Electronic Commerce*, *8*(2), 75–94.

Kollock, P., & Smith, M. (1996). Managing the virtual commons: Cooperation and conflict in computer communities . In Herring, S. (Ed.), *Computer-Mediated Communication: Linguistic, Social, and Cross-Cultural Perspectives* (pp. 109–128). Amsterdam: John Benjamins.

Kraut, R. E., & Rice, R. E. (1998). Varieties of social influence: The role of utility and norms in the success of a new communication medium. *Organization Science*, *9*(4), 437–453. doi:10.1287/orsc.9.4.437

McKenna, K. Y. A., & Green, A. S. (2002). Virtual group dynamics. *Group Dynamics*, *6*(1), 116–127. doi:10.1037/1089-2699.6.1.116

McMillan, D. W., & Chavis, D. M. (1986). Sense of community: A definition and theory. *Journal of Community Psychology*, *14*(1), 6–23. doi:10.1002/1520-6629(198601)14:1<6::AID-JCOP2290140103>3.0.CO;2-I

Meyer, J. P., Allen, N. J., & Smith, C. A. (1993). Commitment to organizations and occupations: Extension and test of a three-component conceptualization. *The Journal of Applied Psychology*, *78*(4), 538–551. doi:10.1037/0021-9010.78.4.538

Meyer, J. P., Becker, T. E., & Van Dick, R. (2006). Social identities and commitments at work: Toward and integrative model. *Journal of Organizational Behavior*, *27*(5), 665–683. doi:10.1002/job.383

Michinov, N., Michinov, E., & Toczek-Capelle, M.-C. (2004). Social identity, group processes, and performance in synchronous computer-mediated communication. *Group Dynamics*, 8(1), 27–39. doi:10.1037/1089-2699.8.1.27

Nahapiet, J., & Ghoshal, S. (1998). Social capital, intellectual capital, and the organizational advantage. *Academy of Management Review*, 23(2), 242–266. doi:10.2307/259373

Obst, P., & White, K. M. (2007). Choosing to belong: The influence of choice on social identification and psychological sense of community. *Journal of Community Psychology*, 35(1), 77–90. doi:10.1002/jcop.20135

Oh, H., Chung, M.-H., & Labianca, G. (2004). Group social capital and group effectiveness: The role of informal socializing ties. *Academy of Management Journal*, 47(6), 860–875. doi:10.2307/20159627

Omoto, A. M., & Malsch, A. M. (2005). Psychological sense of community: Conceptual issues and connections to volunteerism-related activism . In Omoto, A. M. (Ed.), *Processes of Community Change and Social Action* (pp. 83–104). Mahwah, NJ: Lawrence Erlbaum.

Pickering, J. M. K., John Leslie. (1995). Hardwiring weak ties: Interorganizational computer-mediated communication, occupational communities, and organizational change. *Organization Science*, 6(4), 479–486. doi:10.1287/orsc.6.4.479

Postmes, T., Spears, R., & Lea, M. (2000). The formation of group norms in computer-mediated communication. *Human Communication Research*, 26(3), 341–371. doi:10.1111/j.1468-2958.2000.tb00761.x

Postmes, T., Spears, R., Lee, A. T., & Novak, R., J. (2005). Individuality and social influence in groups: Inductive and deductive routes to group identity. *Journal of Personality and Social Psychology*, 89(5), 747–763. doi:10.1037/0022-3514.89.5.747

Putnam, R. D. (1996). Bowling alone: America's declining social capital. *Journal of Democracy*, 6(1), 65–78. doi:10.1353/jod.1995.0002

Redman, T., & Snape, E. (2005). Unpacking commitment: Multiple loyalties and employee behaviour. *Journal of Management Studies*, 42(2), 301–328. doi:10.1111/j.1467-6486.2005.00498.x

Ren, Y., Kraut, R., & Kiesler, S. (2007). Applying common identity and bond theory to design of online communities. *Organization Studies*, 28(3), 377–408. doi:10.1177/0170840607076007

Rheingold, H. (1993). *The virtual community: Homesteading on the electronic frontier*. Reading, MA: Addison-Wesley.

Ridings, C. M., & Gefen, D. (2004). Virtual community attraction: Why people hang out online. *Journal of Computer-Mediated Communication*, 10(1).

Ritekka, M. (2005). Organizational identification: A meta-analysis. *Journal of Vocational Behavior*, 66(2), 358–384. doi:10.1016/j.jvb.2004.05.005

Rothaermel, F. T., & Sugiyama, S. (2001). Virtual Internet communities and commercial success: Individual and community-level theory grounded in the atypical case of TimeZone.com. *Journal of Management*, 27(3), 297–312. doi:10.1016/S0149-2063(01)00093-9

Sarason, S. B. (1974). *The psychological sense of community: Prospects for a community psychology*. San Francisco, CA: Jossey-Bass.

Sassenberg, K. (2002). Common bond and common identity groups on the Internet: Attachment and normative behavior in on-topic and off-topic chats. *Group Dynamics, 6*(1), 27–37. doi:10.1037/1089-2699.6.1.27

Spears, R., Lea, M., & Postmes, T. (2007). CMC and social identity . In Joinson, A. N., McKenna, K. Y. A., Postmes, T., & Reips, U.-D. (Eds.), *The Oxford Handbook of Internet Psychology* (pp. 253–279). London: Oxford University Press.

Sproull, L., & Kiesler, S. (1986). Reducing social context cues: Electronic mail in organizational communication. *Management Science, 32*(11), 1492–1512. doi:10.1287/mnsc.32.11.1492

Tanis, M., & Postmes, T. (2005). A social identity approach to trust: Interpersonal perception, group membership and trusting behaviour. *European Journal of Social Psychology, 35*, 413–424. doi:10.1002/ejsp.256

Turner, J. W., Grube, J. A., & Meyers, J. (2001). Developing an optimal match within online communities: An exploration of CMC support communities and traditional support. *The Journal of Communication, 51*(2), 231–251. doi:10.1111/j.1460-2466.2001.tb02879.x

Van Knippenberg, D., & Sleebos, E. (2006). Organizational identification versus organizational commitment: Self-definition, social exchange and job attitudes. *Journal of Organizational Behavior, 27*(5), 571–584. doi:10.1002/job.359

Walther, J. B. (1996). Computer mediated communication: Impersonal, interpersonal and hyperpersonal interaction. *Communication Research, 22*(1), 33–43.

Walther, J. B., Slovacek, C. L., & Tidwell, L. C. (2001). Is a picture worth a thousand words?: Photographic images in long-term and short-term computer-mediated communication. *Communication Research, 28*(1), 105–134. doi:10.1177/009365001028001004

Wasko, M., & Faraj, S. (2005). Why should I share? Examining social capital and knowledge contribution in electonic networks of practice. *Management Information Systems Quarterly, 29*(1), 247–253.

Weis, R., Stamm, K., Smith, C., Nilan, M., Clark, F., & Weis, J. (2003). Communities of care and caring: The case of MSWatch.com(R). *Journal of Health Psychology, 8*(1), 135–148. doi:10.1177/1359105303008001449

Wellman, B., & Guilia, M. (1999). Net Surfers don't ride alone: Virtual communities as communities . In Wellman, B. (Ed.), *Networks in the Global Village: Life in Contemporary Communities* (pp. 331–366). Boulder, CO: Westview.

Wellman, B., Haase, A. Q., Witte, J., & Hampton, K. (2001). Does the internet increase, decrease, or supplement social capital? Social networks, participation and community commitment. *The American Behavioral Scientist, 45*(3), 437–456. doi:10.1177/00027640121957286

ADDITIONAL READING

Abrams, D., & Hogg, M. A. (2001). Collective Identity: Group Membership and Self-Conception . In Hogg, M. A., & Tindale, R. S. (Eds.), *Blackwell Handbook of Social Psychology: Group Processes* (pp. 425–460). Oxford, UK: Blackwell. doi:10.1002/9780470998458.ch18

Ahuja, M. K., & Galvin, J. E. (2003). Socialization in virtual groups. *Journal of Management, 29*(2), 161–185. doi:10.1177/014920630302900203

Akkirman, A., & Harris, D. (2005). Organizational communication satisfaction in the virtual workplace. *Journal of Management Development, 24*(5), 397–409. doi:10.1108/02621710510598427

Allan, B., & Lewis, D. (2006). The impact of membership of a virtual learning community on individual learning careers and professional identity. *British Journal of Educational Technology*, *37*(6), 841–852. doi:10.1111/j.1467-8535.2006.00661.x

Ardichvili, A. (2008). Learning and knowledge sharing in virtual communities of practice: Motivators, barriers, and enablers. *Advances in Developing Human Resources*, *10*(4), 541–554. doi:10.1177/1523422308319536

Ashforth, B., & Mael, F. (1989). Social identity theory and the organization. *Academy of Management Review*, *14*(1), 20–39. doi:10.2307/258189

Ashforth, B. E., Harrison, S. H., & Corley, K. G. (2008). Identification in organizations: An examination of four fundamental questions. *Journal of Management*, *34*(3), 325–374. doi:10.1177/0149206308316059

Ashforth, B. E., Kreiner, G. E., & Fugate, M. (2000). All in a day's work: Boundaries and micro role transitions. *Academy of Management Review*, *25*(3), 472–491. doi:10.2307/259305

Blanchard, A. (2007). Developing a sense of virtual community measure. *Cyberpsychology & Behavior*, *10*(6), 827–830. doi:10.1089/cpb.2007.9946

Butler, B., Sproull, L., Kiesler, S., & Kraut, R. (2007). Community Effort in online groups: who does the work and why? In Wiesband, S. (Ed.), *Leadership at a distance: Research in Technologically-Supported Work* (pp. 346–362). Hillsdale, NJ: Lawrence Erlbaum and Associates.

Chipuer, H. M., & Pretty, G. H. (1999). A review of the sense of community index: Current uses, factor structure, reliability and further development. *Journal of Community Psychology*, *27*(6), 643–658. doi:10.1002/(SICI)1520-6629(199911)27:6<643::AID-JCOP2>3.0.CO;2-B

Clark, S. C. (2002). Employees' sense of community, sense of control, and work/family conflict in Native American organizations. *Journal of Vocational Behavior*, *61*(1), 92–108. doi:10.1006/jvbe.2001.1846

Constance A. Steinkuehler, D. W. (2006). Where everybody knows your (screen) name: Online games as "third places". *Journal of Computer-Mediated Communication*, *11*(4), 885–909. doi:10.1111/j.1083-6101.2006.00300.x

Culnan, M. J. (2008). Online communities: Infrastructure, relational cohesion and sustainability. In Elliott, M. S., & Kraemer, K. L. (Eds.), *Computerization Movements and Technology Diffusion: From Mainframes to Ubiqutous Computing* (pp. 239–259). Medford, NJ: Information Today.

Fisher, A. T., Sonn, C. C., & Bishop, B. J. (2002). *Psychological sense of community: Research, applications and implications*. New York: Kluwer Academic/Plenum Publishers.

Hogg, M., Sherman, D., Dierselhuis, J., Maitner, A., & Moffitt, G. (2007). Uncertainty, entitativity, and group identification. *Journal of Experimental Social Psychology*, *43*(1), 135–142. doi:10.1016/j.jesp.2005.12.008

Hogg, M., & Terry, D. (2000). Social identity and self-categorization processes in organizational contexts. *Academy of Management Review*, *25*(1), 121–140. doi:10.2307/259266

Jones, Q. (1997). Virtual-communities, virtual settlements & cyber-archaeology: A theoretical outline. *Journal of Computer-Mediated Communication*, *3*(3).

Lea, B. R., Yu, W. B., Maguluru, N., & Nichols, M. (2006). Enhancing business networks using social network based virtual communities. *Industrial Management & Data Systems*, *106*(1), 121–121. doi:10.1108/02635570610641022

Mael, F., & Ashforth, B. (1992). Alumni and their alma mater: A partial test of the reformulated model of organizational identification. *Journal of Organizational Behavior*, *13*(2), 103–123. doi:10.1002/job.4030130202

Obst, P., Smith, S. G., & Zinkiewicz, L. (2002). An exploration of sense of community, Part 3: Dimensions and predictors of psychological sense of community in geographical communities. *Journal of Community Psychology*, *30*(1), 119–133. doi:10.1002/jcop.1054

Obst, P., Zinkiewicz, L., & Smith, S. G. (2002a). Sense of community in science fiction fandom, Part 1: Understanding sense of community in an international community of interest. *Journal of Community Psychology*, *30*(1), 87–103. doi:10.1002/jcop.1052

Obst, P., Zinkiewicz, L., & Smith, S. G. (2002b). Sense of community in science fiction fandom, Part 2: Comparing neighborhood and interest group sense of community. *Journal of Community Psychology*, *30*(1), 105–117. doi:10.1002/jcop.1053

Parker, M. (1997). Dividing organizations and multiplying identities. In Munro, R., & Hetherington, K. (Eds.), *Ideas of difference: Social spaces and the labour of division* (*Vol. 9*, pp. 114–138). Oxford, UK: Blackwell.

Perkins, D. D., & Long, D. A. (2002). This neighborhood sense of community and social capital: A multi-level analysis. In Fisher, A. T., Sonn, C. C., & Bishop, B. J. (Eds.), *Psychological sense of community: Research, applications, and implications* (pp. 291–316). New York: Kluwer Academic/Plenum Publishers.

Prentice, D. A., Miller, D. T., & Lightdale, J. R. (1994). Asymmetries in attachments to groups and to their members: Distinguishing between common-identity and common-bond groups. *Personality and Social Psychology Bulletin*, *20*(5), 484–493. doi:10.1177/0146167294205005

Roberts, L. D., Smith, L. M., & Pollock, C. M. (2002). MOOing till the cows come home: The sense of community in virtual environments. In Fisher, A. T., Sonn, C. C., & Bishop, B. J. (Eds.), *Psychological sense of community: Research, applications, implications* (pp. 223–245). New York: Kluwer Academic/Plenum Publishers.

Snape, E., & Redman, T. (2003). An evaluation of a three-component model of occupational commitment: Dimensionality and consequences among United Kingdom human resource management specialists. *The Journal of Applied Psychology*, *88*(1), 152–159. doi:10.1037/0021-9010.88.1.152

Utz, S. (2008). Social identification with virtual communities. *Mediated Interpersonal Communication*, *1*(1), 252.

Walther, J. (2007). Selective self-presentation in computer-mediated communication: Hyperpersonal dimensions of technology, language, and cognition. *Computers in Human Behavior*, *23*(5), 2538–2557. doi:10.1016/j.chb.2006.05.002

Wellman, B., Salaff, J., Dimitrova, D., Garton, L., Gulia, M., & Haythornthwaite, C. (1996). Computer networks as social networks: Collaborative work, telework, and virtual community. *Annual Review of Sociology*, *22*(1), 213–238. doi:10.1146/annurev.soc.22.1.213

Witt, L., Patti, A., & Farmer, W. (2002). Organizational politics and work identity as predictors of organizational commitment. *Journal of Applied Social Psychology*, *32*(3), 486–499. doi:10.1111/j.1559-1816.2002.tb00226.x

KEY TERMS AND DEFINITIONS

Occupational Commitment: Commitment to a specific profession or occupation beyond any feelings of commitment to a particular organization.

Occupational Identity: Feelings of identity that develop with one's profession or occupation. Super-ordinate identity applied to a particular type of job.

Personal Identity: The development of an understanding of others in the virtual community as well as the creation of one's own identity to be presented to the rest of the group.

Professional Sense of Virtual Community: Sense of virtual community that develops in professional virtual communities.

Sense of Virtual Community: Member's feelings of identity, belonging, and attachment with each other in their online groups.

Sub-Ordinate Identity: Feelings of identity that develop with a particular, interacting group. Although theoretically similar to super-ordinate identity, it is tied to a particular group.

Super-Ordinate Identity: Feelings of identity that develop with large, non-interacting groups (e.g., ethnicity).

Virtual Community: Groups of people who interact primarily through information and communication technologies (ICT).

Chapter 10
Virtual Mentoring

Narissra Maria Punyanunt-Carter
Texas Tech University, USA

Emilio S. Hernandez
Texas Tech University, USA

ABSTRACT

With the proliferation of information technology and its saturation within homes, classrooms, and organizations, the traditional landscape of mentoring relationships is quickly becoming a faceless phenomenon. Virtual mentoring is rapidly being the more preferred way to initiate mentor and protégé relationships because of constraints that prevent people from meeting face-to-face. It is through this computer-mediated method of interaction where benefits surface that increase computer-mediate dialogue, allow for the free exchange of knowledge and information regardless of an individual's role within the interaction, and provides women a channel to voice their opinions and ideas free from gender bias. Outside of these benefits; however, limitations do exist that should be closely monitored so that the continued success of virtual mentoring can remain a viable option.

INTRODUCTION

With computerized technology on the forefront of organizational advancement, and the increased desire for globalization, virtual mentoring is rapidly becoming the preferred method of choice when mentors and protégés communicate with one another. No longer is geographic distance a barrier. Asynchronous technologies promote the development of virtual organizations, let mentors and protégés

DOI: 10.4018/978-1-61520-979-8.ch010

respond to inquiries at convenient times, and provide organizational members an opportunity to influence the current generation by using an assortment of web sites, podcasts, and a myriad of other types of technology to foster creativity. Additionally virtual mentoring programs can serve as virtual voices for women, minorities, and other marginalized and underrepresented groups. It is through this chapter where the prevalence of virtual mentoring will be reviewed.

Mentoring, as a concept, goes back thousands of years to Homer's epic poem *The Odyssey*. Homer tells the story of an elderly and wise sea captain named Mentor, who gives Odysseus's son, Telemachus, guidance while his father is gone on his long journey. In modern times, the word "mentor" has been used to refer to a relationship where one individual with more knowledge and experience aids another individual who has less knowledge and experience (Richmond, Wrench, & Gorham, 2001). Mentoring can be described as the communication relationship where a senior person advises, teaches, and encourages a junior person's professional and sometimes personal development (Hill, Bahniuk, & Dobos, 1989).

Today we see a mentor as "someone who helps someone else learn something that he or she would have learned less well, more slowly, or not at all if left alone" (Bell, 2000, p. 53). One type of mentoring relationship is the virtual mentoring relationship. To date, very little research has been conducted in the area of virtual mentoring (Harrington, 1999). The book chapter examines the realm of virtual mentoring and how it pertains to virtual work. Moreover, this chapter aims to identify mentoring practices and processes underlying virtual organizing. Most importantly, the chapter provides an understanding of the practical implications of mentoring to virtual work.

According to a UK website, called "Mentors Forum", a website devoted to mentoring, mentor provide four key elements in their relationships with their mentees:

- **Coach:** to show the learner how to carry out a task
- **Facilitate:** create opportunities for learners to utilize new skills
- **Counsel:** help learners explore consequences of potential decisions
- **Network:** refer learners to others when mentor's experience is insufficient

Overall, mentors offer many roles to their mentees. This type of relationship often relies on effective communication. It has been demonstrated that mentor-mentee relationships can create more satisfaction, increase productivity, and increase understanding (Conner, 2002).Hence, there are several benefits to mentorship.

For the mentor, there may be some benefits such as:

- Offers knowledge to others
- Offers a new perspective on their current task
- Offers insight for the future
- Offers a personal actualization in one's talent/skill/compentency

For the mentee, there may also be some benefits such as:

- Obtains advice from the mentor
- Obtains assurance from mentor's support
- Obtains personalized attention
- Obtains a new perspective on the current task

The mentor-mentee relationship is valuable for any organization because it also offers many benefits, such as:

- Creating morale
- Fosters creativity and growth
- Increases satisfaction and retention
- Increases productivity
- Increases awareness of the organization

At the same time, the mentor-mentee relationship has some limitations, such as the time and effort required to maintain the relationship. Sometimes, personality differences between the mentor and mentee make the relationship more difficult to maintain. There is little research in this area, which deals with the limitations of mentorship.

Most of the research has been devoted to face-to-face mentoring. The primary difference between the traditional face to face mentorship and a virtual mentorship is that virtual mentoring involves more virtual forms of contact through electronic means, such as e-mail, voice mail, video conferences, and/or instant messaging. One of the biggest obstacles of any mentorship is the availability of time. Face-to-face mentoring requires that both individuals share similar time components. However, virtual mentorship does not require that participants share the same time requirements. It is also suggested that virtual mentorship does not provide enough feedback, because it is usually delivered by electronic means (Harrington, 1999). Virtual mentoring is also known as "e-mentoring" and "online mentoring". The key element in virtual mentoring is the face-to-face contact is substituted with virtual contact. Virtual mentoring can occur with individuals in two very different locations. Thus, it increases the opportunity for two unlikely individuals to form a relationship. Virtual mentoring is usually asynchronous, in which one party can have a delayed response. Face-to-face mentoring is usually synchronous because both parties can offer communication and feedback instantly.

Knouse (2001) noted that mentoring is a significant factor in career development. She noted that several mentees have increased career satisfaction, monetary rewards, and opportunities for promotion. Thus, mentoring is an important function in one's career. Knouse stated that there are two types of mentoring: psychosocial and instrumental. First, psychosocial mentoring deals with decreasing stress, communication interpersonally, and acting as a confidant. Second, instrumental mentoring deals specifically with the career-related activities, such as offering advice, insight, training, and instruction.

Through the rapid development of information technology, and its seamless integration within the workplace environment, the practice of traditional mentoring has virtually entered the technological era. Through the increased desire to obtain information instantaneously and through the normative practice of globalization, virtual mentoring is quickly becoming the preferred way to communicate amongst mentors and protégés. Virtual mentoring provides several key benefits for both the mentor and protégé, which otherwise would not have been thought of, if it were not for the advances in information technology. It is through information technology where the globe is tightly woven together through the internet, computers, and other technologies that make the transmission and dispensation of information easier, faster, and more available to those who are privileged to enjoy such luxury. Despite the many benefits to virtual mentoring; however, problems do exist, which are problematic areas for improvement that should be minimized if the rapidly growing virtual mentoring phenomenon is expected to thrive with success.

The pervasiveness of information technology can be found within the infrastructures of most successful organizations. Information technology controls large communication networks, it provides employees the ability to send and receive e-mail, and information technology provides users access to unprecedented amounts of information that previously would have been difficult to access. The internet, video conferencing, personal digital assistants, and a host of other devices are the digital keys that are continuing to unlock doors within the workplace. From the organizational standpoint, information technology - increases work productivity, provides employees the opportunity to handle an assortment of tasks more efficiently, and provides members of an organization the ability to communicate with one another regardless of geographic distance. It is this final component of globalization that is beneficial and fascinating because virtual mentorship can aid mentors and protégés alike. Additionally, by reviewing the literature surrounding this topic thus far, new topic areas of significance can be expanded upon. The duration of this chapter will primarily call attention to the positive and negative affects of virtual mentoring, compare and contrast the differences and similar trends surrounding traditional mentoring verses virtual mentoring practices, and conclude with an emphasis on the strengths and areas of improvement that encompass this topic.

BACKGROUND

Virtual mentoring has only recently stepped onto the economic landscape, and since that time it has rapidly become the more preferred channel through which mentors and protégés interact with one another. This is largely due to organizations out sourcing manufacturing jobs to foreign countries. For this reason is why traditional mentoring is becoming a less-used method of cultivating mentor and protégé relationships.

It is due to globalization why virtual mentoring is becoming the more practical way of initiating dialogue. Virtual mentoring occurs when a mentor and protégé start corresponding with one another electronically regardless of geographic distance (Bierema & Hill, 2005); (Ramos & Green, 2007). Indicated earlier in this chapter, an assortment of devices can serve as electronic pathways for communication such as, e-mail, video conferencing, blogs, and instant messaging (Bierema & Hill, 2005). Utilizing these computerized channels of communication, allows the mentor and protégé to benefit from the various advantages that exist from virtual mentoring.

An assortment of advantages exists for mentors and protégés who actively engage in virtual mentoring in the workplace. One immediate benefit is the ability to communicate either synchronously or asynchronously by using computer technology. By utilizing instant messaging, e-mail, and other methods of communication greatly increases the opportunity for communication to occur conveniently for either member of the dyad (Guy, 2002). For example, if a new employee is located in Atlanta and a member of a large international organization, but needs mentor support, corresponding with an expert in Phoenix, will give the new employee ease, flexibility, and the convenience of communicating with a colleague

despite physical distance. It is through this innovation where time is no longer a constraint. For instance, if an e-mail is sent at 6:30 PM, it can be read and replied to at 8:30 AM the next morning (Guy, 2002). This eliminates scheduling conflicts and gives each member of the interaction more independence to freely reply to messages when he or she has enough time. No longer is the mentor and protégé confined to face-to-face appointments that are perhaps inconvenient. In prospective to the average college student, this example can be easily compared with a student completing homework on a late night, but who has a question over a particularly difficult problem. By sending his or her professor a message at 2:30 in the morning, and getting a reply at 3:00 the next afternoon is a clear example of asynchronous computer technology use. Outside of this benefit, other important features are of equal significance.

Virtual mentoring provides organizations the opportunity to recruit prospective employees. For example, virtual mentoring provides interested parties to communicate with experienced professionals within a specific area of interest. The ability to engage in virtual mentoring is vital for those in the medical profession. The U.S Department of Labor estimates that approximately by the year 2012, roughly one million jobs will be available for registered nurses. This national concern is why the concept of virtual mentoring is necessary, most especially for students who are seeking possible employment in this profession (Kalisch, Valzetta, & Cook, 2005). Virtual mentoring becomes beneficial as a practical tool for nursing recruitment because the internet is already seen as an invaluable resource for obtaining information. Therefore, it is understandable why high school students and college students in particular, prefer this medium of communication. In terms of seeking prospective nurses, the University of Michigan was sponsored to conduct a pilot program that consisted of developing a web site for nurses and students to visit. This site allowed students to learn about the nursing profession, and provided nurses the opportunity to post a brief biographical sketch and photo of themselves. Additionally, the web site let students view the projected salary outcome, learn about scholarships, and learn about the various roles and positions nursing provides. Moreover, the project let nurses respond to student questions at a convenient point in the day where ample time could be devoted to the response, thus adding the benefit of thoughtful and accurate answers to be given (Kalisch et al., 2005). This benefit to the nursing profession is crucial, but where the increased benefit gives women the opportunity to truly utilize the advent of virtual mentoring is found within the workplace as a practicing professional.

Virtual mentoring for women has positively impacted their occupational outlook within the workplace. Previously, most women were merely relegated to the clerical tasks of a secretary if work outside the home was an option. Since the early periods of allowing women to vote and being recognized as equal to their male counterpart, vast changes have allowed women to step into more promising roles - from Doctors, to policewomen, to College Professors, etc. Virtual mentoring has helped women who are professionals within their occupation by heavily using e-mentoring web sites to help further develop their professional success. Since the integration of such technologies, women have been able to develop their "virtual voice," by networking with others in similar professions or by counseling others who are enduring previously experienced challenges. For example, (www.systers.org) is a web site tailored to be a networking hub due to the lack of female mentors for women working in science-related occupations. Additionally, for those women who are unsure of where to find the best-suited mentor that will help them through their employment experience, (www.ivilliage.com/workingdiva/mentoring/mentor/articles) is an asset that can guide unfamiliar women through the process of obtaining a mentor. Finally, for those women who have a genuine interest in technology-related fields, (www.girlgeeks.

com) is a web site that is specifically targeted for women who is an underrepresented group within this arena (Bierema & Merriam, 2002). Women have largely been underrepresented in occupations, but the foundation for this problem stems from the academic training women endure. For this poor representation within the math and sciences, a web site has been developed to give women an opportunity to advance within their desired careers. WEPAN, Women in Engineering ProActive Network, is a non-profit organization created in 1990. The mission of this educational organization strives to improve the social injustices women face. With an active membership of over 500, WEPAN feverishly works to increase female retention within jobs by providing technical aid to colleges and universities (Muller, 1998). With this understanding of how virtual mentoring can aid women in securing employment and excelling within their respective organizations, the role virtual mentoring plays within the organization is as equally important.

The influence information technology has within the workplace is rapidly becoming an increasing benefit for organizations. Like previously eluded to earlier in this chapter, globalization is continuing to dominate the infustructure of organizations, thus resulting in the virtual organization, which has naturally evolved from a change in the global market coupled with the integration of new technologies (Lavin Colky & Young, 2006); (Manzin & Kodric, 2009). The presence of technology has become such a fixture within organizations that technology is largely responsible for the development of virtual organizations. It is through the virtual organization, which in some instances exists independently from physical companies, where the ability to solidly establish a common definition becomes difficult. Therefore, the virtual organization is the "material organization of time-sharing social practices that work through flows of information – (capital, images, sounds, symbols, and interaction) between organizations and people" (Bekkers, 2003 Pg. 90. More easily explained, the virtual organization operates as though it were an actual fixture n noted within the organization, but when in reality it functions in cyberspace (Bekkers, 2003). Now with this more clear definition, let us now turn our attention towards the benefits virtual mentoring provides the work place.

Virtual mentoring serves as an asset to the workplace environment. With the increasing move to virtual environments where employees can potentially work from home, collaborate with colleagues via video conferencing, and interact with other employees through instant messaging, list serves, etc. The added benefit of virtual teams is perfectly aligned with the concept of virtual workplaces. Where mentoring can be highly beneficial is with problems that arise with virtual teams. By communicating with a team leader and other group members through informal channels will greatly increase the level of cohesiveness and synergy within the group. Furthermore, this informal dialogue will foster a more balanced scale where all group members can learn from one another, while still maintaining the group structure (Boule, 2008). Through the advent of virtual teams, the prospect of mentors rising to the occasion is believed to greatly increase, so the group can remain task-oriented, and accomplish the goal or goals set before them.

Other benefits that have been observed due to virtual mentoring are advantages to the workplace. For instance, as previously conveyed within the chapter, virtual mentoring allows the mentor and protégé to communicate via e-mail, or through other electronic channels. Also, by utilizing asynchronous mediums for communication, gives more mentors and protégés an opportunity to enter the virtual interaction, thus reaching a wider audience. Through the assortment of technologies available to mentors and protégés within the workplace, open and supportive relationships can develop. Due to this relational advantage, virtual coaching is quickly becoming a vital component in this online network. It has been illustrated throughout this chapter how important the role technology has in the development, execution, and success of virtual mentoring. Additionally, due to virtual mentoring virtual coaching is possible. Virtual coaching, like the overarching benefit of communication despite geographic location can now occur via text messaging, e-mail, video conferencing, or via the telephone. Presently, The University of Texas at Dallas, and The International Coach Academy both are active organizations that facilitate virtual coach training (Bennett & Bush, 2009). Additionally, messages can be reviewed and refined before sharing with fellow mentors or mentees, so as to eliminate any miscommunication problems as best as possible (Muller, 1998); (Ragins & Scandura, 1999). Outside of these advantages exists drawbacks.

Some of the drawbacks to virtual mentoring and virtual work are issues, which can erode the mentor and protégé relationship. For instance, a group of men were working effectively and successfully on a project. The communication between al the group members occurred via computerized technology because some of the group members were from California, and others were from Taiwan, and others still were from Maryland. On one occasion one of the group members sent a slightly sarcastic e-mail calling his Taiwanese colleagues cohorts. Unbeknownst to the North American group members, the Taiwanese group members did not take this favorably, and thus several weeks of relational repair were required. Due to this error of miscommunication, or lack of understanding cultural differences halted work productivity, communication practices became inadequate, and inter-team trust was damaged indefinitely (Graf, 2001). This narrative serves as one prime example of how the aforementioned areas can damage virtual working environments.

Another area where problems can arise due to virtual mentoring and virtual workplaces is with employment longevity. No longer is loyalty being regarded as a key force that secures an employee his or her job. No longer is the value of hard work, dedication, or determination principal values to a company. With the changing demographics, globalization, and a push for increased productivity for consumers, the request for more efficient workplaces is in high demand. Due to the rapid integration of virtual mentoring and virtual work, some employees fear losing their jobs due to their inability to operate new technology. In conjunction, these same employees are at a higher risk for job termination due to their age, vulnerability due to high organizational uncertainty, and early retirement (Darwin, 2000). For these reasons and a myriad of others is why virtual mentoring programs coupled with virtual workplaces are disadvantaging to older employees. Also, part time work and contract work are becoming a popular way for organizations to become more cost-effective, which again, diminishes employment longevity. From these disadvantages surrounding virtual mentoring in relation to virtual workplaces, trends and issues are evident.

Since e-mentoring and traditional mentoring operate very similarly, it is likely that trends and problems exist within both contexts. For example, traditional mentoring occurred in the framework of a dyad. However with the advent of computer mediated technology, the limitation of working one-on-one is virtually obsolete. Regardless of either approach used when entering into a mentorship relationship, the general purpose is clear, which aims to be a support network for both the mentor and protégé (Kasprisin, Boyle single, Single, & Muller, 2003); (Packard, 2003). This support network is built on the premise that the protégé should seek guidance from an older person, who is not a parent, and who he or she can turn to for guidance. Furthermore, the mentor is a person of nobility who desires to aid a young person or less-experienced employee excel, so as to help the protégé achieve his or her goals (Hamilton, Hamilton, & Rhodes, 2002). In the context of the virtual mentor, this is more commonly known as grooming-mentoring. Grooming-mentoring is the "special assistance by an older more experienced professional who grooms his or her protégé" (Haring-Hidore, 1987). With these basic trends that are representative of both the traditional mentor relationship and the virtual mentor relationship, problems become evident.

Within traditional mentoring and virtual mentoring relationships respectively, problems exist that are limitations to each mentoring context. For instance, with the traditional mentor, it is possible that the mentor and protégé are incompatible working partners. Also, if the mentor holds pernicious beliefs of leadership, this in conjunction with the aforementioned problem can be greatly detrimental for the protégé (Johnson, 2002). The dysfunction this outlook has on the entire mentor experience can severely scar the protégé's perception of mentoring relationships, thus causing him or her to hold a negative and distasteful attitude about traditional mentoring. Moreover, ample time should be devoted for the insured success of the role the traditional mentor plays in his or her protégé's life. Compounding these problems is the lack of stellar interpersonal communication skills. If the mentor does not have solid skills with which to communicate, then the mentor relationship has a greater propensity of failing. Therefore, this is why it is equally important to devote the required and necessary time to the protégé, so conversations can be forged. In addition to serving as a mentor, the mentor should be very mindful of his or her role in the dyad and let the protégé make decisions on his or her own (Kilburg, 2007). In the context of the virtual mentoring atmosphere problems exist.

One of the more prevalent issues facing virtual mentoring partnerships is the high degree of miscommunication. The nonverbal cues most people rely upon in face-to-face interactions are no longer visible. What further amplifies this problem is the lack of listening cues. The nodding of a head, or eye contact are key message markers, which in virtual mentoring relationships are nonexistent. Due to the lack of these key listening techniques prohibits the receiver of the message to provide empathy or interest. Perhaps it is due to this final issue, which causes the response to a message to be largely misinterpreted. For instance, in some e-mentoring relationships the appearance of responding quickly to a message without having read the entire message can become frustrating. Not to mention sending e-mail is highly risky. By the click of the mouse a message meant for one protégé can be forwarded to several if not hundreds of other protégés or mentors. It is due to this problem, which due to virtual mentoring has caused protégés to feel less inhibited to share information with their mentor (Purcell, 2004). Despite these strengths and weaknesses of traditional mentoring and virtual mentoring, the initiative of virtual mentoring still continues to flourish.

Like a plant that experiences growth through a series of phases, so does virtual mentoring encounter a similar destiny when beginning to cultivate virtual relationships. Initiation, separation, and termination are all important phases for the virtual mentoring to protégé relationship (Hamilton & Scandura, 2003). The initiation phase is perhaps the most important phase of the entire relationship because it is at this moment where the tenor of the entire relationship is defined. For instance, it is during this stage where program rules, norms, expectations, and evaluation procedures are agreed upon. Also, it is at this stage where the expectation is assumed that mentors and protégés will develop a professional relationship that allows for the free exchange of career-advancement strategies, which is a corps principle of virtual mentoring (Hamilton & Scandura, 2003). Through the cultivation of the virtual mentor and protégé relationship, both members of the interaction may reach a plateau, at which time both members of the relationship may decide to terminate the interaction. The added feature that virtual mentoring provides this stage of the relationship is that in most instances where virtual mentoring is used, in most cases the mentor and protégé are already at some geographic distance. Therefore, the separation phase may not always be necessary. The termination phase is

perhaps usually the stage that precedes the cultivation phase. Since most mentors and protégés have some distance between them, this stage is most ideal when deciding to end the virtual relationship. This may occur due to one or both members of the relationship no longer reaping the rewards of the virtual mentoring process. The advantage this provides both members of the interaction is that face-to-face interaction at work as colleagues or face-to-face interaction to officially end the relationship is not needed (Hamilton & Scandura, 2003). However, once a virtual mentoring relationship has been established, the importance of technology plays a crucial role in fostering the relational growth of the interaction, which only stresses the importance of the following benefits associated to virtual mentoring.

Unlike traditional mentoring, which relies heavily on face-to-face interaction, virtual mentoring is utilizing the infrastructure of the internet to initiate mentoring relationships. Presently, the concept of virtual mentoring is defined as email or computer conferencing facilitated interactions where face-to-face interaction is not practical, which links mentors with protégés regardless of geographic location (Bierema & Hill, 2005). This revolutionary avenue of communication is yielding unprecedented benefits for both the mentor and protégé. The most evident benefit of virtual mentoring is that it provides users the ability to communicate with one another independent of distance or other hindrances that would otherwise prevent dialogue from occurring if face-to-face communication was the sole means of interaction. Mentoring relationships can be initiated by using a variety of technological mediums such as, E-mail, list serves, intranets, chat groups, and computer conferencing. Furthermore, the ability to transmit messages using asynchronous message systems is vital for the continued dialogue between the mentor and protégé. For example, the protégé may have a question in the early hours of the morning, or at an otherwise less than ideal time, to which the mentor cannot respond to immediately. By utilizing the aforementioned technologies, the mentor can then reply to the question at a time that is most convenient for him or her (Bierema & Hill, 2005).

Another innovative benefit to virtual mentoring is the continued development of professional relationships. The added element virtual mentoring brings to professional development is that virtual mentoring provides the mentor and protégé the opportunity to increase job performance despite the occupational stage either member of the interaction is currently at. Also, like traditional mentoring practices, virtual mentors and protégés can improve writing skills, which are vitally important and perhaps more crucial when entering into dialogue electronically. Since most communication occurs digitally, the ability to write affectively, convey thoughts clearly and accurately, and do ones best not to mislead or leave responses vague are all important aspects to be mindful of when engaging in virtual mentoring (Bierema & Hill, 2005). Since virtual mentoring can occur practically anywhere at any time, the increased availability to include other prospective protégés or mentors into the virtual infrastructure regardless of personal characteristics that otherwise would detour or limit mentor to protégé availability becomes more feasible. Therefore, when engaging in virtual mentoring, race, gender, sexual orientation, physical limitation, or a myriad of other personal traits are not a concern, which aids in the dismantling of sociocultural barriers (Bierema & Hill, 2005).

Another added benefit to virtual mentoring is the ability to more accurately assign a mentor who is most qualified to oversee a protégé within a specific context. With traditional mentoring practices, the protégé was often limited to communicating with a mentor who had experience, but who often times was older than the protégé. It is through this new and innovative mentoring relationship where virtual mentoring becomes valuable. The value virtual mentoring brings to the mentor and protégé relationship is the simultane-

ous flow of knowledge and information (Bierema & Hill, 2005). Virtual mentoring affords mentors and protégés the ability to become synergetic of one another because the constant flow of information is no longer a one-directional channel, but a dual-directional pathway that allows the mentor and protégé to learn from one another (Bierema & Hill, 2005). For example, by sharing narratives, choices about career decisions, and collaborating on projects, this allows the mentor and protégé to positively impact one another, thus blurring the relational line between mentor and protégé to a minimal degree. It is through this dual-directional exchange of information where further advantages surface for both members and perhaps multiple members of the existing relationship. For instance, psychosocially, advice, trust, and the creation of relational meaning all can be achieved with less effort than traditional mentoring relationships (Hamilton & Scandura, 2003). It is through the virtual channels of e-mentoring where members of the interaction can be more trusting, which is vital when forging virtual relationships because perhaps emotional support can be provided, which only strengthens the bond between mentor and protégé (Hamilton & Scandura, 2003). Role-modeling in traditional mentoring relationships can be mastered through direct observation, and also through the virtual lens of technology role-modeling can be reached. For instance, the mentor may observe the protégé indirectly and thereby give rewards tied to the actions of the protégé, which can serve as a tool of reinforcement and virtual praise (Hamilton & Scandura, 2003).

For women, the ability to enter the world of virtual mentoring opens beneficial doors of possibility for career advancement, and gender equality. Previously, studies indicated that women's views to use a computer were negative, but through the seamless integration of the internet, and computers becoming permanent fixtures within homes and businesses, women's views have changed. Computer affordability and maintenance, and the increasing exposure women have with working with technology are factors that have contributed to the lowering of women's anxiety, thus increasing self-efficacy for women (Hamilton, 2003.).

Women view computer usage as an avenue or channel to receive and disseminate information, whereas men view computer usage as a competitive means to an end. Where virtual mentoring and women positively impact one another is in the aspect of electronic dialogue. For example, women are generally more conversationally-driven, whereas men are not. This is important distinction is beneficial for women because it is through this normative behavior where women are more apt to develop support networks, and increase the level of learning and communication of the entire group. Where this claim is evidently seen is in the transmission of E-mail by women. Women generally view the ability to send and receive e-mail as a contextual building block of relationship development. Another feature virtual mentoring affords women is the ability to converse on an equal level with men. Since most women respond to physical cues, which causes them to allow men to dominate a conversation, the benefit of virtual mentoring eliminates this hindrance (Hamilton & Scandura, 2003). Another barrier for women that virtual mentoring abolishes is the need for organizational hierarchy. By the organizational structure becoming electronically equal, the foundation is set for women to more freely engage in managerial advancement in their careers, which otherwise would have been more difficult if impossible due to the male-dominated organizational culture (Headland, Gosland, & Craig, 2005). In this instance is where utilizing the knowledgeable experience of a mentor is vital because employees regardless of gender need someone to guide them through organizational complexities that so often chain employees to feelings of annoyance and dissatisfaction (Headland et al., 2005).

For the employee who desires to be a "guiding light" for new employees, or for the employee who simply desires to serve as a continued ben-

eficial asset to the organization, programs exist that train people to become virtual mentors. The ability to access massive amounts of information via the internet is an increasing norm in society. It is through this access of previously limited information that allows people to reap the reward of helping others, thus becoming virtual mentors. Various e-mentoring programs have been created; therefore, in order to find the most appropriate program for an individual takes researching various programs in order to find the one of best fit. For instance, GlobalMecca is an online training resource that provides African-Americans with the ability to learn the skills that are vital and necessary to become a successful mentor who desires to interact with protégés electronically. For women, several sites are tailored towards helping women regain entrance into the workplace or continue to enhance their marketability by improving already developed skills. For example, Women in Surgery Training (WITS), is a site that focuses on women who want to share experiences or training techniques that others may find helpful (Knouse, 2001).

Communication, Relational, and Practical Implications

The implications as they are relative to dyadic interaction are visible. Since virtual mentoring is a dialogue facilitated by information technology, the inability for a mentor to actively observe their protégée is troublesome because direct observation is vital for accurate feedback. Due to the computer-mediated method for interaction, interpersonal skills are not able to be refined, thus inhibiting the protégée from developing interpersonal skills necessary when face-to-face interaction is required. Due to women and other marginalized groups seldom finding colleagues in positions of power who can serve as mentors and comprehend their unique concerns, relegates these men and women to use virtual mentoring as an alternative to traditional mentoring (Knouse, 2001). Other challenges are prevalent that could potentially denigrate the purpose of virtual mentoring. For instance, the comfort level of technology users needs to be carefully scrutinized because the necessity to use the computer as a tool and cognitive medium is crucial for virtual mentoring. Also, users may lack the information literacy skills necessary to actively participate in virtual mentoring; therefore, organizations need to tread with caution when deciding to implement such a service. Couple with this lack of skills exists the inability to effectively communicate via an online medium, which can diminish the desired outcome of virtual mentoring. Trust, online privacy, and relational stability are several key concerns that have surfaced as a result of virtual mentoring (Bierema & Hill, 2005).

SOLUTIONS AND RECOMMENDATIONS

Outside of the benefits virtual mentoring provides, setbacks do exist that have the potential to be problematic. For example, the lack of being able to visit the protégé in his or her working environment to provide accurate and detailed feedback through direct observation is presently not possible with the current standards of virtual mentoring. Also, since the entire concept of virtual mentoring is a new area of study, the measurement of its effectiveness is minimal and highly inconclusive (Knouse, 2001). Perhaps an increasing factor that severely limits organizational integration of virtual mentoring programs is the cost associated to starting such a program. For those groups or organizations who desire to implement such a program careful consideration should be given to the overall cost of the technology, training seminars for employee usage, and the ease of learning and operating the associated technologies to engage in such interactions (Bierema & Hill, 2005). Coupled with the inability to use the technology for virtual mentoring exists the issue of miscommunication. The problematic issue that is derived from

miscommunication under the umbrella of virtual mentoring is the lack of understanding of how to correctly navigate through the software program that allow the mentor and protégé to communicate with one another (Bierema & Hill, 2005). Also, with the increasing trend of information technology dominating the organizational landscape is the lack of privacy. Unlike traditional relationships, once the dialogue and interaction is over, it is over, but with virtual mentoring relationships often times, the information being transmitted is usually recorded (Bierema & Hill, 2005).

The limitations surrounding this body of research are areas that can be expanded upon as this area of communication gains wider recognition. Presently, the concept of virtual mentoring is defined as email or computer conferencing facilitated interactions where face-to-face interaction is not either practical (Bierema & Hill, 2005). Presently virtual mentoring is restricted to web sites, where prospective mentors or protégées can link to various sites tailored to a specific interest. Through further development, virtual mentoring has the potential to offer clearinghouses where protégées can go and obtain most of the information about a specific topic so that securing a mentor can be more efficient. By mainstreaming such information, professionals can eventually have access to senior members within their respective organizations (Knouse, 2001).

FUTURE RESEARCH DIRECTIONS

With the newly and rapidly enjoyed concept of virtual mentoring being an engaging topic of discussion and testing, several directions ought to be considered in order to maximize the potential virtual mentoring can have on the entire mentoring process at-large. First, the ability to create clearinghouses where massive amounts of information can be stored, retrieved, and shared with numerous people at any time (Knouse, 2001). Also the ability to develop a team mentoring program is also another viable and possible avenue to pursue. Within this context, many different people can come into a mentoring interaction from different locations within an organization, or different areas on the globe – this may be the next wave of the future for virtual mentoring (Knouse, 2001). With the entire concept of virtual mentoring, it may be highly possible that soon all members within an organization may have a direct link to senior members of a company due to the advent and integration of an assortment of technologies that can make this possible (Knouse, 2001). Through the implementation of such a program; however, it is mindful and wise to consider that the organization in question is prepared to embark on such a journey. In order to be well-prepared for such an event the organization in question must have all the information technology necessary. In accordance with this, it is best to first, run a pilot program to test the program and its believed outcome for future uses by other employees. It will be through the pilot testing of a virtual mentoring program where problems either foreseen or unforeseen can be observed, noted, and remedied (Hamilton & Scandura, 2003). For instance, a problem that can be manageably solved is the training of employees to work with the new software. It is through extensive training programs where employees become familiar with the terminology, technology, and issues that may arise due to their exposure with the computer and software. Also by training employees how to use the technology it will provide them with new and cross-occupational skills that can be used in most organizational settings today (Hamilton & Scandura, 2003).

CONCLUSION

Traditional mentoring is a face-to-face dyadic interaction, but this practice is becoming obsolete. Due to the integration of computerized technology, which is largely responsible for the development and growth of virtual mentoring is the backbone behind the relatively new topic of virtual mentoring. It is because of virtual mentoring women, virtual workplaces and organizations, and e-coaching in addition to other key benefits become modern day fixtures within the virtual landscape of the global economy. However, with traditional and virtual mentoring problems exist. These problems are similar in scope, but uniquely different. Aside from these areas of weakness the strengths far outweigh the costs of mentoring in the general sense. Therefore, with the changing economy, the increased need for globalization, and the need for efficiency it is evident virtual mentoring will continue to be beneficial for the mentor and protégé.

Discussion Questions

1. What is the overarching difference between traditional mentoring verses virtual mentoring?
2. Based on your understanding coupled with information from this chapter, how can traditional mentoring and virtual mentoring complement each other if possible?
3. What are some unique challenges that affect traditional mentoring?
4. What are some unique problems virtual mentoring relationships will inevitably face?
5. How has virtual mentoring altered the organizational infrastructure?
6. What additional implications can be thought of surrounding globalization and virtual mentoring?
7. Have there been moments when you engaged in virtual mentoring either in a personal or professional setting? If so, were you aware you were engaging in virtual mentoring?
8. What are some drawbacks to virtual mentoring?

Virtual mentoring unlike traditional mentoring is rapidly becoming the more preferred way of initiating dialogue with mentors and protégés.

By utilizing information technology, mentors and protégés can communicate with one another across geographic distances that otherwise would have not been possible. Also, by the integration of asynchronous technology, mentors and protégés can send, receive, and reply to message at a time that is most convenient for either member of the interaction. Through the integration of virtual mentoring both members of the interaction will learn to develop solid reading, writing, and overall vital communication skills that will only increase the likelihood that the virtual relationship will be successful. However, limitations exist that can be resolved so that the continued prospect of virtual mentoring can remain a possibility for future people who choose to enter into the virtual world of mentoring electronically. If organizations simply become proactive and are prepared to commit to such a task, then small problems, which can become large mountains to cross, can be easily overcome. For instance, by having all the necessary technology, conducting training seminars, so employees can learn how to use the technology and programs correctly and effectively, instituting a virtual mentor pilot program, and creating a clearinghouse as a general resource bank of information, then many of the aforementioned issues can be resolved with no problem.

REFERENCES

Bekkers, V. (2003). E-governments and the emergence of virtual organizations in the public sector. *The International Journal of Government and Democracy in the Information Age, 8*(3-4), 89–101.

Bell, C. R. (2000). The mentor as partner. *Training & Development, 54*, 52–56.

Bennett, J., & Bush, M. (2009). Coaching in organizations. *Od Practitioner, 41*(1), 2–7.

Bierema, L. L., & Hill, J. R. (2005). Virtual mentoring and hrd. *Advances in Developing Human Resources, 7*(7), 556. doi:10.1177/1523422305279688

Boule, M. (2008). Best practices for working in a virtual team environment. *Library Technology Reports, 44*(1), 28–31.

Darwin, A. (2000). Critical reflections on mentoring in work settings. *Adult Education Quarterly, 50*(3), 197. doi:10.1177/07417130022087008

Graf, T. (2009). The future of od: developing an effective virtual organization for the od Network. *OD Practitioner, 41*(3), 30–36.

Hamilton, B. A., & Scandura, T. A. (2003). E-mentoring: Implications for organizational learning and development in a wired world. *Organizational Dynamics, 3*(4), 388–402. doi:10.1016/S0090-2616(02)00128-6

Hamilton, M., Hamilton, S., & Rhodes, J. (2002). Why mentoring in the workplace works. *New Directions for Youth Development, 93*, 59–89.

Haring-Hidore, M. (1987). Mentoring as a career strategy for women. *Journal of Counseling and Development, 66*(3), 147.

Harrington, A. (1999). E-Mentoring: The advantages and disadvantages of using email to support distance mentoring. *European Social Fund.* Retrieved December 27, 1999 from the World Wide Web: http://www.mentorsforum.co.uk/cOL1/discover.htm

Headlam-Wells, J., Gosland, J., & Craig, J. (2005). There is magic in the web: E-mentoring for women's career development. *International Business, 10*(6), 444–456.

Hill, S. K., Bahniuk, M. H., & Dobos, J. (1989). The impact of mentoring and collegial support on faculty success: An analysis of support behavior, information adequacy, and communication apprehension. *Communication Education, 38*, 15–33. doi:10.1080/03634528909378737

Johnson, W. (2002). The intentional mentor: Strategies and guidelines for the practice of mentoring. *Professional Psychology, Research and Practice, 33*(1), 88. doi:10.1037/0735-7028.33.1.88

Kalisch, B. J., Falzetta, L., & Cook, J. (2005). Group e-mentoring: A new approach to recruitment into nursing. *Nursing Outlook, 53*, 199–205. doi:10.1016/j.outlook.2004.12.005

Kasprisin, C., Boyle Single, P., Single, R., & Muller, C. (2003). Building a better bridge: Testing e-training to improve e-mentoring programs in higher education. *Mentoring and Tutoring: Partnership in Learning, 11*(1), 67. doi:10.1080/1361126032000054817

Kilburg, G. (2007). Three mentoring team relationships and obstacles encountered: A school-based case study. *Mentoring and Tutoring: Partnership in Learning, 15*(3), 293–308. doi:10.1080/13611260701202099

Knouse, S. (2001). Virtual mentoring: Mentoring on the internet. *Journal of Counseling, 38*.

Lavin Colky, D., & Young, W. (2006). Mentoring in the virtual organization: Keys to building successful schools and businesses. *Mentoring and Tutoring: partnership in Learning, 14*(4), 443-447.

Manzin, M., & Kodric,, B. (2009). The influence of outsourcing and information and communication technology on virtualization of the company. *International Research journal, 7*(1), 45-60.

Muller, C. (1998). Mentornet: The national electronic industrial mentoring network for women in engineering and science. Paper presented at the Women in Higher Education Conference (San Francisco, CA, Jan 3-8).

Packard, D. (2003). Web-based mentoring: Challenging traditional models to increase women's access. *Mentoring and Tutoring: Partnership in Learning, 11*(1), 53. doi:10.1080/1361126032000054808

Purcell, K. (2004). Making e-mentoring more effective. *American Journal of Health-System Pharmacy, 61*(3), 284–286.

Ragins, R. B., & Scandura, T, A. (1999). Burden or blessing? Expected costs and benefits of being a mentor. *Journal of Organizational Behavior, 20*(4), 493–509. doi:10.1002/(SICI)1099-1379(199907)20:4<493::AID-JOB894>3.0.CO;2-T

Ramos, M., & Green, R. (2003). Mentoring in libraries. *Library Worklife, 12*(4).

Richmond, V. P., Wrench, J. S., & Gorham, J. (2001). *Communication, learning, and affect in instruction* (3rd ed.). Acton, MA: Tapestry.

ADDITIONAL READING

Ackley, B., & Gall, M. D. (1992). *Skills, strategies and outcomes of successful mentor teachers*. Paper presented at the Annual Meeting of the American Educational Research Association (San Francisco, CA, April 20-24).

Ang, S., & Cummings, L. L. (1994). Panel analysis of feedback-seeking patterns in face-to-face computer-mediated, and computer-generated communication environments. *Perceptual and Motor Skills, 79*(1), 67.

Duarte, D. L. (1999). *Mastering virtual teams: Strategies, tools, and techniques that succeed*. San Francisco, CA: Jossey-Bass.

Edenfield, A. L. (2007). Medical student professionalism at New York University school of medicine. *The Virtual Mentor, 9*(4), 280–284.

El-Shinnawy, M., & Markus, M. (1997). The Poverty of media richness theory: Explaining people's choice of electronic mail versus voice mail. *International Journal of Human-Computer Studies, 46*, 443–467. doi:10.1006/ijhc.1996.0099

Ensher, L. A. (2003). Online mentoring and computer-mediated communication: New directions in research. *Journal of Vocational Behavior, 63*(2), 264–288. doi:10.1016/S0001-8791(03)00044-7

Fisher, K. (2001). *The distance manager: A hands on guide to managing off-site employees and virtual teams.* New York: McGraw-Hill.

Gibson, S. K. (2004). Mentoring in business and industry: The need for a phenomenological perspective. *Mentoring and Tutoring: Partnership and Learning, 12*(2), 259–275. doi:10.1080/1361126042000239974

Gonzales, C. L., & Thompson, V. (1998). Reciprocal mentoring in technology use: Reflecting with a literacy educator. *Journal of Information technology for Teacher Education, 7(*2), 163-178.

Harrington, A. (1999). *E-Mentoring: The advantages and disadvantages of using email to support distance mentoring.* European Social Fund. Retrieved December 27, 1999 from http://www.mentorsforum.co.uk/cOL1/discover.htm

Headlam-Wells, J., Craig, J., & Gosland, J. (2006). Encounters in social cyberspace: E-mentoring for professional women. *Women in Management Review, 21*(6), 483–499. doi:10.1108/09649420610683471

Heller, M. P., & Sindelar, N. W. (1991). Developing an effective teacher mentor program. Bloomington, IND: Phi Delta Kappa Educational Foundation. (ERIC Document Reproduction Service No. ED 332 996).

Lipnack, J., & Stamps, J. (2000). *Virtual teams: people working across boundaries with technology.*

Luna, G., & Cullen, D. (1995). *Empowering the faculty: Mentoring redirected and renewed.* (ERIC Document Reproduction Service No. ED 399888).

Oakley, J. G. (1999). Leadership process in virtual teams and organizations. *Journal of Leadership & Organizational Studies, 5*(3), 3–17. doi:10.1177/107179199900500301

Peterson, R. W. (1989). *Mentor Teacher Handbook.* Retrieved December 28, 1999 from http://apollo.gse.uci.edu/MentorTeacher/Contents.html

Riel, M. (1999). *Tele-Mentoring over the net.* Retrieved December 28, 1999 from the World Wide Web: http://www.igc.org/iearn/circles/mentors.html

Rose Ragins, B., & Kram, K. e. (2007). *The handbook of mentoring at work: Theory, research, and practice.* Los Angeles, CA: Sage Publications.

Russell, J. E. A., & Adams, D. A. (1997). The changing nature of mentoring in organizations: An introduction to the special issue of mentoring in organizations. *Journal of Vocational Behavior, 51*(1), 1–14. doi:10.1006/jvbe.1997.1602

Schlichte, J., Yssel, N., & Merbler, J. (2005). Pathway to burnout: Case studies in teacher isolation and alienation. *Preventing School Failure, 50*(1), 34–40. doi:10.3200/PSFL.50.1.35-40

Seabrooks, J. J., Kenney, S., & LaMontagne, M. (2000). Collaboration and Virtual mentoring: Building relationships between pre-service and in-service special education teachers. *Journal of Information Technology for Teacher Education, 9*(2), 219–236.

Single, P. B., Jaffe, A., & Schwartz, R. (1999). Evaluating programs for recruiting and retaining community faculty. *Family Medicine, 31*(2), 114–121.

Single, P. B., & Muller, C. B. (1999, April). *Electronic Mentoring: Issues to Advance Research and Practice.* Paper presented at the International Mentoring Association Conference, Atlanta, GA.

Single, P. B., & Muller, C. B. (2001). When email and mentoring unite: The implementation of a nationwide electronic mentoring program . In Stromei, L. K. (Ed.), *Creating Mentoring and Coaching Programs*. Alexandria, VA: American Society for Training and Development in Action Series.

Smith, S. C., & Scott, J. J. (1990). *The collaborative school: A work environment for effective instruction* (Report No. ISBN-0-86552-092-5). Reston, VA: National Association of Secondary School Principals. (ERIC Document Reproduction Service No. ED316918)

Southeast Center for Teaching Quality. (2004). *Teaching working conditions are student working conditions.* (ERIC Document Reproduction Service No. ED 485954). University of North Carolina: Wighton, D. J. (1993). *Telementoring: An examination of the potential for an educational network.* USWEST Fellows and Telementoring. Retrieved December 28, 1999 from t http://mentor.creighton.edu/htm/telement.htm

Willbur, J. (1989). Three keys to a structured mentoring system. *Mentoring International, 3*(3), 32–36.

Chapter 11
Politics in Virtual Work

Shawn D. Long
University of North Carolina at Charlotte, USA

Marla D. Boughton
University of North Carolina at Charlotte, USA

Rachel Widener
University of North Carolina at Charlotte, USA

ABSTRACT

Due to their hierarchical structure and limited resources, organizations are inherently political. Employees need to know how to "play the game" in order to get ahead. In this chapter, we provide a background on politics, examining how the study of politics has evolved over time. We also examine the relationship between politics and similar constructs, such as authority, power, and influence. We then apply politics to an increasingly common organizational structure—virtual teams. Based upon research on trust, resource allocation, and influence in virtual teams, we suggest that, rather than being attenuated in the virtual environment, politics may in fact become exacerbated by the use of computer-mediated communication. We end the chapter with suggestions for future research on politics in virtual teams.

INTRODUCTION

Organizational executives are wasting 20 percent of their time dealing with company politics (Communication World, 1995). This statistic indicates not only a decrease in productivity due to organizational politics, but also suggests a potential increase in harmful activities. In order to achieve a desired outcome within their organizations, individuals may go so far as to spread rumors about colleagues, leak sensitive company information to the media, threaten or sabotage coworkers or projects, or bypass their immediate supervisors (Farrell & Petersen, 1982). Clearly, organizational politics present several causes for concern.

Organizational politics are generally considered to be a type of influence process (Mayes & Allen, 1977), which significantly impacts the relational dynamics of superiors and subordinates in an organization. Politics, power and authority are all intertwined communication concepts. Rosabeth Moss Kanter (1979) in her seminal article "Power failure in management circuits" lamented that,

DOI: 10.4018/978-1-61520-979-8.ch011

"Power is America's last dirty word. It is easier to talk about money-and much easier to talk about sex-than it is to talk about power. People who have it deny it; people who want it do not want to appear to hunger for it; and people who engage in its machinations do so secretly (pg. 68)."

"Politics" can easily replace "Power" in the passage above and the spirit of the argument remains the same. Politics is an insidious and seductive, yet oftentimes invisible element in organizational behavior.

Advantages and disadvantages of politics in the workplace have been noted in the literature. Gaining and maintaining access to resources and information and the ability to deliver this information to employees in a timely and secure manner solidifies the political clout of managers in many organizations and certainly facilitates positive relational dynamics with employees in a variety of contexts. However, some studies suggest that subordinates who perceive their supervisors as highly involved in organizational politics are less open in their communication and generally less satisfied with their supervisors than subordinates who perceive their supervisors as moderately or minimally involved in politics (Jablin, 1981, pg. 273). The dearth of studies in organizational politics highlights a neglected, yet critical, aspect of organizational life. This is particularly true given the changing nature of work with the explosion of virtual work and an emerging new social contract between employers and employees of what constitutes "work".

This chapter further advances the discussion of politics in virtual work. Due to the lack of consistent scholarship in the area of politics in virtual work, we approach this topic with a standard overview of authority and power in organizations; offer extant theories and definitions of power and politics in organizations; relocate these concepts to virtual work politics and suggest implications and consequences of engaging in organizational politics in virtual work.

BACKGROUND

Organizations are inherently pluralistic and political, divided into competing interests and differing preferences among organizational members. Politics exist in organizations because individuals seek "some end state or valued outcome" such as additional capital or increased power (Pfeffer, 1982, p. 78). However, before developing an understanding of politics, one must understand the complex conceptions of power and authority intrinsic to politics. Power exists in everyday interactions between individuals and teams, but it is authority that determines where power is situated.

Authority in Organizations

Sources of power within an organization often formally originate from authority, determined by Jones (1997) to be "legitimized by the legal and cultural foundations on which an organization is based" (p. 564). Power within organizations is largely the result of the distribution of authority (Jones, 1997). Organizations are innately comprised of individuals with different agendas and motivations who use their authority to achieve their desired outcomes.

As an operational hierarchy of power is established, organizations determine the amount and type of authority to be given to each individual. Distribution of authority within organizations serves to accomplish consensus and coordinate the activities of members (Mintzberg, 1983). Essentially, by making the choice to participate in an organization, members are consenting to the authority of the organization.

Consensus about the distribution of authority throughout the organization develops both formally and passively. Formal consensus is cultivated through established hierarchies legitimized by members, and passive consensus is achieved as members respond to the demands of authority. As members of a corporate group, individuals are, by virtue of their membership, subject to authority and the control of those in power (Weber, 1947).

Power in Organizations

Power is a fundamental concept in political theories because political behavior is action taken to obtain or maintain power. Definitions of power often incorporate influence, opposition, and dominance (Pfeffer, 1982; Conrad, 1993). Fimbel (1994) relates power to a person's potential for changing another's "attitudes or behavior" (p. 8). In his *Theory of Social and Economic Organization*, Weber (1947) associates power with the probability that an individual will "be in a position to carry out his own will despite resistance" (p. 152). Similarly, Jones (1997) argues that power, in conjunction with other resources, allows individuals to obtain preferred outcomes.

Power is inherent to organizations due to their hierarchical nature. Employees use their power and influence to succeed and advance within the organization. The more an individual's success depends on the performance of others, the more important it becomes for the individual to have power. Power allows the individual to gain the resources and make the decisions necessary to succeed.

It is important to note that power in organizations is not guaranteed (Conrad, 1993). Individuals can only use power and influence if others grant them that ability. This formal power stems from the authority provided by one's position within the organizational hierarchy.

Power and Conflict

In organizations there are intrinsic tensions between the individual and the group (Pfeffer, 1982). Power exists in the conditions of conflict between the interests of the individual and interests of the group. However, power is often used in apparent attempts at satisfying an individual's own personal needs which are unauthorized by

the organization (Mintzberg, 1983). Individuals often use their power to resolve conflicts in organizations. For example, power plays within organizations determine how desired resources are allocated (Morgan, 1996).

Power also provides individuals with a means of preventing conflict from forming. A balance of organizational power involves opportunities for alternative views and solutions where dissenting views can be heard (Jones, 1997). Political behavior is the means by which individuals enact their power to fulfill their needs. The following section will define politics and further describe the construct's relationship with authority, power, and influence.

Defining Politics

The political landscape in organizations is rooted in diversity and the relational dynamics between individuals. Diversity of thoughts, perspectives, backgrounds and motives of individuals results in a tension when people think differently and are determined to act differently (Morgan, 1996). Using and applying politics and authority sometimes eases this tension.

Aristotle first examined organizational politics related to the visible formation of conflict and seedy "wheeling and dealing" negotiation. Politics, according to Aristotle, avoids totalitarian power while maintaining stability and order throughout a diverse environment (Morgan, 1996). The development of order further results in the formation of coalitions and mutual influence within organizations. Politics provide a channel for those with divergent interests to reconcile differences through consultation and negotiation. Politics is also concerned with relationships of control or influence.

More recently, Mintzberg (1983) defined politics as "individual or group behavior that is informal... divisive... illegitimate and unsanctioned by formal authority" (p. 172). This definition recasts the role of formal politics built into the structure of organizations with a somewhat negative connotation but emphasizes the powerful informal role politics plays in daily organizational lives. Politics is often defined as conflict over whose preferences are to prevail or any actions related to organizational power.

Redefining Politics

Although definitions of politics often contain certain negative connotations, some scholars define politics more neutrally as an integral part of an organization (Jones, 1997). Pfeffer suggests that politics occur in organizations when individuals "acquire, develop, and use power and other resources to obtain one's preferred outcomes in a situation" (Fimbel, 1994, p. 9). The more neutral definitions serve in stark contrast to Mintzberg's assertion of politics as illegitimate and unauthorized actions.

Mayes and Allen (1977) conclude that Mintzberg's approach is too narrow to fully capture the robust spirit of organizational politics and propose that contemporary theories of politics operate at both micro, or individual levels, and macro, or organizational levels. They further posit that apart from organizational politics, which relates only to decision-making and resource allocation, definitions must also delineate political and non-political behaviors.

In addition, Mayes and Allen (1977) suggest that definitions of politics need to be comprehensive enough to include more than conflict over policy decisions and should incorporate elements of politics occurring on an ongoing basis within organizations. Towards this end, they define politics as "the management of influence" (Mayes & Allen, 1977, p.675). Throughout the literature, politics is related to the application of both power and influence.

Developing an inclusive conceptualization of politics, Robbins (2002) argues that individuals are engaging in politics whenever power is converted into action and not necessarily as part of their required organizational tasks. These actions are further described as either legitimate, 'everyday' politics or illegitimate, extreme political behavior. Conrad (1993) similarly defines politics as the overt application of power, usually involving actions that will achieve a desired personal advantage or result. Ultimately, organizational politics entails communication in order to construct order amid diversity and conflict.

ORGANIZATIONAL AND TEAM POLITICS

Incorporating the definitions provided above, we define organizational politics as extra-role behavior in which individuals convert their power into action to obtain desired resources or outcomes. When individuals come together in organizations and teams, they engage in politics as a means of gaining and maintaining power and influence. Additionally, political skill allows individuals to use their power effectively. This section of the chapter reviews politics in organizations and teams and compares them to politics in virtual teams.

Politics in Organizations

Organizational politics are extra-role activities that influence the distribution of resources within the organization (Farrell & Peterson, 1982). Both individual and organizational factors contribute to political behavior; however, organizational factors tend to play a greater role. Organizational factors that promote political behavior include competition for scarce resources, changing resource allocation procedures, and opportunities to get ahead in the organization. In addition, some organizational cultures promote political behavior. These cultures are characterized by high levels of ambiguity regarding roles and performance evaluations, unfair rewards/recognition, and low intergroup cooperation (Parker, Dipboye, & Jackson, 1995). At the individual level, those who are more likely to engage in political behavior tend to be high self-monitors, those who possess an internal locus of control, and those with a high need for power.

Success within an organization largely relies on an individual's ability to learn the political ropes and hone their political skills to influence and control decision-making. Such political behaviors might also include "increasing indispensability... building and managing coalitions, controlling the agenda, and bringing in an outside expert" (Jones, 1997, p. 578). Fimbel (1994) further identifies usage of political strategies in order to: cultivate a favorable impression, show competence, express confidence, be well liked, develop a base of support, align oneself with more powerful others, and control access of information.

Politics in Virtual Teams

Currently, there is a dearth of research regarding political behavior in virtual teams. We are attempting to advance this discussion by applying antecedents used in research on politics in face-to-face interactions to individuals who work in virtual teams. Although the work setting differs, many of the approaches and political techniques and consequences found in physical and traditional organizational settings may be similar to those found in computer-mediated virtual work.

The definition of politics provides reason to believe that political behavior is more prevalent in virtual teams, compared to traditional face-to-face teams. Political behavior is consistently defined as activities outside of the formal job role. Compared to face-to-face communication, it is more difficult to determine what activities (assigned or extra-role) others are performing, to track team progress, and to communicate expectations in computer-mediated communication. Below we will describe how the ambiguity inherent to virtual teams allows for increased political behavior in this setting.

First, in virtual teams, it is more difficult for leaders to monitor the progress of team members and therefore reward and recognize them. Team members also may not trust that they will be rewarded for their efforts since it is more difficult to show and document how much effort they are contributing to the project; in a virtual team you cannot demonstrate effort by coming in early or staying late. These factors may lead to an increase in political behavior, such as ingratiation with the team leader, in order to be rewarded.

A second, related point is that a manager may unconsciously favor individuals who work "in the office" versus those who work virtually, and the rewards and behaviors of the manager may reflect this bias. Such actions may include, but are not limited to, stalled upward mobility, lateral only promotions, and the withholding of key and/or lead assignments from virtual employees. The changes brought about by working in the virtual environment can have real, negative consequences for members of virtual teams.

Third, the constraints imposed by computer-mediation (e.g., lack of nonverbal cues, asynchronous communication, increased physical distance, etc.) can affect team members' political behavior. For example, Metiu (2006) found that virtual team members on one continent used informal closure strategies (e.g., sending incomplete documents to India) to obtain and maintain power. The closure strategies led to negative assumptions about the expertise and abilities of the team members in India, which in turn led to the creation of additional closure strategies. This study suggests that physical distance can increase political behavior.

Finally, intergroup cooperation in virtual teams may be lower than in face-to-face teams. This is because trust and cohesion take longer to develop with computer-mediated communication (Walther, 1996). Trust is a key factor in developing close relationships. Without trust, virtual team members may be less willing to cooperate with one another and may engage in more political behaviors.

Due to the lack of physical proximity and the reliance on communication technologies, our understanding of trust in virtual teams is different from the trust in traditional teams (Picherit-Duthler, Long & Kohut, 2004). Meyerson, Weick, and Kramer (1996) coined the term "swift trust" to describe how virtual teams develop a different type of trust than in traditional teams. Due to the shared task orientation rather than the relational dynamics typical in traditional work arrangements, individuals are able to develop trust more quickly (Jarvenpaa & Leidner, 1999). This swift trust may be compromised and potentially eradicated if the political behavior is seen as destructive or power is misplaced in this work arrangement and if there is a perception that working virtually is viewed as being "out of the loop" and disconnected to the power bases of the organization or team. In sum, when antecedents of organizational politics are applied to virtual teams, it seems that political behavior should be, not only prevalent, but more extreme due to the added ambiguity inherent in computer-mediated communication.

Politics and Resource Allocation in Virtual Teams

As the above discussion of influence tactics and politics within teams suggests, organizations are settings which are inherently defined by power. Both the structure of and the communication within an organization are based on power distributions within this entity. As such, politics are highly applicable to the organizational context in which individuals struggle for resources and power. This section will explore how politics affect resource allocation in virtual teams.

Impression Management

In the physical environment, resource allocation can function as a result of impression management. Acquiring scarce resources requires political behavior. Employees who come in early and stay late may be perceived by those who distribute resources as harder workers and as more valuable than their coworkers. These "hard workers" may be rewarded with extra resources (e.g., bonuses, raises, promotions).

Teleworkers or members of virtual teams have more difficulty demonstrating their hard work as there is no one physically present to observe them. Although we are transitioning to more task-focused employment, time is still the primary determinant of the work day structure (Thompson, 1967); as such, employees working in a physical office may garner more resources than those working virtually. Members of virtual teams will need to find ways to ensure that their contributions are recognized by resource allocators at the organization's physical headquarters. The greater difficulty of impression management in a computer-mediated context causes increased difficulties in garnering scarce resources which, in turn, could lead to increased political behavior in virtual teams.

Centrality

Centrality plays a pivotal role in determining how resources are allocated and also provides support for the assertion that political behavior is increased in virtual teams, compared to face-to-face teams. Centrality is defined as how closely a team's purpose aligns with the mission of the organization (Hackman, 1985). For a team that works at the physical headquarters of the organization, centrality is relatively easy to display.

Depending on the construction of the virtual team, displays of centrality may be difficult, if not impossible, to accomplish. This difficulty arises because virtual teams are often comprised of members from different organizations who have come together to accomplish a task. The organizations from which the team members come most likely have different—possibly conflicting—missions, and team members will have to choose whether to align themselves with the mission of the organization or the purpose of the team. When this division is present, resources will most likely be distributed to face-to-face teams that have demonstrated centrality.

Team Composition

Another problem for garnering resources is posed by virtual teams that are comprised of members from different organizations or from different departments within the same organization. As no one organization or unit is responsible for funding the virtual team, it is difficult for the virtual team leader to gather the necessary resources for the team to complete its task. Organizational politics can help virtual team leaders and members acquire the resources they need to ensure that their project is a success.

It can also be difficult for the virtual team to get sufficient members assigned to it. Virtual team members often have additional assignments to complete in their physical office which compete with their virtual work. These tasks are observable to their supervisor, while the work that they do for their virtual teams is less apparent. Because virtual team leaders are different than the members' supervisors, supervisors may not receive updates on the team's progress or accomplishments and may see membership in the virtual team as wasting the employee's time which could be better spent working on assignments for the supervisor. When this is the case, the supervisor may demand that the employee spend less time on the virtual team project or be removed from the project entirely. Political behavior can be used to convince others of the important contributions made by the virtual team and its members.

Influence in Virtual Teams

In organizational research, discussions of politics are closely tied to discussions of power and influence. These concepts are so closely related that Ferris, Russ, and Fandt (1989) defined organizational politics as "a social influence process in which behavior is strategically designed to maximize short-term or long-term self-interest, which is either consistent with or at the expense of others' interests" (p.145). Because organizational politics is defined by influence and is closely related to both power, it is important to examine influence in virtual organizations when looking at politics.

Influence Tactics

While influence tactics are important at the organizational level because they maximize self-interest, they also play a significant role at the team level. In teams, influence tactics can determine "how decisions are made, which strategies and policies are implemented successfully, how motivated the team members will be to achieve the team's goals, and how much cooperation and support will be a significant part of the ways members interact with each other" (Elron & Vigoda-Gadot, 2006, p.298). Influence tactics are examples of political behavior that allow individuals to gain and exert power, garner resources, and attain desired goals.

Several influence tactics have been identified in the organizational research literature. These include rational persuasion, inspirational appeals, consultation, ingratiation, personal appeals, exchange, coalition, legitimating, pressure, sanctions, and upward-appeal (Kipnis, Schmidt, & Wilkinson, 1980; Yukl & Falbe, 1990). These tactics can be separated into hard tactics and soft tactics. Hard tactics include exchange, coalitions, and pressure. Soft influence tactics are personal and inspirational appeals, rational persuasion, and consultation.

In face-to-face interactions, soft influence tactics tend to be more effective than hard influence tactics. According to Yukl et al., (1990) the most effective influence tactics are rational persuasion, inspirational appeals and consultation. The least effective are pressure, coalition and legitimating. Ingratiation, personal appeals and exchange were intermediate in effectiveness (Elron & Vigoda-Gadot, 2006).

Impact of Computer-Mediated Communication

Findings of influence tactics in face-to-face teams may not always apply to virtual teams as these teams operate in different contexts. One of the main differences between computer-mediated communication and face-to-face communication is the lack of physical nonverbal cues available in the virtual world, such as facial expressions, tone, and gestures, outside of emoticons. Walther (1996) argued that a lack of nonverbal cues does not necessarily result in less effective communication; however, it does affect interactions and relationship formation within virtual teams. Because interactions are altered in computer-mediated communication, influence tactics may not function in the same way as they do in face-to-face communication.

Because of the increasing popularity of such work arrangements, it is important to consider how politics and influence tactics may function differently in virtual teams, compared to face-to-face teams. Ferris, Russ, and Fandt's (1989) created a conceptualization of politics in which one of the antecedents of politics is a social interaction and work context that are not rigidly ritualized, scripted, or otherwise constrained. Because a "reasonably high degree of uncertainty or ambiguity" (Ferris et al., p.147) exists regarding how virtual teams are supposed to function, it is reasonable to assume that political behavior would be higher in virtual teams, relative to collocated teams. However, this assumption has not received empirical support.

In a study of global virtual teams, Elron and Vigoda-Gadot (2006) found that limited familiarity/intimacy with team members, high task orientation within the team, and team centrality led to more socially acceptable and effective influence tactics. More specifically, the researchers found

that the most commonly used influence tactics in virtual teams were rational persuasion and consultation, which is similar to findings for face-to-face teams. Further, the researchers found that there was a decrease in political actions within the virtual teams. These results seem counterintuitive, given that individuals are often less inhibited in online interactions (Kiesler & Sproull, 1992).

However, Elron and Vigoda-Gadot's finding of decreased politics makes sense in the more specific context of virtual teams. There is an automatic record of the communications that occur within virtual teams, a running archive of information. Team members, although not necessarily familiar with one another, are not anonymous. Words and actions can be traced back to their originator, hence decrease anonymity. Thus, in virtual teams there is accountability and self-monitoring mechanisms in place for one's virtual work behavior. As such, virtual team members may be more strategic about or think twice before using the more obvious hard influence tactics and instead use the more socially acceptable soft influence tactics or simply avoid political behavior entirely.

Elron and Vigoda-Gadot (2006) showed that virtual team politics differ from face-to-face politics in three distinct ways. The underlying cause of these differences is the lack of information available in virtual teams. First, virtual team members cannot use nonverbal cues to help mask the intent of their political behavior, necessitating the use of more subtle approaches. One difference that arises from this lack of information is that virtual team politics are construed as being milder than face-to-face politics. This is a result of the inherent nature of virtual teams in which there tends to be a lack of familiarity/intimacy among team members, an increase in task orientation, and in which the team forms a more peripheral role in members' organizational identities in comparison to face-to-face teams.

A second difference between the two types of teams is that different influence tactics are used and are effective in the different contexts.

Whereas the most effective tactics for members of face-to-face teams tend to be rational persuasion, inspirational appeals and consultation (Yukl & Falbe, 1990), members of virtual teams are less likely to use any type of influence tactic (Elron & Vigoda-Gadot, 2006).

The final distinction between virtual team politics and face-to-face politics identified in prior research is that the limited familiarity of virtual team members leads to politics becoming less acceptable than it is in face-to-face environments (Elron & Vigoda-Gadot, 2006). This is because cultural and language differences exist in virtual teams that cause team members to be more polite and inhibit harsh responses. Limited familiarity could have the opposite effect, freeing team members from the social mores that typically shape their behaviors. However, this is unlikely to be the case as political behaviors, especially hard influence tactics, are risky behaviors which can have repercussions if noticed. Violators of team norms are subject to sanctioning from group members, leading to a decrease in the effectiveness of the political action.

Implications for Virtual Teams

While politics in face-to-face settings lead to lower job satisfaction, increased job anxiety and stress, and higher turnover (Valle & Witt, 2001), virtual team members may not necessarily suffer from similar outcomes. Previous research has found that overt politics play a minimal role in the functioning of virtual teams (Elron & Vigoda-Gadot, 2006). The lack of politics is especially beneficial for virtual teams who suffer from other obstacles that affect their productivity, such as technical problems, language/cultural barriers, and lack of clarity within their communications. The subsequent result is one less obstacle for virtual team members to overcome.

Where politics become necessary for virtual team members is in the acquisition of resources. Virtual team leaders need to be cognizant of how organizational members who distribute key resources perceive their virtual team. Virtual team leaders and members will need to use influence tactics and impression management on both virtual and collocated individuals in order to garner resources. Thus, focusing political behavior outside of the virtual team can have positive consequences for the team as a whole.

The Political Landscape of Virtual Work

Politics and power, both direct and indirect, in organizations are here to stay. Assuming that the virtual configuration of co-located teams and individuals will eradicate the political nature of organizational functioning is a naïve and false assumption. As computer-mediated communication theory suggests, the virtual environment may actually accelerate politics in work. As more organizations are reducing their physical workplace presence to a more remote virtual infrastructure, battles over resources, limited vertical positions, attention by management of individual work and a host of other implications highlights the need for greater attention to the political landscape of virtual work.

Politics, power and influence are all critical features of organizational life. However, these features operate in a subtle and indirect fashion to manipulate various organizational members, practices and processes. An individual's image, upward mobility and levels of trust by peers, management and subordinates are facilitated by the political moves, whether overt or covert, of the organizational actor. Upward mobility, assignments to prime projects and tasks, and ones position within the organization greatly depends on the type and quality of work but also on how this work is articulated to others in the organization, particularly those who are in a position of power or decision making. To be sure, political behavior in the physical environment is not the same as in virtual work. We suggest that many of the political tasks and political labor that is apparent in traditional face-to-face organizations dissipates in the virtual work environment. It may certainly take a different form, but the techniques and usage of political posturing may not be as evident in virtual work.

Virtual work politics is analogous to a long distance relationship. At first, organizations, much like people in newly developed relationships, are apt to play fair, be committed, and see all the workings of the new relationship (configurations) in all the best possible lights (convenience of working from home; less commute to work; flexible hours; more time with family, friends, etc.; concentration of tasks without interruptions indicative of face-to-face work, etc.). Political posturing is minimized or absent in the initial stages of the relationship. However, as time moves forward and the lack of physical presence facilitates a reduction of individual attention by "the other", so does the commitment and excitement with the relationship. There are increasing levels of suspicion about the commitment of each party and the old adage "out of sight...out of mind" may influence organizational decision makers on resource allocations, promotions, informal communication networks, and other opportunities afforded to those who are "around". This inherently creates a political wedge, although unspoken, between virtual members and physically present members of the organization. This may characterize virtual relationships in terms of connectivity and sustainability, especially for those who have ambitions of being upwardly mobile. When promotions, physical and social contact with peers and supervisors, and informal communication that may lead to increased satisfaction of employees are missing or not overtly available, individuals may seek to regain their organizational agency by relocating to another relationship—organizational or personal.

CONCLUSION AND FUTURE RESEARCH DIRECTIONS

Politics is a ubiquitous feature of organizational life. This ambiguous communication function is an important, yet often abused tool in organizations. There is a dearth of research on the political functions in virtual work. Due to the increasing reliance on technology in organizations and the rapid reconfiguration of traditional work structures to virtual ones, greater attention and scholarship to organizational politics in virtual work should reflect this shift in the organizational aesthetic. The consequences of political maneuvering, or the lack thereof, may have long-reaching impacts on organizations and its members. As indicated in the research provided throughout this chapter, organizational politics is vibrant, although subtle, in most organizational structures. This chapter broadly examined power, authority and politics in organizations, while localizing similar concepts to virtual work. We proposed a "long-distance relationship" metaphor to virtual work, as well as advanced positive and negative implications of working virtually.

It is clear that organizational politics thrive when organizations and people intersect. Further research should empirically examine the nuanced features of organizational politics, contextualizing data-driven consequences and processes, and develop a virtual work typology to better understand the degrees of political maneuvering associated with various virtual organizational structures. As more organizational members situate themselves in virtual working environments, a better understanding of the processes, practices, and implications of working virtually is needed.

REFERENCES

Conrad, C. (1993). *Strategic organizational communication: Toward the twenty-first century* (3rd ed.). Fort Worth: Harcourt Brace College Publishers.

Elron, R., & Vigoda-Gadot, E. (2006). Influence and political processes in cyberspace: The case of global virtual teams. *International Journal of Cross Cultural Management, 6*, 295–317. doi:10.1177/1470595806070636

Farrell, D., & Petersen, J. C. (1982). Patterns of political behavior in organizations. *Academy of Management Review, 7*, 403–412. doi:10.2307/257332

Ferris, G. R., Russ, G. S., & Fandt, P. M. (1989). Politics in organizations . In Giacalone, R. A., & Rosenfeld, P. (Eds.), *Impression Management in the Organization* (pp. 143–170). Hillsdale, NJ: Lawrence Erlbaum Associates.

Fimbel, N. (1994). Communicating realistically: Taking account of politics in internal business communications. *Journal of Business Communication, 31*, 7–26. doi:10.1177/002194369403100101

Jarvenpaa, S. L., & Leidner, D. E. (1999). Communication and trust in global virtual teams. *Organization Science, 3*. http://jcmc.indiana.edu/vol3/issue4/jarvenpaa.html.

Jones, G. R. (1997). *Organizational theory: Text and cases* (2nd ed.). Massachusetts: Addison-Wesley Publishing Company.

Kanter, R. M. (1979). Power failure in management circuits. *Harvard Business Review, 57*(4), 65–75.

Kiesler, S., & Sproull, L. (1992). Group decision making and communication technology. *Organizational Behavior and Human Decision Processes, 52*, 96–123. doi:10.1016/0749-5978(92)90047-B

Kipnis, D., Schmidt, S. M., & Wilkinson, I. (1980). Intraorganizational influence tactics: Exploration in getting one's way. *The Journal of Applied Psychology, 65*, 440–452. doi:10.1037/0021-9010.65.4.440

Mayes, B. T., & Allen, R. W. (1977). Toward a definition of organizational politics. *Academy of Management Review, 1*, 672–676. doi:10.2307/257520

Metiu, A. (2006). Owning the code: Status closure in distributed groups. *Organization Science, 17*, 418–435. doi:10.1287/orsc.1060.0195

Meyerson, D., Weick, K. E., & Kramer, R. M. (1996). Swift trust and temporary groups . In Kramer, R. M., & Tyler, T. R. (Eds.), *Trust in organizations: Frontiers of theory and research* (pp. 166–195). Thousand Oaks, CA: SAGE Publications.

Mintzberg, H. (1983). *Power in and around organizations*. New Jersey: Prentice Hall.

Morgan, G. (1996). *Images of organization* (2nd ed.). London: Sage Publications.

Parker, C. P., Dipboye, R. L., & Jackson, S. L. (1995). Perceptions of organizational politics: An investigation of antecedents and consequences. *Journal of Management, 21*, 891–912. doi:10.1177/014920639502100505

Pfeffer, J. (1982). *Organizations and organization theory*. Boston: Pitman Publishing Inc.

Robbins, S. P. (2002). *Organizational behavior* (10th ed.). New Jersey: Prentice Hall.

Survey quantifies amount of time executives waste in organizational politics. (1995, January/February). *Communication World, 12(1)*, 1-4.

Thompson, E. P. (1967). Time, work-discipline, and industrial capitalism. *Past & Present, 38*, 56–97. doi:10.1093/past/38.1.56

Valle, M., & Witt, L. A. (2001). The moderating effect of teamwork perceptions on the orgainztional politics-job satisfaction relationship. *The Journal of Social Psychology, 141*, 379–388. doi:10.1080/00224540109600559

Walther, J. B. (1996). Computer-mediated communication: Impersonal, interpersonal, and hyperpersonal interaction. *Communication Research, 23*, 3–43. doi:10.1177/009365096023001001

Weber, M. (1947). *Max Weber: The theory of social and economic organization* (Henderson, A. M., & Parsons, T., Trans.). New York: Oxford University Press.

Yukl, G., & Falbe, C. M. (1990). Influence tactics in upward, downward, and lateral influence attempts. *The Journal of Applied Psychology, 76*, 416–423. doi:10.1037/0021-9010.76.3.416

ADDITIONAL READING

Benoit-Barne, C., & Cooren, F. (2009). The accomplishment of authority through presentification. *Management Communication Quarterly, 23*, 5–31. doi:10.1177/0893318909335414

Clegg, S., Courpasson, D., & Phillips, N. (2006). *Power in organizations*. London: Sage.

Dubrovsky, V. J., Kiesler, S., & Sethna, B. N. (1991). The equalization phenomenon: Status effects in computer-mediated and face-to-face decision-making groups. *Human-Computer Interaction, 6*, 119–146. doi:10.1207/s15327051hci0602_2

Ferris, G. R., Russ, G. S., & Fandt, P. M. (1989). Politics in organizations . In Giacalone, R. A., & Rosenfeld, P. (Eds.), *Impression management in the organization* (pp. 143–170). Hillside, NJ: Lawrence Erlbaum Associates.

Hollingshead, A. B. (1996). Information suppression and status persistence in group decision making: The effects of communication media. *Human Communication Research, 23*, 193–219. doi:10.1111/j.1468-2958.1996.tb00392.x

Perrow, C. (1986). *Complex Organizations: A Critical Essay*. New York: Random House.

Pfeffer, J. (1992). *Managing with Power: Power and Influence in Organizations*. Boston: Harvard Business School Press.

Ridgeway, C. L., & Balkwell, J. W. (1997). Group processes and the diffusion of status beliefs. *Social Psychology Quarterly, 60*, 14–31. doi:10.2307/2787009

Ridgeway, C. L., & Berger, J. (1986). Expectations, legitimation, and dominance behavior in task groups. *American Sociological Review, 51*, 603–617. doi:10.2307/2095487

Scott, W. R. (2003). *Organizations: Natural, Rational, and Open Systems* (5th ed.). Upper Saddle River, NJ: Prentice Hall.

Weber, M. (1958). The three types of legitimate rule. *Berkeley Publications in Society & Institutions, 4*(1), 1–11.

Weisband, S. P., Schneider, S. K., & Connolly, T. (1995). Computer-mediated communication and social information: Status salience and status differences. *Academy of Management Journal, 38*, 1124–1151. doi:10.2307/256623

KEY TERMS AND DEFINITIONS

Authority: the legitimization of power.

Computer-Mediated Communication: synchronous or asynchronous communication conducted over a computer. Communication may consist solely of text or may include audio and/ or visual components as well.

Influence: the exertion of power.

Influence Tactics: methods of manipulating others in order to get what one wants.

Organizational Culture: prevailing values and shared meanings unifying members of the organization

Organizational Politics: extra-role behavior in which individuals convert their power into action to obtain desired resources or outcomes.

Power: the ability to control and influence people and resources for personal gain.

Virtual Team: a group of two or more people who work together to complete a task or fulfill a shared purpose. Members of the group are separated geographically (and possibly temporally). Because they rarely, if ever, meet face-to-face, members of virtual teams communicate through other media such as the telephone and the computer.

Section 3
Practices in Virtual Work

Chapter 12
The Amplification of Power Dynamics in Virtual Work

Stephen C. Yungbluth
Northern Kentucky University, USA

Zachary P. Hart
Northern Kentucky University, USA

ABSTRACT

This chapter examines how power dynamics are manifested in virtual work. It starts with a look at how power is demonstrated in traditional decision making, and progresses to an exploration of how some organizations are experimenting with different forms of e-participation. Two cases are presented to illustrate some of the decisions associated with the implementation of information and communication technology (ICT), and the consequences of those choices. The first case looks at President Obama's platform on technology and how his administration has embraced it to expand his vision of democracy in the information age. The second case portrays a utility company seeking to increase the involvement of its stakeholders through the creation of a blog site for the exclusive use of its community council. Both cases reveal a complex view of how organizations attempting to increase participation can paradoxically find themselves stifling it.

INTRODUCTION

Working in virtual environments provides a number of tools that can serve to amplify the power dynamics involved in the relationships among the relevant stakeholders. The internet was developed under a premise of facilitating open information sharing and providing a platform for more equal participation. There are many information and communication technologies (ICTs) that demonstrate the attainment of these ideals. However, there are also many developments in other ICTs that have provided a more sophisticated means of command and control that could signal the arrival of a type of neo-scientific management. At either extreme, it would appear that the ordinary power dynamics associated with the traditional working relationships between employers, employees, customers, suppliers, regulators, and other stakeholders are all amplified by technology that either enhances the

DOI: 10.4018/978-1-61520-979-8.ch012

participation of these stakeholders by increasing the levels of participation in both a quantitative and qualitative sense, or strengthens the capacity of those who desire to monitor and constrain their communication. The objective of this chapter is to identify how these competing organizational paradigms are invoked by engaging organizational stakeholders through the various processes of virtual work and electronic participation.

BACKGROUND

Power is one of the most frequently studied concepts in the social sciences. Accordingly, there are many different perspectives on how power should be conceptualized. One of the most frequently cited frameworks for understanding the various bases of power was provided by French and Raven (1959). Work on this framework has been sustained for almost 50 years (Raven, 2008) and has led to the development of the Power/Interaction Model of Interpersonal Influence. Tompkins and Cheney (1985) utilize Edwards' (1981) historic description of the progression in communicative strategies moving from simple control, to technical control, and then bureaucratic control. They then add concertive control to the list to describe how organizational values continue to unobtrusively influence the behavior of organizational members in the absence of any overt controlling mechanism. Despite the recognition of the multiple bases of power held by members across the organizational hierarchy, the concept of power has mostly been viewed as inherently located within the organizational structure, which thereby produces dominant relationships. Tompkins and Cheney (1985) make a distinction between power and control where power is the capacity to achieve a goal and control is the exercise of that capacity. Barker and Cheney (1994) point out that any form of power is "most meaningful, then not as a commodity (though we commonly reify it metaphorically so: "Her power rose yesterday") but as we exercise

it" (p. 22). Mumby (2001) also advocates a more communicative view that conceptualizes power as the situational accomplishment of actors, which allows for a more open view of how organizations are constructed. This view is particularly valuable when thinking about how the work of organizations is accomplished in virtual environments where the "organization" is no longer bound by physical space or the traditional markers of status. Rather, organizations are beginning to be defined by the relationships between the various stakeholders who share interdependent goals. These relationships do not necessarily require the face-to-face contact traditionally encountered between the hours of 9 to 5 on Mondays through Fridays. These relationships are now constructed in a virtual space that can potentially span the globe as a result of various networked technologies.

There has been a great deal of work on participation in decision making (see review by Seibold & Shea, 2001) that demonstrates some resistance to the dominant power structures by attempting to empower workers to assume more responsibility for organizational outcomes. However, in this approach the ultimate responsibility for empowering or inviting participation still resides in those located in the upper echelons of the hierarchy. This is seen particularly when examining the use of quality circles, which were derived from the implementation of Total Quality Management (TQM). The premise of TQM was to engage in a continual search for the most efficient ways of running a given business. This search was ideally accompanied by the use of data analysis in a manner reminiscent of Taylor's Principles of Scientific Management (1911). This approach was criticized for the inequitable treatment of workers that was attributed to the application of these methods. Although this approach was ultimately replaced by efforts to humanize the workforce, characteristics of these classic organization principles persist in organizations today. New developments in information and communication technology hold the latest promise of being able to provide the tools necessary for leveling the playing field in today's organizations once and for all. Yet Deetz (1992) warns that, "To the extent that particular technologies embody values, hide authority relations, or reify social relations, they participate in domination" (p. 170).

Undoubtedly, information can yield power and it remains to be seen whether the development of ICTs will be utilized to enact a more equitable workplace, or if existing power relationships will be simply reified in the virtual world. Raven (1965) argued for the inclusion of information power as an addition to the five bases of power that are commonly cited from the original source (French & Raven, 1959). This base of power was differentiated from expertise by the prospect that the information could be inherently persuasive regardless of the source, which portrays information as another commodity that essentially renders this base of power as another form of resource control analogous to reward power or coercive power. In the development of network organizations (Monge & Contractor, 2001) power is based on an individual's position in the network. This power is clearly related to the individual's access to valuable information resources and allows for an understanding of how information is exchanged to enact the power structure within a given organizational form.

E-participation is thought of as a way to tap into these latent information resources. ICTs are currently being adopted to enhance participation in government by encouraging two-way communication between a government and its citizens, giving a greater voice and ultimately power to the public. Many of the strategies and tools used in this approach can be applied to non-governmental organizations as well, enhancing interaction between any organization and its stakeholders and potentially altering the power structure in those relationships. However, Deetz (1992) points out that democracy "fails if it becomes the means by which might exerts itself. Public democratic participation in decision making must contribute

to continuous determination of choices for the public good, rather than being reduced to a vote on who will set the boundaries for someone else's determination of our future" (p. 146).

Phang and Kankanhalli (2008) adapted a framework originally proposed by Glass (1979) to match different participatory techniques, in this case ICTs, to different purposes of participation. They argue that e-participation has four primary objectives: information exchange, education and support building, decision making supplementation, and input probing. Similar to Media Richness Theory (Daft & Lengel, 1984), they argue government agents should first identify the objective to be served by the e-participation initiative and then select the best-matching participatory techniques and its associated ICT tools that can support the objective. For example, Glass (1979) argued that public hearings would be the best participatory technique to fulfill the information exchange purpose of citizen participation. Phang and Kankanhalli (2008) argue that in e-participation initiatives, a web portal with an online discussion forum or chat would be the ICT tool that best meets this objective.

Kumar and Vragov (2009) make a similar argument, but identify three somewhat different categories that ICTs fall into as reasons to increase citizen participation. They include the Communication Component, which primarily involves disseminating information about government activities and policies. In the past, traditional mass media tools such as television, radio and printed materials fulfilled this purpose. ICTs such as digitized information made available on government websites can serve this purpose today. A second category Kumar and Vragov identify is the Deliberation Component, which provides feedback and discussion about government activities and policies. In the past, face-to-face meetings with government representatives or town hall meetings would serve this purpose. ICTs such as electronic petitions and blogs can serve this purpose today. The final category they identify is the Voting

Component, through which citizens elect officials and make decisions about government policies. In the past, paper-based ballots and electronic voting systems in physical polling booths served this purpose. Today and in the future, online voting systems can serve this purpose. Each of the technologies has the potential to greatly enhance citizen participation, increasing their power and ability to influence government policies and decisions. However, Fitzpatrick (2002) reminds us that traditional organizational power structures may adjust to and be reconfigured by new information technologies, but tend not to be substantially undermined by them. Despite ICTs potential to enhance democratic ideals, technological advancements in ICTs can just as easily reinforce the existing power structures.

Learning organizations have also been striving to maximize the hidden potential of valuable knowledge resources through a process of knowledge management. Neff (2002) describes how organizations develop online learning communities to produce something resembling a more powerful version of grassroots community-based efforts by coordinating all of the inputs gathered from the organization's various stakeholders. A knowledge management system takes all of the organizational and employee-based knowledge that can be represented symbolically and links them together. However, some knowledge is not easily captured and remains tacit. It has been proposed, therefore, that it might be more valuable to map a network of the individuals who possess relevant knowledge rather than attempting to catalogue that knowledge (Conrad & Poole, 2002). This approach acknowledges that knowledge is not a static entity and will continue to dynamically evolve.

MANAGING POWER IN VIRTUAL WORK

While the *goal* of a learning organization is to harness institutional memory and experience so that the organization can avoid repeating costly mistakes and maximize opportunities for growth, the *design* of a learning organization is intended to create a space for organizational members to become self-sufficient. This design clearly requires empowerment to create the desired self-sufficiency and thereby must avoid the sense of command and control that was ultimately associated with Total Quality Management. The advancement of new technologies enabling the development of knowledge management systems could make the idealistic aspirations arising from the design of the learning organization appear to be a more realistic possibility. For example, some organizations have attempted to capture the personal knowledge of workers that enables them to think and perform in the job (Chan & Garrick, 2003). The application of the various technologies that make this possible produces what we refer to as amplification factors, which essentially intensify existing organizational dynamics. Rice and Gattiker (2001) point out how the early adoption of computerization into the workplace tended to reinforce the status quo. "In organizations that tended toward centralization, the introduction of computers led to increased centralization; in organizations that tended toward decentralization and empowerment, the introduction of computers increased empowerment and decentralization" (Conrad & Poole, 2002, p. 198). It is argued here that the implementation of the ICTs of today will likely be associated with similar effects where the reach of power can be extended for the purposes of command and control or for the encouragement of more open participation and broad-based empowerment. Power dynamics, in particular, are amplified through ICT usage due to factors such as: the availability of workers connected 24 hours a day / 7 days a week allowing both flexible scheduling and extended monitoring and surveillance, the digital divide adding to the further disenfranchisement of those without access to the latest technology, and the questions related to the security of electronic information presenting their own unique challenges.

ISSUES, CONTROVERSIES, PROBLEMS

Rice and Gattiker (2001) point out that organizational structure is best conceptualized as a process that constrains and facilitates human action in organizational contexts, where new structures can arise or be suppressed. Although most approaches reject determinism, there are still those who view the role of ICTs as constructing either technological utopias or technophobias. The excitement of new technologies always seems to bring the promise of the utopian views until the application of the technologies reveal misappropriations that produce the phobias about new technology. So, the question remains whether the increased access to information and tools to collect and organize anonymous input will serve as an equalizing force in today's organizations or not. Rice and Gattiker (2001) cite some studies that have demonstrated how ICT usage has promoted more crossing of traditional work boundaries to open the lines of communication across various departments that would not otherwise allow for the cross-fertilization that results from such information sharing.

Conrad and Poole (2002) point out that "being able to participate does not mean that members have influence in the organization" (p. 198). The challenge of promoting e-participation and effective knowledge management comes from the difficulty of obtaining the needed inputs due to the overwhelming experiences of information overload and the competing demands for the scarce amount of time that people have available. Hudson (2002) refers to this phenomenon as "the jungle syndrome" to suggest the challenge of navigating the unpredictability of the online environment. The unpredictability concern is an issue for many organizations, including political offices that are concerned with controlling how institutional messages are conveyed (Cummings, 2009). Of course, this interest opposes the desire for promoting open exchange and participation in decision making. Hudson argues, "the tougher solution is to discover in the jungle itself the deepest form of learning and the most transformative capabilities of the learning community" (p. 188). Fitzpatrick (2002) contends that if any learning is to occur, that it will not likely be transformative since the expectations that ICTs would level the playing field between managers and employees have not been realized. Instead, it appears that the flow of information about the relatively powerless to the relatively powerful has increased.

As suggested above, there is more to creating effective knowledge management systems than simply arranging the necessary technology and inputting the relevant information. It is perhaps instructive to look at how smaller communities of practice are formed and implemented. A community of practice was originally described as, "a set of relations among persons, activity, and world, over time and in relation with other tangential and overlapping communities of practice (p. 98)" (Lave & Wenger, 1991, as cited in Hildreth, 2004, p. 35). The understanding of what makes effective communities of practice has since evolved to further emphasize the social aspects of organizing. For example, it is suggested that "legitimation of a member in the community comes not from some formal and externally imposed hierarchy but by his/her gaining the acceptance of the other members" (Hildreth, 2004, p. 44).

There are many other social implications that have not been fully articulated in the ICT literature. The next section will present two case studies that highlight how these issues affect the virtual work of organizations. This section will demonstrate how a communicative perspective attends to the choices and consequences associated with the management of these social dimensions.

Communication, Relational, and Practical Implications

Two cases are presented below to illustrate the complexity of how organizations are communicatively constructed in a manner that resists simple categorizations as either "centralized" or "decentralized." Instead, we find that organizations can simultaneously demonstrate both properties through the management of dialectical tensions (Baxter & Montgomery, 1996). Although an organization may avow an open structure inviting input and participation by its members, there may be constraints placed upon the organization that require the implementation of certain controls. The first case examines how the Obama presidency has employed a variety of ICTs in order to organize his constituents in an unprecedented manner with the goal of increasing participation. However, an analysis of this case will also reveal some of the necessary limitations associated with the Office of the President. The second case will present a utility company that has organized a community council to proactively solicit the input of its stakeholders. When this organization decides to incorporate the use of a blog to extend the dialogue of this group, they are confronted with a number of difficult choices regarding the implementation of this technology that paradoxically threaten to actually restrict the dialogue. These cases both illustrate how the choices about ICT usage reveal "deeply embedded assumptions about the way people learn and about the underlying culture of learning" (Hudson, 2002, p. 190).

Obama Case

During the 2008 campaign, presidential candidate Barack Obama made a commitment to create a new level of transparency in the federal government through ICTs. He argued that "cutting-edge" ICTs could change the way business is conducted in Washington by giving Americans the ability to participate in government and making government accountable in ways that had not been previously possible (Obama & Biden, 2008). Obama pledged to use ICTs to reform government and improve the exchange of information between the federal government and its citizens, suggesting that this use of technology would empower citizens more fully than what had been possible before. He appointed the nation's first Chief Technology Officer, Aneesh Chopra, to work with the Chief Information Officer, Vivek Kundra, to ensure the safety of the nation's computer networks, as well as lead an interagency effort to establish best-in-class technologies and share best practices (Obama, 2009a).

Obama has re-conceptualized the work of the United States government as being the work of the people, which requires their democratic participation. His campaign sent out daily e-mails soliciting not only a vote and donations from supporters, but also their assistance in a wide range of campaign activities from the hosting of parties for the viewing of events like his acceptance speech, to helping increase the turnout at campaign rallies. His campaign also encouraged citizen involvement through other new media like Facebook and YouTube. He also directed his presidential staff to extend these efforts from his campaign into his presidency. It is particularly interesting to examine how his staff has embarked on the process of redesigning the WhiteHouse.gov website in order to make it more interactive and encourage citizens to communicate more directly with the Office of the President (BBC News, 2009, Weeks, 2009). They have also initiated the Organizing for America movement hosted by the http://www.barackobama.com website to continue the extensive grassroots organizing network that was created through the Change.gov campaign website in order to bring citizen participation in government to a new level.

Once Obama became president in January, 2009, he issued a memorandum to the heads of all executive departments and agencies on the topic of transparency and open government (Obama,

2009b). In it, he outlined three principles that were to guide government activities, including citizen e-participation, related to transparency and openness. These principles stated the following: (1) Government should be transparent, specifically using new technologies to make information about its operations and decisions easily available by placing it online; (2) Government should be participatory, providing opportunities for Americans to participate in policymaking and provide their knowledge and expertise via ICTs as well as other means; and (3) Government should be collaborative, increasing cooperation through innovative technologies among agencies as well as with the private sector. He directed his Chief Technology Officer, Director of the Office of Management and Budget and the Administrator of General Services to develop an Open Government Directive that instructs government departments and agencies on specific ways the principles could be implemented.

Interestingly, the principles President Obama identified parallel in many ways the purposes of e-participation outlined by Phang and Kankanhalli (2008), as well as Kumar and Vragov (2009) and originally proposed by Glass (1979). The principles of encouraging participation in decision making are certainly not new, but the Obama administration believes the technological tools available today, especially ICTs, make the ability to carry out these principles much greater than was previously possible. At the same time, technological and systemic issues are likely to create hurdles for the implementation of these principles. For example, the platforms for social media (necessary for interactivity) and web content management (necessary for storing official documents) are different and not necessarily compatible (CMS Watch, 2009).

Once in the White House, the Obama administration ran into many issues with the existing White House technology apparatus that threatened to prevent him from implementing the e-participation principles he had outlined (Vargas, 2009).

The White House had an antiquated system that required technological upgrades to do such things as text message. In addition, federal government privacy rules restricted some of the communication activities that had been much easier to do during the campaign (Soller, 2009). Information about presidential activities has not been posted quite as quickly or as completely as had been envisioned in the campaign pledge.

The Obama administration has faced additional difficulties in the implementation of his plan for using technology to encourage citizen's e-participation in government. During the transition period between winning the election and taking the oath of office, Obama made plans to utilize his extensive e-mail network developed during the campaign to mobilize support for his administration's initiatives (Vaidyanathan, 2008). Some 13 million individuals had signed up during the campaign to receive campaign e-mail alerts. Privacy laws prevented him from taking the e-mail list to the White House, but he could ask everyone on the list to sign up with the White House site. This is likely one of the reasons why the www.barackobama.com website was launched in order to administer the Organizing for America movement to supplement the use of the whitehouse.gov website. In addition, Obama planned to use streaming video to a much greater extent, supplementing the traditional weekly radio address with video addresses broadcast by YouTube, but this was not accomplished without first confronting another set of questions regarding the privacy and security of government information (Sandoval, 2009; Soghoian, 2009a; Soghoian, 2009b).

Utility Case

Few organizations face constraints that are as stringent as those facing the White House. Therefore, it could perhaps be more instructive to look at a utility company that has explored the sharing of its decision making process with its multiple stakeholders through the formation of a community council. This group established its purpose and shared goals in face-to-face meetings, but these meetings were held for only a few hours once every quarter or so. Therefore, the utility company attempted to continue the dialogue between meetings by launching a blog site for the council. The development of this blog involved a number of decisions that clearly illustrate the potential for the amplification of power dynamics.

The intention of the organization was clearly to provide additional outlets for participation by the members of this community council. The community council was originally designed to meet several times over the course of a year to provide input on ten-year plans that would impact a wide variety of stakeholders who were represented on the community council including: environmental advocates, farmers, real estate developers, governmental regulators, and retail customers. It was determined that the amount of time available for each of these stakeholders to give voice to their concerns was limited due to the size of the group and the amount of time available for each of their scheduled meetings, especially since the organization wanted to use these meetings to convey vital information, as well as to seek input and feedback on the information being presented. Therefore, they chose to develop the blog exclusively for the use of council members to extend the opportunities for them to provide their feedback.

The first decision to make the blog private rather than public was intended to monitor the public relations concerns for the organization. The blog was used as an additional tool to seek feedback from the community council prior to presenting its plans to the general public. In addition, the blog could also be used to help gain support for the plans, as well as mitigate any conflicts that could otherwise lead into legal battles. The organization told the community council members it would moderate all posts submitted to the blog in order to maintain a respectful tone in the discussion of the contentious issues involved. The availability of these technological

options was essential for allowing this organization to create a desirable virtual work space for their community council to exchange information. However, the limits introduced to this tool intended to increase participation may have the effect of actually restricting participation. Many members of the council expressed how excited they were by the openness of the process in their first meeting. Making the blog private may have signaled a change in the communication climate that could be discouraging to those members of the council who were energized by the promise of a participatory process. The procedures for moderating the posts submitted for inclusion in the blog could lead some members of the council to fear that they would be censored and thereby serve to stifle their voice in the dialogue.

SOLUTIONS AND RECOMMENDATIONS

The two cases described above demonstrate how ICT usage presents a number of different means for enhancing the participation of stakeholders in an organization's decision making process. Of course, there have been many other technological developments that can also be used to constrain the communication of people engaging in virtual work. For instance, there are many ways that employers can monitor the work of employees such as through the surveillance of company e-mail systems, webpage access, and in some cases even the content of personal websites and social networking accounts to ensure that their desired organizational image is maintained. Some companies may decide to restrict employees' access to the internet altogether, which some workers may consider a denial of their individual rights or perhaps an unnecessary limit on their access to resources that could be used to accomplish their job effectively. These organizations may be trying to address some legitimate concerns about productivity, but have reverted to traditional command and control approaches to management rather than transferring more recent approaches to the leadership of learning organizations that would encourage the promotion of a more empowering use of the technological tools available. Neff (2002) suggests that there are some essential elements for an online knowledge community to be effective including: the right size, previous socialization, moderator proficiency, community latency, cultural issues, and support.

It should be evident from the foregoing discussion how ICTs present a number of solutions to some of the existing problems, but the application of these solutions can create a new set of problems of their own. A number of recommendations are presented below based on an analysis of the two cases and an application of relevant theory and research.

1. Virtual organizations need to identify the perspective (impact vs. choice) they are going to take about ICT's role in knowledge sharing and participation.

Nelissen, Wenneker, and Van Selm (2008) proposed two perspectives on the relationship between ICT and knowledge sharing. The first perspective argues that ICT characteristics determine knowledge sharing. This objectivist approach states that the characteristics of ICT can be assigned objectively and the outcome of ICT performance can be predicted beforehand. The second perspective argues that knowledge sharing practices determine the use of ICT. This subjectivist approach states that characteristics of an ICT are subjectively assigned over time and the outcome of ICT performance depends on the users and context. Each of these perspectives offers a different explanation of how ICTs may interact to influence the participatory nature within virtual organizations. It is likely in the first perspective that participation in organizational decision making may be more limited while in the second perspective participation occurs on a wider range of issues.

Nelissen et al. (2008) make reference to Büchel's (2001) three theoretical perspectives to help articulate the relationship between ICT and organizations. The impact perspective states that the amount of knowledge sharing in an organization will be determined by the communication technology available in a given organization. The basis of power in the organization from this perspective appears to reside with the ICT and those who determine which ICT the organization is going to use. The choice and emergent perspectives state that people determine the technological design of organizations and virtual communities will figure out unique ways that the ICTs can help them accomplish their goals. In order to maximize participation, Nelissen et al. (2008) suggest that these communities should "possess a considerable amount of joint enterprise, mutual engagement and a shared repertoire" (p. 94). The basis of power from this perspective must be balanced throughout the virtual organization community since the community determines the role of ICTs.

The effects of ICTs within virtual and brick and mortar organizations beyond the specific knowledge sharing task they are focused on also need to be considered as the organization decides which perspective it will take in its approach to ICTs. The effects can be categorized into two levels (Nelissen et al., 2008). First level effects focus on ICT impact on individual tasks, but the second level effects focus on other issues more directly related to the power structure within the organization. For example, ICTs can bypass formal communication hierarchies and create new communication patterns. New patterns of dependency among organizational members can be established and sometimes the changes to the organizational structure cannot be anticipated. The potential for the organizational power structure to continually change is great as new forms of ICTs come online and the number and size of virtual organizations grow.

2. If virtual organizations plan to enhance stakeholder participation in its activities and decision making processes, they need to consider ways to motivate all stakeholders to use ICTs.

Although the utility company's use of the blog was an excellent way to continue the community council's dialogue, it was evident that it could not replace the quarterly meetings since only a minority of the council members utilized the blog. Another issue that highlights potential power imbalances in relation to access to information centers on the use of public ICT sites. Selwyn's (2003) study of ICT sites in the UK found that public access sites (e.g., computer terminals in a public library) did little to increase access to government online information even for those groups who are marginalized or excluded from the information age due to income, age, or technological limitations. In fact, many members of those groups indicated they had little interest or need to use public ICT sites. This finding indicates power balances resulting from differing levels of access to government online information continue to persist. Selwyn argues that the approach toward increasing public access has failed to make the technology and information relevant to people's lives and until that is done, simply providing more information online through private and public means is not going to make a meaningful difference in the public's participation in government. The same argument can be made for other organizations. If employees and key stakeholders cannot effectively use ICTs to make informed contributions to the organization's decision making process, ICTs will fail to truly change the power balance within organizations to a more democratic one. Although some evidence exists to suggest a shift in the power balance from those who are more comfortable in face-to-face interactions to those with more comfort with a given technology being used to facilitate interaction, after an extensive review of the relevant research Scott

(1999) concludes, "it may well be that influence patterns from FtF [face-to-face] group interaction are carried over, at least partially, into GSS [group support systems] meetings so that status effects and differential influence are still quite possible even with systems designed to minimize them" (p. 461). It seems safe to say that decision making authority will require the knowledge, ability and motivation to use whatever ICT system the organization is supporting as a pre-requisite to retaining that power.

3. Virtual organizations need to be aware of how ICTs create opportunities for exerting new forms of power, creating a paradox between increased control and increased responsibility.

Simons and De Ridder (2004) argue ICTs have several characteristics that affect the formal structure as well as group interaction within organizations. These characteristics have significant implications for all organizations, but especially virtual organizations. ICTs allow work to become time- and place-independent. They make it possible to overcome the inherent boundaries that time, space and distance can create in getting work done. The boundaries also create opportunities for control within organizations and ICTs can lessen that control by eliminating boundaries. ICTs also break down physical and psychological barriers by connecting people, groups, and organizations throughout the world.

At the same time, Simons and De Ridder (2004) point out ICTs offer new possibilities for exerting new forms of power within organizations. "Management workflow systems reduce the need for human intervention and support the entire range of business processes and the control of materials and finance. Humans and objects become both controllable and traceable" (p. 165). This characteristic is even more important in virtual organizations where all work is managed and observed through ICTs and the need for direct in-person supervision (which typically is not capable of monitoring and managing all work) is diminished. They argue that leadership can become more centralized in relation to the use and design of information architecture, but also become less hierarchical because ICTs can facilitate coordination and lessen the need for a single leader. Of course, some critical theorists might argue this is an instance of concertive control (Tompkins & Cheney, 1985). However, Mumby (1997) points out that according to Gramsci's philosophy of praxis, hegemony is supposed "to demonstrate that organizational realities are neither imposed coercively on people, nor emerge spontaneously and consensually as a result of equal participation in the meaning-making process" (p. 344). Essentially, ICTs within virtual and all organizations create a paradox of greater control, but increased responsibility (Pearlson & Saunders, 2001).

4. Transparency has become a foundational business principle, altering the power relationship between organizations and stakeholders. Virtual organizations can do much through the use of social media and other ICTs to fulfill this principle.

Social media such as blogging, Twitter, and YouTube as well as other forms of ICTs have also made it possible to increase the transparency of organizations, giving stakeholders greater access than ever before and potentially altering the balance of power between an organization and its stakeholders. Holtz (2008) states that organizational transparency is increasingly necessary to increase the confidence of investors as well as gain the local community's support. Handling transparency well ultimately impacts a company's reputation and it is becoming a foundational business principle. Holtz argues that transparency can be defined as the extent to which the organization shares information about its leaders, employees, values, culture, business strategy, and all business

results, both the good and the bad. Sharing this information can be accomplished by increasing the accessibility of organizational communicators through the "tools of transparency," as Holtz describes social media. Virtual organizations are especially dependent on these tools to make its stakeholders aware of their activities and plans since little in person observation or participation occurs.

FUTURE RESEARCH DIRECTIONS

The nature of virtual relationships is fragmented by an overabundance of available information and competing demands for attention. The development of mobile technologies will likely continue to increase access to valuable information sources. These technologies can be used to further enhance the potential power of participatory communication processes, but those with power over others can also use these technologies to tighten their control over the actions they want to monitor and influence. Obviously, new technologies will continue to be introduced and future research will need to keep up with the latest technologies and explore the new implications that these technologies bring. It will also be important to examine whether existing theories about the effects of technology generally will need to be revised according to the impact of new technologies.

While the fragmented nature of virtual interaction suggests the presence of a post-modern aesthetic, there may also be evidence to suggest the development of a neo-classical approach found in organizations that embrace virtual work. Future research should be conducted to monitor how power is being enacted in virtual organizations. This research can investigate how technology might be used to coordinate and possibly centralize the many transactions that occur in a given organization.

CONCLUSION

Power is pervasive and can even be seen in the way information and communication technology is adopted in organizations. There are many decisions to be made about which technology should be used, who should be allowed to use it, and how the technology will be used. Each of these decisions represents a site where the members of an organization may assert or contest the amount of influence they have in an organization. Some assert that the technology itself has influence on the organization and where the technology intersects with the social concerns we see an amplification of existing power dynamics. Technology is a tool that can be used for many different purposes, and like all tools, technology provides some sort of advantage for the individual who can use the tool skillfully. So, the answer to the question of whether ICTs level the playing field to remove power inequities has to take into consideration all the different decisions that have gone into the way the technology is being adopted in a given organization. Many ICTs provide means that can move organizations to a more equitable workplace, if that is their desired goal; however, it would be inaccurate to make a blanket statement saying that technology in general has this effect. A more complex view reveals that although some organizations may tend towards centralization and other organizations tend towards decentralization, there are likely going to be elements of both intermingled in any given organization. This more complex view also reveals the paradox of organizations intending to empower stakeholders utilizing strategies that unintentionally reify existing power imbalances.

The two cases presented above both illustrate this phenomenon. Although the Obama administration and the utility company were both effective at mobilizing their constituents to engage in grassroots community-based efforts, the introduction of technology to broaden their capacity has met with mixed results. By examining the social dimensions in addition to the technological capabilities, it can be seen how individuals are overloaded with information and competing responsibilities. When it comes to engaging additional concerns, technology may make it easier to do this, but stakeholders still need to maintain enough of a stake in the cause to warrant taking the time to contribute online. Neff (2002) indicates that the creation of online learning communities requires engagement in two-way dialogue, yet the virtual interaction that is mediated through ICTs is often asynchronous and sometimes representative of one-way communication. Virtual work exists because of people. Certain jobs can be automated and accomplished by technology without the assistance of human operators, but the work is still created and initiated by a human being and it is being done to serve human purposes. It is important to recognize how social dimensions continue to assert themselves in the virtual world of work.

REFERENCES

Barker, J. R., & Cheney, G. (1994). The concept and the practices of discipline in contemporary organizational life. *Communication Monographs*, *61*, 19–43. doi:10.1080/03637759409376321

Baxter, L. A., & Montgomery, B. M. (1996). *Relating: Dialogue and dialectics*. New York: Guilford.

Chan, A., & Garrick, J. (2003). The moral "technologies" of knowledge management. *Information Communication and Society*, *6*, 291–306. doi:10.1080/1369118032000155258

Conrad, C., & Poole, M. S. (2002). *Strategic organizational communication in a global economy* (5th ed.). Ft. Worth, TX: Harcourt.

Cummings, J. (2009, February 5). Obama losing stimulus message war. *Politico*. Retrieved February 5, 2009, from http://www.politico.com/news/stories/0209/18444.html

Daft, R. L., & Lengel, R. H. (1984). Information richness: A new approach to managerial information processing and organization design . In Cummings, L. L., & Staw, B. M. (Eds.), *Research in organizational behavior* (*Vol. 6*, pp. 191–234). Greenwich, CT: JAI Press.

Deetz, S. A. (1992). *Democracy in an age of corporate colonization: Developments in communication and the politics of everyday life*. Albany, NY: SUNY Press.

Fitzpatrick, T. (2002). Critical theory, information society and surveillance technologies. *Information Communication and Society*, *5*, 357–358. doi:10.1080/13691180210159300

French, J. R. P. Jr., & Raven, B. H. (1959). The bases of social power. In D. Cartwright (Ed.), Studies in social power (pp. 150-167). Ann Arbor, MI: Institute for Social Research.

Glass, J. J. (1979). Citizen participation in planning: The relationship between objectives and techniques. *American Planning Association Journal*, *45*, 180–189. doi:10.1080/01944367908976956

Hildreth, P. M. (2004). *Going virtual: Distributed communities of practice*. Hershey, PA: Idea Group Publishing.

Holtz, S. (2008). A clear case of transparency. *Communication World*, *25*(6), 16–20.

Hudson, B. (2002). The jungle syndrome: Some perils and pleasures of learning without walls . In Rudestam, K. E., & Schoenholtz-Read, J. (Eds.), *Handbook of online learning: Innovations in higher education and corporate training* (pp. 185–220). Thousand Oaks, CA: Sage.

Kumar, N., & Vragov, R. (2009). Active citizen participation using ICT tools. *Communications of the ACM*, *52*(1), 118–121. doi:10.1145/1435417.1435444

Monge, P. R., & Contractor, N. S. (2001). Emergence of communication networks . In Jablin, F. M., & Putnam, L. L. (Eds.), *The new handbook of organizational communication: Advances in theory, research, and methods* (pp. 440–502). Thousand Oaks, CA: Sage.

Mumby, D. K. (1997). The problem of hegemony: Rereading Gramsci for organizational communication studies. *Western Journal of Communication*, *61*, 343–375.

Mumby, D. K. (2001). Power and politics . In Jablin, F. M., & Putnam, L. L. (Eds.), *The new handbook of organizational communication: Advances in theory, research, and methods* (pp. 585–623). Thousand Oaks, CA: Sage.

Neff, M. D. (2002). Online knowledge communities and their role in organizational learning . In Rudestam, K. E., & Schoenholtz-Read, J. (Eds.), *Handbook of online learning: Innovations in higher education and corporate training* (pp. 335–352). Thousand Oaks, CA: Sage.

Nelissen, P., Wenneker, M., & Van Slem, M. (2008). ICT performance in processes of knowledge sharing in organizations: A review of the literature. *Communications*, *33*, 91–108. doi:10.1515/COMMUN.2008.005

News, B. B. C. (2009, January 22). White House plans open government. Retrieved March 13, 2009, from http://news.bbc.co.uk/go/pr/fr/-/2/hi/technology/7844280.stm

Obama, B. (2009a, April 18). *Weekly address*. Washington, DC: The White House. Retrieved April 24, 2009, from http://www.whitehouse.gov/the_press_office/Weekly-Address-President-Obama-Discusses-Efforts-to-Reform-Spending-Government-Waste-Names-Chief-Performance-Officer-and-Chief-Technology-Officer/

Obama, B. (2009b). *Memorandum for the heads of executive departments and agencies: Transparency and open government.* Retrieved April 1, 2009, from http://www.whitehouse.gov/the_press_office/TransparencyandOpenGovernment/

Obama, B., & Biden, J. (2008). The Obama-Biden plan: Technology. Retrieved March 13, 2009, from http://change.gov/agenda/technology_agenda/

Pearlson, K. E., & Saunders, C. S. (2001). There's no place like home: Managing telecommuting paradoxes. *The Academy of Management Executive, 15,* 117–128.

Phang, C. W., & Kankanhalli, A. (2008). A framework of ICT exploitation for e-participation initiatives. *Communications of the ACM, 51*(12), 128–132. doi:10.1145/1409360.1409385

Raven, B. H. (1965). Social influence and power . In Steiner, I. D., & Fishbein, M. (Eds.), *Current studies in social psychology* (pp. 371–382). New York: Holt, Rinehart, Winston.

Raven, B. H. (2008). The bases of power and the power/interaction model of interpersonal influence. *Analyses of Social Issues and Public Policy (ASAP), 8,* 1–22. doi:10.1111/j.1530-2415.2008.00159.x

Rice, R. E., & Gattiker, U. E. (2001). New media and organizational structuring . In Jablin, F. M., & Putnam, L. L. (Eds.), *The new handbook of organizational communication: Advances in theory, research, and methods* (pp. 544–581). Thousand Oaks, CA: Sage.

Sandoval, G. (2009, March 3). No, the White House hasn't ditched YouTube. *CNET News.* Retrieved March 13, 2009, from http://news.cnet.com/8301-1023_3-10187099-93.html?tag=mncol

Scott, C. R. (1999). Communication technology and group communication . In Frey, L. R. (Ed.), *The handbook of group communication theory and research* (pp. 432–472). Thousand Oaks, CA: Sage.

Seibold, D. R., & Shea, B. C. (2001). Participation and decision making . In Jablin, F. M., & Putnam, L. L. (Eds.), *The new handbook of organizational communication: Advances in theory, research, and methods* (pp. 664–703). Thousand Oaks, CA: Sage.

Selwyn, N. (2003). ICT for all? Access and use of public ICT sites in the UK. *Information Communication and Society, 6,* 350–375. doi:10.1080/1369118032000155285

Simons, M. E., & De Ridder, J. A. (2004). Renewing connections and changing relations: Use of information and communication technology and cohesion in organizational groups. *Communications, 29,* 159–177. doi:10.1515/comm.2004.011

Soghoian, C. (2009a, March 2). Is the White House changing its YouTube tune? *CNET News.* Retrieved March 13, 2009, from http://news.cnet.com/8301-13739_3-10184578-46.html

Soghoian, C. (2009b, January 23). White House acts to limit YouTube cookie tracking. *CNET News.* Retrieved March 13, 2009, from http://news.cnet.com/8301-13739_3-10148844-46.html

Soller, K. (2009, January 20). Can Obama's new whitehouse.gov deliver all that it promises? *Newsweek.* Retrieved March 13, 2009, from http://www.newsweek.com/id/180719

Taylor, F. W. (1911). *The principles of scientific management.* New York: Harper & Row.

Tompkins, P. K., & Cheney, G. (1985). Communication and unobtrusive control in contemporary organizations . In McPhee, R. D., & Tompkins, P. K. (Eds.), *Organizational communication: Traditional themes and new directions* (pp. 179–210). Beverly Hills: Sage.

Vaidyanathan, R. (2008). Barack Obama's plans for the web. Retrieved March 5, 2009, from http://news.bbc.co.uk/2/hi/americas/7754485.stm

Watch, C. M. S. (2009, March 11). *Obama call for citizen e-participation will encounter technical hurdles* [Press release]. Retrieved April 1, 2009, from http://www.cmswatch.com/About/Press/2009-CMS-Social-Gap/

Weeks, L. (2009, March 13). White House web site: Window into Obama's soul? *National Public Radio*. Retrieved March 13, 2009, from http://www.npr.org/templates/story/story.php?storyId=99794168

ADDITIONAL READING

Berger, C. R. (1994). Power, dominance, and social interaction . In Knapp, M. L., & Miller, G. R. (Eds.), *Handbook of interpersonal communication* (2nd ed., pp. 450–507). Thousand Oaks, CA: Sage.

Chan, A., & Garrick, J. (2003). The moral "technologies" of knowledge management. *Information Communication and Society*, 6, 291–306. doi:10.1080/1369118032000155258

Chawla, S., & Renesch, J. (1995). *Learning organizations: Developing cultures for tomorrow's workplace*. Portland, OR: Productivity Press.

DeSanctis, G., & Monge, P. (1998, June). Communication processes for virtual organizations. *Journal of Computer-Mediated Communication*, 3(4), Editors' introduction. Retrieved May 14, 2007, from http://jcmc.indiana.edu/vol3/issue4/desanctis.html

Drucker, P. (1998). *The coming of the new organization*. Cambridge, MA: Harvard Business School Press.

Fulk, J., & Steinfield, C. (Eds.). (1990). *Organizations and communication technology*. Newbury Park, CA: Sage Publications.

Giddens, A. (1984). *The constitution of society: Outline of the theory of structuration*. Cambridge, UK: Polity Press.

Harris, U. S. (2007). Community informatics and the power of participation. *Pacific Journalism Review*, 13(2), 29–45.

Heaton, L., & Taylor, J. R. (2002). Knowledge management and professional work. *Management Communication Quarterly*, 16, 210–236. doi:10.1177/089331802237235

Huber, G. P. (1990). A theory of the effects of advanced information technologies on organizational design, intelligence, and decision making. *Academy of Management Review*, 15, 47–71. doi:10.2307/258105

Iverson, J. O., & McPhee, R. D. (2002). Knowledge management in communities of practice. *Management Communication Quarterly*, 16, 259–266. doi:10.1177/089331802237239

Jarvenpaa, S. L., & Leidner, D. E. (1998, June). Communication and trust in global virtual teams. *Journal of Computer-Mediated Communication*, 3(4), Article 4. Retrieved May 14, 2007, from http://jcmc.indiana.edu/vol3/issue4/jarvenpaa.html

Lave, J., & Wenger, E. (1991). *Situated learning: Legitimate peripheral participation*. Cambridge, UK: Cambridge University Press.

Miller, P. (1999). How communication can add spice to knowledge management. *Strategic Communication Management*, *3*(3), 12–15.

Peña, J., Walther, J. B., & Hancock, J. T. (2007). Effects of geographic distribution on dominance perceptions in computer-mediated groups. *Communication Research*, *34*, 313–331. doi:10.1177/0093650207300431

Rice, R. E. (1984). *The new media: Communication, research, and technology*. Beverly Hills, CA: Sage Publications.

Senge, P. M. (1994). *The fifth discipline fieldbook: Strategies and tools for building a learning organization*. New York: Currency Doubleday.

Senge, P. M. (2006). *The fifth discipline: The art and practice of the learning organization* (Rev. ed.). New York: Currency Doubleday.

Shah, D. V., Cho, J., Eveland, W. P. Jr, & Kwak, N. (2005). Information and expression in a digital age: Modeling internet effects on civic participation. *Communication Research*, *32*, 531–565. doi:10.1177/0093650205279209

Srinivasan, R. (2006). Where information society and community voice intersect. *The Information Society*, *22*, 355–365. doi:10.1080/01972240600904324

Van Der Velden, M. (2004). From communities of practice to communities of resistance: Civil society and cognitive justice. *Development*, *47*, 73–81. doi:10.1057/palgrave.development.1100004

Walther, J. B., & Anderson, J. F. (1994). Interpersonal effects in computer-mediated interaction. *Communication Research*, *21*, 460. doi:10.1177/009365094021004002

Walther, J. B., & Bazarova, N. N. (2008). Validation and application of electronic propinquity theory to computer-mediated communication in groups. *Communication Research*, *35*, 622–645. doi:10.1177/0093650208321783

Wenger, E. (1998). *Communities of practice, learning, meaning, and identity*. Cambridge, UK: Cambridge University Press.

Yates, J. (1989). *Control through communication: The rise of system in American management*. Baltimore: The John Hopkins University Press.

KEY TERMS AND DEFINITIONS

E-Participation: Broadly describes government efforts (on all levels) to use Internet based technology to facilitate two-way communication between a government and its citizens, enhancing citizen participation in government activities.

Information and Communication Technology (ICT): Technologies, especially Internet based ones, that are meant to improve an organization's ability to share knowledge, communicate internally and externally, and increase stakeholder involvement in organizational processes.

Knowledge Management: Organizational efforts to share information about its processes and experiences in an understandable way with all its stakeholders; ICTs are increasingly used to accomplish this.

Learning Organizations: Organizations which utilize institutional memory and experience to avoid repeating costly mistakes and maximize growth opportunities; they create space for organizational members to become self-sufficient.

Participation in Decision Making: Ideally thought of as involvement of all organizational stakeholders in decision making processes; gives workers increased responsibility for organizational outcomes; technologies of virtual organizations are the latest attempt to fulfill the promise of participation in decision making.

Power: Ability to influence and control others; it has been mostly viewed as inherently located within the organizational structure, producing dominant relationships; in virtual organizations, power no longer operates under boundaries of physical space or traditional markers of status.

Transparency: A major goal of e-participation efforts; government uses ICTs to give citizens greater access to government information than ever before, making government operations and decision making processes open for all to see; increasingly seen as a foundational business practice for all organizations.

Chapter 13
Engineers' Perceptions of Relational Limitations Intrinsic to Virtual Work

Eletra S. Gilchrist
The University of Alabama in Huntsville, USA

ABSTRACT

Virtual work is increasingly prevalent in organizational settings. Many corporations communicate virtually to reduce travel and facility costs and expedite production. Benefits of employees communicating virtually are recognizable and advantageous, but the benefits can come at a price—decreased human interactions. This study explored engineers' perceptions of relational limitations inherent to virtual work. Engineers enrolled in a communication course who use virtual work methods on the job comprised the sample. Qualitative content analysis revealed engineers perceive virtual work as a convenient and easy-to-use medium that bridges geography, curtails expenses, expedites meetings, and allows flex time. Conversely, engineers reported several relational limitations associated with virtual work, including reduced personal interactions, diminished nonverbal cues, increased miscommunications, added interference, and weakened interpersonal skills. Engineers exercise supplemental face-to-face communication, occasional on-site meetings, and social activities to counter virtual relational limitations. A social exchange theoretical perspective explains engineers' continued use of virtual work.

INTRODUCTION

Companies and organizations have always relied upon effective communication to develop products and keep employees and corporate partners informed. Once upon a time, a company's internal and external communications were limited to

personal contact, letters, memos, and newsletters. However, long are the days since employees were confined to snail mail or face-to-face encounters in order to coalesce on projects or conduct meetings. Virtual work, especially in the form of emails, conference calls, and video presentations, has bridged geographical distances in the corporate world and enabled employees to expand their interaction possibilities. Through virtual communication, companies

DOI: 10.4018/978-1-61520-979-8.ch013

have minimized physical challenges, cut costs, and expedited product outflow.

Arguably, engineers rely on virtual work more than most professions. These workers use technology consistently to research, create products, conduct meetings, connect with suppliers, and maintain communication between management and employees. The benefits offered by virtual communication cannot be denied or dismissed and have secured technology's position as a permanent and valued part of engineering. Yet, relational limitations of virtual work abound in the corporate sector. This study explored engineers' (a) motivations for using virtual communication methods and (b) perceptions of the relational limitations intrinsic to working virtually.

BACKGROUND

Interpersonal Benefits of Virtual Communication

Virtual communication is commonly perceived to facilitate task and social exchanges comparatively as well as more traditional communication forms, including face-to-face (Walther & Parks, 2002). The Internet is praised as a medium that aids in establishing and advancing interpersonal relationships. Even in the relatively impersonal environment created by online interactions, researchers assert that it is possible for communicators to form interpersonal relationships through textual and verbal cues (Walther, 1992). Testimonies abound on how virtual communication helps in creating and maintaining friendships and romantic relationships (e.g., Katz & Aspden, 1997; Lenhart, Lewis, & Rainie, 2006; McKenna & Bargh, 2000). Virtual communication, especially in the form of chat rooms, friendship-oriented websites, and support groups, allows individuals to develop new relationships with people they may never meet face-to-face (Barnes, 2006).

Virtual communication is perceived to facilitate and enhance human relationships in part by fostering a sense of social presence. Social presence "is the degree to which we as individuals perceive another as a real person and any interaction between the two of us as a relationship" (Wood & Smith, 2001, p. 72). Social presence implies that the virtual environment can be viewed similarly to the physical environment. In other words, the virtual environment permits individuals in remote locations to feel connected and physically present with one another. Consider a company's representative visiting a partner corporation in another country. The representative gathers data and needs to report back to her company constantly with the latest updates. Technologies, such as email, on-line chat, and conference calls can give the representative social presence by keeping her virtually connected to the home company while physically present at another location, even one outside the country.

An additional benefit of virtual work is its ability to enable socially reticent individuals to develop, build, and enhance their interpersonal skills by removing the social pressures of immediate face-to-face interactions. Introverted and individuals high in communication apprehension can use mediated means to express themselves and contribute to group discussions that they may otherwise view as uncomfortable and intimidating. This virtual benefit is commonly experienced in college classrooms with some introverted students preferring to email their professors rather than communicate in face-to-face situations (Barnes, 2006). In a sense, technology allows socially reticent individuals to share thoughts and ask questions in a shielded environment not available in person-to-person situations.

As an added benefit, virtual technology represents an asynchronous communication tool. In our fast-paced and multi-tasking corporate world, individuals are not always available at the same time for face-to-face interactions, even if they work in side-by-side cubicles. Thus, the atemporality of virtual work allows communicators to offer detailed information free from the pressures of immediate response time (Teske, 2002). Because engineers often communicate with suppliers in different locations and time zones, the asynchronous nature of virtual work makes it ideal for use in corporate America.

Virtual Work and Implications for Engineers

The Internet has essentially opened floodgates of communication potential not limited by the time and space of physical proximity. As a medium that erases geographical borders, technology is increasingly used by engineers for job success. Not only does virtual communication and forums provide engineers with valuable product information, but it allows them to canvass the opinions and advice of thousands of engineers at once. According to Peet and Kren (2005), online industry-specific chat rooms and discussion boards are essential venues for engineers to share information about equipment functionality and related industry-specific application issues. Open virtual discussions regarding a vendor's equipment can also significantly reduce design errors and engineering effort (Peet & Kren, 2005).

Virtual technology in the workplace is further praised for concealing demographic features, such as race, gender, ethnicity, and appearance—physical traits that have been linked to advancing stereotypes, biases, and restricting human interactions (Rheingold, 1993). As a medium that minimizes the effects of demographic features, the Internet can enhance corporate diversity and allow various perspectives to be voiced that might otherwise be muted.

Because virtual work in corporations is commonly used, it is important to understand the implications of technology in the workplace for engineers. Thus, the following research question is raised:

- **RQ1:** *What motivations do engineers report for using virtual work?*

Relational Limitations of Virtual Work

An infamous ode argues that regardless of how flat one makes a pancake, it still has two sides. So although the advantages of technology have made it a thriving and valuable force in the corporate sector, there are limitations, especially related to human interactions, which spark concern.

Interpersonal communication literature stresses that the Internet has made it possible for humans to establish and maintain relationships across the miles in a convenient and relatively safe environment (e.g., Katz & Aspden, 1997; McKenna & Bargh, 2000). Yet, with individuals and corporations relying more and more on electronic transfers of information in lieu of face-to-face communication, there are concerns that our interconnectedness, interdependence, and overall relational lives may suffer.

In the early 1990s, researchers warned that the Internet phenomenon could produce a relationally limited society that some might consider "a nation of strangers" (Katz & Aspden, 1997, p. 81). Commentators particularly predicted the potential destruction of community and social integration (Turkel, 1995) and decreased friendship enjoyment and commitment (Stoll, 1995). Teske (2002) argued that on the one hand the Internet can widen our world and make it more inclusive, but on the other hand it can "shrink our sense of relationship and personhood" (p. 678).

Virtual communication often occurs with much anonymity, which has mixed consequences. In one sense, anonymity can foster self-disclosure, intimacy, and nonverbal immediacy (Teske, 2002). Conversely, the natural degree of anonymity provided by virtual communication can open the door for individuals to incur less consequences and accountability online. Anonymous conditions in the virtual world can contribute to deindividuation (Joinson, 1998). When communicators are deindividualized, they may experience weakened self regulation, emotional reactivity, reduced awareness of others' responses, increased impulsiveness, and greater bluntness, hostility, and aggression (Teske, 2002). Suler (2004) added that anonymous and deindividualized communicators can compartmentalize their online and offline selves, which suggest online participants can divorce themselves from their actions. Additional research in this area has noted the link between deindividuation and flaming, the "aggressive, hostile, or profanity-laced interactions via e-mail and in online discussion groups" (O'Sullivan & Flanagin, 2003, p. 70; Joinson, 1998).

In a related vein, individuals can experience a lack of privacy when communicating virtually. Hertzel (2000) noted that many people are worried about the potential misuse of their personal information on the Internet, and there is strong evidence indicating they should be concerned. Research by Gartner Incorporated, an information technology research and advisory company, revealed that approximately 15 million Americans were victimized by some sort of identity-theft related fraud in 2006. These figures represent more than a 50 percent increase since 2003 when the Federal Trade Commission (FTC) reported 9.9 million American adult identity theft victims (Pettey, 2007).

Along with questionable online privacy, a chief relational limitation of virtual work is the lack of nonverbal communication. Approximately 65-93 percent of all meaning is nonverbal (Burgoon & Hoobler, 2002). Tone of voice, eye contact, facial expressions, gestures, body movement, and touch are all relied on to communicate meaning. We are symbolic individuals who depend on nonverbal cues to complement, repeat, accent, and sometimes substitute for verbal meanings (Burgoon & Hoobler, 2002). Emoticons and other online signals serve a somewhat nonverbal function in online interactions (Barnes, 2006), but virtual work is primarily void of nonverbal cues. Thus,

it is often difficult to gage if people are listening, comprehending, approving, disapproving, or even bored with a message.

Because virtual work generally occurs in a nonverbal-depleted environment, communicators are required to draw conclusions about message reception and shared understanding with minimal information conveyed via text-based interactions (Walther & Parks, 2002). Consequently, virtually formed relationships occur at a slower pace because they require a longer time to develop trust and communicate closeness compared to face-to-face relationships (Lea & Spears, 1995).

In essence, relational limitations of virtual work are plentiful; yet, companies consistently require employees to work virtually. To explore engineers' perspectives of communicating in a virtual work environment, the following research questions are advanced:

- **RQ2:** What relational limitations do engineers report from virtual work?
- **RQ3:** How do engineers overcome the relational limitations associated with virtual work?

ENGINEERS AND VIRTUAL WORK

Participants and Data Collection

Participants included a sample of introductory-level engineers employed at an internationally-known engineering company located in a mid-size Southern city in which engineering is the dominant professional career. The participants were enrolled in a communication course that emphasized effective communication and presentation skills taught by me, the principal investigator. The engineers enrolled in this course use technology and virtual work to deliver presentations, give reports, make proposals, and communicate with management and colleagues both on and off the company's site. Because engineering companies are becoming increasingly aware of the importance of their employees having effective communication skills, especially when it comes to the use of virtual communication, more and more engineering companies are offering training avenues, such as the effective presentation course taken by the participants in this course.

During the virtual communication unit of the corporate training course, the 15 participating engineers completed a 12-item open-ended survey for class discussion and analysis. The survey initially obtained information on the engineers' corporate responsibilities. Then, the employees reported on the types and uses of virtual communication exercised in their corporation. The survey further inquired about the participants' perceptions of the strengths, weaknesses, and relational implications of virtual work (see Appendix).

This study's objective was to explore the meaning of the messages contained in the engineers' written responses; thus qualitative content analysis was used to analyze the data. Qualitative content analysis was the appropriate method because it looks at the meaning of the message (Frey, Bottan, & Creps, 2000), and a qualitative approach focuses both on "explicit and implicit concepts and empowers the researcher to use his or her judgment in determining, on a case by case basis, whether a particular linguistic token references a particular concept in the given context" (Bazerman & Prior, 2004, p. 15).

Qualitative content analysis allows researchers to act as tools for analyzing the data (Hoepfl, 1997). Thus, the class members and I performed the qualitative content analysis by following the process outlined by Auerbach and Silverstein (2003). After the participating engineers completed the open-ended survey questions, we examined the written answers and looked for *repeating ideas*, which are defined as concepts "expressed in relevant text by two or more research participants" (p. 54). The information was then categorized into *thematic constructs*, which are viewed as abstract concepts that organize a group of themes by plac-

ing them into a theoretical framework (Auerbach & Silverstein, 2003).

Results and Discussion

The engineers participating in this study all labeled virtual communication as a required and necessary part of their work. Engineers reported consistently using eight virtual communication methods in the workplace: emails, teleconferences, video conferences, web meetings, instant messages/chat, wikis, blogs, and text messaging.

- **RQ1 asked:** What motivations do engineers report for using virtual work?
  - Respondents indicated that engineering companies use the previously mentioned eight communication methods for six reasons: (1) to overcome geographical distances, (2) cut costs, (3) expedite meeting times, (4) permit flex time, (5) convenience, and (6) ease of use.

Overcome Geographical Distances

Engineers indicated that their suppliers are all across the United States, and some of them are internationally based. Thus, communicating with them can present geographical challenges and time zone differences. Virtual work serves to bridge space and time constraints, thus allowing the engineers to overcome geographical limitations and expedite product output without always having to be physically present for meetings.

Cut Costs

As our nation currently faces one of its worst recessions, nearly everyone is seeking to maximize profits while minimizing expenses—engineering companies are no exception. Traveling to off-site suppliers can be very expensive after factoring in transportation, lodging, and food expenditures.

However, an email, audio conference, or even video conference represent much more cost effective means of communication for companies. As stated by one engineer, "The cost savings benefits of technology are priceless to companies."

Expedite Meeting Time

According to one respondent, "Time is money in the corporate world." Aligning employees' schedules, setting up a meeting time when everyone is available, and reserving a meeting place for face-to-face discussions can prove a time-consuming task. In contrast, emails, wikis, blogs, and text messages facilitate quick information dissemination without requiring immediate participation from all participants. This benefit of virtual work mirrors the findings of Ober (1995), who reported that Boeing has reduced its meeting time by more than 50 percent since mandating employee use of virtual workgroups in the 1990s.

Flex Time

One engineer reported that she and 90 percent of her team primarily work from home. Working from home and flexible working schedules are becoming more of the norm in corporate America. Engineering companies are increasingly aware of the family and home responsibilities of their employees. Thus, virtual work allows engineers to work from home, off-site, or with more sporadic hours than in years past. According to one respondent, virtual work has minimized the stress level of many parents by allowing them to stay home with their children who may be sick or out of school.

Convenience

Many engineering companies supply their new employees with lap tops, cell phones, and hand-held computer devices. These devices equip engineers with immediate, constant, and convenient access to company business. As one engineer stated, "Technology is at our fingertips...it's quick and convenient to use." In other words, engineers do not always have to be at the office or in front of a desktop computer to conduct business. Portable computer devices allow engineers the convenience of working from anywhere at anytime.

Ease of Use

We are currently living in the "instant-message generation" in which teens readily email, chat, and text with little effort (Lenhart et al., 2006). These teens grow up and bring their knowledge-level of technology into the workplace. The engineers in this study reported that it is very easy to send a colleague an email or to chat with a supplier online. When new programs or operating systems are launched employees commonly receive training on how to use the equipment via web or video conferences. As a whole, the engineers reported that working virtually is relatively easy to learn and uncomplicated to operate.

In sum, engineers perceive virtual work as a convenient and easy-to-use medium that overcomes geographical distances, cuts costs, expedites meeting times, and permits flex time. These benefits, on the one hand, encourage engineers to view virtual work very positively. On the other hand, engineers acknowledge relational limitations linked to technology on the job.

- **RQ2 asked:** What relational limitations do engineers report from virtual work?
  - Content analysis indicated engineers recognize five inherent relational limitations associated with virtual work: (1) less personal, (2) lack of nonverbal cues (3) increased miscommunications, (4) more noise/interference, and (5) reduced interpersonal competence.

Less Personal

Engineers consistently reported that virtual communication has depersonalized their workplace. As one engineer stated, "That aspect (face-to-face) of the work environment has diminished. The personal interactions with other coworkers are now limited." Respondents also reported that it takes longer to build trust and develop personal relationships in a virtually driven corporation. Essentially, the engineering workplace resembles what Katz and Aspden (1997) labeled "a nation of strangers" (p. 81). The engineers testified that they often have lengthy conversations with suppliers and colleagues that they have never met. Per respondents' comments, this depersonalized work environment makes it more challenging to develop and maintain social relationships on the job, as stressed in previous research (e.g., Lea & Spears, 1995).

Lack of Nonverbal Cues

In addition to creating a depersonalize work environment, virtual communication creates an atmosphere primarily devoid of nonverbal cues. Eye contact, gestures, and body language are primarily missing from text-based interactions, such as email exchanges, instant messaging, wikis, and blog communications. As insinuated by Walther and Parks (2002), a lack of nonverbal cues can easily limit virtual communication to impersonal and task-oriented exchanges whereby communicators are unaware of message reception and understanding. One engineer put it bluntly: "Nonverbal communication just doesn't exist in most of our virtual work. We basically go off of our past experiences to establish meaning." Engineers essentially compensate for missing nonverbal cues by drawing conclusions and inferring meaning.

Miscommunication

As much as 90 percent of meaning can be linked to nonverbal cues (Burgoon & Hoobler, 2002); thus, communicators often look for nonverbal markers to regulate communication outflow and create shared meaning. In the absence of eye contact, facial expressions, gestures, body movements, tone of voice etc., miscommunications can occur. Per the engineers' comments, they experience more miscommunications in virtual work compared to face-to-face encounters. Miscommunications occur, in part, because engineers often compensate for the lack of nonverbal cues by relying on their assumptions and prior knowledge. As one engineer articulated, "You don't know what the person looks like. So you sometimes guess. Also, sometimes there can be mixed signals through email and how they [the signals] are perceived." Another engineer echoed this sentiment by stating, "I'm always concerned that someone will misinterpret what I say, and when I receive an email in all caps I think the person is mad and screaming at me." The ultimate goal of communication is to create *shared meaning* among communicators (Lucas, 2009). Virtual work appears to operate adversely to this objective because it requires communicators to play a guessing game and assume underlying meaning, which can lead to misunderstandings.

Increased Noise/Interference

The traditional speech model informs that shared meaning among communicators can be interrupted due to noise or interference occurring in either internal (e.g., stereotypes, biases, sickness etc.) or external (e.g., static, outside conversations, ringing cell phones etc.) forms (Lucas, 2009). Noise can block the clear transmission of messages, thus leading to inaccurate communication. Engineers reported increased external noise associated with virtual work. One engineer said, "If the equipment has static, loses a signal, or malfunctions, you can lose the entire team's attention in a heartbeat."

Another respondent commented how distracting it is when a cell phone rings during an audio conference. Additionally, the anonymity provided by virtual work can cause participants to engage in outside tasks, such as checking email or texting to friends, during important web or video conferences.

Reduced Interpersonal Competence

Since the 1970s, relationship scholars have advocated enhancing interpersonal communication competence by engaging in opportunities that exercise relational skills (Beatty & Beatty, 1976). In other words, to become a more effective interpersonal communicator, one must participate in face-to-face communication. Virtual work has reduced the quantity of person-to-person communication in the workforce. Accordingly, engineers report a decrease in the quality of interpersonal skills among colleagues. As an engineer expressed, "Virtual work has made people become lazy communicators. Some people are not comfortable communicating face-to-face anymore because they hide behind technology." This relational limitation expressed by engineers contradicts the belief that virtual work enables socially reticent individuals to develop and improve interpersonal skills by removing the social pressures associated with synchronous face-to-face encounters (Barnes, 2006). Instead of allowing introverted individuals to express themselves in a comfortable environment, virtual work appears to reduce interpersonal competence and foster meager communication skills.

Essentially, engineers rely on virtual work to successfully perform their tasks; however, these employees are quite cognizant of the intrinsic relational limitations linked to technology. The relational challenges associated with virtual work (i.e., less personal, lack of nonverbal cues, greater risk of miscommunication, increased noise/interference, and reduced interpersonal competence) motivate engineers to employ coping strategies.

- **RQ3 asked:** How do engineers overcome the relational limitations associated with virtual work?
  - Content analysis results suggest that engineers use three strategies to facilitate effective interpersonal relationships in virtually-driven corporations: (1) supplemental face-to-face communication, (2) site visits, and (3) socialization.

Supplemental Face-to-Face Communication

Engineers agree that virtual work can accomplish significant amounts of job-related tasks. On the flipside, engineers report that it is sometimes necessary to supplement virtual work with face-to-face communication. One respondent said, "Sometimes we just need to meet physically to get answers to hard questions and address other issues related to our area of work." Another engineer commented, "We work face-to-face in the more interactive cases." In the engineering field, employees concur that the limitations of virtual work are best mitigated with supplemental face-to-face communication. Although virtual work tends to be the preferred method, communication moments are evaluated on a situational basis. Topics that require detail explanations, nonverbal communication, and human contact are conducted in dyadic or small group settings. As one respondent said, "Some things just can't be discussed via a computer."

Site Visits

Budgetary cuts, a downward economy, and rising travel costs are chief motivators for working virtually. Yet, engineering companies are often willing to spend additional funds in the present to offset potential future expenses. "Sometimes site visits are just necessary, in spite of how much they cost," articulated by one engineer. Accordingly, engineering companies commonly conduct annual, semi-annual, or even quarterly on-site meetings. As reported by one respondent, "These meetings are essential to keeping employees informed and maintaining the human element of our work."

Socialization

Engineers further cope with virtual relational limitations by socializing outside of the corporate environment. As stated by one engineer, "The best way to maintain human relationships in a virtually-driven corporation is to attend company functions, volunteer to participate with co-workers in community activities, call each other, and visit co-workers' work locations (cubes, offices, labs etc.) during breaks." Engineers also use technology to enhance their work relationships by exchanging jokes/funny emails, texting personal notes, and chatting about non-work related topics, such as family, politics, and recreational activities. Engineers additionally commented that they periodically have lunch together, attend after-work cocktail settings, and even allow their children to have "play dates" together. As summed up by one engineer, "Work can be fun if you allow it to be so."

Overall findings from this study imply that in spite of the relational limitations of virtual work, engineers find technology useful and necessary for task completion and are, therefore, motivated to cope with the decreased human elements presented by virtual work. One engineer described virtual work as having "drawbacks on issues such as eliminating human face to face meetings for most decisions…but the cost savings are critical and very essential to the existence of the private sectors." Another engineer referred to virtual work as "second nature and impossible to work without." Other comments labeled corporate technology as "useful," "very beneficial," and "the best thing ever invented".

Findings suggest an application of the social exchange theory (SET) as a framework for under-

standing engineers' perceptions of virtual work. SET is a behavioral theory that triggers positive or negative dispositions towards a behavior based on costs and rewards. People strive to minimize costs and maximize rewards. From a SET perspective, individuals essentially evaluate an exchange relative to the personal benefits and costs associated with the interaction, and this assessment affects their overall opinion, attitude, and behavior concerning the exchange (Thibault & Kelley, 1952).

In the context of this study, SET stipulates that virtual work occurs in engineering companies because of positive exchange. In other words, the positive benefits engineers obtain from virtual work (i.e., overcoming geographical distances, reduced costs, expedited meeting times, flexible work schedules, convenience, and ease of use) outweigh the perceived relational limitations of virtual work (i.e., less personal, lack of nonverbals, more miscommunications, increased noise/interference, and reduced interpersonal competence). The positive exchanges provided by virtual work have apparently secured technology's future in the workplace. As articulated by one engineer, "If we haven't already, we might as well get used to it; virtual communication is here to stay."

FUTURE RESEARCH DIRECTIONS

Findings from this study suggest that virtual work is vital to the engineering profession. Many companies now find it an inconceivable idea to divorce themselves from virtual work, especially since virtual workgroups have expanded geographical borders and saved corporations valuable resources including time, money, and effort (Ober, 1995). Future research concerning employees' perceptions of virtual work should correct some of this study's limitations and explore relationship-enhancing possibilities in the corporate sector.

Sample size is perhaps one limitation of this study because data were collected from only 15 engineers. Future research should seek a larger sample of engineers to increase the findings' validity. Additionally, the participating engineers were enrolled in an effective communication course and completed the open-ended survey for class discussion and analysis during the course's virtual communication unit. Because the participants were taking a communication course, they may have been extra sensitive to the intrinsic relational limitations of virtual work. To enhance the findings' generalizability, forthcoming research should diversify the sample by surveying engineers from different companies not enrolled in a communication course.

Apart from the study's limitations, findings indicate that virtual work weakens the human element. Engineers overwhelmingly paired virtual work with decreased human relationships, reduced face-to-face interactions, and diminished interpersonal competence among employees. The engineers' testimonies validate the need for workplace relationship-enhancing opportunities. Engineering team leaders and communication scholars should consider more partnership possibilities, whereby workshops, short courses, or training programs are incorporated in the workforce to help facilitate interpersonal communication competence among employees. Implementing relationship-enhancing possibilities in the corporate sector could function as an additional coping strategy for alleviating intrinsic relational limitations of virtual work.

CONCLUSION

In the late 1960s, Licklider and Taylor (1968) made the following bold statement: "In a few years, men will be able to communicate more effectively through a machine than face to face" (p. 21). Licklider and Taylor were correct in their assumption that virtual technology would be widespread and prevalent in both our personal and work lives. This study's findings revealed engineers perceive virtual work as a convenient and

easy-to-use medium that mitigates geographical distances, minimizes expenses, expedites meeting times, and permits flexible working hours.

Findings from this study also concur with previous research (e.g., Katz & Aspden, 1997; McKenna & Bargh, 2000; Teske, 2002) by suggesting that virtual work breeds a multitude of relational limitations. Engineers' responses linked technology with fewer face-to-face interactions, diminished nonverbal cues, increased risks of miscommunications, added noise/interference, and reduced interpersonal skills among colleagues. Engineers cope with these relational limitations by supplementing virtual work with face-to-face communication, periodically having on-site meetings, and socializing in relaxed and informal settings.

Social exchange theory suggests that the benefits of virtual work outweigh the inherent relational costs and, therefore, motivate engineers to communicate in a technologically driven atmosphere. It is probable that virtual work will continue its reign as an integral part of engineering task completion. The challenge remains for engineers to negotiate an equitable balance between virtual work as a tool that both facilitates quality product output and enhances healthy employee relationships.

REFERENCES

Auerbach, C. F., & Silverstein, L. B. (2003). *Qualitative data: An introduction to coding and analysis*. New York: New York University Press.

Barnes, S. B. (2006). Internet interpersonal relationships. In Galvin, K. M., & Cooper, P. J. (Eds.), *Making connections: Readings in relational communication* (4th ed., pp. 347–354). Los Angeles, CA: Roxbury.

Bazerman, C., & Prior, P. (Eds.), *What writing does and how it does it: An introduction to analyzing texts and textual practices*. Mahwah, NJ: Lawrence Earlbaum.

Beatty, M. J., & Beatty, P. J. (1976). Interpersonal communication anxiety. *Theory into Practice*, *15*, 368–372. doi:10.1080/00405847609542660

Burgoon, J. K., & Hoobler, G. D. (2002). Nonverbal signals. In Knapp, M. L., & Miller, G. R. (Eds.), *Handbook on Interpersonal Communication* (3rd ed., pp. 240–299). Thousand Oaks, CA: Sage.

Frey, L., Botan, C., & Kreps, G. (2000). *Investigating communication: An introduction to research methods* (2nd ed.). Boston: Allyn & Bacon.

Hertzel, D. A. (2000). Don't talk to strangers: An analysis of government and industry efforts to protect a child's online privacy. *Federal Communications Law Journal*, *52*, 429–451.

Hoepfl, M. (1997). Choosing qualitative research: A primer for technology education researchers. *Journal of Technology Information*, *9*, 47–63.

Joinson, A. (1998). Causes and implications of disinhibited behavior on the Internet . In Gackenbach, J. (Ed.), *Psychology and the Internet: Intrapersonal, interpersonal, and transpersonal implication* (pp. 43–60). New York: Academic Press.

Katz, J. E., & Aspden, P. (1997). A nation of strangers? *Communications of the ACM*, *40*, 81–86. doi:10.1145/265563.265575

Lea, M., & Spears, R. (1995). Love at first byte? Building personal relationships over computer networks . In Wood, J. T., & Duck, S. (Eds.), *Understudied relationships: Off the beaten track* (pp. 197–233). Beverly Hills, CA: Sage.

Lenhart, A., Lewis, O., & Rainie, L. (2006). Teenage life online: The rise of the instant-message generation and the Internet's impact on friendships and family relationships . In Galvin, K. M., & Cooper, P. J. (Eds.), *Making connections: Readings in relational communication* (4th ed., pp. 355–362). Los Angeles, CA: Roxbury.

Licklider, J. C. R., & Taylor, R. W. (1968). The computer as a communication device. *Science & Technology*, *76*, 21–31.

Lucas, S. E. (2009). *The art of public speaking* (10th ed.). Boston: McGraw Hill.

McKenna, K. Y. A., & Bargh, J. A. (1999). Causes and consequences of social interaction on the Internet: A conceptual framework. *Media Psychology*, *1*, 249–269. doi:10.1207/s1532785xmep0103_4

McKenna, K. Y. A., & Bargh, J. A. (2000). Plan 9 from cyberspace: The implications of the Internet for personality and social psychology. *Personality and Social Psychology Review*, *4*, 57–75. doi:10.1207/S15327957PSPR0401_6

O'Sullivan, P. B., & Flanagin, A. J. (2003). Reconceptualizing 'flaming' and other problematic messages. *New Media & Society*, *5*, 69–94. doi:10.1177/1461444803005001908

Ober, S. (1995). *Contemporary Business Communication* (2nd ed.). Boston: Houghton Mifflin.

Peet, T., & Kren, L. (2005). Online communities and discussion boards are critical to today's design engineers. *Machine Design*, *77*, 133.

Pettey, C. (2007). *Gartner says number of identity theft victims has increased more than 50 percent since 2003*. Retrieved April 25, 2009, from www.gartner.com/it/page.jsp?id =501912.

Rheingold, H. (1993). *The virtual community: Homesteading on the electronic frontier*. Reading, MA: Addison-Wesley.

Stoll, C. (1995). *Silicon Snake Oil*. New York: Doubleday.

Suler, J. (2004). The online disinhibition effect. *CyberPsychololgy & Behavior*, *7*, 321–326. doi:10.1089/1094931041291295

Teske, J. A. (2002). Cyberpsychology, human relationships, and our virtual interiors. *Zygon: Journal of Religion & Science*, *37*, 677–700.

Thibault, J. W., & Kelley, H. H. (1952). *The Social Psychology of Groups*. New York: John Wiley & Sons.

Turkle, S. (1995). *Life on the screen: Identity in the age of the Internet*. New York: Simon and Schuster.

Walther, J. B. (1992). Interpersonal effects in computer-mediated interaction: A relational perspective. *Communication Research*, *19*, 52–89. doi:10.1177/009365092019001003

Walther, J. B., & Parks, M. R. (2002). Cues filtered out, cues filtered in: Computer-mediated communication and relationships . In Knapp, M. L., & Daly, J. A. (Eds.), *Handbook of interpersonal communication* (3rd ed., pp. 529–563). Thousand Oaks, CA: Sage.

Wood, A. F., & Smith, M. J. (2001). *Online communication: Linking technology, identity, and culture*. Mahwah, NJ: Lawrence Erlbaum Associates.

ADDITIONAL READING

Barnes, S. B. (2001). *Online connections: Internet interpersonal relationships*. Cresskill, NJ: Hampton Press.

Barnes, S. B. (2003). *Computer-mediated communication: Human-to-human communication across the internet*. Boston: Allyn & Bacon.

Bryden, M., & McCorkle, D. (2005). Virtual engineering. *Mechanical Engineering (New York, N.Y.)*, *127*, 138–167.

Cornwell, B., & Lundgren, D. C. (2001). Love on the Internet: Involvement and misrepresentation in romantic relationships in cyberspace vs. realspace. *Computers in Human Behavior*, *17*, 197–211. doi:10.1016/S0747-5632(00)00040-6

Deiner, E. (1980). De-individuation: The absence of self-regulation and self-awareness in group members . In Paulus, P. (Ed.), *The psychology of group influence* (pp. 1160–1171). Hillsdale, N.J.: Erlbaum.

Emerging technology disappointments. (2007). *eWeek, 24,* 46.

Flaherty, L. M., Pearce, K. J., & Rubin, R. B. (1998). Internet and face-to-face communication: Not functional alternative. *Communication Quarterly*, *46*, 250–268.

Hinds, P., & Kiesler, S. (1995). Communication across boundaries: Work, structure, and use of communication technologies in a large organization. *Organization Science*, *6*, 373–393. doi:10.1287/orsc.6.4.373

Joachim, D. (2001). Virtual engineering teams grapple with tech change. *Long Island Business News*, *48*, 40A.

Jones, S. (Ed.). (1997). *Virtual culture: Identity and communication in cybersociety*. Thousand Oaks, CA: Sage.

Katz, J. E., & Rice, R. E. (2002). *Social consequences of internet use: Access, involvement, and interaction*. Cambridge, MA: MIT Press.

Kong, L. X., Hunter, S. L., & Lin, G. C. I. (2007). An advanced virtual program in engineering education for research and teaching excellence. *International Journal of Mechanical Engineering Education*, *35*, 148–165.

Kraut, R., Patterson, M., Lundmark, V., Kiesler, S., Mukopadhyay, T., & Scherlis, W. (1998). Internet paradox: A social technology that reduces social involvement and psychological well-being? *The American Psychologist*, *53*, 1017–1031. doi:10.1037/0003-066X.53.9.1017

Mazur, M. A., Burns, R. J., & Emmers-Sommer, T. M. (2000). Perceptions of relational interdependence in online relationships: The effects of communication apprehension and introversion. *Communication Research Reports, 17,* 397–406.

McKenna, K. Y. A., Green, A. S., & Gleason, M. E. J. (2002). Relationship formation on the Internet: What's the big attraction? *The Journal of Social Issues, 58,* 9–31. doi:10.1111/1540-4560.00246

Paradis, J. G., & Zimmerman, M. L. (1997). *The MIT guide to science and engineering.* Cambridge, MA: The MIT Press.

Parks, M. R., & Floyd, K. (1996). Making friends in cyberspace. *The Journal of Communication, 46,* 80–97. doi:10.1111/j.1460-2466.1996.tb01462.x

Postmes, T., Spears, R., & Lea, M. (2000). The formation of group norms in computer-mediated communication. *Human Communication Research, 26,* 341–371. doi:10.1111/j.1468-2958.2000. tb00761.x

Rabby, M. K., & Walther, J. B. (2003). Computer-mediated communication effects on relationship formation and maintenance . In Canary, D. J., & Dainton, M. (Eds.), *Maintaining relationships through communication: Relational, contextual, and cultural variations* (pp. 141–184). Mahwah, NJ: Lawrence Erlbaum Associates.

Ramirez, A. Jr, & Wang, Z. (2008). When online meets offline: An expectancy violations theory perspective on modality switching. *The Journal of Communication, 58,* 20–39. doi:10.1111/j.1460-2466.2007.00372.x

Ramirez, A. Jr, & Zhang, S. (2007). When on-line meets off-line: The effect of modality switching on relational communication. *Communication Monographs, 74,* 287–310. doi:10.1080/03637750701543493

Rintel, E. S., & Pittam, J. (1997). Strangers in a strange land: Interaction management on internet relay chat. *Human Communication Research, 23,* 507–534. doi:10.1111/j.1468-2958.1997. tb00408.x

Sampson, E. E. (1988). The debate on individualism: Indigenous psychologies of the individual and their role in personal and societal functioning. *The American Psychologist, 43,* 15–22. doi:10.1037/0003-066X.43.1.15

Stefanick, L., & LeSage, E. J. (2005). Limitations to developing virtual communities in the public sector: A local government case study. *Canadian Public Administration, 48,* 231–250. doi:10.1111/j.1754-7121.2005.tb02189.x

Tidwell, L. C., & Walther, J. B. (2002). Computer-mediated communication effects on disclosure, impressions, and interpersonal evaluations: Getting to know one another a bit at a time. *Human Communication Research, 28,* 317–348. doi:10.1111/j.1468-2958.2002.tb00811.x

Trevino, L. K., & Webster, J. (1992). Flow in computer-mediated communication. *Communication Research, 19,* 539–573. doi:10.1177/009365092019005001

Turkle, S. (2004). How computers change the way we think. *The Chronicle of Higher Education, 50,* B26–B28.

Wallace, P. (1999). *The psychology of the internet.* New York: Cambridge University Press.

Walther, J. B. (1996). Computer-mediated communication: Impersonal, interpersonal, and hyperpersonal interaction. *Communication Research, 23,* 3–43. doi:10.1177/009365096023001001

Walther, J. B., & Burgoon, J. K. (1992). Relational communication in computer-mediated interaction. *Human Communication Research, 19,* 50–88. doi:10.1111/j.1468-2958.1992.tb00295.x

Walther, J. B., Slovacek, C., & Tidwell, L. C. (2001). Is a picture worth a thousand words? Photographic images in long term and short term virtual teams. *Communication Research, 28*, 105–134. doi:10.1177/009365001028001004

Whittle, D. B. (1997). *Cyberspace: The human dimension.* New York: W. H. Freeman and Company.

Williams, R., & Rice, R. E. (1983). Communication research and new media technologies . In Bostrom, R. (Ed.), *Communication Yearbook, 7* (pp. 200–224). Beverly Hills, CA: Sage Publications.

Witmer, B. G., & Singer, M. J. (1998). Measuring presence in virtual environments: A presence questionnaire. *Presence (Cambridge, Mass.), 7*, 225–240. doi:10.1162/105474698565686

Wrench, J. S., & Punyanunt-Carter, N. M. (2007). The relationships between computer-mediated-communication competence, apprehension, self-efficacy, perceived confidence, and social presence. *The Southern Communication Journal, 72*, 355–378.

APPENDIX

Employees' Perceptions of Organizational Virtual Communication

Instructions: This survey seeks to better understand the role of virtual communication in your company and your perception of its effectiveness. Please write out your answers to the following questions in as much detail as needed.

1. Briefly describe your corporate responsibilities.
2. How long have you been employed in this line of work?
3. What virtual communication methods are used at your place of employment? Please list all virtual communication methods that apply, such as e-mail, chat, audioconference, videoconference etc.
4. What are the primary reasons for using the virtual communication methods you listed in question #3?
5. Is communicating virtually required for your position, or is it optional?
6. Did you receive on-the-job training on how to communicate virtually? If so, briefly describe the training you received.
7. Did your education prepare you how to communicate virtually? If so, briefly tell how?
8. How has communicating virtually impacted the human or face-to-face component of your work?
9. How do you work to maintain healthy and appropriate human or face-to-face relationships in a virtually-driven corporation?
10. What do you perceive as the greatest strengths associated with communicating virtually in the corporate sector?
11. What do you perceive as the greatest negatives associated with communicating virtually in the corporate sector?
12. What is your overall perception of virtual communication in the corporate sector?

Chapter 14

Power and Trust in the Virtual Workplace:
Team Development as Communities-of-Practice

Ardis Hanson
University of South Florida Library System, USA

Eric Paul Engel
Ketchcom Development, Inc.

Sheila Gobes-Ryan
University of South Florida, USA

ABSTRACT

How we work in an increasingly computer-mediated world requires new ways of understanding the construction of teams, their co-construction of tacit knowledge to make sense of the organization, and their use of emergent technologies. We posit an alternative research perspective –that of the communities of practice construct – allows a fuller understanding of the relationships of power and trust in team behaviors and processes. The communities of practice model provides an avenue to examine the intricate dance that trust and power perform in virtual environments, with people as the focal point. It is how people interact with each other, with in technology, to be or become successful virtually that is the focus of this chapter. We explore trust and power in virtual or blended work environments using a reflexive autoethnographic narrative, comprised of three case studies, grounded in the larger context of the organizational communication literature.

INTRODUCTION

"One should expect trust to be increasingly in demand as a means of enduring the complexity of the future which technology will generate" (Luhmann, 1979, p. 16).

DOI: 10.4018/978-1-61520-979-8.ch014

Organizations formally codify and informally communicate explicit knowledge with varying levels of effectiveness. However, tacit knowledge—such as operational knowledge, decision-making judgment in the absence of data, or interpersonal skills embodied in individuals—is not easily achieved. The tacit knowledge of each team member must be accessible for knowledge creation to occur (Nonaka & Takeuchi, 1995). Although work teams contain jobs that are interrelated through project tasks and milestones, they also contain a social structure linking the individual team members in such a way that successful completion of each member's job is necessary to achieve larger goals and desired outcomes.

In an increasingly complex environment, we posit that teams function as *de facto* communities-of-practice. They exhibit three characteristics: (1) valuation of work roles, (2) the degree of participation in "peripheral" learning permitted under working conditions, and (3) opportunities for participation in innovative implementations (Wenger, 1998). Virtual work is such an innovation. It requires members to engage creatively in new ways of working. Hence, members learn through praxis (Brown & Duguid, 2002). Teams range the gamut from physically collocated teams (everyone in the same space/place), blended teams (people located in both physical place and virtual space), and virtual teams (everyone in virtual space). For the purposes of this chapter, the use of the phrase virtual teams may also be considering blended teams. All teams use a variety of technologies to work and to innovate.

However, the real innovation in virtual work is in communication, not technology. Technology can make communication faster and more efficient. Unfortunately, technology does not enhance the social interaction required by team members to clarify, create, or trust. For it is the communication of both the explicit and the tacit knowledge possessed by an organization and its members that is the critical challenge in the transition to or blending of virtual and physical work (Belanger & Allport, 2008; Polyani, 1966). Because of this, within daily team praxis are embedded the relationship and the contextualization of power and trust.

Effective communication in blended work teams requires trust, as "Virtuality requires trust to make it work: Technology on its own is not enough" (Handy, 1995, p. 44). This "trust rela-

tionship" is constructed through the content and frequency of formal and informal content communication (Panteli & Duncan, 2004). Trust not only enables cooperation, it also becomes the means for complexity reduction or disambiguation (Eisenberg, 2007). Trust is especially valuable in alliances, such as inter-firm, joint ventures, or contracted work, because firms, teams, and individuals rely on their partners' performance and are vulnerable to partners' actions (Kumar, 1996).

However, as part of an analysis of trust, we suggest it is imperative to consider power. Power is an important contextual factor. Power creates unilateral dependencies or unbalanced relationships. These affect the trust of a team with its organization, as well as among team members or the team members and team leader. Bachmann (2001) suggests that trust and power together are the means of coordinating organizational relationships at the interpersonal and the structural levels. If that is true, how does one make sense of virtual work, trust, and power within a communication framework of praxis and theory? That is the goal of this chapter.

We begin with a theoretical overview of the research on virtual teams, quickly segueing into a review of power and trust. After the more traditional literature review and analysis, we then offer a narrative of our individual experiences as members of virtual teams. We believe this narrative (autoethnographic) approach as virtual workers *and* as researchers writing this chapter allows us to provide a more integrative, analytic perspective of theory and praxis. After all, if narratives are sites for the production of situated 'accountings-for' (explaining why we behave the way we do), then narrative as data gives us privileged insights into how people conceptualize and engage in relationships (Baker, 2004). The narrative is comprised of three lived experiences. The first narrator was one of four virtual employees in a business unit of a large corporation based in multiple locations. The second narrator explores the experiences of a national software training team as they navigate the political perils and pitfalls of virtual work amidst a brick-&-mortar organizational mentality. The third narrator addresses her experiences on the work of a blended virtual team in the implementation of a multi-year, multi-campus virtual library project. We conclude with recommendations for improving practice, as well as for those individuals who lead, manage, or work in these new blended work environments. Although these narratives address three diverse settings over three different times, (1995-1998; 1999-2000, and 2007-2008), the issues of 'virtual' work, teams, power and trust seem to be constant, regardless of time, place, or space.

A REVIEW OF POWER AND TRUST IN VIRTUAL TEAMS

Powell and Piccoli (2004) conducted a review of the 1991-2002 organizational literature on virtual teams. They found fifteen different theoretical perspectives; however, there was no one unifying theory available. When Mazor et al. (2004) examined important factors in virtual teams, they organized them into four categories: inputs, processes, outcomes, and performance moderators. Another review performed by Schiller and Mandviwalla (2007) found twenty-five virtual team theories, which they organized into three categories: team inputs, team processes, and team outputs. According to Schiller & Mandviwalla, team inputs were divided into members and context, team processes were divided into communication and social interaction, and team outputs were divided into task performance and effectiveness. As one examines the categorization done by Mazur and colleagues and Schiller and Mandviwalla, a majority of the models developed by these researchers to examine virtual teams primarily addressed social interaction. From our perspective as communication researchers, social interaction is a key construct in research on virtual teams, allowing multiple theoretical perspectives and avenues of study. If social interaction creates community and teams

are communities-of-practice; then we suggest the social interaction of such a community creates a team. Hence, within the frameworks of context, social interaction, and performance, we begin our investigation of teams as communities-of-practice, followed by an examination of issues of power and trust in teams.

Work teams are teams embedded in organizations that exist to accomplish tasks (Ilgen, 1999). The literature abounds with examples of how teams accomplish tasks (Clark & Wheelwright, 1992; Durst & Kabel, 2001), the import of strong project managers (Henderson, 2004; Kodama, 2005; Norrgren & Schaller, 1999; Trevino, Hartman, & Brown, 2000; Wheelwright & Clark, 1992), cross-functional team structures (Lam, Bischoff, Higgins, & Persing, 1999; McDonough, 2000; Patrashkova & McComb, 2004; Zolin et al., 2004), and the design process (Hong et al., 2005; Rangarajan et al., 2004). Hence, the structure of team, the reasons why a team was created, the knowledge each team member brings to the team and/or the knowledge created by the team, and the product created by team processes (interaction) are critical components in the understanding of the virtual or blended teams.

Virtual or blended teams can be set up as temporary structures with fluid membership, can exist only to complete a specific task, or can be permanent structures working on core business processes. Whether the team is an "action team" (Kozlowski et al., 1996) or a "distributed expertise team" (Hollenbeck et al., 1995), each team member possesses specific information or expertise to contribute to the team task as well as a shared situational awareness and mutual knowledge (Cramton, 2001). Further, team members possess contextual task and team information that are essential content to be communicated to and understood by other team members (Lam et al., 1999). In addition, the accuracy and similarity of shared mental models among team members is predictive of the quality of team processes and performance (Driskell et al., 2006).

Teams, as innovative communities-of-practice, exist as complex, adaptive learning systems (Arrow & Cook, 2007; Wenger, 1998). After all, as team norms and roles evolve, new structures and opportunities emerge that allow the group to expand individual and collective knowledge to achieve its goal. All teams develop processes for sharing knowledge, experiences, and insights critical for accomplishing their missions. These processes ensure the dissemination of existing knowledge among team members and acquisition of new knowledge from the external environment into the team. If learning occurs at both process and outcomes levels, then the more interdependent the team is, the more successful the team will be in accomplishing both personal and team goals.

Is a virtual team different from a physically situated team? A team is traditionally a

collection of individuals who are interdependent in their tasks, who share responsibility for outcomes, who see themselves and who are seen by others as an intact social entity embedded in one or more larger social systems, and who manage their relationship across organizational boundaries (Cohen & Baily, 1997, p. 241).

In the past, if a team was not physically collocated, it was not considered a 'real' team. Although a virtual team may not be seen as an intact social entity within the organization due to its location in 'space' not 'place,' a virtual team meets most of the defining features of a team—its unity of purpose, its identity as a social structure, and its members' shared responsibility for outcomes. This has implications for the evolution of virtual teams into communities-of-practice, particularly when addressing competence, structure, and governance.

Bogenrieder and Nooteboom (2004) provide a different way to understand the need for open communication and trust in the competence of team members that affect the successful development of virtual or blended teams as communities-

of-practice. They see competence encompassing different types of knowledge, learning, and trade-offs between team stability and flexibility of relations. The structure of a team can be examined by looking at a team's network density, the strength of its network ties, its structural 'holes,' and the stability of the group. Team governance focuses on risk, i.e., psychological risk (reputation or legitimation), career risk, risk of competition, and risk of 'lock-in into the group.' Further, they see trust as the basis for dealing with the risks involved in being a member of a team as well as a way to create a successful structure built on the competence of its members (Bogenrieder & Nooteboom, 2004). After all, explicit factors found in physical 'place' (such as organizational norms and rewards, physical space within an office building, and organizational routines) may not offer value or community-building to members in virtual or blended teams. Within the context of virtual teams, shared and collectively created knowledge is the 'physical' explicit factor transformed into a virtual counterpart. Organizational knowledge, after all, is a communal or public good collectively owned by members of the teams or practice communities.

Therefore, as teams become or are born as virtual teams, they become communities-of-practice. They develop a variety of knowledge-sharing mechanisms and interactions using numerous technologies, ranging from voice and text, to groupware and knowledge mining. Expected to be high achievers – after all, they are defined by technology and knowledge creation, virtual teams need to operate with high reliability. Along with other high performance organizations, "They have no choice but to function reliably. If reliability is compromised, severe harm results" (Weick & Sutcliffe, 2001, p. xiii). Further, Bachmann (2001) argues that the interpersonal and structural patterns of trust and power affect the quality of micro- and macro-relationships. Hence, managers, including project managers, should be aware of the significant impacts trust and power have on team reliability, especially on their interpersonal and organizational relationships (Schiller & Mandviwalla, 2007). With online, distributed teams, issues of trust and power become even more salient.

TRUST

Everyone 'knows' what trust is. However, there are many definitions of trust, ranging from those used in social psychology (Lindskold & Bennett, 1973), sociology (Strub & Priest, 1976), economics (Dasgupta, 1988) and marketing (Moorman, Zaltman, & Deshpande, 1992). However, all of these definitions suggest trust involves specific expectations that each party can be depended upon to act in a mutually beneficial way, since that dependence involves risk (Ba, 2001, Siau & Shen, 2003). We particularly like Paul and Mc-Daniel's definition because it addresses the most basic concerns common across definitions of trust throughout the many disciplines exploring trust. They suggest that trust is

... based on confident expectations and beliefs that another party will act in a certain manner, and that the trusting party must in some way be vulnerable under condition of risk and interdependency to actions by the other party (Paul & McDaniel, 2004)

Further, "to reap the benefits of newer work relationships" particularly in regard to virtual teams, "organizations must address interpersonal trust factors" (Paul & McDaniel, 2004, p. 184). Since we claim that social interaction is crucial to the successful development of team and team as community-of-practice, a review of interpersonal trust factors is essential to understanding how teams work. This section will look at types or stages of interpersonal trust, the process needed for trust, the development of trust, trust constructs, trust and social capital, and technology and trust. Next we look at how trust is viewed in the organisational

literature. Having a larger perspective of the types of trust and how trust is developed provides practitioners a frame for developing more effective virtual team practices. One essential caveat is that the 'trust in virtual teams' literature is still heavily grounded in the ways of viewing and measuring trust in 'physically collocated' and/or 'blended' teams. Hence, our review of trust addresses both the physical and virtual team literature. We feel this is acceptable because trust forms through social interaction in all three instances.

The organizational literature discusses three distinct types or levels of trust development–deterrence-based, cognition-based trust and affect-based (Ba, 2001; McAllister, 1995; Lander et al. 2004). Paul & McDaniel (2004) identify similar but more distinct types of interpersonal trust as calculative trust, competence trust, and relational trust. In addition, within each of these constructs, it is important to remember that the types of trust can have a relationship to each other (Paul & Mc-Daniel, 2004; Mayer, Davis, & Schoorman, 1995).

Deterrent-based trust is based on a desire to avoid undesired outcomes (Ba, 2001; Lander et al, 2004). Other researchers see this as a substitute for trust and not trust itself (Rousseau, 1998; Paul & McDaniel, 2004). They define a more specific type of trust for this level, i.e., calculative trust. This market-oriented trust involves economic exchange and contractual agreement.

Cognition-based trust is built on an individual's behavior, specifically, role performance. A cognitive reasoning process is based on one's self-perception and self-interest of the performance, direct interactions, and accomplishments of partners (McAllister 1995). If an individual is impressed with another team member's professional and educational training, his or her experience, or how well he or she performs a designated role, then the individual tends to trust that team member. Information- or knowledge-based trust is similar to cognition-based trust in that it is based on familiarity. Predictable behavior of the other lowers an individual's sense of uncertainty and risk (Ba, 2001; Lander et al, 2004; Panteli & Duncan, 2004). Cognition-based trust also has a technology component, in that underlying technology infrastructure and control mechanisms are capable of facilitating work and transactions among team members or firms.

Paul and McDaniel (2004) prefer a more specific identification of trust at this level, i.e., competence trust. Competence, the ability to do the job, is the specific measure of trustworthiness here. Ratnasingam (2005) indicates this type of trust is important for virtual teams. Abrams et al. (2003) concur, with their analyses of virtual workplaces as social networks. They also suggest that trust results from a person's competence *and* benevolence (affect-based trust).

Identification-based trust, or affect-based trust, occurs when there are emotional bonds between individuals in which each believes in the intrinsic value of the relationship and each believes his or her sentiments are reciprocated (Lander et al., 2004; McAllister, 1995). In such cases, people have developed strong interpersonal relationships and shared identities that enable them to work together and create collective strengths (Panteli & Sockalingam, 2005). McAllister (1995) indicates that in addition to competence and responsibility, reliability and dependability also are measures for interpersonal trust development. Interpersonal trust is often founded in the emotional bonds between individuals. Again, for this level of trust Paul & McDaniel (2004) differ somewhat identifying this type as relational trust. For this type of trust, benevolence and fairness become important for a trust relationship that is based on a feeling of connection to the other.

Trust is produced by a gradual process of interpersonal interactions and norms (Homans, 1950). In fact, confident expectations and a "willingness to be vulnerable" (Mayer et al., 1995) continue to emerge in many of the definitions of trust in this literature review. Cultivating trust is a dynamic, time-consuming, and iterative process, i.e., trust is developed through repeated interactions over time or through social networks that people establish (Ba, 2001; Ring & van de Ven, 1992; Zaheer et al., 1998). The social interaction that creates trust sustains trust, "Trust is created through dialogue and conversation and through gestures, looks, smiles, handshakes and touches" (Bruhn, 2001, p. 22). Rousseau et al. (1998) suggest that trust is a matter of the 'culture of shared worlds'; whatever that culture may be, be it team-, organization-, work- or project-related, developing shared cultural values is often the first step in establishing a trust relationship.

Trust can be an outcome, antecedent, and mediator (Rousseau et al, 1998). For example, trust is the outcome of a past collaboration and is an antecedent of future collaboration. In addition, the relationships of different types of trust, the trust stage, and the changes of trust over time are important. The initial stage and mature stages of trust (Jarvenpaa & Leidner, 1999), occur through development of trust in interaction and knowledge (Paul & McDaniel, 2004; Rousseau et al., 1988). Several researchers (Ba, 2001; Lander et al., 2004; Panteli & Sockalingam, 2005) argue that trust is dynamic and has a distinctive character as one moves through the different stages of a working relationship (professional or personal). Because trust is not static, Siau & Shen (2003) propose an awareness of trust development as a continuous process. Continuous trust development is much like continuous quality improvement. Cummings & Bromiley (1996) assert that trust between individuals and groups must have three components and stress the important of its development over time, as each team member

(a) makes a good-faith effort to behave in accordance with any commitments both explicit or implicit, (b) is honest in whatever negotiations preceded such commitments, and (c) does not take excessive advantage of another even when the opportunity is available (Cummings & Bromiley, 1996, p. 303).

Finally, if stages of trust follow a sequential iteration process, then the achievement of trust at one level enables the development of trust at the next level (Panteli & Sockalingam, 2005). After all, although trust is easier to maintain than to create, it is never difficult to destroy trust (Baier, 1986).

Trust also emerges from an individual's social capital, i.e., trust emerges from the network of relationships possessed by an individual or emerges from within a social network and the set of resources in which it is embedded (Olk & Elvira, 2001). In examining trust from a social capital perspective, one examines cognitive (shared representation, interpretations, and systems of meaning among parties), relational (the type of personal relationships developed through a history of interactions), and structural (the overall pattern of connections between actors) attributes (Nahapiet & Ghoshal, 1998). Bandura (1989) suggests that social cognitive theory addresses how individuals are able to increase the depth, breadth, and efficiency of mutual knowledge exchange through behaviors in their respective networks. Other researchers combine social capital and social cognitive theory to capture the complexity of social interaction ties, trust, norms of reciprocity, identification, shared vision, and shared language vis-à-vis outcome expectations in trust relationships (Chiu, Hsu, & Wang, 2006; Hsu, Ju, Yen, & Chang, 2007). The role of affect- and cognition-based trust in complex knowledge sharing is a primary factor in self-efficacy and outcomes of virtual teams (Chowdhury, 2005). In their study of cognitive complexity of groups and trust, Curseu, Schruijer, & Boros (2007) find that cognitive disparity, i.e., not having shared mental models, has a negative impact on group cognitive complexity. Further, they suggest a high quality of group interactions engender the highest cognitive complexity of both individuals and groups.

Trust exists along a continuum, i.e., trust is built, trust is stable, or trust declines. If we add in culture, language, and gender, the process and behaviors required to build, to sustain, or

to dissolve trust becomes increasingly complex. Many of the studies cited in this section focus on a particular phase in the trust continuum. It is essential to remember that trust acts as an independent variable, a dependent variable, or as an interaction variable. In simpler terms, trust is the cause, the effect, or the condition for a work or social relationship. Individual trust relations may be constrained or enhanced by organisational processes. The converse also holds true, i.e., organizations may be constrained or enhanced by individual relationships.

Finally, trust in technology and technology's impact on trust formation and maintenance are critical for virtual teams, again from the interpersonal and organisational perspectives. Lin & Huang (2008) extend social-cognitive theory and 'task technology fit' as barriers or access to trust in knowledge sharing, hence our position that virtual teams are communities-of-practice due to their innovative use of emergent technology. Therefore, we should consider two perspectives. The first perspective examines the 'how, why, and if' members of teams trust the hardware and software components of the technology. The second perspective addresses the trust in the technology support staff and the organizational management providing the technology. Therefore, any examination of virtual teams should include a review of practices possible vis-à-vis the framework of technology and the people providing or supporting technology.

Studies also show that the influence of organizational context (competitive versus cooperative) and introductory meeting medium (face-to-face versus online) affect trust and collaborative behaviors (Fuller, Hardin, & Davison, 2006; Guo, D'ambra, Turner, & Zhang, 2009; Hill, Bartol, Tesluk, & Langa, 2009). Finally, Li, Hess, and Valacich (2008) examine factors outside the team to explain trust formations, which may also change individuals' initial trust in technology. They suggest there are eight trusting base factors. Of the eight, three best address the focus of this paper –

cognitive (as in cognitive-based trust), technology, and organizational. These three factors emerge in the narrative later in this chapter and again as major talking points of lessons learned.

PREDICTORS OF BEHAVIOR: TRUST AND POWER

At an *interpersonal* level, trust is an implicit set of beliefs that the other party will behave in a dependent manner and will not take advantage of the situation. As each team member interacts with him or herself and as the team interacts, new information is related to their previous information and knowledge structure (Hernes & Bakken, 2003). In this iterative interrelationship, "not only does the organization construct the employee, but the employee constructs the organization" (Gabriel, 1999, p. 190). We posit that trust exists because the parties involved understand and appreciate each other's wants. As trust develops, this 'mutual understanding' develops to such a degree that each can effectively act for the other. Trust therefore encourages strong individual inter-relationships and a shared identity, allowing individuals to work together successfully as a team. Power affects communication, trust, team identity, and cooperative activities. There are as many forms of power as there are of trust, and the intertwining of these two complex, multi-layered constructs is the focus of this section.

Moving to the team level, if members of distributed groups are going to engage in cooperative activities, they must either trust each other or be able to monitor each other. Although Ouchi (1981, p.101) describes trust as expectations about consistent or reliable behavior, the virtual workplace is not an online reality event. One of the issues that arises without the daily observations and interactions of virtual team members is that they may become 'invisible' to the home office or other remote sites. This "behavioral invisibility" (Sheppard & Sherman, 1998) also carries additional risks to the

trust inherent among and between the team and its effectiveness, including misinterpretation and (mis)anticipation of team member actions. Further, such invisibility affects the larger organizational structure, reduces organizational complexity, and fails to allow for a comprehensive understanding of interpersonal/professional characteristics of all members of the organization (Anand, Clark, & Zellmer-Bruhn, 2003; Cross, 2002; Gibson & Cohen, 2003). Invisibility has consequences for trust and for the effective use and abuse of power.

Embedded within many of the trust discussions in the literature noted above are the implicit and explicit notions and uses of power. From the asymmetrical relationships between supervisor and employee to the shifts in power dynamics among team members, the issue of power affects knowledge construction, self- and team-efficacies, productivity, and work/social outcomes. Within an organisational setting, there are formal and informal structures used to create, sustain, or enhance communication among team members. According to Katzenbach and Smith (2001), virtual teams may require different 'rules of engagement' that address their concerns and ways of working. However, similar to physical teams, virtual teams may be provided formalized manners of communication (e.g., ethical codes, process requirements) designed to accommodate their virtual processes and communication styles. Hence, members will interpret the rules and protocols in similar manners, thereby promoting cohesiveness.

As virtual workers assume new roles within virtual environments, ethical codes take on more importance (Kuntze et al., 2002). Within teams, the project manager assumes a formal power position. The complexity of a manger's scope of duties can be overwhelming, i.e., managing risks, stakeholders, and resources (Lee, 2008). A manager's style and competence directly affects team and organisational effectiveness (Turner & Mûller, 2005). Further, team effectiveness is correlated to management practices addressing goals, tasks, and outcomes, particularly in interdependent projects (Hertel, Konradt, & Orlikowski, 2004), which may require different strategies between physical and virtual work teams. However, numerous power factors affect teams, such as coercion (Kirschner et al., 2008; Kohlberg, 1969), control (Trevino, 1986; Trevino et al., 2000), motives (DePaulo, DePaulo, Tang, & Swaim, 1989), and Machiavellianism (Giacalone & Knouse, 1990; Winter et al., 2004).

The first of these factors, coercion, is behavior predicated on a lack of moral reasoning (or judgment), not within the basic principles of fairness (Kohlberg, 1969). Coercive behaviors are often more subtle while bullying behaviors are more overt. Coercion often is framed inappropriately as a tool for negotiation and for shared sense-making, i.e., a 'common ground' (Kirschner et al., 2008). Communication, whether face-to-face or virtual, also allow the emergence of aggressive and reciprocal bullying behaviors (Cranford, 1996). However, both behaviors create an uncaring environment through isolation, lack of motivation, reduction, or loss of loyalty to the team and the project, lack of commitment by the team or its individual members to the project, and failed communication. Any or all of these factors can contribute directly to project failure (Kliem, 2004). Hence, facilitating and maintaining communication is a primary responsibility of managers as a way to avoid coercive or bullying behaviors. It may mean changes in behavior and power dynamics, when weighing in these social costs, so teams can remain connected with each other.

Control is an essential attribute of power, whether it is self-control or control of others. An individual's need for a sense of control is foundational in how he or she interacts with others. An internal locus of control addresses an individual's belief that he or she controls his or her destiny (Lefcourt, 1966). Derived from social learning theory, locus of control also addresses adaptability, a trait critical in virtual environments. Someone with a strong internal locus of control, for example, often has a larger capacity to trust,

and is willing to share power or use power wisely. Trevino (1986) suggests that how managers think about ethical concerns requires them to ground their decision-making in 'real world' terms. Hence, strengthening cognitive and behavioral approaches to decision-making would encourage positive behaviors, such as positive reinforcement, having congruent rules for team members, congenial organisational cultures, and increased appreciation of the differences in virtual, blended, and physical work environments. Trevino et al. (2000) further expand on the benefits of understanding 'control' in a positive fashion, resulting in increased employee satisfaction, commitment, and ethical conduct from both the management and employee point of view.

Power is also motive-driven. How do we determine motives of managers and team members? Determining motives of team members or management depends upon the frequency of interaction and the impression that members of teams have of one another (Goffman, 1971). However, the social cues we use face-to-face are missing in virtual interaction. How do virtual teams cue into behaviors or deduce motives behind behaviors and communication at a distance? Technology is not the panacea. As Rockmann and Norcraft (2008, p. 106) found, "Video-mediated communication solves some, but not all, of the problems inherent when interacting via communication technology." Numerous studies examining social identity and relationship between and among group members show that individuals have a variety of self-identities (personal and social) which emerge as needed (Somers, 1994; Cunningham & Chelladurai, 2004; Pratt, 2003; Tanis & Postmes, 2008). Impression management, or how others view us, portrays our preferred identities to others (Goffman, 1971). Virtual workers, like workers in a physical environment, have a variety of strategies to elicit motives. These strategies include "interrogation, self-disclosure, deception detection, environmental structuring, and deviation testing" to gather information about team members (Walther, 1992, p.71). Other studies have addressed attributional or self-serving biases among members (Walther 2007).

Finally, any discussion of power must address Machiavellianism (covert manipulative behaviors). The 'cues filtered-out' (the lack of face-to-face) communication (Culnan & Markus, 1987) among virtual teams makes deception detection difficult to determine, creating environments conducive to covert, or Machiavellian, behaviors (Riva, 2002). These behaviors often manifest as contestation or exploitation of institutionalized power and authority, covert conflict in material and symbolic forms, and social (in)visibility (Morrill, Zald, and Rao, 2003), making teams vulnerable and contributing to failure. Giacalone and Knouse (1990) found, in their study of sabotage behavior, that high Machiavellian individuals manipulate others into defining ethically acceptable behavior in ways that are consistent with the Machiavellian interpretation of organizational or personal goals.

Winter, Stylianou, and Gialcone (2004) found that Machiavellianism interacts with the situations in which people find themselves. High-level impression management often is the tool used to present behaviors that the target audience wants to see, with rewards and emulation as possible outcomes for such behavior. Hence, an organization's ethical climate, or a manger's ethical practice, can significantly influence the accepted behavior of the organization or the team.

However, to neutralize dissent and resistance and to secure resources for their teams, managers themselves need to develop better 'back stage' skills and strategies to counteract Machiavellianism (Jackson, 2001). 'Front stage' engagement shows normative behaviors and expectations. However, 'back stage', managers can lobby for appropriate behaviors, negotiate issues surrounding boundary management and inaccurate perceptions of individual, team, or work behaviors, and (re)generate member and team involvement (Jackson, 2001).

Hence, in any examination of trust and power in virtual or blended teams, it is incumbent upon managers to be aware of and appropriately address team dynamics, especially in the areas of coercion, control, motives, and Machiavellianism.

A CONVERSATION AMONG PEERS: CASE STUDIES IN POWER, TRUST, AND VIRTUAL WORK

Early on, we had agreed to a format blending a traditional literature review with a bit of narrative ethnography, incorporating our personal case studies as a storied text. We'd each read through at least one draft of our own virtual work stories, and we'd come together this afternoon to discuss our findings and engage in some sensemaking. "So, where do we start?" Sheila began. "We've got a literature review and we've each written up our own stories, our own experiences with power and trust in virtual work teams. What next?"

"A big part of what made it interesting for the three of us to work together was that each of us found ourselves situated in virtual work differently" Eric opened the conversation.

Ardis added, "And each of these situations also offers examples of the challenges and successes of creating communities of practice in a new way.

"Well, why don't we first provide a concise review of our personal experiences, our own autoethnographic case studies? Our individual stories abstracted in short form for efficient, palatable consumption. Then we could provide a review of our own reflexive lessons learned," Eric suggested.

"Well that's easy enough for me," Sheila laughed. "I struggled with the details, so paring it down shouldn't be that difficult." Sheila glanced at the digital recorder on the table. "Fine," she began, smiling at Ardis. "As you know, I titled my case study, 'Alone in a Group.' Basically, I was hired on as a virtual employee by an organization of almost entirely physically situated employees even though it didn't officially permit virtual work."

"When people don't normally work entirely virtually, trust between the organization and a virtual employee can be complicated," Sheila paused to take a drink of water. "Mutual engagement in a common shared work environment may be unavailable to the person working virtually. In my case, I was a virtual employee dependent on the technology the organization already had in place. The technology was supposed to enable the interactions that I needed to become a trusted team member.

Ardis inquired, "In the lit review for the paper, we referenced Wenger and Paul & Duguid to build a case for teams as communities-of-practice. Did you find that to be true in your case?"

"The work group I was in developed a number of strong communities-of-practice within it, divided by geography, expertise groups, and a number of project/client teams. The shared repertoire changed for each one, and learning it was largely based in mutual engagement in a shared physical work environment. There was a core senior team that shared a common history dispersed among offices that provided a certain base reification to the community.

Starting in a new organization requires some initial trust from both sides: they trust I will be capable to do the work I committed to and I trust that they will provide the tools – both co-workers and technology – that I need to do the job. Due to the newness of virtual work, the organization expected I'd bear the entire burden of developing a successful work process that was outside that of the co-present employees. Although this was never formally stated before or after I started, the actions of the organization indicated it strongly. On the other hand, I expected that they would meet their 'promise' to for me to be able to work virtually by having the tools and viable processes in place," Sheila responded.

"Promises, promises," Eric grinned. "Give me an example."

Sheila sighed, "I felt like it was an opportunity lost, "I reported for work my first day, expecting to work in a company location, just not one of the locations with my work-group. The staff there said the office had no room for me. They were quick to inform me, had they been asked, they would have told my group *not* to hire me because they had no space. I didn't have a desk, a telephone, or a computer. I didn't even have a filing cabinet. My supervisor, who worked in a different office, was nowhere to be found; he'd assumed someone else would get me started."

Eric inserted "Ah, assumptions. A classic source of organizational frustration. Not the kind of welcome you'd expected, I'm sure. The initial grounding that participation plays in making you part of a practice was missing. So what did you do?"

"There was a week of getting stacks of paper from the receptionist, for me to do my work on my own personal computer, before I got a two-year old hand-me-down from a senior employee. I spent two weeks moving stacks of paper, sometimes several times a day; finally, I suggested to my project manager, that the only way for me to get work done was to set up an office space at home. It was almost two months before I got a cell phone. I couldn't figure out the process to order one, and no one saw it as their job to help me. You see, it was normally handled by someone in your work group, who worked in your location. It was three months before I met with IT and my supervisor to get instructions on how the technology security system worked. The way I had gotten it to work wasn't correct or consistent." Sheila paused, rolling her eyes back as she remembered the events of her first months. "It was another month before IT figured out that the hardware on the hand-me-down computer was the problem. It was four months before I got a new, working computer."

"Interesting, you lacked the technology to participate in the only process you had available. Back to the trust you had for the organization, but what about their trust, or better yet, their expectations of trust, with you?" Ardis noticed.

Sheila thought and then continued, "The organization wasn't inherently untrustworthy, and I certainly wasn't lacking in the skill required to do the work, but neither of us understood the difference between being out of the office, even regularly, and working virtually on a routine basis. Neither of us had really thought it through and both expected the other to carry the burden of making the 'different way' of working work. In order to save the cost of a new laptop, they wasted months of man-hours – mine and the company's. This negatively impacted my ability to gain the trust of my co-workers, much less successfully complete work. Now this would've been a bad enough problem in a shared work environment, but in a virtual one, it was disastrous. The trust I needed to build with co-workers was eroded when all they heard was problems.

Ardis insisted, "Do you think, in retrospect, that you could've fixed the situation? If trust is essential to create a shared knowledge, it doesn't sound like there was much hope."

"I have to admit I've replayed that in my head a few times. "Sheila recalled. "At the time I worked for them there was not a virtual work environment possible, due to the technology limits. I believe it was essential to be collocated physically with co-workers so we could develop those organizational relationships that enable tacit learning. Especially in becoming part of a community."

Eric questioned, "So what was the result?"

"The unpreparedness of both the organization and me to work in the new way rapidly destroyed the initial trust we placed in each other," Sheila remembered sadly.

"Did the problem extend to your ability to interact with co-workers using the available technology?" Eric asked.

"Yes," Sheila indicated, "The tools we used were really designed for the transfer of information and not for an interactive collaboration. Much more like a linear, or transmission, model of communication."

"How did that impact your ability to establish trust relationships with your project community of practice? It sounds like you were missing the mutual engagement required to establish trust? Eric asked.

"Yes, that's true. I didn't get to be involved because the process of mutual engagement for this community of practice existed only in the shared physical work environment," Sheila replied. "Enabling virtual work as a member of a community of practice requires involvement in a common place, be it physical or virtual, at least to establish your membership in the community." Sheila paused before going on, "we were going to have to depend on one another to get work done yet we, no – *I* did not share a place to participate in the iterative process needed for trust. Because the tools for virtual interaction were cumbersome, physically situated employees preferred to keep their use to a minimum."

Sheila then added, "In the past, in a shared work environment, my coworkers and I developed trust from mutual engagement in joint enterprises. They knew my skills and talents through formal assignments and in day-to-day challenges and support. When I wasn't physically collocated, my co-workers never learned what I could do."

Ardis interjected, "your coworkers were never able to become familiar enough with you to know what could be expected of you, so you remained a risk to work with."

Sheila replied, "Yes, that's it. I also lacked a virtual 'break room'—the down times, the informal conversation where I got to know others as people and they got to know me. This informal interaction is a critical factor in becoming a community of practice. An important example was my interaction with the IT people. Working with someone 'off site' was more complicated for them. My interactions with them broke into two distinct periods: the before my office visit and the after. It was more than just seeing me; while they were working on my laptop, I was able to share stories with them. For example, once I became a 'just another guy' to IT, they stopped being just "the IT guys" to me and became Mark and Bruce. That annoyance factor that my off-site problem negotiation had posed then became an interesting challenge to them. Before I had been 'not really their responsibility. After they gave me their cell phone numbers, providing me help outside of office hours when I was traveling and needed help."

"What about *you*? What about *your* story, *your* case study?" Sheila suddenly shined the spotlight onto Eric, as she left to bring in more food to the group.

"Once upon a time, over a decade ago," Eric began, "I was a member of a national software training team as we navigated the political perils and pitfalls of virtual work amidst a bricks-and-mortar organizational mentality. Despite our team's internal cohesion and productivity employing the company's proprietary online publishing communication and community building software, a dearth of trust among the organization's senior management ultimately resulted in forced face time at the home office. For me, the experience highlighted the dynamic tensions between a managerial mindset rooted in traditional co-present work relations and a virtual team at home in cyberspace working with blended communication technologies and practices."

Leaning back in his chair, he continued, "It was back during the dot com boom, and I was hired by a small online publishing outfit as one of two new trainers. My boss, the training manager, had previously managed all of the company's training needs by himself. As the number of clients around the country grew, however, so did training needs. The first couple of months were spent becoming familiar with the company's propriety online publishing software. Five days a week, I commuted 30-45 minutes in highway traffic to a small office in a non-descript office building. In my third month, however, I was tasked with taking the show on the road. For the next six months, I trained over 250 clients in major media markets – including New York, San Francisco, Philadelphia, Boston,

and Atlanta – on how to employ and strategically deploy the company's publishing software as a community development and media marketing tool. As I noted before, the first few months were spent in the company's bricks-and-mortar headquarters. After that, it wasn't uncommon to be on the road two to three weeks per month."

"After roughly six months on the job," I continued, "my boss explained that even when we were in town, when we were local, we no longer needed to report to the office. Thus, for a short time, my position became relatively *virtual*, whether I was working from home or Hoboken.

"Unlike Sheila's story, your story addresses a transition to being virtual," Ardis pointed out. "That must have created a very different sense of trust among your team and the organization?"

"Between instant messaging and data from the company's proprietary software showing our login and logout times, our boss knew that the other training specialist and I were working between 60 and 80 hours a week. He knew how much we valued time at home in contrast to being on the road, and he also appreciated how we resented time lost to traffic twice a day during the daily commute—particularly since ours was an online communication tool! He could see the fruits of our labor in the training products we created both online and in print as well as in positive client feedback regarding our training methods and practices. I was online night and day, instantly available to my boss, my co-workers, and my training clients in the field who frequently confronted deadline driven dilemmas cropping up in the wee hours. Our team was cohesive and our trust was solid. Unfortunately, the organization had a different perspective. Soon after, things became bumpy around the office. We began to experience the downfalls of physical non-presence even though we actively maintained virtual co-presence through frequent and numerous phone calls and emails with colleagues and clients. It felt like management didn't trust us."

"In part, I question my boss's ability at navigating office politics. Unfortunately, I don't think he necessarily had the greatest relationship with senior management. I'm not saying it was his fault per se, but rather that he could only insulate us so much from the larger organizational sentiment and actions. In many ways, it seemed like being out of *sight* also meant being out of *mind*."

"Behavioral invisibility," Sheila interjected.

"Exactly! Even though ours was an *online* company, management practices were still firmly rooted in traditional bricks-and-mortar organizing. To be working meant being seen around the office. Our absence from the office became problematic for senior management, and ultimately we were required to once again report to the office whenever in town for 'normal' office hours."

Leaning back to stretch, hands clasped squarely behind his head, Eric continued. "Reflecting on the experience, power and trust seem naturally coupled with politics and control. Whether senior management didn't trust us, the training department, I'll never know. I left the company shortly thereafter. What struck me about the experience was the pivotal role a manager can play in the office politics for a virtual worker. Even though my company's publishing product was online, the company itself was still firmly entrenched in co-present business practices. Managerial expectations and corporate policies colluded in maintaining bricks-and-mortar relations, ultimately undermining the training department's experiment with telecommuting and virtual work. Since I was just a trainer and thus not privy to the company's strategic plans, I'll never know why we were forced to cease and desist our virtual work. Part of me thinks it was office politics rooted in managerial power and control issues. There was a norm to be maintained, and that meant being *at* work with everyone else. It meant geographic co-presence. At that time, working from home was often seen as slacking off, perhaps largely because connection speeds were still dial-up slow and telecommuting was relatively uncommon."

"Anything else?" Sheila queried.

"No," Eric confirmed, "that's my story in short form, abstracted lessons and all.

"Your story reminds me of Foucault's panopticon – the notion of continuous external and internal monitoring by the powers that be," Ardis stated, "with a twist. If they can't see you, you can't be monitored."

"Including his notion of power-knowledge," Sheila added, "That definitely seems applicable here."

Sheila paused to take a drink before turning the attention to Ardis. "So what about your story?"

"What *about* my story?" Ardis skillfully volleyed the conversational ball back into her court.

"Well, for one thing," Eric interjected, "I'd be curious to know more about *your* experience, Ardis

"How so?" Ardis responded.

"Well," Eric continued, "in reading and rereading your story and Sheila's story, I noticed that where Sheila's story was quite personal, storied as a first-person experiential contribution, your story of events was more organizational, more third-person. In committing your experience to the page, your reflections addressed *organizational* lessons learned. In contrast, reading Sheila's story struck me as reflecting both organizational *and* interpersonal lessons learned."

"Such is the nature of my mysterious ways," Ardis responded wryly.

Sheila took the conversational floor. "Speaking of *your* story, why don't you share your abstracted narrative with the class?" Sheila grinned as she motioned to the digital recorder at the center of the table.

"*My* story might perhaps be more appropriately framed as *our* story insofar as it involves not just me but the staff of the five libraries on three campuses comprising the University of South Florida Library System. My story really looks at multi-library, multi-campus, multi-team virtual work processes. In 1995, the USF Virtual Libraries Planning Committee prepared a proposal, which we called the *Blueprint,* for a university-wide virtual library. With the adoption of the *Blueprint* as a guiding document, the members of the planning committee morphed into the Virtual Library Implementation Team. What had been a handful of nine core group members mushroomed into eight project teams, roughly 40 faculty and staff across five libraries, with many individuals having membership in more than one geographically dispersed work team." Ardis paused to take a sip of her drink.

"This was the first time the USF libraries had collaborated on a system-wide project of this scope too, right?" Sheila asked for confirmation.

"Right, we saw this as a complex and adaptive project," Ardis acknowledged. "For the USF Virtual Library Project to succeed, we had organizational factors that had to be addressed. First, we had to develop a plan to build the virtual library. We had to develop an inter- and intra-library team structure that let us have buy-in from all the libraries, from administrators to front-line staff, from faculty to student workers. We needed to develop work processes for all the different functional areas of the libraries that addressed the ways virtual collections and services would be done. Let me finish the story about the project and you'll see the virtual processes of the project, becoming a community of practice, as well as the issues of power and trust in what became a virtual organization paralleling a bricks-and-mortar one."

Sheila queried, "What did you see as critical organisational factors?"

"From an organizational perspective, we needed a reliable and advanced networked infrastructure as well as true programmatic cooperative decision-making among the libraries regarding any facility and financial decisions. Next, each of the libraries had to be fully committed to the project, from its administration to its faculty and staff. And this also had to have University commitment. Finally, somehow we had to transcend existing barriers based on territoriality and distance. After all, the libraries were located on campuses in St. Petersburg, Sarasota, and Tampa. Driving

logistics for eight teams across four campuses to come in for meetings were a nightmare. The way this was going to succeed was to move to virtual workspaces and telecommunications to make this project get off the ground."

Eric asked slowly, "And how did that work out? Sheila's story of technical support, or lack of, just for her makes me wonder if this story has a happy ending?"

"The technology story has mixed results. For example, Ed and I had shared whiteboard and editing capacities on NetMeeting, so we set up meetings two or three times a week between ourselves and asked other team members to meet with us online. Even though this technology was available to all the teams, we found that most team members relied upon an older, more reliable online tool—the telephone conference call. Transparency was also an issue since not all staff or administration were on teams. So each of the project teams and VLIT had team websites with agenda, minutes, timeline, shared readings, and a comments and questions section to make the doings of the teams open to everyone. Like Sheila, we also had to trust that those of us with subject, technical, or process expertise were going to be aware of those cutting-edge technologies and apply them appropriately. These technologies hopefully could assist in the execution of the team projects or in new work processes that would result from creating the virtual library, which was really a blended library environment of place and space."

"OK, so those were the challenges," Sheila acknowledged. "What were the lessons learned? What was your experience with regard to trust and power in the development of virtual teams and virtual work?"

"Well, creating ownership among and within the libraries' staff was a major focus," Ardis responded. "Trust among management and staff of the various libraries wasn't immediate. Rather, it had to be built and, more importantly, *earned* through time, through working together. One interesting development was the emphasis some members placed on trust in competence, rather than interpersonal trust. Sometimes, unfortunately, personality or organizational history is a hard hurdle to surmount."

Eric interjected, "What about behavioral invisibility? In such a long-term, multi-player project, what happened to the power dynamics?"

"Ah, yes, power dynamics absolutely was a factor" Ardis replied. "They had to change for the project to move forward, much less to succeed. The advent of teleconferencing allowed for the creation of a more democratic planning committee, for example, with nearly equal representation from all the libraries involved. This was a double-edged sword for the Tampa Library. As the largest of the libraries, the Tampa campus library dominated committees and work groups, however, in this case, its size worked against it. While the other libraries had no choice but to enlist all or nearly all of their staff in order to cover the multifunctional teams created for implementation purposes, the Tampa campus library had a large percentage of staff who chose not to participate at all. As a result, unlike the smaller libraries, the Tampa campus library *en toto* really didn't benefit from the cohesiveness engendered by the shared experience."

Ardis paused to sip her drink, flipping through some more of her notes. "Another change was in committee structures and assignments. The traditional committee structure wasn't effective anymore. Previously, committee memberships were often based on job position or status. Now, staff self-identified their interests and helped build assignments cooperatively. Probably one of the most important components that changed committee membership and participation was the simple fact that location no longer governed the composition of the teams. There was a real effort to create a shared yet distributed workload based on expertise or interest."

"Not to say there weren't interpersonal issues or attempts to reestablish old patterns of behaviors, but overall I would have to say 'our'", as Ardis

paused to 'air quote' for emphasis, "virtual team experience was positive. However, probably the most interesting aspect of the virtual library project, for me, was how we became a community-of-practice. Brown and Duguid say that 'The central issue in learning is *becoming* a practitioner not about learning *practice.*' Valuation of work roles – every person who participated had a contribution to make. Peripheral learning required each of us to share what we knew, either from conference attendance or from 'best practice' in the literature, which we shared using a distribution list, first as members of the Planning Committee, then as members of VLIT. And, of course, participation in innovative implementations. Earning and retaining trust and keeping balances of power were two ways that we were able to cohere as a virtual team as well as to became a community of practitioners."

"Anything else?" Eric inquired.

"Not really, other than communication is paramount, especially in an innovative and multi-year project." Ardis replied. "The major lesson learned is that in any virtual or blended environment, it is essential to recognize the impact and process of change. We needed to monitor the place of the team within the organization as the goals and structure of the organization changed during the five years of the project. Bottom line, to stay aligned, teams need to talk to one another and to the organization."

"And that's *my* story, or rather *our* story, in a nutshell."

"So what now?" Sheila continued. "You've captured our stories," she said, pointing at the digital recorder, "now what are we going to *do* with them?"

"First, I'll transcribe our conversation," Eric explained, "then I'll email you both a copy of the transcripts. We can do some keyword coding of the text, then extrapolate lessons learned to inform our chapter's conclusion."

"After that," Ardis chimed in, "It's your turn, Sheila. Bearing in mind our review of the literature and our individual case studies, all you'll need to do is stitch together our final remarks. That's it," Ardis smiled confidently.

"That's it, she says!" Sheila smiled.

And with that, the conversation was concluded. We gathered our materials, Ardis closed up her office, and we made our way out into the parking lot to our cars.

CONCLUSION

We as researchers have an interest in the way we construct ourselves socially while also constructing objects ('out there') in our research (Steier, 1991). This chapter intertwined a traditional review of the literature on trust and power in virtual teams with a more reflective (reflexive) approach. Reflexivity can result in an episteme, or a historical *a priori*, which structures and organizes that which we come to consider knowledge, or in organisational terms, 'the ways of working.' This interpretive-reflective approach we use acknowledges theory, interpretation, and the (dis)ambiguity of 'data' offered by narratives to build a coherent, sensible (sense-making) understanding of the relationships of power and trust among virtual teams, members, and organizational settings. From our perspectives as academics, "…as individuals negotiate identity boundary permeability, they are, in essence, (re) producing individual identity as well as opening it up to an identity completeness external to themselves that can potentially reside in aspects of organizational identity" (Kreiner, Hollensbe, & Sheep, 2006, p. 1333). In short, identity—as an individual, as a member of a team, as a manger, as an organization—is critical in the building of trust in persons, in the team, in a manager and in an organization. So what are some of the lessons learned about trust and power?

Trust can be an outcome, antecedent, and mediator. This addresses the dynamic, continuous process nature of trust, It is the 'outcome of a past collaboration and is an antecedent of future

collaboration' (Rousseau et al., 1998). Therefore, trust is not just something that one acquires but that it also must be maintained. Virtual work doesn't mean that everyone goes off to the mountaintop and works hermetically, rather it is a constant back-and-forth of talk and text and process. However, to create and maintain trust, one must be aware of the power dynamics involved in team and management relationships. Power, in itself, is not a bad thing; however, in virtual work it is something that must be (re)considered as to how it is (re)constructed in organizational behaviors.

Another important element for the three of us was that trust required consistent and reliable expectations. In each of the case studies, expectations played a prominent role, whether the expectation was from each of us to the rest of the team or to management or management's often unexpressed expectations of us. One of the things that really struck us is the role of emergent and evolving technologies. As new technologies continue to become available, so is the process of working together in concert with technology an emergent process, which makes expectation in virtual environments an ongoing construct and process. Assumptions based on previous work and team processes need to be viewed recursively and iteratively to allow virtual workers to engage effectively with new ways of working.

Virtual teams have different 'rules of engagement' (Katzenbach & Smith, 2001). The distinction between doing the same job and having a different role is subtle, though substantial. It argues whether it is a new way of doing work or a new way of perceiving the 'organizational identity' of the individual. Working virtually allows, no, it demands a higher level of complexity in how we think about the discrete tasks that comprise an activity, or the process, or the relationships in which we engage to create a product.

It is not sufficient to define new roles as specific technical or administrative skill sets. The converse it true. New roles must be examined and understood as a set of capabilities. These capabilities must respond quickly and effectively be applied whenever and to whatever new need or opportunity arises (Hanson et al., 2003). How trust and power are perceived and created in the development and performances of these new roles are certainly worth reviewing in these 'rules of engagement.'

Earlier in the chapter, we describe our view of teams as communities-of-practice. We believe that this construct provides us a tool for evaluating an emergent work process to understand if the components necessary for successful teamwork are present. Communication provides us the tools to make sense of joint enterprise, shared repertoire, and mutual engagement, all common elements in communities-of-practice (Wenger, 1998). These concepts are certainly extensible to the study of virtual teams and their inherent or innate processes.

We often simplify complexity in organizations to dichotomous constructs, e.g., physical place and virtual space. Technology is seen as the simple answer to a complex environment comprised of people, relationships, tools, and processes. However, simplification often leads to behavioral invisibility, as members of virtual teams are not seen as 'situated organizationally.' This invisibility creates problems of access to shared organizational knowledge or of being seen as a vital contributor to that knowledge.

Technology is not a panacea nor is it a monolithic construct. Different experiences with technology often focus on ramping up directly into projects. Organizations often use the technology at hand, rather than seeking the optimal task-technology fit. Teams often are not allowed the luxury of creating that tacit understanding of what they will be doing, why they are doing it, or how they will be doing it. The rules by which they work may be created on the spot, fall together serendipitously, or emerge expeditiously. Technology comprises such a variety of tools. Therefore, a new technology requires new understanding, new constructs, from a cognitive, a process, and a collaborative perspective. It is not just technol-ogy; it is also the people and the relationships they create to do work.

If we were to list some take-away lessons for practitioners, we would offer the following. First, an organization's clarity of vision is critical. Since it is subject to change based upon external forces, (mission, vision, and values), it is critical that institutional and team priorities are in congruence. Second, never underestimate the power of personal relationships in building and maintaining trust, in using power effectively, by establishing positive control, and reducing coercive and bullying behaviors. Teams need to trust one another—and their organization—to be honest, capable, and committed to joint goals. Third, innovation is not an ideology. Persons who see themselves or their team as *the* change agents may be unable to integrate effectively into other teams and projects or organizations. Fourth, the organization should not ignore the team or discount team members;' requests for assistance or interaction. As in Sheila's story, it was too easy to dismiss her as the only virtual worker in the group. Conversely, the team should not ignore the rest of the organization. Both situations lead to violation of territory and lack of awareness to environmental factors of change and process. Finally, communication is the cornerstone. Without clear communication to all members of a team or organization as to goals and outcomes, accountability devolves rapidly into power trips and destroys trust.

Unfortunately, the "build it and they will come" mantra and its brother "technology can replace face-to-face interaction" response are myths that have concrete and adverse effects on work processes and interactions (Dixon, 2000). Constraints surrounding knowledge sharing, such as trust, time, technology, power, and culture, also contribute to team failure (Rosen, Furst, & Blackburn, 2007). However, the key elements in knowledge sharing, from a communication perspective, are not hardware and software, but rather the people in the process co-constructing communities-of-practice.

REFERENCES

Abrams, (2003). Nurturing interpersonal trust in knowledge-sharing networks. *The Academy of Management Executive, 17*(4), 64–77.

Anand, V., Clark, M. A., & Zellmer-Bruhn, M. (2003). Team knowledge structures: Matching task to information environment. *Journal of Managerial Issues, 15*(1), 15–31.

Arrow, H., & Cook, J. (2007). Configuring and reconfiguring groups as complex learning systems . In Sessa, V. I., & London, M. (Eds.), *Work group learning: Understanding, improving and assessing how groups learn in organizations* (pp. 45–72). Boca Raton, FL: CRC Press/ Lawrence Erlbaum.

Axelrod, R. (1984). *The evolution of cooperation.* New York: Basic Books.

Ba, S. (2001). Establishing online trust through a community responsibility system. *Decision Support Systems, 31*(4), 323–336. doi:10.1016/S0167-9236(00)00144-5

Bachmann, R. (2001). Trust, power and control in trans-organizational relations. *Organization Studies, 22*(2), 337–365. doi:10.1177/0170840601222007

Baier, A. (1986). Trust and antitrust. *Ethics, 96,* 231–260. doi:10.1086/292745

Baker, C. (2004). Membership categorization and interview accounts . In Silverman, D. (Ed.), *Qualitative research: Theory, method, practice* (2nd ed., pp. 162–176). London: Sage.

Bandura, A. (1989). Social cognitive theory . In Vasta, R. (Ed.), *Annals of Child Development* (pp. 1–60). Greenwich, CT: Jai Press LTD.

Belanger, F., & Allport, C. D. (2008). Collaborative technologies in knowledge telework: An exploratory study. *Information Systems Journal, 18*(1), 101–121. doi:10.1111/j.1365-2575.2007.00252.x

Bogenrieder, I., & Nooteboom, B. (2004). Learning groups: What types are there? A theoretical analysis and an empirical study in a consultancy firm. *Organization Studies, 25*(2), 287–313. doi:10.1177/0170840604040045

Brown, J. S., & Duguid, P. (2002). Local knowledge: Innovation in the networked age. *Management Learning, 33*(4), 427–438. doi:10.1177/1350507602334002

Bruhn, J. (2001). *Trust and health of organizations.* New York: Kluwer.

Chiu, C.-M., Hsu, M.-H., & Wang, E. T. G. (2006). Understanding knowledge sharing in virtual communities: An integration of social capital and social cognitive theories. *Decision Support Systems, 42*(3), 1872–1888. doi:10.1016/j.dss.2006.04.001

Chowdhury, S. (2005). The role of affect- and cognition-based trust in complex knowledge sharing. *Journal of Managerial Issues, 17*(3), 310–326.

Clark, K. B., & Wheelwright, S. C. (1992). Organising and leading heavyweight development teams. *California Management Review,* (34): 9–28.

Cohen, S. G., & Bailey, D. E. (1997). What makes teams work: Group effectiveness research from the shop floor to the executive suite. *Journal of Management, 23*(3), 239–290. doi:10.1177/014920639702300303

Cramton, C. D. (2001). The mutual knowledge problem and its consequences for dispersed collaboration. *Organization Science, 12,* 346–371. doi:10.1287/orsc.12.3.346.10098

Cranford, M. (1996). The social trajectory of virtual reality: Substantive ethics in a world without constraints. *Technology & Society, 18*(1), 79–92. doi:10.1016/0160-791X(95)00023-K

Cross, R. '. L. (2002). The people who make organizations go – or stop. *Harvard Business Review, 80*(6), 104–112.

Culnan, M. J., & Markus, M. L. (1987). Information technologies. In F. M. Jablin, L.L. Putnam, L.L., K. H. Roberts, et al. (eds.), Handbook of organizational communication: An interdisciplinary perspective. Newbury Park, CA: Sage, pp. 420–443.

Cummings, L. L., & Bromiley, P. (1996). The Organizational Trust Inventory (OTI): Development and validation . In Kramer, R. M., & Tyler, T. R. (Eds.), *Trust in organizations: Frontiers of theory and research* (pp. 302–330). Thousand Oaks, CA: Sage Publications.

Cunningham, G. B., & Chelladurai, P. (2004). Affective reactions to cross-functional teams: The impact of size, relative performance, and common in-group identity. *Group Dynamics*, *8*(2), 83–97. doi:10.1037/1089-2699.8.2.83

Curseu, P. L., Schruijer, S., & Boros, S. (2007). The effects of groups' variety and disparity on groups' cognitive complexity. *Group Dynamics*, *11*(3), 187–206. doi:10.1037/1089-2699.11.3.187

Dasgupta, P. (1988). Trust as a commodity . In Gambetta, D. (Ed.), *Trust: Making and breaking cooperative relations* (pp. 47–72). New York: Basil Blackwell.

DePaulo, P. J., DePaulo, B. M., Tang, J., & Swaim, G. (1989). Lying and detecting lies in the organization . In Giacalone, R. A., & Rosenfeld, P. (Eds.), *Impression management in the organization* (pp. 377–396). Hillsdale, NJ: Erlbaum.

Dixon, N. M. (2000). *Common knowledge: How companies thrive by sharing what they know*. Boston, MA: Harvard Business School Press.

Driskell, J. E., Goodwin, G. F., Salas, E., & O'Shea, P. G. (2006). What makes a good team player? Personality and team effectiveness. *Group Dynamics*, *10*(4), 249–271. doi:10.1037/1089-2699.10.4.249

Durst, R., & Kabel, D. (2001). Cross-functional teams in a concurrent engineering environment: Principles, model, and methods . In Beyerlein, M. M., Johnson, D. A., & Beyerlein, S. T. (Eds.), *Advances in interdisciplinary studies of work teams: Virtual teams* (8th ed., pp. 167–214). Greenwich, CT: JAI.

Eisenberg, E. (2007). *Strategic ambiguities: Essays on communication, organization, and identity*. Thousand Oaks, CA: Sage.

Fuller, M. A., Hardin, A. M., & Davison, R. M. (2006). Efficacy in technology-mediated distributed teams. *Journal of Management Information Systems*, *23*(3), 209–235. doi:10.2753/MIS0742-1222230308

Gabriel, Y. (1999). Beyond happy families: A critical reevaluation of the control-resistance-identity triangle. *Human Relations*, *52*(2), 179–203. doi:10.1177/001872679905200201

Giacalone, R. A., & Knouse, S. B. (1990). Justifying wrongful employee behavior: The role of personality in organizational sabotage. *Journal of Business Ethics*, *9*, 55–61. doi:10.1007/BF00382564

Gibson, C. B., & Cohen, S. G. (2003). *Virtual teams that work: Creating conditions for virtual team effectiveness*. New York: Jossey-Bass.

Goffman, E. (1971). *The presentation of self in everyday life*. New York: Penguin.

Guo, Z. X., D'ambra, J., Turner, T., & Zhang, H. Y. (2009). Improving the effectiveness of virtual teams: A comparison of video-conferencing and face-to-face communication in China. *IEEE Transactions on Professional Communication*, *52*(1), 1–16. doi:10.1109/TPC.2008.2012284

Handy, C. (1995). Trust and the virtual organization. *Harvard Business Review*, *73*(3), 40–50.

Hanson, A., Levin, B. L. L., Heron, S., & Burker, M. (2003). Technology, organizational change, and virtual libraries . In Hanson, A., & Levin, B. L. (Eds.), *Building a virtual library* (pp. 1–18). Hershey, PA: Information Science Publishing.

Henderson, L. S. (2004). Encoding and decoding communication competencies in project management: An exploratory study. *International Journal of Project Management*, 22(6), 469–476. doi:10.1016/j.ijproman.2004.01.004

Hernes, T., & Bakken, T. (2003). Implications of self-reference: Niklas Luhmann's autopoiesis and organization theory. *Organization Studies*, 24(9), 1511–1535. doi:10.1177/0170840603249007

Hertel, G., Konradt, U., & Orlikowski, B. (2004). Managing distance by interdependence: Goal setting, task interdependence, and team-based rewards in virtual teams. *European Journal of Work and Organizational Psychology*, 13(1), 1–28. doi:10.1080/13594320344000228

Hill, N. S., Bartol, K. M., Tesluk, P. E., & Langa, G. A. (2009). Organizational context and face-to-face interaction: Influences on the development of trust and collaborative behaviors in computer-mediated groups. *Organizational Behavior and Human Decision Processes*, 108(2), 187–201. doi:10.1016/j.obhdp.2008.10.002

Hollenbeck, J. R., Ilgen, D. R., Sego, D., Heldund, J., Major, D., & Phillips, J. (1995). Multilevel theory of team decision making: decision performance in teams incorporating distributed expertise. *The Journal of Applied Psychology*, 80(2), 292–316. doi:10.1037/0021-9010.80.2.292

Homans, G. (1950). *The human group*. New York: Harcourt.

Hong, P., Vonderembse, M. A., Doll, W. J., & Nahm, A. Y. (2005). Role change of design engineers in product development. *Journal of Operations Management*, 24(1), 63–79. doi:10.1016/j.jom.2005.03.002

Hsu, M.-H., Ju, T. L., Yen, C.-H., & Chang, C.-M. (2007). Knowledge sharing behavior in virtual communities: The relationship between trust, self-efficacy, and outcome expectations. *International Journal of Human-Computer Studies*, 65(2), 153–169. doi:10.1016/j.ijhcs.2006.09.003

Ilgen, D. R. (1999). Teams embedded in organizations. *The American Psychologist*, 54, 129–139. doi:10.1037/0003-066X.54.2.129

Jackson, P. J. (2001). Organizational change and virtual teams: strategic and operational integration. *Information Systems Journal*, 9(4), 313–332. doi:10.1046/j.1365-2575.1999.00066.x

Jarvenpaa, S., & Leidner, D. (1999). Communication and trust in global virtual teams. *Organization Science*, 10(6), 791–815. doi:10.1287/orsc.10.6.791

Katzenbach, J. R., & Smith, D. K. (2001). The discipline of virtual teams. *Leader to Leader, Fall* (22). Retrieved March 1, 2009 from http://www.leadertoleader.org/knowledgecenter/journal.aspx?ArticleID=112.

Kirschner, P. A., Beers, P. J., Boshuizen, H. P. A., & Gijselaers, W. H. (2008). Coercing shared knowledge in collaborative learning environments: Part Special Issue: Cognition and Exploratory Learning in Digital Age. *Computers in Human Behavior*, 24(2), 403–420. doi:10.1016/j.chb.2007.01.028

Kliem, R. (2004). *Leading high-performance projects*. Boca Raton, FL: J. Ross Publishing Inc.

Kodama, M. (2005). Knowledge creation through networked strategic communities: Case studies on new product development in Japanese companies. *Long Range Planning*, 38(1), 27–49. doi:10.1016/j.lrp.2004.11.011

Kohlberg, L. (1969). Stage and sequence: The cognitive-developmental approach to socialization . In Goslin, D. A. (Ed.), *Handbook of socialization theory and research* (pp. 347–480). Chicago, IL: Rand McNally.

Kozlowski, S. W. J., Gully, S. M., McHugh, P. P., Salas, E., & Cannon-Bowers, J. A. (1996). A dynamic theory of leadership and team effectiveness: Developmental and task contingent leader roles. G. R. Ferris (Ed.), Research in personnel and human resources management (pp. 253-305). Greenwich, CT: JAI Press.

Kreiner, G. E., Hollensbe, E. C., & Sheep, M. L. (2006). On the edge of identity: Boundary dynamics at the interface of individual and organizational identities. *Human Relations*, *59*(10), 1315–1341. doi:10.1177/0018726706071525

Kuntze, M. F., Stoermer, R., Mueller-Spahn, F., & Bullinger, A. H. (2002). Ethical codes and values in a virtual world. *Cyberpsychology & Behavior*, *5*(3), 203–206. doi:10.1089/109493102760147187

Lam, L. W., Bischoff, S. J., Higgins, L. V. H., & Persing, D. L. (1999). Implementing effective cross-functional teams: A multilevel framework for analysis . In Woodman, R. W., & Pasmore, W. A. (Eds.), *Research in organizational change and development* (12th ed., pp. 171–203). Greenwich, CT: JAI.

Lander, M. C., Purvis, R. L., McCray, G. E., & Leigh, W. (2004). Trust building mechanisms utilized in outsourced IS development project: a case study. *Information & Management*, *41*(4), 509–558. doi:10.1016/j.im.2003.10.001

Lee, M. R. (2008). E-ethical leadership for virtual project teams. *International Journal of Project Management,* E-print.

Lefcourt, H. M. (1966). Internal versus external control of reinforcement: A review. *Psychological Bulletin*, *64*(4), 206–220. doi:10.1037/h0023116

Li, X., Hess, T. J., & Valacich, J. S. (2008). Why do we trust new technology? A study of initial trust formation with organizational information systems. *The Journal of Strategic Information Systems*, *17*(1), 39–71. doi:10.1016/j.jsis.2008.01.001

Lin, T.-C., & Huang, C.-C. (2008). Understanding knowledge management system usage antecedents: An integration of social cognitive theory and task technology fit. *Information & Management*, *45*(6), 410–417. doi:10.1016/j.im.2008.06.004

Lindskold, S., & Bennett, R. (1973). Attributing trust and conciliatory intent from coercive power capability. *Journal of Personality and Social Psychology*, *28*, 180–186. doi:10.1037/h0035734

Luhmann, N. (1979). *Trust and power*. Chichester, UK: Wiley.

Mayer, R. C., Davis, J. H., & Schoorman, F. D. (1995). An integrative model of organizational trust. *Academy of Management Review*, *20*(3), 709–734. doi:10.2307/258792

Mazor, K. M., Simon, S. R., Yood, R. A., Martinson, B. C., Gunter, M. J., & Reed, G. W. (2004). Health plan members' views about disclosure of medical errors. *Annals of Internal Medicine*, *140*(6), 409–418.

McAllister, D. (1995). Affect and cognition-based trust as foundations for interpersonal cooperation in organizations. *Academy of Management Journal*, *38*(1), 24–59. doi:10.2307/256727

McDonough, E. F. (2000). Investigation of factors contributing to the success of cross-functional teams. *Journal of Product Innovation Management*, *17*(3), 221–235. doi:10.1016/S0737-6782(00)00041-2

Moorman, C., Zaltman, G., & Deshpande, R. (1992). Relationships between providers and users of market research: The dynamics of trust within and between organizations. *JMR, Journal of Marketing Research, 29*, 314–328. doi:10.2307/3172742

Morrill, C. (2003). Covert political conflict in organizations: challenges from below. *Annual Review of Sociology, 29*(1), 391–415. doi:10.1146/annurev.soc.29.010202.095927

Nahapiet, J., & Ghoshal, S. (1998). Social capital, intellectual capital, and the organizational advantage. *Academy of Management Review, 23*(2), 242–266. doi:10.2307/259373

Nonaka, I., & Takeuchi, H. (1995). *The knowledge-creating company: How Japanese companies create the dynamics of innovation*. New York: Oxford University Press.

Norrgren, F., & Schaller, J. (1999). Leadership style: its impact on cross-functional product development. *Journal of Product Innovation Management, 16*(4), 377–384. doi:10.1016/S0737-6782(98)00065-4

Olk, P., & Elvira, M. (2001). Friends and strategic agents: The role of friendship and discretion in negotiating strategic alliances. *Group & Organization Management, 26*(2), 124–164. doi:10.1177/1059601101262002

Ouchi, W. G. (1981). *Theory Z: How American business can meet the Japanese challenge*. Reading, MA: Addison-Wesley.

Panteli, N., & Duncan, E. (2004). Trust and temporary virtual teams: alternative explanations and dramaturgical relationships. *Information Technology & People, 17*(4), 423–441. doi:10.1108/09593840410570276

Panteli, N., & Sockalingam, S. (2005). Trust and conflict within virtual inter-organizational alliances: A framework for facilitating knowledge sharing. *Decision Support Systems, 39*(4), 599–617. doi:10.1016/j.dss.2004.03.003

Patrashkova, R. R., & McComb, S. A. (2004). Exploring why more communication is not better: Insights from a computational model of cross-functional teams. [Special Issue: Research on the Human Connection in Technological Innovation]. *Journal of Engineering and Technology Management, 21*(1-2), 83–114. doi:10.1016/j.jengtecman.2003.12.005

Paul, D. L., & McDaniel, R. R., Jr. (2004). A field study of the effect of interpersonal trust on virtual collaborative relationship performance. *MIS Quarterly, 28*(2), [HTML]. Retrieved March 24, 2009 from http://www.misq.org/archivist/vol/no28/issue2/PaulMcDaniel.html.

Polyani, D. M. (1966). *The tacit dimension*. London, England: Routledge and Kegan Paul.

Powell, A., & Piccoli, G. I. B. (2004). Virtual teams: a review of current literature and directions for future research. *ACM SIGMIS Database, 35*(1), 6–36. doi:10.1145/968464.968467

Pratt, M. G. (2003). Disentangling collective identities . In Polzer, J. T. (Ed.), *Identity issues in groups: Research on managing groups and teams* (*Vol. 5*, pp. 161–188). Boston, MA: Elsevier Science. doi:10.1016/S1534-0856(02)05007-7

Rangarajan, D., Chonko, L. B., Jones, E., & Roberts, J. A. (2004). Organizational variables, sales force perceptions of readiness for change, learning, and performance among boundary-spanning teams: A conceptual framework and propositions for research. *Industrial Marketing Management, 33*(4), 289–305. doi:10.1016/S0019-8501(03)00072-5

Ratnasingam, P. (2005). Trust in inter-organizational exchanges: A case study in business to business electronic commerce. *Decision Support Systems*, *39*(3), 525–544. doi:10.1016/j.dss.2003.12.005

Ring, P. S., & van de Ven, A. H. (1992). Structuring cooperative relationships between organizations. *Strategic Management Journal*, *13*(7), 483–498. doi:10.1002/smj.4250130702

Riva, G. (2002). The sociocognitive psychology of computer-mediated communication: The present and future of technology-based interactions. *Cyberpsychology & Behavior*, *5*(6), 581–598. doi:10.1089/109493102321018222

Rockmann, K. W., & Northcraft, G. B. (2008). To be or not to be trusted: The influence of media richness on defection and deception. *Organizational Behavior and Human Decision Processes*, *107*(2), 106–122. doi:10.1016/j.obhdp.2008.02.002

Rosen, B., Furst, S., & Blackburn, R. (2007). Overcoming barriers to knowledge sharing in virtual teams. *Organizational Dynamics*, *36*(3), 259–273. doi:10.1016/j.orgdyn.2007.04.007

Rousseau, D. M., Sitkin, S. B., Burt, R. S., & Camerer, C. (1998). Not so different after all: A cross-discipline view of trust. *Academy of Management Review*, *23*(3), 393–404.

Schiller, S. Z., & Mandviwalla, M. (2007). Virtual team research - an analysis of theory use and a framework for theory appropriation. *Small Group Research*, *38*(1), 12–59. doi:10.1177/1046496406297035

Sheppard, B. H., & Sherman, D. M. (1998). The grammars of trust: A model and general implications. *Academy of Management Review*, *23*, 422–437. doi:10.2307/259287

Siau, K., & Shen, Z. (2003). Building customer trust in mobile commerce. *Communications of the ACM*, *46*(4), 91–94. doi:10.1145/641205.641211

Somers, M. R. (1994). The narrative constitution of identity: A relational and network approach. *Theory and Society*, *23*(5), 605–649. doi:10.1007/BF00992905

Steier, F. (1991). Research as self-reflexivity, self-reflexivity as social process . In Steier, F. (Ed.), *Research and reflexivity* (pp. 1–11). London: SAGE Publications.

Strub, P. J., & Priest, T. B. (1976). Two patterns of establishing trust: The marijuana user. *Sociological Focus*, *9*, 399–411.

Tanis, M., & Postmes, T. (2008). Cues to identity in online dyads: Effects of interpersonal versus intragroup perceptions on performance. *Group Dynamics*, *12*(2), 96–111. doi:10.1037/1089-2699.12.2.96

Trevino, L. K. (1986). Ethical decision making in organizations: A person–situation interactionist model. *Academy of Management Review*, *11*, 601–617. doi:10.2307/258313

Trevino, L. K., Hartman, L. P., & Brown, M. E. (2000). Moral person and moral manager: How executives develop a reputation for ethical leadership. *California Management Review*, *42*(4), 128–143.

Turner, J. R., & Müller, R. (2005). The project manager's leadership style as a success factor on projects: a literature review. *Project Management Journal*, *36*(2), 49–61.

Weick, K. E., & Sutcliffe, K. (2001). *Managing the unexpected: Assuring high performance in an age of complexity*. San Francisco, CA: Jossey-Bass.

Wenger, E. (1998). *Communities of practice: Learning, meaning and identity*. Cambridge, UK: Cambridge University Press.

Wheelwright, S. C., & Clark, K. B. (1992). *Revolutionizing product development: Quantum leaps in speed, efficiency, and quality*. New York: Free Press.

Winter, S. J., Stylianou, A. C., & Gialcone, R. A. (2004). Individual differences in the acceptability of unethical information technology practices: The case of Machiavellianism and ethical ideology. *Journal of Business Ethics*, *54*(3), 275–296. doi:10.1007/s10551-004-1772-6

Zaheer, A., McEvily, B., & Perrone, V. (1998). Does trust matter? Exploring the effects of interorganizational and interpersonal trust on performance. *Organization Science*, *9*(2), 141–159. doi:10.1287/orsc.9.2.141

Zolin, R., Hinds, P. J., Fruchter, R., & Levitt, R. E. (2004a). Interpersonal trust in cross-functional, geographically distributed work: A longitudinal study. *Information and Organization*, *14*(1), 1–26. doi:10.1016/j.infoandorg.2003.09.002

Chapter 15

Structuring a Local Virtual Work Ecology for a Collaborative, Multi-Institutional Higher Educational Project:
A Case Study

Shalin Hai-Jew
Kansas State University, USA

ABSTRACT

This chapter focuses on a multi-institutional shared curricular-build project (2009) out of Kansas State University, Johnson County Community College, Kansas City Kansas Community College, and Dodge City Community College. This project involved the building of a range of digital learning objects for modules for an online course that will be taught at the various institutions in both online and hybrid formats. This collaboration is unique in that it brought together experts from cross-functional domains (from both the empirical sciences and the humanities) for an interdisciplinary freshman level course. The team collaborated virtually through computer mediated communications and built e-learning based on instructional design precepts. The curriculum was built to the standards of the public health domain field, the Quality Matters™ rubric (for e-learning standards), federal accessibility guidelines, intellectual property laws, and technological interoperability standards (with the curriculum to be delivered through four disparate learning / course management systems). This chapter focuses on the socio-technical structuring of a local virtual work ecology to support this "Pathways to Public Health" project.

INTRODUCTION

In higher education, with the geographical dispersion of talents and skill sets, many more subject matter experts work on virtual teams. A more recent phenomena has been that of local (vs. global) virtual teams, with peers from institutions of higher education that are within reasonable commuting distances, similar time zones, and even some co-located members. Demanding schedules make it difficult to meet face-to-face, but collegial and interdisciplinary work requires collaboration and shared decision-making. The nature of the work

DOI: 10.4018/978-1-61520-979-8.ch015

and team will determine some of the strategies for structuring the local virtual work ecology, which includes both a shared electronic environment and structured interactions between the team members. This chapter will be based on the research literature and practitioner research based on one recent case.

REVIEW OF THE LITERATURE

With growing interorganizational alliances, virtual teams have become commonplace (Kahai, Carroll, & Jestice, 2007). Virtual teams are generally defined as those where team members are not co-located, but are distributed geographically and connected via computer-mediated technologies to collaborate on a shared work project.

Virtual teams are "groups of geographically, organizationally and/or temporally dispersed individuals brought together by information and telecommunications technologies to accomplish one or more organizational tasks" (Powell, Piccoli, & Ives, 2004). There may be differing levels of team virtualization. Zigurs proposes four dimensions of virtuality: "temporal dispersion," "geographic dispersion," "organizational dispersion," and "cultural dispersion" (Sarker, Sarker, & Schneider, 2009, p. 77). A local virtual work ecology refers to the interactions between virtual team members and their technological and physical environments.

VIRTUAL TEAM STRUCTURES

Differing levels of team virtualization may exist, with some virtual teams including sub-group co-location. Baskerville and Nandhakumar cite Mowshowitz's concept of a virtual workgroup as a basis for their thinking, which plays with the meaning of "virtual" as in virtual memory: "A team's virtuality regards the potential for an imagined team to become a real team, giving the

organization the ability to assemble teams on an as-needed basis for highly specific purposes" (Baskerville & Nandhakumar, 2007, p. 18). Virtual teams are new organizational forms enabled by more powerful computer technologies (Powell, Piccoli, & Ives, 2004, p. 6). Partially distributed teams (PDTs) involve sub-teams of co-located members working from different geographic locations (Peters, Ocker, & Rosson, 2008, p. 273). Dyadic teams are those that are formed by two people and have been found to result in higher team satisfaction, which is a predictor of virtual team effectiveness (Karayaz & Keating, 2007, p. 2593). The way work is designed may be one of the five critical factors that may support high creativity (Nemiro, 2004, p. xxvii).

THE CHALLENGES OF VIRTUAL TEAMING

The research on virtual teaming highlights a range of supervisory challenges that extend beyond typical management duties. These include:

- difficulty establishing trust (Coppola, Hiltz, & Rotter, 2004; Jarvenpaa & Leidner, 1999; Jarvenpaa et al., 2004);
- difficulty establishing a shared team identity (Armstrong & Cole, 2002; Cramton, 2001);
- managing conflict (Hinds & Bailey, 2003; Hinds & Mortensen, 2005; Montoya-Weiss, Massey & Song, 2001);
- maintaining awareness of members' activities (Hinds & Mortensen, 2005);
- coordinating team member efforts (Maznevski & Chudoba, 2001; Malhotra et al., 2001; Sarkey & Shay, 2002);
- effective leadership (Bell & Kozlowski, 2002; Kayworth & Leidner, 2001);
- knowledge sharing (Cramton, 2001, Griffith et al., 2003); and

- determining the appropriate task technology fit (Qureshi & Vogel, 2001, as cited in Ocker & Fjermestad, 2008, p. 52).

Virtual teams may experience the forming of fragmentation and in-groups (particularly among collocated members vs. the distributed or distant ones). This researcher switched some team members' locations halfway through the experiment to see what effect it would have on in-groups:

People who changed from being isolated 'telecommuters' to collocators very quickly formed new collaborative relationships. People who were moved out of a collocated room had more trouble adjusting, and tried unsuccessfully to maintain previous ties. Overall, collocation was a more powerful determiner of collaboration patterns than previous relationships (Bos, Olson, Cheshin, Kim, Nan, & Shami 2005, p. 1917).

The concept of resilience in virtual teaming is critical especially after intended or unintended disruptions, with some findings of high human adaptability and "bounce back" (Mark & Semann, 2008, p. 137). Virtual teaming requires on-going sense-making through technology mediation (Bansler & Havn, 2003, p. 135).

VIRTUAL LEADERSHIP

Virtual leadership requires an ability to create a virtual ecology. The supervisory work requires a mix of high engagement at times and hands-off interactivity at others. Leaders have to get a team established "on a good trajectory and then to make small adjustments along the way to help members succeed, not to try to continuously manage team behavior in real time." Applied to a virtual team context, the work ecology is this context for the team's work success. Hackman suggests that successful teams need "a compelling direction, an enabling team structure, a supportive organiza-

tional context, and expert team coaching" (*Leading Teams*, 2002, p. ix). Leadership on virtual teams may be explicit and implicit, with the conclusion that good coordination involves a "subtle mixture of both approaches" (Boulthier, Charoy, Perrin, Saliou, Bignon, Halin, & Malcurat, 2001, p. 135).

According to the literature, different types of leadership may be brought into play in virtual spaces.

- *Participative leadership* is defined as the equalization of power and sharing of problem solving with followers by consulting them before making a decision.
- *Directive leadership* is defined as providing and seeking compliance with directions for accomplishing a problem-solving task. Participative leadership and directive leadership are considered parallel to transformational leadership and transactional leadership respectively (Zhang, Fjermestad, & Tremaine, 2005, pp. 1 - 2).

Managers often find a greater need to troubleshoot virtual team challenges (Thomas, Bostom, & Gouge, 2007; Crowston, Howison, Masango, & Eseryel, 2007; Sarker, Sarker, & Schneider, 2009, p. 75). Team conflicts may arise from "differences, discrepancies, incompatible wishes or irreconcilable desires" (Paul, Seetharaman, Samarah, & Mykytyn, 2005, p. 1). They may mitigate conflicts through video-conferencing (Rutkowski, Vogel, van Genuchten, Bemelmans, & Favier, 2002, p. 227). For those in some industries, the amount of work done virtually affects their satisfaction with their work lives and their retention (Ferratt, Enns, & Prasad, 2001). There have been gender preferences found in the virtual team experience (Lind, 1999, p. 280).

Technologies may be brought into play to replace some on-site leadership. Kerr and Jermier (1978) offered a leader substitutes theory that suggests certain enhancements of leadership through "mechanisms and alternatives for the various functions of the formal leader." Enhancers augment the leader-outcome relationship; supplements contribute to the varied "effects on the subordinates' performance but do not cancel out or augment the leader's direct effects," and substitutes make "the leadership impossible or unnecessary" (Bass, 1990, pp. 682 – 683). Applied to virtual teaming, the leadership substitute theory shows that technologies may "stand in" for a present physical team leader.

However, there are built-in constraints to virtual teaming that may make "effective coordination, visibility, communication and cooperation" more challenging (Casey & Richardson, 2006, p. 66). The more interdependency and the more complex the work flows, the more reciprocal coordination and collaboration are needed (Corbitt, Gardiner, & Wright, 2004). Virtual teaming may be used in both low-risk and high-risk situations. The research literature includes descriptions of tense interchanges and misunderstandings in time- and safety-critical situations that were mediated virtually (Bayerl & Lauche, 2008, p. 424).

Virtual leadership in the Internet Age "*is* communication" (Skovolt, 2009, p. 1). Individuals' communications styles, which stem from personality factors (Balthazard, Potter, & Warren, 2002), may be categorized as constructive, passive, and aggressive styles.

The constructive style is characterized by a balanced concern for personal and group outcomes, cooperation, creativity, free exchange of information, and respect for others' perspectives. The constructive style enables group members to fulfill both needs for personal achievement as well as needs for affiliation. The passive style places greater emphasis on fulfillment of affiliation goals only, maintaining harmony in the group, and limiting information sharing, questioning and impartiality. The aggressive style places greater emphasis on personal achievement needs, with personal ambitions placed above concern for group outcome. Aggressive groups are charac-

terized by competition, criticism, interruptions, and overt impatience" (Balthazard, Potter, & Warren, 2002).

Tensions stemming from outsourcing may also cause stresses on virtual teams. Challenges communicating the requirements for a project may be compounded "by cultural and language differences, lack of communication, distance from the customer, different process maturity levels, testing tools, standards, technical ability and experience" (Casey & Richardson, 2006, p. 66).

THE SELECTION OF COMPUTER MEDIATED COMMUNICATIONS (CMC) TECHNOLOGIES

Information Technology (IT) must help a virtual team maintain a sense of continuous communications discourse (Albin-Clark, 2008). There must be connective richness without overwhelming complexity. People may generally be assumed to function on the so-called Principle of Least Effort when it comes to computer mediated communications (Bos, Shami, Olson, Cheshin, & Nan, 2004, p. 430). Technologies have to fit in with the leaders' choices (Samarah, Paul, & Tadisina, 2007) in the virtual team and must also be accessible (Sivunen & Valo, 2006, p. 57).

Successful virtual teams tend to have high message frequency characterized by positive messages and "appropriate feedback." Such teams prefer a variety of communication media (Dekker & Rutte, 2007, p. 3). High performing virtual teams "out-communicate" low performing ones (Ocker & Fjermestad, 2000, p. 1). Rich dialogue techniques help teams make up for the loss of "proxemic, haptic, and environmental cues" (Guo, D'Ambra, Turner, & Zhang, 2009, p. 3) and may promote team cohesion (Guo, D'Ambra, Turner, & Zhang, 2009, p. 5) and a sense of "mutuality and shared frame" (Sarker, Sarker, Nicholson, & Joshi, 2005, p. 201). Teams that are homogeneous in terms of "shared backgrounds, interests, attitudes, and values" may find it easier to be cohesive (Panteli & Davison, 2005, p. 192) but may have greater challenges with innovations.

TECHNOLOGIES FOR INTERCOMMUNICATIONS

Social presence theory suggests that the perceivable physical presence of partners in a communication would have better interpersonal relationships via greater apparent presence (Short, et al., 1976, as cited in Ehsan, Mirza, & Ahmad, 2008, n.p.). Social exchange theory suggests that individuals engage in social interactions for financial and social rewards, which might suggest reciprocity behaviors on virtual teams such as knowledge sharing (Chen, Zhang, Vogel, & Zhao, 2009, p. 2).

Media Richness Theory suggests that the greater the range of communications cues, the more an individual may personalize a message and control the interactions. Media richness is defined as the ability of information to change understanding within time interval (Dekker & Rutte, 2007, pp. 1 - 2). The richness of a medium is focused around five functions: the immediacy of feedback, symbol variety, parallelism, rehearsability, and reprocessability:

Immediacy of feedback is the extent to which the medium enables users to give rapid feedback on the communication they receive. Symbol variety is very similar to multiplicity of cues from Media Richness Theory. Parallelism is the number of communications that can exist simultaneously. Rehearsability is the ability to go over the message before communicating it to the sender. Finally, Reprocessability is the ability to reexamine the message within the communication event (Dekker & Rutte, 2007, p. 2).

Medium-richness theory (Daft & Langel, 1986) suggests that two factors are critical for rich communications: "(1) The ability of communication medium to transmit personality cues of interaction partners. (2) The extent of the immediate feedback" (Ehsan, Mirza, & Ahmad, 2008, n.p.).

Without media richness or nonverbal cues, some researcher suggest a possible "downward spiral of decreased trust and commitment in a group," less information-sharing, misinterpreted messages, and eventually "conflict, damage group cohesion, and lower trust" (dePillis & Furumo, 2007, p. 93). These then would result in higher transaction costs, with team members double-checking each other and taking fewer creative risks. Fear and social inequities also have negative effects on a virtual team's innovativeness and team cohesion (Casey & Richardson, 2008, p. 170). Social dominance by group members may result in low levels of team creativity (Ocker, 2007, p. 204).

Mutual trust is built on the exchange of information (Alexander, 2002, p. 68). Recursiveness in interactions and interchanges may lead to the building up and maintenance of trust (Baskerville & Nandhakumar, 2007). Shared expressed and ethically-justifiable values may enhance trust and also bring a group closer (Xiao & Wei, 2008). High levels of trust can exist on virtual teams particularly in initial relationships among members but will need to be maintained through confidence-building measures and non-exploitation of members (Hung, Dennis, & Robert, 2004).

Face-to-face (F2F) is the richest communication medium, and is followed "by Telephone, Email, Letter, Note, Memo, Bulletin etc. in the medium richness hierarchy" (Ehsan, Mirza, & Ahmad, 2008, n.p.). Different types of messages require different mediums. Technologies may de-individuate individuals by restricting the amount of identifying information about each other: "Lack of information regarding interpersonal differences among group members causes them to be more sensitive to available information about their personal or social identity" (Kahai, Carroll, & Jestice, 2007, p. 64). Group cohesion has been found to support group performance (Salisbury, Carte, & Chidambaram, 2006, p. 147), so a lack of human connectedness via the formal and informal communications may be inhibiting of virtual team work (p. 148).

Synchronicity may play a role in presence (Dennis & Valacich, 1999, as cited in Ehsan, Mirza, & Ahmad, 2008) and immediacy. Synchronous interactions on a team may often be done for collaborating on a common task; promoting group well-being, and supporting members in difficult situations, according to the Time, Interaction, and Performance theory (McGrath, 1991, as cited in Mirza & Ahmad, 2008, n.p.).

Research later found that the technologies used for computer-mediated groups could be more social than F2F interaction, via the Social Identity model of De-Individuation Effects (Postmes, Spears, & Lea, 1999; Reicher, Separs, & Postmes, 1995; Spears & Lea, 1994, as cited in Ehsan, Mirza, & Ahmad, 2008). Others argued that the human interactions and organizational contexts affect the richness of media (Dekker & Rutte, 2007, p. 2). Virtual teams' preferences for particular media often resulted in a particular rhythm in media selected and used.

Immersive 3D spaces may also provide a venue for human-embodied avatar-based intercommunications. Here, the human imagination makes virtual worlds more potent and social, with engaging sense of telepresence and social presence. "The objective of virtual worlds was to achieve a feeling of telepresence, immersion and participation from a distance" (Jäkälä & Pekkola, 2007, p. 12). Cooperative online game experiences "even without any direct communication interactions" can impact people's liking for others (Dabbish, 2008, p. 353), and immersive virtual games have been employed as team ice breakers (Ellis, Luther, Bessiere, & Kellogg, 2008).

The research unequivocally suggests the importance of intercommunications, with a continual flow of creating, assessing and exchanging information around both task-driven and social-driven needs (Wang, Huang, & Wang, 2006, n.p.). Virtual team members co-build shared cultures (Andrews & Starke-Meyerring, 2005, p. 26). The social aspects of virtual collaboration are so critical that researchers conduct social network analyses to understand virtual teams (Lin & Chen, 2004, p. 1). Some collaborative technologies "facilitate ad hoc contact with remote professional expertise within the organization…as well as beyond the organization at reduced costs" (Sole & Applegate, 2000, p. 581).

UNDERSTANDING / NOT MISUNDERSTANDING … SILENCE

How team members understand others' silence depends in part on the understanding of what else is taking the time of team members or "distractions". The accuracy of the attribution of silence depends on information sharing and access (TerBush, 2006). While such cues may be instituted into socio-technical collaboration systems, the author notes: "Participants themselves can improve their virtual team experience by learning to build and maintain mental maps about the environments of their remote partners and recognizing that environmental factors may be responsible for their partner's periods of silence. By starting with situational attributions, group efficacy may be improved" (TerBush, 2006, p. 8). For others, silence comes from social politeness and cultural expectations but may be misread as agreement (Anawati & Craig, 2006, pp. 50 - 51).

Computer mediated communications involve both synchronous and asynchronous interactions, and light and media-rich interactivity. Optimally, socio-technical systems need to offer the greatest ranges of freedom of expression (Nunamaker, 1999) for greatest utility.

SHARED MENTAL MODELS, COORDINATION, VISUALIZATION AND MODELING, AND KNOWLEDGE-SHARING AND LEARNING

The technologies employed not only promote communications but the building of shared mental models of the work. Per Dourish & Bellotti's work, group awareness refers to "an understanding of the activities of others which provides a context for your own activity"; technologically, this awareness is achieved synchronously with presence indicator widgets (such as on instance messaging systems), user lists, and remote viewports (Schümmer & Lukosch, 2006). Virtual team members have a need for on-going sense-making (Bansler & Havn, 2003).

Technologies may help team members coordinate their schedules and collaborative strategies. They may help individuals be aware of the work processes (Dustdar & Gall, 2002). They may indicate the different phases of teamwork. They may help with the structuring of tasks and work flows. Project management methods and tools need to be built into systems to benefit virtual teams and to accommodate for various types of diversity in the team members (Beise, 2004). In systems where these are not yet coded in to the software, human coordination has to be stand in the gap.

They may promote the exploration of creative and "outlandish" ideas (Ocker & Fjermestad, 2008, p. 53), their multi-dimensional visualization, and digital modeling. There needs to be a virtual team climate to support innovation, with a tolerance of diverse opinions and constructive conflict. Research into computer-supported collaborative work (CSCW) offers some insights on virtual spaces that support co-design, for example. Technologies extend the affordances of human endeavors.

Technological systems may raise team members' awareness of knowledge possessed by their co-workers, which may be valuable for "team effectiveness in learning, viability, and overall performance" (Shen, 2007, p. 228). Information sharing has a positive effect on virtual team performance and satisfaction (Dekker & Rutte, 2007, p. 3). The designs of socio-technical systems may foster knowledge sharing (Powell, Piccoli, & Ives, 2004). Information exchanges need to be technologically secure (Pripužić, Gjenero, & Belani, 2006, p. 266) to maintain virtual team trust.

Trust or the extent to which a person is confident in another—has been linked to "virtual team efficiency, collaboration and performance" and the sharing of various information types (Mogan & Wang, 2007, p. 43). The ability to create trust may be seen as a virtual skill: "The work by Jarvenpaa & Leidner (1998) suggests that factors associated with online competence, responsiveness, leadership and performance, as well as communication aimed at socialisation become inextricably involved in the process of creating trust in GVTs" (global virtual teams). (Clear & Kassabova, 2005, p. 55).

Discovered knowledge has to flow back into the virtual environment (Biuk-Aghai & Simoff, 2001, p. 61). Virtual work needs to be structured in a space and environment to create a "landscape of work artifacts" (Churchill & Bly, 1999, p. 40). The credibility of the knowledge transfer information is based on trust and reputation (Sarker, Sarker, Nicholson, & Joshi, 2005, p. 204).

Virtual teams also need to capture events and decisions taken by one subgroup or the main group, with sufficient details for later review (Bayerl & Lauche, 2008, p. 425). Such collaboration systems may help in the archival and delivery of digital resources and artifacts. Researchers point to the importance of learning collaboration and also learning while collaborating (Kildare, Williams, & Hartnett, 2006).

SOME CRITIQUES OF VIRTUAL COLLABORATION SYSTEMS

There have been various criticisms of the technologies supporting virtual team ecologies. The design of collaborative virtual spaces may involve insufficient consideration for the "exigencies of living with the system" (Tan & Kondoz, 2008, p. 2046), which may force a virtual team to be more adaptable. Others suggest that collaborative technologies need to create symbioses between "project management tools and collaborative ones" for effective virtual project management (Donker & Blumberg, 2008, p. 41). Others suggest that bridging the socio-technical gap will require new computing paradigms, potentially without "rules, hierarchies and control" (daSilva, de Souza, Prates, & Nicolaci-da-Costa, 2003, p. 145).

THE IMPORTANCE OF TEAM CONTINUITY

Continuity is seen in the research as something positive in terms of team trust and mutual understandings (Panteli & Davison, 2005, pp. 192-193). Researchers have found risks to short-duration virtual projects: "Our results indicate that at least for projects of short duration, virtual teams yield significantly lower performance, lower satisfaction, and a lower results-to-effort ratio. Virtual teams appear to excel only at lowering commitment, morale, and performance..." (dePillis & Furumo, 2007, p. 95).

Teams that have a sense of continuity outperform new teams. "Members develop familiarity with one another, their collective work, and the work setting, so they are able to settle in and focus on working together rather than waste time and energy getting oriented to new coworkers or circumstances. They develop a shared mental model of the performance situation, one that, with time and experience, is more integrative than the individual models with which they began. They

develop a shared pool of knowledge, accessible to all, and build what social psychologist Dan Wegner calls 'transactive memory' (that is, members themselves serve as memory aids to one another, providing the possibility of collective recollection that exceeds the capacity of any single individual)" (Hackman, *Leading Teams,* 2002, pp. 55 - 56).

Teams also seem to have a mid-point inflection in terms of performance. This is a time of a major transition.

In a concentrated burst of changes, they dropped old patterns of behavior, reengaged with outside supervisors, and adopted new perspectives on their work. Following the midpoint transition, groups entered a period of focused task execution, which persisted until very near the project deadline, at which time a new set of issues having to do with termination processes arose and captured members' attention" (Gersick, as cited in Hackman, Leading Teams, 2002, pp. 177 – 178).

Time seems to be a critical factor in bringing virtual team members together: "In the case of computer-supported groups it has been shown that given adequate time teams will exchange enough social information to develop strong relational links" (Beranek, "A comparison of...," 2005, p. 1; Casey & Richardson, Project management with..., 2006). Relationship history has also been found "to positively impact openness, trust, and information sharing in computer-mediated teams" (Lojeski, Reilly, & Dominick, 2007, p. 3); this shared past affects current work (Hung, Dennis, & Robert, 2004, p. 1).

Researchers have found more "deadbeats" with non-contributing behavior and "deserters" on virtual teams (dePillis & Furumo, 2006, p. 318). Others note the loss of "organizational memory, corporate history and process knowledge" with ad hoc virtual teams (Sengupta & Zhao, 1998). Bringing on the team members with the right skill sets, virtual teaming skills and level of commitment is critical (Cordes & Spine, 2007). Virtual team members need to have an ability to work independently and to execute on the promised work by deadline. There are also motivational patterns in virtual team collaboration (Clear & Kassabova, 2005).

Managers should consider the full lifecycle of social ties in terms of virtual teaming between local and remote sites. This is especially true for projects which unify professionals in a state with staff members who represent elite and mission-critical skill sets, as was this case with the Pathways to Public Health endeavor. Oshri, Kotlarsky, and Willcocks suggest that development of social ties move from Introduction to Build-up to Renewal. They also suggest that F2F meetings are not a panacea for distributed teams (2008, p. 78). Mixed factors may contribute to virtual team success (Paré & Dubé, 1999, p. 480)—technologies, project context, team dynamics and processes, leadership and project management, and even wildcard factors.

PATHWAYS TO PUBLIC HEALTH: THE PROJECT'S BACKGROUND

The project involved the collaboration between Kansas State University and three colleges (Johnson County Community College, Kansas City Kansas Community College, and Dodge City Community College) to build a freshman-level public health course. This would be an entry-level semester-long course to draw learners into this field to fill a deep personnel gap in Kansas; this would optimally bring in those who are working in the field with plenty of experience but potentially little formal training. This would be an online prototype, the first course of an undergraduate program and then a graduate program, all in development, as part of a state-wide endeavor. This would also serve as an anchor in the statewide endeavor to professionalize and establish credentials for public health. The processes, the forms, and the relationships formed during this project would have large potential impacts into the future.

One way to understand a project is to understand its progress "trajectory" and shared local virtual team experiences. Important project milestones may be analyzed. Nemiro (2004) highlights three work design approaches used in the creative process. The Wheel Approach focuses on the use of one individual to be the hub for communications, and that individual is usually a high-powered one. The Modular Approach begins with a brainstorming approach by the group and then individual teams breaking up to address different parts of the build. The Iterative Approach involves back-and-forth development cycles where work is presented to the team, critiqued, and returned to the individual developers to revise (pp. 15 – 16). All three methods were used, except The Wheel Approach did not use a high-status team member but rather an outside support staff member. This was by necessity given the busy schedules of the principal investigators. Figure 1: A Composite of Images from the Virtual Work Ecology represents the complexity of the curricular elements at play. The logo represents the branding endeavor. A screenshot of Axio™ L/CMS evokes some of the work spaces. Some stills from video presentations and interviews highlight the expert contributions from across campus. The slide captures show the global nature of public health with open copyright releases from world health organizations. Another screenshot shows the deep structure of the various modules and the rich mix of HTML-delivered directions, audio-narrated slideshows, transcripts, videos, and learning activities.

IMPORTANT "PATHWAYS" PROJECT MILESTONES

The Creation of the Team

An interesting challenge with dispersed virtual teams is that the members hail from different institutions with different organizational mandates, stakeholders, and authorizing environments. Orga-

Figure 1. A composite of images from the virtual work ecology

nizational culture plays a role in the "acceleration of virtual world technology adoption" (Fuller, Hardin, & Scott, 2007, p. 43) and the adaptivity to virtual spaces. Some members are full-time faculty at their universities or colleges, and others are full-time staff who are sub-contracting on the project. In a sense, this organizational structure fits with Weick's definition of a loosely coupled system, with relatively autonomous and independent units that influence each other and little need for coordination. A loosely coupled system may allow for a greater "number of mutations and novel solutions" to problems given that "the identity, uniqueness, and separateness of elements is preserved" (Weick, 1976, p. 7). Orton and Weick note that a loose coupling is not a decoupling with less "connectedness, responsiveness, and interdependence" (1990, p. 207); rather, these connections are a critical part of the virtual structure promoting both the strategic cohesions and sparks of innovation. Such social modularity reduces "the number of necessary relationships" (Page-Jones, as cited in Orton & Weick, 1990, p. 210), which implies streamlined efficiencies.

A Centralized Digital Ecology

The virtual work ecology for this half-year multi-institutional curricular build focused on the Axio™ Learning / Course Management System (L/CMS). The technological setup allowed collaborators from off-campus to create accounts and to have full access to the socio-technical system. Using a democratic participative leadership model, all the principal investigators on the four campuses would need full ability to act as primary instructors (in terms of role-based access)—to build contents to the shared course. This access level would mean each member could ostensibly edit anyone else's contents, and each could actually delete the entire work site. (The Axio™ system's "indestructible" back-up would actually protect all contents though in case of a total work site deletion.) This team used a loosely coupled and flat structure. If the control of communications and information is a form of virtual leadership (Skovolt, 2009), then it's critical that all members of the distributed participative team have equal access and equal voice—even at risk to the larger project. After all, each of the campuses would be taking ownership of the shared course, once completed.

Technologically, this site would provide plenty of collaboration tools: a third-party Wimba Classroom™ web conferencing tool, an asynchronous text message board, built-in audio capture and distribution capabilities, a shared calendar, and grouping tools. It also offered a space for the archival of digital learning objects, their annotation, and their organization into modules. There was a shared announcement board. There was a built-in survey system to allow for the surveying of live learners. A broadcast email system is also built into Axio™. The extensive context-sensitive help system made the acclimating easier for those new to the system.

Getting the team onto the work site early on was important, particularly with the need for early successes (Weick's concept of "small wins") to raise user confidence and self-efficacy. This involved posting necessary contents online but also making it available through email and other means.

Lean Communications Channels

Lean-channel communications technologies—telephones, emails, electronic mailing lists—were also tapped to enhance the connectivity of the development team. The different institutions had their own ways of maximizing the co-location of their team members, through electronic mailing lists, face-to-face meetings, and others. The idea was to have both formal and informal channels for information sharing, to promote both.

Researchers point to the importance of structure in virtual teaming (Rutkowski, Vogel, Ven Genuchten, Bemelmans, & Favier, 2002). That need for structure applies to role definitions; work definition; socio-technological structures, and policies.

Shared Curricular Design

Team members had met face-to-face to determine the contents of the co-created curriculum. Once this was designed, the various faculty and their campus teams worked with their respective curricular committees to get the courses approved. This was a critical part of the project in terms of shaping shared academic aims. This also gave all members a voice at the table, so their expertise would be represented in the curriculum. The curriculum was designed as follows:

- Module 1: Overview and Basic Principles
- Module 2: Epidemiological Principles
- Module 3: Population Health Tools
- Module 4: Disease and Disability: Determinants, Burdens, and Interventions
- Module 5: Healthcare and Public Health Systems (Public Health Administration)
- Module 6: Special Topic Areas (These areas included ones focused on One Health; Infectious Disease and Zoonosis; Food Safety, Security, and Defense—Food Chain Security, Public Health Nutrition and Physical Activity, and Public Health Future Direction and Challenges.)

A Pre-module was proposed but was eventually folded into some other modules. The concept of the Pre-module was to offer "scaffolding" for learners totally new to the field with a particular focus on the biological sciences, biostatistics, and e-learning.

Stylebook Design

A critical step in the curriculum design was meeting face-to-face to co-create a stylebook, which would set the standards and expectations for the work; define accessibility and intellectual property guidelines; set technological expectations, and start the clock on the distributed development. The Quality Matters rubric standards would also be integrated, with the needs for curricular coherence and segues. This stylebook also recorded the importance of building and infusion of diversity and learning scaffolding for both novices (freshman students) and "experts" (those who may have worked in public health for years but not studied formally in the academic field or a related field) in the curriculum.

The stylebook was created also to have a "common language to facilitate the work" (Suchan & Hayzak, 2001, p. 174). Virtual teams need a clear sense of mutual purpose (Keyzerman, 2003) and role coordination (Sutanto, Phang, Kuan, Kankanhalli, & Tan, 2005, p. 1), which the stylebook recorded. Determining understandings early was done to head off wasted effort. For example, the team members were trained on intellectual property, to head off possible illegalities in the use of information, imagery, audio, or video. The team also reviewed the importance of maintaining raw footage and imagery for possible non-lossy uses.

A stylebook works as an evolving document. It supports the planning stages, the curricular build, and the standards design for future changes to a curriculum. For example, this particular stylebook has projections into possibly building tangibles (such as CDs or DVDs), related e-books, and an instructional handbook. Considering options—depending on the time, energy, and resources available once the core curricular build was done—was motivating to the group.

Distributed Digital Learning Object (DLO) Development

The various distributed teams then met on their own to develop their portions of the curriculum, usually either whole modules or whole modules with additional segments. People concurrently worked in small-teams on their campuses and through computer mediated communications with a centralized instructional designer.

Virtual and F2F Meetings

The team met virtually to discuss progress and concerns once the first deadline for initial digital learning objects had been met. This meeting set future "soft" deadlines for intermediate work against the backdrop of hard grant-driven deadlines. Team decision-making was created using virtual voting procedures, an approach that suggests a more democratic approach (Ferscha & Scheiner, 1999). A "checklist" of quality factors were captured at this meeting and distributed to the team.

Another critical point came with the structured critique of the different modules. Here, the team used their self-created "checklist" that had been co-created in a collaborative virtual meeting in order to create feedback for their colleagues.

This team found it helpful to have several core "go-to" people for various basic functionalities: project oversight and logistics, technology troubleshooting, funding, and subject matter expertise.

Curricular Revisions

The critiques resulted in a flurry of discussions among the team members. Based on the specific feedback, the team members revised their curriculum. They added audio files as over-lays to existing slideshows. They filled in the missing contents.

As the main modules were getting near finalizing, the project leaders came up with new ideas for more value-added learning. One endeavor involved the use of video captures of leading experts in related fields. The other involved the creation of Web-based automated mysteries highlighting aspects of the content domain. The group had created a culture of flexibility, innovation and efficiency that allowed these add-ons to be included into the final curricular build. Near the end of the build, the team decided to add student guides to help learners navigate the curriculum through the selection of important learning points.

The finalized curriculum was aligned with the Quality Matters™ standards, with a special focus on the annotation and flow of contents and on accessibility standards. Extra contents would be used for other electronic trainings in public health.

Alpha and Beta Testing

Alpha testing involved in-house testing of the technologies and curriculum among the team members. Beta testing involved taking the e-learning out to a larger public, with live-testing of learners in a blended course in the summer of 2009. Continuing information collection and formal testing would involve datamining (of the L/CMS) and continuing learner surveys. (These were not formally addressed before the submittal of this chapter.)

ELEMENTS OF A LOCAL VIRTUAL TEAM ECOLOGY

The factors that created the virtual work ecology for this local virtual team involved four main elements:

1. social elements (both formal role structures and social relationships),
2. time elements (shared mutual time, asynchronous time, and deadlines),
3. informational elements (domain knowledge structures and quality standards), and

4. socio-technical elements (virtual spatial structures and communications channels).

A structured ecology enables a group to collaborate by setting shared expectations, upholding group standards, promoting professional rapport and camaraderie, and guiding and enabling the shared work. A local virtual team ecology supports individual and shared work across time and through digital environments. These four factors are represented in Figure 2: Elements of a Local Virtual Team Ecology.

LEARNING ABOUT LOCAL VIRTUAL TEAMING

While the members of the team were all professionals in their respective fields, there was a range of attitudes towards e-learning and collaborative technologies. The research suggests that technology acceptance depends on computer self-efficacy and perceived usefulness of IT support mechanisms for group work (Yager, 1999, p. 73). One rural-based campus had continual issues with low Internet connectivity, and another was getting rewired with a new security system which caused connectivity challenges. A web conferencing meeting was missed by one local team because of scheduling challenges, and others who did participate had latency challenges.

Outsider Leverage and Distributed Hubs of Expertise

The concept of social capital appeared in this virtual team experience, with an "outsider" brought in to support the e-learning curriculum design, in part to preserve the social relationships of the subject matters experts who will be collaborating well into the future.

Figure 2. Elements of a local virtual team ecology

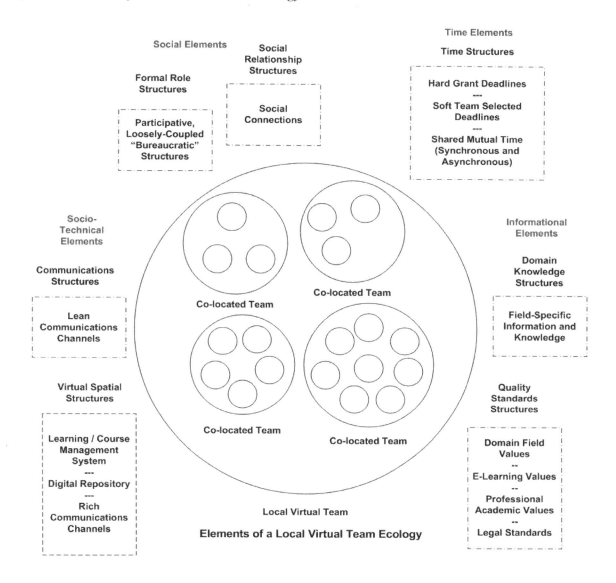

Elements of a Local Virtual Team Ecology

Changes to the Virtual Work Ecology

The virtual work site (on the Axio™ L/CMS) evolved over time, with much activity just prior to, during and after shared deadlines. The work site was the center for all the shared work. In the building and co-design phases, the work folders got congested and a little disorderly. However, when it came time to formally present curriculum to colleagues, the work areas were tidied, with raw

files and research moved so as not to confuse those critiquing the work. The work site also changed before the various co-located teams were about to download the curricular contents to their various L/CMSes. A work site's purposes are very different than a cleaned-up ready-to-go-live site, so much of the development materials and raw files were archived and hidden away for the master course (the pristine version that would be maintained by one of the partners and which would be revised over time based on the best practices by each of the teams). While team members' names played a major role in the development of the contents early on (for clear work assignments), the team decided to remove their names from each of the respective slideshows (but not the videos) and instead have an "Introduction to the Pathways Development Team" form developed, which included brief biographies, headshots, contact information, and data about what each member contributed to the course.

Uploading onto L/CMSes

Once the curriculum was finalized, the curriculum was uploaded on the four learning / course management systems (L/CMSes). The lack of interoperability between these systems meant tedious manual uploading and deployment of contents using zipped files. Each of the "playable" elements had to be re-tested in each system. The e-learning trajectory and branding also had to be rebuilt in each course, along with the assessments, message boards, and grade books. In another endeavor, the master course had to be moved onto a different server, so one of the teams from a college could use teach using this more flexible platform. While the move went smoothly, the master worksite was essentially erased off the server, and all the team members had to be re-enrolled in a back-up master of the finalized course. Some interchanges and messages, though, would be unrecoverable from the Message Board.

The Human Touch

Interestingly, the various team members seemed to prefer communicating in-person or by telephone and email. They used the online site to share and archive their digital learning artifacts but not so much for direct collaboration or communications (synchronous or asynchronous). The direct human touch played an important role in team bonding and collaborating. The collaborators chose to meet face-to-face to wrangle through some difficult curricular decisions, such as what parts of the draft course to keep in the final version and what revisions had to be made to each other's work. This reluctance to use the L/CMS mediated resources for direct communications may have been a factor of the poor connectivity of some of the colleges to the Internet. Some of the collaborators had never taught online before and were familiarizing themselves with the L/CMS technologies as the collaboration proceeded.

Open Source Contents

The team had challenges pursuing "public domain" contents made available through federal agencies and some non-governmental health organizations, both in getting documentation of release and in getting the actual digital contents. These involved alt-texted imagery, videos, audio podcasts, and transcripts of these multimedia contents.

Consistency and Expectations Management

Templates of slideshows were used to offer some consistency and quality standards. While guidelines were created for the building of various contents, most development teams needed actual live samples and critiques of those samples to understand what was desirable (based on their peers' insights). Templates were also used to maintain a design look-and-feel consistency for each module, as multiple members of distributed teams would contribute to each of the modules.

Building for the Hand-off

One central practice of the project was to archive and protect all the work created by each team member for the eventuality of a hand-off. During the 6-month curricular build, there were occasions for the sharing of work, but no major team member dislocations occurred.

IT'S A WRAP: INTRODUCTION TO PUBLIC HEALTH

The course was finalized in the summer, and two sections of it were offered at two of the colleges for Fall Semester 2009. An external office has been enlisted to formally evaluate this course to identify ways to strengthen the curriculum and learner experience—based on learner feedback at the end of this first semester. The launch of a One Health Kansas site later that summer hailed the beginning of a long-term publicity plan. A playlist off of the K-State portal on YouTube™ was under consideration at press time, to showcase some of the expert videos captured for this course.

A multi-year schedule has been tentatively planned for this course, and other endeavors to build up a public health track are in the works. This course will be a central introductory and feeder course for this undergraduate and graduate public health series. In-house at Kansas State University, this course is also used as a model for developing other courses in epidemiology and public health. The standards of e-learning quality, accessibility, intellectual property, documentation, and faculty comfort will be carried over to other online courses.

CONCLUSION

Local virtual teaming offers a hybridized way of collaborating with colleagues who are within a reasonable interactional distance from each other. This combination of realities offers opportunities to maximize the co-location (Saxenian's concept of "regional advantage") of team members as well as the distance of distributed colleagues. Examining local virtual teaming also shows the collaborative need in the selection of technologies. This chapter highlights the importance of setting up team member expectations and structures based around social, time, socio-technical and informational elements to support the work and frame the virtual ecology. This also shows the benefits of the loose coupling of a team at a higher abstract level but with tighter coupling up close on particular campuses to actualize the work.

ACKNOWLEDGMENT

This project was supported by the United States Department of Agriculture Cooperative State Research, Education, and Extension Service under Higher Education Challenge Grant number 2008-38411-19052.

I am deeply appreciative of the project principal investigators (PIs) Drs. Beth Montelone and Lisa Freeman, for their support and professionalism. There's a lot to be said for the complex factors that comprise leadership for virtual teaming—to have the room to innovate and explore and to form long-term professional alliances. I appreciated the gentle and direct supervision of Dr. Kimathi Choma, the humor of Dr. Mary McElroy, and the encouragement of Dr. Deanna "Go for It!" Retzlaff. Kent H. Nelson and Joseph D. Chapes provided superb videography work. The many members of the virtual team were creative and hard-working, and it was a pleasure to work with them all; however, they are too many to name. Well after the completion of this chapter, Drs. Cindy Shuman and Valerie K. York (of the Office of Educational Innovation and Evaluation) conducted a debriefing of the communications and collaboration aspects of this work, and their interview reaffirmed the specialness of this local virtual collaboration for me. Thanks to R. Max.

REFERENCES

Alexander, P. M. (2002). Teamwork, time, trust and information. [ACM.]. *SAICSIT, 2002,* 65–74.

Anawati, D., & Craig, A. (2006). Behavioral adaptation with cross-cultural virtual teams. *IEEE Transactions on Professional Communication, 49*(1), 44–56. doi:10.1109/TPC.2006.870459

Andrews, D., & Starke-Meyerring, D. (2005). Making connections: An intercultural virtual team project in professional communication. In *2005 IEEE International Professional Communication Conference Proceedings* (pp. 26-31). IEEE.

Balthazard, P. A., Potter, R. E., & Warren, J. (2002). The effects of extraversion and expertise on virtual team interaction and performance. In *Proceedings of the 35th Hawaii International Conference on System Sciences*. IEEE.

Bansler, J. P., & Havn, E. (2003). Technology-use mediation: Making sense of electronic communication in an organizational context. [Sanibel Island, Florida. ACM.]. *Group, 03*, 135–143.

Baskerville, R., & Nandhakumar, J. (2007). Activating and perpetuating virtual teams: Now that we're mobile, where do we go? *IEEE Transactions on Professional Communication, 50*(1), 17–34. doi:10.1109/TPC.2006.890849

Bass, B. (1990). *Bass & Stogdill's handbook of leadership: Theory, research & managerial Applications* (3rd ed., pp. 682–683). New York: The Free Press.

Bayerl, P. S., & Lauche, K. (2008). Coordinating high-interdependency tasks in asymmetric distributed teams. In CSCW '08 (pp. 417-426). San Diego, California. 4

Beise, C. M. (2004). IT project management and virtual teams. In SIGMIS '04 (pp. 129-133). Tuscon, Arizona. ACM.

Beranek, P. M. (2005). A comparison of relational and trust training techniques for virtual team communication: How much training is enough? In *Proceedings of the 38th Hawaii International Conference on System Sciences 2005* (pp. 1-10). IEEE.

Biuk-Aghai, R. P., & Simoff, S. J. (2001). An integrative framework for knowledge extraction in collaborative virtual environments. [Boulder, Colorado. ACM.]. *Group, 01*, 61–70.

Bos, N., Olson, J., Cheshin, A., Kim, Y.-S., Nan, N., & Shami, N. S. (2005). Traveling blues: The effect of relocation on partially distributed teams. In CHI 2005 (pp. 1917-1920). Portland, Oregon. ACM.

Bos, N., Shami, N. S., Olson, J. S., Cheshin, A., & Nan, N. (2004). In-group / out-group effects in distributed teams: An experimental simulation. In CSCW '04 (pp. 429-436). Chicago, Illinois. ACM.

Casey, V., & Richardson, I. (2006). *Project management within virtual software teams.* Paper presented at IEEE International Conference on Global Software Engineering.

Casey, V., & Richardson, I. (2006). Uncovering the reality within virtual software teams. In GSD '06 (pp. 66-72). Shanghai, China. ACM.

Casey, V., & Richardson, I. (2008). The impact of fear on the operation of virtual teams. In *2008 IEEE International Conference on Global Software Engineering. ICGSE 2008* (pp. 163-172). IEEE.

Chang, K. T., & Ehrlich, K. (2007). *Out of sight but not out of mind? Informal networks, communication and media use in global software teams* (pp. 1-12). IBM Corporation. Chen, Z., Zhang, X., Vogel, D., & Zhao, D. (2009). Encouraging knowledge sharing in global virtual teams: The interaction effect of individual difference and perceived sharing benefits. In *Proceedings of the 42nd Hawaii International Conference on System Sciences* (pp. 1-10).

Churchill, E. F., & Bly, S. (1999). It's all in the words: Supporting work activities with lightweight tools. [Phoenix, Arizona. ACM.]. *Group, 99*, 40–49.

Clear, T., & Kassabova, D. (2005). Motivational patterns in virtual team collaboration. Australasian Computing Education Conference 2005. New Castle, Australia. *Conferences in Research and Practice in Information Technology, 42*, 51 – 58.

Corbitt, G., Gardiner, L. R., & Wright, L. K. (2004). A comparison of team developmental stages, trust, and performance for virtual versus face-to-face teams. In *Proceedings of the 37th Hawaii International Conference on System Sciences* (pp. 1-8). IEEE.

Cordes, R. E., & Spine, T. M. (2007). *Transcending organizational boundaries: Virtual team approach in UI guideline development*. Paper presented at CHIMIT '07. Cambridge, Massachusetts. ACM.

Crowston, K., Howison, J., Masango, C., & Eseryel, U. Y. (2007). The role of face-to-face meetings in technology-supported self-organizing distributed teams. *IEEE Transactions on Professional Communication, 50*(2), 185–203. doi:10.1109/TPC.2007.902654

Da Silva, E. J., de Souza, C. S., Prates, R. O., & Nicolaci-da-Costa, A. M. (2003). What they want and what they get: A study of light-weight technologies for online communities. *ACM International Conference Proceeding Series, 46,* 135-146. Rio de Janeiro, Brazil. Retrieved Apr. 12, 2009, from http://delivery.acm.org/10.1145/950000/944534/p135-silva.pdf?key1=944534&key2=6531759321&coll=GUIDE&dl=GUIDE&CFID=30071228&CFTOKEN=14469905.

Dabbish, L. A. (2008). Jumpstarting relationships with online games: Evidence form a laboratory investigation. In CSCW '08 (pp. 353-356). San Diego, California.

De Pillis, E., & Furumo, K. (2007). Counting the costs of virtual teams: Studying the performance, satisfaction, and group dynamics of virtual and face-to-face teams. *Communications of the ACM, 50*(12), 93–95.

Dekker, D. M., & Rutte, C. G. (2007). Effective versus ineffective communication behaviors in virtual teams. In *Proceedings of the 40th Hawaii International Conference on System Sciences* (pp. 1-10). IEEE.

Donker, H., & Blumberg, M. (2008). Collaborative process management and virtual teams. In CHASE '08 (pp. 41-43). Leipzig, Germany. ACM.

Ehsan, N., Mirza, E., & Ahmad, M. (2008). *Impact of computer-mediated communication on virtual teams' performance: An empirical study*. IEEE.

Ellis, J.B., Luther, K., Bessiere, K., & Kellogg, W.A. (2008). Games for virtual team building.

Ferscha, A., & Scheiner, C. (1999). Collective choice in virtual teams. In *IEEE 8th International Workshops on Enabling Technologies: Infrastructure for Collaborative Enterprises (WETICE '99)*. Retrieved Apr. 12, 2009, from http://www.soft.uni-linz.ac.at/Research/Publications/Documents/WETICE99.ps

Fuller, M. A., Hardin, A. M., & Scott, C. L. (2007). Diffusion of virtual innovation. *The Data Base for Advances in Information Systems, 38*(4), 40–44.

Godart, C., Bouthier, C., Canalda, P., Charoy, F., Molli, P., & Perrin, O. (2001). *Asynchronous coordination of virtual teams in creative applications (co-design or co-engineering): Requirements and design criteria* (pp. 135–142). IEEE.

Guo, Z., D'Ambra, J., Turner, T., & Zhang, H. (2009). Improving the effectiveness of virtual teams: A comparison of video-conferencing and face-to-face communication in China. *IEEE Transactions on Professional Communication, 52*(1), 1–16. doi:10.1109/TPC.2008.2012284

Hackman, J. R. (2002). *Leading teams: Setting the stage for great performances*. Boston: Harvard Business School Press.

Huang, H., & Ocker, R. (2006). Preliminary insights into the in-group / out-group effect in partially distributed teams: An analysis of participant reflections. In SIGMIS-CPR '06 (pp. 264-271). Claremont, California. ACM.

Hung, Y.-T. C., Dennis, A. R., & Robert, L. (2004). Trust in virtual teams: Towards an integrative model of trust formation. In *Proceedings of the 37ᵗʰ Hawaii International Conference on System Sciences* (pp. 1-11). IEEE.

Ignat, C.-L., Papadopoulou, S., Oster, G., & Norrie, M. C. (2008). Providing awareness in multi-synchronous collaboration without compromising privacy. In CSCW '08 (pp. 659-668). San Diego, California. ACM.

In, D. I. S. 2008 (pp. 295-304). Cape Town, South Africa. ACM.

Jäkälä, M., & Pekkola, S. (2007). From technology engineering to social engineering: 15 years of research on virtual worlds. *The Data Base for Advances in Information Systems, 38*(4), 11–16.

Kahai, S. S., Carroll, E., & Jestice, R. (2007). Team collaboration in virtual worlds. *The Data Base for Advances in Information Systems, 38*(4), 61–68.

Karayaz, G., & Keating, C. B. (2007). Virtual team effectiveness using dyadic teams. In PICMET 2007 Proceedings (pp. 2593-2603). Portland, Oregon.

Keyzerman, Y. (2003). *Trust in virtual teams* (pp. 391–400). IEEE.

Kildare, R., Williams, R. N., & Harnett, J. (2006). *An online tool for learning collaboration and learning while collaborating.* Paper presented at the Australian Computer Society, Inc. Eighth Australasian Computing Education Conference 2006. Hobart, Tasmania, Australia.

Lin, F.-r., & Chen, C.-h. (2004). Developing and evaluating the social network analysis system for virtual teams in cyber communities. In *Proceedings of the 37ᵗʰ Hawaii International Conference on System Sciences* (pp. 1-8). IEEE.

Lind, M. R. (1999). The gender impact of temporary virtual work groups. *IEEE Transactions on Professional Communication, 42*(4), 276–285. doi:10.1109/47.807966

Lind, M. R. (2007). Collective team identification in temporary teams. In *Proceedings of the 40ᵗʰ Hawaii International Conference on System Sciences* (pp. 1-9). IEEE.

Lojeski, K. S., Reilly, R., & Dominick, P. (2007). Multitasking and innovation in virtual teams. In *Proceedings of the 40ᵗʰ Hawaii International Conference on System Sciences* (pp. 1-9). IEEE.

Mark, G., & Semaan, B. (2008). Resilience in collaboration: Technology as a resource for new patterns of action. In CSCW '08 (pp. 137-146). San Diego, California. ACM.

Mogan, S., & Wang, W. (2007). A study into user perceptions of information sharing and trust in virtual teams. In *HT '07* (pp. 43–44). Manchester, United Kingdom: ACM.

Nemiro, J. E. (2004). *Creativity in Virtual Teams: Key Components for Success* (pp. 15–16). San Francisco: John Wiley & Sons.

Nunamaker, J. F. (1999). *The case for virtual teaming systems. IT Pro* (pp. 52–57). IEEE.

Ocker, R. J. (2005). Influences on creativity in asynchronous virtual teams: A qualitative analysis of experimental teams. *IEEE Transactions on Professional Communication, 48*(1), 22–30. doi:10.1109/TPC.2004.843294

Ocker, R. J. (2007). A balancing act: The interplay of status effects on dominance in virtual teams. *IEEE Transactions on Professional Communication, 50*(2), 204–218. doi:10.1109/TPC.2007.902656

Ocker, R. J., & Fjermestad, J. (2000). High versus low performing virtual design teams: A preliminary analysis of communication. In *Proceedings of the 33rd Hawaii International Conference on System Sciences* (pp. 1-10). IEEE.

Ocker, R. J., & Fjermestad, J. (2008). Communication differences in virtual design teams: Findings from a multi-method analysis of high and low performing experimental teams. *The Data Base for Advances in Information Systems, 39*(1), 51–67.

Orton, J. D., & Weick, K. E. (1990). Loosely coupled systems: A reconceptualization. *Academy of Management Review, 15*(2), 203–223. doi:10.2307/258154

Oshri, I., Kotlarsky, J., & Willcocks, L. (2008). Missing links: Building critical social ties for global collaborative teamwork. *Communications of the ACM, 51*(4), 76–81. doi:10.1145/1330311.1330327

Panteli, N., & Davison, R. M. (2005). The role of subgroups in the communication patterns of global virtual teams. *IEEE Transactions on Professional Communication, 48*(2), 101–200. doi:10.1109/TPC.2005.849651

Paré, G., & Dubé, L. (1999). Virtual teams: An exploratory study of key challenges and strategies. *International Conference on Information Systems* (pp. 479-483). Charlotte, North Carolina. ACM. Retrieved Apr. 12, 2009, from http://delivery.acm.org/10.1145/360000/352978/p479-pare.pdf?key1=352978&key2=5845759321&coll=GUIDE&dl=GUIDE&CFID=30868979&CFTOKEN=74505829

Paul, S., & Ray, S. (2009). Cultural diversity, perception of work atmosphere, and task conflict in collaboration technology supported global virtual teams: Findings from a laboratory experiment. In *Proceedings of the 42nd Hawaii International Conference on System Sciences* (pp. 1-10). IEEE.

Paul, S., Seetharaman, P., Samarah, I., & Mykytyn, P. (2005). Understanding conflict in virtual teams: An experimental investigation using content. In *Proceedings of the 38th Hawaii International Conference on System Sciences* (pp. 1-10). IEEE.

Peters, M. R., Ocker, R. J., & Rosson, M. B. (2008). Collaboration in a distributed world: Technological support for partially distributed teams. *Eighth IEEE International Conference on Advanced Learning Technologies* (pp. 273-277). IEEE.

Powell, A., Piccoli, G., & Ives, B. (2004). Virtual teams: A review of current literature and directions for future research. *The Data Base for Advances in Information Systems, 35*(1), 6–36.

Pripužić, K., Gjenero, L., & Belani, H. (2006). Improving virtual team communication.

Regenbrecht, H., Ott, C., Wagner, M., Lum, T., Kohler, P., Wilke, W., & Mueller, E. (2003). An augmented virtuality approach to 3D videoconferencing. In *Proceedings of the Second IEEE and ACM International Symposium on Mixed and Augmented Reality* (pp. 1-2). IEEE.

Rutkowski, A. F., Vogel, D. R., Van Genuchten, M., Bemelmans, T. M. A., & Favier, M. (2002). E-Collaboration: The reality of virtuality. *IEEE Transactions on Professional Communication, 45*(4), 219–230. doi:10.1109/TPC.2002.805147

Salisbury, W. D., Carte, T. A., & Chidambaram, L. (2006). Cohesion in virtual teams: Validating the perceived cohesion scale in a distributed setting. *The Data Base for Advances in Information Systems, 37*(2-3), 147–155.

Samarah, I., Paul, S., & Tadisina, S. (2007). Collaboration technology support for knowledge conversion in virtual teams: A theoretical perspective. In *Proceedings of the 40th Hawaii International Conference on System Sciences* (pp. 1-10). IEEE.

Sarker, S., Sarker, S., Nicholson, D. B., & Joshi, K. D. (2005). Knowledge transfer in virtual systems development teams: An exploratory study of four key enablers. *IEEE Transactions on Professional Communication*, *48*(2), 201–218. doi:10.1109/TPC.2005.849650

Sarker, S., Sarker, S., & Schneider, C. (2009). Seeing remote team members as leaders: A study of US–Scandinavian teams. *IEEE Transactions on Professional Communication*, *52*(1), 75–94. doi:10.1109/TPC.2008.2007871

Schümmer, T., & Lukosch, S. (2006). The absent participant. Paper presented at PLoP '06. Portland, Oregon. ACM.

Sengupta, K., & Zhao, J. L. (1998). Designing workflow management systems for virtual organizations: An empirically grounded approach. In *Proceedings of the 31ˢᵗ Hawaii International Conference on System Sciences* (pp. 365-373). Retrieved Apr. 12, 2009 from http://ieeexplore.ieee.org/stamp/stamp.jsp?arnumber=00655293

Shen, Y. (2007). Transactive memory system development in virtual teams: The potential role of shared identity and shared context. In SIGMIS-CPR 07 (pp. 228-230). St. Louis, Missouri. ACM.

Sivunen, A., & Valo, M. (2006). Team leaders' technology choice in virtual teams. *IEEE Transactions on Professional Communication*, *49*(1), 57–68. doi:10.1109/TPC.2006.870458

Skovolt, K. (2009). Leadership communication in a virtual team. In *Proceedings of the 42ⁿᵈ Hawaii International Conference on System Sciences* (pp. 1-12).

Software in Telecommunications and Computer Networks2006. SoftCOM 2006 (pp. 266-270). IEEE. Retrieved Apr. 12, 2009, at http://ieeexplore.ieee.org/stamp/stamp.jsp?arnumber=04129918. 266 – 270.

Sole, D., & Applegate, L. (2000). Knowledge sharing practices and technology use norms in dispersed development teams. *International Conference on Information Systems* (pp. 581-587). Retrieved Apr. 12, 2009, from http://delivery.acm.org/10.1145/360000/359821/p581-sole.pdf?key1=359821&key2=5790759321&coll=GUIDE&dl=GUIDE&CFID=30070776&CFTOKEN=39968476

Suchan, J., & Hayzak, G. (2001). The communication characteristics of virtual teams: A case study. *IEEE Transactions on Professional Communication*, *44*(3), 174–186. doi:10.1109/47.946463

Sutanto, J., Phang, C. W., Kuan, H. H., Kankanhalli, A., & Tan, B. C. Y. (2005). Vicious and virtuous cycles in global virtual team role coordination. In *Proceedings of the 38ᵗʰ Hawaii International Conference on System Sciences* (pp. 1-10). IEEE.

Tan, A., & Kondoz, A. M. (2008). Barriers to virtual collaboration. In CHI 2008 Proceedings (pp. 2045-2052). Florence, Italy.

Tan, B. C. Y., Wei, K.-K., Huang, W. W., & Ng, G.-N. (2000). A dialogue technique to enhance electronic communication in virtual teams. *IEEE Transactions on Professional Communication*, *43*(2), 153–165. doi:10.1109/47.843643

Ter Bush, R. F. (2006). Silence, attribution accuracy and virtual environments: Implications for developers and facilitators. In *Proceedings of the 39ᵗʰ Hawaii International Conference on System Sciences* (pp. 1-9). IEEE.

Thomas, D. M., Bostrom, R. P., & Gouge, M. (2007). Making knowledge work in virtual teams. *Communications of the ACM*, *50*(11), 85–90. doi:10.1145/1297797.1297802

Wang, Q., Huang, H., & Wang, X. (2006). Intelligent virtual team in collaborative design. Computer-Aided Industrial Design and Conceptual Design 2006. IEEE. Retrieved Apr. 12, 2009, from http://ieeexplore.ieee.org/stamp/stamp.jsp?arnumber=04127026

Weick, K. E. (1976). Educational organizations as loosely coupled systems. *Administrative Science Quarterly, 21*, 1–19. doi:10.2307/2391875

Xiao, W., & Wei, Q.-Q. (2008). A study on virtual team trust mechanism and its construction strategies. *2008 International Conference on Information Management, Innovation Management and Industrial Engineering* (pp. 315-319). IEEE.

Yager, S. E. (1999). Using information technology in a virtual work world: Characteristics of collaborative workers. In SIGCPR '99 (pp. 73-78). New Orleans, Louisiana. ACM.

Zhang, S., Fjermestad, J., & Tremaine, M. (2005). Leadership styles in virtual team context: Limitations, solutions and propositions. In *Proceedings of the 38ᵗʰ Hawaii International* Conference on System Sciences (pp. 1-10). IEEE.

KEY TERMS AND DEFINITIONS

Accessibility: The nature of being attainable or able to be used; meeting guidelines for being usable (in a technological and human sensory sense).

Attribution: Interpreting, assigning a quality or idea to someone or some action.

Co-location: The state of being in the same vicinity.

Collaboration: The act of working together on a shared project, from planning to development to critique; teamwork.

Critique: A criticism or constructive feedback.

Discourse: A formal conversation.

Dispersed: Spread over a wide geographical area.

Ecology: The interdependence of people within a particular environment, and their interactions with that environment.

Hybrid: A blend of types, usually referring to electronic learning (e-learning) and face-to-face (F2F) learning.

Inflection: A point of change; a turning.

Intercommunication: Mutual communications between people.

Interdisciplinary: Combining two or more fields of study, consisting of the influences of multiple disciplines.

Leverage: Power.

Local: Close by geographically; nearby.

Loose Coupling: The concept of less interdependence between entities for greater adaptivity in an organization or organizational unit.

Media Richness: The state of having high communications cues through mediated communications.

Mental Model: The conceptualization of a particular system, held by individuals (vs. conceptual models, which are held by subject matter experts in a particular knowledge domain).

Milestone: A significant event or stage in a process.

Module: A separate stand-alone learning component that may be interchangeable with others.

Non-Verbal Cues: Body language as a tool of communications.

Rehearsable: The ability to go over a message before sending it out.

Reprocessibility: The ability to re-examine a message within a particular communications event.

Resilience: The power to recover from difficulty.

Rubric: An assessment device that is characterized by its presentation via tables with informational cells.

Social Exchange: The relationships between people as a basis for work and interactions.

Stylebook: A document used in digital project management that defines standards.

Trajectory: A particular path or course.

Transactional: A type of relationship based on mutual exchanges.

Virtual Teaming: The work collaboration by individuals who are geographically (and often temporally) dispersed.

APPENDIX A

Draft Stylebook for the Pathways to Public Health

Subject Matter Experts (SMEs) and Developers

A stylebook guides the development of the curriculum and digital learning objects. It is unique to a project and is co-created by the members of the team. (**Redaction**: The team members' names, contact information, institutional affiliations, and areas of domain expertise were deleted here. A "To Do" list specific to the project and work flows also were redacted. A table of deadlines was also omitted.)

1. Team Work Flow

Note: A separate workflow is annotated and color-coded to show the three main phases of the project: (1) development, (2) alpha and beta testing, and (3) deployment and archival. Also, that included annotations of where decisions would get made and by whom—to assign responsibilities and to ensure clear cross-team understandings.

Note: The above flow communicates the general steps to the online course design process. The project-specific due dates have been redacted.

Figure 3. A team work flow

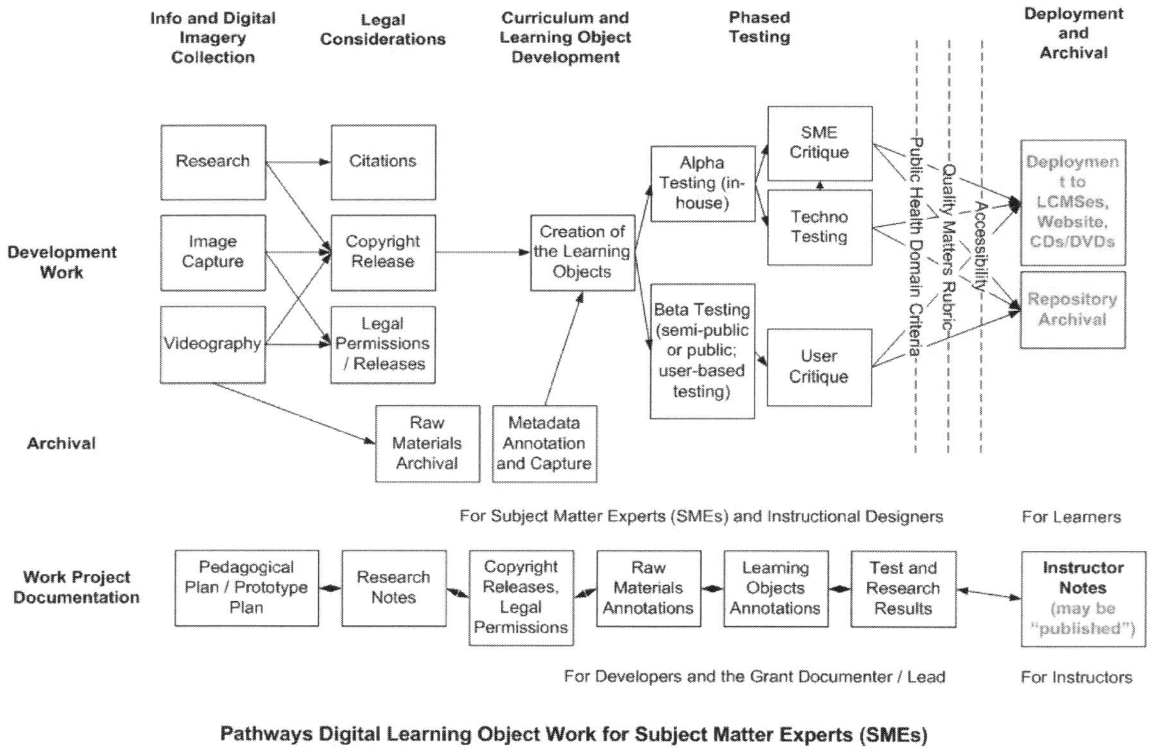

Pathways Digital Learning Object Work for Subject Matter Experts (SMEs)

Figure 4. General steps to the online course design process

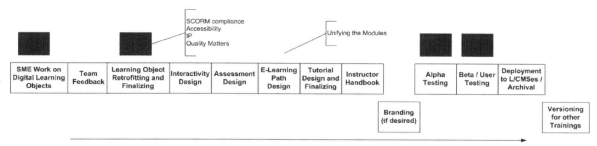

General Steps to the Online Course Design Process

2. Modular Contents

This segment set expectations for the team about the sizes of the modules in terms of the hours that learners would spend on each and the length of each module (two weeks of learning per module for 9 hours of learning per week—or 3 hours online and 6 hours of homework).

The group defined the modular contents, so there would be a shared understanding of what was being built:

Based on the face-to-face meeting by the project subject matter experts, the curriculum was divided into a pre-module (to help novice learners acclimate to both online learning and the subject matter), and six other modules. There were learning outcomes linked to each module, and there were chapters of a shared textbook linked to each.

Table 1.

Defined Learning Objectives: Learning objectives (5-10 total) (related to the digital learning objects, activities and assessments)
Self-Explanatory Topical Slideshows: 1-3 slideshows (approximately 20 – 25 slides each, with between 4-8 images per each slideshow)
Multimedia: Audio and / or video files
Relevant External Links: 2-5 links to professional, related resources on the WWW (simulations, immersive learning, videos, slideshows, informative websites, and other contents)
Discussion / Interactivity Plans: case studies, current events, controversial issues
Field Study Ideas: Field trips, site visits
Practice Exercises: based on learner opt-in (flashcards, crosswords, automated multiple-choice, true-false, matching, and other exercises)
Assessments: An objective assessment (multiple choice, true/false, matching, etc.)

3. Development / Authoring Technologies

Tech Standards and Tools: Given the technological standards of the project, this part set the URL for the work site. It also pointed to various freeware that could add value to the project—such as a site that allows for the low-cost easy-moving of large digital files. The authoring tool software programs and their versions (2007), digital file types (for text, slideshows, still images, audio, video, automation, and others) were defined specifically. Included also were specs on imagery in terms of file sizes, for the greatest flexibility in terms of versioning. The three learning / course management systems that would be used in the execution of this project were also listed.

    Raw Files: Content creators were asked to keep proper raw video, photos, diagrams, and other elements in their modular folders for possible later use and for the most information-rich versions of the files (before compression and / or integration into a polished, finalized digital learning object or experience).

4. Course Development Standards

To develop this online course, it was critical to have clear definition of standards. A special segment at the end addressed issues of copyright and intellectual property, and another addressed federal Section 508 compliance for accessibility.

    Annotation, Record-keeping and Citations: All subject matter experts and content creators were asked to annotate imagery for alt text. They were asked to keep records of all intellectual property / copyright releases. Citations were to be done using the American Psychological Association (APA) citation method. Guidelines for the labeling of diagrams were included.

    File Naming Protocols: This section addressed how to name files in a consistent way without limiting how the digital files could be used. (The idea of modularization is not to lock individuals into a set curriculum but to make digital learning objects interchangeable to different e-learning and hybrid-learning situations.)

    Credits: Another segment explored how to add a credits page at the end of a digital learning object, if desired.

    Instructor Telepresence Strategies: A way for an inheriting faculty member to create telepresence was addressed. A digital instructor's manual would be created to go along with this curriculum.

    Quality Matters™ Curricular Standards: A live URL link to the Quality Matters™ rubric was offered as part of the standards setting along with a brief overview of the contents of the QM standards.

5. Course and Module Assessment and Feedback Loops

This section addressed a survey feedback instrument to gather user feedback from learners (See Appendix C.) during the summer hybrid test-run of the course. A version of this survey instrument could be used with each course offering for continuing feedback loops and revisions. (Logistically, there would have to be one "pristine" master course, which all members of the team would have access to…and a way to capture changes and have those delivered to learners.) This noted, too, that datamining would be set up on the various learning / course management systems to observe learner behaviors and to gather information about how to improve the course and the student learning.

Stylebook Appendix A: Why IP in E-Learning?

A segment addressed intellectual property issues in terms of the rationale behind intellectual property, Creative Commons® releases, and public domain objects. The tenets of intellectual property and the various laws [the US Copyright Act (1976); "fair use" via Section 107 of the Copyright Act, 1976; the Digital Millennium Copyright Act (1998); the Technology, Education and Copyright Harmonization Act (TEACH Act, 2002) related to performances; trademark tenets; patent tenets, and trade secret protections were all covered. There was a tips section for faculty to help in their establishing provenance of information. The proposed "orphaned works" legislation was not addressed given a lack of an official decision. The subject matter experts also were given links to open cost-free educational resources that could offer topic-specific resources which they could use in this curriculum. They were also asked to use links to various sites.

Stylebook Appendix B: Accessibility

Lastly, there were tips given to make courses accessible. These involved efforts to use universal product format file types and versioning file types for more robust accessibility. Text documents would not be digital image graphics but text-readable files. Documents would be tagged for document structure and markup, so users may understand headers from body text. The language would be clear, simple English, to help those using computerized language translators or reading the English as a second or foreign language. Informational graphics needed alt text labeling, and all audio and video needed transcription. PowerPoint slideshows would have to be made accessible based on using their extant templates instead of inserting text boxes (which are skipped over by some text readers). Color needed to be accessible for those who have low vision or color-blindness, so the use of color *alone* to communicate was discouraged. Data tables had to be summarized and created in a screen-readable way for clarity. Live events that were planned for the course needed to be accessible, with preliminary, during-event, and post-event work. If automations or sequenced actions were created, these had to be controllable by users to the largest extent possible.

APPENDIX B

Peer Feedback on the Modular Contents

1. Based on the **Pathways to Public Health Check List for Course Materials** (in the Stylebook Criteria folder in the online workspace), did you find (a) **anything missing** or (b) **needing revision** from the module? (**Note:** Please be specific. Name the lecture or item, and note the exact slide. If referring to a video, refer to an exact time. Provide specific suggestions for improvement.)
2. Based on **the Quality Matters rubric** in the Stylebook Criteria folder in the online workspace), did you find the following elements in the module you assessed? And did these come up to the course standards? If any parts do not come up to course standards, list below and specifically state why they do not. Provide suggestions to help bring them up to course standards. Please be specific in your comments.

Table 2.

	Quality Matters review: (See Project Stylebook at K-State Online. Use QM Best Practice Guidelines)	
	Module Overview and Introduction	
	Learning Objectives	
	Assessment and Measurement	
	Resources and Materials	
	Learner Engagement	
	Course Technology (see -- stylebook pgs. 10, 12 and 13)	
	Learner Support	
	Accessibility (see Pathways stylebook)	

3. Based on the **subject matter for the module**, did you find any curricular **information missing?** If so, what would you add?

4. Did you have any **technological problems** accessing the curricular contents? Please describe these in depth. (What were the file types?)

Submittal: Please keep a copy of this for your team, and make sure to send a copy to ---. She'll make sure that all the developers for a particular module receive a copy of the comments. She'll also maintain an archive of the critiques in the online workspace.

If you and your team have suggestions for the overall development of the modules, feel free to share that with the team. (You may email all team members via the Roster area of the worksite.) Thanks. (**Note:** A separate form will be used for critiquing the overall course later on.)

APPENDIX C

Proposed Learner Survey for Pathways to Public Health Curriculum Assessment

This 24-question survey will be used to enhance the online course "Pathways to Public Health." The first section consists of a series of statements, which may be evaluated based on your learning experience.

The second short section consists of two short-answer questions. This survey may take about 10 minutes to complete. Your help is appreciated.

Directions: Please read the following statements. Rank how true each statement is with the following scale.

LEARNER BACKGROUND:

1. I had the proper amount of prior knowledge to understand the contents of this introductory public health course.

Table 3.

N/A	1	2	3	4	5
Non-applicable	Disagree	Somewhat disagree	Neutral	Somewhat agree	Agree

LEARNER NEEDS:

2. I needed more materials in order to understand the subject matter of this course.
3. My learning styles or preferences were met in this course.

CLARITY OF COURSE EXPECTATIONS:

4. I was clear about the course expectations early on (through the syllabus and course postings).

TECHNOLOGIES:

5. I was able to access all the digital files related to this course.
    If not, I had problems with the following file types:
    Images
    Slideshows
    Audio
    Video
    Animated tutorials
    Simulations
6. The learning / course management system (the software through which you accessed the online course) was user-friendly.

COURSE CURRICULUM:

7. The course curriculum was clear.
8. I had sufficient opportunities to apply the learning during this course.
9. The course materials related clearly to the course textbook.
10. The case studies helped me understand some real-world aspects of public health.
11. The field trips (if applicable) helped me better understand public health.
12. I have a better understanding of careers in public health.
13. My interest in public health careers has been enhanced.
14. I felt the learning showed diverse populations in an inclusive way.
15. The course assessments (quizzes, tests) aligned with the learning.

16. The textbook was helpful for my learning.
17. The external readings (in addition to the textbook) were helpful to my learning.

INTERACTIVITY:

18. I felt engaged and interested throughout this course.
19. I experienced sufficient communications with my fellow students / peers.
20. I experienced sufficient communications with my instructor.

INSTRUCTOR SUPPORT:

21. The instructor(s) was / were responsive to my learning needs.
22. The instructor(s)' response time and availability to answer my questions was adequate.

Short Answer Questions

23. Were there topics you wanted to learn more about in this introductory --- course that were not addressed? If so, please list them below.
24. Any suggestions on ways that this online course may be improved for future learners?

Thanks for your participation in this course and survey. If you would like to be contacted by a faculty member, please include your email below:

Chapter 16

Aided System of Competence Management for Virtual Team Building Adapted to Specific Needs of Design Projects

Marinita Schumacher
Ecole Centrale Paris, France

Julie Stal Le Cardinal
Ecole Centrale Paris, France

Jean-Claude Bocquet
Ecole Centrale Paris, France

ABSTRACT

Virtual instruments and tools are future trends in Engineering which are due to the growing complexity of engineering tasks. Individuals who are working in Virtual Teams must be equipped with spanning competencies that provide a basis for Virtual Team building. In the first step this chapter gives a broad insight to the field of Competence Management and Virtual Teams. The second step responds to the need of a method of Competence Management to build Virtual Teams that are active in virtual design projects in the area of New Product Development (NPD). Due to the systemic approach of the functional analysis, we present an Aided Competence Management for Virtual Team Building System (Aided CMVTB System) that permits to be adapted not only to organizations but also to design projects without a real organizational structure. The focus of this work is set on the generic aspect to highlight the adaptability and flexibility of the system.

INTRODUCTION

Today's economic prosperity depends on generating new knowledge, innovation and technological

DOI: 10.4018/978-1-61520-979-8.ch016

progress. As prospective partners and customers are spread out across the globe, organizations need access to worldwide communication to aspire worldwide competitiveness. In light of the increasing de-centralization and globalization of work processes, many organizations have responded to their dynamic environments by introducing Virtual Teams, in which members are geographically dispersed and coordinate their work mainly through electronic information and communication technologies (Grenier & Metes, 1995). The focus of this work is set in providing an Aided Competence Management for Virtual Team Building System (Aided CMVTB System). Those Virtual Teams are active in virtual design projects in the area of New Product Development (NPD). The Aided CMVTB System should improve the NPD process by providing Virtual Teams whose competencies assign the best to the requirements of design projects.

According to the systemic approach, our method is considered as a system that is described by functions. The importance of them depends on the specific needs of an organization or particular design projects. It is measured in a qualitative way with a tool called "hierarchical tree" that represents the system in a hierarchical form. By preparing the hierarchical tree and identifying the most important functions, we aim to represent the Aided CMVTB System to be better understood, to provide substantiated recommendations and to be realized in a further step. We like to ensure that the functions are partitioned in an appropriate manner and to show interfaces between them. The hierarchical functional decomposition of the system shall ensure traceability between functional requirements throughout all the levels. By using the tool of the hierarchical tree we aim to find a formulation of a framework that fits for each context.

The chapter is organized as follows:

- Firstly, we give an overview of our topic and a conceptualization for Virtual Teams and Competence Management is proposed. Furthermore, we give a brief overview of the positioning of our Aided CMVTB System.
- Secondly, we present briefly the systemic approach to provide the Aided CMVTB

System based on the functional analysis that helps us to get a holistic picture of our topic from a systemic point of view.

- In a third step we present the tool of the hierarchical tree. Based on our key findings, in this contribution we aim to measure the importance of the key functions as a final step of the functional analysis. We are concentrating on the hierarchical structure of the functions that we have identified to describe our system in a qualitative way.

To provide a first basic hierarchical structure we refer in a fourth step to a model of CEISAR called "Enterprise Architecture Cube". We adapted its principle to our system that helps us to bring a first structure in our functions and to prepare the hierarchical tree.

Next we aspire to provide clear visibility of the large number of functions making up our system by the hierarchical tree. The importance of the key functions will be represented.

We finish in a last step with our concluding remarks and some perspectives for future work. Building on this systemic analysis makes it possible for us to give guidelines, best practices and recommendations to implement a system like ours in industry.

BACKGROUND

Global competition, mass customization, and strong international collaborations on the international market are some of the trends that currently drive organizational changes and a rising value of Virtual Teams (Grenier & Metes, 1995). But what do we understand exactly by a Virtual Team? Earlier research on Virtual Teams gravitated around comparing Virtual Teams to conventional teams (Archer, 1990; Hollingshead et al. 1993; Warkentin et al. 1997). However, recent arguments have stressed that the line between calling a team conventional or traditional and one that is virtual

Figure 1. Similarities and differences of virtual team and traditional teams–a proposal based on the state of the art

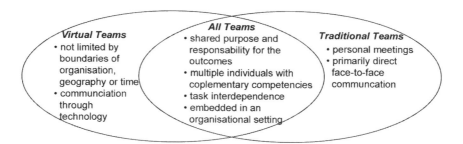

is becoming increasingly blurred. Fewer teams are remaining collocated, without any reliance upon technology for support of communication; and Virtual Teams may periodically meet face-to-face while undertaking tasks. Researchers instead have turned to discussion on the extent that teams engage in virtual methods of collaboration, or the extent of virtuality that any team employs (Griffith et al. 2003). A clear picture of the general similarities and differences between those two forms of teams is given in Figure 1.

Many authors have provided their own definition of Virtual Teams and the concept of Virtual Team lacks a universally accepted definition (Griffith, 2003; Schmidt et al., 2001; Rezgui, 2007). From these definitions, we derived the following description of a Virtual Team that consists of Individuals that are geographically and temporally dispersed and act interdependently through technology to achieve a common goal. The changing nature of teams has brought on a need to identify the competencies that are necessary to work effectively in a Virtual Team environment (Schumacher et al. 2008a). Competence is seen as the basis of competitiveness, it enables a company to offer products and valued services to customers and to innovatively generate new products and services. Indeed this "new" way of considering human resource requires a more precise formalization of concepts like competence or skills, in order to be able to identify the com-

petencies needed to work effectively in a Virtual Team environment and to assign employees' competencies efficiently to process activities. One of the strategic reasons for Virtual Teams is to combine different core competencies of experts from different locations to take advantage of market opportunities. The strategic management field is focusing on the role of competencies and resources that accumulate within an organization (Leiponen 2000; Heene & Sanchez 1997; Harzallah & Vernadat 1999). This implies according to Tuma (1998) a mechanism of concentration for each partner on its strategic competencies.

Figure 2 shows our model of "Competence Management" that is explained in detail in following paragraph.

The model emphasises that competencies are always carried out in a context that is derived from the requirements of a product or a service. We adapted our model of Competence Management to its context and defined it by different aspects. The list of considered aspects is not exhaustive and can be enriched according to every organization's specific need. In our model are five aspects considered describing the context in which the required knowledge and competencies are set. We define the procedural, organizational, economic, informational and physical aspects.

The model represents at the same time the relation between knowledge and competency that is visualized as a ladder. It takes into account that

Figure 2. Our understanding of competence management

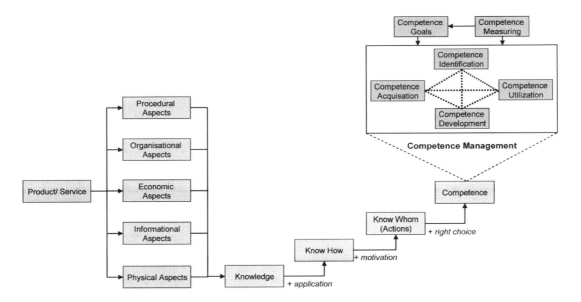

knowledge is only valuable for an organization if knowledge ("know what") will be transformed into "know-how". This happens in the moment of application. Hence, knowledge is only measurable in form of actions (know-whom). The know-how enables one to act, but without motivation it does not turn in action. With the right choice what means if the action is adjusted to the requirements of the respective situation, indicates competency. We refer to North who declaims that competencies are substantiated in the moment of knowledge application which means that competencies only exist when the knowledge meets a task (North, 2002). This means that competencies are always related to an action and thus established in the moment of knowledge application. Hence, competencies do only exist when the knowledge meets a task. Accordingly, we speak of competence in the context of interpreted knowledge that is contextualized by an individual or a group that confers an aptitude of decision to a respective action (Bocquet and Stal-Le Cardinal, 2005). Also Teece et al. (1997) distinguishes that knowledge builds the basis for competencies and that competencies are composed

of knowledge, which occurs from learning that takes place within the organizational context.

Furthermore our model copes with the demand of a holistic concept of Competence Management as it structures the management process in logical tasks and provides clues for intervention. Broadly spoken, Competence Management comprises identification, acquisition, development, and use of competencies and is the way how organizations manage the competencies of the organization, teams and individuals by goal-setting and measurement. Our concept of Competence Management has its seeds in a model of Probst called "Building Blocks of Knowledge Management" that is widely accepted in the domain of knowledge management (Probst et al. 1999). We translated it to our framework of Competence Management. Its arrangement follows certain principles. An inner cycle consists of the building blocks of identification, acquisition, development, and use of competencies. An outer cycle consists of all these activities plus goal-setting and measurement. This feedback cycle clarifies the importance of

Table 1. Processes of competence management according to the building blocks

Organization Sector	Building Blocks of Competence Management					
	Goals	**Identification**	**Aquisitation**	**Development**	**Utilization**	**Measuring**
Personal Department	Define job profiles and objectives of each employee	Appraisal Interviews	Recruiting	Personal Development, Succession Planning	As-is and To-be- Analysis to fill a job with a competent Employee.	Appraisal Interviews, Employee grading system
Knowledge Management	Define objectives in the field of KM	Profiling Experts Yellow pages	Experts Retrieval	Personal Development to assign missing competencies	Experts Assignment	Comparison of As-is and To-be- Analysis
Project Management	Define request of competencies	Profiling Experts	Experts Retrieval, Recruiting	Personal Development to assign missing competencies	Assigning of requirements and competencies	Analysis of gaps
Strategic Management	Define core competencies, Define indicators for their objectives	As-is-analysis	Recruiting	Try to meet the To-be-analysis	Strategic management by using the strengths and weaknesses Analysis	Comparison of As-is and To-be- Analysis (SMART-Analysis)

measuring the measurable variables in order to focus on goal-oriented interventions.

Following listing describes the functions of each building block:

- Competence Goals point the way for Competence Management activities and determine the objectives in the field of Competence Management.
- Competence Identification is the process of analyzing and describing the organizations competence environment. Competence sources are localized and their importance for the execution of tasks is evaluated.
- Competence Acquisition refers to which kind of expertise the organization should acquire missing competencies from outside through relationship with customers, suppliers, competitors and partners.
- Competence Development complements the process of Competence Acquisition. Its focus is on generating new competencies to implement new products, better ideas and more efficient processes.

- Competence Utilization consists of carrying out activities to make sure that the existing competencies are well applied for the benefit of all.
- Competence Measuring completes the cycle, providing the essential data for the strategic control of Competence Management. It is responsible for the regular adjustment between competence objectives and evaluated results of the sub-processes of Competence Management.

Due to the section of the organization the conversion of the processes of Competence Management can vary according to the respective building block. We identify four organization sectors where Competence Management plays a significant role: Personnel Department, Knowledge Management, Project Management and Strategic Management. The respective processes according to the Building Blocks are presented in Table 1.

As the Aided CMVTB System is situated in the organization sector of Project Management we are focusing on this sector in our research.

Figure 3. Positioning of the aided CMVTB system

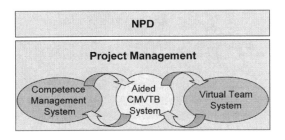

The following paragraph deals with issues, controversies and problems of our topic and paraphrases more in detail the importance of Competence Management for Virtual Teams.

Issues, Controversies, Problems

NPD comprises numerous knowledge intensive tasks and thus, the need for highly skilled employees. The "new" way of considering human resource requires a more precise formalization of concepts like competencies or skills, in order to be able to identify the competencies needed to work effectively in a Virtual Team environment and to link employees efficiently to tasks. Communication, Relationships, and Practices in Virtual Work are based on competencies of team members, which is why it is important to define them and to assign the frame.

In our research we are focusing on gaps between existing competencies and required competencies for current or future needs. In this case Competence Management occurs in the moment where a task and its required competencies are linked to an Individual and his acquired competencies (Schumacher et al., 2008b). One of the major benefits of a Competence Management system is that individuals can be assigned with specific jobs or tasks as they arise. Competence assigning is invaluable, for example, when a project leader asks for assistance in building a team for a new assignment. According to Horvarth and Tobin empirically-based prescriptions, guidelines and specifications for Virtual Team competencies are often missing (Horvarth & Tobin 2001). One of the major benefits of a Competence Management system for Virtual Teams is to combine different competencies of experts from different locations to take advantage of market opportunities (Harzallah & Vernadat, 1999). Individuals can be assigned with specific jobs or tasks which are invaluable in the field of NPD that comprises numerous knowledge intensive tasks and thus, the need for highly skilled employees. Due to costs, such experts are a rare resource which has to be applied in order to achieve innovative products and thereby competitive advantage.

The Virtual Teams which we handle are active in virtual design projects in the area of NPD. Figure 3 gives an overview of our positioning. It handles the domain of NPD as the context and the aspect of Project Management as the kind of organization of our work.

Due to our systemic approach the domain of Competence Management and the domain of Virtual Teams are considered as systems that are in interrelation with the Aided CMVTB System.

Figure 3 shows the positioning of the Aided CMVTB System.

The figure highlights that the Aided CMVTB System is in interaction with the Virtual Team System. The Aided CMVTB System functions as method that supports the Virtual Team System to create virtual teams. On the other hand the experience of the Virtual Team System can enhance the Aided CMVTB System by giving recommendations. Both systems are integrated as sub-systems in the domain of Project Management that functions as organization sector and is canopied by the context of the NPD. In our work we are considering the virtual aspect in NPD processes that claim other demands than traditional design projects in the domain of project management. Our focus is set on the Aided CMVTB System that supports the Virtual Team System by giving best practices, guidelines and recommendations for competence management for virtual teams

Figure 4. Steps of the functional analysis according to our study

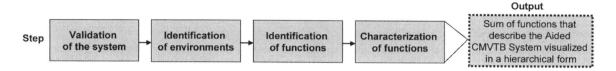

building. This is important for the functioning of the Project Management and thereby as well for the NPD.

A SYSTEMIC APPROACH OF COMPETENCE MANAGEMENT FOR VIRTUAL TEAMS

For understanding and mastering the complexity of the Aided CMVTB System we need a holistic approach which helps to identify needs and requirements, shows interrelations and leads to the establishment of sustainable research results.

In a former study we decided to use the functional analysis that is, referring to Snodgrass, often chosen as an instrument of NPD processes. Its power lies in its ability to take different ideas and apply a united symbolism and theory to deal with the important central features of the problem (Snodgrass 1986, Schumacher et al. 2008). It helps to gain a clear picture about functionalities and usability of a new product or services and assists in identifying main actors in the field (Schumacher 2009). The functional analysis is the tool that we use to be as objective, generic and exhaustive as possible. According to the systemic approach the method of Competence Management for Virtual Team Building is considered a system that is described by functions. This study focuses on the last step of the functional analysis, the hierarchical tree, which facilitates the characterization of the functions describing our system. To define the main categories of the hierarchical tree we refer to a model of CEISAR that is described briefly in the second part of this paragraph.

Functional Analysis

Referring to the APTE® formalism for conducting a Value Analysis it takes into consideration the various points of view of different research domains as well as the environmental aspects influencing a system (Apte 2000). Functional analysis is a technique of identifying and describing all the functions of an intended system (Yosida 1978). The analysis is performed to establish the system's functions, to define the key functions related to the system and to control the distribution and maintenance of these functions in a systematic and useful manner.

We have pursued the following steps that are presented in Figure 4. The focus of this work is set on the Characterization of the functions that helps to classify the sum of the functions that describe the Aided CMVTB System in a hierarchical form. This hierarchical form helps to provide a model that is adaptable at each specific context.

Through this approach the functional analysis provided us following key findings (Schumacher et al. 2008). In the step of the "validation of the system" we got a first impression about the system itself, its target group, application areas and limits, as well as the reason for its existence and its intention. We identified that its target groups are design projects, service providers, clients and end users. The reason for existence of our system is the need to react on the growing complexity of engineering tasks and the improvements in the NPD and project management process. The system's intention is to provide a method that intends to improve the NPD process by providing a vir-

Figure 5. Environments and extract of interfaces according to the aided CMVTB system

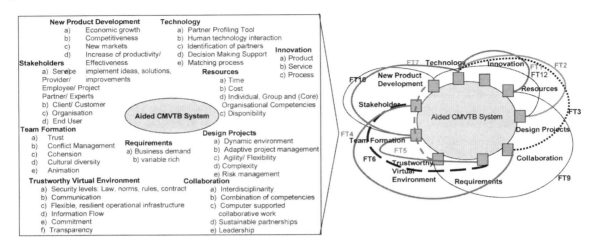

tual team whose competencies assign the best to the requirements of design projects.

We passed a validity control and analyzed the cause of the system (*Virtual Teams could be more effective if we moved ahead in the field of Competence Management; Competencies have to be available just when it is needed to rapidly complete required tasks, irrespective of where they are situated; There is a need of virtually access to new and larger markets, know-how and technology*, the objectives it aims for *(to enable design projects to develop more sophisticated and innovative products and services; to provide a method allowing to assign requirements with coherent competencies)*, and the risks of evolution or disappearance of the need (*development of new tools, which make web-based communication systems needless*).

In the step of identification of environments we defined 10 main environments and 43 subenvironments. This step was done in a multidisciplinary brainstorming process based on the literature review. The defined environments permit us to take different concepts, critical terms and conditions into consideration. They are shown on the left side of following Figure 5.

In the step of the identification of functions we established interfaces between those environ-

ments. According to Snodgrass each component of an open and living system interacts constantly with its environment by means of information and matter-energy exchanges (Snodgrass, 1986). This means that it is not enough to take only the system itself into account, but the whole interaction between the system and the environment in which it is acting to ensure consideration of the whole system. One of the most important benefits of the functional analysis for this study is that it puts the focus on the environment of the system. This fosters to get a holistic picture of all decisive components that have an important impact on our Aided CMVTB System. The fact that it is considered as a whole settles our claim of a holistic approach. By putting the different environments of our system in relation we are going to provide the functions that describe our Aided CMVTB System. Those functions describe the optimum behavior of the system and its terms of usability. We identified 243 transfer functions and 38 constraint functions.

An extract of interfaces to provide functions is seen on the right side of the figure. In visual terms, the sub-clusters are not listed in this figure but they interact with other sub-clusters or main clusters in the same way as main clusters do.

There are two kinds of functions: the transfer functions (FT) which are at least two different environments that interact by the means of the system, and the constraint functions (FC) which are generated by only one environment and that the system has to respect absolutely (Apte 2000).

An example of those FT and FC functions that have been detected is shown in the following listing to make a clearer picture.

- FT12: The system should make sure that the execution of **design projects** is based on knowledge and skills of the **service providers**.
- FC13: The system should provide that **employees** offer voluntary their individual competencies and their disponibilities.

In a collaborative negotiation process we have defined key functions that represent main aspects of the system. Based on our key findings, in the final step of our functional analysis, the importance of the key functions is measured with a tool called "hierarchical tree" to provide substantiated qualitative recommendations.

The hierarchical tree of the functions that describe the Aided CMVTB System is the focus of this study. The tree structure provides a clear visibility of the large number of functions making up the system. It helps us to measure the importance of the functions in a qualitative way and to represent the system in a hierarchical form.

In a first step different categories should be established at the top level that helps to cluster several functions. Those categories imply several functions that are regrouped in the hierarchical tree.

To determine the different basic categories of the highest level of the hierarchical tree we leaned on a model called CEISAR Enterprise Architecture Cube that is explained briefly in the following paragraph.

CEISAR Enterprise Architecture Cube

The approach of CEISAR focuses on "Enterprise Architecture" and tries to support organizations to develop their adaptivity in a proactive way. According to Weill et al. (2006) Enterprise Architecture provides an organizing structure for business processes and IT infrastructure that reflect organizations' operating model by integration and standardization of their requirements. According to CEISAR, Enterprise Architecture is seen as a new discipline that restructures systems and aligns them to the business strategy to accelerate transformation (CEISAR, 2008).

As our virtual teams consist of actors in a virtual environment that is considered by us in an abstract way as virtual enterprise we use the CEISAR Enterprise Architecture Cube as framework that is easily adaptable to our system. We consider that building a virtual team implies the same structures for business processes and IT infrastructure that reflect an enterprise in its operating model by integration and standardization of their requirements.

In our study we are focusing on the CEISAR Enterprise Architecture that defines organizations in three dimensions: Complexity, Agility, and Synergy. These are the key business concerns of each organization and according to CEISAR the most important challenges. As seen in the following Figure 6, they comprise complying with CEISAR as well as the other six proposed aspects: Strategy, Human Resources, Communication, Globalization, Productivity, and Marketing.

Each of those three main concerns Complexity, Agility and Synergy is regarded from two different perspectives that define the content. Concerning Complexity CEISAR makes the difference between "real world execution" and "model". By separating the real world execution from the global model CEISAR tries to master the complexity. By focusing on global maps of processes, solutions, functions, services, and

Figure 6. Three main concerns of the CEISAR enterprise architecture cube

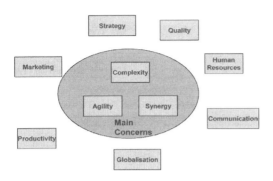

Figure 7. CEISAR enterprise architecture cube

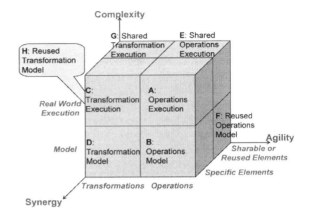

entities this global model helps to understand the complexity of an organization and how the organization works.

Concerning Agilty the two perspectives are "transformations" and "operations". Synergy considers "sharable or reused elements" and "specific elements.

As result of these three main concerns which are each split in two denominations, we obtain eight different dimensions that form the CEISAR Enterprise Architecture Cube. It is shown in Figure 7.

The CEISAR Enterprise Architecture Cube builds the fundament of our hierarchical clustering of functions. The primary purpose of describing the architecture of an enterprise is to improve the effectiveness and efficiency of the structure itself. By referring to the model of the CEISAR Enterprise Architecture Cube we intend to comprise as soon as possible the different dimensions to provide an Aided CMVTB System that is adaptable to each context.

In our study we aim to translate the eight dimensions of the cube to our main functions that are concerned by the dimensions. In a second step we try to adapt also the listed aspects of Figure 2 in our hierarchical tree to get a better understanding of in which field the functions are collocated.

Solutions and Recommendations

To give consideration in a holistic way to the concept of the CEISAR model and its three main concerns Complexity, Agility and Synergy we incorporated the eight dimensions of the CEISAR Enterprise Architecture Cube in our hierarchical tree and adapted them to the Aided CMVTB System and its corresponding functions. Table 2 takes the eight different dimensions of the cube into account, explains briefly the perspectives and presents our translation to our system and its corresponding functions.

While dimension A "Operations Execution" stands for operations and actions in the real world and focuses on the operations that are done in an organization, dimension B "Operations Model" regards the way organizations are doing those operations. We adapted dimension A to our functions with the focus "What do I do". Dimension B is translated to our functions in terms of "How do I do". Dimension C "Transformation Execution" considers the execution of the real world to evolve the way of doing. Due to pure functions we are focusing on the question "What makes me evolving the model to integrate the evolution". Dimension D "Transformation Model" takes the question of "How I make evolving the model to integrate the evolution?" into account. While

Table 2. Adaption of the CEISAR enterprise architecture cube to the aided CMVTB system

	Dimension	Perspective	Translation to our functions
A	Operations Execution	Real World Execution, Specific Elements, Operations	"What do I do"
B	Operations Model	Model, Specific Elements, Operations	"How do I do"
C	Transformation Execution	Real World Execution, Specific Elements, Transformations	"What makes me evolving my way of doing"
D	Transformation Model	Model, Specific Elements, Transformations	"How I make evolving the model to integrate the evolution"
E	Shared Operations Execution	Real World Execution, Sharable or Reused Elements, Operations	"What do I share with others"
F	Reused Operations Model	Model, Sharable or Reused Elements, Operations	"How I generalise and form this model"
G	Shared Transformation Execution	Real World Execution, Sharable or Reused Elements, Transformations	"What do I explain and form how to make evolving"
H	Reused Transformation Model	Model, Sharable or Reused Elements, Transformations	"How do I explain how to make evolving"

(Table title row: *Adaption of the CEISAR Enterprise Architecture Cube to our system*)

Dimension E examines sharable elements of the execution and focuses on "What do I share with others" is dimension F "Reused Operations Model" concerned in our translation by the generalization and the forming of the model. "Shared and Transformation Execution" looks at transformations of the real world execution to "explain and form how to make evolving". The last dimension H "Reused Transformation Model" contemplates "How do I explain how to make evolving".

Due to these eight dimensions and their adaption to our functions we obtain following basis of our approach of the hierarchical tree according to our system. It is presented in Figure 8.

In order to facilitate the visuality we neglect the intermediate step of the CEISAR Enterprise Architecture Cube and our translation of the main concerned function that is concerned by the dimension in further figures and illustrate only our translated main functions as categories A–H.

The model of CEISAR that has been presented earlier proposes a cartography of three main concerns regarding the entire organization: Complexity, Agility and Synergy.

That generic representation of an entire organization allowed us to consider these three main categories as well as the other six as specifications for the Aided CMVTB System. We translated the eight dimensions to our functions. In this step we try to relate them to the specifications as further categories.

Furthermore, we added six own categories due to our systemic approach of the functional analysis. These categories contain the constraint functions FC of our functional analysis: Simplicity of Use, Innovation, Universality, Costs, Quality and Technology. The categories of the CEISAR Enterprise Architecture Cube due to our functional analysis are shown in Figure 9.

Hierarchical clustering is widely used to cluster several elements into groups based on their expression similarity. We intend to use our translation of the eight dimensions of the CEISAR Enterprise Architecture Cube as a first structure to establish different categories of the highest top level of the hierarchical tree. At the second level we draw on the specifications of the three main concerns that have been presented in Figure 5 and adapted them to our system in Figure 8. This

Figure 8. Basis of the hierarchical tree according to the aided CMVTB system

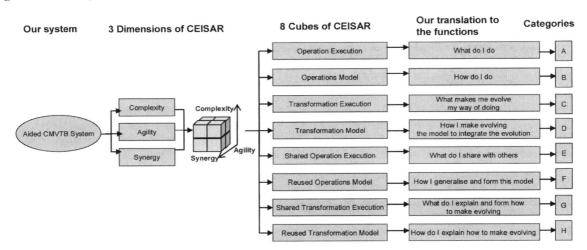

Figure 9. Categories of the CEISAR enterprise architecture cube due to our functional analysis

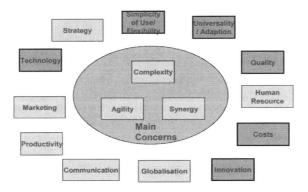

second level of categories permits us to cluster our functions also from a different perspective. We analyzed our key functions of the respective categories A–H to range them to these 12 specifications. Due to our key functions we neglected the categories communication and globalization because they have not had any effects on our functions.

To cluster the functions in this way helps us to describe them also on a second level. Figure 10 shows the results of the clustering. In terms of visibility we are obliged to neglect the respective key functions on this state. A detailed example will be presented in the following paragraph.

When the functions contain a clear "structure" in terms of clusters of elements that are similar to each other, this structure is reflected as distinct branches in the hierarchical tree. A hierarchical structure starts at a top level and breaks down the functions to lower levels due to different branches. This method first constructs a tree. Next this tree is partitioned into sub trees by cutting all edges at some level, thereby inducing a clustering. A function, which is passed to a lower level, is a higher level function for the recipient level.

A hierarchical structure starting at a top level working down in detail shall allow verification that the functions of the lower levels are consistent

Figure 10. Top levels of categories of the hierarchical tree according to our system (simplified view)

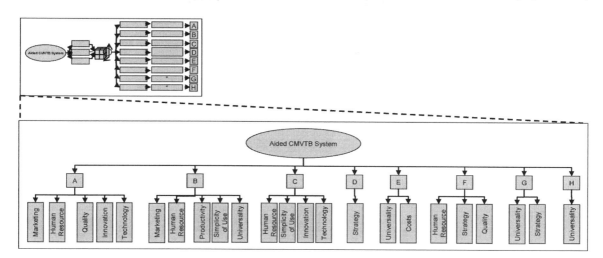

with functions of this top level. The hierarchical tree allows the functions to be regrouped and the interrelations between functions to be established. In the first step we needed to define the top level functions and decompose them to lower level functions. A function of a lower level can be required by a number of main functions which means that it may appear several times in the hierarchical tree. Functions may either be at a high level where they were derived or may be passed to a lower level.

Figure 11 gives only a brief extract the branch A "What do I do" of our hierarchical tree with the categories Marketing, Human Resource, Quality, Innovation and Technology.

For reasons of visualization this figure shows only the first and second level of functions. The percentages are noted as an example in this figure. They depend on the purpose of the specific needs of the organization or the design project. They are defined during the constitution of the virtual team, and they depend on its particular needs. It is self evident that the functions are broken down to several levels. The figure presents exclusively the first and the second level of branch A.

Only in one example the figures breaks the functions down up to the fourth level. While the beforehand presented function FT12 is situated in the first level of the category "Quality", function FC13 is on the fourth level of category "Human Resource". They are both classified in this branch. But nevertheless they are positioned in different levels what implicates different importance. FT12 is in the first level with fixed 0,5%. FC13 is situated in the fourth level with 0,01%. While the percentages depend on the purpose of the specific needs is the hierarchy of the function determined. Nevertheless, we can say that they decrease from the left to right with each lower level. The fact of having defined a structure of importance permits that the Aided CMVTB System is applicable to a wide range of organizations in the domain of NPD. It can apply to various application domains and to different design projects, with the weighting in terms of percentages varying according to the point of view of the stakeholder. There might be an organization that likes to concentrate more on the aspect of dimension C "How I make evolving my way of doing" or another one that set the focus on the aspect of further dimension. This flexibility of varying the percentages permits us to provide a global Aided CMVTB System that is adaptable to each context by pointing out different specific aspects.

Figure 11. Extract of branch A "What do I do" of the hierarchical tree according to our system

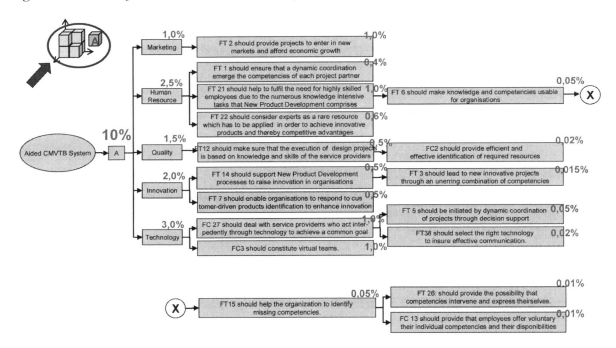

CONCLUSION

We demonstrated that the generic aspect of our Aided CMVTB System is based on the flexibility of our model. Any priorities to which a stakeholder might aspire, the model is adaptable to the respective demands.

Based on the systemic approach of the functional analysis we provided holistic picture of all decisive components that have an important impact on our Aided CMVTB System. We described all functions of our methodology that reflect requirements and ensured that they are partitioned in an appropriate manner. We were as objective, generic and exhaustive as possible. We identified interrelations and a hierarchical structure among the functions. The hierarchical tree allows the functions to be regrouped and their traceability. Predicated on the CEISAR Enterprise Architecture Cube the hierarchical tree the most important reasons for the generality of the Aided CMVTB System. The tree structure provides a clear visualization of the

large number of functions making up the system. A hierarchical structure starts at the higher level function and works down in detail that allows verification that the lower level functions are consistent with the top-level functions. Both types of functions may be either solved internally within the high level or refined to be met at some lower level. Thus, some functions have different levels of importance associated with them depending on how and they where originated.

This graphical hierarchical structure seems especially useful for us as we are in the process of the initial decomposition and structuring of functional requirements. As a result of a successful analysis with this tool, we detected branches of functions and were able to interpret them. It enables us to detect errors, neglects, inconsistencies and duplications through the branches. Before having used this method we did not have a clear picture of the importance of the specific functions of our system that have to be taken into consideration to provide the Aided CMVTB

Table 3. Extract of building blocks of competence management due to the functions according to project management

Building Blocks of Competence Management						
	Goals	Identification	Acquisition	Development	Utilization	Measuring
Project Management *Functions*	Define request of competencies **FT12**, FT9, FT19, FT4,	Profiling Experts FT22, FT15, FT6, FT16, FT17, FT4, FT2, FT19	Experts Retrieval, Recruiting FT21, FT22, FT4, FT19, **FC13**	Personal development to assign missing competencies FT1, FT4	Assigning of requirements and competencies FT27,**FT12**, FT24, FT6, FT18, FT11, FT3, FT25, FT4, FT20, FT13, **FC13**	Analysis of gaps FT9, FT4, FC11, FC4

System. In our example the tool of the hierarchical tree helped us to work with our ideas and to find substantiated guidelines in order to provide a holistic picture of the system that should be applicable to each context. New perceptions are attained like for example that the system should be capable of dealing with the challenge that characteristics of individual competencies as well as characteristics of the tasks and their activities for a new design are imprecise data that are hard to measure. Another guideline is that the end of our dynamic system should be the realization of the conception of the innovative product or service and not its industrialization.

Furthermore, the hierarchical structure permits us to make the reasoning of the Building Blocks (Table 1) due to the respective functions. A brief extract is shown in Table 3 that highlights the according functions to Project Management. In terms of visualization, functions are not explained in detail. Table 3 helps to get more information about the respective functions. We are focusing on the two beforehand presented functions FT12 and FC13 to give an overview of the use of the table.

With the help of our approach, functions are better described and dedicated as our beforehand presented examples of FT 12 and FC13 shows in the following listing.

- FT12 The system should make sure that the execution of design projects is based on knowledge and skills of the service providers.

  - *Hierarchical Tree: Branch A, Quality*
  - *Building Blocks (Project Management): Goals and Utilization*
- FC13 The system should provide that employees offer voluntary their individual competencies and their disponibilities.

  - *Hierarchical Tree: Branch A, Human Resource,*
  - *Building Blocks (Project Management): Acquisition and Utilization*

Next to the varying percentages of the hierarchical tree, there might be also different priorities concerning the Building Blocks. As the Aided CMVTB System should be applicable to a wide range of organizations in the domain of NPD, as well as to various application domains and to different design projects, the focus could vary according to the priorities of the stakeholder. There might be an organization that likes to concentrate more on the aspect of the different dimensions of the Enterprise Architecture Cube of CEISAR or another one that set the focus on the aspect of the building blocks. This flexibility of varying the point of view permits us to provide a global Aided CMVTB System that is adaptable to each context by pointing out different specific aspects. Important is, that the relation between Building Blocks and the hierarchical tree due to the CEISAR Enterprise Architecture Cube are coherent. That is why the point of view can be handled flexible.

The variations are flexible and depend on the need of the respective organization or design project

FUTURE RESEARCH DIRECTIONS

In further research we aim to determine our Aided CMVTB System. In this work we have defined key functions and their hierarchy that build the framework of our system. In the next step the detected key functions should be realized and translated in applicable solutions that could be implemented in the industrial practice. We are looking for a tool that helps us to find existing concepts and techniques of competence management and virtual team building to realize the key functions. We need a tool that permits to use the fixed importance of the hierarchical tree as fundamental input and to translate the key functions in applicable solution (Schumacher et al. 2009). On the one hand, this helps to find out strengths and weaknesses of the existent concepts and techniques due to the demand of the functions that could be adapted easily to our Aided CMVTB System. On the other hand, through this approach we get information about those functions whose demands are apparently difficult to achieve. Functions that are not satisfied because there are solutions missing in the literature are treated with specific attention. It is up to us to propose concepts and techniques that answer as quality characteristics to the need of the customer requirements.

To be as inclusive as possible we aim to provide an interrogation platform where concepts and techniques of already well-developed methodologies could be consolidated. One of our near-term objectives is to interview experts of the Centre Francilien d'Innovation that are familiar with the work in Virtual Teams to validate the hierarchy of our key functions. In a second steps we will interrogate them about practical concepts and techniques that answer to the needs of our theoretical functions. Those concepts and techniques will be an essential part of our Aided CMVTB System.

They give best practises and recommendations how to build a Virtual Team under consideration of Competence Management.

In a further step the Aided CMVTB System must be applied to the industrial reality and especially to innovative organizations in the domain of new services, processes or product development. It should be applicable to a wide range of organizations in the domain of NPD and to various application domains and to different design projects. The generic aspect of the Aided CMVTB System that is adaptable to each specific context, to each organization or particular design project will help us to apply it to the industrial reality. We are in contact with some of the design projects of the Centre Francilien d'Innovation to validate our model in a future step.

REFERENCES

Apte (2000). La Méthode APTE (®) d'AV/AF, Petrelle.

Archer, N. P. (1990). A comparison of computer conferences with face-to-face meetings for small group business decisions. *Behaviour & Information Technology*, *9*(4), 307–317. doi:10.1080/01449299008924246

Bocquet, J.-C., & Stal-Le Cardinal, J. (2005). Definitions and temporal positioning of concepts linked to decision making in industrial project design- DIKCORAC. *International Conference on Engineering Design, ICED 05*, Melbourne.

Ceisar, E. C. P. (2008, April). Center of Excellence in Enterprise Architecture [White Paper]. *Business Process Modeling*. Retrieved April 6, 2008, from http://www.ceisar.org

Ceisar, E. C. P. (2008, April). Center of Excellence in Enterprise Architecture [White Paper]. *Enterprise Modelling*. Retrieved April 29, 2008, from http://www.ceisar.org

Grenier, R., & Metes, G. (1995). *Going virtual: Moving our organsiation in the 21st Century.* Upper Saddle River, NJ: Prentice Hall.

Griffith, T. L., Sawyer, J. E., & Neale, M. A. (2003). Virtualness and knowledge in teams: Managing the love triangle in organizations. *Management Information Systems Quarterly, 27,* 265–287.

Harzallah, M., & Vernadat, F. (1999). Human resource competency management in enterprise engineering. In *14th IFAC World Congress of Information Control in Manufacturing,* Beijing, China.

Heene, A., & Sanchez, R. (1997). *Competence-based strategy management.* Chichester, UK: Wiley.

Hollingshead, A., McGrath, J., & O'Connor, K. (1993). Group task performance and communication technology: A longitudinal study of computer-mediated versus face-to face groups. *Small Group Research, 24*(3), 307–333. doi:10.1177/1046496493243003

Horvarth, L., & Tobin, T. J. (2001). Twenty-first century teamwork: Defining competencies for Virtual Teams. *Virtual Teams, 8,* 239–258. doi:10.1016/S1572-0977(01)08026-8

Leiponen, A. (2000). Competencies, innovation and profitability of firms . *Economics of Innovation and New Technology, 9,* 1–24. doi:10.1080/10438590000000001

Probst, G., & Romhardt, K. (1999). *Bausteine des Wissensmanagements - ein praxisorientierter Ansatz. Handbuch Lernende Organization.* Wiesbaden: Gabler.

Probst, G. J. B., Raub, S., & Romhardt, K. (1999). *Managing Knowledge.* Berlin, Heidelberg: Springer-Verlag.

Rezgui, Y. (2007). Exploring virtual team-working effectiveness in the construction sector. *Interacting with Computers, 19,* 96–112. doi:10.1016/j.intcom.2006.07.002

Schmidt, J. B., Montoya-Weiss, M. M., & Massey, A. P. (2001). New product development decision-making effectiveness: Comparing individuals, face-to-face teams, and virtual teams. *Decision Sciences, 32*(4). doi:10.1111/j.1540-5915.2001.tb00973.x

Schumacher, M., Le Stal-Cardinal, J., & Bocquet, J. C. (2009). Towards a methodology for managing competencies in virtual teams–A systemic approach . In Camarinha-tos, L. M., Paraskasis, I., & Afsarmanesh, H. (Eds.), *Levering Knowledge for Innovation in Collaborative Networks* (pp. 235–244). Heidelberg: Springer. doi:10.1007/978-3-642-04568-4_25

Schumacher, M., Stal-Le Cardinal, J., & Mekhilef, M. (2008a). Competence Management for Virtual Team Building: A survey. *International Conference on Integrated, Virtual and Interactive Engineering for fostering Industrial Innovation - IDMME 2008,* Peking.

Schumacher, M., Stal-Le Cardinal, J., & Mekhilef, M. (2008b). A Competence Management Methodology for Virtual Teams–A systemic approach to support innovation processes in SMEs. *International Design Conference–Design 2008,* Dubrovnik.

Snodgrass, T. J. (1986). *Function Analysis–The Stepping Stones to Good Value. CVS at KASI; Muthiah.* CVS.

Teece, D. J., Pisano, G., & Shuen, A. (1997). Dynamic capabilities and strategic management. *Strategic Management Journal, 18*(7), 509–533. doi:10.1002/(SICI)1097-0266(199708)18:7<509::AID-SMJ882>3.0.CO;2-Z

Tuma, A. (1998). Configuration and coordination of virtual production networks. *International Journal of Production Economics, 56-57*, 641–648. doi:10.1016/S0925-5273(97)00146-1

Warkentin, M. E., Sayeed, L., & Hightower, R. (1997). Virtual teams versus face-to-face teams: An exploratory study of a web-based conference system. *Decision Sciences, 28*(4), 975–996. doi:10.1111/j.1540-5915.1997.tb01338.x

Webster, J., & Staples, D. S. (2006). Comparing virtual teams to traditional teams: An identification of new research opportunities. *Research in Personnel and Human Resources Management, 25*, 181–215. doi:10.1016/S0742-7301(06)25005-9

Weill, P., Ross, J. W., & Robertson, D. C. (2006). *Enterprise Architecture as a Strategy*. Boston, MA: Harvard Business School Press.

Yosida, K. (1978). *Functional analysis* (5th ed.). Berlin, Heidelberg: Springer-Verlag.

ADDITIONAL READING

Alajoutsijärvi, K., & Tikkanen, H. (2000). Competence-based business processes within industrial networks: A theoretical and empirical analysis. *Advances in Business Marketing and Purchasing, 9*, 1–49. doi:10.1016/S1069-0964(00)09002-5

Alam M., Gale A., Brown, M., & Kidd C. (2008). The development and delivery of an industry led project management professional development programme: A case study in project management education and success management. *International Journal of Project Management.*

Belkadi, F., Bonjour, E., & Dulmet, M. (2007). Competency characterisation by means of work situation modelling. *Computers in Industry, 58*(2), 164–178. doi:10.1016/j.compind.2006.09.005

Berio, G., & Harzallah, M. (2007). Towards an integrating architecture for competence management . *Computers in Industry, 58*, 199–209. doi:10.1016/j.compind.2006.09.007

Coates, T. T., & McDermott, M. C. (2002). An exploratory analysis of new competencies: a resource based view perspective. *Journal of Operations Management, 20*(5), 435–450. doi:10.1016/S0272-6963(02)00023-2

Drejer, A. (2001). How can we define and understand competencies and their development? *Technovation, 21*(3), 135–146. doi:10.1016/S0166-4972(00)00031-6

Erpenbeck, J., & Heyse, V. (1999). *Die Kompetenzbiographie*. Münster: Waxmann.

Harmsen, H., Grunert, K. G., & Bove, K. (2000). Company competencies as a network: the role of product development. *Journal of Product Innovation Management, 17*(3), 194–207. doi:10.1016/S0737-6782(00)00039-4

Harzallah, M., Berio, G., & Vernadat, F. (2006). Analysis and modelling of individual competencies: toward better management of human resources . *IEEE Transactions on Systems, Man, and Cybernetics, 36*(1).

Hollenbeck, G. P., & McCall, M. W. (2003). Competence, not competenvies: making global executive development work. *Advances in Global Leadership, 3*, 101–119. doi:10.1016/S1535-1203(02)03005-8

Jussupova-Mariethoz, Y., & Probst, A.-R. (2007). Business concepts ontology for an enterprise performance and competences monitoring. *Computers in Industry, 58*(2), 118–129. doi:10.1016/j.compind.2006.09.008

Kjellberg, A. (1999). Teams–What's Next? From Fragmentation and Consciousness to Responsiveness by Competence Management for Modular Manufacturing Learning. *CIRP Annals - Manufacturing Technology, 48*(2), 599-609.

Kjellberg, A., & Werneman, A. (2000). Business Innovation–Innovative Teams, Competence Brokers and Beehive Structures–in a Sustainable Work Organization. *CIRP Annals - Manufacturing Technology, 49*(1), 355-358.

Krause, F.-L., Hacker, W., Debitz, U., Kind, C., & Strebel, M. (2006). Competence Management for the Optimisation of Product Development Processes. *CIRP Annals - Manufacturing Technology, 55*(1), 135-138.

Lee-Kelley, L., & Sankey, T. (2008). Global virtual teams for value creation and project success: A case study. *International Journal of Project Management, 26*(1), 51–62. doi:10.1016/j.ijproman.2007.08.010

Martins, L. L., Gilson, L. L., & Maynard, M. T. (2004). Virtual teams: What do we know and where do we go from here? *Journal of Management, 30*(6), 805–835. doi:10.1016/j.jm.2004.05.002

McDonough, E. F. III, Kahn, K. B., & Barczak, G. (2001). An investigation of the use of global, virtual, and colocated new product development team. *Journal of Product Innovation Management, 18*(2), 110–120. doi:10.1016/S0737-6782(00)00073-4

Nicolin, C. (2002). The power of competency in industrial development. *Technology in Society, 5*(3-4), 167–170. doi:10.1016/0160-791X(83)90018-0

Pandian, J. R., & McKiernan, P. (2004). Competence-based management and strategic alliances. *Advances in Applied Business Strategy, 8*, 135–146. doi:10.1016/S0749-6826(04)08006-0

Peña-Mora, F., Hussein, K., Vadhavkar, S., & Benjamin, K. (2001). CAIRO: a concurrent engineering meeting environment for virtual design teams. *Journal of Product Innovation Management, 18*(2), 110–120.

Pépiot, G., Cheikhrouhou, N., Fürbringer, J.-M., & Glardon, R. (2008). A fuzzy approach for the evaluation of competence. *International Journal of Production Economics, 112*(1), 336–353. doi:10.1016/j.ijpe.2006.08.025

Prahalad, C. K., & Hamel, G. (1990). The core competence of the organization . *Harvard Business Review*, 79–91.

Robey, D., Khoo, H., & Powers, C. (2000). Situated learning in cross-functional virtual teams. *IEEE Transactions on Professional Communication, 43*(1), 51–66. doi:10.1109/47.826416

Schumacher, M. (2009). A systemic approach of knowledge development to create service innovation . In Kazi, A. S. (Eds.), *Supporting Service Innovation through Knowledge Management: Practical Insights and Case Studies* (pp. 280–299). Zürich: SKMF and KnowledgeBoard.

Sharma, M., & Raja, V. Fernando, & T. (2006, July). Collaborative design review in a distributed environment. *2nd IPROMS Virtual International Conference* (pp.65-70).

Zülch, G., & Becker, M. (2007). Computer-supported competence management: Evolution of industrial processes as life cycles of organizations. *Computers in Industry, 58*(2), 143–150. doi:10.1016/j.compind.2006.09.012

KEY TERMS AND DEFINITIONS

Virtual Team: Consists of Individuals that act interdependently through technology to achieve a common goal.

Competencies: Are always related to an action and thus established in the moment of knowledge application. From an organizational point of view they are always carried out in a context that is derived from the requirements of a product or a service.

Competence Management: Comprises identification, acquisition, development, and utilization of competencies and is the way how organizations manage the competencies of the organization, teams and individuals by goal-setting and measurement.

Functional Analysis: Functional analysis is a technique of identifying, describing an evaluating functions of an intended system. Each component of an open and living system interacts constantly with its environment. This interaction is recorded in form of functions that give substantiated recommendations about the system.

CEISAR: Center of Excellence in Enterprise Architecture

Enterprise Architecture: Describes how an organization works through the Enterprise Model which covers actors, actions and information and transform it by defining a model that is in line with the organization's strategy and then moving to it.

Hierarchical Tree: Final step of the Functional Analysis that provides a hierarchical structure of the large number o

Compilation of References

Aakhus, M. (2007). Communication as design. Communication Monographs, 74, 112–117. doi:10.1080/03637750701196383

Abrams, (2003). Nurturing interpersonal trust in knowledge-sharing networks. The Academy of Management Executive, 17(4), 64–77.

Adkins, L. (1999). Community and economy: A retraditionalization of gender? Theory, Culture & Society, 16, 119–139.

Adkins, L. (2005). The new economy, property and personhood. Theory, Culture & Society, 22, 111–130. doi:10.1177/0263276405048437

Adler, P. S., & Kwon, S.-W. (2002). Social capital: prospects for a new concept. Academy of Management Review, 22(1), 17–40. doi:10.2307/4134367

Aiello, J. R., & Kolb, K. J. (1995). Electronic performance monitoring: A risk factor for workplace stress . In Stauter, S. L., & Murphy, L. R. (Eds.), Organizational Risk Factors for Job Stress (pp. 163–180). Washington, D.C.: American Psychological Association. doi:10.1037/10173-010

Alder, G. S. (1998). Ethical issues in electronic performance monitoring: A consideration of deontological and teleological perspectives. Journal of Business Ethics, 17, 729–743. doi:10.1023/A:1005776615072

Alder, G. S., Noel, T. W., & Ambrose, M. L. (2006). Clarifying the effects of internet monitoring on job attitudes: The mediating role of employee trust. Information & Management, 43, 894–903. doi:10.1016/j.im.2006.08.008

Alder, G. S., Schminke, M., & Noel, T. W. (2007). The Impact of Individual Ethics on Reactions to Potentially Invasive HR Practices. Journal of Business Ethics, 75(2), 201. doi: 1337619411.

Alexander, P. M. (2002). Teamwork, time, trust and information. [ACM.]. SAICSIT, 2002, 65–74.

Alexander, S. C., Peterson, J. L., & Hollingshead, A. B. (2003). Help is at your keyboard: Support groups on the internet . In Frey, L. R. (Ed.), Group communication in context: Studies of bona fide groups (pp. 309–335). Hillsdale, NJ: Lawrence Erlbaum Associates.

Allen, T. J. (1977). Managing the flow of technology: Technology transfer and the dissemination of technological information within the R&D organization. Cambridge, MA: MIT Press.

Alvesson, M. (2001). Knowledge work: Ambiguity, image, and identity. Human Relations, 54, 863–886. doi:10.1177/0018726701547004

Alvesson, M., & Willmott, H. (2002). Identity regulation as organizational control: Producing the appropriate individual. Journal of Management Studies, 39, 619–644. doi:10.1111/1467-6486.00305

Amason, A. (1996). Distinguishing the effects of functional and dysfunctional conflict on strategic decision making: Resolving a paradox for top management teams. Academy of Management Journal, 39, 123–148. doi:10.2307/256633

Ambrose, M., Arnaud, A., & Schminke, M. (2008, February). Individual moral development and ethical climate: The influence of person-organization fit on job attitudes. Journal of Business Ethics, 77(3), 323–333. .doi:10.1007/s10551-007-9352-1

American Management Association. (2006). 2006 Workplace E-Mail, Instant Messaging & Blog Survey. New York: Author.

Amick, B. C., & Smith, M. J. (1992). Stress, computer-based work monitoring and measurement systems: A conceptual overview. Applied Ergonomics, 23(11), 6–16. doi:10.1016/0003-6870(92)90005-G

Anand, V., Clark, M. A., & Zellmer-Bruhn, M. (2003). Team knowledge structures: Matching task to information environment. Journal of Managerial Issues, 15(1), 15–31.

Anawati, D., & Craig, A. (2006). Behavioral adaptation with cross-cultural virtual teams. IEEE Transactions on Professional Communication, 49(1), 44–56. doi:10.1109/TPC.2006.870459

Andersen, J. (1979). Teacher immediacy as a predictor of teaching effectiveness . In Nimmo, D. (Ed.), Communication yearbook 3 (pp. 543–559). New Brunswick, NJ: Transaction Books.

Anderson, A. H., McEwan, R., Bal, J., & Carletta, J. (2007). Virtual team meetings: An analysis of communication and context. Computers in Human Behavior, 23, 2558–2580. doi:10.1016/j.chb.2007.01.001

Andrews, D., & Starke-Meyerring, D. (2005). Making connections: An intercultural virtual team project in professional communication. In 2005 IEEE International Professional Communication Conference Proceedings (pp. 26-31). IEEE.

Anson, R., & Munkvold, B. E. (2004). Beyond face-to-face: A field study of electronic meetings in different time and place modes. Journal of Organizational Computing and Electronic Commerce, 14, 127–152. doi:10.1207/s15327744joce1402_03

Apte (2000). La Méthode APTE (®) d'AV/AF, Petrelle.

Arbaugh, J. B. (2001). How instructor immediacy behaviors affect student satisfaction and learning in web-based courses. Business Communication Quarterly, 64, 42–54. doi:10.1177/108056990106400405

Archer, N. P. (1990). A comparison of computer conferences with face-to-face meetings for small group business decisions. Behaviour & Information Technology, 9(4), 307–317. doi:10.1080/01449299008924246

Argandona, A. (2003). The new economy: Ethical issues. Journal of Business Ethics, 44(1), 3-22. doi: 470202181.

Arrow, H., & Cook, J. (2007). Configuring and reconfiguring groups as complex learning systems . In Sessa, V. I., & London, M. (Eds.), Work group learning: Understanding, improving and assessing how groups learn in organizations (pp. 45–72). Boca Raton, FL: CRC Press/ Lawrence Erlbaum.

Ashforth, B. E., & Kreiner, G. E. (1999). "How can you do it?": Dirty work and the challenge of constructing a positive identity. Academy of Management Review, 24(3), 413–434. doi:10.2307/259134

Aubert, B. A., & Kelsey, B. L. (2003). Further understanding of trust and performance in virtual teams. Small Group Research, 34, 574–618. doi:10.1177/1046496403256011

Auerbach, C. F., & Silverstein, L. B. (2003). Qualitative data: An introduction to coding and analysis. New York: New York University Press.

Axelrod, R. (1984). The evolution of cooperation. New York: Basic Books.

Ba, S. (2001). Establishing online trust through a community responsibility system. Decision Support Systems, 31(4), 323–336. doi:10.1016/S0167-9236(00)00144-5

Bachmann, R. (2001). Trust, power and control in trans-organizational relations. Organization Studies, 22(2), 337–365. doi:10.1177/0170840601222007

Baier, A. (1986). Trust and antitrust. Ethics, 96, 231–260. doi:10.1086/292745

Bailey, D. E., & Kurland, N. B. (2002). A review of telework research: Findings, new directions and lessons for the study of modern work. Journal of Organizational Behavior, 23, 383–400. doi:10.1002/job.144

Bain, P., & Taylor, P. (2000). Entrapped by the 'electronic panopticon:' Worker resistance in the call centre. New Technology, Work and Employment, 15(1), 2–18. doi:10.1111/1468-005X.00061

Baker, C. (2004). Membership categorization and interview accounts . In Silverman, D. (Ed.), Qualitative research: Theory, method, practice (2nd ed., pp. 162–176). London: Sage.

Baker, P. M. A., Moon, N. W., & Ward, A. C. (2006). Virtual exclusion and telework: Barriers and opportunities of technocentric workplace accommodation policy. Work (Reading, Mass.), 27, 421–430.

Bakhtin, M. M. (1981). The dialogic imagination: Four essays (Holquist, M., Trans.). Austin, TX: University of Texas Press.

Baldwin, G. (1994). The student as customer: The discourse of 'quality' in higher education. Journal of Tertiary Educational Administration, 16, 125–133.

Balthazard, P. A., Potter, R. E., & Warren, J. (2002). The effects of extraversion and expertise on virtual team interaction and performance. In Proceedings of the 35th Hawaii International Conference on System Sciences. IEEE.

Bandura, A. (1989). Social cognitive theory . In Vasta, R. (Ed.), Annals of Child Development (pp. 1–60). Greenwich, CT: Jai Press LTD.

Bansler, J. P., & Havn, E. (2003). Technology-use mediation: Making sense of electronic communication in an organizational context. [Sanibel Island, Florida. ACM.]. Group, 03, 135–143.

Barett, A. (2008, October 17). Making telecommuting work. Business Week SmallBiz. Retrieved September 29, 2009, from http://www.businessweek.com/magazine/content/08_70/s0810048750962.htm?chan=smallbiz_smallbiz+index+page_best+of+small+biz+magazine

Bargh, J. A., & Ferguson, M. J. (2000). Beyond behaviorism: On the automaticity of higher mental processes. Psychological Bulletin, 126, 925–945. doi:10.1037/0033-2909.126.6.925

Barker, J. R., & Cheney, G. (1994). The concept and the practices of discipline in contemporary organizational life. Communication Monographs, 61, 19–43. doi:10.1080/03637759409376321

Barnes, S. B. (2002). Computer-mediated communication: Human-to-human communication across the Internet. Boston: Allyn & Bacon.

Barnes, S. B. (2006). Internet interpersonal relationships . In Galvin, K. M., & Cooper, P. J. (Eds.), Making connections: Readings in relational communication (4th ed., pp. 347–354). Los Angeles, CA: Roxbury.

Barney, J. B., & Hansen, M. H. (1994). Trustworthiness as a source of competitive advantage. Strategic Management Journal: Special Issue, 15, 175. doi: 8926192.

Baruch, Y. (2001). The state of research on teleworking and an agenda for future research. International Journal of Management Reviews, 3, 113–129. doi:10.1111/1468-2370.00058

Baskerville, R., & Nandhakumar, J. (2007). Activating and perpetuating virtual teams: Now that we're mobile, where do we go? IEEE Transactions on Professional Communication, 50(1), 17–34. doi:10.1109/TPC.2006.890849

Bass, B. (1990). Bass & Stogdill's handbook of leadership: Theory, research & managerial Applications (3rd ed., pp. 682–683). New York: The Free Press.

Baxter, L. A., & Montgomery, B. M. (1996). Relating: Dialogues & dialectics. New York: Guildford Press.

Bayerl, P. S., & Lauche, K. (2008). Coordinating high-interdependency tasks in asymmetric distributed teams. In CSCW '08 (pp. 417-426). San Diego, California. 4

Baym, N. (1997). Interpreting soap operas and creating community: Inside an electronic fan culture . In Keisler, S. (Ed.), Culture of the Internet (pp. 103–120). Manhaw, NJ: Lawrence Erlbaum Associates.

Bazerman, C., & Prior, P. (Eds.), What writing does and how it does it: An introduction to analyzing texts and textual practices. Mahwah, NJ: Lawrence Earlbaum.

Beatty, M. J., & Beatty, P. J. (1976). Interpersonal communication anxiety. Theory into Practice, 15, 368–372. doi:10.1080/00405847609542660

Beise, C. M. (2004). IT project management and virtual teams. In SIGMIS '04 (pp. 129-133). Tuscon, Arizona. ACM.

Bekkers, V. (2003). E-governments and the emergence of virtual organizations in the public sector. The International Journal of Government and Democracy in the Information Age, 8(3-4), 89–101.

Belanger, F., & Allport, C. D. (2008). Collaborative technologies in knowledge telework: An exploratory study. Information Systems Journal, 18(1), 101–121. doi:10.1111/j.1365-2575.2007.00252.x

Bell, B. S., & Kozlowski, S. J. (2002). A typology of virtual teams: Implications for effective leadership. Group & Organization Management, 27, 14–49. doi:10.1177/1059601102027001003

Bell, C. R. (2000). The mentor as partner. Training & Development, 54, 52–56.

Bennett, J., & Bush, M. (2009). Coaching in organizations. Od Practitioner, 41(1), 2–7.

Benoit, A. A., & Kelsey, B. L. (2003). Further understanding of trust and performance in virtual teams. Small Group Research, 34, 575–618. doi:10.1177/1046496403256011

Bentham, J. (1791). Outline for the construction of a panopticon penitentiary house . In Mack, M. (Ed.), A Bentham Reader. New York: Pegasus.

Bentham, J. (1995). The Panopticon Writings. (Miran Bozovic, Ed.; pp. 29-95). London: Verso.

Beranek, P. M. (2005). A comparison of relational and trust training techniques for virtual team communication: How much training is enough? In Proceedings of the 38th Hawaii International Conference on System Sciences 2005 (pp. 1-10). IEEE.

Berger, C. R., & Calabrese, R. J. (1975). Some explorations in initial interaction and beyond: Toward a developmental theory of interpersonal communication. Human Communication Research, 1, 99–112. doi:10.1111/j.1468-2958.1975.tb00258.x

Berger, J., Cohen, B. P., & Zelditch, M. Jr. (1972). Status characteristics and social interaction. American Sociological Review, 37, 241–255. doi:10.2307/2093465

Berger, J., Rosenholtz, S. J., & Zelditch, M. Jr. (1980). Status organizing processes. Annual Review of Sociology, 6, 479–508. doi:10.1146/annurev.so.06.080180.002403

Berger, P. L., & Luckmann, T. (1967). The social construction of reality: A treatise in the sociology of knowledge. New York: Anchor.

Bergquist, M., & Ljungberg, J. (2001). The power of gifts: Organizing social relationships in open source communities. Information Systems Journal, 11(4), 305–320. doi:10.1046/j.1365-2575.2001.00111.x

Bierema, L. L., & Hill, J. R. (2005). Virtual mentoring and hrd. Advances in Developing Human Resources, 7(7), 556. doi:10.1177/1523422305279688

Biuk-Aghai, R. P., & Simoff, S. J. (2001). An integrative framework for knowledge extraction in collaborative virtual environments. [Boulder, Colorado. ACM.]. Group, 01, 61–70.

Bixoux, T. (2009). Making connections. BizEd, January/February, 16-22.

Black, D. (1976). The behavior of law. New York: Academic Press.

Black, D. (1984). Social control as a dependent variable . In Black, D. (Ed.), Toward a general theory of social control (Vol. 1, pp. 1–36). New York: Academic Press.

Blalock, H. (1957). Percent non-white and discrimination in the South. American Sociological Review, 22, 677–682. doi:10.2307/2089197

Blanchard, A. L. (2004a). Blogs as Virtual Communities: Identifying sense of community in the Julie/Julia Project . In Gurak, L., Antonijevic, S., Johnson, L., Ratliff, C., & Reyman, J. (Eds.), Into the Blogosphere: Rhetoric. Community and Culture.

Blanchard, A. L. (2004b). The effects of dispersed virtual communities on face-to-face social capital . In Huysman, M., & Wulf, V. (Eds.), Social Capital and Information Technology (pp. 53–74). Cambridge: MIT Press.

Blanchard, A. L. (2008). Testing a model of sense of virtual community. Computers in Human Behavior, 24(5), 2107–2123. doi:10.1016/j.chb.2007.10.002

Blanchard, A. L., & Markus, M. L. (2004). The experienced "sense" of a virtual community: Characteristics and processes. The Data Base for Advances in Information Systems, 35(1), 65–79.

Blau, P. M. (1977). Inequality and heterogeneity. New York: Free Press.

Bobek, D., & Radtke, R. (2007, Fall). 2007). An experiential investigation of tax professionals' ethical environments. [from Business Source Complete database.]. Journal of the American Taxation Association, 29(2), 63–84. Retrieved April 19, 2009. doi:10.2308/jata.2007.29.2.63

Bocquet, J.-C., & Stal-Le Cardinal, J. (2005). Definitions and temporal positioning of concepts linked to decision making in industrial project design- DIKCOR-AC. International Conference on Engineering Design, ICED 05, Melbourne.

Bogenrieder, I., & Nooteboom, B. (2004). Learning groups: What types are there? A theoretical analysis and an empirical study in a consultancy firm. Organization Studies, 25(2), 287–313. doi:10.1177/0170840604040045

Bordia, P. (1997). Face-to-face versus computer-mediated communication: a synthesis of the experimental literature. Journal of Business Communication, 34(1), 99–120. doi:10.1177/002194369703400106

Bordia, P., DiFonzo, N., & Chang, A. (1999). Rumor as group problem solving: Development patterns in informal computer-mediated groups. Small Group Research, 30, 8–28. doi:10.1177/104649649903000102

Bormann, E. G. (1980). Communication theory. New York: Holt, Rinehart & Winston.

Bos, N., Olson, J., Cheshin, A., Kim, Y.-S., Nan, N., & Shami, N. S. (2005). Traveling blues: The effect of relocation on partially distributed teams. In CHI 2005 (pp. 1917-1920). Portland, Oregon. ACM.

Bos, N., Shami, N. S., Olson, J. S., Cheshin, A., & Nan, N. (2004). In-group / out-group effects in distributed teams: An experimental simulation. In CSCW '04 (pp. 429-436). Chicago, Illinois. ACM.

Boshier, R., & Onn, C. M. (2000). Discursive constructions of Web learning and education. Journal of Distance Education, 15, 1–16.

Boule, M. (2008). Best practices for working in a virtual team environment. Library Technology Reports, 44(1), 28–31.

Boyer, E. (1990). Scholarship reconsidered: Priorities of the professoriate. Princeton, NJ: Carnegie Foundation for the Advancement of Teaching.

Brady, F. N. (1985). A Janus-headed model of ethical theory: Looking two ways at business/society issues. Academy of Management Review, 10, 568–576. doi:10.2307/258137

Brady, F. N., & Wheeler, G. E. (1996). An empirical study of ethical predispositions. Journal of Business Ethics, 15, 927–940. doi:10.1007/BF00705573

Brief, A. P., Dukerich, P. R., & Doran, L. I. (1991). Resolving ethical dilemmas in management: Experimental investigations of values, accountability, and choice'. Journal of Applied Social Psychology, 21, 380–396. doi:10.1111/j.1559-1816.1991.tb00526.x

Brien, A. (1998). Professional ethics and the culture of trust. Journal of Business Ethics, 17(4), 391-409. doi:27409633.

Brown, J. S., & Duguid, P. (2002). Local knowledge: Innovation in the networked age. Management Learning, 33(4), 427–438. doi:10.1177/1350507602334002

Bruhn, J. (2001). Trust and health of organizations. New York: Kluwer.

Bullis, C., & Bach, B. W. (1989). Socialization turning points: An examination of change in organizational identification. Western Journal of Speech Communication, 53, 273–293.

Burgoon, J. K., & Hoobler, G. D. (2002). Nonverbal signals . In Knapp, M. L., & Miller, G. R. (Eds.), Handbook on Interpersonal Communication (3rd ed., pp. 240–299). Thousand Oaks, CA: Sage.

Burroughs, S. M., & Eby, L. T. (1998). Psychological sense of community at work: A measurement system and explanatory framework. Journal of Community Psychology, 26(6), 509–532. doi:10.1002/(SICI)1520-6629(199811)26:6<509::AID-JCOP1>3.0.CO;2-P

Byrne, D. (1971). The attraction paradigm. New York: Academic Press.

Cambell, J. E., & Carlson, M. (2002). Panopticon. com: Online surveillance and the commodification of privacy [Electronic version]. *Journal of Broadcasting & Electronic Media, 46,* 586–606. doi:10.1207/s15506878jobem4604_6

Carlone, D. (2008). The contradictions of communicative labor in service work. *Communication and Critical . Cultural Studies, 5,* 158–179.

Carlson, J. R., & Zmud, R. W. (1999). Channel expansion theory and the experiential nature of media richness perceptions. *Academy of Management Journal, 42,* 153–170. doi:10.2307/257090

Carte, T. A., Chidambaram, L., & Becker, A. (2006). Emergent leadership in self-managed virtual teams. *Group Decision and Negotiation, 15,* 323–343. doi:10.1007/s10726-006-9045-7

Casey, V., & Richardson, I. (2006). Project management within virtual software teams. Paper presented at IEEE International Conference on Global Software Engineering.

Casey, V., & Richardson, I. (2006). Uncovering the reality within virtual software teams. In GSD '06 (pp. 66-72). Shanghai, China. ACM.

Casey, V., & Richardson, I. (2008). The impact of fear on the operation of virtual teams. In 2008 IEEE International Conference on Global Software Engineering. ICGSE 2008 (pp. 163-172). IEEE.

Castor, T. (2007). Language use during school board meetings: Understanding controversies of and about communication. *Journal of Business Communication, 44,* 111–136. doi:10.1177/0021943606298828

Ceisar, E. C. P. (2008, April). Center of Excellence in Enterprise Architecture [White Paper]. Business Process Modeling. Retrieved April 6, 2008, from http://www.ceisar.org

Chan, A., & Garrick, J. (2003). The moral "technologies" of knowledge management. *Information Communication and Society, 6,* 291–306. doi:10.1080/1369118032000155258

Chan, S. (2002). Getting the virtual work contract done - Practicalities and organizational dynamics. *Employment Relations Today, 28*(4), 27-35. doi: 108932704.

Chang, K. T., & Ehrlich, K. (2007). Out of sight but not out of mind? Informal networks, communication and media use in global software teams (pp. 1-12). IBM Corporation. Chen, Z., Zhang, X., Vogel, D., & Zhao, D. (2009). Encouraging knowledge sharing in global virtual teams: The interaction effect of individual difference and perceived sharing benefits. In Proceedings of the 42nd Hawaii International Conference on System Sciences (pp. 1-10).

Charmaz, K. (2000). Grounded theory: objectivist and constructivist methods . In Denzin, N. K., & Lincoln, Y. S. (Eds.), Handbook of qualitative research (pp. 509–535). Thousand Oaks, CA: Sage.

Chavis, D. M., & Pretty, G. H. (1999). Sense of community: Advances in measurement and application. *Journal of Community Psychology, 27*(6), 635–642. doi:10.1002/(SICI)1520-6629(199911)27:6<635::AID-JCOP1>3.0.CO;2-F

Chen, A.Y. S., Sawyers, R. B.,& Williams, P. F. (1997). Reinforcing ethical decision making through corporate culture. *Journal of Business Ethics, 16*(8), 855-865. doi: 12622777.

Cheney, G. (1983). The rhetoric of identification and the study of organizational communication. *The Quarterly Journal of Speech, 69,* 145–158. doi:10.1080/00335638309383643

Cheney, G., McMillan, J. J., & Schwartzman, R. (1997). Should we buy the 'student-as-consumer' metaphor? *The Montana Professor, 8*(3), 8–11.

Chidambaram, L. (1996). Relational development in computer-supported groups. *Management Information Systems Quarterly, 20*(2), 143–165. doi:10.2307/249476

Chiu, C.-M., Hsu, M.-H., & Wang, E. T. G. (2006). Understanding knowledge sharing in virtual communities: An integration of social capital and social cognitive theories. *Decision Support Systems, 42*(3), 1872–1888. doi:10.1016/j.dss.2006.04.001

Chowdhury, S. (2005). The role of affect- and cognition-based trust in complex knowledge sharing. *Journal of Managerial Issues, 17*(3), 310–326.

Christophel, J. L. (1990). The relationships among teacher immediacy behaviors, student motivation and learning. Communication Education, 39, 323–340. doi:10.1080/03634529009378813

Chudoba, K. M., Wynn, E., Lu, M., & Watson-Manheim, M. B. (2005). How virtual are we? Measuring virtuality and understanding its impact on a global organization. Information Systems Journal, 15, 279–306. doi:10.1111/j.1365-2575.2005.00200.x

Churchill, E. F., & Bly, S. (1999). It's all in the words: Supporting work activities with lightweight tools. [Phoenix, Arizona. ACM.]. Group, 99, 40–49.

Clark, K. B., & Wheelwright, S. C. (1992). Organising and leading heavyweight development teams. California Management Review, (34): 9–28.

Clear, T., & Kassabova, D. (2005). Motivational patterns in virtual team collaboration. Australasian Computing Education Conference 2005. New Castle, Australia. Conferences in Research and Practice in Information Technology, 42, 51 – 58.

Cohen, B. P., & Zhou, X. (1991). Status processes in enduring work groups. American Sociological Review, 56, 179–188. doi:10.2307/2095778

Cohen, S. G., & Bailey, D. E. (1997). What makes teams work: Group effectiveness research from the shop floor to the executive suite. Journal of Management, 23(3), 239–290. doi:10.1177/014920639702300303

Connaughton, S. L., & Daly, J. A. (2003). Long distance leadership: Communicative strategies for leading virtual teams . In Pauleen, D. J. (Ed.), Virtual teams: Projects, protocols, and processes (pp. 116–144). Hershey, PA: Idea Group Inc.

Connaughton, S. L., & Daly, J. A. (2004). Leading from afar: Strategies for effectively leading virtual teams . In Godar, S. H., & Ferris, S. P. (Eds.), Virtual and collaborative teams: Process, technologies, and practice (pp. 49–75). Hershey, PA: Idea Group Publishing.

Connaughton, S. L., & Daly, J. A. (2005). Leadership in the new millennium: Communicating beyond temporal, spatial, and geographical boundaries . In Kalbfleisch, P. (Ed.), Communication yearbook, 29 (pp. 187–213). Mahwah, NJ: Erlbaum.

Connaughton, S. L., & Shuffler, M. (2007). Multinational multicultural distributed teams: A review and future agenda. Small Group Research, 38, 387–412. doi:10.1177/1046496407301970

Conrad, C., & Poole, M. S. (2002). Strategic organizational communication in a global economy (5th ed.). Ft. Worth, TX: Harcourt.

Constant, D., Sproull, L., & Kiesler, S. (1996). The kindness of strangers: On the usefulness of electronic weak ties for technical advice. Organization Science, 7(2), 119–135. doi:10.1287/orsc.7.2.119

Conway, M., Pizzamiglio, M. T., & Mount, L. (1996). Status, communality, and agency: Implications for stereotypes of gender and other groups. Journal of Personality and Social Psychology, 71, 25–38. doi:10.1037/0022-3514.71.1.25

Cooley, C. H. (1902). Human nature and the social order. New York: Scribner's.

Corbin, J., & Strauss, A. (2008). Basics of qualitative research (3rd ed.). Thousand Oaks, CA: Sage.

Corbitt, G., Gardiner, L. R., & Wright, L. K. (2004). A comparison of team developmental stages, trust, and performance for virtual versus face-to-face teams. In Proceedings of the 37th Hawaii International Conference on System Sciences (pp. 1-8). IEEE.

Cordes, R. E., & Spine, T. M. (2007). Transcending organizational boundaries: Virtual team approach in UI guideline development. Paper presented at CHIMIT '07. Cambridge, Massachusetts. ACM.

Corman, S. R. (2006). On being less theoretical and more technological in organizational communication. Journal of Business and Technical Communication, 20, 325–338. doi:10.1177/1050651906287256

Cramton, C. D. (2001). The mutual knowledge problem and its consequences for dispersed collaboration. Organization Science, 12, 346–371. doi:10.1287/orsc.12.3.346.10098

Cramton, C. D. (2002). Finding common ground in dispersed collaboration. Organizational Dynamics, 30, 356–367. doi:10.1016/S0090-2616(02)00063-3

Cramton, C. D., & Hinds, P. J. (2004). Subgroup dynamics in internationally distributed teams: Ethnocentrism or cross-national learning? Research in Organizational Behavior, 26, 231–263. doi:10.1016/S0191-3085(04)26006-3

Cranford, M. (1996). The social trajectory of virtual reality: Substantive ethics in a world without constraints. Technology & Society, 18(1), 79–92. doi:10.1016/0160-791X(95)00023-K

Creswell, J. W. (2003). Research design: Qualitative, quantitative, and mixed methods approaches (2nd ed.). Thousand Oaks, CA: Sage.

Cropanzano, R., & Mitchell, M. S. (2005). Social exchange theory: An interdisciplinary review. Journal of Management, 31(6), 874–900. doi:10.1177/0149206305279602

Cross, R. '. L. (2002). The people who make organizations go – or stop. Harvard Business Review, 80(6), 104–112.

Crossman, A., & Lee-Kelley, L. (2004). Trust, commitment and team working: The paradox of virtual organizations. Global Networks, 4, 375–390. doi:10.1111/j.1471-0374.2004.00099.x

Crowston, K., Howison, J., Masango, C., & Eseryel, U. Y. (2007). The role of face-to-face meetings in technology-supported self-organizing distributed teams. IEEE Transactions on Professional Communication, 50(2), 185–203. doi:10.1109/TPC.2007.902654

Culnan, M. J., & Markus, M. L. (1987). Information technologies. In F. M. Jablin, L.L. Putnam, L.L., K. H. Roberts, et al. (eds.), Handbook of organizational communication: An interdisciplinary perspective. Newbury Park, CA: Sage, pp. 420–443.

Cummings, J. (2009, February 5). Obama losing stimulus message war. Politico. Retrieved February 5, 2009, from http://www.politico.com/news/stories/0209/18444.html

Cummings, L. L., & Bromiley, P. (1996). The Organizational Trust Inventory (OTI): Development and validation . In Kramer, R. M., & Tyler, T. R. (Eds.), Trust in organizations: Frontiers of theory and research (pp. 302–330). Thousand Oaks, CA: Sage Publications.

Cunningham, G. B., & Chelladurai, P. (2004). Affective reactions to cross-functional teams: The impact of size, relative performance, and common in-group identity. Group Dynamics, 8(2), 83–97. doi:10.1037/1089-2699.8.2.83

Currid, E. (2007). The Warhol economy: How fashion, art, and music drive New York City. Princeton, NJ: Princeton University Press.

Curseu, P. L., Schruijer, S., & Boros, S. (2007). The effects of groups' variety and disparity on groups' cognitive complexity. Group Dynamics, 11(3), 187–206. doi:10.1037/1089-2699.11.3.187

Curtis, F. (2001). Ivy-covered exploitation: Class, education, and the liberal arts college . In Gibson-Graham, J. K., Resnick, S., & Wolff, R. (Eds.), Re/Presenting class: Essays in postmodern Marxism (pp. 81–104). Durham, NC: Duke.

Cutrona, C. E., & Russell, D. W. (1990). Type of social support and specific stress: Toward a theory of optimal matching . In Sarason, I. G., Sarason, B. R., & Pierce, G. R. (Eds.), Social support: An interactional view (pp. 319–366). Oxford, England: John Wiley & Sons.

D'Urso, S. C. (2006). Toward a structural-perceptual model of electronic monitoring and surveillance in organizations. Communication Theory, 16, 281–303. doi:10.1111/j.1468-2885.2006.00271.x

Da Silva, E. J., de Souza, C. S., Prates, R. O., & Nicolaci-da-Costa, A. M. (2003). What they want and what they get: A study of light-weight technologies for online communities. ACM International Conference Proceeding Series, 46, 135-146. Rio de Janeiro, Brazil. Retrieved Apr. 12, 2009, from http://delivery.acm.org/10.1145/950000/944534/p135-silva.pdf?key1=944534&key2=6531759321&coll=GUIDE&dl=GUIDE&CFID=30071228&CFTOKEN=14469905.

Dabbish, L. A. (2008). Jumpstarting relationships with online games: Evidence form a laboratory investigation. In CSCW '08 (pp. 353-356). San Diego, California.

Daft, R. L., & Lengel, R. H. (1984). Information richness: A new approach to managerial information processing and organization design . In Cummings, L. L., & Staw, B. M. (Eds.), Research in organizational behavior (Vol. 6, pp. 191–234). Greenwich, CT: JAI Press.

Daft, R. L., & Lengel, R. H. (1986). Organizational information requirements, media richness, and structural design. Management Science, 32, 554–571. doi:10.1287/mnsc.32.5.554

Daft, R. L., & Lengel, R. K. (1984). Information richness: A new approach to managerial information processing and organizational design . In Cummings, L. L., & Staw, B. M. (Eds.), Research in organizational behavior (pp. 191–234). Greenwich, CT: JAI.

Darwin, A. (2000). Critical reflections on mentoring in work settings. Adult Education Quarterly, 50(3), 197. doi:10.1177/07417130022087008

Dasgupta, P. (1988). Trust as a commodity . In Gambetta, D. (Ed.), Trust: Making and breaking cooperative relations (pp. 47–72). New York: Basil Blackwell.

De Koster, W., & Houtman, D. (2008). 'Stormfront is like a second home to me': On virtual community formation by right-wing extremists. Information . Communication and Technology, 11(8), 1155–1176.

De Lara, P. Z. M. (2006). Fear in organizations: Does intimidation by formal punishment mediate the relationship between interactional justice and workplace internet deviance? Journal of Managerial Psychology, 21(6), 580–592. doi:10.1108/02683940610684418

De Pillis, E., & Furumo, K. (2007). Counting the costs of virtual teams: Studying the performance, satisfaction, and group dynamics of virtual and face-to-face teams. Communications of the ACM, 50(12), 93–95.

Deetz, S. A. (1992). Democracy in an age of corporate colonization: Developments in communication and the politics of everyday life. Albany, NY: SUNY Press.

Deetz, S. A. (1995). Transforming communication, transforming business: Building responsive and responsible workplaces. Cresskill, NJ: Hampton.

Deetz, S. A. (1998). Discursive formations, strategized subordination and self-surveillance . In McKinley, A., & Starkey, K. (Eds.), Foucault, management and organizational theory (pp. 151–172). London: Sage.

Dekker, D. M., & Rutte, C. G. (2007). Effective versus ineffective communication behaviors in virtual teams. In Proceedings of the 40th Hawaii International Conference on System Sciences (pp. 1-10). IEEE.

Dekker, D. M., Rutte, C. G., & Van den Berg, P. T. (2008). Cultural differences in the perception of critical interaction behaviors in global virtual teams. International Journal of Intercultural Relations, 32, 441–452. doi:10.1016/j.ijintrel.2008.06.003

DePaulo, P. J., DePaulo, B. M., Tang, J., & Swaim, G. (1989). Lying and detecting lies in the organization . In Giacalone, R. A., & Rosenfeld, P. (Eds.), Impression management in the organization (pp. 377–396). Hillsdale, NJ: Erlbaum.

DeSanctis, G., & Poole, M. S. (1994). Capturing the complexity in advanced technology use: Adaptive structuration theory. Organization Science, 5, 121–147. doi:10.1287/orsc.5.2.121

DeSanctis, G., Poole, M. S., & Zigurs, I. (2008). The Minnesota GDSS research project: Group support systems, group processes, and group outcomes. Journal of the Association for Information Systems, 9, 551–608.

Deshpande, S., & Joseph, J. (2009, April). Impact of emotional intelligence, ethical climate, and behavior of peers on ethical behavior of nurses. Journal of Business Ethics, 85(3), 403–410. .doi:10.1007/s10551-008-9779-z

Dixon, N. M. (2000). Common knowledge: How companies thrive by sharing what they know. Boston, MA: Harvard Business School Press.

Donaldson, S. A. (2002). Who should work from home? Black Enterprise, 33(1), 42.

Donker, H., & Blumberg, M. (2008). Collaborative process management and virtual teams. In CHASE '08 (pp. 41-43). Leipzig, Germany. ACM.

Douglas, P.C., Davidson, R. A., & Schwartz, B.N. (2001). The effect of organizational culture and ethical orientation on accountants' ethical judgements. Journal of Business Ethics, 34(2), 101-121. doi: 90060318.

Draves, W. A. (2000). Teaching online. River Falls, WI: LERN Books.

Driskell, J. E., Goodwin, G. F., Salas, E., & O'Shea, P. G. (2006). What makes a good team player? Personality and team effectiveness. Group Dynamics, 10(4), 249–271. doi:10.1037/1089-2699.10.4.249

Driskell, J. E., Radtke, P. H., & Salas, E. (2003). Virtual teams: Effects of technological mediation on team performance. Group Dynamics, 7, 297–323. doi:10.1037/1089-2699.7.4.297

du Gay, P. (1996). Consumption and identity at work. London: Sage.

Duarte, D., & Snyder, N. (2006). Mastering virtual teams: Strategies, tools, and techniques that succeed (3rd ed.). San Francisco, CA: John Wiley & Sons, Inc.

Dube, L., & Pare, G. (2004). The multifaceted nature of virtual teams . In Pauleen, D. J. (Ed.), Virtual teams: Projects, protocols, and processes (pp. 1–39). Hershey, PA: Idea Group Publishing.

DuBrin, A. J. (1991). Comparison of the job satisfaction and productivity of telecommuters versus in-house employees: A research note on work in progress. Psychological Reports, 68, 1223–1234. doi:10.2466/PR0.68.4.1223-1234

Durst, R., & Kabel, D. (2001). Cross-functional teams in a concurrent engineering environment: Principles, model, and methods . In Beyerlein, M. M., Johnson, D. A., & Beyerlein, S. T. (Eds.), Advances in interdisciplinary studies of work teams: Virtual teams (8th ed., pp. 167–214). Greenwich, CT: JAI.

Ehsan, N., Mirza, E., & Ahmad, M. (2008). Impact of computer-mediated communication on virtual teams' performance: An empirical study. IEEE.

Eisenberg, E. (2007). Strategic ambiguities: Essays on communication, organization, and identity. Thousand Oaks, CA: Sage.

Eisenberg, E. M. (1984). Ambiguity as strategy in organizational communication. Communication Monographs, 51, 227–242. doi:10.1080/03637758409390197

Ellis, J.B., Luther, K., Bessiere, K., & Kellogg, W.A. (2008). Games for virtual team building.

Ellison, N. B. (1999). Social impacts: New perspectives on telework. Social Science Computer Review, 17, 338–356. doi:10.1177/089443939901700308

Elron, R., & Vigoda-Gadot, E. (2006). Influence and political processes in cyberspace: The case of global virtual teams. International Journal of Cross Cultural Management, 6, 295–317. doi:10.1177/1470595806070636

Farrell, D., & Petersen, J. C. (1982). Patterns of political behavior in organizations. Academy of Management Review, 7, 403–412. doi:10.2307/257332

Feldman, D. C. (1984). The development and enforcement of group norms. Academy of Management Review, 9, 47–53. doi:10.2307/258231

Fernandez, W. D. (2004). Trust and the trust placement process in metateam projects . In Pauleen, D. J. (Ed.), Virtual teams: Projects, protocols, and processes (pp. 40–69). Hershey, PA: Idea Group Publishing.

Ferris, G. R., Russ, G. S., & Fandt, P. M. (1989). Politics in organizations . In Giacalone, R. A., & Rosenfeld, P. (Eds.), Impression Management in the Organization (pp. 143–170). Hillsdale, NJ: Lawrence Erlbaum Associates.

Ferscha, A., & Scheiner, C. (1999). Collective choice in virtual teams. In IEEE 8th International Workshops on Enabling Technologies: Infrastructure for Collaborative Enterprises (WET ICE '99). Retrieved Apr. 12, 2009, from http://www.soft.uni-linz.ac.at/Research/Publications/Documents/WETICE99.ps

Fimbel, N. (1994). Communicating realistically: Taking account of politics in internal business communications. Journal of Business Communication, 31, 7–26. doi:10.1177/002194369403100101

Finholt, T., & Sproull, L. (1988). Electronic groups at work. Organization Science, 1(1), 41–64. doi:10.1287/orsc.1.1.41

Fiol, C. M., & O'Connor, E. J. (2005). Identification in face-to-face, hybrid, and pure virtual teams: Untangling the contradictions. Organization Science, 16, 19–32. doi:10.1287/orsc.1040.0101

Fisek, M. H., & Ofshe, R. (1970). The process of status evolution. Sociometry, 33, 327–346. doi:10.2307/2786161

Fisek, M. H., Berger, J., & Norman, R. Z. (1995). Evaluations and the formation of expectations. American Journal of Sociology, 101, 721–746. doi:10.1086/230758

Fitzpatrick, T. (2002). Critical theory, information society and surveillance technologies. Information Communication and Society, 5, 357–358. doi:10.1080/13691180210159300

Ford, R.C., & Richardson, W. D. (1994). Ethical decision making: A review of the empirical literature. Journal of Business Ethics, 13(3), 205. doi: 572059.

Foucault, M. (1977). Discipline and punishment: The birth of the prison. New York: Pantheon Books.

French, J. R. P. Jr., & Raven, B. H. (1959). The bases of social power. In D. Cartwright (Ed.), Studies in social power (pp. 150-167). Ann Arbor, MI: Institute for Social Research.

Frey, L. R. (Ed.). (2003). Group communication in context: Studies of bona fide groups. Hillsdale, NJ: Lawrence Erlbaum Associates.

Frey, L., Botan, C., & Kreps, G. (2000). Investigating communication: An introduction to research methods (2nd ed.). Boston: Allyn & Bacon.

Friedman, B., & Reed, L. (2007). Workplace privacy: Employee relations and legal implications of monitoring employee e-mail use. Employee Responsibilities and Rights Journal, 19(2), 75–83. .doi:10.1007/s10672-007-9035-1

Fuller, M. A., Hardin, A. M., & Davison, R. M. (2006). Efficacy in technology-mediated distributed teams. Journal of Management Information Systems, 23(3), 209–235. doi:10.2753/MIS0742-1222230308

Fuller, M. A., Hardin, A. M., & Scott, C. L. (2007). Diffusion of virtual innovation. The Data Base for Advances in Information Systems, 38(4), 40–44.

Gabriel, Y. (1999). Beyond happy families: A critical reevaluation of the control-resistance-identity triangle. Human Relations, 52(2), 179–203. doi:10.1177/001872679905200201

Gajendran, R. S., & Harrison, D. A. (2007). The good, the bad, and the unknown about telecommuting: Meta-analysis of psychological mediators and individual consequences. The Journal of Applied Psychology, 92, 1524–1541. doi:10.1037/0021-9010.92.6.1524

Garrett, R. K., & Danziger, J. N. (2007). Which telework? Defining and testing a taxonomy of technology-mediated work at a distance. Social Science Computer Review, 25, 27–47. doi:10.1177/0894439306293819

Gersick, C. J. G. (1988). Time and transition in work teams: Toward a new model of group development. Academy of Management Journal, 31, 9–41. doi:10.2307/256496

Giacalone, R. A., & Knouse, S. B. (1990). Justifying wrongful employee behavior: The role of personality in organizational sabotage. Journal of Business Ethics, 9, 55–61. doi:10.1007/BF00382564

Gibbs, J. L. (2009). Dialectics in a global software team: Negotiating tensions across time, space, and culture. Human Relations, 62, 905–935. doi:10.1177/0018726709104547

Gibbs, J. L., Nekrassova, D., Grushina, Y., & Abdul Wahab, S. (2008). Reconceptualizing virtual teaming from a constitutive perspective: Review, redirection, and research agenda . In Beck, C. S. (Ed.), Communication yearbook, 32 (pp. 187–229). New York: Routledge.

Gibson, C. B., & Cohen, S. G. (2003). Virtual teams that work: Creating conditions for virtual team effectiveness. New York: Jossey-Bass.

Gibson, C. B., & Gibbs, J. L. (2006). Unpacking the concept of virtuality: The effects of geographic dispersion, electronic dependence, dynamic structure, and national diversity on team innovation. Administrative Science Quarterly, 51, 451–495.

Giddens, A. (1984). Constitution of society: Outline of the theory of structuration. Cambridge: Polity Press.

Giroux, H. A., & Myrsiades, K. (Eds.). (2001). Beyond the corporate university: Pedagogy, culture, and literary studies in the new millennium. Lanham, MD: Rowman and Littlefield.

Glass, J. J. (1979). Citizen participation in planning: The relationship between objectives and techniques. American Planning Association Journal, 45, 180–189. doi:10.1080/01944367908976956

Gluesing, J. C., Alcordo, T. C., Baba, M. L., Britt, D., Wagner, K. H., & McKether, W. (2003). The development of global virtual teams . In Gibson, C. B., & Cohen, S. G. (Eds.), Virtual teams that work: Creating conditions for virtual team effectiveness (pp. 59–86). San Francisco, CA: Jossey-Bass.

Godart, C., Bouthier, C., Canalda, P., Charoy, F., Molli, P., & Perrin, O. (2001). Asynchronous coordination of virtual teams in creative applications (co-design or co-engineering): Requirements and design criteria (pp. 135–142). IEEE.

Goffman, E. (1959). The presentation of self in everyday life. Garden City, NY: Doubleday Anchor.

Golden, T. D. (2006). The role of relationships in understanding telecommuter satisfaction. Journal of Organizational Behavior, 27, 319–340. doi:10.1002/job.369

Golden, T. D., & Veiga, J. F. (2005). The impact of extent of telecommuting on job satisfaction: Resolving inconsistent findings. Journal of Management, 31, 301–318. doi:10.1177/0149206304271768

Golden, T. D., Veiga, J. F., & Simsek, Z. (2006). Telecommuting's differential impact on work-family conflict: Is there no place like home? The Journal of Applied Psychology, 91, 1340–1350. doi:10.1037/0021-9010.91.6.1340

Goluboff, N. B. (2006, August 6). Taxing telecommuters. New York Times. Retrieved September 30, 2009, from http://www.nytimes.com/2006/08/06/opinion/nyregionopinions/06CTgolubuff.html

Gonzalez, C. (2009). Conceptions of, and approaches to, teaching online: A study of lecturers teaching postgraduate distance courses. Higher Education, 57, 299–314. doi:10.1007/s10734-008-9145-1

Gossett, L., & Kilker, J. (2005). My job sucks: Counter-institutional websites as locations for organizational member voice, dissent, and resistance. Management Communication Quarterly, 20, 63–90. doi:10.1177/0893318906291729

Graf, T. (2009). The future of od: developing an effective virtual organization for the od Network. OD Practitioner, 41(3), 30–36.

Green, S. (1999). A plague on the panopticon: Surveillance and power in the global information economy [Electronic version]. Information Communication and Society, 2, 26–44. doi:10.1080/136911899359745

Greene, R. W. (2004). Rhetoric and capitalism: Rhetorical agency as communicative labor. Philosophy and Rhetoric, 37, 188–206. doi:10.1353/par.2004.0020

Grenier, R., & Metes, G. (1995). Going virtual: Moving our organsiation in the 21st Century. Upper Saddle River, NJ: Prentice Hall.

Griffith, T. L., Sawyer, J. E., & Neale, M. A. (2003). Virtualness and knowledge in teams: Managing the love triangle in organizations. Management Information Systems Quarterly, 27, 265–287.

Grossberg, L. (2005). Caught in the crossfire: Kids, politics, and America's future. Boulder, CO: Paradigm.

Grosse, C. U. (2002). Managing communication within virtual intercultural teams. Business Communication Quarterly, 65(4), 22–38. doi:10.1177/108056990206500404

Guidi, M. E. L. (2004). My own utopia. The economics of Bentham's panopticon. European Journal of the History of Economic Thought, 11(3), 405–431. doi:10.1080/0967256042000246485

Guo, Z. X., D'ambra, J., Turner, T., & Zhang, H. Y. (2009). Improving the effectiveness of virtual teams: A comparison of video-conferencing and face-to-face communication in China. IEEE Transactions on Professional Communication, 52(1), 1–16. doi:10.1109/TPC.2008.2012284

Habermas, J. (1987). The theory of communicative action: Vol. 2. Lifeworld and system. Cambridge, MA: MIT Press.

Hackman, J. R. (2002). Leading teams: Setting the stage for great performances. Boston: Harvard Business School Press.

Hakonen, M., & Lipponen, J. (2008). Procedural justice and identification with virtual teams: The moderating role of face-to-face meetings and geographical dispersion. Social Justice Research, 21, 164–178. doi:10.1007/s11211-008-0070-3

Halford, S. (2005). Hybrid workspace: Re-spatialisations of work, organization and management. New Technology, Work and Employment, 20, 19–33. doi:10.1111/j.1468-005X.2005.00141.x

Hambley, L. A., O'Neill, T. A., & Kline, T. B. (2007). Virtual team leadership: The effects of leadership style and communication medium on team interaction styles and outcomes. Organizational Behavior and Human Decision Processes, 103, 1–20. doi:10.1016/j.obhdp.2006.09.004

Hamilton, B. A., & Scandura, T. A. (2003). E-mentoring: Implications for organizational learning and development in a wired world. Organizational Dynamics, 3(4), 388–402. doi:10.1016/S0090-2616(02)00128-6

Hamilton, M., Hamilton, S., & Rhodes, J. (2002). Why mentoring in the workplace works. New Directions for Youth Development, 93, 59–89.

Handy, C. (1995). Trust and the virtual organization. Harvard Business Review, 73(3), 40–50.

Hanson, A., Levin, B. L. L., Heron, S., & Burker, M. (2003). Technology, organizational change, and virtual libraries . In Hanson, A., & Levin, B. L. (Eds.), Building a virtual library (pp. 1–18). Hershey, PA: Information Science Publishing.

Haring-Hidore, M. (1987). Mentoring as a career strategy for women. Journal of Counseling and Development, 66(3), 147.

Harrington, A. (1999). E-Mentoring: The advantages and disadvantages of using email to support distance mentoring. European Social Fund. Retrieved December 27, 1999 from the World Wide Web: http://www.mentorsforum.co.uk/cOL1/discover.htm

Harrison, T. R., & Doerfel, M. L. (2006). Competitive and cooperative conflict communication climates: The influence of ombuds processes on trust and commitment to the organization. The International Journal of Conflict Management, 17, 129–153. doi:10.1108/10444060610736611

Harrison, T. R., & Morrill, C. (2004). Ombuds processes and disputant reconciliation. Journal of Applied Communication Research, 32(4), 318–342. doi:10.1080/0090988042000276005

Harry, B., Sturges, K. M., & Klinger, J. K. (2005). Mapping the process: An exemplar of process and challenge in grounded theory analysis. Educational Researcher, 34, 3–13. doi:10.3102/0013189X034002003

Hart, R. K., & McLeod, P. L. (2003). Rethinking team building in geographically dispersed teams: One message at a time. Organizational Dynamics, 31, 352–361. doi:10.1016/S0090-2616(02)00131-6

Harvey, M., Novicevic, M. M., & Garrison, G. (2004). Challenges to staffing global virtual teams. Human Resource Management Review, 14, 275–294. doi:10.1016/j.hrmr.2004.06.005

Harzallah, M., & Vernadat, F. (1999). Human resource competency management in enterprise engineering. In 14th IFAC World Congress of Information Control in Manufacturing, Beijing, China.

Hayes-Brown, T., & Massiello, L. (2009). Keep your virtual employees IN THE LOOP. [Retrieved from Business Source Complete database.]. Incentive, 183(6), 34–35.

Haythornwaite, C. (2002). Strong, weak, and latent ties and the impact of new media. The Information Society, 18(5), 385–401. doi:10.1080/01972240290108195

Headlam-Wells, J., Gosland, J., & Craig, J. (2005). There is magic in the web: E-mentoring for women's career development. International Business, 10(6), 444–456.

Heene, A., & Sanchez, R. (1997). Competence-based strategy management. Chichester, UK: Wiley.

Henderson, L. S. (2004). Encoding and decoding communication competencies in project management: An exploratory study. International Journal of Project Management, 22(6), 469–476. doi:10.1016/j.ijproman.2004.01.004

Henry, K. B., Arrow, H., & Carini, B. (1999). A tripartite model of group identification: Theory and measurement. Small Group Research, 30, 558–581. doi:10.1177/104649649903000504

Herbert, M. (2006). Staying the course: A study in online student satisfaction and retention. Online Journal of Distance Learning Administration, 9(4). Retrieved March 28, 2009 from http://www.westga.edu/~distance/ojdla/winter94/herbert94.htm

Hernes, T., & Bakken, T. (2003). Implications of self-reference: Niklas Luhmann's autopoiesis and organization theory. Organization Studies, 24(9), 1511–1535. doi:10.1177/0170840603249007

Hertel, G., Geister, S., & Konradt, U. (2005). Managing virtual teams: A review of current empirical research [Electronic version]. Human Resource Management Review, 15, 69–95. doi:10.1016/j.hrmr.2005.01.002

Hertel, G., Konradt, U., & Orlikowski, B. (2004). Managing distance by interdependence: Goal setting, task interdependence, and team-based rewards in virtual teams. European Journal of Work and Organizational Psychology, 13(1), 1–28. doi:10.1080/13594320344000228

Hertzel, D. A. (2000). Don't talk to strangers: An analysis of government and industry efforts to protect a child's online privacy. Federal Communications Law Journal, 52, 429–451.

Hewett, B. L., & Powers, C. E. (2007). Guest editors' introduction: Online teaching and learning: Preparation, development, and organizational communication. Technical Communication Quarterly, 16, 1–11. doi:10.1207/s15427625tcq1601_1

Hildreth, P. M. (2004). Going virtual: Distributed communities of practice. Hershey, PA: Idea Group Publishing.

Hill, N. S., Bartol, K. M., Tesluk, P. E., & Langa, G. A. (2009). Organizational context and face-to-face interaction: Influences on the development of trust and collaborative behaviors in computer-mediated groups. Organizational Behavior and Human Decision Processes, 108(2), 187–201. doi:10.1016/j.obhdp.2008.10.002

Hill, S. K., Bahniuk, M. H., & Dobos, J. (1989). The impact of mentoring and collegial support on faculty success: An analysis of support behavior, information adequacy, and communication apprehension. Communication Education, 38, 15–33. doi:10.1080/03634528909378737

Hinds, P. J., & Bailey, D. E. (2003). Out of sight, out of sync: Understanding conflict in distributed teams. Organization Science, 14, 615–632. doi:10.1287/orsc.14.6.615.24872

Hinds, P. J., & Mortensen, M. (2005). Understanding conflict in geographically distributed teams: The moderating effects of shared identity, shared context, and spontaneous communication. Organization Science, 16, 290–307. doi:10.1287/orsc.1050.0122

Hoepfl, M. (1997). Choosing qualitative research: A primer for technology education researchers. Journal of Technology Information, 9, 47–63.

Hogg, M. A., & Terry, D. J. (2000). Social identity and self-categorization processes in organizational contexts. Academy of Management Review, 25, 121–140. doi:10.2307/259266

Hogg, M. A., Abrams, D., Otten, S., & Hinkle, S. (2004). The social identity perspective: intergroup relations, self-conception and small groups. Small Group Research, 35(3), 246–276. doi:10.1177/1046496404263424

Hollenbeck, J. R., Ilgen, D. R., Sego, D., Heldund, J., Major, D., & Phillips, J. (1995). Multilevel theory of team decision making: decision performance in teams incorporating distributed expertise. The Journal of Applied Psychology, 80(2), 292–316. doi:10.1037/0021-9010.80.2.292

Hollingshead, A., McGrath, J., & O'Connor, K. (1993). Group task performance and communication technology: A longitudinal study of computer-mediated versus face-to face groups. Small Group Research, 24(3), 307–333. doi:10.1177/1046496493243003

Holloway, D. (2007). Gender, telework and the reconfiguration of the Australian family home [Electronic version]. Journal of Mass Media and Cultural Studies, 21, 33–44. doi:10.1080/10304310601103919

Holman, D., Chissick, C., & Totterdell, P. (2002). The effect of performance monitoring on emotional labor and well-being in call centers. Motivation and Emotion, 26(1), 57–82. doi:10.1023/A:1015194108376

Holmes, D. (2001). From iron gaze to nursing care: Mental health nursing in the era of panopticism. Journal of Psychiatric and Mental Health Nursing, 8, 7–15. doi:10.1046/j.1365-2850.2001.00345.x

Holtz, S. (2008). A clear case of transparency. Communication World, 25(6), 16–20.

Homans, G. (1950). The human group. New York: Harcourt.

Hong, P., Vonderembse, M. A., Doll, W. J., & Nahm, A. Y. (2005). Role change of design engineers in product development. Journal of Operations Management, 24(1), 63–79. doi:10.1016/j.jom.2005.03.002

Horner, D., & Day, P. (1995). Labour and the information society: Trade union policies for teleworking. Journal of Information Science, 21, 333–341. doi:10.1177/016555159502100501

Horvarth, L., & Tobin, T. J. (2001). Twenty-first century teamwork: Defining competencies for Virtual Teams. Virtual Teams, 8, 239–258. doi:10.1016/S1572-0977(01)08026-8

Hoskins (2006, July 10). Understanding the importante of a telecommuting policy. Retrieved May 7, 2009 from http://articles.tecrepublic.com.com/5100-10878_11-6070340.html

Hsu, M.-H., Ju, T. L., Yen, C.-H., & Chang, C.-M. (2007). Knowledge sharing behavior in virtual communities: The relationship between trust, self-efficacy, and outcome expectations. International Journal of Human-Computer Studies, 65(2), 153–169. doi:10.1016/j.ijhcs.2006.09.003

Huang, H., & Ocker, R. (2006). Preliminary insights into the in-group / out-group effect in partially distributed teams: An analysis of participant reflections. In SIGMIS-CPR '06 (pp. 264-271). Claremont, California. ACM.

Hudson, B. (2002). The jungle syndrome: Some perils and pleasures of learning without walls . In Rudestam, K. E., & Schoenholtz-Read, J. (Eds.), Handbook of online learning: Innovations in higher education and corporate training (pp. 185–220). Thousand Oaks, CA: Sage.

Hughes, J., O'Brien, J., Randall, D., Rouncefield, M., & Tolmie, P. (2001, March). Some 'real' problems of 'virtual' organisation. [from Business Source Premier database.]. New Technology, Work and Employment, 16(1), 49. Retrieved March 11, 2009. doi:10.1111/1468-005X.00076

Hughes, S. S. (2007). Global panopticon: Looking at human rights in light of the U.S. and international laws [Electronic version]. Conference Paper: National Communication Association.

Hung, Y.-T. C., Dennis, A. R., & Robert, L. (2004). Trust in virtual teams: Towards an integrative model of trust formation. In Proceedings of the 37th Hawaii International Conference on System Sciences (pp. 1-11). IEEE.

Huysman, M., Steinfield, C., Chyng-Chang, J., Kenneth, D., & Huis, I., M., Jan, P., & Ingrid, M. (2003). Virtual teams and the exploration of communication technology: Exploring the concept of media stickiness. Computer Supported Cooperative Work: The Journal of Collaborative Computing, 12, 411–437. doi:10.1023/A:1026145017609

Hylmo, A., & Buzzanell, P. (2002). Telecommuting as viewed through cultural lenses: An empirical investigation of the discourses of utopia, identity and mystery. Communication Monographs, 69, 329–356. doi:10.1080/03637750216547

Igbaria, M., & Tan, M. (Eds.). (1998). The virtual workplace. Hershey, PA: Idea Group.

Ignat, C.-L., Papadopoulou, S., Oster, G., & Norrie, M. C. (2008). Providing awareness in multi-synchronous collaboration without compromising privacy. In CSCW '08 (pp. 659-668). San Diego, California. ACM.

Ilgen, D. R. (1999). Teams embedded in organizations. The American Psychologist, 54, 129–139. doi:10.1037/0003-066X.54.2.129

In, D. I. S. 2008 (pp. 295-304). Cape Town, South Africa. ACM.

Jablin, E. M. (1987). Organizational entry, assimilation, and exit . In Jablin, E. M., Putnam, L. L., Roberts, K. H., & Porter, L. W. (Eds.), Handbook of organizational communication: An interdisciplinary perspective (pp. 679–740). Newbury Park, CA: Sage.

Jablin, F. M. (1984). Assimilating new members into organizations . In Bostrom, R. (Ed.), Communication Yearbook 8 (pp. 594–626). Beverly Hills, CA: Sage.

Jablin, F. M. (1987). Organizational entry, assimilation and exit . In Jablin, F. M., Putnam, L. L., Roberts, K. H., & Porter, L. W. (Eds.), Handbook of organizational communication (pp. 679–740). Beverly Hills, CA: Sage.

Jackson, P. J. (2001). Organizational change and virtual teams: strategic and operational integration. Information Systems Journal, 9(4), 313–332. doi:10.1046/j.1365-2575.1999.00066.x

Jackson, S. (1998). Disputation by design. Argumentation, 12, 183–198. doi:10.1023/A:1007743830491

Jäkälä, M., & Pekkola, S. (2007). From technology engineering to social engineering: 15 years of research on virtual worlds. The Data Base for Advances in Information Systems, 38(4), 11–16.

James, M., & Ward, K. (2001). Leading a multinational team of change agents at Glaxo Wellcome (now Glaxo SmithKline). Journal of Change Management, 2, 148–159. doi:10.1080/714042500

Jarvenpaa, S. L., & Leidner, D. E. (1999). Communication and trust in global virtual teams. Organization Science, 10, 791–815. doi:10.1287/orsc.10.6.791

Jarvenpaa, S. L., Knoll, K., & Leidner, D. (1998). Is anybody out there? Antecedents of trust in global virtual teams. Journal of Management Information Systems, 14, 29–64.

Jarvenpaa, S. L., Shaw, T. R., & Staples, D. S. (2004). Toward contextualized theories of trust: The role of trust in global virtual teams. Information Systems Research, 15, 250–264. doi:10.1287/isre.1040.0028

Jarvenpaa, S., & Leidner, D. (1999). Communication and trust in global virtual teams. Organization Science, 10(6), 791–815. doi:10.1287/orsc.10.6.791

Jian, G. (2007). "Omega is a four-letter word": Toward a tension-centered model of resistance to information and communication technologies. Communication Monographs, 74, 517–540. doi:10.1080/03637750701716602

Jian, G., & Rosiek, S. (2009, May). Understanding the paradox of autonomy and control: Toward a dialectical model of telework. Paper presented at annual conventions of the International Communication Association, Chicago, IL.

Johnson, W. (2002). The intentional mentor: Strategies and guidelines for the practice of mentoring. Professional Psychology, Research and Practice, 33(1), 88. doi:10.1037/0735-7028.33.1.88

Joinson, A. (1998). Causes and implications of disinhibited behavior on the Internet . In Gackenbach, J. (Ed.), Psychology and the Internet: Intrapersonal, interpersonal, and transpersonal implication (pp. 43–60). New York: Academic Press.

Jones, G. R. (1997). Organizational theory: Text and cases (2nd ed.). Massachusetts: Addison-Wesley Publishing Company.

Jones, T., & Bowie, N. (1998, April). Moral hazards on the road to the virtual corporation. [from Business Source Complete database.]. Business Ethics Quarterly, 8(2), 273–292. Retrieved January 29, 2009. doi:10.2307/3857329

Kahai, S. S., Carroll, E., & Jestice, R. (2007). Team collaboration in virtual worlds. The Data Base for Advances in Information Systems, 38(4), 61–68.

Kalisch, B. J., Falzetta, L., & Cook, J. (2005). Group e-mentoring: A new approach to recruitment into nursing. Nursing Outlook, 53, 199–205. doi:10.1016/j.outlook.2004.12.005

Kanter, R. M. (1979). Power failure in management circuits. Harvard Business Review, 57(4), 65–75.

Karayaz, G., & Keating, C. B. (2007). Virtual team effectiveness using dyadic teams. In PICMET 2007 Proceedings (pp. 2593-2603). Portland, Oregon.

Kasprisin, C., Boyle Single, P., Single, R., & Muller, C. (2003). Building a better bridge: Testing e-training to improve e-mentoring programs in higher education. Mentoring and Tutoring: Partnership in Learning, 11(1), 67. doi:10.1080/1361126032000054817

Katz, J. E., & Aspden, P. (1997). A nation of strangers? Communications of the ACM, 40, 81–86. doi:10.1145/265563.265575

Katzenbach, J. R., & Smith, D. K. (2001). The discipline of virtual teams. Leader to Leader, Fall (22). Retrieved March 1, 2009 from http://www.leadertoleader.org/knowledgecenter/journal.aspx?ArticleID=112.

Kayworth, T. Leidner, D. (2000). The global virtual manager: A prescription for success. European Management Journal, 18(2), 183-194. doi: 53926014.

Kayworth, T. R., & Leidner, D. E. (2001/2002). Leadership effectiveness in global virtual teams. Journal of Management Information Systems, 18, 7–40.

Kelley, D., & Gorham, J. (1988). Effects of immediacy on recall information. Communication Education, 37, 198–207. doi:10.1080/03634528809378719

Kelly, L., Keaten, J., & Finch, C. (2004). Reticent and non-reticent college students' preferred communication channels for interacting with faculty. Communication Research Reports, 21, 197–209.

Kennedy, F. A., Loughry, M. L., Klammer, T. P., & Beyerlein, M. M. (2009). Effects of organizational support on potency in work teams: The mediating role of team processes. Small Group Research, 40, 72–93. doi:10.1177/1046496408326744

Keyzerman, Y. (2003). Trust in virtual teams (pp. 391–400). IEEE.

Khaifa, M., & Davidson, R. (2000). Exploring the telecommuting paradox. Communications of the ACM, 43(3), 29–31. doi:10.1145/330534.330554

Kiesler, S., & Sproull, L. (1992). Group decision making and communication technology. Organizational Behavior and Human Decision Processes, 52, 96–123. doi:10.1016/0749-5978(92)90047-B

Kiesler, S., Siegel, J., & McGuire, T. W. (1984). Social psychological aspects of computer-mediated communication. The American Psychologist, 39, 1123–1134. doi:10.1037/0003-066X.39.10.1123

Kilburg, G. (2007). Three mentoring team relationships and obstacles encountered: A school-based case study. Mentoring and Tutoring: Partnership in Learning, 15(3), 293–308. doi:10.1080/13611260701202099

Kildare, R., Williams, R. N., & Harnett, J. (2006). An online tool for learning collaboration and learning while collaborating. Paper presented at the Australian Computer Society, Inc. Eighth Australasian Computing Education Conference 2006. Hobart, Tasmania, Australia.

Kim, K.-J., & Bonk, C. J. (2006). The future of online teaching and learning in higher education: The survey says…. Educause Quarterly, 29(4). Retrieved March 28, 2009 from http://www.educause.edu/EDUCAUSE+Quarterly/EDUCAUSEQuarterlyMagazineVolum/TheFutureofOnlineTeachingandLe/157426

Kipnis, D., Schmidt, S. M., & Wilkinson, I. (1980). Intraorganizational influence tactics: Exploration in getting one's way. The Journal of Applied Psychology, 65, 440–452. doi:10.1037/0021-9010.65.4.440

Kirby, E. L., & Krone, K. J. (2002). "The policy exists but you can't really use it": Communication and the structuration of work-family policies. Journal of Applied Communication Research, 30, 50–77. doi:10.1080/00909880216577

Kirkman, B. L., Rosen, B., Tesluk, P. E., & Gibson, C. B. (2004). The impact of team empowerment on virtual team performance: The moderating role of face-to-face interaction. Academy of Management Journal, 47, 175–192. doi:10.2307/20159571

Kirkman, B., & Mathieu, J. (2005). The dimensions and antecedents of team virtuality. Journal of Management, 31, 700–718. doi:10.1177/0149206305279113

Kirschner, P. A., Beers, P. J., Boshuizen, H. P. A., & Gijselaers, W. H. (2008). Coercing shared knowledge in collaborative learning environments: Part Special Issue: Cognition and Exploratory Learning in Digital Age. Computers in Human Behavior, 24(2), 403–420. doi:10.1016/j.chb.2007.01.028

Kitto, S. (2003). Transplanting and electronic panopticon: Educational technology and the re-articulation of lecture-student relations in online learning. Information Communication and Society, 6(1), 1–23. doi:10.1080/1369118032000068796

Kliem, R. (2004). Leading high-performance projects. Boca Raton, FL: J. Ross Publishing Inc.

Knoll, K., & Jarvenpaa, S. L. (1998). Working together in global virtual teams . In Igbaria, M., & Tan, M. (Eds.), The virtual workplace (pp. 2–23). Hershey, PA: Idea Group Publishing.

Knottnerus, J. D. (1988). A critique of expectation states theory: Theoretical assumptions and models of social cognition. Sociological Perspectives, 31, 420–445.

Knouse, S. (2001). Virtual mentoring: Mentoring on the internet. Journal of Counseling, 38.

Kodama, M. (2005). Knowledge creation through networked strategic communities: Case studies on new product development in Japanese companies. Long Range Planning, 38(1), 27–49. doi:10.1016/j.lrp.2004.11.011

Koh, J., & Kim, Y.-G. (2003). Sense of virtual community: A conceptual framework and empirical validation. International Journal of Electronic Commerce, 8(2), 75–94.

Kohlberg, L. (1969). Stage and sequence: The cognitive-developmental approach to socialization . In Goslin, D. A. (Ed.), Handbook of socialization theory and research (pp. 347–480). Chicago, IL: Rand McNally.

Kohlberg, L. (1984). The psychology of moral development. San Francisco: Harper & Row.

Kollock, P., & Smith, M. (1996). Managing the virtual commons: Cooperation and conflict in computer communities . In Herring, S. (Ed.), Computer-Mediated Communication: Linguistic, Social, and Cross-Cultural Perspectives (pp. 109–128). Amsterdam: John Benjamins.

Koskela, H. (2000). 'The gaze without eyes': Video-surveillance and the changing nature of urban space. Progress in Human Geography, 24(2), 243–265. doi:10.1191/030913200668791096

Kozlowski, S. W. J., Gully, S. M., McHugh, P. P., Salas, E., & Cannon-Bowers, J. A. (1996). A dynamic theory of leadership and team effectiveness: Developmental and task contingent leader roles. G. R. Ferris (Ed.), Research in personnel and human resources management (pp. 253-305). Greenwich, CT: JAI Press.

Kramer, M. W. (1993). Communication and uncertainty reduction during job transfers: Leaving and joining processes. Communication Monographs, 60, 178–198. doi:10.1080/03637759309376307

Kramer, R. M. (1999). Trust and distrust in organizations: Emerging perspectives, enduring questions. Annual Review of Psychology, 50, 569–598. doi:10.1146/annurev.psych.50.1.569

Krauss, F., & Ally, M. (2005). A study of the design and evaluation of a learning object and implications for content development. Interdisciplinary Journal of Knowledge and Learning Objects, 1, 1–22.

Kraut, R. E., & Rice, R. E. (1998). Varieties of social influence: The role of utility and norms in the success of a new communication medium. Organization Science, 9(4), 437–453. doi:10.1287/orsc.9.4.437

Krebs, S. A., Hobman, E. V., & Bordia, P. (2006). Virtual teams and group member dissimilarity: Consequences for the development of trust. Small Group Research, 37, 721–741. doi:10.1177/1046496406294886

Kreiner, G. E., Hollensbe, E. C., & Sheep, M. L. (2006). On the edge of identity: Boundary dynamics at the interface of individual and organizational identities. Human Relations, 59(10), 1315–1341. doi:10.1177/0018726706071525

Krikorian, D., & Kiyomiya, T. (2003). Bona fide groups as self-organizing systems: Applications to electronic newsgroups . In Frey, L. R. (Ed.), Group communication in context: Studies of bona fide groups (pp. 335–367). Hillsdale, NJ: Lawrence Erlbaum Associates.

Kumar, N., & Vragov, R. (2009). Active citizen participation using ICT tools. Communications of the ACM, 52(1), 118–121. doi:10.1145/1435417.1435444

Kuntze, M. F., Stoermer, R., Mueller-Spahn, F., & Bullinger, A. H. (2002). Ethical codes and values in a virtual world. Cyberpsychology & Behavior, 5(3), 203–206. doi:10.1089/109493102760147187

Kurland, N. B., & Bailey, D. E. (1999). Telework: The advantages and challenges of work here, there, anywhere, and anytime. Organizational Dynamics, 28, 53–67. doi:10.1016/S0090-2616(00)80016-9

Lam, L. W., Bischoff, S. J., Higgins, L. V. H., & Persing, D. L. (1999). Implementing effective cross-functional teams: A multilevel framework for analysis . In Woodman, R. W., & Pasmore, W. A. (Eds.), Research in organizational change and development (12th ed., pp. 171–203). Greenwich, CT: JAI.

Lander, M. C., Purvis, R. L., McCray, G. E., & Leigh, W. (2004). Trust building mechanisms utilized in outsourced IS development project: a case study. Information & Management, 41(4), 509–558. doi:10.1016/j.im.2003.10.001

Lange, M. C. S., & Nelson, M. D. (2005, March 29). Preservation perils: Updating your corporation's document retention policy for the digital age. Retrieved on November 2, 2008 from http://swmicropublishing.com/wpdload/preserv-perils.pdf

Larson, C. E., & LaFasto, F. M. (1989). Teamwork: What must go right/what can go wrong. Newbury Park, CA: Sage.

Lautsch, B. A., Kossek, E. E., & Eaton, S. C. (2009). Supervisory approaches and paradoxes in managing telecommuting implementation. Human Relations, 62, 795–827. doi:10.1177/0018726709104543

Lavin Colky, D., & Young, W. (2006). Mentoring in the virtual organization: Keys to building successful schools and businesses. Mentoring and Tutoring: partnership in Learning, 14(4), 443-447.

Lazzarato, M. (1996). Immaterial labor . In Virno, P., & Hardt, M. (Eds.), Radical thought in Italy: A potential politics (pp. 133–147). Minneapolis: University of Minneapolis Press.

Lea, M., & Spears, R. (1995). Love at first byte? Building personal relationships over computer networks . In Wood, J. T., & Duck, S. (Eds.), Understudied relationships: Off the beaten track (pp. 197–233). Beverly Hills, CA: Sage.

Lee, M. R. (2008). E-ethical leadership for virtual project teams. International Journal of Project Management, E-print.

Lefcourt, H. M. (1966). Internal versus external control of reinforcement: A review. Psychological Bulletin, 64(4), 206–220. doi:10.1037/h0023116

Legreco, M. E. (2007). Consuming policy: Organizing school meal programs to promote healthy eating practices. Doctoral dissertation, Arizona State University. Retrieved September 24, 2009 from Dissertations & Theses: A&I (Publication No. AAT 3270597).

Leiponen, A. (2000). Competencies, innovation and profitability of firms . Economics of Innovation and New Technology, 9, 1–24. doi:10.1080/10438590000000001

Lenhart, A., Lewis, O., & Rainie, L. (2006). Teenage life online: The rise of the instant-message generation and the Internet's impact on friendships and family relationships . In Galvin, K. M., & Cooper, P. J. (Eds.), Making connections: Readings in relational communication (4th ed., pp. 355–362). Los Angeles, CA: Roxbury.

Leonard, D. A., Brand, P. A., Edmondson, A., & Fenwick, J. (1998). Virtual teams: Using communications technology to manage geographically dispersed development groups . In Bradley, S. P., & Nolan, R. L. (Eds.), Sense & Respond: Capturing value in the network era (pp. 285–298). Boston: Harvard Business School Press.

Leung, C. (2008). Handling teleworkers. [from ABI/INFORM Global database.]. Canadian Business, 81(5), 34. Retrieved March 21, 2009.

Lewis, J. D., & Weigart, A. (1985). Trust as a social reality. Social Forces, 63, 967–985. doi:10.2307/2578601

Li, X., Hess, T. J., & Valacich, J. S. (2008). Why do we trust new technology? A study of initial trust formation with organizational information systems. The Journal of Strategic Information Systems, 17(1), 39–71. doi:10.1016/j.jsis.2008.01.001

Licklider, J. C. R., & Taylor, R. W. (1968). The computer as a communication device. Science & Technology, 76, 21–31.

Lin, F.-r., & Chen, C.-h. (2004). Developing and evaluating the social network analysis system for virtual teams in cyber communities. In Proceedings of the 37th Hawaii International Conference on System Sciences (pp. 1-8). IEEE.

Lin, T.-C., & Huang, C.-C. (2008). Understanding knowledge management system usage antecedents: An integration of social cognitive theory and task technology fit. Information & Management, 45(6), 410–417. doi:10.1016/j.im.2008.06.004

Lincoln, Y. S., & Guba, E. G. (1985). *Naturalistic inquiry*. Beverly Hills, CA: Sage.

Lind, M. R. (1999). The gender impact of temporary virtual work groups. *IEEE Transactions on Professional Communication*, 42(4), 276–285. doi:10.1109/47.807966

Lind, M. R. (2007). Collective team identification in temporary teams. In *Proceedings of the 40th Hawaii International Conference on System Sciences* (pp. 1-9). IEEE.

Lindlof, T. R., & Taylor, B. C. (2002). *Qualitative communication research methods*. Thousand Oaks, CA: Sage.

Lindskold, S., & Bennett, R. (1973). Attributing trust and conciliatory intent from coercive power capability. *Journal of Personality and Social Psychology*, 28, 180–186. doi:10.1037/h0035734

Lipnack, J., & Stamps, J. (1997). *Virtual teams: Reaching across space, time, and organizations with technology*. New York: John Wiley.

Liu, X., Magjuka, R. J., & Lee, S. (2008). An examination of the relationship among structure, trust, and conflict management styles in virtual teams. *Performance Improvement Quarterly*, 21, 77–93. doi:10.1002/piq.20016

Llewellyn, K., & Hoebel, E. A. (1983). *The Cheyenne Way: Conflict and Case Law in Primitive Jurisprudence*. Norman, OK: Oklahoma University Press.

Lojeski, K. S., Reilly, R., & Dominick, P. (2007). Multitasking and innovation in virtual teams. In *Proceedings of the 40th Hawaii International Conference on System Sciences* (pp. 1-9). IEEE.

Lopez, Y., Rechner, P., & Olson-Buchanan, J. (2005, September 15). Shaping ethical perceptions: An empirical assessment of the influence of business education, culture, and demographic factors. *Journal of Business Ethics*, 60(4), 341–358. .doi:10.1007/s10551-005-1834-4

Lu, M., Watson-Manheim, M., Chudoba, K. M., & Wynn, E. (2006). Virtuality and Team Performance: Understanding the Impact of Variety of Practices. *Journal of Global Information Technology Management*, 9(1), 4-23. doi: 999471691.

Lucas, S. E. (2009). *The art of public speaking* (10th ed.). Boston: McGraw Hill.

Luhmann, N. (1979). *Trust and power*. Chichester, UK: Wiley.

Lyon, D. (1994). *The electronic eye: The rise of surveillance society*. Minneapolis, MN: University of Minnesota Press.

Lyon, D. (2001). *Surveillance society: Monitoring everyday life*. Philadelphia, PA: Open University Press.

Lyon, D., & Zureik, E. (Eds.). (2006). *Computers, surveillance, and privacy*. Minneapolis, MN: University of Minnesota Press. "Management by walking around." *A Dictionary of Business and Management*. Oxford University Press. 2006. Retrieved January 06, 2010 from Encyclopedia.com: http://www.encyclopedia.com/doc/1O18-managementbywalkingaround.html

MacDonald, C. J., Stodel, E., Thompson, T. L., Muirhead, B., Hinton, C., Carson, B., & Banit, E. (2005). Addressing the eLearning contradiction: A collaborative approach for developing a conceptual framework learning object. *Interdisciplinary Journal of Knowledge and Learning Objects*, 1, 79–98.

Maclagan, P. (2007, January). Hierarchical control or individuals' moral autonomy? Addressing a fundamental tension in the management of business ethics. *Business Ethics . European Review (Chichester, England)*, 16(1), 48–61. .doi:10.1111/j.1467-8608.2006.00468.x

Majchrzak, A., Rice, R. E., Malhotra, A., King, N., & Ba, F. (2000). Technology adaptation: The case of a computer-supported inter-organizational virtual team. *Management Information Systems Quarterly*, 24, 569–599. doi:10.2307/3250948

Major, D. A., Verive, J. M., & Joice, W. (2008). Telework as a dependent care solution: Examining current practice to improve telework management strategies. *The Psychologist Manager Journal*, 11, 65–91. doi:10.1080/10887150801967134

Makower, J. (2009, February 2). In recession, business keeps going green. *Business Week*. Retrieved September, 29, 2009 from http://www.businessweek.com/bwdaily/dnflash/content/feb2009/db2009022_982216.htm

Malhotra, A., Majchrzak, A., & Rosen, B. (2007, February). Leading virtual teams. [from Business Source Premier database.]. The Academy of Management Perspectives, 21(1), 60–70. Retrieved March 11, 2009.

Manzin, M., & Kodric,, B. (2009). The influence of outsourcing and information and communication technology on virtualization of the company. International Research journal, 7(1), 45-60.

Mark, G., & Semaan, B. (2008). Resilience in collaboration: Technology as a resource for new patterns of action. In CSCW '08 (pp. 137-146). San Diego, California. ACM.

Marques, J. M., Abrams, D., Paez, D., & Hogg, M. A. (2001). Social categorization, social identification and rejection of deviant group members . In Hogg, M. A., & Tindale, R. S. (Eds.), Blackwell handbook of social psychology: Group Processes (Vol. 3, pp. 400–424). Oxford: Blackwell. doi:10.1002/9780470998458.ch17

Martin, L. G., & Ross-Gordon, J. M. (1990). Cultural diversity in the workplace: Managing a multicultural workforce. New Directions for Adult and Continuing Education, 48, 45–54. doi:10.1002/ace.36719904806

Martin, R., & Hewstone, M. (2003). Majority versus minority influence: When, not whether, source status instigates heuristic or systematic processing. European Journal of Social Psychology, 33, 313–330. doi:10.1002/ejsp.146

Martins, L. L., Gilson, L. L., & Maynard, M. T. (2004). Virtual teams: What do we know and where do we go from here? Journal of Management, 30, 805–835. doi:10.1016/j.jm.2004.05.002

Marx, K. (1967). Capital: Vol. 1. A critical analysis of capitalist production. New York: International.

Marx, K. (1978). Economic and philosophic manuscripts of 1844 . In Tucker, R. C. (Ed.), The Marx-Engels reader (2nd ed., pp. 66–125). (Milligan, M., Trans.). New York: Norton.

Massey, A. P., Montoya-Weiss, M. M., & Hung, Y. (2003). Because time matters: Temporal coordination in global virtual project teams. Journal of Management Information Systems, 19, 129–155.

Mayer, R. C., Davis, J. H., & Schoorman, F. D. (1995). An integrative model of organizational trust. Academy of Management Review, 20(3), 709–734. doi:10.2307/258792

Mayes, B. T., & Allen, R. W. (1977). Toward a definition of organizational politics. Academy of Management Review, 1, 672–676. doi:10.2307/257520

Mazor, K. M., Simon, S. R., Yood, R. A., Martinson, B. C., Gunter, M. J., & Reed, G. W. (2004). Health plan members' views about disclosure of medical errors. Annals of Internal Medicine, 140(6), 409–418.

McAllister, D. (1995). Affect and cognition-based trust as foundations for interpersonal cooperation in organizations. Academy of Management Journal, 38(1), 24–59. doi:10.2307/256727

McCarthy, M. J. (1999, October 21). Virtual Morality: A New Workplace Quandary. Wall Street Journal (Eastern Edition), p. B1. doi: 45699514.

McCloskey, D. W., & Igbaria, M. (1998). A review of the empirical research on telecommuting and directions for future research . In Igbaria, M., & Tan, M. (Eds.), The virtual workplace (pp. 338–358). Hershey, PA: Idea Group.

McCrehin, C. (2008, September). GSA, AFGE sign national agreement on telework. American Society for Public Administration, 13.

McCuddy, M. K., Reichardt, K. E., & Schroeder, D. L. (1993). Ethical pressures: Fact or fiction? Management Accounting, 74(10), 57. doi: 654037.

McDonald, T. (1999). A whole new ball game. Successful Meetings, 48, 19.

McDonough, E. F. (2000). Investigation of factors contributing to the success of cross-functional teams. Journal of Product Innovation Management, 17(3), 221–235. doi:10.1016/S0737-6782(00)00041-2

McGrew, J. F., Bilotta, J. G., & Deeney, J. M. (1999). Software team formation and decay: Extending the standard model for small groups. Small Group Research, 30, 209–234. doi:10.1177/104649649903000204

McKenna, K. Y. A., & Bargh, J. A. (1999). Causes and consequences of social interaction on the Internet: A conceptual framework. Media Psychology, 1, 249–269. doi:10.1207/s1532785xmep0103_4

McKenna, K. Y. A., & Bargh, J. A. (2000). Plan 9 from cyberspace: The implications of the Internet for personality and social psychology. Personality and Social Psychology Review, 4, 57–75. doi:10.1207/S15327957P-SPR0401_6

McKenna, K. Y. A., & Green, A. S. (2002). Virtual group dynamics. Group Dynamics, 6(1), 116–127. doi:10.1037/1089-2699.6.1.116

McLeod, P. L., Baron, R. S., Marti, M. W., & Yoon, K. (1997). The eyes have it: Minority influence in face-to-face and computer-mediated group discussion. The Journal of Applied Psychology, 82, 706–718. doi:10.1037/0021-9010.82.5.706

McMillan, D. W., & Chavis, D. M. (1986). Sense of community: A definition and theory. Journal of Community Psychology, 14(1), 6–23. doi:10.1002/1520-6629(198601)14:1<6::AID-JCOP2290140103>3.0.CO;2-I

McMillan, J. J., & Cheney, G. (1996). The student as consumer: The implications and limitations of a metaphor. Communication Education, 45, 1–15. doi:10.1080/03634529609379028

Mehrabian, A. (1971). Silent messages. Belmont, CA: Wadsworth.

Meier, C. (2003). Doing "groupness" in a spatially distributed work groups: The case of videoconferences at Technics. In L. R. Frey (Ed.), Group communication in context: Studies of bona fide groups (pp. 367-399). Hillsdale, NJ: Lawrence Erlbaum Associates.

Mello, J. A. (2007). Managing telework programs effectively. [from ABI/INFORM Global database.]. Employee Responsibilities and Rights Journal, 19(4), 247. Retrieved March 21, 2009. doi:10.1007/s10672-007-9051-1

Metiu, A. (2006). Owning the code: Status closure in distributed groups. Organization Science, 17, 418–435. doi:10.1287/orsc.1060.0195

Meyer, J. P., Allen, N. J., & Smith, C. A. (1993). Commitment to organizations and occupations: Extension and test of a three-component conceptualization. The Journal of Applied Psychology, 78(4), 538–551. doi:10.1037/0021-9010.78.4.538

Meyer, J. P., Becker, T. E., & Van Dick, R. (2006). Social identities and commitments at work: Toward and integrative model. Journal of Organizational Behavior, 27(5), 665–683. doi:10.1002/job.383

Meyer, K. A. (2002). Quality in distance education: Focus on on-line Learning ([). San Francisco: Jossey-Bass.]. ASHE-ERIC Higher Education Report, 29(4).

Meyerson, D., Weick, K. E., & Kramer, R. M. (1996). Early trust and temporary groups . In Kramer, R. M., & Tyler, T. R. (Eds.), Trust in organizations: Frontiers of theory and research (pp. 166–195). Thousand Oaks, CA: Sage.

Meyerson, D., Weick, K. E., & Kramer, R. M. (1996). Swift trust and temporary groups . In Kramer, R. M., & Tyler, T. R. (Eds.), Trust in organizations: Frontiers of theory and research (pp. 166–195). Thousand Oaks, CA: SAGE Publications.

Michinov, N., Michinov, E., & Toczek-Capelle, M.-C. (2004). Social identity, group processes, and performance in synchronous computer-mediated communication. Group Dynamics, 8(1), 27–39. doi:10.1037/1089-2699.8.1.27

Miller, C. C. (2009). Sharing consumers' tastes in cellphone web surfing. New York Times, Retrieved February 23, 2009 from http://www.nytimes.com/2009/02/23/technology/23buzz.html?th=&emc=th&pagewanted=print.

Miller, V. D., & Jablin, F. M. (1991). Information seeking during organizational entry: Influences, tactics and a model of the process. Academy of Management Review, 16, 92–120. doi:10.2307/258608

Mills-Senn, P. (2006). Can home work work? H&HN . Hospitals & Health Networks, 80(6), 24.

Mintzberg, H. (1983). Power in and around organizations. New Jersey: Prentice Hall.

Mogan, S., & Wang, W. (2007). A study into user perceptions of information sharing and trust in virtual teams . In HT '07 (pp. 43–44). Manchester, United Kingdom: ACM.

Mokhtarian, P. L. (2009). If telecommunication is such a good substitute for travel, why does congestion continue to get worse? Transportation Letters: The International Journal of Transportation Research, 1, 1–17. doi:10.3328/TL.2009.01.01.1-17

Mokhtarian, P. L., Salomon, I., & Choo, S. (2005). Measuring the measurable: Why can't we agree on the number of telecommuters in the U.S.? Quality & Quantity, 39, 423–452. doi:10.1007/s11135-004-6790-z

Monge, P. R., & Contractor, N. S. (2001). Emergence of communication networks . In Jablin, F. M., & Putnam, L. L. (Eds.), The new handbook of organizational communication: Advances in theory, research, and methods (pp. 440–502). Thousand Oaks, CA: Sage.

Montoya-Weiss, M. M., Massey, A. P., & Song, M. (2001). Getting it together: Temporal coordination and conflict management in global virtual teams. Academy of Management Journal, 44, 1251–1262. doi:10.2307/3069399

Moorman, C., Zaltman, G., & Deshpande, R. (1992). Relationships between providers and users of market research: The dynamics of trust within and between organizations. JMR, Journal of Marketing Research, 29, 314–328. doi:10.2307/3172742

Morgan, D. L. (1997). Focus groups as qualitative research. Thousand Oaks, CA: Sage.

Morgan, D. L., & Krueger, R. A. (1993). When to use focus groups and why . In Morgan, D. L. (Ed.), Successful Focus Groups: Advancing the State of the Art. Thousand Oaks, CA: Sage.

Morgan, G. (1996). Images of organization (2nd ed.). London: Sage Publications.

Morrill, C. (1995). The executive way: Conflict management in corporations. Chicago: University of Chicago Press.

Morrill, C. (2003). Covert political conflict in organizations: challenges from below. Annual Review of Sociology, 29(1), 391–415. doi:10.1146/annurev.soc.29.010202.095927

Morrison, E. (2002). Newcomers' relationships: The role of social network ties during socialization. [Retrieved from Business Source Complete database.]. Academy of Management Journal, 45(6), 1149–1160. doi:10.2307/3069430

Mortensen, M., & Hinds, P. J. (2001). Conflict and shared identity in geographically distributed teams. The International Journal of Conflict Management, 12, 212–238. doi:10.1108/eb022856

Moustafa-Leonard, K. (2007). Trust and the manager-subordinate dyad: Virtual work as a unique context. [from ABI/INFORM Global database.]. Journal of Behavioral and Applied Management, 8(3), 197–201. Retrieved January 23, 2009.

Mueller, M., & Lentz, B. (2004). Revitalizing communication and information policy research. The Information Society, 20, 155–157. doi:10.1080/01972240490456773

Muller, C. (1998). Mentornet: The national electronic industrial mentoring network for women in engineering and science. Paper presented at the Women in Higher Education Conference (San Francisco, CA, Jan 3-8).

Mumby, D. K. (1997). The problem of hegemony: Rereading Gramsci for organizational communication studies. Western Journal of Communication, 61, 343–375.

Mumby, D. K. (2001). Power and politics . In Jablin, F. M., & Putnam, L. L. (Eds.), The new handbook of organizational communication: Advances in theory, research, and methods (pp. 585–623). Thousand Oaks, CA: Sage.

Murphy, P. (2004). Trust, rationality, and the virtual team . In Pauleen, D. J. (Ed.), Virtual teams: Projects, protocols, and processes (pp. 317–343). Hershey, PA: Idea Group.

Nahapiet, J., & Ghoshal, S. (1998). Social capital, intellectual capital, and the organizational advantage. Academy of Management Review, 23(2), 242–266. doi:10.2307/259373

Naquin, C. E., Kurtzburg, T. R., & Belkin, L. Y. (2008). E-mail communication and group cooperation in mixed motive contexts. *Social Justice Research, 21*, 470–489. doi:10.1007/s11211-008-0084-x

Neff, M. D. (2002). Online knowledge communities and their role in organizational learning . In Rudestam, K. E., & Schoenholtz-Read, J. (Eds.), *Handbook of online learning: Innovations in higher education and corporate training* (pp. 335–352). Thousand Oaks, CA: Sage.

Nelissen, P., Wenneker, M., & Van Slem, M. (2008). ICT performance in processes of knowledge sharing in organizations: A review of the literature. *Communications, 33*, 91–108. doi:10.1515/COMMUN.2008.005

Nelson, P., Safirova, E., & Walls, M. (2007). Telecommuting and environmental policy: Lessons from the ecommute program. *Transportation Research Part D, Transport and Environment, 12*(3), 195–207. doi:10.1016/j.trd.2007.01.011

Nemiro, J. E. (2004). *Creativity in Virtual Teams: Key Components for Success* (pp. 15–16). San Francisco: John Wiley & Sons.

News, B. B. C. (2009, January 22). *White House plans open government*. Retrieved March 13, 2009, from http://news.bbc.co.uk/go/pr/fr/-/2/hi/technology/7844280.stm

Nilles, J. (1998). *Managing telework: Strategies for managing the virtual workforce*. New York: John Wiley.

Nissenbaum, H. (1998). Protecting privacy in an information age: The problem of privacy in Public [Electronic version]. *Law and Philosophy, 17*, 559–596.

Nonaka, I., & Takeuchi, H. (1995). *The knowledge-creating company: How Japanese companies create the dynamics of innovation*. New York: Oxford University Press.

Norrgren, F., & Schaller, J. (1999). Leadership style: its impact on cross-functional product development. *Journal of Product Innovation Management, 16*(4), 377–384. doi:10.1016/S0737-6782(98)00065-4

Novaco, R. W., Kliewer, W., & Broquet, A. (1991). Home environmental consequences of commute travel impedance. *American Journal of Community Psychology, 19*, 881–909. doi:10.1007/BF00937890

Nunamaker, J. F. (1999). The case for virtual teaming systems. *IT Pro* (pp. 52–57). IEEE.

O'Hara-Devereaux, M., & Johansen, R. (1994). *Global work: Bridging distance, culture, and time*. San Francisco: Jossey-Bass.

O'Leary, C., & Pangemanan, G. (2007, October 15). The effect of groupwork on ethical decision-making of accountancy students. *Journal of Business Ethics, 75*(3), 215–228. .doi:10.1007/s10551-006-9248-5

O'Sullivan, P. B., & Flanagin, A. J. (2003). Reconceptualizing 'flaming' and other problematic messages. *New Media & Society, 5*, 69–94. doi:10.1177/1461444803005001908

Obama, B. (2009a, April 18). *Weekly address*. Washington, DC: The White House. Retrieved April 24, 2009, from http://www.whitehouse.gov/the_press_office/Weekly-Address-President-Obama-Discusses-Efforts-to-Reform-Spending-Government-Waste-Names-Chief-Performance-Officer-and-Chief-Technology-Officer/

Obama, B. (2009b). *Memorandum for the heads of executive departments and agencies: Transparency and open government*. Retrieved April 1, 2009, from http://www.whitehouse.gov/the_press_office/TransparencyandOpenGovernment/

Obama, B., & Biden, J. (2008). *The Obama-Biden plan: Technology*. Retrieved March 13, 2009, from http://change.gov/agenda/technology_agenda/

Ober, S. (1995). *Contemporary Business Communication* (2nd ed.). Boston: Houghton Mifflin.

Obst, P., & White, K. M. (2007). Choosing to belong: The influence of choice on social identification and psychological sense of community. *Journal of Community Psychology, 35*(1), 77–90. doi:10.1002/jcop.20135

Ocker, R. J. (2005). Influences on creativity in asynchronous virtual teams: A qualitative analysis of experimental teams. *IEEE Transactions on Professional Communication, 48*(1), 22–30. doi:10.1109/TPC.2004.843294

Ocker, R. J. (2007). A balancing act: The interplay of status effects on dominance in virtual teams. *IEEE Transactions on Professional Communication, 50*(2), 204–218. doi:10.1109/TPC.2007.902656

Ocker, R. J., & Fjermestad, J. (2000). High versus low performing virtual design teams: A preliminary analysis of communication. In Proceedings of the 33rd Hawaii International Conference on System Sciences (pp. 1-10). IEEE.

Ocker, R. J., & Fjermestad, J. (2008). Communication differences in virtual design teams: Findings from a multi-method analysis of high and low performing experimental teams. The Data Base for Advances in Information Systems, 39(1), 51–67.

Oh, H., Chung, M.-H., & Labianca, G. (2004). Group social capital and group effectiveness: The role of informal socializing ties. Academy of Management Journal, 47(6), 860–875. doi:10.2307/20159627

Olk, P., & Elvira, M. (2001). Friends and strategic agents: The role of friendship and discretion in negotiating strategic alliances. Group & Organization Management, 26(2), 124–164. doi:10.1177/1059601101262002

Omoto, A. M., & Malsch, A. M. (2005). Psychological sense of community: Conceptual issues and connections to volunteerism-related activism . In Omoto, A. M. (Ed.), Processes of Community Change and Social Action (pp. 83–104). Mahwah, NJ: Lawrence Erlbaum.

Orton, J. D., & Weick, K. E. (1990). Loosely coupled systems: A reconceptualization. Academy of Management Review, 15(2), 203–223. doi:10.2307/258154

Oshri, I., Kotlarsky, J., & Willcocks, L. (2008). Missing links: Building critical social ties for global collaborative teamwork. Communications of the ACM, 51(4), 76–81. doi:10.1145/1330311.1330327

Ouchi, W. G. (1981). Theory Z: How American business can meet the Japanese challenge. Reading, MA: Addison-Wesley.

Packard, D. (2003). Web-based mentoring: Challenging traditional models to increase women's access. Mentoring and Tutoring: Partnership in Learning, 11(1), 53. doi:10.1080/1361126032000054808

Panteli, N., & Davison, R. M. (2005). The role of subgroups in the communication patterns of global virtual teams. IEEE Transactions on Professional Communication, 48(2), 101–200. doi:10.1109/TPC.2005.849651

Panteli, N., & Duncan, E. (2004). Trust and temporary virtual teams: alternative explanations and dramaturgical relationships. Information Technology & People, 17(4), 423–441. doi:10.1108/09593840410570276

Panteli, N., & Sockalingam, S. (2005). Trust and conflict within virtual inter-organizational alliances: A framework for facilitating knowledge sharing. Decision Support Systems, 39(4), 599–617. doi:10.1016/j.dss.2004.03.003

Paré, G., & Dubé, L. (1999). Virtual teams: An exploratory study of key challenges and strategies. International Conference on Information Systems (pp. 479-483). Charlotte, North Carolina. ACM. Retrieved Apr. 12, 2009, from http://delivery.acm.org/10.1145/360000/352978/p479-pare.pdf?key1=352978&key2=5845759321&coll=GUIDE&dl=GUIDE&CFID=30868979&CFTOKEN=74505829

Parker, C. P., Dipboye, R. L., & Jackson, S. L. (1995). Perceptions of organizational politics: An investigation of antecedents and consequences. Journal of Management, 21, 891–912. doi:10.1177/014920639502100505

Patrashkova, R. R., & McComb, S. A. (2004). Exploring why more communication is not better: Insights from a computational model of cross-functional teams. [Special Issue: Research on the Human Connection in Technological Innovation]. Journal of Engineering and Technology Management, 21(1-2), 83–114. doi:10.1016/j.jengtecman.2003.12.005

Paul, D. L., & McDaniel, R. R., Jr. (2004). A field study of the effect of interpersonal trust on virtual collaborative relationship performance. MIS Quarterly, 28(2), [HTML]. Retrieved March 24, 2009 from http://www.misq.org/archivist/vol/no28/issue2/PaulMcDaniel.html.

Paul, S., & Ray, S. (2009). Cultural diversity, perception of work atmosphere, and task conflict in collaboration technology supported global virtual teams: Findings from a laboratory experiment. In Proceedings of the 42nd Hawaii International Conference on System Sciences (pp. 1-10). IEEE.

Paul, S., Samarah, I. M., Seetharaman, P., & Myktyn, P. P. (2005). An empirical investigation of collaborative conflict management style in group support system-based global virtual teams. *Journal of Management Information Systems, 21*, 185–222.

Paul, S., Seetharaman, P., Samarah, I., & Mykytyn, P. (2005). Understanding conflict in virtual teams: An experimental investigation using content. In *Proceedings of the 38th Hawaii International Conference on System Sciences* (pp. 1-10). IEEE.

Pauleen, D. J. (2004). *Virtual teams: Projects, protocols and processes*. Hershey, PA: Idea Group Publishing.

Paulre, B. (2000). *Is the New Economy a Useful Concept?* Matisse UMT CNRS No. 8595, Paris.

Pearlson, K. E., & Saunders, C. S. (2001). There's no place like home: Managing telecommuting paradoxes. *The Academy of Management Executive, 15*, 117–128.

Peet, T., & Kren, L. (2005). Online communities and discussion boards are critical to today's design engineers. *Machine Design, 77*, 133.

Pepper, G. L., & Larson, G. S. (2006). Cultural identity tensions in a post-acquisition organization. *Journal of Applied Communication Research, 34*, 49–71. doi:10.1080/00909880500420267

Perez, M. P., Sanchez, A. M., & Carnicer, M. (2003). Top manager and institutional effects on the adoption of innovations: The case of teleworking. *Prometheus, 21*, 59–73. doi:10.1080/0810902032000051018

Perrolle, J. A. (2006). Privacy and surveillance in computer-supported cooperative work . In Lyon, D., & Zureik, E. (Eds.), *Computers, surveillance, and privacy* (pp. 47–65). Minneapolis, MN: University of Minnesota Press.

Peters, M. R., Ocker, R. J., & Rosson, M. B. (2008). Collaboration in a distributed world: Technological support for partially distributed teams. *Eighth IEEE International Conference on Advanced Learning Technologies* (pp. 273-277). IEEE.

Peters, T. J., & Waterman, R. H. (1982). *In search of excellence: Lessons from America's best-run companies*. New York: Harper and Row.

Pettey, C. (2007). *Gartner says number of identity theft victims has increased more than 50 percent since 2003*. Retrieved April 25, 2009, from www.gartner.com/it/page.jsp?id =501912.

Pfeffer, J. (1982). *Organizations and organization theory*. Boston: Pitman Publishing Inc.

Phang, C. W., & Kankanhalli, A. (2008). A framework of ICT exploitation for e-participation initiatives. *Communications of the ACM, 51*(12), 128–132. doi:10.1145/1409360.1409385

Picherit-Duthler, G., Long, S. D., & Kohut, G. F. (2004). Newcomer assimilation in virtual team socialization . In Godar, S., & Ferris, S. P. (Eds.), *Virtual & collaborative teams: Process, technologies, & practice* (pp. 115–132). Hershey, PA: Idea Group Inc.

Pickering, J. M. K., John Leslie. (1995). Hardwiring weak ties: Interorganizational computer-mediated communication, occupational communities, and organizational change. *Organization Science, 6*(4), 479–486. doi:10.1287/orsc.6.4.479

Pinsonneault, A., & Boisvert, M. (2001). The impacts of telecommuting on organizations and individuals: A review of the literature . In Johnson, N. J. (Ed.), *Telecommuting and virtual offices: Issues and opportunities* (pp. 163–185). Hershey, PA: Idea Group.

Pitts, M. J., Fowler, C., Kaplan, M. S., Nussbaum, J., & Becker, J. C. (2009). Dialectical tensions underpinning family farm succession planning. *Journal of Applied Communication Research, 37*, 59–79. doi:10.1080/00909880802592631

Pollach, I. (2006). Privacy statements as a means of uncertainty reduction in WWW interactions. *Journal of Organizational and End User Computing, 18*, 23–49.

Polsani, P. R. (2003). Use and abuse of reusable learning objects. *Journal of Digital Information, 3*(4). Retrieved June 14, 2005 from http://jodi.ecs.soton.ac.uk/Articles/v03/i04/Polsani/

Polyani, D. M. (1966). *The tacit dimension*. London, England: Routledge and Kegan Paul.

Pondy, L. R. (1967). Organizational conflict: Concepts and models. *Administrative Science Quarterly, 12*, 296–320. doi:10.2307/2391553

Poole, M. S., & DeSanctis, G. (1992). Microlevel structuration in computer-supported group decision making. Human Communication Research, 19, 5–49. doi:10.1111/j.1468-2958.1992.tb00294.x

Poole, M. S., & Van de Ven, A. (1989). Using paradox to build management and organizational theories. Academy of Management Review, 14, 562–578. doi:10.2307/258559

Poole, M. S., & Zhang, H. (2005). Virtual teams . In Wheelan, S. A. (Ed.), The handbook of group research and practice (pp. 363–386). Thousand Oaks, CA: Sage Publications.

Postmes, T., Spears, R., & Lea, M. (2000). The formation of group norms in computer-medicated communication. Human Communication Research, 26, 341–371. doi:10.1111/j.1468-2958.2000.tb00761.x

Postmes, T., Spears, R., Lee, A. T., & Novak, R., J. (2005). Individuality and social influence in groups: Inductive and deductive routes to group identity. Journal of Personality and Social Psychology, 89(5), 747–763. doi:10.1037/0022-3514.89.5.747

Powell, A., Piccoli, G., & Ives, B. (2004). Virtual teams: A review of current literature and directions for future research. The Data Base for Advances in Information Systems, 35(1), 6–36.

Pratt, M. G. (2003). Disentangling collective identities . In Polzer, J. T. (Ed.), Identity issues in groups: Research on managing groups and teams (Vol. 5, pp. 161–188). Boston, MA: Elsevier Science. doi:10.1016/S1534-0856(02)05007-7

Prince, M. (2000). Telecommuters present unique risks to employers. Business Insurance, 34(20), 22–23.

Pripužić, K., Gjenero, L., & Belani, H. (2006). Improving virtual team communication.

Probst, G. J. B., Raub, S., & Romhardt, K. (1999). Managing Knowledge. Berlin, Heidelberg: Springer-Verlag.

Probst, G., & Romhardt, K. (1999). Bausteine des Wissensmanagements - ein praxisorientierter Ansatz. Handbuch Lernende Organization. Wiesbaden: Gabler.

Purcell, K. (2004). Making e-mentoring more effective. American Journal of Health-System Pharmacy, 61(3), 284–286.

Putnam, L. L., & Boys, S. (2006). Revisiting metaphors of organizational communication . In Clegg, S., Hardy, C., & Nord, W. (Eds.), Handbook of organizational studies (2nd ed., pp. 541–576). London: Sage.

Putnam, L. L., & Fairhurst, G. T. (2001). Discourse analysis in organizations: Issues and concerns . In Jablin, F. M., & Putnam, L. L. (Eds.), The new handbook of organizational communication (pp. 78–136). Thousand Oaks, CA: Sage.

Putnam, L. L., & Poole, M. S. (1987). Conflict and negotiation . In Jablin, F. M., Putnam, L. L., Roberts, K. H., & Porter, L. W. (Eds.), Handbook of Organizational Communication: An Interdisciplinary perspective (pp. 549–599). Newbury Park, CA: Sage Publications.

Putnam, L. L., & Stohl, C. (1990). Bona fide groups: A reconceptualization of groups in context. Communication Studies, 41, 248–265.

Putnam, L. L., & Stohl, C. (1996). Bona fide groups: An alternative perspective for communication and small group decision making . In Hirokawa, R. Y., & Poole, M. S. (Eds.), Communication and group decision making (2nd ed., pp. 147–177). Thousand Oaks, CA: Sage Publications.

Putnam, R. D. (1996). Bowling alone: America's declining social capital. Journal of Democracy, 6(1), 65–78. doi:10.1353/jod.1995.0002

Ragins, R. B., & Scandura, T, A. (1999). Burden or blessing? Expected costs and benefits of being a mentor. Journal of Organizational Behavior, 20(4), 493–509. doi:10.1002/(SICI)1099-1379(199907)20:4<493::AID-JOB894>3.0.CO;2-T

Ramos, M., & Green, R. (2003). Mentoring in libraries. Library Worklife, 12(4).

Rangarajan, D., Chonko, L. B., Jones, E., & Roberts, J. A. (2004). Organizational variables, sales force perceptions of readiness for change, learning, and performance among boundary-spanning teams: A conceptual framework and propositions for research. Industrial Marketing Management, 33(4), 289–305. doi:10.1016/S0019-8501(03)00072-5

Rasters, G., Vissers, G., & Dankbear, B. (2002). An inside look – Rich communication through lean media in a virtual research team. *Small Group Research, 33,* 718–734. doi:10.1177/1046496402238622

Ratnasingam, P. (2005). Trust in inter-organizational exchanges: A case study in business to business electronic commerce. *Decision Support Systems, 39*(3), 525–544. doi:10.1016/j.dss.2003.12.005

Raven, B. H. (1965). Social influence and power . In Steiner, I. D., & Fishbein, M. (Eds.), Current studies in social psychology (pp. 371–382). New York: Holt, Rinehart, Winston.

Raven, B. H. (2008). The bases of power and the power/interaction model of interpersonal influence. *Analyses of Social Issues and Public Policy (ASAP), 8,* 1–22. doi:10.1111/j.1530-2415.2008.00159.x

Ravlin, E. C., & Thomas, D. C. (2005). Status and stratification processes in organizational life. *Journal of Management, 31,* 966–987. doi:10.1177/0149206305279898

Ravlin, E. C., Thomas, D. C., & Ilsev, A. (2000). Beliefs about values, status, and legitimacy in multicultural groups: Influences on intragroup conflict. In P.C. Earley & H. Singh (Eds.), Innovations in international and cross-cultural management (pp. 17-51). Thousand Oaks, CA: Sage.

Redman, T., & Snape, E. (2005). Unpacking commitment: Multiple loyalties and employee behaviour. *Journal of Management Studies, 42*(2), 301–328. doi:10.1111/j.1467-6486.2005.00498.x

Regan, P. M. (2006). Genetic testing and workplace surveillance: Implications for privacy . In Lyon, D., & Zureik, E. (Eds.), Computers, surveillance, and privacy (pp. 21–46). Minneapolis, MN: University of Minnesota Press.

Regenbrecht, H., Ott, C., Wagner, M., Lum, T., Kohler, P., Wilke, W., & Mueller, E. (2003). An augmented virtuality approach to 3D videoconferencing. In Proceedings of the Second IEEE and ACM International Symposium on Mixed and Augmented Reality (pp. 1-2). IEEE.

Reid, S. A., & Hogg, M. A. (2005). Uncertainty reduction, self enhancement, and ingroup identification. *Personality and Social Psychology Bulletin, 31,* 804–817. doi:10.1177/0146167204271708

Reidenbach, R. E., & Robin, D. P. (1991). A conceptual model of corporate moral development. *Journal of Business Ethics, 10*(4), 273. doi: 572503.

Ren, Y., Kraut, R., & Kiesler, S. (2007). Applying common identity and bond theory to design of online communities. *Organization Studies, 28*(3), 377–408. doi:10.1177/0170840607076007

Rezgui, Y. (2007). Exploring virtual team-working effectiveness in the construction sector. *Interacting with Computers, 19,* 96–112. doi:10.1016/j.intcom.2006.07.002

Rheingold, H. (1993). The virtual community: Homesteading on the electronic frontier. Reading, MA: Addison-Wesley.

Rice, R. E., & Gattiker, U. E. (2001). New media and organizational structuring . In Jablin, F. M., & Putnam, L. L. (Eds.), The new handbook of organizational communication: Advances in theory, research, and methods (pp. 544–581). Thousand Oaks, CA: Sage.

Richmond, V. P. (1990). Communication in the classroom: Power and motivation. *Communication Education, 45,* 293–305.

Richmond, V. P., Wrench, J. S., & Gorham, J. (2001). Communication, learning, and affect in instruction (3rd ed.). Acton, MA: Tapestry.

Ridings, C. M., & Gefen, D. (2004). Virtual community attraction: Why people hang out online. *Journal of Computer-Mediated Communication, 10*(1).

Ring, P. S., & van de Ven, A. H. (1992). Structuring cooperative relationships between organizations. *Strategic Management Journal, 13*(7), 483–498. doi:10.1002/smj.4250130702

Ritekka, M. (2005). Organizational identification: A meta-analysis. *Journal of Vocational Behavior, 66*(2), 358–384. doi:10.1016/j.jvb.2004.05.005

Ritzer, G. (1996). The McDonaldization of society (Rev. ed.). Thousand Oaks, CA: Pine Forge Press.

Riva, G. (2002). The sociocognitive psychology of computer-mediated communication: The present and future of technology-based interactions. Cyberpsychology & Behavior, 5(6), 581–598. doi:10.1089/109493102321018222

Robbins, S. (2005). Organizational Behavior. In Capella University (Ed.), Managing and Organizing People (11th ed.). Boston, MA: Pearson Custom Publishing.

Robbins, S. P. (2002). Organizational behavior (10th ed.). New Jersey: Prentice Hall.

Rockmann, K. W., & Northcraft, G. B. (2008). To be or not to be trusted: The influence of media richness on defection and deception. Organizational Behavior and Human Decision Processes, 107(2), 106–122. doi:10.1016/j.obhdp.2008.02.002

Roethelisberger, F. J. (1939). Management and the worker; an account of a research program conducted by the Western electric company, Hawthorne works. Cambridge, MA: Harvard University Press.

Rosen, B., Furst, S., & Blackburn, R. (2007). Overcoming barriers to knowledge sharing in virtual teams. Organizational Dynamics, 36(3), 259–273. doi:10.1016/j.orgdyn.2007.04.007

Rosenberg, M. J. (2001). E-learning: Strategies for delivering knowledge in the digital age. New York: McGraw-Hill.

Rothaermel, F. T., & Sugiyama, S. (2001). Virtual Internet communities and commercial success: Individual and community-level theory grounded in the atypical case of TimeZone.com. Journal of Management, 27(3), 297–312. doi:10.1016/S0149-2063(01)00093-9

Rousseau, D. M., Sitkin, S. B., Burt, R. S., & Camerer, C. (1998). Not so different after all: A cross-discipline view of trust. Academy of Management Review, 23(3), 393–404.

Russell, T. L. (2001). The no significant difference phenomenon (5th ed.). Montgomery, AL: International Distance Education Certification Center.

Rutkowski, A. F., Vogel, D. R., Van Genuchten, M., Bemelmans, T. M. A., & Favier, M. (2002). E-Collaboration: The reality of virtuality. IEEE Transactions on Professional Communication, 45(4), 219–230. doi:10.1109/TPC.2002.805147

Ryan, G. W., & Bernard, H. R. (2003). Data management and analysis methods . In Denzin, N. K., & Lincoln, Y. S. (Eds.), Collecting and interpreting qualitative materials (pp. 259–309). Thousand Oaks, CA: Sage.

Sacks, P. (1996). Generation X goes to college. Chicago: Open Court.

Salisbury, W. D., Carte, T. A., & Chidambaram, L. (2006). Cohesion in virtual teams: Validating the perceived cohesion scale in a distributed setting. The Data Base for Advances in Information Systems, 37(2-3), 147–155.

Samarah, I., Paul, S., & Tadisina, S. (2007). Collaboration technology support for knowledge conversion in virtual teams: A theoretical perspective. In Proceedings of the 40th Hawaii International Conference on System Sciences (pp. 1-10). IEEE.

Sandoval, G. (2009, March 3). No, the White House hasn't ditched YouTube. CNET News. Retrieved March 13, 2009, from http://news.cnet.com/8301-1023_3-10187099-93.html?tag=mncol

Santilli, S., & Beck, V. (2005). Graduate faculty perceptions of online teaching. Quarterly Review of Distance Education, 6, 155–160.

Sarason, S. B. (1974). The psychological sense of community: Prospects for a community psychology. San Francisco, CA: Jossey-Bass.

Sarker, S., Sarker, S., & Schneider, C. (2009). Seeing remote team members as leaders: A study of US–Scandinavian teams. IEEE Transactions on Professional Communication, 52(1), 75–94. doi:10.1109/TPC.2008.2007871

Sarker, S., Sarker, S., Nicholson, D. B., & Joshi, K. D. (2005). Knowledge transfer in virtual systems development teams: An exploratory study of four key enablers. IEEE Transactions on Professional Communication, 48(2), 201–218. doi:10.1109/TPC.2005.849650

Sassenberg, K. (2002). Common bond and common identity groups on the Internet: Attachment and normative behavior in on-topic and off-topic chats. Group Dynamics, 6(1), 27–37. doi:10.1037/1089-2699.6.1.27

Sayer, A. (1999). Valuing culture and economy . In Ray, L., & Sayer, A. (Eds.), Culture and economy after the cultural turn (pp. 53–75). London: Sage.

Schiller, S. Z., & Mandviwalla, M. (2007). Virtual team research - an analysis of theory use and a framework for theory appropriation. Small Group Research, 38(1), 12–59. doi:10.1177/1046496406297035

Schlenkrich, L., & Upfold, C. (2009). A guideline for virtual team managers: the key to effective social interaction and communication. [Retrieved from Business Source Complete database.]. Electronic Journal of Information Systems Evaluation, 12(1), 109–118.

Schmidt, J. B., Montoya-Weiss, M. M., & Massey, A. P. (2001). New product development decision-making effectiveness: Comparing individuals, face-to-face teams, and virtual teams. Decision Sciences, 32(4). doi:10.1111/j.1540-5915.2001.tb00973.x

Schminke, M., & Wells, D. (1999). Group processes and performance and their effects on individuals' ethical frameworks. Journal of Business Ethics, 18(4), 367-381. doi: 40195392.

Schminke, M., Ambrose, M. L., & Noel, T. W.. (1997). The effect of ethical frameworks on perceptions of organizational justice. Academy of Management Journal, 40(5), 1190-1207. doi: 22006305.

Schoenfeld-Tacher, R., & Persichitte, K. A. (2000). Differential skills and competencies required of faculty teaching distance education courses. International Journal of Educational Technology, 2(1). Retrieved April 1, 2009 from: http://www.outreach.uiuc.edu/ijet/v2n1/schoenfeld-tacher/index.html

Schumacher, M., Le Stal-Cardinal, J., & Bocquet, J. C. (2009). Towards a methodology for managing competencies in virtual teams–A systemic approach . In Camarinha-tos, L. M., Paraskasis, I., & Afsarmanesh, H. (Eds.), Levering Knowledge for Innovation in Collaborative Networks (pp. 235–244). Heidelberg: Springer. doi:10.1007/978-3-642-04568-4_25

Schumacher, M., Stal-Le Cardinal, J., & Mekhilef, M. (2008a). Competence Management for Virtual Team Building: A survey. International Conference on Integrated, Virtual and Interactive Engineering for fostering Industrial Innovation - IDMME 2008, Peking.

Schumacher, M., Stal-Le Cardinal, J., & Mekhilef, M. (2008b). A Competence Management Methodology for Virtual Teams–A systemic approach to support innovation processes in SMEs. International Design Conference–Design 2008, Dubrovnik.

Schümmer, T., & Lukosch, S. (2006). The absent participant. Paper presented at PLoP '06. Portland, Oregon. ACM.

Schwartzman, R. (1995). Are students customers? The metaphoric mismatch between management and education. Education, 116, 215–222.

Schwartzman, R. (2006). Virtual group problem solving in the basic communication course: Lessons for online learning. Journal of Instructional Psychology, 33, 3–14.

Schwartzman, R. (2007a). Electronifying oral communication: Refining the conceptual framework for online instruction. College Student Journal, 41, 37–49.

Schwartzman, R. (2007b). Refining the question: How can online instruction maximize opportunities for all students? Communication Education, 56, 113–117. doi:10.1080/03634520601009728

Schwartzman, R., Runyon, D., & von Holzen, R. (2007). Where theory meets practice: Design and deployment of learning objects . In Koohang, A., & Harman, K. (Eds.), Learning objects: Theory, praxis, issues, and trends (pp. 1–44). Santa Rosa, CA: Informing Science Press.

Scott, C. R. (1999). Communication technology and group communication . In Frey, L. R. (Ed.), The handbook of group communication theory and research (pp. 432–472). Thousand Oaks, CA: Sage.

Scott, C. R., & Choi, S. (2009, May). Communication policies in the workplace: Tensions surrounding identifiability and anonymity of technology users. Paper presented at the annual convention of the International Communication Association, Chicago, IL.

Scott, C. R., & Timmerman, C. E. (1999). Communication technology use and multiple workplace identifications among organizational teleworkers with varied degrees of virtuality. IEEE Transactions on Professional Communication, 42, 240–260. doi:10.1109/47.807961

Sedgewick, R. (2009, June 1). Green and beyond: The hard and soft benefits of telecommuting. ITBusinessEdge. Retrieved September 28, 2009, from http://www.itbusinessedge.com/cm/community/features/guestopinions/blog/green-and-beyond-the-hard-and-soft-benefits-of-telecommuting/?cs=32987

Seibold, D. R., & Shea, B. C. (2001). Participation and decision making . In Jablin, F. M., & Putnam, L. L. (Eds.), The new handbook of organizational communication: Advances in theory, research, and methods (pp. 664–703). Thousand Oaks, CA: Sage.

Selwyn, N. (2003). ICT for all? Access and use of public ICT sites in the UK. Information Communication and Society, 6, 350–375. doi:10.1080/1369118032000155285

Sengupta, K., & Zhao, J. L. (1998). Designing workflow management systems for virtual organizations: An empirically grounded approach. In Proceedings of the 31st Hawaii International Conference on System Sciences (pp. 365-373). Retrieved Apr. 12, 2009 from http://ieeexplore.ieee.org/stamp/stamp.jsp?arnumber=00655293

Seo, M., Putnam, L. L., & Bartunek, J. M. (2004). Dualities and tensions of planned organizational change . In Poole, M. S., & van de Ven, A. H. (Eds.), Handbook of organizational change and innovation (pp. 73–107). New York: Oxford University Press.

Shedletsky, L. J., & Aitken, J. E. (2001). The paradoxes of online academic work. Communication Education, 50, 206–217. doi:10.1080/03634520109379248

Shen, Y. (2007). Transactive memory system development in virtual teams: The potential role of shared identity and shared context. In SIGMIS-CPR 07 (pp. 228-230). St. Louis, Missouri. ACM.

Sheppard, B. H., & Sherman, D. M. (1998). The grammars of trust: A model and general implications. Academy of Management Review, 23, 422–437. doi:10.2307/259287

Shils, E. (1975). Center and periphery: Essays in macrosociology. Chicago: University of Chicago Press.

Shin, Y. (2005). Conflict resolution in virtual teams. Organizational Dynamics, 34, 331–345. doi:10.1016/j.orgdyn.2005.08.002

Short, J., Williams, E., & Christie, B. (1976). The social psychology of telecommunications. New York: John Wiley.

Shuler, S., & Sypher, B. D. (2000). Seeking emotional labor: When managing the heart enhances the work experience. Management Communication Quarterly, 14, 50–89. doi:10.1177/0893318900141003

Siau, K., & Shen, Z. (2003). Building customer trust in mobile commerce. Communications of the ACM, 46(4), 91–94. doi:10.1145/641205.641211

Siau, K., Nah, F. F., & Teng, L. (2002). Acceptable Internet use policy. Communications of the ACM, 45, 75–79. doi:10.1145/502269.502302

Sidanius, J., Pratto, F., & Rabinowitz, J. L. (1994). Gender, ethnic status, and ideological asymmetry. Journal of Cross-Cultural Psychology, 25, 194–216. doi:10.1177/0022022194252003

Simbulan, M. S. R. (2004). Internet access practices and employee attitudes toward Internet usage policy implementation in selected Philippines financial institutions. Gadjah Mada International Journal of Business, 6, 193–224.

Simmers, C. A. (2002). Aligning Internet usage with business priorities. Communications of the ACM, 45, 71–74. doi:10.1145/502269.502301

Simons, M. E., & De Ridder, J. A. (2004). Renewing connections and changing relations: Use of information and communication technology and cohesion in organizational groups. Communications, 29, 159–177. doi:10.1515/comm.2004.011

Sinclair, A. (1993). Approaches to organisational culture and ethics. Journal of Business Ethics, 12(1), 63. doi: 571826.

Compilation of References

Sivunen, A. (2006). Strengthening identification with the team in virtual teams: The leaders' perspective. Group Decision and Negotiation, 15, 345–366. doi:10.1007/s10726-006-9046-6

Sivunen, A., & Valo, M. (2006). Team leaders' technology choice in virtual teams. IEEE Transactions on Professional Communication, 49(1), 57–68. doi:10.1109/TPC.2006.870458

Skovolt, K. (2009). Leadership communication in a virtual team. In Proceedings of the 42nd Hawaii International Conference on System Sciences (pp. 1-12).

Skow, L., & Whitaker, T. (1996). It's what you say and what you do! Nonverbal immediacy behaviors: A key to effective communication. NASSP Bulletin, 80(584), 90–95. doi:10.1177/019263659608058414

Snare, C. E. (2000). An alternative end-of-semester questionnaire. PS: Political Science and Politics, 33, 823–825. doi:10.2307/420922

Snodgrass, T. J. (1986). Function Analysis–The Stepping Stones to Good Value. CVS at KASI; Muthiah. CVS.

Software in Telecommunications and Computer Networks2006. SoftCOM 2006 (pp. 266-270). IEEE. Retrieved Apr. 12, 2009, at http://ieeexplore.ieee.org/stamp/stamp.jsp?arnumber=04129918. 266 – 270.

Soghoian, C. (2009a, March 2). Is the White House changing its YouTube tune? CNET News. Retrieved March 13, 2009, from http://news.cnet.com/8301-13739_3-10184578-46.html

Soghoian, C. (2009b, January 23). White House acts to limit YouTube cookie tracking. CNET News. Retrieved March 13, 2009, from http://news.cnet.com/8301-13739_3-10148844-46.html

Sole, D., & Applegate, L. (2000). Knowledge sharing practices and technology use norms in dispersed development teams. International Conference on Information Systems (pp. 581-587). Retrieved Apr. 12, 2009, from http://delivery.acm.org/10.1145/360000/359821/p581-sole.pdf?key1=359821&key2=5790759321&coll=GUIDE&dl=GUIDE&CFID=30070776&CFTOKEN=39968476

Soller, K. (2009, January 20). Can Obama's new whitehouse.gov deliver all that it promises? Newsweek. Retrieved March 13, 2009, from http://www.newsweek.com/id/180719

Somers, M. R. (1994). The narrative constitution of identity: A relational and network approach. Theory and Society, 23(5), 605–649. doi:10.1007/BF00992905

Spears, R., Lea, M., & Postmes, T. (2007). CMC and social identity . In Joinson, A. N., McKenna, K. Y. A., Postmes, T., & Reips, U.-D. (Eds.), The Oxford Handbook of Internet Psychology (pp. 253–279). London: Oxford University Press.

Sproule, M. J. (1988). The new managerial rhetoric and the old criticism. The Quarterly Journal of Speech, 74, 468–486. doi:10.1080/00335638809383854

Sproule, M. J. (1989). Organizational rhetoric and the public sphere. Communication Studies, 40, 258–265.

Sproule, M. J. (1990). Organizational rhetoric and the rational-democratic society. Journal of Applied Communication Research, 18, 129–140.

Sproull, L., & Kiesler, S. (1986). Reducing social context cues: Electronic mail in organizational communication. Management Science, 32(11), 1492–1512. doi:10.1287/mnsc.32.11.1492

Steier, F. (1991). Research as self-reflexivity, self-reflexivity as social process . In Steier, F. (Ed.), Research and reflexivity (pp. 1–11). London: SAGE Publications.

Stohl, C., & Cheney, G. (2001). Participatory processes/paradoxical practices: Communication and the dilemmas of organizational democracy. Management Communication Quarterly, 14, 349–407. doi:10.1177/0893318901143001

Stohl, C., & Putnam, L. L. (1994). Group communication in context: Implications for the study of bona fide groups . In Frey, L. R. (Ed.), Group communication in context: Studies of natural groups (pp. 248–292). Hillsdale, NJ: Lawrence Erlbaum Associates.

Stohl, C., & Putnam, L. L. (2003). Communication in bona fide groups: A retrospective and prospective account . In Frey, L. R. (Ed.), Group communication in context: Studies of bona fide groups (pp. 399–414). Hillsdale, NJ: Lawrence Erlbaum Associates.

Stoll, C. (1995). Silicon Snake Oil. New York: Doubleday.

Strauss, A. L., & Corbin, J. (1990). Basics of qualitative research: Grounded theory procedures and techniques. Newbury Park, CA: Sage.

Strub, P. J., & Priest, T. B. (1976). Two patterns of establishing trust: The marijuana user. Sociological Focus, 9, 399–411.

Suchan, J., & Hayzak, G. (2001). The communication characteristics of virtual teams: A case study. IEEE Transactions on Professional Communication, 44(3), 174–186. doi:10.1109/47.946463

Suitecommute (no date). Suitecommute: A complete telework solutions provider. Retrieved May 7, 2009 from http://www.suitecommute.com.

Suler, J. (2004). The online disinhibition effect. CyberPsycholology & Behavior, 7, 321–326. doi:10.1089/1094931041291295

Survey quantifies amount of time executives waste in organizational politics. (1995, January/February). Communication World, 12(1), 1-4.

Sutanto, J., Phang, C. W., Kuan, H. H., Kankanhalli, A., & Tan, B. C. Y. (2005). Vicious and virtuous cycles in global virtual team role coordination. In Proceedings of the 38th Hawaii International Conference on System Sciences (pp. 1-10). IEEE.

Swidler, A. (1986). Culture in actions: Symbols and strategies. American Sociological Review, 51, 273–286. doi:10.2307/2095521

Tajfel, H. (1978). Differentiation between social groups. London: Academic Press.

Tajfel, H., & Turner, J. C. (1986). The social identity theory of intergroup behavior . In Worchel, S., & Austin, W. G. (Eds.), Psychology of intergroup relations (2nd ed., pp. 7–24). Chicago: Nelson-Hall.

Tan, A., & Kondoz, A. M. (2008). Barriers to virtual collaboration. In CHI 2008 Proceedings (pp. 2045-2052). Florence, Italy.

Tan, B. C. Y., Wei, K.-K., Huang, W. W., & Ng, G.-N. (2000). A dialogue technique to enhance electronic communication in virtual teams. IEEE Transactions on Professional Communication, 43(2), 153–165. doi:10.1109/47.843643

Tanis, M., & Postmes, T. (2005). A social identity approach to trust: Interpersonal perception, group membership and trusting behaviour. European Journal of Social Psychology, 35, 413–424. doi:10.1002/ejsp.256

Tanis, M., & Postmes, T. (2008). Cues to identity in online dyads: Effects of interpersonal versus intragroup perceptions on performance. Group Dynamics, 12(2), 96–111. doi:10.1037/1089-2699.12.2.96

Taylor, F. W. (1911). The principles of scientific management. New York: Harper & Row.

Teece, D. J., Pisano, G., & Shuen, A. (1997). Dynamic capabilities and strategic management. Strategic Management Journal, 18(7), 509–533. doi:10.1002/(SICI)1097-0266(199708)18:7<509::AID-SMJ882>3.0.CO;2-Z

Telework Enhancement Act of 2009. Retrieved October 1, 2009, from govtrack.us website http://frwebgate.access.gpo.gov/cgi-bin/getdoc.cgi?dbname=111_cong_bills&docid=f:s707is.txt.pdf

Ter Bush, R. F. (2006). Silence, attribution accuracy and virtual environments: Implications for developers and facilitators. In Proceedings of the 39th Hawaii International Conference on System Sciences (pp. 1-9). IEEE.

Teske, J. A. (2002). Cyberpsychology, human relationships, and our virtual interiors. Zygon: Journal of Religion & Science, 37, 677–700.

Thibault, J. W., & Kelley, H. H. (1952). The Social Psychology of Groups. New York: John Wiley & Sons.

Thibodeaux, P. (2003). Telecommuters weather storm. Computerworld, 37(8), 1–2.

Thomas, D. C. (1999). Cultural diversity and work group effectiveness: An experimental study. Journal of Cross-Cultural Psychology, 30, 242–263. doi:10.1177/0022022199030002006

Thomas, D. M., Bostrom, R. P., & Gouge, M. (2007). Making knowledge work in virtual teams. *Communications of the ACM*, 50(11), 85–90. doi:10.1145/1297797.1297802

Thompson, E. P. (1967). Time, work-discipline, and industrial capitalism. *Past & Present*, 38, 56–97. doi:10.1093/past/38.1.56

Thrift, N. (2006). Re-inventing invention: New tendencies in capitalist commodification. *Economy and Society*, 35, 279–306. doi:10.1080/03085140600635755

Tietze, S. (2002). When "work" comes "home": Coping strategies of teleworkers and their families [Electronic version]. *Journal of Business Ethics*, 41, 385–396. doi:10.1023/A:1021236426657

Timmerman, C. E., & Scott, C. R. (2006). Virtually working: Communicative and structural predictors of media use and key outcomes in virtual work teams. *Communication Monographs*, 73, 108–136. doi:10.1080/03637750500534396

Tompkins, P. K. (2005). *Apollo, Challenger, Columbia: The decline of the space program*. Los Angeles: Roxbury.

Tompkins, P. K., & Cheney, G. (1985). Communication and unobtrusive control in contemporary organizations. In McPhee, R. D., & Tompkins, P. K. (Eds.), *Organizational communication: Traditional themes and new directions* (pp. 179–210). Beverly Hills: Sage.

Townsend, A. M., & Bennett, J. T. (2003). Privacy, technology, and conflict: Emerging issues and action in workplace privacy. *Journal of Labor Research*, 24, 195–205. doi:10.1007/BF02701789

Tracy, S. J. (2004). Dialectic, contradiction, or double bind? Analyzing and theorizing employee reactions to organizational tensions. *Journal of Applied Communication Research*, 32, 119–146. doi:10.1080/0090988042000210025

Tretheway, A., & Ashcraft, K. L. (2004). Special issue introduction. Practicing disorganization: The development of applied perspectives on living with tension. *Journal of Applied Communication Research*, 32, 81–88.

Trevino, L. K. (1986). Ethical decision making in organizations: A person–situation interactionist model. *Academy of Management Review*, 11, 601–617. doi:10.2307/258313

Trevino, L. K., Hartman, L. P., & Brown, M. E. (2000). Moral person and moral manager: How executives develop a reputation for ethical leadership. *California Management Review*, 42(4), 128–143.

Trevino, L., Butterfield, K., & McCabe, D. (1998, July). The ethical context in organizations: Influences on employee attitudes and behaviors. [from Business Source Premier database.]. *Business Ethics Quarterly*, 8(3), 447–476. Retrieved March 10, 2009. doi:10.2307/3857431

Trkman, P., Jerman-Blazic, B., & Turk, T. (2008). Factors of broadband development and the design of a strategic policy framework. *Telecommunications Policy*, 32, 101–115. doi:10.1016/j.telpol.2007.11.001

Tuckman, B. (1965). Developmental sequence in small groups. *Psychological Bulletin*, 63, 384–399. doi:10.1037/h0022100

Tuckman, B., & Jensen, M. (1977). Stages of small group development. *Group and Organizational Studies*, 2, 419–427. doi:10.1177/105960117700200404

Tuma, A. (1998). Configuration and coordination of virtual production networks. *International Journal of Production Economics*, 56-57, 641–648. doi:10.1016/S0925-5273(97)00146-1

Turkle, S. (1995). *Life on the screen: Identity in the age of the Internet*. New York: Simon and Schuster.

Turner, J. R., & Müller, R. (2005). The project manager's leadership style as a success factor on projects: a literature review. *Project Management Journal*, 36(2), 49–61.

Turner, J. W., Grube, J. A., & Meyers, J. (2001). Developing an optimal match within online communities: An exploration of CMC support communities and traditional support. *The Journal of Communication*, 51(2), 231–251. doi:10.1111/j.1460-2466.2001.tb02879.x

UNC Tomorrow Commission. (2007). University of North Carolina Tomorrow Commission final report. Chapel Hill, NC: University of North Carolina General Administration.

University of North Carolina Board of Governors. (2004). Report on expanding access to higher education through state-funded distance education programs. Retrieved March 27, 2009 from http://intranet.northcarolina.edu/docs/aa/planning/reports/DERpt2004.pdf

Vaidyanathan, R. (2008). Barack Obama's plans for the web. Retrieved March 5, 2009, from http://news.bbc.co.uk/2/hi/americas/7754485.stm

Valentine, S., & Barnett, T. (2007, Fall). 2007). Perceived organizational ethics and the ethical decisions of sales and marketing personnel. [from Business Source Complete database.]. Journal of Personal Selling & Sales Management, 27(4), 373–388. Retrieved April 19, 2009. doi:10.2753/PSS0885-3134270407

Valle, M., & Witt, L. A. (2001). The moderating effect of teamwork perceptions on the orgainztional politics-job satisfaction relationship. The Journal of Social Psychology, 141, 379–388. doi:10.1080/00224540109600559

Van Echtelt, P., Glebbeek, A., Lewis, S., & Lindenberg, S. (2009). Post-Fordist work: A man's world?: Gender and working overtime in the Netherlands. Gender & Society, 23, 188–214. doi:10.1177/0891243208331320

van Eemeren, F. H., Grootendorst, R., Jackson, S., & Jacobs, S. (1993). Reconstructing argumentative discourse. Tuscaloosa: University of Alabama Press.

van Es, R., & French, W., & Stellmaszek, F. (2004). Resolving Conflicts Over Ethical Issues: Face-to-face Versus Internet Negotiations. Journal of Business Ethics: Building Ethical Institutions for Business, 165-172. doi: 707261411.

Van Knippenberg, D., & Sleebos, E. (2006). Organizational identification versus organizational commitment: Self-definition, social exchange and job attitudes. Journal of Organizational Behavior, 27(5), 571–584. doi:10.1002/job.359

Vanhorn, S., Pearson, J. C., & Child, J. T. (2008). The online communication course: The challenges. Qualitative Research Reports in Communication, 9, 29–36. doi:10.1080/17459430802400332

Varca, P. E. (2006). Telephone surveillance in call centers: Prescriptions for reducing strain. Managing Service Quality, 16(3), 290–305. doi:10.1108/09604520610663507

Veblen, T. (1976). The higher learning . In Lerner, M. (Ed.), The portable Veblen (pp. 507–528). New York: Penguin. (Original work published 1918)

Velasquez, M. (2006). Business Ethics Concepts and Cases. New Jersey: Pearson Prentice Hall.

Verbos, A., Gerard, J., Forshey, P., Harding, C., & Miller, J. (2007, November 15). The positive ethical organization: Enacting a living code of ethics and ethical organizational identity. Journal of Business Ethics, 76(1), 17–33. .doi:10.1007/s10551-006-9275-2

Wallace, P. (2004). The internet in the workplace: How new technology is transforming work. New York: Cambridge University Press.

Walls, J. A. Jr, & Callister, R. R. (1995). Conflict and its management. Journal of Management, 21, 515–558. doi:10.1177/014920639502100306

Walther, J. B. (1992). Interpersonal effects in computer-mediated interaction: A relational perspective. Communication Research, 19, 52–89. doi:10.1177/009365092019001003

Walther, J. B. (1996). Computer mediated communication: Impersonal, interpersonal and hyperpersonal interaction. Communication Research, 22(1), 33–43.

Walther, J. B., & Bunz, U. (2005). The rules of virtual groups: Trust, liking, and performance in computer-mediated communication. The Journal of Communication, 55, 828–846. doi:10.1111/j.1460-2466.2005.tb03025.x

Walther, J. B., & Parks, M. R. (2002). Cues filtered out, cues filtered in: Computer-mediated communication and relationships . In Knapp, M. L., & Daly, J. A. (Eds.), Handbook of interpersonal communication (3rd ed., pp. 529–563). Thousand Oaks, CA: Sage.

Walther, J. B., Slovacek, C. L., & Tidwell, L. C. (2001). Is a picture worth a thousand words?: Photographic images in long-term and short-term computer-mediated communication. *Communication Research*, 28(1), 105–134. doi:10.1177/009365001028001004

Wang, Q., Huang, H., & Wang, X. (2006). Intelligent virtual team in collaborative design. *Computer-Aided Industrial Design and Conceptual Design 2006*. IEEE. Retrieved Apr. 12, 2009, from http://ieeexplore.ieee.org/stamp/stamp.jsp?arnumber=04127026

Ward, C., Leong, C.-H., & Low, M. (2004). Personality and sojourner adjustment: An exploration of the Big Five and the cultural fit proposition. *Journal of Cross-Cultural Psychology*, 35, 137–151. doi:10.1177/0022022103260719

Warkentin, M. E., Sayeed, L., & Hightower, R. (1997). Virtual teams versus face-to-face teams: An exploratory study of a web-based conference system. *Decision Sciences*, 28(4), 975–996. doi:10.1111/j.1540-5915.1997.tb01338.x

Warschauer, M. (1999). *Electronic literacies: Language, culture, and power in online education*. Mahwah, NJ: Lawrence Erlbaum.

Wasko, M., & Faraj, S. (2005). Why should I share? Examining social capital and knowledge contribution in electonic networks of practice. *Management Information Systems Quarterly*, 29(1), 247–253.

Watch, C. M. S. (2009, March 11). Obama call for citizen e-participation will encounter technical hurdles [Press release]. Retrieved April 1, 2009, from http://www.cmswatch.com/About/Press/2009-CMS-Social-Gap/

Weber, M. (1947). *Max Weber: The theory of social and economic organization* (Henderson, A. M., & Parsons, T., Trans.). New York: Oxford University Press.

Webster, J., & Staples, D. S. (2006). Comparing virtual teams to traditional teams: An identification of new research opportunities. *Research in Personnel and Human Resources Management*, 25, 181–215. doi:10.1016/S0742-7301(06)25005-9

Weeks, L. (2009, March 13). White House web site: Window into Obama's soul? *National Public Radio*. Retrieved March 13, 2009, from http://www.npr.org/templates/story/story.php?storyId=99794168

Weick, K. E. (1976). Educational organizations as loosely coupled systems. *Administrative Science Quarterly*, 21, 1–19. doi:10.2307/2391875

Weick, K. E. (1979). *The social psychology of organizing* (2nd ed.). New York: McGraw-Hill, Inc.

Weick, K. E. (1995). *Sensemaking in organizations*. Thousand Oaks, CA: Sage.

Weick, K. E., & Sutcliffe, K. (2001). *Managing the unexpected: Assuring high performance in an age of complexity*. San Francisco, CA: Jossey-Bass.

Weill, P., Ross, J. W., & Robertson, D. C. (2006). *Enterprise Architecture as a Strategy*. Boston, MA: Harvard Business School Press.

Weis, R., Stamm, K., Smith, C., Nilan, M., Clark, F., & Weis, J. (2003). Communities of care and caring: The case of MSWatch.com(R). *Journal of Health Psychology*, 8(1), 135–148. doi:10.1177/1359105303008001449

Wellman, B., & Guilia, M. (1999). Net Surfers don't ride alone: Virtual communities as communities . In Wellman, B. (Ed.), *Networks in the Global Village: Life in Contemporary Communities* (pp. 331–366). Boulder, CO: Westview.

Wellman, B., Haase, A. Q., Witte, J., & Hampton, K. (2001). Does the internet increase, decrease, or supplement social capital? Social networks, participation and community commitment. *The American Behavioral Scientist*, 45(3), 437–456. doi:10.1177/00027640121957286

Wenger, E. (1998). *Communities of practice: Learning, meaning and identity*. Cambridge, UK: Cambridge University Press.

Wheelwright, S. C., & Clark, K. B. (1992). *Revolutionizing product development: Quantum leaps in speed, efficiency, and quality*. New York: Free Press.

Whitman, M. E., Townsend, A. M., & Alberts, R. J. (1999). Considerations for an effective telecommunications-use policy. Communications of the ACM, 42(6), 101–108. doi:10.1145/303849.303868

Wiesenfeld, B. M., Raghuram, S., & Garud, R. (1999). Communication patterns as determinants of organizational identification in a virtual organization. Organization Science, 10, 777–790. doi:10.1287/orsc.10.6.777

Wiesenfeld, B.M., Raghuram, S., Garud, R. (1999). Managers in a Virtual Context: The Experience of Self-threat and its Effects on Virtual Work Organizations. Journal of Organizational Behavior: Trends in Organizational Behavior, 6, 31-44. doi: 1393566161.

Wimbush, J. C., & Shepard, J. M. (1994). Toward an understanding of ethical climate: Its relationship to ethical behavior and supervisory influence. Journal of Business Ethics, 13, 637–647. doi:10.1007/BF00871811

Winter, S. J., Stylianou, A. C., & Gialcone, R. A. (2004). Individual differences in the acceptability of unethical information technology practices: The case of Machiavellianism and ethical ideology. Journal of Business Ethics, 54(3), 275–296. doi:10.1007/s10551-004-1772-6

Witt, P. L., & Schrodt, P. (2006). The influence of instructional technology use and teacher immediacy on student affect for teacher and course. Communication Reports, 19, 1–15. doi:10.1080/08934210500309843

Wood, A. F., & Smith, M. J. (2001). Online communication: Linking technology, identity, and culture. Mahwah, NJ: Lawrence Erlbaum Associates.

World Wide Waves. (1999, October). Policy makers need the facts on global effects of telework . Management Services, 43(10), 7.

WorldatWork. (2009). Telework trendlines 2009: A survey brief. Scottsdale, AZ: WorldatWork.

Wray-Bliss, E. (2001). Representing customer service: Telephones and texts . In Sturdy, A., Grugulis, I., & Wilmott, H. (Eds.), Customer service: Empowerment and entrapment (pp. 38–59). New York: Palgrave.

Wulff, S., Hanor, J., & Bulik, R. J. (2000). The roles and interrelationships of presence, reflection, and self-directed learning in effective world wide web-based pedagogy . In Cole, R. A. (Ed.), Issues in web-based pedagogy: A critical primer (pp. 143–160). Westport, CT: Greenwood Press.

Xiao, W., & Wei, Q.-Q. (2008). A study on virtual team trust mechanism and its construction strategies. 2008 International Conference on Information Management, Innovation Management and Industrial Engineering (pp. 315-319). IEEE.

Yager, S. E. (1999). Using information technology in a virtual work world: Characteristics of collaborative workers. In SIGCPR '99 (pp. 73-78). New Orleans, Louisiana. ACM.

Yoo, Y., & Alavi, M. (2004). Emergent leadership in virtual teams: What do emergent leaders do? Information and Organization, 14, 27–58. doi:10.1016/j.infoandorg.2003.11.001

Yosida, K. (1978). Functional analysis (5th ed.). Berlin, Heidelberg: Springer-Verlag.

Yukl, G., & Falbe, C. M. (1990). Influence tactics in upward, downward, and lateral influence attempts. The Journal of Applied Psychology, 76, 416–423. doi:10.1037/0021-9010.76.3.416

Zaccaro, S. J., Ardison, S. D., & Orvis, K. L. (2004). Leadership in virtual teams . In Day, D., Zaccaro, S., & Halpins, S. (Eds.), Leader development for transforming organizations (pp. 267–292). Mahwah, NJ: Lawrence Erlbaum.

Zaheer, A., McEvily, B., & Perrone, V. (1998). Does trust matter? Exploring the effects of interorganizational and interpersonal trust on performance. Organization Science, 9(2), 141–159. doi:10.1287/orsc.9.2.141

Zelditch, M. Jr, & Walker, H. A. (1989). Legitimacy and the stability of authority. Advances in Group Processes, 1, 1–25.

Zetter, K. (2006, October). Employers crack down on personal net use. PC World Magazine.

Zhang, S., Fjermestad, J., & Tremaine, M. (2005). Leadership styles in virtual team context: Limitations, solutions and propositions. In Proceedings of the 38th Hawaii International Conference on System Sciences (pp. 1-10). IEEE.

Zigurs, I. (2003). Leadership in virtual teams: Oxymoron or opportunity? Organizational Dynamics, 31, 339–351. doi:10.1016/S0090-2616(02)00132-8

Zigurs, I., Poole, M. S., & DeSanctis, G. L. (1988). A study of influence in computer-mediated group decision making. Management Information Systems Quarterly, 12, 625–644. doi:10.2307/249136

Zolin, R., Hinds, P. J., Fruchter, R., & Levitt, R. E. (2004a). Interpersonal trust in cross-functional, geographically distributed work: A longitudinal study. Information and Organization, 14(1), 1–26. doi:10.1016/j.infoandorg.2003.09.002

About the Contributors

Shawn D. Long (Ph.D., University of Kentucky; M.P.A., Tennessee State University) is the Director of Graduate Studies and Associate Professor of Communication Studies and Associate Professor of the Interdisciplinary Organizational Science Doctoral Program at the University of North Carolina at Charlotte. His teaching and research interests include organizational communication, organizational dialogue, virtual work, diversity communication, virtual- team assimilation and socialization, virtual work, health communication and interpretive methods associated with the study of organizational culture and symbolism. His primary research methods have employed interpretative phenomenology, case study approach, and grounded theory. Long was co-investigator of a $1.5 million federal grant that investigated the influence of families, media, organizational structure and interpersonal communication on an individual's decision to discuss and participate in the organ donation process. Additionally, Dr. Long has studied the utility, development, and communication practices of virtual teams within a variety of organizations. He has consulted several local, regional and national organizations on communication, culture, diversity, and structure. Prior to arriving at UNC-Charlotte, Shawn D. Long was a Southern Regional Educational Board Doctoral Scholar and Lyman T. Johnson Doctoral Fellow at the University of Kentucky. He has been recognized with several professional awards including the Chancellor's Award for Outstanding Teaching at the University of Kentucky, The Multicultural Summer Fellowship at the University of Nebraska-Lincoln, Outstanding Teaching Assistant in the College of Communication and Information Studies at the University of Kentucky, Outstanding Graduate Teaching Assistant recognized by the International Communication Association, and Who's Who Among American Teachers. He and his colleagues have recently been honored with the Southern States Communication Association's Minority Recruitment and Retention Award. He has written, presented and published several papers on issues of organizational diversity, organizational discourse, virtual teams in organizations, health communication, and organizational culture. He has appeared as a featured guest on Charlotte Talks with Mike Collins, a NPR affiliate broadcast. His most recent research appears in Communication Monographs, Clinical Transplantation, Health Communication, Journal of Health Psychology, Journal of Health Communication, Communication Teacher, Health Communication, Information and Science Technology, The Encyclopedia of Organizational/Industrial Psychology, Case Studies for Organizational Communication: Understanding Communication Processes (1, 2, and 3rd editions), and Virtual and Collaborative Teams. He is currently a board member on the Special Issues on Qualitative Research in the Southern Communication Journal, an ad-hoc member on the editorial board for the International Journal of Cases on Electronic Commerce, reviewer for The Journal of the National Medical Association, International Communication Association and the National Communication Association. Dr. Long is currently a Divisional Officer of the National Communication Association and Coordinator of The Organizational Science Summer Institute.

* * *

Rachel Byers and was born, raised, and currently lives in Daphne, Alabama. She received a Bachelor of Science degree in Accounting with a minor in Computer Science as well as a Master's degree in Accounting from the University of Alabama. She graduated with Honors and was offered a full time position with Pricewaterhouse Coopers but declined and chose to complete my masters. After college, she immediately sat for and passed the CPA Exam and is currently a practicing Certified Public Accountant in Alabama. She teaches part time as an adjunct instructor at the University of South Alabama and online for Devry University. Her love for teaching led her to go back to school to complete her doctoral degree. She is currently in the dissertation phase of her program and hopes to finish by August of this year.

Rachel Widener is currently pursuing her Masters of Arts in Communication with an emphasis in organizational communication at University of North Carolina in Charlotte. Apart from her duties as a Graduate research and teaching assistant, Rachel is Vice President of the Communication Studies Graduate Student Association. At this time, Rachel is working on her thesis, examining volunteer participation and workplace democracy. Her interest in organizational communication involves overlapping organizational commitments and responsibilities in our lives: how these are balanced and negotiated; how they shape our identities, and how individuals deal with competing identification. Upon completing her Masters degree, Rachel will be continuing her academic pursuits in a doctoral program.

Chase Clow received his Master's Degree in Industrial/Organizational Psychology from the University of North Carolina at Charlotte in 2007. Currently, Chase is a doctoral student at Arizona State University, studying Organizational Communication. His research interests include organizational surveillance, religious organizational rhetoric and persuasion, spirituality, and the diffusion of narratives. Additionally, Chase is a research assistant for the Consortium for Strategic Communication, where he studies the spread of extremist narratives through contested areas. Chase is also an associate editor for Mindful Heresy, an online journal that explores a variety of perspectives, methodologies and contexts for the communication of spiritual practices in contemporary life.

Elizabeth C. Ravlin is Associate Professor of Organizational Behavior and Management on the faculty of the Moore School of Business, University of South Carolina. She received her Ph.D. from Carnegie Mellon University. Her research examines multicultural interactions, interpersonal and team processes, work values, and status influences in organizations. Her publications have appeared in such journals as Journal of Applied Psychology, Personnel Psychology, Journal of Management, and Journal of Organizational Behavior. Dr. Ravlin currently serves on the editorial board of the Journal of Management, and has also served on the boards of the Academy of Management Journal and the Academy of Management Review. She is a Research Fellow of the Centre for Global Workforce Strategy in the Segal Graduate School of Business, Simon Fraser University.

Eletra S. Gilchrist received her Ph.D. (2004) from The University of Memphis and her M.A. and B.A. degrees from The University of Alabama. She is an Assistant Professor in the Communication Arts Department at The University of Alabama in Huntsville. Her research focuses on communication pedagogy, interpersonal communication, and cultural studies from both quantitative and qualitative perspectives. She teaches classes in Fundamentals of Communication, Media Writing I & II, Small Group Communication, Senior Seminar, Interpersonal Communication, Research Methods, African American Communication, Persuasion, and the Dark Side of Interpersonal Communication. Gilchrist also teaches Effective Presentation Skills as a Professional and Continuing Education course on the corporate level.

Narissra Maria Punyanunt-Carter, is an associate professor of Communication Studies at Texas Tech University in Lubbock, Texas. She teaches the basic interpersonal communication course. She is a protégé of Drs. Rebecca Rubin & Alan Rubin, who are considered to be two of the most notable researchers in communication studies. Her research areas include mass media effects, father-daughter communication, mentoring, advisor-advisee relationships, family studies, religious communication, humor, and interpersonal communication. She has published over 30 articles that have appeared in several peer-reviewed journals, such as Communication Research Reports, Southern Journal of Communication, and Journal of Intercultural Communication Research. She has also published numerous instructional ancillaries and materials.

Emilio S. Hernandez received his Bachelor's Degree in May 2008, from Buena Vista University in Storm Lake, Iowa. Currently, Mr. Hernandez is a graduate student and teaching assistant at Texas Tech University in the Department of Communication Studies. His research interests include: family communication, interpersonal communication, and computer-mediated communication and information technology.

Dipl. **Päd. Marinita Schumacher** studied Organisational Pedagogy at University of Hildesheim in Germany where she graduated in the fields of human resource management, organisational development and communication science. During her studies she has had a part time job as junior consultant where she acquired profound knowledge in the field of quality management. She has written her diploma thesis in collaboration with Volkswagen AG concerning the implementation of a skill management system. Her research interests include developing new methodologies of design and management in an industrial context, especially in the domain of competence management and virtual team building. Currently she is preparing her PhD at Ecole Centrale Paris to develop an Aided Competence Management System for Virtual Team Building. At Ecole Centrale Paris she has been in charge of several EU projects in the domain of knowledge management and innovation management funded under FP6.

Julie Stal-Le Cardinal is Associate Professor, HDR, in the Industrial Engineering Laboratory at Ecole Centrale Paris, France. She has been working on decision-making support, at the intersection between knowledge management and project management since 1997. Her research topics include knowledge management and lessons learned for technical decisions, decision-making improvement with a project (choice of actor, collaborative decisions, and risks management) and strategic decisions leading to new king of organization (working in network, in virtual team). Julie Stal-Le Cardinal works as well as a consultant for supporting companies that want to reach a project oriented organization.

Jean-Claude Bocquet is Head of the Laboratory LGI – Industrial Engineering Department that includes 100 persons, therein 35 PhD students. The Laboratory has been classified with the degree "A" by the French Ministry of Research, which is the best evaluation. The research domains of Jean-Claude Bocquet contain the modelling of organisational and complex systems for value creation as well as the constitution and management of teams.

Roy Schwartzman is a Professor of Communication Studies at the University of North Carolina at Greensboro. His research interests include computer-mediated communication, online teaching and learning, rhetoric of science and technology, figurative language, and Holocaust studies. He is founding co-editor of the Journal of Applied Learning in Higher Education and serves on the editorial review boards of several IT journals, including Informing Science Journal and the Journal of Information Technology Education. His research is published in many journals and anthologies, including Communication Education, College Student Journal, the Journal of Communication and Media Research, and the Journal of Instructional Psychology. He is the author of Fundamentals of Oral Communication (Kendall/Hunt).

David Carlone is an Associate Professor of Communication Studies at the University of North Carolina at Greensboro. His research interests lie at the intersection of organizational communication and cultural studies. His ongoing research program examines the new economy as a social, cultural, and political phenomenon. Within this research program, he has recently focused on the representation and practice of communication in service and knowledge intensive work, and the implications of these for the creation of social and economic forms of value. His research has appeared in Communication and Critical/Cultural Studies, Management Communication Quarterly, and the Western Journal of Communication.

Dr. **Shalin Hai-Jew** works as an instructional designer at Kansas State University; in addition, she works as an online instructor for WashingtonOnline. She has worked on a range of instructional design projects in a number of fields: biosecurity, college policy, emotional health, nonprofit fund-raising, leadership studies, and learning theories. She has BAs in English and psychology, and an MA in English from the University of Washington; she has earned an Ed.D. in Educational Leadership (with a focus on public administration) from Seattle University (2005), where she was a Morford Scholar. She serves as a peer reviewer for Educause Quarterly and MERLOT's Journal of Online Learning and Teaching. She led the team that founded the ELATEwiki (the E-Learning and Teaching Exchange wiki) in 2009 and founded the Instructional Design Open Studio (IDOS) blog in 2006. She is interested in simulations, immersive learning, mixed reality learning, and the nature of re-learning, un-learning, and negative learning.

Tyler R. Harrison (University of Arizona, 1999) is an Associate Professor in the Department of Communication at Purdue University. His primary areas of research focus on organizational communication and health communication with a special interest in how organizational and relational structures influence perceptions, enactments, and consequences of conflict and health related decisions for individuals and organizations. He has served as past Chair for the National Communication Association Peace and Conflict Communication Division. Examples of his work can be found in such journals as International Journal of Conflict Management, Conflict Resolution Quarterly, Journal of Communication, Journal of Applied Communication Research, and Health Communication.

Elizabeth A. Williams (M.A., Purdue University, 2007) is a doctoral candidate in the Department of Communication at Purdue University. Her research interests include identification and leadership in a variety of organizational contexts, including distributed teams, multi-team systems, organizations experiencing change, and health organizations. Her work has been published in *Journal of Communication* and *Health Communication* and she has conducted communication workshops in a variety of corporate and academic settings. In 2007, she was awarded Purdue University's College of Liberal Arts Distinguished Masters Thesis Award.

Richie Goodman is a masters student in the Communication Studies Department at the University of North Carolina at Charlotte. He uses a critical lens to study underrepresented and/or voiceless groups in organizations with a particular interest on impacts of interpersonal communication. Current projects revolve around diversity in organizations, public relations/communication campaigns with minorities, and organizational branding.

Marla Boughton is a doctoral candidate in the Organizational Science PhD program at the University of North Carolina at Charlotte. She is currently working on her dissertation on the topic of power and influence in virtual teams. Her other research interests include: feelings of identity, belonging, and attachment in virtual communities and teams, the effects of identity technologies on feelings of entitativity in virtual communities and teams, and the effects of sense of community on health outcomes in online support groups.

Jennifer L. Gibbs is an Assistant Professor of Communication at Rutgers University. She earned her Ph.D. from the Annenberg School for Communication at the University of Southern California in 2002. Her research interests include collaboration and identification in virtual teams and virtual work arrangements as well as online self-presentation and relationship formation. Her work has been published in Administrative Science Quarterly, Communication Research, Communication Yearbook, Human Relations, and Journal of Computer-Mediated Communication, among others. She currently serves on the editorial boards for Communication Quarterly, the Journal of Computer-Mediated Communication, International Journal of Communication and Media, and Women's Studies in Communication.

Craig R. Scott (Ph.D., Arizona State University) is an Associate Professor of Communication and Director of the Ph.D. program in the Rutgers School of Communication & Information. His research examines communication technology use, identification, and anonymous communication in the workplace. His work related to communication technology use by organizational members has been published in Communication Monographs, Communication Research, Management Communication Quarterly, Journal of Computer-Mediated Communication, IEEE Transactions on Professional Communication, Western Journal of Communication, Communication Quarterly, Small Group Research and several current and forthcoming book chapters. He has been on the top paper panel at international, national, and regional conferences 13 different times. He currently serves on the editorial boards for Human Communication Research, Communication Monographs, and Management Communication Quarterly.

Young Hoon Kim is a doctoral student in the School of Communication and Information at Rutgers University. He earned his M.A. from the department of Telecommunication, Information, & Media Studies at Michigan State University. His research interests center on the relationship between people's communicative behaviors and their use of information and communication technologies. Currently, his research interests focus on the interaction taking place among computer-mediated group participants in organizational settings. In addition, he is also interested in exploring the impact of anonymity/deindividuation on an individual's communicative behaviors in computer-mediated communication. His work has been published in Journal of Organizational and End User Computing.

Sun Kyong Lee is currently a doctoral student in School of Communication and Information at Rutgers University and a Research Associate for the Center for Mobile Communication Studies at Rutgers. She earned her M.A. from Kansas State University. Her research interests include mobile communication, social networks, and communication technology uses in organizational settings. She has presented her work at national and international conferences and her paper on structurational processes of virtual work will be published in International Journal of the Humanities.

Stacey L. Connaughton (Ph.D. The University of Texas at Austin, 2002), is an Associate Professor in the Department of Communication at Purdue University. Her research interests include identification and leadership in geographically distributed contexts, particularly as these issues relate to virtual teams/ organizations and political parties. Her published work has appeared in the Small Group Research, Journal of Communication, Management Communication Quarterly, Communication Studies, Communication Yearbook, The Howard Journal of Communications, Corporate Communication: An International Journal, Knowledge Management Review, and her book, Inviting Latino Voters: Party Messages and Latino Party Identification, was published in 2005 by Routledge. She has been invited to present her research on virtual teams and virtual leadership to industry, military, and higher educational audiences, and has facilitated workshops and written guidebooks in the areas of virtual teams, leadership, team-building, and strategic planning in the United States, Canada, and China.

Elizabeth A. Williams (M.A., Purdue University, 2007), is a doctoral candidate in the Department of Communication at Purdue University. Her research interests include identification and leadership in a variety of organizational contexts, including distributed teams, multi-team systems, organizations experiencing change, and health organizations. Her work has been published in Journal of Communication and Health Communication and she has conducted communication workshops in a variety of corporate and academic settings. In 2007, she was awarded Purdue University's College of Liberal Arts Distinguished Masters Thesis Award.

Jennifer S. Linvill (MA, Purdue University, 2008) is a doctoral student in the Department of Communication and a Counselor for International Scholars at Purdue University. Her research interests include identification, leadership, and workplace incivility, particularly in the context of organizations. She has presented her work at national and international conferences and was awarded Purdue University's 2009 College of Liberal Arts Distinguished Masters Thesis Award.

Elizabeth J. O'Connor (B.A. Purdue University, 2009), is a graduate student in the Department of Communication at Purdue University. Her primary area of interest is organizational communication with specific focus on communication in geographically distributed contexts as well as gendered and cross-cultural communication in work contexts. Elizabeth has conducted research on young women's agreeableness and relational aggression, as well as communication and leadership among geographically distributed teams.

Troy G. Hayes (Psy.D. Alliant International University) works within the Human Resource function at the Ingersoll Rand Company, Security Technologies sector. While he started his career in clinical psychology, the majority of his professional experience has been spent working within large corporations. In his work, he emphasizes a strong connection to the business strategy as he engages senior executives in evaluating and developing leadership capabilities, and guiding organizational design decisions. He has extensive experience around the globe and lived in Europe for several years. He worked for several years for RHR International as a consultant to many large companies prior to joining Ingersoll Rand four years ago. He has had several opportunities to present his work in various psychology and business forums and has been published in the Journal of Business Strategy and the Detroiter.

Stephen Yungbluth is an assistant professor in the Department of Communication at Northern Kentucky University. He earned his Ph.D. and M.A. in Communication from the University of Kentucky, and his B.A. in Organizational Communication from Xavier University. His primary areas of study include Interpersonal, Organizational, and Small Group Communication with a special emphasis in the area of conflict management. He is a trained mediator and serves on the Advisory Board for the Alternative Dispute Resolution Center at Northern Kentucky University. His research addresses the communication of respect in the context of conflict interaction and dialogue. He has also analyzed programs that target the development of character education and social-emotional learning skills in middle schools.

Zachary Hart is an associate professor and Undergraduate Studies Director in the Department of Communication at Northern Kentucky University. He earned his Ph.D. in Organizational Communication from Michigan State University, his M.S. in Journalism from the University of Illinois at Urbana-Champaign, and his B.A. in Mass Communication from Western Illinois University. His research focuses on organizational socialization and workplace relationship development, particularly among employees with disabilities. His work has been published in Human Communication Research, Communication Studies, Rehabilitation Education and the Journal of Applied Communication Research. He previously taught at Concordia University-Chicago and worked in public relations/marketing at the Chicago Symphony Orchestra.

Huiyan Zhang (Ph.D, Texas A&M University) lived in the U.S. for nearly ten years and has taught in several universities, including Texas A&M University, University of Maryland, and Temple University. Dr. Zhang interests include organizational communication, group communication, leadership, organizational culture, and conflict. Dr. Zhang now lives in Beijing, China and work as a trainer and consultant with a focused interest in soft skills and leadership development.

Marshall Scott Poole (Ph.D, University of Wisconsin-Madison) is a Professor in the Department of Communication, Senior Research Scientist at the National Center for Supercomputing Applications, and Director of the Institute for Computing in the Humanities, Arts, and Social Sciences at the University of Illinois Urbana-Champaign. He is the author or editor of ten books and over 150 articles and book chapters. Recent books include Theories of Small Groups: Interdisciplinary Perspectives and Organizational Change and Innovation Processes: Theory and Methods for Research. His research interests include group and organizational communication, organizational change, and information technology, particularly its implementation and impacts.

Ardis Hanson is the head of the Research Library at the Louis de la Parte Florida Mental Health Institute at the University of South Florida (USF). She has been involved in a number of virtual projects [http://lib.fmhi.usf.edu/aboutus.html#projects]. An adjunct instructor in the School of Library and Information Science and the College of Public Health at USF, Ms. Hanson teaches classes on mental health informatics. A member of the USF Virtual Library Planning Committee, the Implementation Team, the Interface Design Project Group, and the Metadata Team, she continues to work virtually and employ new technologies whenever possible. Ms. Hanson is currently a doctoral candidate in the Department of Communication at the University of South Florida.

Sheila Gobes-Ryan has worked as a strategic planning workplace consultant for numerous government and corporate clients to efficiently and effectively support teleworkers. Sheila has served as the Co-Chair of the Work Environments Network of the Environmental Design Research Association (EDRA) for the past decade. Based upon her architectural and design experience designing workplaces, she has also served as the organizer for a special topic session on workplaces for the annual EDRA conference. Her interest in examining the integration of virtual and physical work environments has motivated her to pursue a PhD. and she is currently doing graduate work in the Department of Communication at the University of South Florida.

Eric Paul Engel is executive director of Ketchcom Development, Inc. (www.ketchcom.net), an organizational communication development practice that helps professionals increase the effectiveness, efficiency, and productivity of their written and spoken communication. Mr. Engel has provided organizational learning and communication development training, facilitation, and consulting services for over a decade to private, government, and non-profit organizations including the Pentagon's Information Technology Agency, Purdue University, St. Petersburg College, and Ringling College of Art & Design. As of fall 2009, Mr. Engel is nearing completion of his doctorate in Communication at the University of South Florida. He can be reached by phone (1-727-823-5809) and email (epengel@ketchcom.net).

Anita Blanchard is an associate professor of Psychology and Organization Science at the University of North Carolina Charlotte. She studies the effects of technology on online group members' identity with and attachment to each other. In particular, she is interested in sense of virtual community in virtual communities, how virtual communities affect organizations and face-to-face communities, and the technological influences on behavior, affect and cognition on virtual community members.

David Askay is a doctoral student in the Organizational Science program at the University of North Carolina Charlotte. He studies how technology is changing the way people interact and how online organizing is influenced by the social and technological structures of virtual organizations. Current projects include examining trust, reputation, and information exchange among members of virtual communities.

Katherine Frear is a doctoral student in the interdisciplinary Organizational Science program at the University of North Carolina at Charlotte. She studies personality and identity with regard to low-wage and underemployed workers, with an emphasis on examining ways to enhance employment opportunities. She is also interested in how technology and virtual communities can be used to assist workers who struggle in the labor market. As an interdisciplinary student, her research on employment integrates theory and methodology from sociology, psychology, and communication studies.

Index